BLOOMSBURY
DICTIONARY OF DIFFICULT WORDS

BLOOMSBURY

Dictionary of
Difficult Words

Laurence Urdang

BLOOMSBURY

First published in 1993
by Bloomsbury Publishing Limited
2 Soho Square, London W1V 5DE

This paperback edition first published 1994

The moral right of the author has been asserted

Copyright © Laurence Urdang Inc 1993
ISBN 0 7475 1672 3

A copy of the CIP entry for this book is available from the
British Library.

Designed by Geoff Green
Typeset by Market House Books Ltd and Florencetype Ltd
Printed and bound in Britain by Cox & Wyman Ltd,
Reading, Berkshire

Foreword

It will immediately become apparent to users of this dictionary that some of the words defined are not 'difficult' – that is, not difficult for those who know what they mean and how they are pronounced. Indeed, as a professional lexicographer who has dealt with hundreds of thousands of words for most of my working life, I could not prepare an adequate, meaningful defence of what a 'difficult' word is. Yet, despite my familiarity with many words, I am forced to admit that the meanings of some low-frequency terms do not spring readily to mind, so I look them up in the dictionary. Then, like many people, when I see the definition I say, 'Oh, yes. Of course. I knew that!' Generally, as can be seen from this Foreword, I eschew arcane and recondite sesquipedalianisms in my own writing, introducing them only for the sake of humour and, sometimes, for effect. But the writings of others, often replete with ephemera, are not always quite so felicitous.

On the whole, the words are those encountered in general reading; omitted are the common words that occupy a huge amount of space in general dictionaries, the meanings of which everyone knows and never looks up. Every effort has been made to provide definitions that are succinct yet full enough to make the term understandable. Because of our obsession with ailments as well as the medications we take, the names of afflictions, (generic) drugs, and related terms have been included; also included are some terms from biology, genetics, computer terminology, together with a handful from finance, for these crop up continually in newspapers and popular periodicals.

The pronunciation of each uncommon word is given in a simple and easy-to-use respelt form.

Laurence Urdang

Pronunciation Key

In the speech of England, Scotland, Wales, and other areas are reflected many pronunciations, and it would be impossible to record all the valid variants in a book of such limited scope. The pronunciations shown are generally those of the Southern British educated user. Speakers of other dialects may refer to the key words accompanying the symbols that follow.

Vowels

a	at, bat
ā	aim, made, stay
ä	art, father
e	etch, bet
ē	east, seed, we
e'ə	air, pair
ē'ə	ear, beard, near
i	it, bit
ī	isĺand, might, deny
o	omelette, pot, bottom
ō	over, rove, though
ô	ought, caught, flaw
oi	ointment, joint, boy
o͞o	book, foot
o͞o	ooze, pool, woo
ou	out, loud, now
u	up, cup
û	bird (bûd), fur (fû) [in positions where r is not pronounced in Received Pronunciation]
ə	[in unstressed syllables only:] alone (əlōn'), upon (əpon'), bottle (bot'əl), etc.

Consonants

b	baby, nab
CH	church, pitcher
d	deed
f	for, offer, staff
g	good, beggar, log
h	hat, behind
j	jury, major, hedge
k	kill, liquor, quick
l	long, miller, nail
m	mat, hammer, calm
n	night, banner, can
NG	sing, hanger
p	pale, copper, snap
r	red, berry
s	see, mist, ice
SH	shout, mashed, cash
t	tea, better, bet
th	thin, math
TH	then, mother, writhe
v	voice, never, live
w	win, owing
y	yellow, few (fyo͞o)
z	zero, hazel, maze
ZH	treasure, beige

Foreign Sounds

KH	*Scottish* loch, *German* ach, ich
N	(nasalizes preceding vowel) *French* bon (bôN), vin (vaN)
Y	*French* tu, *German* über

Stress

Unmarked syllables are (relatively) unstressed. Primary stress marks (') and secondary stress marks (,) follow the syllable they affect: **dec·a·li·tre** (dek'əlē,tə)

A

aard·vark (äd'väk), *n.* an African anteater.

Aaron's rod (er'ənz), (in the Bible) a staff, marked with the name Aaron, that blossomed. Numbers 17:8.

ab·a·cus (ab'əkəs), *n.*, *pl.* **ab·a·cus·es, ab·a·ci** (ab'əsī, ab'əkī). **1.** a frame having several rows of beads strung across it on stiff wires: used in the orient as a calculating device and in some elementary schools for teaching arithmetic. **2.** a square slab at the top of an architectural column.

ab·a·lo·ne (abəlō'nē), *n.* a large, edible snail, common in California, whose shell is a source of mother-of-pearl.

à·bas (äbä'), *French.* down with, as *A bas la tyrannée!* (Down with tyranny!).

a·bate (əbāt'), *v.* **1.** to diminish or cause to moderate or lessen. *Law.* **2.** to stop an action. **3.** to put an end to (a nuisance). —**a·bate'ment**, *n.*

ab·a·tis, ab·at·tis (ab'ətē, ab'ətis), *n.*, *pl.* **ab·a·tis, ab·at·tis** (ab'ətēz, əbat'ēz) or **ab·a·tis·es, ab·at·tises.** a barricade of felled trees with sharpened branches directed towards an advancing enemy.

a·bat·jour (əbäˈzHŌŌr), *n.* an aperture, as a skylight, or a device, as a reflector, for directing light into a room or building.

ab·at·toir (abətwä'), *n.* a slaughterhouse.

ab·di·cate (ab'dəkāt), *v.* to give up or renounce, formally and voluntarily, an office or responsibility. —**ab·di·ca'tion**, *n.*

ab·duct (abdukt'), *v.* to kidnap. —**ab·duc'tion,** *n.*

ab·duc·tor (abduk'tər), *n.* **1.** a kidnapper. **2.** a muscle that controls movement away from the body. See also **adductor.**

a·be·ce·da·ry (ābēsē'dərē), *n.*, *pl.* **abe·ce·da·ries.** a book arranged in alphabetical order.

ab·er·rant (aber'ənt), *adj.* deviating; differing, in some characteristics, from others of the same class. —**ab·er'rance,** *n.*

ab·er·ra·tion (abərā'sHən), *n.* **1.** a wandering away, esp. from normal behaviour, thought processes, etc. **2.** (in astronomy) apparent displacement of a heavenly body caused by the observer's motion.

a·bet (əbet'), *v.* to help or aid. —**a·bet'tor,** *n.*

abhor (abhô'), *v.* to hate; detest. —**ab·hor'rence,** *n.* —**ab·hor'rent,** *adj.*

ab in·it·i·o (ab inisH'ēō), *Latin.* from the beginning.

ab intra (ab in'trə), *Latin.* from within.

ab·i·o·gen·e·sis (ā,bīōjen'isis), *n.* generation of living organisms from inanimate matter, as the laboratory creation of a virus from a complex protein molecule.

ab·ir·ri·tant (abir'ətənt), *n.* a soothing drug or medication.

ab·ject (ab'jekt), *adj.* so low as to be hopeless; utterly humiliated.

ab·jure (abjŌōr'), *v.* to withdraw from formally; renounce; retract. See also **adjure.**

ab·la·tion (ablā'sHən), *n.* a wearing away, as of a glacier by erosion or the nose cone of a rocket by the heat of high-speed re-entry into the atmosphere.

ab·le·gate (ab'ləgāt), *n.* a papal envoy to newly appointed cardinals or civil dignitaries.

ab·lu·tion (ablŌō'sHən), *n.* a ritual or ceremonial washing or cleansing.

ab·ne·gate (ab'nəgāt,), *v.* to deny oneself (something); renounce. —**ab·ne·ga'tion,** *n.*

ab·o·ma·sum (abəmā'səm), *n.*, *pl.* **ab·o·ma·sa** (abəmā'sə). the fourth of the four stomachs of a ruminant. See also **rumen, reticulum, omasum.**

ab·o·rig·i·nal (abərij'inəl), *adj.* **1.** pertaining to aborigines; primitive. —*n.* **2.** an aborigine.

ab·o·rig·i·ne (abərij'inē), *n.* an original, primitive native of a region. [from Latin **ab origine**, 'from the beginning']

a·bor·ti·cide (əbôr'tisīd), *n.* destruction of a fetus in the uterus.

a·bor·ti·fa·cient (əbôr,təfā'sHənt), *n.* **1.** a drug that causes abortion. —*adj.* **2.** tending to cause abortion.

a·bou·li·a (əbŌŌ'lēə), *n.* See **abulia.**

ab o·vo (ab ō'vō), *Latin.* from the beginning; literally, from the egg.

ab·re·act (ab,rēakt'), *v.* to remove a psychological complex by abreaction.

ab·re·ac·tion (ab,rēak'sHən), *n.* removal of a psychological complex by expressing, by word or act, a repressed experience.

ab·ro·gate (ab'rəgāt), *v.* to repeal, abolish, or annul. —**ab·ro·ga'tion,** *n.*

ab·rup·tion (abrup'sHən), *n.* the breaking off of a portion or part from a mass.

ab·scess (ab'ses, ab'sis), *n.* a collection of pus in the tissues of the body, usually caused by an infection.

ab·scond (abskond'), *v.* to run away suddenly and secretly, in order to avoid legal action.

ab·sinthe (ab'sin*th*), *n.* a bitter, aromatic liqueur prepared from wormwood and tasting of liquorice.

absolute zero, the lowest temperature that could occur in nature; the temperature (-273° C) at which particles whose motion constitute heat would be at rest.

ab·so·lu·tion (absəlōō'sHən), *n.* release from consequences, obligations, or penalties, esp. from the penal consequence of sin.

ab·solve (abzolv'), *v.* to grant absolution to.

ab·sor·be·fa·cient (abzôr,bəfā'sHənt), *n.* 1. a substance that causes absorption. —*adj.* 2. causing absorption.

ab·stain (abstān'), *v.* to refrain from indulging one's passions or appetites, as to abstain from eating meat.

ab·ste·mi·ous (abstē'mēəs), *adj.* moderate in eating and drinking.

ab·sten·tion (absten'sHən), *n.* the act of abstaining.

ab·sterge (abstûrj'), *v.* to cleanse by wiping or washing. —**ab·ster'gent,** *adj., n.*

ab·sti·nent (ab'stinənt), *adj.* refraining from indulging one's desire for something, esp. for alcoholic drinks. —**ab'sti·nence,** *n.*

abstract art, a form of 20th-century art that appeals to an emotional appreciation of colour, shape, texture, material, and their interrelations rather than to realistic or concrete representations.

ab·struse (abstrōōs'), *adj.* difficult to understand.

a·bu·li·a (əbōō'lēə, əbyōō'lēə), *n.* a mental disorder characterized by loss of will power. Also spelled **aboulia.**

a·bys·mal (əbiz'məl), *adj.* like an abyss; unfathomable; profound; immeasurable. —**a·bys'mal·ly,** *adv.*

a·byss (əbis'), *n.* an immeasurably deep space. —**a·byss'al,** *adj.*

ac·a·dem·ic (akədem'ik), *adj.* 1. pertaining to an advanced institution of learning. 2. unrealistic; impractical; theoretical. 3. conventional; conforming to set rules and traditions; not imaginative or innovative.

a·cal·cul·i·a (ākal,kyōōl'ēə), *n.* the inability to perform simple mathematical calculations.

a cap·pel·la (ä käpel'lä), (of singing) without musical accompaniment. Also **alla cappella.**

ac·a·ri·a·sis (akarī'əsis), *n.* infestation by mites.

a·car·i·cide (əkar'isīd), *n.* a substance that kills mites.

a·cat·a·lec·tic (ākat'əlek'tik), *adj.* (of a verse) having the full number of syllables.

ac·ci·den·tal (ak,siden'təl), *n.* a sign put before a musical note to show a change of pitch.

ac·claim (əklām'), *v.* 1. to applaud. —*n.* 2. acclamation.

ac·cla·ma·tion (akləmā'sHən), *n.* 1. a shout, applause, or other demonstration of assent or approbation. 2. spontaneous approval or adoption of a measure by oral vote, applause, etc., in place of a formal ballot.

ac·cli·mate (əklī'mit, ak'ləmāt), *v.* to acclimatize.

ac·cli·ma·tize (əklī'mətīz,), *v.* to accustom or adapt to a new climate or environment.

ac·cliv·i·ty (əkliv'itē), *n.* an upward slope (from the observer's point of view). See also declivity.

ac·co·lade (akəlād'), *n.* praise; commendation for quality.

ac·cord·ant (əkor'dənt), *adj.* in conformity; agreeing.

ac·cost (əkost'), *v.* 1. to approach with a greeting. 2. to approach brazenly. 3. (of prostitutes) to solicit for sexual purposes.

ac·cou·tre, ac·cou·ter (əkōō'tər), *v.* to equip or furnish.

ac·cou·tre·ments, ac·cou·ter·ments (əkōō'trəmənts), *n. pl.* (rarely used in sing.) nonessential features that superficially characterize and identify something.

ac·cred·it (əkred'it), *v.* to approve the credentials of (a school, individual, etc.). —**ac·cred·i·ta'tion,** *n.*

ac·cre·tion (əkrē'sHən), *n.* an increase by natural growth, esp. by addition of external parts.

ac·cru·al (əkrōō'əl), *n.* accretion; act or process of accruing.

ac·crue (əkrōō'), *v.* to happen or result as a natural growth.

ac·cul·tu·ra·tion (əkul,cHərā'sHən), *n.* the adoption of the culture of another social group. —**ac·cul'tu·rate,** *v.*

a·cer·bic (əsur'bik), *adj.* sharp; harsh. Also a·cerb'. —**a·cer'bi·ty,** *n.*

ac·e·tyl·sal·i·cyl·ic acid (a,sētilsal,isil'ik), *n.* the chemical name for aspirin.

ach·ro·mat·ic (ak,rəmat'ik), *adj.* (of a camera or telescope lens) corrected for chromatic aberration.

a·cid·u·lous (əsid'yələs), *adj.* having a sour, harsh, caustic disposition or expression. Also a·cid'u·lent.

ac·o·lyte (ak'əlīt), *n.* an attendant or assistant.

a·cou·asm (əkōō'azm), *n.* an imagined ringing in the head.

a·cous·tics (əkōō'stiks), *n.* the science of hearing or of sound. —**acous'tic,** *adj.*

ac·qui·esce (ak,wēes'), *v.* to agree or consent quietly; comply or submit. —**ac,qui·es'cence,** *n.* —**ac,qui·es'cent,** *adj.*

ac·quired im·mune de·fi·cien·cy syn·drome *n.* See AIDS.

ac·rid (ak'rid), *adj.* bitter, sharp, or irritating to taste or smell.

ac·ri·mo·ny (ak'rəmō,nē), *n.* harshness or bitterness, esp. stemming from resentment, anger, or bad disposition. —ac,ri·mo'ni·ous, *adj.*

ac·ro·ceph·a·ly (ak,rōsef'əlē, ak,rōkef'əlē), *n.* a malformation in which the head is somewhat pointed. Also **hypsicephaly.** —ac·ro·ce·phal'ic, *adj.*

ac·ro·lith (ak'rəli*th*), *n.* a sculptured figure having the head and extremities carved in stone and the rest usually of wood.

ac·ro·meg·a·ly (ak,rōmeg'əlē), *n.* abnormal enlargement of the head and the extremities owing to dysfunction of the pituitary gland. —ac,ro·me·gal'ic, *adj.*

ac·ro·nym (ak'rənim), *n.* a pronounceable word made up from the initial letters or parts of words in a phrase, title, company name, or the like: *Nabisco* from *Na(tional) Bis(cuit) Co(mpany)*; *radar* from *ra(dio) d(etecting) a(nd) r(anging).*

ac·ro·pho·bi·a (ak,rəfō'bēə), *n.* a dread of being in or looking down from high places.

ACTH, adrenocorticotrophic hormone; a hormone, secreted by the pituitary gland, which stimulates the adrenal cortex to generate corticosteroids.

ac·ti·nism (ak'tiniz,əm), *n.* the property of radiation to produce chemical changes.

ac·tion·a·ble (ak'sHənəbəl), *adj.* furnishing sufficient ground for legal action.

ac·tiv·ist (ak'təvist), *n.* one who takes an energetic, active part in political or social causes.

ac·tu·ar·y (ak'cHōoerē), *n.* an expert on life expectancy and the statistics of insurance. —ac·tu·ar'i·al, *adj.*

ac·u·men (ak'yəmən), *n.* keen perception; penetrating insight.

a·cu·mi·nate (əkyōo'mənit, əkyōo'mināt), *adj.* tapering to a point.

ac·u·punc·ture (ak'yəpuNGk,cHər), *n.* a practice, developed in China, in which delicate needles are inserted into the tissues to cure illness.

ad·age (ad'ij), *n.* a saying, proverb, or maxim.

ad·a·mant (ad'əmənt), *adj.* obstinately firm despite appeal; unyielding.

ad·den·dum (əden'dəm), *n., pl.* **ad·den·da** (əden'də). something to be added; appendix.

ad·duce (ədyōos'), *v.* to present as evidence.

ad·duc·tor (əduk'tər), *n.* a muscle that controls movement of parts towards one another or to a common centre. See also **abductor.**

a·de·no·vi·rus (ad,inōvī'rəs), *n.* a coldlike virus which irritates the upper respiratory tract and the lymph nodes.

a·deph·a·gous (ədef'əgəs), *adj.* gluttonous; having a voracious appetite.

a·dept (ədept'), *adj.* **1.** skilled; proficient. —*n.* **2.** one who is skilled or proficient.

a·di·aph·o·re·sis (ā,dīəfərē'sis), *n.* lack of perspiration.

a·di·aph·o·ret·ic (ā,dīəfəret'ik), *n.* **1.** a drug

that prevents perspiration; antiperspirant. —*adj.* **2.** preventing perspiration.

ad in·fi·ni·tum (ad' infinī'təm), *Latin.* to infinity; limitlessly.

ad in·ter·im (ad' in'tərim), *Latin.* for the time being.

ad·i·po·pex·i·a (ad,əpōpek'sēə), *n.* lipopexia. Also **ad·i·po·pex·is** (ad,əpōpek'sis).

ad·i·pose (ad'ipōs, ad'ipōz), *adj.* fatty; consisting of or resembling fat. —ad·i·pos'i·ty, *n.*

ad·join (əjoin'), *v.* to be next to or in contact with.

ad·journ (əjurn'), *v.* to put off or postpone. —ad·journ'ment, *n.*

ad·ju·di·cate (əjōō'dikāt), *v.* to pronounce judgment upon. —ad·ju·dica'tion, *n.*

ad·junct (ad'juNGkt), *n.* something added to another but not necessarily a part of it.

ad·jure (əjōōr'), *v.* to command, entreat, or order, usually with appeal to God or by the invocation of a curse; beseech. See also **abjure.** —ad·ju·ra'tion, *n.*

ad·ju·vant (aj'əvənt), *adj.* **1.** contributory; auxiliary, as an adjuvant drug. —*n.* **2.** something that helps or assists.

ad lib (ad' lib'), to the extent of one's wishes; freely.

ad·mon·ish (admon'isH), *v.* **1.** to warn or caution (someone). **2.** to rebuke or reprimand (someone). —ad,mo·ni'tion, *n.*

ad·re·nal (ədrē'nəl), *adj.* located near the kidneys.

ad·ren·er·gic (adrənû'jik) *adj.* **1.** activated by or releasing adrenaline or a similar substance. **2.** resembling adrenaline.

a·droit (ədroit'), *adj.* skilful or dexterous; ingenious.

ad·sci·ti·tious (ad,sitisH'əs), *adj.* supplemental; additional; unessential.

ad·u·la·tion (ad,yəlā'sHən), *n.* excessive devotion; exaggerated praise. —ad'u·late,, *v.*

ad·um·brate (adum'brāt), *v.* to foreshadow; give a faint shadow of; outline. —ad·um·bra'tion, *n.*

ad va·lo·rem (ad' vəlôr'əm), *Latin.* according to the value (applied to import duties based on the declared value of merchandise).

ad·ven·ti·tious (ad,ventisH'əs), *adj.* accidentally or casually acquired; added from another source.

ad·verse (ad'vûs, advûs'), *adj.* antagonistic; hostile; unfavourable; unfortunate. See also **averse.**

ad·ver·si·ty (advû'sitē), *n.* an unfortunate, calamitous, or distressful state or occurrence.

ad·vo·cate (ad'vəkit), *n.* one who defends a cause; one who defends another in a court; an intercessor.

ae·gis (ē'jis), *n.* protection; sponsorship.

ae·on, e·on (ē'on), *n.* a period of time comprising at least two geological eras.

aer·o·bic (erō'bik), *adj.* living in air (applied to an organism).

aer·o·bics (erō'biks), *n.* a form of exercise that stimulates deep breathing, thus increasing the intake of oxygen.

aer·o·stat (er'əstat,), *n.* a lighter-than-air craft; balloon or dirigible.

aes·the·sia, es·the·sia (ēsthē'ziə), *n.* sensitivity; ability to feel.

aes·the·si·om·e·ter (ēsthē,zēom'itə), *n.* a device to measure the degree of tactile sensitivity.

aes·the·si·om·e·try (ēsthē,zēom'itrē), *n.* the process of using an aesthesiometer.

aes·the·sis, es·the·sis (ēsthē'sis), *n.* feeling; sensation.

aes·thete, es·thete (ēs'thēt), *n.* a lover of beautiful things, esp. to the scornful exclusion of practicalities.

aes·thet·ic, es·thet·ic (ēsthet'ik), *adj.* concerning or having sensitivity towards beauty or towards what is beautiful.

aes·ti·val, es·ti·val (ēstī'vəl, es'tivəl), *adj.* of the summer.

aes·ti·vate, es·ti·vate (ēs'tivāt,, es'tivāt), *v.* to pass the summer, as in a certain place. —**aes·ti·va'tion, es·ti·va'tion,** *n.*

aet. *Abbr. for* **anno aetatis suae.**

ae·the·re·al (ithēr'ēəl), *adj.* See **ethereal.**

ae·ti·ol·o·gy, e·ti·ol·ogy (ē,tēol'əjē), *n.* any study of causes, esp. of causes of disease.

af·fa·ble (af'əbəl), *adj.* having a kind, benevolent manner; hence, easy and pleasant to talk to or deal with. —**affa·bil'i·ty,** *n.* —**af·fa·bly,** *adv.*

af·fec·ta·tion (afəktā'sHən), *n.* a striving to produce an effect, esp. with an artificiality of manner or behaviour. —**af·fect'ed,** *adj.*

af·fer·ent (af'ərənt), *adj.* (in physiology) carrying to or towards or inward, as a nerve carrying an impulse to a centre. See also **efferent.**

af·fil·i·ate (əfil'ēit), *n.* a company or corporation owned partly or wholly by another.

af·fin·i·ty (əfin'itē), *n.* an attraction for a person or thing; sense of relationship.

af·fla·tus (əflā'təs), *n.* inspiration; knowledge or understanding.

af·flu·ent (af'lōōənt), *adj.* **1.** wealthy. —*n.* **2.** a tributary stream. —**af'fluence,** *n.*

af·for·est (əfor'ist), *v.* to convert bare or cultivated land into a forest. —**af,for·es·ta'tion,** *n.*

af·front (əfrənt'), *n.* **1.** an insult; an offence to one's dignity, sense of justice or of what is proper, etc. —*v.* **2.** to insult (someone or someone's dignity, etc.).

a·fi·ci·o·na·do (əfisн,yənä'dō), *n.*, *pl.* **a·fi·ci·o·na·dos.** a fan or devotee.

Af·ri·kaans (af,rikäns'), *n.* a language, resembling Dutch, spoken in South Africa.

Af·ri·kan·der (af,rikän'də), *n.* a native of South Africa born of white European parents.

Af·ro (af'rō), *n.*, *pl.* **Af·ros.** a large bushy hairdo, sometimes worn by blacks and other people with kinky hair.

af·ter·burn·er (af'təbur,nə), *n.* a device in the exhaust system of a jet or internal combustion engine to increase its power.

af·ter·care (af'təke,), *n.* the treatment of a patient during convalescence.

af·ter·ef·fect (af'təəfekt,), *n.* an effect produced or felt after the removal of a stimulus.

af·ter·im·age (af'təim,ij), *n.* an image seen after the removal of a stimulus; for example, staring at a red light produces a green afterimage.

a·ga·ve (əgā'vē), *n.* a genus of American plants grown for economic or ornamental purposes.

a·gen·da (əjen'də), *n.* *pl.*, *sing.* **agen·dum** (əjen'dəm). things to be done, usually listed in a formal manner for a meeting.

a·gent pro·voc·a·teur (äzнän' prōvokätu'), *pl.* **a·gents pro·voc·ateurs.** a police or political spy who provokes suspicious people to perform an illegal action that will get them arrested.

ag·glom·er·ate (əglom'ərit), *n.* **1.** (in geology) rock composed of angular volcanic fragments. **2.** any collection or accumulation of miscellaneous materials. —**ag·glom,e·ra'tion,** *n.*

ag·glu·ti·nate (əglōō'tinät,), *v.* (in linguistics) to form and express grammatical relationships by the continued addition of strings of meaningful elements, as in Turkish. —**ag·glu'ti·na'tion,** *n.* —**ag·glu'ti·na,tive,** *adj.*

ag·gran·dize (əgran'dīz), *v.* to enlarge, broaden, or increase in wealth, power, rank, or honour. —**ag·gran'dize·ment,** *n.*

ag·gra·vate (ag'rəvät,), *v.* **ag·gra·vat·ed, ag·gra·vat·ing.** to make worse, as *My cold was aggravated by a throat infection.* —**ag,gra·va'·tion,** *n.*

ag·grieve (əgrēv'), *v.* **ag·grieved, ag·griev·ing.** to cause grief or distress to.

a·ghast (əgäst'), *adj.* horrified; overcome with fright.

ag·i·o (aj'ēō). *n.*, *pl.* **ag·i·os.** a fee charged by money brokers for exchanging coin for paper currency or one currency for another.

ag·it·prop (aj'itprop,), *n.* agitation and propaganda. [from Russian *Agitpropbyuro, agit-(atsiya) prop(aganda)byuro*]

ag·nate (ag'nāt), *n.* a kinsman whose relationship is traceable only through males; any male relation on the father's side. See also **cognate.** —**ag·na'tion,** *n.*

ag·nos·tic (agnos'tik), *n.* one who denies knowledge of God. —**ag·nos'tic·ism,** *n.*

ag·o·ra·pho·bi·a (ag,ərəfō'bēə), *n.* a dread of being in open spaces.

a·grar·i·an (əgrer'ēən), *adj.* concerning land, esp. public or agricultural land.

a·gres·tal (əgres'təl), *adj.* (of weeds) growing in cultivated areas.

a·gres·tic (əgres'tik), *adj.* **1.** rural, rustic. **2.** uncouth.

ag·ri·ol·ogy (ag,rēol'əjē), *n.* the comparative study of the customs of uncivilized man.

ag·ro·bi·ol·ogy (ag,rōbīol'əjē), *n.* the study of the biology of crops in relation to soil. —**ag,ro·bi·o·log'i·cal,** *adj.*

a·grol·o·gy (əgrol'əjē), *n.* soil science. —**ag,ro·log'i·cal,** *adj.*

a·gron·o·my (əgron'əmē), *n.* the study of soil science in relation to crop management. —**ag,ro·nom'ic,** *adj.*

a·gryp·ni·a (əgrip'nēə), *n.* sleeplessness; insomnia.

AID *Abbr. for* **artificial insemination (by) donor.**

AIDS (ādz), *acronym for* **acquired immune deficiency syndrome:** a disease of humans, caused by a virus, in which certain cells of the immune system are destroyed, resulting in diminished ability to fight infections.

ai·lu·ro·phile (īlōōr'əfīl), *n.* one who is fond of cats; a cat fancier.

ai·lu·ro·phil·i·a (īlōōr,əfil'ēə), *n.* love of cats.

ai·lu·ro·phobe (īlōōr'əfōb,), *n.* one who fears cats.

ai·lu·ro·pho·bi·a (īlōōr,əfō'bēə), *n.* dread of cats.

air·brush (eə'brusH,), *n.* an atomizer used to spray paint.

air·foil (eə'foil,), *n.* any surface on an aircraft for controlling or aiding its motion.

air·speed (eə'spēd,), *n.* the speed of an aircraft with respect to the air through which it is flying. See also **groundspeed.**

ait (āt), *n.* a small island in a river or lake.

à jour (ä zHōōə'), (of decorative objects) pierced to let through light, as a screen.

a·kim·bo (əkim'bō), *adj., adv.* (of the arms) bent outward at the elbow when the hands are on the hips, as *She stood, arms akimbo, and demanded to know why I'd come.*

a·la (ā'lə), *n., pl.* **a·lae** (ā'lē). (in zoology and botany) a wing or winglike part.

a·lac·ri·ty (əlak'ritē), *n.* liveliness; readiness; cheerful willingness.

al·a·nine (al'ənēn), *n.* an amino acid; discovered to be present in a 1970 meteorite.

a·lar·ums (əlar'əmz) **and excursions,** a stage direction used in early modern English theatre (15th and 16th century) to call for the sound effects of a battle, with trumpets, clash of arms, etc.

a·late (ā'lāt), *adj.* (in botany and zoology) having alae.

a lat·ti·ci·nio (älät,tēcHē'nyô), *Italian.* (of

ornamental glass) having the transparent body decorated with embedded lines or bands of opaque milky-white glass.

Al·bi·on (al'bēən), *n.* an old, poetic name for Britain.

al·cal·de (alkal'dē), *n.* (in Spain and S.W. U.S.) a mayor with authority as a justice of the peace.

al·che·my (al'kəmē), *n.* medieval chemistry concerned chiefly with transmuting baser metals into gold. —**al·chem'i·cal,** *adj.*

a·le·a·to·ry (ā'lēətôr,ē), *adj.* depending on a contingent event; uncertain; dependent on chance.

a·lex·i·a (əlek'sēə), *n.* inability to read because of aphasia.

al·fres·co (alfres'kō), *adv., adj.* out of doors; in the open air.

al·go·rism (al'gərizm), *n.* **1.** the Arabic system of counting based on tens. **2.** the ability to count using numerals. —**al,go·ris'mic,** *adj.*

al·go·rithm (al'gəriTHm), *n.* a method for computing or for solving a particular problem.

al·ien·ate (āl'yənāt,), *v.* to estrange; ward off; keep at a distance, esp. someone who was formerly a friend or close associate.

al·ion·a·tion (āl,yənā'sHən), *n.* **1.** a state of feeling withdrawn from the world. **2.** derangement; insanity, esp. legal insanity.

al·ien·ist (āl'yənist), *n.* an expert in the study of mental disease.

al·i·ment (al'əmənt), *n.* nourishment; food. —**al·i·men'ta·ry,** *adj.*

alimentary canal, the system of organs in the body through which food passes.

al·i·quant (al'əkwənt), *adj.* (of a number) not dividing evenly into a larger number, as *6 is an aliquant part of 16.* See also **aliquot.**

al·i·quot (al'əkwot), *adj.* (of a number) dividing evenly into a larger number, as *6 is an aliquot part of 18.* See also **aliquant.**

al·ka·hest (al'kəhest), *n.* the universal solvent sought by alchemists.

al·ka·li (al'kəlī), *n.* a chemical that neutralizes acids. —**al'ka·line,** *adj.*

al·ka·lize (al'kəlīz), *v.* to change (an acid) into an alkali.

al·la cap·pel·la (äl'lä käpel'lä). See **a cappella.**

al·lay (əlā'), *v.* **1.** to pacify, quiet, or appease, as an agitated person. **2.** to relieve or ease, as misery or pain.

al·lege (əlej'), *v.* to assert, declare, or affirm. —**al,le·ga'tion,** *n.*

al·leged (əlejd'), *adj.* **1.** stated to be as maintained (used in journalism to avoid possible libel action for declaring a person a criminal, as *the alleged killer*). **2.** supposed; questionable, as an alleged cure for cancer.

al·le·go·ry (al'əgôr,ē), *n.* a story, drama, or other treatment in which the subject is not mentioned but is represented symbolically. —**al·le·gor'i·cal**, *adj.* —**al,le·gor'i·cal·ly**, *adv.*

al·lele (əlēl'), *n.* a form of gene causing hereditary variation. Also **al·lelo·morph** (əlē'ləmôrf,).

al·ler·gen (al'əjen,), *n.* something that produces an allergic reaction. —**al·ler·gen'ic**, *adj.*

al·ler·gy (al'əjē), *n.* an abnormal reaction resulting from sensitivity towards a germ or substance. —**al·ler·gic** (əlû'jik), *adj.*

al·le·vi·ate (əlē'vēāt,), *v.* to lighten, ease, or relieve, as pain, burdens, sorrow, worry, etc.

al·li·a·ceous (al,ēā'sHəs), *adj.* smelling or tasting of garlic, onions, or the like.

al·lit·er·a·tion (əlit,ərā'sHən), *n.* the repetition of the same sound at the beginning of two or more words in a phrase, verse of poetry, etc., as *Tippecanoe and Tyler, too.* —**al·lit'er·a·tive**, *adj.*

al·loch·tho·nous (əlok'thənəs), *adj.* not native to the region where found. See also **autochthonous**.

al·lo·cu·tion (al,əkyōō'sHən), *n.* a formal speech, esp. one intended to advise or exhort.

al·lop·a·thy (əlop'əthē), *n.* the principle of treating disease by using agents that produce effects different from the symptoms of the disease treated. See also **homeopathy**. —**allop'a·thist, al'lo·path**, *n.*

al·lo·trope (al'ətrōp,), *n.* one of the two or more forms in which an element exists, as *Diamond is an allotrope of carbon.* —**al·lo·trop'ic**, *adj.*

al·lot·ro·py (əlot'rəpē), *n.* a property of certain chemical elements to exist in more than one form, as *Carbon exhibits allotropy.*

al·lude (əlōōd'), *v.* to refer casually or indirectly. —**al·lu'sion**, *n.*

al·lu·vi·um (əlōō'vēəm), *n.*, *pl.* **allu·vi·ums, al·lu·vi·a** (əlōō'vēə). sedimentary deposit of a river or flood.

Al·ni·co (alnē'kō), *n.* a trademark for an alloy used in making permanent magnets.

al·o·pe·cia (al,əpē'sHə), *n.* baldness.

Al·pha Cen·tau·ri (al'fə sentô'rē), the first-magnitude star nearest the sun (4.3 light-years).

alpha particle, a positively charged particle; the nucleus of the helium atom.

al·to·re·lie·vo (äl,tōrilē'vō), *n.*, *pl.* **al·to·re·lie·vos.** a kind of sculpture in relief in which the highest points are above the level of the original surface. See also **bas-relief**.

al·tru·ism (al'trōōiz,əm), *n.* an attitude of charitable regard for others, esp. by doing something for someone with no thought of reciprocal favour. —**al'tru·ist**, *n.*

a·mal·gam (əmal'gəm), *n.* a mixture, esp. a silver-mercury mixture used as a dental filling.

a·man·u·en·sis (əman,yōōen'sis), *n.*, *pl.* **a·man·u·en·ses** (əman,yōōen'sēz). a secretary who can write rapidly enough to record dicta-

tion; one employed to copy what another has written.

am·a·ranth (am'əranth), *n.* an imaginary flower that never fades or withers. —**am·a·ran'·thine**, *adj.*

am·ba·gious (ambā'jəs), *adj.* not straightforward; devious; circumlocutory; roundabout.

am·bi·ance, am·bi·ence (am'bēəns), *n.* atmosphere; environment, as *an ambience of mystery.*

am·bi·ent (am'bēənt), *adj.* surrounding; encompassing, as *The ambient air was redolent with perfume.*

am·big·u·ous (ambig'yōōəs), *adj.* uncertain or doubtful; unclear and indefinite. —**am,bi·gu'·i·ty**, *n.*

am·bit (am'bit), *n.* limit, boundary, or extent.

am·biv·a·lent (ambiv'ələnt), *adj.* uncertain or doubtful; unable or not caring to choose among two or more alternatives. —**am·biv'a·lence**, *n.*

am·bu·la·to·ry (am,byōōlā'təri), *adj.* capable of walking, said esp. of a patient who is not bedridden.

a·me·ba (amē'bē), *n.* See **amoeba**.

a·mel·io·rate (əmēl'yərāt), *v.* to improve or make better. —**a·mel,iora'tion**, *n.* —**a·mel'io·ra,·tive**, *adj.*

a·me·na·ble (əmē'nəbəl), *adj.* agreeable; tractable; willing to answer, yield, or submit.

a·mend (əmend'), *v.* to change for the better; improve. See also **emend**.

a·merce (əmûs'), *v.* to punish by an arbitrary fine not provided for by statute; mulct. —**a·merce'ment**, *n.*

American plan, a system of paying for both hotel rooms and meals at one fixed rate.

a·mi·a·ble (ā'mēəbəl), *adj.* (of a person) showing a friendly character and disposition.

am·i·ca·ble (am'ikəbəl), *adj.* (of an agreement, relationship, etc.) characterized by cordiality and by goodwill; friendly.

a·mi·cus cu·ri·ae (əmē'kəs kyōōr'iē), (in law) a disinterested person who volunteers or is invited to advise the court in a proceeding. [from Latin, 'a friend of the court']

a·mi·no acid (əmē'nō), a class of organic chemical compounds from some of which proteins are constructed.

am·i·ty (am'itē), *n.* harmony; peacefulness; friendliness; friendship.

am·nes·ty (am'nistē), *n.* **1.** a general or conditional pardon for a crime or for a class of offences. —*v.* **2.** to grant amnesty to; pardon.

am·ni·o·cen·te·sis (am,nēōsentē'sis), *n.* the technique of sampling amniotic fluid via the abdominal wall during pregnancy to test for abnormalities of the fetus.

am·ni·ot·ic fluid (am,nēot'ik), the fluid in which an unborn fetus floats.

a·moe·ba, a·me·ba (amē'bə), *n.*, *pl.* **a·moe-**

·bae, a·me·bae (əmē'bē), a·moe·bas, a·me·bas. a one-celled, microscopic animal. —amoe'bic, a·me'bic, adj.

a·mok (əmuk', əmok'), adv. used chiefly in the expression run amok: to run about wildly, attacking everyone indiscriminately.

a·mon·til·la·do (əmon,tilä'dō), n. a medium dry Spanish sherry, less pale than fino.

a·mor·al (āmôr'əl, amôr'əl), adj. having no moral sense; unable to distinguish between moral and immoral quality or behaviour.

a·mor·phous (əmô'fəs), adj. having no distinct shape or structure.

a·mour·propre (āmŏŏə'prôpr'), n. self-respect.

am·pere (am'pēə), n. a measure of amount of electric current: one volt acting through a resistance of one ohm. See also **ohm, volt.** —am·per·age (am'pərij), n.

am·per·sand (am'pəsand,), n. the name for the symbol '&'.

am·phet·a·mine (amfet'əmēn, amfet'əmin), n. a drug that stimulates the central nervous system, used in treatment of depressive states.

am·phi·bol·o·gy (am,fəbol'əjē), n. the use of ambiguous or quibbling phrases or statements. Also **amphib'o·ly.**

am·phig·e·an (amfij'ēən), adj. extending around the earth in approximately the same latitudes, as certain botanical species.

am·phi·gor·y (am'figəri), n. a meaningless hotchpotch; a nonsensical parody. —am,phi·gor'ic, adj.

am·pho·ra (am'fərə), n., pl. am·pho·ras, am·pho·rae (am'fərē). a tall, two-handled vessel, usually made of clay and having a pointed base for insertion into a stand or the ground, used by the Greeks and Romans for storage of grain, honey, wine, etc.

am·yl·ase (am'ilās), n. an enzyme capable of splitting up starches.

a·nab·a·sis (ənab'əsis), n., pl. a·nab·a·ses (ənab'əsēz). a military expedition. See also **katabasis.**

an·a·bat·ic (an,əbat'ik), adj. (of a wind) rising upward because of local heating. See also **katabatic.**

an·a·bi·o·sis (an,əbīō'sis), n. reanimation; recovery to consciousness after seeming death. —an,a·bi·ot'ic, adj.

a·nab·o·lism (ənab'əliz,əm), n. constructive metabolism, a process in which a substance is transformed into another that is more complex or more highly organized and energetic. See also **catabolism.** —an,abol'ic, adj.

a·nach·ro·nism (ənak'rəniz,əm), n. a person or event misplaced in time, as if a Shakespearian character were to quote Lincoln. See also **pa·rachronism, prochronism.** —a·nach·ronis'tic, adj.

A·nac·re·on·tic (ənak,rēon'tik), adj. pertaining to the praise of love and wine.

a·nad·ro·mous (ənad'rəməs), adj. denoting fish, like the salmon, that swim from the sea up a fresh-water river to spawn. See also **catadromous, diadromous.**

an·aer·obe (aner'ōb), n. an organism able to live without air or oxygen or unable to live in their presence. —an·aer·ob·ic (an,erōb'ik), adj.

an·a·glyph (an'əglif), n. **1.** a picture printed in two, slightly overlapping colours so that, when viewed through lenses with corresponding colours, it appears to be three-dimensional. **2.** any form of carving in low relief.

an·a·gram (an'əgram), n. **1.** the rearrangement of the letters of a word or sentence to form a new word, as ward from draw or stare down from don't swear. **2.** the word formed.

an·a·lects (an'əlekts), n. pl. (rarely used in sing.) selected passages or extracts from the writings of one or more authors.

an·a·lep·tic (an,əlep'tik), adj. restorative; invigorating; giving strength during convalescence.

an·al·ge·sic (an,əljē'zik), n. **1.** any drug that relieves pain. —adj. **2.** serving to remove pain. —an·al·ge·si·a (anəljē'zēə), n.

an·a·logue, an·a·log (an'əlog,), n. something bearing a resemblance or proportion to another thing or things: an electric wire as an analogue of a nerve. —a·nal·o·gy (ənal'əjē), n. —a·nal·o·gous (ənal'əgəs), adj.

analogue computer, a computer that uses properties of known physical processes (like the voltage, amperage, resistance of electric current) to solve mathematical problems. See also **digital computer, hybrid computer.**

a·nal·o·gy (ənal'əjē), n. a likeness between two things in certain respects; something partially similar to another.

a·nal·y·sand (ənal'isand,), n. a person undergoing psychoanalysis.

an·am·ne·sis (an,əmnē'sis), n., pl. an·am·ne·ses (an,əmnē'sēz). reminiscence of the past, esp. of a previous existence of the soul. —an·am·nes·tic (an,əmnes'tik), adj.

an·a·mor·phic (an,əmôr'fik), adj. having or making unequal magnifications along two perpendicular axes.

an·a·mor·phism (an,əmôr'fizəm), n. a change under the earth's surface which changes simple minerals into complex ones. See also **katamorphism.**

an·a·mor·pho·sis (an,əmôr'fəsis, an,əmôrfō'sis), n. an image distorted so as to appear natural when reflected in a curved mirror or viewed from a certain angle.

an·ar·chy (an'ərkē), n. absence of government or law in a society; political and social disorder. —an·ar'chic, adj.

an·ash·er (an'əsHər), *n.* a blend of fine marijuana from India.

an·as·tig·mat (ənas'tigmat, an,astig'mat), *n.* a lens that corrects astigmatism. **—an,as·tig·mat'-ic**, *adj.*

a·nath·e·ma (ənath'əmə), *n.* a person or thing hated, loathed, or detested.

an·chor·ite (aNG'kərīt), *n.* a hermit; recluse.

an·cil·lar·y (ansil'ərē), *adj.* auxiliary; subordinate; extra.

an·dro·cen·tric (an,drōsen'trik), *adj.* dominated by males, as *an androcentric culture.*

an·droc·ra·cy (androk'rəsē), *n.* rule by males. **—an·dro·crat·ic** (an,drōkrat'ik), *adj.*

an·drog·y·nous (androj'ənəs), *adj.* exhibiting both male and female sexual characteristics.

an·droid (an'droid), *n.* a robot resembling a human being.

an·dro·sphinx (an'drəsfiNGks), *n.* a sphinx with the head of a man.

an·e·cho·ic (an,ekō'ik), *adj.* (of a recording studio, etc.) having echoes reduced to a minimum.

an·e·mom·e·ter (an,əmom'ətər), *n.* an instrument for measuring wind velocity.

an·er·oid (an'əroid), *adj.* noting a kind of barometer consisting of a box containing a partial vacuum and having a flexible diaphragm on one side to which a pointer is attached. The pointer, when calibrated, indicates the atmospheric pressure.

an·eu·rysm (an'yəriz,əm), *n.* dilatation of an artery caused by a weakening of its wall through disease.

an·frac·tu·ous (anfrak'CHŌŌəs), *adj.* having turnings and windings. **—an·frac,tu·os'i·ty,** *n.*

an·gi·na pec·to·ris (anjī'nə pek'təris), a condition characterized by intense pain below the sternum caused by lack of blood supply to the heart.

angst (aNGst), *n.* dread; anxiety; anguish.

ang·strom unit (aNG'strəm), a unit of length used to express electromagnetic wave lengths, equal to one tenth of a millimicron.

an·i·mad·ver·sion (an,əmadvû'zHən), *n.* criticism; censure; adverse comment.

an·i·mal·cule (an,imal'kyōōl), *n.* a microscopic animal.

an·i·mism (an'imiz,əm), *n.* the belief that inanimate objects, like natural phenomena, possess souls or consciousness.

an·i·mos·i·ty (an,imos'itē), *n.* active ill-will or enmity.

an·i·mus (an'iməs), *n.* 1. animosity; hostility; antagonism. 2. an animating spirit.

ankh (aNGk), *n.* a cross with a loop on top: an ancient Egyptian symbol of life.

an·ky·lo·sis (aNGkilō'sis), *n.* the consolidation of articulating joints, forming a stiff joint.

an·nals (an'əlz), *n.* 1. a yearly record of events. 2. historical records.

an·neal (ənēl'), *v.* to toughen (as glass or metal) by heating and gradually cooling.

an·nex (aneks'), *v.* to add (something) in order to enlarge a thing that is larger or more important.

an·nexe, an·nex (an'eks), *n.* 1. a structure added to a building. 2. an item added or annexed, esp. to a document.

an·no ae·ta·tis su·ae (an'nō ītä'tis sōō'ī), *Latin.* in the year of his age; aged. *Abbr.:* **aet.**

an·nul (ənul'), *v.* to abolish; invalidate; cancel. **—an·nul'ment,** *n.*

an·nu·lar (an'yələr), *adj.* having a ringlike form.

an·nun·ci·ate (ənun'sēāt,), *v.* announce. **—an·nun,ci·a'tion,** *n.*

an·ode (an'ōd), *n.* 1. a positive electrode, emitting positive ions in a cell, etc. 2. the positive pole of a battery. 3. a positive plate in an electron tube.

an·o·dize (an'ədīz), *v.* to coat a metal with a protective film.

an·o·dyne (an'ədīn), *n.* anything, esp. a medicine, that relieves pain and soothes or tranquilizes.

a·nom·a·ly (ənom'əlē), *n.* 1. variation from the common form. 2. an irregularity or incongruity. 3. (in astronomy) the angular distance of a planet from its perihelion. **—a·nom'a·lous,** *adj.*

an·o·mie (an'əmē), *n.* the condition of an uprooted race, of individuals, or of their society, characterized by a breakdown of accepted values.

an·o·rex·i·a (an,ərek'sēə), *n.* an abnormal, often psychological inability to eat.

an·ox·aem·i·a, an·ox·em·i·a (an,oksē'mēə), *n.* lack of oxygen in the blood.

an·ox·i·a (anok'sēə), *n.* lack of sufficient oxygen in the blood.

An·schluss (an'sHlōōs), *n.* annexation, as the forced union of Austria and Germany in 1938.

Ant·a·buse (an'təbyōōs), *n.* a trade name for the drug disulfiram, used in the treatment of alcoholism by creating unpleasant reactions when combined with liquor.

An·tar·es (anter'ēz), *n.* a red supergiant star of the first magnitude in the constellation of Scorpius.

an·te·bel·lum (an,tēbel'əm), *adj.* before the war, especially the American War between the States.

an·te·ced·ent (an,təsē'dənt), *n.* 1. something or someone that has gone before, in time or in placement, as an ancestor or a word in a sentence to which another, later word refers. **—adj.** 2. going before; preceding; earlier in time or ahead in placement.

an·te·di·lu·vi·an (an,tēdilōō'vēan), *adj.*

before the (Biblical) flood; hence, ancient, antiquated.

an·te par·tum (an'tē pär'təm), pertaining to the period before childbirth. See also **post partum**.

an·te·pe·nult (an,tēpē'nult), *n*. **1**. the third from the last syllable of a word, as *te* in *antepenult*. **2**. the third from the last in any series. —an,te·pe·nul'ti·mate, *adj*.

an·te·ri·or (antē'rēə), *adj*. situated in or near the front. See also **posterior**.

an·thel·min·tic (an,thəlmin'tik, ant,helmin'-tik), *n*. an agent that destroys or expels parasitic worms, esp. from the gut. Also **an,thel·min'thic** (an,thəlmin'thik, ant,helmin'thik).

an·thro·po·cen·tric (an,thrəpōsen'trik), *adj*. assuming man to be the focal point of the universe. —an,thro·po·cen'trism, *n*.

an·thro·pom·e·try (an,thrəpom'itrē), *n*. the comparative study of the measurements of the human body. —an,thro·po·met'ri·cal. *adj*.

an·thro·po·mor·phic (an,thrəpōmôr'fik), *adj*. ascribing human form and attitudes as to a god. —an,thropo·mor'phism, *n*.

an·thro·poph·a·gi (an,thrəpof'əjī), *n. pl*. cannibals.

an·thro·pos·co·py (an,thrəpos'kəpē), *n*. See **physiognomy**.

an·thro·pos·o·phy (an,thrəpos'əfē), *n*. a philosophy emphasizing study of the nature of man, based on the teachings of Rudolf Steiner. —an,thro·po·soph'i·cal, **an,thro·po·soph'ic**, *adj*.

an·ti·bi·ot·ic (an,tēbīot'ik), *n*. a substance, as penicillin, produced by mould or fungi, that inhibits the growth of bacteria or other microorganisms.

an·ti·bo·dy (an'tibodē), *n*. a protein in blood plasma that reacts to overcome bacterial toxins and viruses.

an·ti·cryp·tic (an,tēkrip'tik), *adj*. concealing an animal from its prey. See also **procryptic**.

an·ti·cy·clone (an,tēsī'klōn), *n*. the circulation of winds round an area of high barometric pressure; clockwise in the Northern Hemisphere; counterclockwise in the Southern Hemisphere. See also **cyclone**. —an,ti·cy·clon'ic, *adj*.

an·ti·fer·ro·mag·net·ic (an,tēfer,ōmagnet'-ik), *adj*. pertaining to a substance the magnetic moments of whose adjacent atoms point in opposite directions at low temperatures. See also **diamagnetic, ferromagnetic, paramagnetic**.

an·ti·he·ro (an'tēhē,rō), *n*. in literature, etc., a central figure who lacks heroic attributes and noble qualities.

an·ti·his·ta·mine (an,tēhis'təmēn), *n*. any of certain medicines used in the treatment of allergies. See also **histamine**.

an·ti·knock (an,tēnok'), *adj*. pertaining to substances added to internal combustion engine fuel to minimize knock.

an·ti·mat·ter (an'tēmat,ər), *n*. matter composed of antiparticles.

an·ti·nov·el (an'tinov,əl), *n*. a work of prose fiction that discards traditional features of the novel.

an·ti·par·ti·cle (an'tēpä,tikəl), *n*. an elementary particle that annihilates a corresponding particle of the same mass upon collision.

an·tip·a·thy (antip'əthē), *n*. a settled aversion; a basic repugnance. —an,ti·pa·thet'ic, *adj*.

an·tip·o·des (antip'ədēz), *n. pl*. places diametrically opposite on the globe. —an·tip·o·de,-an (antip'ədēən), *adj., n*.

an·tith·e·sis (antith'əsis), *n., pl*. **an·tith·e·ses** (antith'əsēz). complete contrast or opposite. —an·ti·thet·ic (an,təthet'ik), —an,ti·thet'i·cal, *adj*.

an·ti·trust (an,tētrust'), *adj*. opposing the formation of commercial trusts that would tend to create monopolies.

an·ti·ven·in (an,tēven'in), *n*. an anti-toxin formed in blood following repeated injections of venom; hence, an antitoxic serum obtained from this blood.

an·to·no·ma·sia (an,tənəmā'ZHə), *n*. the use of a title or epithet, instead of a name, to identify a person. —an·to·no·mas·tic (an,tənəmas'tik), *adj*.

an·to·nym (an'tənim), *n*. a word that is opposite or nearly opposite in meaning to another, as *black* and *white, tall* and *short*, and *happy* and *sad*. See also **synonym**. —an·ton'y·mous, *adj*.

a·part·heid (əpät'hīt), *n*. the policy of racial segregation in the Republic of South Africa.

ap·a·tet·ic (ap,ətet'ik), *adj*. (of animals) assuming colours that afford camouflage.

ap·a·thet·ic (ap,əthet'ik), *adj*. having or showing mental or emotional indifference.

ap·a·thy (ap'əthē), *n*. an absence or lack of emotion, interest, or concern.

a·per·i·ent (əpēr'ēənt), *adj*. **1**. laxative. —*n*. **2**. a laxative food or medicine.

a·pha·sia (əfā'ziə, əfā'ZHə), *n*. impairment or loss of speech or the power to understand written or spoken language.

a·pha·si·ac (əfā'zēak), *n*. **1**. Also **apha·sic** (əfā'zik). a person suffering from aphasia. —*adj*. **2**. losing the power of speech or the ability to understand written or spoken language.

a·phe·li·on (əphē'liən, əfēl'yən), *n., pl*. **a·phe·li·a** (əphēliə, əfēl'yə). the point of a planet's or comet's orbit farthest from the sun. See also **perihelion**.

aph·o·rism (af'əriz,əm), *n*. a short, pithy maxim embodying a general truth. —aph·o·ris'-tic, *adj*.

aph·ro·dis·i·ac (af,rōdiz'ēak), *n*. an agent, as a drug, arousing sexual excitement.

a·pi·ar·y (ā'pēerē), *n*. a place for keeping bees. —a'pi·a·rist, *n*.

ap·i·cal (ap'ikəl), *adj.* pertaining to the tip or apex.

ap·i·cul·ture (ap'ikul,CHər), *n.* beekeeping.

a·plomb (əplum'), *n.* self-assurance and self-confidence, esp. when it enables one to retain his dignity and remain unperturbed.

a·poc·a·lypse (əpok'əlips), *n.* revelation, discovery, or disclosure, esp. through Scripture.

a·poc·a·lyp·tic (əpok,əlip'tik), *adj.* prophesying total destruction or great disasters.

ap·o·ca·tas·ta·sis (ap,ōkətas'təsis), *n.* restitution or reestablishment. —**ap·o·cat·a·stat·ic** (ap,-ōkat,əstat'ik), *adj.*

a·poc·o·pe (əpok'əpē), *n.* omission of the last letter or syllable of a word.

a·poc·ry·phal (əpok'rəfəl), *adj.* of false or doubtful origin.

ap·o·dic·tic (ap,ədik'tik), *adj.* incontrovertible; incontestable.

a·pod·o·sis (əpod'əsis), *n., pl.* **a·pod·o·ses** (əpod'əsēz). the consequence clause in a conditional sentence, beginning with *then.* See also **protasis.**

ap·o·gee (ap'əjē), *n.* **1.** the point where the moon or an earth satellite is farthest from the earth. See also **perigee. 2.** the climax, as of a career.

ap·o·logue (ap'əlog), *n.* a moral fable.

ap·o·mix·is (ap,əmik'sis), *n.* any of several kinds of asexual reproduction. —**ap·o·mic·tic** (ap,əmik'tik), *adj.*

ap·o·pemp·tic (ap,əpemp'tik), *adj.* pertaining to dismissal or departing.

ap·o·phthegm (ap'əthem), *n.* See **apothegm.** —**ap·o·phtheg·mat·ic** (ap,əthegmat'ik), *adj.*

a·poph·y·ge (əpof'əjē), *n.* (in architecture) a curve joining the base to the shaft of a column. Also **hypophyge.**

a·pos·ta·sy (əpos'təsē), *n.* a rejection of one's religion, allegiance, party, principles, etc.

a·pos·tate (əpos'tāt), *n.* **1.** one who rejects his faith, allegiance, party, principles, etc. —*adj.* **2.** characterized by apostasy.

a pos·te·ri·o·ri (ā' postē,rēôr'ī), **1.** proceeding from effect to cause. **2.** based upon observation. See also **a priori.**

ap·os·tol·ic delegate (ap,əstol'ik), a papal representative in a country where no diplomatic relations with the Vatican exist. See also **nuncio.**

ap·o·thegm (ap'əthəm) *n.* a pithy saying; maxim. Also **apophthegm.** —**ap·o·theg·mat·ic** (ap,əthegmat'ik), *adj.*

a·poth·e·o·sis (əpoth,ēō'sis), *n.* the raising of a person to be a god or an ideal.

ap·o·tro·pa·ic (ap,ōtrəpā'ik), *adj.* having power to ward off evil.

ap·pall·ing (əpôl'iNG), *adj.* horrifying; shocking; revolting. —**ap·pal** or *U.S.* **ap·pall,** *v.*

ap·pa·rat·chik (ap,əraCH'ik), *n.* secret agents, esp. when considered as part of the Soviet government.

ap·pease (əpēz'), *v.* **ap·peased, ap·peas·ing.** to pacify, esp. by making concessions. —**ap·pease'·ment,** *n.*

ap·pel·lant (əpel'ənt), *n.* (in law) one who appeals, esp. to a higher court.

ap·pel·late (əpel'it), *adj.* (in law) pertaining to or reviewing appeals, as a court.

ap·pel·la·tion (ap,əlā'sHən), *n.* a name or designation of someone or something.

ap·per·ceive (ap,əsēv'), *v.* (in psychology) to be conscious of perceiving. —**ap·per·cep·tion** (ap,əsep'sHən), *n.*

ap·pe·tence (ap'ətəns), *n.* intense natural desire; craving.

ap·pos·ite (ap'əzit, ap'əzīt), *adj.* pertinent; appropriate; suitable.

ap·pre·hend (ap,rəhend'), *v.* **1.** to arrest and take into custody, as a suspect. **2.** to understand or perceive. —**ap,pre·hen'sion,** *n.*

ap·pre·hen·sive (ap,rəhen'siv), *adj.* fearful or wary, esp. of something felt to be imminent.

ap·pur·te·nance (əpur'tənəns), *n.* something subordinate to another thing; accessory; appendage.

a pri·o·ri (ā' prīôr'ī, ä' prēôr'ē), **1.** proceeding from cause to effect. **2.** not based on observation; nonanalytic. See also **a posteriori.**

ap·te·ri·um (aptēr'ēəm), *n., pl.* **ap·te·ri·a** (aptēr'ēə). the part of a bird's body having no feathers. See also **pteryla.**

aq·ui·cul·ture (ak'wəkul,CHər), *n.* the cultivation of plants in a solution, not soil; hydroponics.

a·rach·noid (ərak'noid), *adj.* **1.** like a spider's web. **2.** like a spider or other member of the same class. **3.** the membrane forming the middle of three coverings of the spinal cord and brain. See also **dura mater, pia mater.**

ar·bi·ter (ä'bitər), *n.* a judge or one acting as a judge in deciding a dispute.

ar·bi·trage (ä'biträzH), *n.* the buying and selling simultaneously of securities, currencies, etc. in different places to profit by the different prices. —**ar·bi·tra·geur** (ä,biträzHù'), *n.*

ar·bit·ra·ment (äbit'rəmənt), *n.* arbitration; the deciding of a dispute by an agreed authority.

ar·bi·trar·y (ä'bitrer,ē), *adj.* decided in each instance by individual choice; unpredictable, because it is not governed by rule or law; random; capricious; not based on reason.

ar·bo·re·al (äbôr'ēəl), *adj.* **1.** pertaining to trees. **2.** living in trees.

ar·cane (äkān'), *adj.* obscure; secret; esoteric.

arch (äCH), *adj.* **1.** a chief, important, or principle one of its kind, as an *archfiend.* **2.** cunning, sly, or shrewd; too clever.

ar·che·type (ä'kətīp), *n.* a prototype from

which copies are made; original pattern or model. —ar,che·ty'pal, ar,che·typ'i·cal, adj.

ar·chi·tec·ton·ic (ä,kitekton'ik), adj. pertaining to architecture, esp. the principles of architecture.

ar·ci·fin·i·ous (ä,səfin'ēəs), adj. having a border that forms a natural barrier, as from invasion.

ar·col·o·gy (äkol'əjē), n. a combination of the fields of architecture and ecology. —ar·col'o·gist, n.

ar·cu·ate (ä'kyōoit, ä'kyōoāt), adj. curved or bent like a bow.

ar·du·ous (ä'jōoəs), adj. difficult; involving great labour or effort.

are (eə, ä), n. a unit of area measurement equalling 100 square metres.

ar·e·ca nut (ar'əkə, ərē'kə), the nut of a palm growing in tropical Asia, esp. the betel palm.

ar·e·na·ceous (ar,ənā'sHəs), adj. sandy. Also ar'e·nose.

a·rête (ərāt'), n. a sharp ridge of a mountain.

ar·got (ä'gō, ä'gət), n. a slang belonging to a group or class, esp. the private language of thieves.

ar·id (ar'id), adj. 1. dry or parched. 2. unimaginative; sterile; dull.

ar·ith·man·cy (ar'ithman,sē), n. prophecy by numbers, esp. the number of letters in names.

ar·ith·met·ic progression (ar,ithmet'ik), a series of numbers, as 2, 4, 6, 8, 10, etc., obtained by adding a constant number to the preceding number. See also **geometric progression, harmonic progression.**

Ar·ma·ged·don (ä,məged'ən), n. scene of the final battle between good and evil, esp. the battle on the Day of Judgment.

ar·ma·men·tar·i·um (ä,məmentâr'ēəm), n., pl. **ar·ma·men·tar·i·a.** the full array of techniques and equipment available for use, esp. by a physician.

ar·mip·o·tent (ämip'ətənt), adj. strong in arms; possessing powerful weapons.

ar·mo·man·cy (ä'məman,sē), n. prophecy by the shoulder bones of animals.

ar·mor·ist (ä'mərist), n. an expert in heraldry.

ar·rack (ar'ək), n. any of various spirituous liquors distilled from molasses, rice, etc.

ar·raign (ərān'), v. to accuse as before a court or tribunal. —ar·raign'ment, n.

ar·rant (ar'ənt), adj. absolute; complete, as an arrant idiot.

ar·rhyth·mi·a (əriTH'mēə), n. a disturbance in the rhythm of the heart-beat. —ar·rhyth'mic, adj.

ar·rière-pen·sée (äryer,pänsā'), French. a hidden motive.

ar·ri·viste (ar,ēvēst'), n. one who has acquired success or money by dubious methods.

ar·ro·gance (ar'əgəns), n. an attitude or pattern of behaviour resulting from a superior opinion of oneself; offensive conduct. —ar'ro·gant, adj.

ar·ro·gate (ar'əgāt), v. **ar·ro·gat·ed, ar·ro·gat·ing.** to take or claim (something) for oneself without justification.

ar·roy·o (əroi'ō), n. a small watercourse, dry except after rain, esp. in the SW U.S.

ars gra·ti·a ar·tis (äz grä'tēə ä'tis), Latin. art for art's sake.

ars lon·ga, vi·ta brev·is (äz loNG'gə vē'tə brev'is), Latin. art is long, life is short.

Art Dec·o (dek'ō). See **moderne.** Also **Art Dec·o·ra·tif** (dek,ərätēf'), **Art Dec·or** (dekôr').

ar·te·fact, ar·ti·fact (ä'təfakt), n. anything made by man.

ar·tel (ätel'), n. (in the former U.S.S.R.) a workers' cooperative.

ar·te·ri·o·scle·ro·sis (ätēr,ēosklerō'sis), n. a disease characterized by thickening of the artery walls. See also **atherosclerosis.** —ar·te,rio·scle·rot'ic, adj.

art·ful (ät'fəl), adj. 1. adroit; expert. 2. cunning; shrewd; clever to the point of deceit.

ar·tic·u·late (ätik'yəlāt,), v. 1. to express clearly and adroitly, as an idea, the pronunciation of a word, etc. —adj. (ätik'yəlit). 2. able to express oneself clearly, adroitly, and in few words.

ar·ti·fice (ä'təfis), n. a trick or wile.

art·less (ät'ləs), adj. 1. unskilful; without art or taste. 2. innocently naive; simple and sincere; unsophisticated; guileless.

Art Nou·veau (nōōvō'), a style of the late 19th and early 20th centuries, characterized by highly stylized patterns of vines and entwined flowers.

as·bes·to·sis (as,bestō'sis), n. a condition of the lung caused by inhaling asbestos dust.

as·cend·er (əsen'də), n. (in lowercase letters) the part extending upwards above the top of an 'x' of the same size and typeface. See also **descender.**

as·cer·tain (as,ətān'), v. to discover, determine, or find out, as He ascertained the reason why the car wouldn't start.

as·ce·sis (əsē'sis), n., pl. **as·ce·ses** (əsē'sēz). the practising of self-discipline.

as·cet·ic (əset'ik), n. 1. one who practises severe self-denial, as for religious reasons. —adj. 2. austere; self-denying. —as·cet'i·cism, n.

a·scribe (əskrīb'), v. **a·scribed, ascrib·ing.** to assign, esp. after determining, as She ascribed the origin of the text to the ancient city of Ur. —a·scrip'tion, n.

a·sep·sis (əsep'sis, āsep'sis), n. absence of sepsis as in wounds. —a·sep'tic, adj.

Ashcan School, a group of artists of the early 20th century in America who painted scenes of city life in a sardonic style.

Ash·ke·na·zim (äsн,kənä'zim), *n. pl.* Jews of central and eastern Europe or their descendants.

ash·lar (asн'lə), *n.* a square-cut building stone; such stones collectively.

as·i·nine (as'ənīn), *adj.* stupid; silly; idiotic.

a·skance (əskans'), *adv.* 1. with disapproval or mistrust. 2. obliquely; sidewise.

a·so·ma·tous (əsō'mətəs), *adj.* bodiless; incorporeal.

as·par·tic acid (əspä'tik), an amino acid, recently identified in a meteorite, used in the preparation of culture media.

as·per·i·ty (asper'ətē), *n.* 1. sharpness of manner. 2. unevenness of surface.

as·perse (əspûs'), *v.* 1. to slander or attack with damaging charges. 2. to spatter.

as·per·sion (əspər'zнən), *n.* a statement or comment blaming another for something bad; a criticism.

as·pire (əspīə'), *v.* **as·pired, as·piring.** to hope or yearn for (something or a stated condition), as *She aspired to be the first to climb Annapurna* or *He aspired to recognition for his scholarship.* **—as,pi·ra'tion,** *n.*

as·sen·ti·ent (əsen'sнēənt), *adj.* 1. agreeing or sanctioning. **—n.** 2. one who assents.

as·sev·er·ate (əsev'ərāt), *v.* to affirm earnestly; aver. **—as·sev,er·a'tion,** *n.*

as·si·du·i·ty (as,idyōō'itē), *n.* constant perseverance; industry.

as·sid·u·ous (əsid'yōōəs), *adj.* persevering; constant; unremitting.

as·sig·na·tion (asəgnä'sнən), *n.* an arrangement to meet, esp. a secret lovers' meeting.

as·sim·i·la·ble (əsim'ələbəl), *adj.* that may be assimilated.

as·sim·i·late (əsim'əlāt), *v.* 1. to take in; absorb; understand fully. 2. to digest and convert (food) for absorption into the system. 3. to adapt or adjust; become like. See also **dissimilate. —as·sim,i·la'tion,** *n.* **—assim'i·la,tive,** *adj.*

as·suage (əswāj'), *v.* to relieve; ease; soothe.

as·ter·oid (as'təroid), *n.* any of the thousands of minor planets revolving round the sun between the orbits of Mars and Jupiter.

as·then·ic (asthen'ik), *adj.* relating to or denoting a physical type characterized by a tall, narrow, lean build. See also **athletic, leptosome, pyknic.**

as·tig·ma·tism (əstig'mətiz,əm), *n.* a defect of vision resulting from irregular curvature of the cornea.

as·tra·pho·bi·a (as,trəfō'bēə), *n.* an abnormally intense fear of thunder and lightning.

as·tro·gate (as'trəgāt), *v.* to navigate a spacecraft in space. **—as,tro·ga'tion,** *n.*

as·tro·man·cy (as'trəman,sē), *n.* prophecy by means of the stars.

as·tro·naut (as'trənôt,), *n.* one who has trav-

elled beyond the earth's atmosphere. Also **cosmonaut.**

as·tro·nau·tics (as,trənô'tiks), *n.* the science of space travel.

as·tro·phys·ics (as,trōfiz'iks), *n.* the branch of astronomy dealing with the physical properties of celestial bodies. **—as,tro·phys'i·cist,** *n.*

a·stute (əstyōōt'), *adj.* characterized by intelligent, discerning insight, as *an astute remark.*

at·a·rax·i·a (at,ərak'sēə), *n.* a calm and tranquil state free from anxiety. **—at,a·rac'tic, at,a·rax'ic,** *adj.*

at·a·vism (at'əviz,əm), *n.* the exhibiting of traits or characteristics of an ancestor; a return to an early or original type. **—at,a·vis'tic,** *adj.*

at·e·lier (ətel'yā), *n.* a craftsman's workshop or an artist's studio.

ath·er·o·scle·ro·sis (ath,ərōsklərō'sis), *n.* a form of arteriosclerosis characterized by fatty substances in the intima. See also **arteriosclerosis. —ath,er·o·scle·rot'ic,** *adj.*

ath·let·ic (athlet'ik), *adj.* relating to or denoting a physical type characterized by a sturdy, well-proportioned build. See also **asthenic, leptosome, pyknic.**

at·las (at'ləs), *n.,* *pl.* **at·lan·tes** (atlan'tēz). a male figure serving as a supporting column. See also **caryatid.**

atmospheric boundary layer. See **surface boundary layer.**

at·ra·bil·i·ous (at,rəbil'ēəs), *adj.* morose; gloomy; sad.

a·tri·um (ā'trēəm), *n.* either of the two heart chambers that receive blood from the veins.

at·ro·phy (at'rəfē), *n.* 1. a withering away of an organ in the body. **—v.** 2. to waste away, as from lack of use. **—a·troph·ic** (ətrof'ik), *adj.*

at·ta·ché (atasн'ā), *n.* a diplomatic official employed in a technical capacity on the staff of an embassy, as *a military attaché.*

at·tain (ətān'), *v.* to reach or obtain, as to attain glory. **—at·tain'ment,** *n.*

at·ten·u·ate (əten'yōōāt), *v.* 1. to make slender or thin. 2. to reduce in force or value. **—adj.** 3. slender; tapering. **—at·ten,u·a'tion,** *n.*

at·test (ətest'), *v.* to confirm, verify, or certify, as *She attested to the truth of his remarks.*

at·ti·tu·di·nize (at,ityōō'dinīz), *v.* to pose; strike an attitude.

at·tra·hent (at'rəhənt), *adj.* drawing to; attracting.

at·trib·ute (ətrib'yōōt), *v.* **at·trib·ut·ed, at·trib·ut·ing.** 1. to assign or identify as a source, reason, etc., as *He attributed his sleepiness to the medicine.* **—n.** (at'rəbyōōt). 2. a characteristic or identifying feature; something representative of a person or thing. **—at,tri·bu'tion,** *n.*

at·trite (ətrīt'), *v.* to wear away as by harassment or by friction. **—at·tri'tion** (ətrisн'ən), *n.*

a·typ·i·cal (ātip'ikəl), *adj.* deviating from type; not typical; irregular.

au con·traire (ō kəntreə'), *French.* on the contrary.

au cou·rant (ō kōōräN'), *French.* up-to-date; aware of the latest trends, news, etc.

auc·to·ri·al (awktôr'ēəl), *adj.* relating to an author.

au·di·ent (ô'dēənt), *adj.* hearing; listening.

au·di·o·phile (ô'dēəfīl,), *n.* an enthusiast in listening to high-fidelity sound reproduction of recorded or broadcast music.

au·di·o·vis·u·al (ô,dēôvizH'ōōəl), *adj.* simultaneously involving hearing and sight.

au fait (ō fe'), *French.* versed, expert, or knowledgeable in something.

Au·ge·an (ôjē'ən), *adj.* extremely filthy or corrupt, as the stables of King Augeas which, according to Greek mythology, remained uncleaned for 30 years.

aug·ment (ôgment'), *v.* to increase in size or extent, amount or degree.

au·gur (ô'gər), *n.* **1.** a soothsayer or prophet. —*v.* **2.** to foretell the future. —**au·gu·ry** (ô'gyərē), *n.*

au·gust (ôgust'), *adj.* majestic; noble; very eminent.

au na·tu·rel (ō natərel'), *French.* **1.** naked. **2.** cooked simply. **3.** uncooked.

au·re·ate (ôr'ēət, ôr'āt,), *adj.* **1.** of a golden colour or gilded. **2.** (of speech or writing) excessively ornate or elaborate; pompous.

au·re·ole (ôr'ēōl), *n.* **1.** a halo. **2.** the sun's corona during a total eclipse.

au·ric·u·lar (ôrik'yələr), *adj.* **1.** relating to or using the ear or sense of hearing. **2.** resembling an ear. **3.** relating to the upper chamber of the heart.

au·rif·er·ous (ôrif'ərəs), *adj.* (of rock) bearing gold.

au·rist (ôr'ist), *n.* an ear specialist; otologist.

aus·cul·tate (ôs'kəltāt), *v.* to examine internal organs by listening to them through a stethoscope. —**aus,cul·ta'tion,** *n.*

aus·pi·cious (ôspisH'əs), *adj.* favourable; propitious; predicting success.

aus·tere (ôstēə'), *adj.* **1.** stern and reserved in manner, attitude, or appearance; serious; solemn. **2.** simple; without luxury, decoration, or ornament, as a lifestyle, writing style, etc.

aus·tral (ô'strəl), *adj.* southerly; pertaining to the south or the south wind. See also **boreal, occidental, oriental.**

aut·e·col·o·gy (ôtikol'əjē), *n.* the ecology of a community of plants and animals regarded as individual species. See also **synecology.**

au·toch·tho·nous (ôtok,thənəs), *adj.* pertaining to the original inhabitants or plants of a region. See also **allochthonous.**

au·to·ci·dal (ôt,ōsī'dəl), *adj.* describing a form of pest control in which genetically altered or sterile individuals are introduced to the wild population.

au·to·clave (ô'tōklāv), *n.* an apparatus for sterilization by steam at high pressure

au·toc·ra·cy (ôtok'rəsē), *n.* **1.** government by one absolute ruler. **2.** a state so governed. —**au·to·crat·ic** (ô,təkrat'ik), *adj.*

au·to·crat (ô'təkrat), *n.* a person, esp. one in a position of power, who exercises stern authority over others. —**au·toc'ra·cy,** *n.* —**au,to·cra'tic,** *adj.*

au·to·da·fé (ô,tōdäfā'), *n., pl.* **autos·da·fé.** the public burning of heretics condemned by the Spanish Inquisition. [literally, 'act of faith']

au·to·di·dact (ô'tōdī,dakt), *n.* a self-taught person.

au·to·e·rot·ic (ô,tōirot'ik), *adj.* producing sexual excitement without another person. —**au·to·er·o·tism** (ô,tōer'ətizm), *n.*

au·to·mate (ô'təmāt), *v.* to introduce the use of automatic devices to processes formerly either performed or controlled by people. —**au,to·ma'tion,** *n.*

au·tom·a·ton (ôtom'əton), *n., pl.* **au·tom·a·ta.** **1.** a mechanical figure or device which moves itself. **2.** a person who acts mechanically.

au·to·nom·ic nervous system (ô,tənom'ik), the nervous system that controls the involuntary functions of the heart, blood vessels, etc.

au·ton·o·my (ôton'əmē), *n.* self-government; the power or right of self-government. —**au·ton'o·mous,** *adj.*

au·to·nym (ô'tənim), *n.* one's real name; an author's own name.

au·to·troph (ô'tətrof), *n.* a micro-organism using carbon dioxide as its source of carbon. See also **heterotroph.** —**au,to·troph'ic,** *adj.*

au·tres temps, au·tres moeurs (ōtrə täN' ōtrə mûs'), *French.* other times, other customs.

aux·e·sis (ôgzē'sis, ôksē'sis), *n.* induction of cell division, esp. by the influence of a chemical agent. See also **merisis.**

aux·o·car·di·a (ôk,sōka'dēə), *n.* enlargement of the heart.

a·vant·garde (a,voNgäd'), *adj.* **1.** characterized by unorthodox and experimental treatment of visual, literary, or musical material. —*n.* **2.** the radical group in these fields.

av·a·tar (avətä'), *n.* **1.** (in Hindu mythology) an incarnation of a god. **2.** the manifestation or display of an attitude or principle.

a·ver (əvû'), *v.* **1.** to declare with confidence; to affirm strongly. **2.** (in law) to assert as a fact. —**a·ver'ral,** *n.*

a·verse (əvûs'), *adj.* having a feeling of repugnance; opposed; disinclined. See also **adverse.**

a·ver·sion (əvû'zHən), *n.* a strong dislike for something, as *an aversion to stewed prunes.*

a·vi·an (ā'vēən), *adj.* pertaining to birds.

a·vi·ar·y (ā'vēerē), *n*. a large cage, or building, containing cages for housing birds.

a·vi·cul·ture (ā'vikul,CHər), *n*. the breeding or keeping of birds.

av·id (av'id), *adj*. energetically eager. —**a·vid'·i·ty**, *n*.

av·i·ga·tion (av,igā'SHən), *n*. aerial navigation.

a·vi·on·ics (ā,vēon'iks), *n*. the science and application of electronics in aviation.

av·o·ca·tion (av,ōkā'SHən), *n*. a hobby or pastime.

a·vow (əvou'), *v*. to attest or declare openly and directly; acknowledge or admit. —**a·vow·al**, *n*.

a·vun·cu·lar (əvuNG'kyələr), *adj*. **1.** pertaining to or characteristic of an uncle. **2.** kind; cheerful.

a·wry (ərī'), *adj*. crooked; askew; not set straight or properly.

ax·i·om (ak'sēəm), *n*. a generally accepted principle or proposition; a self-evident truth. —**ax,i·o·mat'ic**, *adj*.

ax·on (ak'son), *n*. a nerve fibre of the neuron which transmits impulses away from the cell. Also **neurite**. See also **neuron**.

a·zon·ic (āzō'nik), *adj*. not local; not restricted to a particular zone.

az·y·gous (az'igəs), *adj*. not forming one of a pair, as a leaf or a bodily organ.

B

Bab·bitt (bab'it), *n.* a complacent person who conforms unthinkingly to middle-class standards.

Ba·bel·ize (bā'bəlīz), *v.* to make confused or unintelligible.

Ba·bin·ski effect (bəbin'skē), a reflex upward (instead of downward) movement of the big toe, caused by stroking the sole of the foot.

bab·ka (bäb'kə), *n.* a sweet-flavoured yeast cake, spongy in texture and made with raisins.

ba·boon·er·y (baboō'nərē), *n.* uncouth or stupid behaviour.

ba·bush·ka (bəboōsh'kə), *n.* a woman's scarf, worn as a head covering with the ends tied under the chin.

bac·ca·lau·re·ate (bak,əlôr'ōit), *n.* **1.** a bachelor's degree. **2.** a religious service at a university or other educational institution.

bac·cha·nal (bak'ənəl), *n.* **1.** a drunken reveller. **2.** a drunken orgy or feast.

bac·chant (bak'ənt), *n.* a devotee of Bacchus, the ancient Greek god of wine; a drunken reveller.

Bac·chic (bak'ik), *adj.* pertaining to Bacchus, the ancient Greek god of wine; riotously drunk.

bac·cif·er·ous (baksif'ərəs), *adj.* bearing or yielding berries.

bac·ci·form (bak'sifôəm), *adj.* shaped like a berry; coccoid.

bac·civ·or·ous (baksiv'ərəs), *adj.* feeding on berries.

bac·il·lar·y (bəsil'ərē), *adj.* **1.** shaped like a rod or bacillus. **2.** pertaining to or produced by bacilli.

ba·cil·lus (bəsil'əs), *n.* any of various rod-shaped bacteria producing spores in the presence of free oxygen.

back bench, any of the seats reserved for backbenchers. See also **front bench.**

back·bench·er (bak'ben'CHər), *n.* any member of the British House of Commons who does not sit on the front benches reserved for those holding ministerial posts and for opposition party spokesmen.

back·lash (bak'lasH), *n.* any sudden or violent reaction, esp. one against a movement of reform, etc.

back·sheesh (bak,sHēsH'), *n.* See **baksheesh.**

back·ward·a·tion (bak,wərdā'sHən), *n.* a fee paid by a seller of stock on the London Stock Exchange to the buyer in compensation for its deferred delivery. See also **contango.**

bac·te·ri·a (baktēr'ēə), *n. pl., sing.* **bac·te·ri·um** (baktēr'ēəm). any of numerous microscopic organisms found in organic matter and causing putrefaction, fermentation, disease, etc.

bac·te·ri·cide (baktēr'isīd), *n.* something capable of destroying bacteria.

bac·te·ri·ol·o·gy (baktēr,ēol'əjē), *n.* the science or study of bacteria.

bac·te·ri·ol·y·sis (baktēr,ēol'isis), *n.* the destruction or dissolution of bacteria.

bac·te·ri·o·phage (baktēr'ēəfāj), *n.* a virus that attacks certain bacteria.

bac·te·ri·os·co·py (baktēr,ēos'kəpē), *n.* the examination of bacteria under a microscope.

bac·te·ri·o·sta·sis (baktēr,ēəstā'sis), *n.* the inhibition of the growth of bacteria without destroying them.

bac·te·ri·o·stat (baktēr'ēəstat), *n.* anything that inhibits the growth of bacteria.

bac·ter·oid (bak'təroid), *n.* **1.** any of the rodlike or branched organisms found in the root nodules of nitrogen-fixing plants. —*adj.* **2.** resembling bacteria. Also **bac·te'ri·oid.**

bac·te·roi·des (bak,təroi'dēz), *n., pl.* **bac·te·roi·des.** any of a number of rodlike bacteria found in man and animals.

ba·cu·li·form (bəkyoō'lifôəm,), *adj.* shaped like a rod.

bac·u·line (bak'yəlin), *adj.* pertaining to the cane or rod or its use as a means of punishment.

ba·di·geon (bədij'ən), *n.* a substance used to repair superficial defects in woodwork or masonry.

bad·i·nage (bad'inäzн,), *n.* light, playful repartee or banter; teasing; raillery.

ba·gasse (bəgas'), *n.* the residue left after making sugar from sugar cane or beets.

bag·a·telle (bagətel'), *n.* **1.** an unimportant trifle; something of little value. **2.** a short, light piece of music. **3.** a game, similar to billiards, played on an oblong board with a cue and balls.

ba·gel (bā'gəl), *n.* a hard roll shaped like a doughnut, made of leavened dough that has been boiled before baking.

bagn·io (ban'yō), *n.* **1.** a brothel. **2.** an Oriental prison for slaves. **3.** a public bath or bathing house.

ba·guette (baget'), *n.* **1.** a gem cut in a rectangular shape; this shape. **2.** (in architecture) a small moulding.

ba·hu·vri·hi (bä,hōōvrē'hē), *n.* a compound noun or adjective comprising two parts, the first, which is adjectival, describing the second, which is substantival, as *fairminded, redeye*.

bail·iff (bā'lif), *n.* **1.** (in Britain) an officer employed by a sheriff to serve writs, make arrests, etc. **2.** (in Britain) the overseer or manager of an estate or farm. **3.** (in the U.S.) a minor officer in some courts.

bail·i·wick (bā'liwik), *n.* **1.** The area in which a bailiff has jurisdiction. **2.** one's sphere of interest, skill, authority, or responsibility.

bain-ma·rie (ban,mərē'), *n.*, *pl.* **bains-marie** (ban,mərē'). a vessel containing hot water inside which another vessel, usually containing food, is placed for heating.

ba·kla·va (bäk'ləvä,), *n.* a pastry, originating in Near Eastern countries, made of thin dough filled with nuts and honey.

bak·sheesh, back·sheesh (bak,SHēSH'), *n.* (in Eastern countries) a gratuity, tip; alms.

bal·a·cla·va (bal,əklä'və), *n.* a close-fitting woollen covering for the head and ears.

bal·a·lai·ka (bal,əlī'kə), *n.* a Russian musical instrument, similar to a guitar, having a triangular shaped body.

balance of payments, the difference between a country's total payments to foreign nations and its total income from them.

balance of power, the distribution of forces among two or more countries to prevent any one of them from becoming the dominant power.

balance of trade, the difference in monetary value between a country's imports and exports.

bal·a·noid (bal'ənoid), *adj.* having the shape of an acorn.

bal·a·ta (bal'ətə), *n.* a gum obtained from the latex of the bully tree, used in making golf balls, machinery belts, etc.

ba·laus·tine (bəlôs'tin), *n.* the dried flowers of the pomegranate used in the preparation of medicines.

bal·brig·gan (balbrig'ən), *n.* a cotton fabric used in underwear and hosiery.

bal·co·net (bal,kənet'), *n.* a railing outside a window giving the effect of a balcony.

bal·da·chin, bal·da·quin (bal'dəkin), *n.* **1.** a silk fabric embroidered with gold or silver threads. **2.** a canopy carried over an important person or sacred object in religious processions. **3.** a canopy over an altar, etc.

bal·der·dash (bôl'dərdaSH), *n.* a meaningless or nonsensical verbal hotchpotch.

bal·dric (bôl'drik), *n.* a belt, often ornamented, worn over one shoulder to support a sword, etc.

ba·leen (bəlēn'), *n.* whalebone.

bale·ful (bāl'fəl), *adj.* having a deadly or malicious influence; harmful; pernicious.

Balkan frame, a frame over a bed for supporting a broken limb in a splint in traction.

Bal·kan·ize (bôl'kənīz), *v.* to split up a large region or country into small relatively impotent and often mutually conflicting states. **—Bal,-kan·i·za'tion,** *n.*

balk·y, baulk·y (bô'kē, bôl'kē), *adj.* liable to stop suddenly.

bal·let·o·mane (balet'əmān), *n.* a lover of the ballet.

bal·lis·tic (bəlis'tik), *adj.* pertaining to the study of the motion of projectiles.

bal·lis·to·car·di·o·graph (bəlis,tōkä'dēəgräf,), *n.* a device used in medicine to ascertain cardiac output. **—bal·lis,to·car'di·o·gram,,** *n.*

bal·lotte·ment (bəlot'mənt), *n.* a technique for detecting a floating object in a fluid-filled part of the body, esp. the fetus in the womb. A sharp tap is given to the body wall using the fingers, causing the object to move through the fluid and give a characteristic rebound tap on the body wall.

bal·lot·tine (bal'ətēn), *n.* a dish of meat, poultry, or fish, prepared as a kind of galantine, usually served hot.

bal·ly·hoo (bal'əhōō), *n.* exaggerated or blatant publicity on behalf of a cause; clamour; outcry.

bal·ma·caan (bal,məkän'), *n.* a short overcoat for men, usually of rough wool and with raglan shoulders.

bal·ne·al (bal'nēəl), *adj.* pertaining to baths or bathing.

bal·ne·ol·o·gy (bal,nēol'əjē), *n.* the science or study of the therapeutic use of baths and bathing.

bal·op·ti·con (balop'tikon), *n.* an apparatus used for projecting images of objects by reflected light; overhead projector.

bal·us·ter (bal'əstə), *n.* one of a series of upright supports for a banister.

bal·us·trade (bal'əsträd), *n.* a banister with its supporting row of balusters.

ba·nal (bənäl'), *adj.* lacking originality; trite; commonplace; stereotyped.

ba·naus·ic (bənô'sik), *adj.* of practical use only; utilitarian; functional.

ban·deau (bandō'), *n.* a band or ribbon worn around the forehead for ornamentation or for binding the hair.

ban·de·ril·la (ban,dərē'ə), *n.* a barbed, decorated dart used by banderilleros in bullfighting.

ban·de·ril·le·ro (ban,dərēer'ō), *n.*, *pl.* **ban·de·ril·le·ros** (ban,dərēer'ôs). (in bullfighting) a matador's assistant who sticks banderillas in the back of the bull's neck.

ban·dog (ban'dog,), *n.* any dog kept chained, esp. a mastiff or bloodhound.

ban·do·leer (ban,dəlēr'), *n.* a belt worn over the shoulder, having small pockets or loops for holding cartridges. Also **ban,do·lier'**.

ban·dy (ban'dē), *v.* to exchange; pass from one to another; convey to and fro.

bane (bān), *n.* a cause of death or disaster; a curse.

Ban·ga·lore torpedo (baNG,əlôr'), a metal pipe containing an explosive mixture and used for making gaps in barbed wire, detonating mines, etc.

banns (banz), *n.* a proclamation, esp. one given in church, of an intended marriage.

ban·tam·weight (ban'təmwāt,), *n.* a boxer whose maximum weight for his class does not exceed 118 pounds.

ban·ter (ban'tə), *n.* **1.** light, playful teasing. —*v.* **2.** to speak in a teasing or playful manner; make fun of.

ban·zai (bänzī'), *interj., n.* a Japanese patriotic cry or cheer of triumph. [literally, '(may you live) 10,000 years']

bar·aes·the·sia (bäris*th*ē'z*ē*ə), *n.* the ability to perceive pressure. Also **bar·es·the·sia.**

bar·ag·no·sis (bar,əgnō'sis), *n.* lack or loss of ability to judge the weight of an object. See also **barognosis.**

bar·bi·tone (bä'bi,tōn), *n.* a hypnotic drug. Also **bar·bi·tal** (bä'bital).

bar·bi·tu·rate (bäbit'yurit, bäbit'yurāt), *n.* any of a group of organic compounds used as sedatives or hypnotics.

bar·bi·tur·ism (bäbit'yəriz,əm), *n.* poisoning resulting from excessive use of barbiturates.

bar·ca·role, bar·ca·rolle (bä'kərōl), *n.* a Venetian boat song or a piece of music in imitation of this.

bar·chan (bäkän'), *n.* a sand dune formed in the shape of a crescent, with the ends pointing away from the direction of the wind.

bar·es·the·sia (bäris*th*ē'zēə), *n.* See **baraesthesia.**

bar·ghest (bä'gest), *n.* an evil spirit appearing as an omen of death or misfortune.

Bar·me·cid·al (bä,misī'dəl), *adj.* providing an illusion of plenty or abundance; illusory.

bar mitz·vah (bä, mits'və), **1.** a ceremony marking the formal admittance of a boy as an adult member of the Jewish community. **2.** the boy himself. See also **bath mitzvah.**

barn (bän), *n.* a unit used for measuring cross-sectional areas of atomic nuclei. 10^{-24} sq. cm.

bar·og·no·sis (bar,əgnō'sis), *n.* the ability to judge variations in weight of an object. See also **baragnosis.**

bar·o·gram (bar'əgram), *n.* a graph traced by a barograph.

bar·o·graph (bar'əgräf), *n.* a barometer which records automatically.

ba·rom·e·ter (bərom'itə), *n.* an instrument which indicates relative changes in atmospheric pressure.

bar·on·et (bar'ənit), *n.* (in England) a member of a hereditary order below a baron and above a knight.

ba·roque (bərōk', bərok'), *n.* an extravagant style in European art and architecture, often characterized by elaborate and even grotesque ornamentation, prevalent in the 17th and early 18th centuries.

bar·o·ther·mo·graph (ba,əthur'məgräf,), *n.* an instrument that automatically records atmospheric pressure and temperature.

bar·o·ther·mo·hy·gro·graph (bar,əthur,-məhī'grəgräf,), *n.* an instrument that automatically records atmospheric pressure, temperature, and humidity.

bar·o·trau·ma (bar,ətrô'mə), *n., pl.* **bar·o·trau·ma·ta** (bar,ətrô'mətə, bar,ətrōmä'tə), **bar·o·trau·mas.** injury to the eardrum caused by a change in atmospheric pressure.

bar·ra·tor (bar'ətə), *n.* one who commits barratry.

bar·ra·try (bar'ətrē), *n.* **1.** a fraudulent or negligent action by the captain or crew of a ship at the expense of the owners. **2.** frequent instigation of quarrels and lawsuits, considered as an illegal action. **3.** traffic in ecclesiastical promotions or offices of state.

bar·rel·house (bar'əlhous,), *n.* a vigorous, rough and crude style of jazz.

bar·rio (bär'ryô), *n.* **1.** (in Spain and Spanish-American countries) one of the sections into which a town or city is divided. **2.** (in other countries, esp. the U.S.) an area in a city occupied by Latin Americans.

ba·sal (bā'səl), *adj.* relating to or constituting the base; basic; essential; minimal.

ba·salt (bas'ôlt), *n.* a dark-coloured, dense, igneous rock of volcanic origin, often found in the form of hexagonal columns.

bash·i·ba·zouk (bas*H*'ēbəzŏŏk'), *n.* a member of an irregular force of mounted troops in the Ottoman Empire.

bas·i·lar (bas'ilə), *adj.* relating to, growing from, or situated at, the base. Also **bas'i·lar,y.**

ba·sil·ic (bəsil'ik), *adj.* pertaining to a king; regal; royal.

ba·sil·i·ca (bəsil'ikə), *n.* an early Christian or medieval church.

bas·i·lisk (bas'əlisk), *n.* **1.** a mythical reptile said to have a fatal breath and glance. **2.** a small lizard of tropical America.

bas·i·net, bas·ci·net (bas'init, bas'inet,), *n.* a light steel helmet worn under a larger helmet.

ba·so·phil, ba·so·phile (bā'zōfil), *n.* **1.** a cell, esp. a white blood cell, that stains with basic dyes. —*adj.* **2.** describing cells or cell contents that stain with basic dyes. *Adj.* also **ba‚so·phil'ic.**

bas·re·lief (bä‚rəlēf', bas‚rilēf'), *n.* a kind of sculpture in which the projecting parts stand out only slightly from the surrounding surface. Also **bas·so·ri·lie·vo** (bas‚ōrilē'vō). See also **alto·rilievo.**

bastard title. See **half title.**

bas·ti·na·do (bas‚tənā'dō), *n., pl.* **bas·ti·na·does.** a blow or a beating with a stick, esp. as applied to the soles of the feet as a method of punishment.

bas·tion (bas'tiən, bas'chən), *n.* a fortress or strongpoint.

bath mitz·vah, bas mitz·vah (bäs, mits'·və), **1.** a ceremony marking the formal admittance of a girl as an adult member of the Jewish community. **2.** the girl herself. See also **bar mitzvah.**

ba·thos (bā'thos), *n.* **1.** a descent from the sublime to the ludicrous or from the exalted to the commonplace. **2.** sentimentality; pathos lacking sincerity.

bath·y·al (bath'ēəl), *adj.* pertaining to the ocean depths.

bath·y·met·ric (bath‚əmet'rik), *adj.* pertaining to the measurement of depths of water in oceans, seas, and lakes. **—ba·thym'e·trist,** *n.* **—ba·thym'e·try,** *n.*

bath·y·pe·lag·ic (bath‚əpəlaj'ik), *adj.* pertaining to the deeper parts of an ocean.

bath·y·scaphe (bath'iskāf), *n.* a submersible sphere used for exploring the depths of the ocean. Also **bathy·scaph** (bath'əskaf), **bath·y·scape** (bath'əskāp).

bath·y·sphere (bath'isfēr), *n.* a spherical diving chamber for deep-sea observation.

ba·tik, bat·tik (bətēk', bat'ik), *n.* a method of preparing fabrics for hand-dyeing by coating with wax the parts which are not to be dyed.

ba·tiste (bətēst'), *n.* a fine, usually sheer fabric of plain weave.

bat·man (bat'mən), *n.* the soldier servant of a British army officer.

ba·tra·chi·an (bətrā'kēən), *adj.* pertaining to the vertebrate amphibians, as frogs, toads, etc.

bat·tol·o·gize (bətol'əjīz), *v.* to repeat words or phrases excessively in speech or writing.

bat·tol·o·gy (bətol'əjē), *n.* the constant, tiresome repetition of words in speech or writing.

baud (bôd), *n.* a measure, equivalent to one unit per second, used to ascertain the speed of signalling.

Bau·haus (bou'hous,), *adj.* pertaining to a school of design established in Germany in 1918 that emphasized chiefly the functional aspect of design.

bau·xite (bôk'sīt), *n.* a rock, the chief ore of aluminium.

ba·var·dage (bav‚ädäzh'), *n.* foolish or nonsensical talk.

bawd (bôd), *n.* a prostitute; a woman who keeps a brothel.

bawd·y (bô'dē), *adj.* indecent; obscene; salacious.

bay·ou (bī'ōō), *n.* a creek, tributary, or outlet of a river, etc.

ba·zoo·ka (bəzōō'kə), *n.* a portable rocket launcher, for destroying tanks and other armoured vehicles.

bea·dle (bē'dəl), *n.* **1.** an official who supervises ceremonial processions at British universities. **2.** a minor parish official.

bear·ish (ber'ish), *adj.* marking or tending towards a decline in stock exchange prices; economically unfavourable, occasioning investors' cautious retreat. See also **bullish.**

beat generation, those who matured after World War II, and who, through disillusionment, rejected traditional moral standards and sought refuge in mysticism and the relaxation of social tensions.

beat·nik (bēt'nik), *n.* one who rejects traditional standards and adopts unconventional behaviour, dress, etc.

beau geste (bō, zhest'), *pl.* **beaux gestes** (bō, zhest'). a graceful or conciliatory gesture, esp. one intended only for effect.

beau monde (bō, mônd'), the world of fashionable society.

bec·que·rel (bek‚ərel'), *n.* the SI unit of radioactivity.

be·dight (bidīt'), *adj.* decorated; ornamented.

be·di·zen (bidī'zən), *v.* to ornament or dress gaudily or vulgarly.

be·fall (bifôl'), *v.* **be·fell, be·falling.** *Chiefly literary.* to happen (to); occur (to); take place, as *It befell that I was at home when a message arrived.*

be·guile (bigīl'), *v.* to deceive or influence by trickery; charm; captivate.

be·gum (bē'gəm), *n.* a Muslim woman or widow of high rank.

be·half (bihäf'), *n.* interest, benefit, or advantage of someone, as *He spoke up on her behalf.*

be·hav·iour·ism (bihā'vyəriz‚əm), *n.* a theory in psychology that emphasizes the importance of the objective study of facts of behaviour and actual responses.

be·he·moth (bihē'məth), *n.* a huge and powerful animal or man.

be·laud (bilôd'), *v.* to bestow lavish praises upon, esp. with the aim of causing ridicule.

bel·dam (bel'dəm), *n.* an old woman; a hag.

be·lea·guer (bilē'gər), *v.* to beset with troubles; annoy; afflict.

bel·es·prit (belesprē'), *n., pl.* **beauxes·prits** (bōzesprē'). a witty or intellectually gifted person.

be·lie (bilī'), v. to give a false impression of; prove false; contradict.

be·lit·tle (bilit'əl), v. be·lit·tled, be·lit·tling. to reduce in reputation or importance, as *You must not belittle the importance of the farmer or She belittles her husband in front of his friends.*

belles·let·tres (bel'let'rə), n. pl., *literally* fine literature; literature viewed as an aesthetic end in itself, ignoring any considerations of entertainment, information, etc. Also **bel·le·tris·tics** (bel,ətris'tiks). —**bellet'rist**, n. —**bel,le·tris'tic**, adj.

bel·li·cose (bel'ikōs), adj. aggressive; quarrelsome; warlike.

bel·lig·er·ent (bəlij'ərənt), adj. **1.** aggressive; hostile; waging war. —n. **2.** a nation in a state of war. —**bel·lig'er·ence**, n.

bell·weth·er (bel'weTH,ər), n. one who takes the lead or initiative, as a male sheep which leads the flock, usually carrying a bell round its neck.

bel·o·man·cy (bel'əman,sē), n. foretelling the future by the use of arrows.

bel·o·noid (bel'ənoid), adj. shaped like a needle or stylus.

be·lu·ga (bəlōō'gə), n. the white sturgeon.

be·muse (bimyōōz'), v. to bewilder; confuse; stupefy.

be·mused (bimyōōzd'), adj. bewildered, confused; preoccupied; lost in thought.

bench warrant, a warrant issued by a judge or court for the apprehension of an accused or guilty person.

bends (bendz), n. pl. See **decompression sickness.**

bend sinister, a diagonal band running across an escutcheon from top left to bottom right, supposedly a sign of bastardy.

ben·e·di·ci·te (ben,ədis'itē), n. a blessing or grace, esp. in the Christian church.

ben·e·dic·tion (ben,idik'sHən), n. **1.** the conferring of a blessing in a formal manner. **2.** a special service in the Roman Catholic Church.

ben·e·fac·tor (ben'əfak,tər), n. one who gives help to others; one who provides financial assistance for a cause, institution, etc.

be·nef·ic (binef'ik), adj. doing or causing good.

ben·e·fice (ben'əfis), n. **1.** an ecclesiastical office or living held by an Anglican clergyman. **2.** the revenue derived from this.

be·nef·i·cent (binef'isənt), adj. doing or producing good; kindly; generous. —**be·nef'i·cence**, n.

be·nev·o·lent (binev'ələnt), adj. characterized by a desire to do good; showing good will; well-wishing. —**be·nev'o·lence**, n.

be·night·ed (binī'tid), adj. **1.** ignorant; backward. **2.** overtaken by darkness or night.

be·nign (binīn'), adj. **1.** kindly; well disposed; gentle. **2.** (of a tumour, etc.) not malignant; mild.

be·nig·nant (binig'nənt), adj. kind, gracious; beneficial.

be·nig·ni·ty (binig'nitē), n. kindness; goodness.

ben·ny (ben'ē), n. *Slang.* any amphetamine tablet, esp. Benzedrine.

ben·thos (ben'thos), n. the animals and plants that live at the bottom of the sea.

ben·zo·di·az·e·pine (ben,zōdīā'zəpēn,), n. any of a class of drugs commonly used as tranquillizers, including Librium and Valium.

be·queath (bikwēth'), v. to give, leave, or dispose of by will; transmit; pass on to.

be·quest (bikwest'), n. something bequeathed; a legacy.

be·rate (birāt'), v. to scold; chide angrily; rebuke.

ber·ceuse (beə'sœz), n. a lullaby, esp. an instrumental composition in six-eight time.

ber·dache (bərdasH'), n. an American Indian tribesman who adopts the clothing and duties of a woman.

be·reave (birēv'), v. to deprive, esp by death; leave destitute; make disconsolate; rob.

be·reft (bireft'), adj. deprived; destitute.

be·rhyme (birīm'), v. to commemorate in verse.

Berke·le·ian (bäklē'ən), adj. **1.** of or relating to the works or the ideas of the Irish philosopher, George Berkeley. —n. **2.** an adherent of Berkeley's philosophy.

ber·ke·li·um (bûkē'lēəm, bû'klēəm), n. a metallic element, symbol Bk.

berm (bûm), n. a path or edge alongside a road, canal, etc.

ber·serk (bəzûk', bəsûk'), adj. in a murderous rage; frenziedly destructive.

be·seech (bisēcH'), v. to plead urgently; implore; appeal humbly.

be·seem (bisēm'), v. to be worthy, suitable, or fitting.

be·smirch (bismûcH'), v. to detract from the good name of; sully or tarnish.

be·sot (bisot'), v. to make intoxicated; stupefy with drink.

be·speak (bispēk'), v. to suggest; signify; indicate.

be·spoke (bispōk'), adj. (in Britain) (of clothing) custom-made.

bes·tial (bes'tēəl, bes'cHəl), adj. cruel; inhuman; barbarous.

bes·ti·al·i·ty (bes,tēal'itē, bēs,cHēal'itē), n. **1.** bestial behaviour or character. **2.** gratification of brutish or animal instincts, appetites, etc. **3.** sexual relations between a human being and an animal.

bes·ti·ar·y (bes'tēəri, bes'cHēer,ē), n. a collection of moralizing stories using animals as the characters.

be·ta·tron (bē'tətron, bā'tətron), n. a device

that accelerates electrons to high energy by varying a magnetic field.

be·tel nut (bē'təl), the areca nut, chewed by people of southeastern Asia.

bête noire (bet' nwär'), *pl.* **bêtes noires** (bet 'nwärz'). a person or thing regarded with particular loathing or fear.

be·think (bithiNGk'), *v.* to consider, think or reflect; recall; resolve or determine.

be·tide (bitīd'), *v.* to happen; come to pass.

be·times (bitīmz'), *adj.* early; soon.

bê·tise (betēz'), *n.* a stupid or foolish remark or act.

be·to·ken (bitō'kən), *v.* to signify, portend; be an indication or evidence of; show.

be·tray (bitrā'), *v.* to give away a secret; reveal a confidence; act in a treacherous or disloyal way, esp. to one's country. —**be·tray'al,** *n.*

bev·a·tron (bev'ətron), *n.* (in physics) a device for accelerating protons to very high energies.

bey (bā), *n.* 1. a provincial governor under the Ottoman Empire. 2. a title of respect given to high-ranking Turkish dignitaries.

bez·el (bez'əl), *n.* a groove in a setting for holding a gem.

bhang, bang (baNG), *n.* the leaves and stalks of Indian hemp used as a narcotic or an intoxicant.

bhees·ty, bhees·tie (bē'stē), *n.* (in India) a water-carrier.

bi·a·ly (bēä'lē), *n.* a roll made of white flour and flavoured with onion.

bi·an·nu·al (bīan'yōōəl), *adj.* 1. occurring twice a year. 2. (sometimes) occurring every two years. See also **biennial.**

bi·be·lot (bib'lō), *n.* a small decorative object having aesthetic value or prized for its rarity.

bib·li·o·clast (bib'lēəklast,), *n.* one who destroys books.

bib·li·og·o·ny (bib,lēog'ənē), *n.* the production and publication of books.

bib·li·o·klept (bib'lēəklept,), *n.* one who steals books.

bib·li·ol·a·try (bib,lēol'ətrē), *n.* an exaggerated respect for the Bible.

bib·li·o·man·cy (bib'lēəman,sē), *n.* prophecy or divination from verses chosen from the Bible at random.

bib·li·o·ma·ni·a (bib,lēōmā'nēə), *n.* excessive zeal for acquiring books.

bib·li·op·e·gy (bib,lēop'əjē), *n.* the art of bookbinding.

bib·li·o·phage (bib'lēəfāj,), *n.* a person with a passion for reading.

bib·li·o·phile (bib'lēəfīl,), *n.* a book-lover; one who is fond of collecting books. Also **bib·li·oph'-i·list.**

bib·li·o·phobe (bib'lēəfōb,), *n.* one who distrusts or dreads books.

bib·li·o·pole (bib'lēəpōl,), *n.* a dealer in books, esp. rare books. Also **bib,li·op'o·list.**

bib·li·o·taph, bib·li·o·taphe (bib'lēətaf,), *n.* one who hoards books.

bib·li·o·the·ca (bib'lēōthē'kə), *n.* a library.

bib·li·o·ther·a·py (bib,lēōther'əpē), *n.* the use of reading as a means of psychiatric therapy.

bib·u·lous (bib'yələs), *adj.* given to alcoholic drinking.

bi·cam·er·al (bīkam'ərəl), *adj.* having or consisting of two branches or chambers, as a legislative body.

bi·cen·te·nary (bī,sentē'nəri), *adj.* 1. lasting 200 years. 2. occurring every 200 years. —*n.* 3. a 200th anniversary. Also *chiefly U.S.*, **bi·cen·ten·ni·al** (bī,senten'ēəl).

bi·cip·i·tal (bīsip'itəl), *adj.* possessing two heads.

bick·er (bik'ə), *v.* to argue, esp. in an unpleasant way, concentrating on trivialities.

bi·cor·po·ral (bīkôə'pərəl), *adj.* possessing two bodies, divisions, etc.

bi·di·rec·tion·al (bī,direk'sHənəl), *adj.* operating or functioning in two different directions.

Bie·der·mei·er (bē'dəmī,ə), *adj.* denoting or relating to a style of interior decoration, furnishing, etc., found in German-speaking countries in the 19th century and characterized by ebony inlays and veneers of fruitwood used in a simplified style resembling French Empire.

bi·en·ni·al (bīen'ēəl), *adj.* occurring every two years; lasting two years. See also **biannual.**

bi·fa·cial (bīfā'sHəl), *adj.* having two faces; having opposite surfaces alike.

bi·fid (bī'fid), *adj.* separated by a cleft into two parts.

bi·flex (bī'fleks), *adj.* having a bend at two different places.

bi·fo·cal (bīfō'kəl), *adj.* (of spectacle lenses) having two parts one above the other, the lower for near and the upper for distant vision. See also **trifocal.**

bi·form (bī'fôəm), *adj.* having or combining the forms of two different kinds of individual; hybrid.

bi·fur·cate (bī'fəkāt), *v.* 1. to divide into two parts or branches. —*adj.* 2. divided into two parts; split; forked.

big·a·mist (big'əmist), *n.* one who commits the crime of marrying a second time while still legally married. —**big'a·my,** *n.*

big·ar·reau (big'ərō,), *n.* a heart-shaped sweet cherry.

big bang theory, a theory that the universe began with an enormous explosion and is still expanding. See also **steady state theory.**

big·gin (big'in), *n.* a silver coffee pot with a separate container for holding the coffee while it is being heated.

big·ot (big'ət), *n.* a person prejudiced against any belief or opinion different from his own.

bi·jou·te·rie (hēzнōō'tərē), *n.* a collection of jewellery.

bi·lat·er·al (bīlat'ərəl), *adj.* of or relating to two sides or parties; symmetrical; two-sided.

bil·bo (bil'bō), *n., pl.* **bil·boes.** an iron bar with sliding cuffs formerly used for fastening the ankles of prisoners.

bil·let-doux (bil,ēdōō'), *n., pl.* **bil·lets-doux** (bil,ēdōōz'). a love letter.

bil·lings·gate (bil'iNGzgāt), *n.* coarse or abusive language.

bi·lo·ca·tion (bī,lōkā'sнən), *n.* being in two places simultaneously.

bim·a·nous (bim'ənəs), *adj.* two-handed.

bi·men·sal (bīmen'səl), *adj.* happening once every two months.

bi·mes·tri·al (bīmes'trēəl), *adj.* **1.** happening every two months. **2.** lasting two months.

bi·met·al·ism (bīmetəliz,əm), *n.* the use of two metals, chiefly gold and silver, as a monetary standard with each having its value fixed in relation to the other. See also **symmetallism.**

bi·na·ry (bī'nərē), *adj.* pertaining to a system of numbers having 2 as its base.

binary star, (in astronomy) a double star system in which two stars orbit a common centre of gravity.

bin·au·ral (bīnôr'əl), *adj.* pertaining to, using, or adapted for two ears.

binaural broadcasting, a system of radio broadcasting designed to achieve a stereophonic effect.

bi·o·as·say (bī,ōəsā'), *n.* **1.** a means of calculating the relative strength of a substance by testing its effect on an organism. —*v.* **2.** to test in such a way.

bi·o·as·tro·nau·tics (bī,ōastrənô'tiks), *n.* the study of the effects of space travel upon animal and plant life.

bi·o·coe·nol·o·gy, bi·o·ce·nol·o·gy (bī,ōsēnol'əjē), *n.* the study of the interactions between the members of an ecological community.

bi·o·de·gra·da·ble (bī,ōdigrā'dəbəl), *adj.* noting a substance, esp. a household cleaner, that is easily disposed of by bacterial decomposition, thus reducing pollution.

bi·o·dy·nam·ics (bī,ōdīnam'iks), *n.* the study of living organisms in relation to their activity.

bi·o·ecol·o·gy (bī,ōēkol'əjē), *n.* the study of the interrelationship between living organisms and their environment.

bi·o·gen·e·sis (bī,ōjen'isis), *n.* the evolution of living forms from other living forms.

biological sociology, 1. the study of the development of social behaviour in correlation with the study of living organisms. **2.** the study of social behaviour treated as a phenomenon

deriving from physiological structure. Also **biosociology.**

bi·o·lu·mi·nes·cence (bī,ōlōō,mənes'əns), *n.* the generation of light by living organisms. —**bi,o·lu,mi·nes'cent,** *adj.*

bi·ol·y·sis (bīol'isis), *n.* the destruction or dissolution of a living organism.

bi·o·mass (bī'ōmas,), *n.* the amount of living matter in a given plane or cubic unit of habitat.

bi·o·med·i·cine (bī,ōmed'isin), *n.* medicine concerned with the relationship of body chemistry and function. —**bi,o·med'i·cal,** *adj.*

bi·om·e·try (bīom'itrē), *n.* the study of the probable length of human life. —**bi,o·met'ric,** *adj.* —**bi,o·me·tri'cian,** *n.*

bi·o·mor·phic (bī,ōmôr'fik), *adj.* (in fine arts) producing or evoking images of living organisms.

bi·on·ics (bīon'iks), *n.* the study of certain functions of man and animals and the application of the derived findings to the designing of computers.

bi·o·nom·ics (bīənom'iks), *n.* See **ecology.**

bi·on·omy (bīon'əmē), **1.** See **physiology. 2.** See **ecology.**

bi·o·phys·ics (bī,ōfiz'iks), *n.* the study of the application of the methods of physics to biological problems.

bi·op·sy (bī'opsē), *n.* the removal of tissue, cells, etc., from a living body for examination.

bi·o·psy·chic (bī,ōsī'kik), *adj.* relating to or denoting the interaction of biological and psychological phenomena.

bi·o·so·cial (bī,ōsō'sнəl), *adj.* relating to or denoting the interaction of biological and social phenomena.

bi·o·so·ci·ol·o·gy (bī,ōsō,sēol'əjē), *n.* See **biological sociology.**

bi·o·sphere (bī'əsfēr), *n.* that part of the world in which living organisms can exist.

bi·o·stat·ics (bī,ōstat'iks), *n.* the study of living organisms in relation to their function and structure.

bi·o·syn·the·sis (bī,ōsin'thisis), *n.* the formation of chemical compounds by a living organism.

bi·o·tech·nol·o·gy (bī,ōteknol'əjē), *n.* the study of the relationship between human beings and machines.

bi·ot·ic (bīot'ik), *adj.* relating or pertaining to life.

biotic potential, the capacity of an organism or species to reproduce and survive in an optimum environment.

bi·o·type (bī'ətīp), *n.* a group of organisms sharing genetic characteristics.

bip·ar·ous (bip'ərəs), *adj.* giving birth to offspring in pairs.

bi·par·ti·san (bīpä'tizn), *adj.* representing,

agreed upon, or supported by two parties, esp. political parties.

bi·par·tite (bīpä'tīt), *adj.* **1.** having two parts or divided into two. **2.** shared by two.

bi·ped (bī'ped), *n.* **1.** an animal with two feet. —*adj.* **2.** having two feet. Also **bi·ped·al** (bī'-pēdəl).

bi·pod (bī'pod), *n.* a two-legged stand or support.

bi·pro·pel·lant (bī,prəpel'ənt), *n.* a rocket propellant consisting of fuel and oxidizer which are kept separate until they are ignited in the combustion chamber.

bi·ra·mous (bīrā'məs), *adj.* having or divided into two branches. Also **bira·mose** (bīrā'mōs).

bird·ie (bûr'dē), *n.* (in golf) one stroke under par on a hole. See also **bogey, eagle.**

bi·sect (bīsekt'), *v.* to divide or cut into two, usually equal, parts; split into two; fork.

bi·sex·u·al (bīsek'sHŌōəl), *adj.* **1.** having both male and female reproductive organs. **2.** (of people) sexually attracted to both sexes. —*n.* **3.** one having the reproductive organs of both sexes. **4.** one who is sexually attracted to both sexes.

bis·sex·tile (bīseks'til), *adj.* having or denoting February 29, the extra day of a leap year.

bis·sex·tus (bīseks'təs), *n.* February 29 considered as the extra day added every four years to the Julian calendar.

bi·sym·met·ri·cal (bī,simet'rikəl), *adj.* denoting or having two planes of symmetry at right angles to each other.

biv·ou·ac (biv'ŏŏak), *n.* **1.** a temporary encampment, esp. a military one, providing very little protection. —*v.* **biv·ou·acked, biv·ou·acking. 2.** to sleep or rest in such an encampment.

bi·zarre (bizär'), *adj.* strange; outlandish; unusual; queer.

black paternoster, an incantation used for attracting evil spirits and black magic. See also **white paternoster.**

black powder, an explosive composed of saltpetre, sulphur, and powdered charcoal, used in fireworks, etc.

Black Shirt, a member of a Fascist organization wearing a black shirt as a distinctive part of its uniform.

blanch (blanCH), *v.* (in cookery) to scald or parboil in order to whiten or skin.

blanc·mange (bləmänj'), *n.* a jellylike pudding made with milk, cornstarch, and gelatin, and flavoured with rum, vanilla, etc.

blan·dish (blan'dīsH), *v.* to seek to influence with flattering words; coax; cajole; flatter.

blan·dish·ments (blan'dīsHmənts), *n. pl.* **1.** flattering speech or action, expressing affection, that is intended to win a person. **2.** anything pleasing or alluring.

blan·quette (bläNket'), *n.* a stew of veal, lamb,

or chicken prepared in a white sauce, served with cooked onions, mushrooms, etc.

blas·pheme (blasfēm'), *v.* to speak about God or sacred things without respect or reverence; curse; revile; swear.

blas·phe·mous (blas'fəməs), *adj.* uttering or containing profane language; irreverent.

blas·phe·my (blas'fəmē), *n.* an impious or profane utterance about God or sacred things; irreverent attitude towards anything considered sacred; abusive speech.

bla·tant (blā'tənt), *adj.* flagrantly obvious; disagreeably noisy; conspicuous in a vulgar or offensive manner.

blath·er·skite (blaTH'ərskīt), *n.* one given to blustering or empty talk.

Blau·e Rei·ter (blou'ə rī'tər), a group of artists employing free form and unconventional colours, active in Munich in the early 20th century.

bleak (blēk), *adj.* cold and desolate; dismal; depressing.

blench (blenCH), *v.* to flinch; shy away through lack of courage; quail.

blight (blīt), *n.* **1.** a disease that causes plants to wither. **2.** a pernicious or malignant influence. —*v.* **3.** to cause to wither. **4.** destroy; shatter.

blithe (blīTH), *adj.* **1.** joyful; cheerful; glad. **2.** carefree; heedless of responsibility.

blood count, the number of blood cells in a given volume of blood.

bloom·e·ry (blŏŏ'mərē), *n.* a forge where, formerly, bar-shaped iron blooms were produced.

blous·on (blŏŏ'zōn), *n.* a woman's blouselike outer garment drawn in at the waist.

blow·out (blō'out,), *n.* See **flameout.**

blowz·y (blou'zē), *adj.* **1.** having a coarse reddish-coloured complexion. **2.** untidy in appearance; unkempt; sluttish.

blue laws, *U.S. history* a number of rigorous, puritanical laws designed to regulate morals, forbidding such activities as dancing, drinking, etc.

blue·nose (blŏŏ'nōz,), *n.* a prudish, censorious or puritanical person.

blue-ribbon jury, *U.S.* a jury of better educated or more intelligent people selected to try especially difficult or complex cases.

blue-sky law, *U.S.* any law providing for the regulation of the sale of securities.

blue·stock·ing (blŏŏ'stokiNG), *n.* a woman who devotes herself to scholarly or literary pursuits.

blus·ter (blus'tər), *v.* **1.** to brag or protest loudly and in a menacing, bullying manner. —*n.* **2.** a noisy, bullying, wildly improbable show, esp. of protest.

B'nai B'rith (bənä' brith'), a Jewish organization which promotes the educational and cultural improvement of Jews.

boat·el (bōtel'), *n.* a hotel at or near the waterside with docking space, providing accommodation for people travelling by private boat.

bo·cage (bōkäzh'), *n.* (in the arts) a decorative pattern consisting of foliage, trees, branches, etc.

boc·cie (boch'ē), *n.* a kind of lawn bowls played by Italians in a narrow court.

bock beer, *U.S., Canada* a variety of strong, dark beer.

bo·de·ga (bōdē'gə, bōdä'gə, *Sp.* bôthe'gä), *n.* (in Spanish America) a grocery store.

bod·kin (bod'kin), *n.* a sharp, slender instrument for making holes in leather, cloth, etc.

boff (bof), *n.* (in the theatre) a humorous remark or saying which causes the audience to laugh.

bo·gey (bō'gē), *n.* (in golf) one stroke over par on a hole. See also **birdie, eagle.**

bog·gle (bog'əl), *v.* to be dismayed or alarmed; shrink from; hesitate; waver.

bo·gie (bō'gē), *n.* a wheel assembly unit of a railway undercarriage.

bo·gus (bō'gəs), *adj.* 1. sham; not genuine; false. —*n.* 2. (in printing) matter set by a compositor which duplicates material already supplied.

Bo·he·mi·an (bōhē'mēən), *n.* a person, esp. one with artistic pretensions, who scorns conventional social behaviour.

boil·er·mak·er (boil'lərmā,kər), *n.* whisky drunk with beer as a chaser.

bois·ter·ous (boi'strəs), *adj.* rowdy and noisy.

boîte (bwat), *n.* a nightclub.

bo·la (bō'lə), *n.* (in South America) a missile consisting of a length of cord with two or more heavy balls at each end, thrown so as to entangle the legs of cattle, etc.

bo·lide (bō'līd), *n.* a large meteor; a fireball.

bo·lo (bō'lō), *n.* a heavy, machete-like knife with a single cutting edge used in the Philippines.

Bol·she·vik (bol'shəvik), *n.* 1. a member of the extreme wing of the Russian Social-Democratic party that seized power in 1917. 2. a member of a Communist party in any country. —**Bol'she·vism,** *n.*

bo·lus (bō'ləs), *n.* (in medicine) a large pill, usually in the form of a sphere.

Bo·marc (bō'mäk), *n.* a type of U.S. surface-to-air missile.

bom·bast (bom'bast), *n.* pompous or pretentious language. —**bom·bas' tic,** *adj.*

Bombay duck, a small fish used when dried as a relish with curries, etc. Also **bummalo.**

bombe (bom, bomb), *n.* a frozen dessert made in a round mould and consisting of ice cream, mousse, etc.

bom·bé (bombā'), *adj.* (of furniture) curving or bulging outwards.

bo·na fi·de (bō'nə fī'di), in good faith; without intention to deceive.

bon·ho·mie (bon'əmē), *n.* kindliness; good nature; joviality.

bon·ho·mous (bon'əməs), *adj.* displaying bonhomie.

bon mot (bon' mō'), *pl.* **bons mots** (bon' mōz'). an apt or clever remark; a witty saying.

bon·ny·clab·ber (bon'ēklab,ər), *n.* *U.S.* thick, sour milk.

bon·sai (bon'sī), *n.,* *pl.* **bon·sai.** 1. a potted plant, usually a tree, which has been dwarfed by special methods of cultivation, pruning, etc. 2. the art of growing such plants, developed in Japan.

bon vi·vant (bôn' vēvän'), one who takes pleasure in good food and drink; an epicure.

boon·docks (bōōn'doks), *n.* an uninhabited area, esp. one overgrown with vegetation; any remote area, esp. in the countryside.

boon·dog·gle (bōōn'dogəl), *n.* 1. trivial or useless work, carried out to give the appearance of being busy. —*v.* 2. to perform such work.

boot·less (bōōt'lis), *adj.* of no avail; fruitless; useless.

bo·rax (bôr'aks), *n.* cheap or shoddy merchandise, esp. furniture.

bor·bo·ryg·mus (bôə,bərig'məs), *n.* the technical word for rumbling or gurgling in the stomach, a natural sound. —**bor,bo·ryg'mic,** *adj.*

bor·del·lo (bôədel'ō), *n.* a brothel.

bor·de·reau (bôə,dərō'), *n.,* *pl.* **bor·de·reaux** (bôə,dərōz'). a detailed note, esp. one listing documents.

bo·re·al (bôr'ēəl), *adj.* pertaining to the north or the north wind. See also **austral, occidental, oriental.**

bore·cole (bô'kōl), *n.* kale.

borscht (bôəsht), *n.* a Russian soup of beef stock flavoured with cooked beets.

borscht circuit, (in theatrical use) the nightclubs and other entertainments in the Catskill Mountains, considered as a Jewish resort area.

bor·stal (bôə'stəl), *n.* (in England) a reformatory for young delinquents.

bos·cage (bos'kij), *n.* a thicket; a growth of trees or shrubs.

bos·ket (bos'kit), *n.* a thicket or grove. —**bosk·y** (bos'kē), *adj.*

bot·an·o·man·cy (bot'ənəman,sē), *n.* prophecy based on examination of plants.

bot·te·ga (bōtä'gə), *n.,* *pl.* **bot·tegas, bot·te·ghe** (bōtä'gē). the studio of an artist of repute where students and apprentices learn.

bot·u·lin (bot'yōōlin, boch'əlin), *n.* the toxin produced by botulinus, the cause of botulism.

bot·u·li·nus (bot,yōōlī'nəs, boch·əlī'nəs), *n.,* *pl.* **bot·u·li·nus·es.** the bacterium *Clostridium botulinum,* which secretes botulin.

bot·u·lism (bot'yōōliz,əm, boch'əliz,əm), *n.*

acute food poisoning caused by the presence of botulin in food.

bou·chée (bōōSHā'), *n.* a small, cup-shaped piece of puff pastry used as a receptacle for an hors d'oeuvre, etc.

bou·clé (bōō'klāy), *n.* **1.** a three-stranded looped yarn or fabric made of this yarn. —*adj.* **2.** denoting such yarn or fabric.

bou·clée (bōō'klā), *n.* (in billiards) a loop made with the thumb and first finger for supporting the cue and through which it slides.

bouf·fant (bōōfän', bōōfänt'), *adj.* full, puffed out, as a skirt, sleeves, hairdo, etc.

bou·gie (bōō'zHē), *n.* (in medicine) a hollow or solid cylindrical instrument used for penetrating body passages, to aid diagnosis, administer drugs, etc.

bouil·la·baisse (bōō,yəbās'), *n.* a kind of soup or stew made of various kinds of fish.

bou·le·var·dier (bōōl,əvädyä'), *n.* a man-about-town who frequents fashionable places.

bou·le·ver·se·ment (bōō,ləversmäN'), *n.* a turning upside down; upset.

bound·en (boun'dən), *adj.* under an obligation; morally obliged.

bou·quet (bōōkā'), *n.* the distinctive aroma of a wine.

bou·quet gar·ni (bōōkä' gärnē'), a selection of herbs, tied in a cloth bag, used for flavouring soups, sauces, stews, etc.

bour·geois (bōōrzHwä'), *n.*, *pl.* **bour·geois. 1.** a member of the middle class, esp. a merchant or businessman. **2.** one whose outlook is supposedly determined chiefly by private property interests. —*adj.* **3.** consisting of or belonging to the middle class. **4.** conventional or limited in outlook; lacking in taste.

bour·geoi·sie (bōōr,zHwäzē'), *n.* the middle class, esp. as contrasted with the proletariat or wage earners.

bour·rée (bô'rā), *n.* **1.** a traditional French dance with quick tempo and two beats per bar, or a composition with a similar rhythm. **2.** a type of ballet step: **pas de bourrée.**

bouse, bowse (bous, bouz), *n.* a spree; a drinking bout.

bou·stro·phe·don (bōō,strəfē'dən), *n.* writing in which alternate lines read in opposite directions.

bou·tique (bōōtēk'), *n.* a small shop that sells fashionable clothes or luxury items.

bo·va·rism (bō'vəriz,əm), *n.* a distortedly magnified opinion of one's own abilities; conceit.

bo·vine (bō'vīn), *adj.* resembling an ox; sluggish, stolid, or dull.

bovine somatotrophin, a hormone that occurs naturally in cattle and promotes growth. Injections of the hormone or its synthetic counterpart may be given to boost milk production. *Abbr.:* **B.S.T.**

bovine spongiform encephalopathy, a fatal degenerative nervous disease of cattle caused by a virus-like agent. *Inf. name* **mad cow disease.**

Bow bells (bō), the bells of the church of St. Mary-le-Bow, in the East End of London: the only true Cockneys are traditionally those born within sound of them.

bowd·ler·ize (boud'lərīz, bōd'lərīz), *v.* to expurgate (a book, play, etc.) prudishly, by omitting passages considered indecent or immodest.

bo·yar (boi'yə, bō'yə), *n.* a member of the old Russian nobility, abolished by Peter the Great. Also **bo·yard'.**

bra·ce·ro (brəser'o), *n.*, *pl.* **bra·ceros.** *U.S.* a Mexican labourer who does seasonal farmwork in the U.S.

brach·y·ce·phal·ic (brak,isifal'ik, brak,ikifal'ik), *adj.* **1.** having a short broad head. —*n.* **2.** an individual with such a head. Also **brach·y·ceph·a·lous** (brak,isef'ələs). See also **dolichocephalic.** —**brach,y·ceph'a·lism, brach,y·ceph'·a·ly,** *n.*

bra·chyl·o·gy (brəkil'əjē), *n.* brevity of speech; a concise means of expression.

brack·ish (brak'isH), *adj.* slightly salty.

brad·y·aux·e·sis (brad,ēôgzē'sis), *n.* (in an organism) the growth of a part at a slower rate than the whole. See also **isauxesis, tachyauxesis.** —**brad·y·aux·et'ic,** *adj.*

brad·y·car·di·a (brad,ikä'dēə), *n.* an abnormally slow pulse rate.

brad·y·ki·net·ic (brad,ikinet'ik), *adj.* moving very slowly; having a slow rate of motion.

brad·y·tel·ic (brad,itel'ik), *adj.* having a slower rate of evolution than normal for a specific group, species, etc. See also **horotelic, tachytelic.**

brag·ga·do·ci·o (brag,ədō'sHēō), *n.* **1.** one who boasts; a braggart. **2.** empty boasting.

brag·gart (brag'ət), *n.* a boastful or bragging person.

Braille (brāl), *n.* a system that enables the blind to read, using combinations of raised dots as symbols.

brain·sick (brān'sik,), *adj.* resulting from or relating to insanity; crazy; demented.

brain·storming (brān'stôəm,iNG), *n.* a technique in which a group of people hold a spontaneous discussion in order to stimulate creative thinking, develop new ideas, etc.

brain·wash·ing (brān'wosH,iNG), *n.* a forcible, systematic method of indoctrination used to undermine a person's political or religious beliefs and to compel him to accept contrary ones.

braise (brāz), *v.* to cook slowly in a little liquid in a closed pan.

bran·dish (bran'dısн), *v.* to shake or wave in a menacing or ostentatious manner.

bran·dreth (bran'dri*th*), *n.* **1.** a wooden railing or fence around a wall. **2.** a three-legged stand of iron placed over a fire.

bran·ni·gan (bran'əgən), *n.* a squabble or brawl; a spree.

brash (brasн), *adj.* reckless, impetuous, rash; impudent; tactless.

brass·age (bras'ij), *n.* a charge levied by a mint to cover the cost of coining money.

bras·sard (bras'äd), *n.* an armlet or badge worn on the upper arm; a piece of armour worn to protect the arm.

bras·se·rie (bras,ərē'), *n.* a restaurant, saloon, etc., providing food or alcoholic drinks.

brat·tle (brat'əl), *n.* **1.** a clattering or rattling noise. —*v.* **2.** to make such a noise.

brat·wurst (brat'wûst), *n.* a sausage made of pork, spices, etc.

bra·va·do (brəvä'dō), *n.* an ostentatious display of courage; a swaggering pretence of bravery.

bra·vu·ra (brəvyōōr'ə), *n., pl.* **bra·vu·ras.** a display of brilliance or daring in the performance of something.

bray (brā), *v.* to crush or pound into fine pieces or powder.

bra·zen (brā'zən), *adj.* **1.** made of brass. **2.** resembling brass in colour, sound, etc. **3.** shameless; insolent; impudent.

bread (bred), *n. Slang.* money.

breakbone fever. See dengue.

brec·ci·a (brecн'ēə), *n.* a rock consisting of sharp fragments of older rock embedded together in a matrix.

breech delivery, a birth in which the baby's posterior or feet are presented first.

breeches buoy, a lifebuoy fitted with canvas breeches and moving on a rope, enabling a person to be hauled from a ship to shore or to another ship.

brems·strah·lung (bremz'sнträ,lənG), *n.* a form of x-radiation emitted when a charged particle, as an electron, is slowed by an electric field, esp. one surrounding an atomic nucleus.

bre·telle (britel'), *n.* an ornamental shoulder strap.

bre·vet (brev'it), *n.* a commission granting a military officer higher rank without extra pay.

bri·cole (brikōl', brik'əl), *n.* **1.** a surprising move or action. **2.** (in billiards) a shot in which the cue ball hits the cushion between striking the object ball and another ball. **3.** a large catapult formerly used in battle.

Brie (brē), *n.* a variety of soft, white, self-ripening cheese originated in France.

bri·gand (brig'ənd), *n.* a bandit who lives by robbing travellers, esp. in forests and mountains.

brig·and·age (brig'əndij), *n.* the work of brigands; robbery; plunder.

brink·man·ship (brinGk'mənsнip), *n.* the art of following a dangerous course of action to the limits of safety in order to achieve one's ends.

bri·oche (brēosн', brēōsн'), *n.* a roll or sweet bun made from eggs and yeast.

bri·quette, bri·quet (briket'), *n.* a block of compressed coal dust, charcoal, etc. used for fuel.

bri·sance (brē'zəns), *n.* the shattering power of high explosive.

bris·ket (bris'kit), *n.* the breast of an animal, esp. that part lying nearest the ribs and considered as a cut of meat.

broach (brōcн), *v.* **1.** to introduce or mention for the first time. **2.** to break the surface of water from below.

broad-spec·trum (brôd,spek'trəm), *adj.* denoting an antibiotic that is effective against a number of organisms.

bro·cade (brōkād'), *n.* a heavy fabric having an elaborate raised pattern in silver or gold.

broc·a·tel, broc·a·telle (brok,ətel'), *n.* a kind of brocade having a pattern woven in high relief.

bro·chette (brōsнet'), *n.* a small spit or skewer used in cooking.

bro·gan (brō'gən), *n.* a coarse, strongly made shoe, esp. one reaching to the ankle.

brogue (brōg), *n.* **1.** a strongly made, comfortable shoe, often with decorative perforations. **2.** English spoken with a pronounced Irish accent.

bro·mide (brō'mīd), *n.* **1.** a trite or platitudinous remark. **2.** a tiresome or boring person.

Bronze Age, a period in human culture, occurring between the Stone Age and the Iron Age, characterized by the use of bronze tools and weapons.

brook (brŏŏk), *v.* to put up with; bear; tolerate.

Brook Farm, a farm in West Roxbury, Massachusetts, the scene of an experiment in communistic living during 1841-7.

broth·el (brotн'əl), *n.* a house for prostitution.

brou·ha·ha (brŏŏ'hähä), *n.* uproar; hubbub; turmoil.

brown dwarf *n.* a celestial body bigger than a large planet and smaller than a star.

brown goods *pl. n.* (in marketing) consumer items such as hi-fi equipment, televisions, and video recorders. See also **white goods.**

bruit (brŏŏt), *v.* to spread a rumour.

bru·lé (brŏŏlā'), *n.* a forest region destroyed by fire.

bru·mal (brŏŏ'məl), *adj.* occurring in winter; wintry.

brume (brŏŏm), *n.* mist; fog.

brum·ma·gem (brum'əjəm), *adj.* gaudy, cheap, and inferior.

brunch (brunCH), *n.* a meal taken late in the morning combining both breakfast and lunch.

brusque (brŏŏsk, brusk), *adj.* having a curt or abrupt manner; rough; blunt.

brus·que·rie (brŏŏs'kərē, brus'kərē), *n.* a display of brusque manners.

brut (brŏŏt), *adj.* (of champagne) very dry.

brux·ism (bruk'siz,əm), *n.* the grinding of teeth, esp. during sleep.

bubble chamber, an apparatus containing heated liquid designed to make visible the paths of ionizing particles as a row of bubbles.

bu·bon·ic plague (byŏŏbon'ik), a virulent form of plague characterized by the growth of inflammatory swellings called buboes.

buc·cal (buk'əl), *adj.* relating to the cheek, the sides of the mouth or the mouth itself.

buc·ca·ro (bŏŏkär'ō), *n.* a kind of unglazed pottery.

buc·co·lin·gual (buk,əliNG'gwəl), *adj.* relating to the cheek and tongue.

bu·cen·taur (byŏŏsen'tôə), *n.* the state barge formerly used by the doge of Venice for the ritual of wedding the state to the Adriatic Sea.

Buch·man·ism (bŏŏk'məniz,əm), *n.* the principles and beliefs of the Moral Rearmament Movement, formerly the Oxford Group, which advocated strict observance of high moral standards both publicly and privately.

buck·a·roo (buk,ərŏŏ'), *n.* a cowboy.

bucket shop, a broker's establishment that speculates fraudulently against its customers' interests.

buck·eye (buk'ī,), *n.* a work of art, esp. a painting, produced as a saleable commodity and generally lacking intrinsic worth.

buck·ram (buk'rəm), *n.* a durable, plain-woven cotton cloth used for binding books, making interlinings, etc.

bu·col·ic (byŏŏkol'ik), *adj.* relating to shepherds or the countryside; pastoral; rural.

Bud·dhism (bŏŏd'izəm), *n.* a religion of southern and eastern Asia, teaching that suffering is an essential characteristic of life and that liberation can be achieved only through enlightenment and self-purification.

budg·er·i·gar (buj'ərēgä,), *n.* a small parakeet of Australia.

buff·er (buf'ə), *n.* a unit designed to store computer data until they can be fed into their appropriate unit for processing.

buffer state, a small state lying between two powerful states, esp. one which by its position lessens the risk of conflict between them.

buf·fet[1] (buf'it), *v.* to strike with the hand; push against or strike repeatedly.

buf·fet[2] (bu'fā), *n.* **1.** a china cupboard or sideboard; a counter or bar for refreshments. **2.** a meal set out on a table, etc., usually offering a choice of dishes to be eaten informally.

bu·lim·i·a (byŏŏlim'ēə), *n.* a morbid and constant hunger; an unnatural craving for food.

bull (bŏŏl), *n.* a document issued by a pope.

bul·la (bŏŏl'ə), *n.,* *pl.* **bul·lae** (bŏŏl'ē). a seal attached to a papal bull.

bul·lion (bŏŏl'yən), *n.* gold and silver considered as bulk, and not as manufactured articles.

bull·ish (bŏŏl'isH), *adj.* (in a stock market, etc.) marked by, conducive to, or tending towards a rise in prices, occasioning investors' optimism. See also **bearish.**

bully tree, any of various tropical American trees which yield balata.

bul·wark (bŏŏl'wûk), *n.* any protection from or defence against an enemy, danger, etc., as a fortification.

bum·boat (bum'bōt,), *n.* a small boat used to ferry provisions to ships lying in harbour.

bum·ma·lo (bum'əlō), *n.* See **Bombay duck.**

bump·tious (bump'sHəs), *adj.* excessively and unpleasantly self-assertive.

Bund (bŏŏnd), *n.* a pro-Nazi organization in the U.S. before World War II.

Bun·des·rat (bŏŏn'dəsrät,), *n.* **1.** the upper chamber of the parliament of the German Federal Republic. **2.** the federal council of Switzerland.

Bun·des·tag (bŏŏn'dəstäg,), *n.* the lower chamber of the parliament of the German Federal Republic.

bung (buNG), *n.* a plug or stopper for the hole in a wooden barrel.

bung·start·er (buNG'stä,tə), *n.* a hammer for removing a bung.

bun·ko, bun·co (buNG'kō), *n.,* *pl.* **bun·kos.** *U.S. Slang* a confidence trick or swindle in a gambling game, etc.

bunko steerer, *U.S. Slang* a swindler, esp. one who entices a victim into a gambling game in which he will be cheated.

bun·kum (buNG'kəm), *n. Chiefly U.S.* deceitful speechmaking by a politician calculated to impress his constituents.

bur·geon (bû'jən), *v.* to expand quickly; flourish.

bu·rin (byŏŏr'in), *n.* a steel cutting tool used for engraving metal, marble, etc.

burke (bûk), *v.* to murder, as by smothering, so as to leave no traces of violence.

bur·nish (bû'nisH), *v.* **1.** to polish by friction so as to make smooth and shiny. **2.** (in engraving) to rub (the dots of a halftone) so as to flatten and enlarge them.

bur·noose, bur·nous (bənŏŏs'), *n.* a hooded cloak worn by Arabs.

burn·out (bûn'out,), *n.* the stage in the flight of a rocket engine when the propellant fuel ceases to provide power.

bur·sar (bû'sər), *n.* an official at a university,

etc., having charge of financial matters. —bur·sar·i·al (bəser'ēəl), *adj.*

burse (bûs), *n.* a small receptacle as a pouch, purse, etc.

bus·by (buz'bē), *n.* a tall fur cap with a bag hanging down from the top, worn by certain British Army regiments.

bus·kin (bus'kin), *n.* 1. a high shoe with thick soles worn by actors in ancient Greek drama. 2. tragedy; the tragic style of acting.

butterfly effect, the notion, used in chaos theory, that a tiny change in a physical system can ultimately result in much larger changes.

but·tress (but'ris), *v.* to strengthen something, as a structure, argument, etc., by adding support.

buzz·word (buz'wûd,), *n.* a word or expression that is currently fashionable in and indicative of familiarity with the latest trends in a particular field, as *user friendly*. It usually becomes a cliché.

bys·si·no·sis (bis,inō'sis), *n.* a lung disease of textile workers caused by long-term inhalation of fibrous dust.

byte (bīt), *n.* a unit of machine-readable information, usually equal to eight bits.

byz·an·tine (bizan'tīn, bizan'tēn; bīzan'tīn, bīzan'tēn; biz'əntīn, biz'əntēn), *adj.* highly complicated, esp. in design and embellishment; intricately complex and involved, as a plot.

C

ca·bal (kəbal'), *n.* a small group of persons engaged in secret plotting, as against a government, etc.

cab·a·la, cab·ba·la, kab·a·la, kab·ba·la (kəbä'lə), *n.* an esoteric theosophical system based on a mystical interpretation of the Scriptures.

cab·a·lism (kab'əliz,əm), *n.* the doctrines or the interpretation of the cabala. —**cab'a·list,** *n.*

cabinet wine, a German wine of good quality.

cab·o·chon (kab'ə,sнon), *n.* a rounded, polished but not faceted precious stone.

ca·bo·clo (kəbô'klōō, kəbô'klô), *n.* a Brazilian Indian.

ca·boo·dle (kəbōō'dəl), *n.* the whole collection; the lot.

cab·o·tage (kab'ətäzн,), *n.* 1. navigation or trade restricted to coastal waters. 2. the restriction of air transport within a country's borders to that country's aircraft.

ca'can·ny (kôkan'ē), *n.* (in Britain) a work slowdown by employees in a factory, etc., in order to reduce production.

cac·chi·na·tion (kak,inā'sнən), *n.* loud, noisy laughter.

cac·cia·to·re (kaсн,ətôr'ē), *adj.* (of an Italian dish) containing or prepared with tomatoes, mushrooms, herbs, etc. Also **cac,cia·to'ra.**

cach·a·lot (kasн'əlot), *n.* See **sperm whale.**

cache (kasн), *n.* 1. a hiding place for treasure, stores, etc. 2. something so hidden.

cache·pot (kasнpō', kasн'pot), *n.* a decorative container for concealing a flower pot.

ca·chet (kasнā'), *n.* a mark or sign of approval or distinction, esp. as conferred by a person in authority.

ca·chex·i·a (kəkek'sēə), *n.* general poor health accompanied by emaciation as the result of chronic disease.

cach·in·nate (kak'ənāt), *v.* to laugh noisily or excessively.

ca·chou (kəsнōō'), *n.* a pill eaten to sweeten the breath.

ca·cique (kəsēk'), *n.* the head man of an Indian tribe in Mexico or the West Indies.

cac·o·de·mon (kak,ədē'mən), *n.* a demon or evil spirit.

cac·o·ep·y (kəkō'ipē), *n.* poor or faulty pronunciation.

cac·o·ë·thes (kak,ōē'thēz), *n.* an insatiable desire; mania.

cac·o·gen·ic (kak,ōjen'ik), *n.* See **dysgenic.**

ca·cog·ra·phy (kakog'rəfē), *n.* 1. inartistic or illegible handwriting. See also **calligraphy.** 2. bad spelling. See also **orthography.**

ca·col·o·gy (kəkol'əjē), *n.* defective speech.

ca·coph·o·ny (kəkof'ənē), *n.* harshness or discordance in sound. See also **euphony.** —**ca·coph'o·nous,** *adj.*

ca·cu·mi·nal (kəkyōō'mənəl), *adj.* articulated with the tip of the tongue turned up to touch the roof of the mouth under the hard palate. Also **cerebral, retroflex.**

ca·das·tral (kədas'trəl), *adj.* of or pertaining to property boundaries, land divisions, etc.

ca·das·tre, ca·das·ter (kədas'tə), *n.* an official register of property, giving details of ownership, etc.

ca·dence (kā'dəns), *n.* 1. the beat or measure of any rhythmical motion. 2. (in music) a sequence of chords showing the end of a section or phrase.

ca·dent (kā'dənt), *adj.* having rhythm or cadence.

ca·den·tial (kāden'sнəl), *adj.* denoting or relating to a cadence in music.

ca·den·za (kəden'zə), *n.* an elaborate, ostentatious passage for a solo instrument or voice in a concerto, aria, etc.

ca·dre (kä'də), *n.* a nucleus of skilled people who train others in an expanding organization, military unit, etc.

ca·du·ce·us (kədyōō'sēəs), *n.* the symbolic staff carried by Mercury as herald of the gods, now used as a symbol for the medical profession.

ca·du·ci·ty (kədyōō'sitē), *n.* 1. senility. 2. the quality of being transitory; impermanence.

cae·cum, ce·cum (sē'kəm), *n., pl.* **cae·ca, ce·ca** (sē'kə). (in anatomy) a cavity open at one end, esp. at the beginning of the large intestine.

cae·no·gen·e·sis, ce·no·gen·e·sis (sē,nōjen'isis), *n.* (in biology) the introduction, in the development of an individual, of characteristics which differentiate it from the earlier phylogeny of its race or stock. See also **palingenesis.**

cae·su·ra (sizyōō'rə), *n., pl.* **cae·su·ras, cae·su·rae.** a break or pause in the middle of a line of verse.

ca·fard (kafar'), *n.* a mood of melancholy or deep depression.

ca·fé au lait (kaf'ā ō lā'), coffee with hot milk in equal proportions.

ca·fé bru·lot (kaf'ā brōōlō'), black coffee flavoured with sugar, lemon, spices, and brandy, ignited briefly before being drunk.

caf·tan, kaf·tan (kaf'tan), *n.* a coatlike garment with long sleeves and tied at the waist.

ca·hier (kayā'), *n.* a report of the proceedings, transactions, etc., of an official body.

Cai·no·zo·ic (kī'nōzō'ik), *n.* See **Cenozoic.**

ca·ique (kīēk'), *n.* **1.** a long slender rowing boat used in the Bosphorus. **2.** any of several sailing vessels of the E. Mediterranean.

cairn (keən), *n.* a heap of stones serving as a landmark, memorial, etc. Also **carn.**

cais·son disease (kā'sən, kəsōōn'). See decompression sickness.

cai·tiff (kā'tif), *n.* **1.** a contemptible or cowardly person. —*adj.* **2.** base; despicable.

ca·jole (kəjōl'), *v.* to coax or persuade with flattery; deceive with false promises. —**ca·jol'·er·y,** *n.*

cakes and ale, the pleasures of life; enjoyment of material things.

cak·ra·var·tin, chak·ra·var·tin (CHuk,-rəvä'tin), *n.* (in Indian philosophy) one who rules the world perfectly, bringing justice and peace to all.

cal·a·boose (kal'əbōōs), *n. U.S. Inf.* a prison; jail.

cal·a·man·co (kal,əmaNG'kō), *n.* a glossy woollen, fabric brocaded in the warp so as to produce a pattern on one side only, common in the 18th century.

cal·a·thi·form (kal'əthəfôəm), *adj.* shaped like a cup.

cal·car·e·ous (kalker'ēəs), *adj.* consisting of or containing calcium carbonate; chalky.

calced (kalst), *adj.* having shoes on the feet; shod.

cal·ci·fi·ca·tion (kal,sifikā'sHən), *n.* the action of changing into lime, esp. by the deposition of lime salts in tissue.

cal·ci·fy (kal'sifī), *v.* to make hard, as by the deposition of calcium salts; make or become intransigent or unyielding.

cal·ci·mine (kal'simīn), *n.* a white or tinted wash for distempering walls, ceilings, etc.

cal·cine (kal'sīn), *v.* to change into calx through the action of heat.

calc·tu·fa (kalk'tōō,fə), *n.* See **tufa.** Also **caltuff.**

cal·cu·lous (kal'kyələs), *adj.* pertaining to or caused by a calculus, or small stone.

cal·cu·lus (kal'kyələs), *n., pl.* **cal·cu·li** (kal'·kyəlī). **1.** (in mathematics) a systematic method of calculation using a special symbolic notation. **2.** a stony mass sometimes found in the kidneys,

gall bladder, etc., and usually made up of layers of mineral salts.

cal·de·ra (kalder'ə), *n.* a large crater formed by the collapse of the centre of the cone of a volcano.

cal·e·fa·cient (kal,əfā'sHənt), *n.* a medicinal substance producing a feeling of warmth.

cal·e·fac·tion (kal,əfak'sHən), *n.* the act of heating; the state of being heated.

cal·e·fac·to·ry (kal,əfak'tərē), *adj.* producing heat.

cal·en·dar (kal'əndə), *n.* a list of motions for consideration; agenda.

ca·les·cent (kəles'ənt), *adj.* increasing in heat.

Cal·i·ban (kal'əban), *n.* a man showing brutal and bestial characteristics.

cal·i·brate (kal'ibrāt), *v.* to ascertain or check the graduations of (an instrument, etc.).

cal·i·bre, cal·i·ber (kal'əbə), *n.* **1.** the internal diameter of a hollow cylinder, esp. of the barrel of a gun. **2.** degree of merit or importance.

cal·i·cle (kal'ikəl), *n.* a cuplike shape, esp. as found in corals.

cal·i·duct (kal'idukt), *n.* a pipe used for conveying a means of heating, as hot air or water.

cal·i·pash (kal'ipasH), *n.* an edible greenish-coloured gelatinous substance lying inside the upper shell of a turtle.

cal·i·pee (kal'əpē), *n.* an edible, yellowish-coloured gelatinous substance inside the lower shell of a turtle.

ca·liph, ca·lif, ka·lif, ka·liph (kā'lif, kal'·if), *n.* a religious or civil ruler in Muslim countries.

cal·iph·ate (kal'ifāt), *n.* the rank, office, or area of jurisdiction of a caliph.

cal·is·then·ics (kal,isthen'iks), *n.* physical exercises designed to develop bodily strength and grace of movement.

calk (kôk), *n.* an attachment to a shoe designed to prevent slipping on ice, snow, etc. Also **cal·kin** (kô'kin, kal'kin).

cal·let (kal'it, kä'lit), *n.* (in British dialect) **1.** a prostitute; a woman of loose morals. **2.** a shrewish, sharp-tongued woman.

cal·lig·ra·phy (kəlig'rəfē), *n.* the art of fine handwriting; penmanship. See also **cacography.**

cal·li·pyg·i·an (kal,ipij'ēən), *adj.* having well-formed buttocks. Also **cal,li·py'gous.**

cal·los·i·ty (kəlos'itē), *n.* the condition of being callous.

cal·lous (kal'əs), *adj.* unfeeling; insensitive; hardened; brutal.

cal·low (kal'ō), *adj.* lacking maturity; inexperienced.

cal·lus (kal'əs), *n.* **1.** a piece of skin which has become thick or hard. **2.** a substance issuing from the ends of broken bone, which helps to join them.

cal·ma·tive (kal'mətiv, kä'mətiv), *adj.* **1.** tending to calm or soothe. —*n.* 2. that which calms or soothes; a sedative.

cal·o·re·cep·tor (kal'ōrisep,tə), *n.* a receptor which is stimulated by heat.

cal·o·res·cence (kal,əres'əns), *n.* incandescence resulting from the absorption by a body of radiation with a frequency less than that of visible light.

ca·lor·ic (kəlor'ik, kal'ərik), *adj.* relating to calories or to heat.

ca·lor·i·fa·cient (kəlor,ifā'sнənt), *adj.* pertaining to heat-producing foods.

cal·o·rif·ic (kal,ərif'ik), *adj.* producing heat.

cal·o·rim·e·ter (kal,ərim'itə), *n.* an instrument which measures quantities of heat.

cal·o·rim·e·try (kal,ərim'itrē), *n.* the measurement of heat.

ca·lotte (kəlot'), *n.* 1. a skullcap, esp. as worn by Roman Catholic clerics. 2. a small dome.

calque (kalk), *n.* the borrowing by one language from another of a construction in which the structure remains the same but the meaningful elements are replaced by those of the native language.

cal·trop (kal'trəp), *n.* a small spiked iron device used to obstruct the passage of cavalry. Also **cal·throp** (kal'throp), **cal·trap** (kal'trap).

cal·tuff (kal'tuf), *n.* See **tufa**.

cal·u·met (kal'yəmet), *n.* an ornamented ceremonial pipe used by North American Indians. Also **peacepipe**.

ca·lum·ni·ate (kəlum'nēāt), *v.* to malign; accuse falsely; spread malicious reports about. —**ca·lum,ni·a'tion,** *n.*

cal·um·ny (kal'əmnē), *n.* a false statement; a malicious report intended to injure another's reputation. —**ca·lum'ni·ous,** *adj.*

calve (käv), *v.* 1. (of a mass of ice) to become detached; break up. 2. to split off a division or other corporate unit from a conglomerate.

cal·vi·ti·es (kalvisн'ēēz), *n.* the state of being bald.

cal·vous (kal'vəs), *adj.* bald.

calx (kalks), *n.,* *pl.* **calx·es, cal·ces** (kal'sēz). lime.

cam (kam), *n.* an irregularly shaped disc or cylinder used for changing rotary into reciprocating motion, etc.

ca·ma·ra·de·rie (kam,ərä'dərē), *n.* loyalty and goodwill among comrades or friends.

cam·ber (kam'bə), *v.* 1. to curve upwards in the middle. —*n.* 2. a slight curving or arching upwards.

cam·bi·on (kam'bēən), *n.* the offspring of an incubus and a succuba.

cam·bist (kam'bist), *n.* one who deals in bills of exchange; one versed in foreign exchange.

Cam·bri·an (kam'brēən), *adj.* relating to the oldest geologic period, characterized by the preservation of many fossils in rocks.

ca·mel·o·pard (kəmel'əpäd), *n.* a giraffe.

Cam·em·bert (kam'əmbeə), *n.* a strong-smelling, soft, self-ripening, rich cheese.

cam·e·o (kam'ēō), *n.* 1. a method of engraving in relief upon a gem, stone, etc. 2. the gem or stone engraved in this way. 3. a short piece of detailed polished writing, dramatic scene, etc., which gives a vivid presentation of its subject.

cam·er·al (kam'ərəl), *adj.* of or relating to a judicial or legislative chamber.

ca·mi·no re·al (kämē'nô reäl'), *pl.* **ca·mi·nos re·a·les** (kämē'nôs reä'les). (in Spanish) a highway or main road.

cam·i·on (kam'ēən), *n.* a wagon or truck used for carrying heavy loads.

ca·mise (kəmēz'), *n.* a loose-fitting shirt or gown.

cam·i·sole (kam'isōl), *n.* a woman's underbodice.

cam·let (kam'lit), *n.* a kind of hardwearing, waterproof cloth.

ca·mou·flet (kam,əflā'), *n.* a bomb, mine, etc., exploded underground, which makes a cavity but does not break the surface.

cam·ou·fleur (kam'əflû), *n.* one who disguises objects by the use of camouflage.

camp (kamp), *n.* 1. exaggeration or extravagance in gesture or style, speech or writing, etc., esp. when inappropriate to the surroundings, context, etc. 2. one who possesses these characteristics. —*adj.* 3. of or relating to these characteristics or to one who possesses them. —*v.* 4. to make an ostentation or flamboyant display, often in self-parody.

cam·pa·ni·le (kam,pənē'lē), *n.* a bell tower, esp. one separated from surrounding buildings.

cam·pa·nol·o·gy (kam,pənol'əjē), *n.* the technique or art of bell ringing or of making bells.

cam·pan·u·late (kampan'yəlit), *adj.* shaped like a bell.

camp·er (kam'pər), *n.* *U.S.* a portable accommodation unit, carried on a vehicle for use in camping, etc.

cam·pes·tral (kampes'trəl), *adj.* pertaining to the countryside.

cam·pim·e·ter (kampim'itə), *n.* an apparatus for testing the field of vision of the human eye.

camp·y (kam'pē), *adj.* extravagant or exaggerated in speech, gesture, etc., esp. as implying homosexual tendencies.

can·a·pé (kan'əpā, kan'əpē), *n.* a piece of bread or toast topped with anchovies, caviar, or some other spread.

ca·nard (kənäd'), *n.* a false report or rumour; a hoax.

can·dent (kan'dənt), *adj.* heated to a white-hot state.

can·des·cent (kandes'ənt), *adj.* glowing, esp. as a result of intense heat; incandescent.

can·did (kan'did), *adj.* outspoken; sincere; frank; unreserved; straightforward.

can·dour, can·dor (kan'dər), *n.* frankness; forthrightness; sincerity in speech or action.

can·na·bis (kan'əbis), *n.* a preparation of Indian hemp smoked as a drug; hashish.

can·nel·lo·ni (ka,nəlō'nē), *n. pl.* cylindrical pieces of pasta filled with meat or cheese. Also **can·ne·lons** (kan'əlonz).

can·ni·bal·ize (kan'ibəlīz), *v.* to dismantle (a machine, motor vehicle, etc.) in order to provide spare parts for use elsewhere.

can·non·ade (kan,ənād'), *n.* continuous, heavy artillery fire.

can·ny (kan'ē), *adj.* cautious; prudent; knowing; shrewd.

can·on (kan'ən), *n.* **1.** a set of accepted principles or standards by which the practitioners in a particular field function. **2.** any standard against which other things of the same class are measured.

ca·non·i·cal (kənon'ikəl), *adj.* orthodox; recognized; standard.

can·on·ize (kan'ənīz), *v.* **1.** to include within a canon, esp. of sacred writings. **2.** to treat as holy or sacrosanct.

Ca·no·pic jar (kanō'pik), a vase used by the ancient Egyptians to hold the entrails of a deceased person.

ca·no·rous (kənôr'əs), *adj.* pleasant sounding; melodious.

cant (kant), *n.* the specialized jargon of a particular class, trade, or profession.

can·tan·ker·ous (kantaNG'kərəs), *adj.* ill-natured; quarrelsome.

can·thar·i·des (kanthar'idēz), *n.* See **Spanish fly.**

can·thus (kan,thəs), *n.* either of the angles formed by the junction of the upper and lower eyelids.

can·ti·cle (kan'tikəl), *n.* a hymn or song of praise.

can·ti·le·na (kan,tilā'nə), *n.* a simple melody.

can·ti·lev·er (kan'tilē,və), *n.* a beam or member projecting from a vertical support and secured firmly only at one end.

can·til·late (kan'tilāt), *v.* to intone or chant. —**can·til·la'tion,** *n.*

canting arms, a coat of arms with a rebuslike heraldic device that makes a punning allusion to the name of the owner, as a picture of a derrick for a family named Crane.

can·tle (kan'təl), *n.* **1.** a slice or portion. **2.** the rear part of a saddle, usually projecting upward.

can·to (kan'tō), *n., pl.* **can·tos.** one of the main divisions of a long poem.

can·tor (kan'tə), *n.* an official in a synagogue who leads the singing or sings the solo parts.

caou·tchouc (kou'CHOok), *n.* the natural milky juice of rubber trees, a highly elastic solid substance; rubber.

ca·pa (kä'pə), *n.* the red cloak carried by a bullfighter.

ca·pa·cious (kəpā'sHəs), *adj.* roomy; having sufficient space inside for something specified.

cap·a·pie (kap,əpē'), *adj.* from head to foot. Also **cap·à·pié.**

ca·par·i·son (kəpar'isən), *n.* **1.** an ornamental covering for a horse. —*v.* **2.** to dress or deck out in a sumptuous or ornate fashion.

ca·pe·a·dor (kä,pēədôə'), *n.* one who assists a matador by waving his red cloak at the bull in order to distract it.

cap·il·lar·i·ty (kap,ilar'itē), *n.* the action by which the surface of a liquid in contact with a solid is raised or lowered, depending on surface tension and the forces of cohesion and adhesion.

cap·il·lar·y (kəpil'əri), *adj.* **1.** relating to or occurring in a tube having a very small bore. —*n.* **2.** one of the tiny blood vessels connecting arteries with veins.

cap·i·tal·ism (kap'itəliz,əm), *n.* an economic system based on the ownership by private individuals of the means of production, distribution, and exchange.

cap·i·tal·ist (kap'itəlist), *n.* one who makes use of his wealth for business ventures.

cap·i·tal·is·tic (kap,itəlis'tic), *adj.* relating to or practising capitalism.

cap·i·ta·tion (kap,itā'sHən), *n.* a method of assessment or enumeration on the basis of individuals.

ca·pi·teux (kapētœ'), *adj.* French. (of wine) heady.

ca·pit·u·lar (kəpit'yōōlə, kəpiCH'ələ), *adj.* relating to an ecclesiastical chapter.

ca·pit·u·late (kəpit'yōōlāt, kəpiCH'əlāt), *v.* to surrender on agreed terms; surrender unconditionally. —**ca·pit·u·la'tion,** *n.*

cap·o·ral (kap'əräl), *n.* a variety of coarse tobacco.

ca·pote (kəpōt'), *n.* a long hooded cloak.

cap·puc·ci·no (kap,ōōCHē'nō), *n.* espresso coffee served with milk and sometimes cream.

ca·pric·ci·o (kəprē'CHēō), *n., pl.* **ca·pric·ci·os, ca·pric·ci** (kəprē'CHē). a frolic, caper, or prank.

ca·price (kəprēs'), *n.* a sudden whim or fancy; an abrupt and unpredictable change.

ca·pri·cious (kəprisH'əs), *adj.* characterized by whim or changeability; unpredictable; unsteady.

cap·ri·ole (kap'rēōl), *n.* a spring, leap, or caper.

cap·si·cum (kap'səkəm), *n.* common garden pepper.

cap·stan (kap'stən), *n.* a winch for moving heavy weights by winding a cable around a vertical drum which is rotated by hand or mechanically.

cap·tious (kap'sнəs), *adj.* characterized by a tendency to find faults; hard to please; critical.

cap·ti·vate (kap'tivāt), *v.* to enchant; to enthral by some special charm; to appeal irresistibly.

car·a·pace (kar'əpās), *n.* the tough upper part of a turtle's shell.

car·a·van·se·rai *n.* (kar,əvan'sərī), (in the East) an inn with a courtyard providing accommodation for caravans. Also **car·a·van·sa·ry** (kar,əvan'sərē).

car·a·vel (kar'əvel), *n.* a small, two or three-masted vessel, used by the Spanish and Portuguese during the 15th and 16th centuries.

car·bine (kär'bīn), *n.* a short rifle, esp. as formerly used by mounted troops.

car·bo·nade (käbənäd', käbənäd'), *n.* a beef stew with beer and onions. Also **car·bon·nade**.

Car·bon·if·er·ous (kä,bənif'ərəs), *adj.* of a period occurring from 270 million to 350 million years ago, noted for its vegetation, from which modern coal is mined.

car·boy (kä'boi), *n.* a large container, usually of glass and protected by basketwork, for holding corrosive acids, etc. See also **demijohn**.

car·bun·cle (kä'buNGkəl), *n.* **1.** a local inflammation of the skin resulting in the discharge of pus and sloughing of dead tissue. **2.** a rounded, unfaceted garnet.

car·ca·net (kä'kənet), *n.* an ornamental jewelled circlet or neckband.

car·cin·o·gen (käsin'əjin), *n.* a substance which produces cancer. —**car,cin·o·gen'ic**, *adj.*

car·ci·no·ma (ka,sənō'mə), *n., pl.* **car·ci·no·mas, car·ci·no·ma·ta** (ka,sənō'mətə). a malignant tumour; a cancer.

car·da·mom (kä'dəməm), *n.* the aromatic seed of various Asian plants used as a spice or condiment and in medicine. Also **car'da·mum**.

car·di·ac (kä'dēak), *adj.* **1.** relating to the heart. **2.** relating to the anterior portion of the stomach.

car·di·al·gi·a (kä,dēal'jēə), *n.* heartburn. See **cardiodynia**.

car·di·ec·to·my (kä,dēek'təmē), *n.* **1.** excision of the heart. **2.** excision of the cardiac portion of the stomach.

car·di·o·dyn·i·a (kä,dēōdin'ēə), *n.* pain in or near the heart.

car·di·oid (kä'dēoid), *n.* a mathematical curve in the shape of a heart.

car·di·ol·o·gy (ka,dēol'əjē), *n.* the study of the heart and its functions.

car·di·o·meg·a·ly (kä,dēōmeg'əlē), *n.* pathological enlargement of the heart.

car·di·o·vas·cu·lar (kä,dēōvas'kyələ), *adj.* relating to or affecting the heart and blood vessels.

card punch. See **key punch**.

car·i·ous (ker'ēəs), *adj.* (of teeth or bones) affected by caries.

cark·ing (kä'kiNG), *adj.* **1.** disturbed; worried; anxious. **2.** penny-pinching; stingy; miserly.

car·min·a·tive (kä'minətiv), *n.* a drug which relieves flatulence.

car·mine (kä'mīn), *n.* a rich crimson colour.

carn (kän), *n.* See **cairn**.

car·nage (kä'nij), *n.* the killing of large numbers of people; massacre.

car·nal (kä'nəl), *adj.* **1.** worldly; unspiritual. **2.** pertaining to the desires of the flesh; sensual.

car·ne·ous (kä'nēəs), *adj.* resembling or having the colour of flesh.

car·net (kä'nā), *n., pl.* **car·nets** (kä'nāz). a customs licence permitting a motor vehicle to be taken from one country to another.

car·ni·fi·ca·tion (kä'nifikä'sнən), *n.* the conversion into flesh of other tissue.

car·nose (kä'nōs), *adj.* relating to flesh; fleshlike.

ca·rot·id (kərot'id), *n.* either of the two main arteries in the neck.

carp (käp), *v.* to find fault unreasonably; complain in a querulous manner.

car·pal (kä'pəl), *adj.* of or relating to the wrist.

car·pe di·em (kä'pi dē'em), *Latin.* enjoy the present; get the most out of life while ignoring the future.

car·pel (kä'pəl), *n.* a pistil, or gynoecium, in the form of a modified leaf.

car·phol·o·gy (käfol'əjē), *n.* See **floccillation**.

car·pol·o·gy (käpol'əjē), *n.* a branch of botany dealing with the study of seeds and fruits. —**car·po·log·i·cal** (kä,pəloj'ikəl), *adj.* —**car·pol'o·gist**, *n.*

car·poph·a·gous (käpof'əgəs), *adj.* fruit-eating.

car·re·four (kar'əfoor), *n.* a junction or crossroads; public square.

car·rel, car·rell (kar'əl), *n.* a small alcove in a library reserved for individual study.

car·ri·on (kar'ēən), *n.* dead and rotting flesh.

carte blanche (kät, blansн'), *pl.* **cartes blanches** (käts, blansн'). full and unconditional power of action.

car·tel (kätel'), *n.* an organization of business interests designed to regulate output and prices.

car·tel·ist (kä'telist), *n.* a member of a cartel.

car·tel·ize (kä'təlīz), *v.* to form into a cartel.

car·ti·lag·i·nous (kä'tilaj'ənəs), *adj.* relating to or resembling cartilage.

car·to·gram (kä'təgram), *n.* the presentation of statistics on a map base.

car·to·man·cy (kä'təman,sē), *n.* fortune-telling or divination by the use of playing cards.

car·touche, car·touch (kätoōsн'), *n.* an oblong or oval design enclosing characters representing a sovereign's name, as on ancient Egyptian monuments.

car·vel-built (kä'vəlbilt,), *adj.* (of a ship) built

with the planks meeting flush at the seams and not overlapping. See also **clinker-built.**

car·y·at·id (kar,ēat'id), *n.*, *pl.* **cary·at·ids, car·y·at·i·des** (kar,ēat'idēz). (in architecture) a draped female figure serving as a supporting column. See also **atlas.**

cas·ca·bel (kas'kəbel), *n.* a projection behind the breech of a muzzleloading cannon.

ca·se·ate (kā'sēāt), *v.* to be converted into a cheeselike substance. —**ca,se·a'tion,** *n.*

ca·se·fy (kā'səfī), *v.* to turn into or become like cheese.

ca·sern (kəsûn'), *n.* an army barracks.

cash·ier (kasHēr'), *v.* to dismiss with ignominy from a position of responsibility, esp. in military service.

casque (kask), *n.* a head covering resembling a helmet in shape.

cas·sa·tion (kasā'sHən), *n.* cancellation; abrogation; annulment.

cas·sol·ette (kas,əlet'), *n.* a receptacle in which individual portions of food are cooked and then served; a casserole.

cas·sou·let (kas,əlā'), *n.* a stew, originally French, made of white beans, pork, garlic sausage, etc.

cas·tel·lan (kas'tilən), *n.* the warden or governor of a fort or castle.

cas·tel·la·ny (kas'tilā,nē), *n.* **1.** the office or dominion of a castellan. **2.** the land belonging to a castle.

cas·tel·lat·ed (kas'tilā,tid), *adj.* having turrets and battlements like a castle.

cas·ti·gate (kas'tigāt), *v.* to chastise, punish, or reprove severely.

cas·tra·me·ta·tion (kas,trəmətā'sHən), *n.* the art of planning or the act of setting up a military camp.

cas·tra·to (kasträ'tō), *n.* (formerly) a male singer castrated in boyhood to preserve his soprano or contralto voice.

cas·u·al·ism (kaz'yōōəliz,əm), *n.* a philosophical doctrine holding that all events occur by chance.

cas·u·ist (kaz'yōōist), *n.* one skilled in the application of general moral rules to specific cases, esp. one who reasons speciously or dishonestly.

cas·u·is·tic (kaz,yōōis'tik), *adj.* relating to casuists or casuistry; specious or intellectually dishonest.

cas·u·ist·ry (kaz'yōōistrē), *n.* the application of general moral rules to specific cases, esp. dishonestly or speciously.

ca·sus bel·li (kä'sōōs bel'lē), *pl.* **casus bel·li.** *Latin.* an event which leads to or justifies a declaration of war.

ca·tab·a·sis (kətab'əsis), *n.*, *pl.* **ca·tab·a·ses** (kətab'ə,sēz). a descent or downward progression; decline. —**cat·a·bat·ic** (kat,əbat'ik), *adj.*

ca·tab·o·lism, ka·tab·o·lism (kətab'əliz,-əm), *n.* destructive metabolism; a process in which a complex substance is transformed into a simpler one. See also **anabolism.** —**cat,a·bol'-ic,** *adj.*

cat·a·chre·sis (kat,əkrē'sis), *n.* the misuse or wrong use of words.

cat·a·clysm (kat'əkliz,əm), *n.* a violent change or upheaval, esp. one involving sweeping political or social changes.

cat·a·clys·mic (kat,əkliz'mik), *adj.* relating to, resulting from, or having the effect of a cataclysm.

cat·a·drom·ous (kətad'rəməs), *adj.* denoting fish, like the eel, that swim from a fresh-water river down to the sea to spawn. See also **anadromous, diadromous.**

cat·a·falque (kat'əfalk), *n.* a raised platform on which the coffin of a dead person is laid.

cat·a·lep·sy (kat'əlep,sē), *n.* a physical condition associated with a mental or nervous disorder and characterized by complete muscular rigidity, loss of sensation, etc. Also **cataleptic seizure.**

ca·ta·logue rai·son·né (kat'əlog rez,ənä'), *pl.* **ca·ta·logues rai·son·nés** (kat'əlogz rez,ənä'). a catalogue with annotations on or detailed descriptions of the items listed.

ca·tal·y·sis (kətal'isis), *n.*, *pl.* **ca·tal·y·ses** (kətal'isēz). an increase in the rate of a chemical reaction by the introduction of a substance which does not itself undergo permanent change.

cat·a·lyst (kat'əlist), *n.* a substance that brings about catalysis.

cat·a·lyse (kat'əlīz), *v.* to subject to or act upon by catalysis.

cat·a·mite (kat'əmīt), *n.* a boy kept for taking part in homosexual activities.

cat·am·ne·sis (kat,amnē'sis), *n.*, *pl.* **cat·am·ne·ses** (kat,amnē'sēz). the medical history of a sick person.

cat·a·pha·sia (kat,əfā'zHə), *n.* a disorder of speech marked by constant repetition of a word or phrase.

cat·a·pho·re·sis (kat,əfərē'sis), *n.* the action of passing medicinal substances through living tissue in the direction of a positive electric current; electrophoresis.

cat·a·phract (kat'əfrakt), *n.* **1.** an armed warship of ancient Greece. **2.** a Roman soldier in mail.

cat·a·pla·sia, kat·a·pla·sia (kat,əplā'zēə), *n.* degeneration of cells or tissues or reversion to a more primitive form.

cat·a·plasm (kat'əplaz,əm), *n.* a poultice.

cat·arrh·ine (kat'ərin,), *adj.* **1.** having a thin nose. —*n.* **2.** a person or animal with such a nose. Also **lep·tor·rhine** (lep'tərīn,).

ca·tas·ta·sis (kətas'təsis), *n.*, *pl.* **catas·ta·ses** (kətas'təsēz). that part of a play immediately preceding the climax. See also **catastrophe, epitasis, protasis.**

ca·tas·tro·phe (kətas'trəfē). *n.* the decisive point in a play, esp. a tragedy. See also **catastasis, epitasis, protasis.**

catastrophe theory *n.* a mathematical theory concerning the form of surfaces; its concepts have found wider application in describing abrupt discontinuities or sudden changes.

ca·tas·tro·phism (kətas'trəfiz,əm). *n.* the theory that important geological alterations in the structure of the earth were caused by catastrophes rather than by gradual development.

cat·a·to·ni·a, kat·a·to·ni·a (kat,ətō'nēə). *n.* a mental disorder marked by catalepsy.

catch-22 (kaCH'twen,tētōō'). a paradoxical problem for which the apparent solutions in fact offer no advantage or relief, as *You can't work unless you're a member of the union; you can't join the union unless you're working.* [an allusion to the novel *Catch-22,* by Joseph Heller]

catch·ment (kaCH'mənt). *n.* **1.** something that collects water, as a reservoir. **2.** the water thus collected.

cat·e·che·sis (kat,əkē'sis). *n.* oral instruction in the doctrines of Christianity. —**cat·e·chet·i·cal** (kat,əket'ikəl). *adj.*

cat·e·chism (kat'əkiz,əm). *n.* a manual of instruction in the doctrines of Christianity, esp. in question and answer form. —**cat'e·chist,** *n.*

cat·e·chize (kat'əkīz). *v.* to teach doctrines, esp. those of Christianity, by means of question and answer.

cat·e·chu·men (kat,əkyōō'mən). *n.* one who is receiving instruction in the basic elements of Christianity.

cat·e·gor·i·cal (kat,əgor'ikəl). *adj.* without qualification; unconditional; absolute.

ca·te·na (kətē'nə). *n., pl.* **ca·te·nae** (kətē'nē). a connected series of related things, esp. extracts from the writings of the fathers of the Church.

cat·e·nar·y (katē'nərē). *n.* a curve formed by a cord hanging freely from two fixed points.

cat·e·nate (kat'ināt). *v.* to connect in a series; link together.

ca·thar·sis, ka·thar·sis (kəthä'sis). *n.* **1.** (in medicine) purging; evacuation. **2.** the relieving of emotions through the effects of tragic drama.

ca·thar·tic (kəthä'tik). *adj.* **1.** relating to catharsis. —*n.* **2.** a purgative medicine.

cath·e·ter (kath'itə). *n.* a tube designed to drain fluids from the body, esp. urine from the bladder.

ca·thex·is (kəthek'sis). *n., pl.* **ca·thex·es** (kəTHek'sēz). the concentration of mental energy on a specific object, as a person or idea. —**ca·thec·tic** (kəthek'tik). *adj.*

cathode ray tube (kath'ōd). a vacuum tube in which cathode rays in the form of spots or lines can be observed on a fluorescent screen.

cath·o·lic (kath'əlik). *adj.* **1.** relating to the Christian Church as a whole. **2.** of general or universal interest. **3.** broad-minded or liberal in tastes, views, etc.

cat·o·lyte (kat'əlīt,). *n.* (in electronics) the region of the electrolyte surrounding the cathode in an electrolytic cell. Also **cath·o·lyte** (kath'əlīt,).

cat's-paw (kats'pô,). *n.* one used by another as a tool; a dupe.

cau·cus (kô'kəs). *n., pl.* **cau·cus·es** (kô'kəsiz). *Chiefly U.S. and Canadian* **1.** a meeting of persons belonging to a political party to nominate or elect candidates, decide on policy, etc. —*v.* **2.** to come together in a caucus.

cau·dal (kô'dəl). *adj.* relating to, or situated at or near the tail.

cau·dle (kô'dəl). *n.* a warm drink for invalids made from wine, brandy, etc., mixed with bread, gruel, eggs, sugar, and spices.

cau·sa·tion (kôzā'SHən). *n.* the act of causing; cause; the relationship between cause and effect.

cause cé·lè·bre (kôz' səleb'rə). *pl.* **causes cé·lè·bres** (kôz' səleb'rə). any event that creates widespread interest, esp. a famous trial.

cau·se·rie (kō'zərē). *n.* a chat; an informal discussion.

caus·tic (kôs'tik). *adj.* having a corrosive effect; biting or sarcastic.

cau·ter·ize (kô'tərīz). *v.* to burn with a hot iron, esp. in order to sear or destroy tissue. —**cau'ter·y,** *n.*

ca·vate (kā'vāt). *adj.* hollowed out so as to form a cave, etc.

ca·ve·at (kā'vēat, kav'ēat). *n.* a legal notice to a court to suspend proceedings temporarily.

caveat emp·tor (emp'tôr). the principle that the buyer of goods buys at his own risk unless the goods are covered by a warranty.

ca·ve ca·nem (kā'vē kä'nem). *Latin.* beware of the dog.

cav·il (kav'il). *v.* **1.** to raise trivial objections; quibble; find fault unnecessarily. —*n.* **2.** an irritating and pointless objection.

cav·i·ta·tion (kav,itā'SHən). *n.* the formation of partial vacuums in a flowing liquid in areas of very low pressure.

ca·vo·re·lie·vo (kä,vōrilē'vō). *n., pl.* **ca·vo·re·lie·vos.** a kind of sculpture in relief in which the highest points are beneath the level of the original surface. See also **alto-relievo, mezzo-relievo.**

ca·vort (kəvôət'). *v.* to leap about in a playful way; caper.

ce·cum (sē'kəm). *n., pl.* **ce·ca** (sē'kə). See **caecum.**

cede (sēd). *v.* to give up, surrender, or yield.

ce·dil·la (sidil'ə). *n.* a mark placed under a

letter, usually indicating a sibilant pronunciation, as in *garçon*.

ceil (sēl), *v.* to overlay with wood or plaster, as the ceiling of a room, etc.

cei·lidh (kā'lē), *n.* a social gathering for dancing and singing, esp. in traditional Scottish or Irish forms.

cel·a·don (sel'ədon), *n.* a porcelain having a light green glaze.

cel·a·ture (sel'əCHŌŌr), *n.* the process of embossing metal.

cel·e·brant (sel'əbrənt), *n.* the priest who officiates at the Eucharist.

ce·ler·i·ty (səler'itē), *n.* rapidity; speed.

ce·les·tial (səles'tiəl, səles'CHəl), *adj.* of or relating to heaven or to the heavens, or sky.

celestial mechanics, the application of Newton's law of gravitation and the laws of dynamics to the movements of celestial bodies.

celestial navigation, navigation by observation of the position of celestial bodies, without reference to Earth.

ce·li·ac disease (sē'lēak). See **coeliac disease.**

cel·i·ba·cy (sel'əbəsē), *n.* the state of being unmarried, esp. as the result of a religious vow.

cel·i·bate (sel'əbət), *n.* **1.** one who does not marry, esp. as the result of a religious vow. —*adj.* **2.** unmarried.

cel·lar·et, cel·lar·ette (sel,əret'), *n.* a cabinet or cupboard in which bottles of wine are stored.

Cel·si·us (sel'sēəs), *n.* See **centigrade.**

cel·ure (sel'yər), *n.* a decorated canopy for a bed, throne, etc.

ce·men·ti·tious (sē,mentisH'əs), *adj.* having the properties of cement.

cen·a·cle, coen·a·cle (sen'əkəl), *n.* the room in which the Last Supper was held.

ce·nes·the·sia (sē,nis*th*ē'zēə), *n.* See **coenesthesia.**

ce·no·gen·e·sis (se,nəjen'isis), *n.* See **caenogenesis.**

cen·o·taph (sen'ətaf), *n.* a tomb or monument erected as a memorial to a deceased person who is buried elsewhere.

Ce·no·zo·ic, Cae·no·zo·ic (sē,nōzō'ik), *adj.* relating to the present or tertiary geological era, marked by the evolution of mammals. Also **Cainozoic.**

cense (sens), *v.* to perfume with a censer; burn incense near.

cen·ser (sen'sər) *n.* a receptacle for holding burning incense.

cen·sure (sen'sHə), *n.* **1.** strong condemnation or disapproval. —*v.* **2.** to blame or condemn; criticize severely.

cen·te·nar·y (sentē'nərē), *adj.* **1.** relating to a period of 100 years. —*n.* **2.** a 100th anniversary.

cen·ten·ni·al (senten'ēəl), *adj.* **1.** relating to or

marking the completion of 100 years. —*n.* **2.** *U.S.* a centenary.

cen·tes·i·mal (sentes'əməl), *adj.* relating to or characterized by a division into hundredths.

cen·ti·grade (sen'tigrād), *adj.* relating to a scale of temperature in which 100 equal degrees are fixed between the freezing point and boiling point of water.

cen·ti·gram (sen'tigram), *n.* 1/100th of a gram.

cen·ti·li·tre (sen'tilē,tə), *n.* 1/100th of a litre.

cen·ti·me·tre (sen'timē,tə), *n.* 1/100th of a metre.

cen·ti·me·tre-gram-sec·ond (sen'timē,tə-gram'sek'ənd), *adj.* relating to the system of measurement in which the centimetre, gram, and second are the basic units of length, mass, and time, respectively. *Abbrev.*: **cgs.**

centre of gravity, that point of a body at which it will balance if supported.

cen·trif·u·gal (sen,trifyŌŌ'gəl, sentrif'yəgəl), *adj.* proceeding or acting in a direction away from the centre.

cen·tri·fuge (sen'trifyŌŌj), *n.* an apparatus which uses centrifugal force to separate substances having different densities.

cen·trip·e·tal (sentrip'itl), *adj.* proceeding towards or acting upon the centre.

cen·tu·ple (sen'tyəpəl), *adj.* a hundredfold; one hundred times as great.

ce·phal·ic (səfal'ik, kəfəl'ik), *adj.* relating to the head.

ceph·a·lo·pod (sef'ələpod), *n.* a class of molluscs including the squid, octopus, etc., having tentacles on the head.

ce·ra·ceous (sərā'sHəs), *adj.* resembling wax in appearance or feel.

ce·ram·ic (səram'ik), *adj.* relating to the manufacture of products from clay, etc.

cer·at·ed (sēr'ātid), *adj.* covered with wax.

cer·a·tin (ser'ətin), *n.* See **keratin.**

cer·a·toid (ser'ətoid), *adj.* horny; resembling horn.

cer·e·bel·lum (ser,əbel'əm), *n.*, *pl.* **cer·e·bel·lums, cer·e·bel·la** (ser,əbel'ə). part of the hindbrain which coordinates movement and helps balance.

cer·e·bral (ser'ibrəl), *adj.* relating to the cerebrum. See **cacuminal.**

cerebral palsy, a kind of paralysis caused by injury or defect to the brain.

cer·e·brate (ser'ibrāt), *v.* to think; use one's mind.

cer·e·bro·spi·nal meningitis (ser,ibrōspī'-nəl), inflammation of the meninges of the brain and the spinal cord.

cer·e·bro·to·ni·a (ser,ibrōtō'nēa), *n.* the personality pattern usually associated with the ectomorphic body type, characterized by sensitivity and concern and involvement with intellectual matters. See also **somatotonia, viscerotonia.**

cer·e·brum (ser'ibrəm), *n.* the larger, anterior part of the brain concerned with conscious and voluntary mental processes.

cere·cloth (sēə'kloth,, sēə'klôth,), *n.* a wax-coated, waterproof cloth, used as a winding sheet.

cere·ment (sēə'mənt), *n., usually pl.* a cerecloth used as a shroud for the dead.

ce·rif·er·ous (sərif'ərəs), *adj.* producing wax.

ce·ro·graph (sēr'ōgräf), *n.* an engraving on a wax surface. —**ce·rog'ra·phy,** *n.*

ce·ro·plas·tic (sēr,ōplas'tik), *adj.* relating to modelling in wax.

ce·rous (sēr'əs), *adj.* of or containing the element cerium, esp. in its trivalent state.

cer·ti·o·ra·ri (sûr,sHēərer'ī), *n.* a writ issued by a higher court calling for review of the records of the proceedings of a lower court.

ce·ru·le·an (sərōō'lēən), *adj.* deep blue; resembling the blue of the sky.

ce·ru·men (sərōō'mən), *n.* a waxy secretion from the glands of the external ear.

cer·ve·lat (sû'vəlat), *n.* a smoked sausage made of pork and beef. Also **cer've·las.**

cer·vi·cal (sû'vikəl, sûvī'kəl), *adj.* relating to the cervix or the neck.

cer·vine (sû'vīn), *adj.* relating to deer; deerlike.

cer·vix (sû'viks), *n., pl.* **cer·vix·es, cer·vi·ces** (sû'visēz). the neck or any part resembling a neck, esp. the narrow outer end of the uterus.

ces·sion (sesH'ən), *n.* the act of yielding something to another; surrender.

ce·ta·cean (sitā'sHən), *adj.* **1.** belonging to a marine mammal family including whales, dolphins, etc. —*n.* **2.** a cetacean mammal.

cete (sēt), *n.* a group of badgers.

ce·te·ris pa·ri·bus (set'əris par'ibəs), *Latin.* other things being equal.

ce·tol·o·gy (sētol'əjē), *n.* the branch of zoology that deals with whales.

cha·bouk, cha·buk (cHäbōōk), *n.* a whip used in eastern countries to inflict corporal punishment.

cha·cun à son goût (sHakuN' a sôN gōō'), *French.* everyone to his own taste.

chad (cHad), *n.* the paper removed when holes are perforated in a card or tape.

chae·toph·o·rous (kitof'ərəs), *adj.* bristly; having bristles.

chaff (cHaf), *n.* strips of metal dropped by aircraft to confuse enemy radar systems. Also **window.**

cha·grin (sHag'rin), *n.* **1.** disappointment, vexation. —*v.* **2.** to cause disappointment or vexation to.

chak·ra·var·tin (cHukrəvär'tin), *n.* See **cak·ravartin.**

chal·ced·o·ny (kalsed'ənē), *n.* a translucent variety of quartz, often pale blue or grey in colour.

chal·cog·ra·phy (kalkog'rəfē), *n.* the technique of engraving on copper or brass.

chal·co·lith·ic (kal,kəlith'ik), *adj.* relating to or characteristic of the Copper Age.

chal·lah (κΗälə), *n., pl.* **chal·lahs, chal·loth** (κΗälôt'). a kind of Jewish bread containing eggs.

chal·lis (sHal'ē), *n.* a soft woollen or cotton fabric.

chal·one (kal'ōn), *n.* a secretion of the endocrine glands that tends to depress activity.

cha·lyb·e·ate (kəlib'ēit), *adj.* (of a mineral spring, etc.) impregnated with salts of iron.

cha·made (sHəmäd'), *n.* (formerly) a signal sounded on a drum calling an enemy to a truce or parley.

cham·ber·lain (cHäm'bəlin), *n.* an attendant upon a king or noble in his bedchamber; an official in charge of a royal household; a treasurer.

cham·bré (sHäN'brā), *adj.* (of a wine) at room temperature.

cham·fer (cHam'fə), *n.* an oblique surface cut into the corner of a board, usually at an angle of 45°; a groove.

cham·paign (sHampān'), *n.* an expanse of open country.

cham·per·ty (cHam'pûtē), *n.* a device whereby a party who promotes litigation illegally shares in the proceeds.

cham·pi·gnon (sHam,pēnyôN', sHampin'yən), *n., pl.* **cham·pi·gnons.** a mushroom.

champ·le·vé (sHäNləvä'), *n.* a technique for making jewellery and other small objects in which enamel is fused onto designs on a metal base.

chan·cel (cHan'səl), *n.* the area around the altar of a church, reserved for the clergy, choir, etc.

chan·cel·ler·y (cHan'sələrē), *n.* the building or room in which the office of a chancellor is situated.

chan·cel·lor (cHan'sələr), *n.* (in some countries) a title of various high-ranking officials, as judges, finance ministers, etc.

chan·cre (sHaNG'kər), *n.* a sore or ulcer caused by syphilis.

chan·croid (sHaNG'kroid), *n.* a soft venereal sore.

chan·dler (cHand'lə), *n.* **1.** one who deals in naval stores or provisions. **2.** one who makes or sells candles.

chan·dler·y (cHand'lərē), *n.* the warehouse, storeroom, or business of a chandler.

change·ling (cHānj'liNG), *n.* a child substituted for another in infancy; a strange or ugly child, esp. one supposedly left by fairies.

cha·no·yu (cHä'nôyōō'), *n.* a Japanese tea ceremony.

chan·son (SHÄNSÔN', SHan'sən), *n.*, *pl.* **chan-sons.** a song, esp. as sung in French cabaret or music-hall.

chan·son de geste (SHÄNSÔN də ZHest'), *pl.* **chan-sons de geste** (SHÄNSÔN də ZHest'). a medieval French epic poem.

chan·son·nier (SHänsənyā'), *n.*, *pl.* **chan·son·niers** (SHänsənyāz'). a nightclub entertainer who combines singing with telling stories, jokes, etc.

chan·teuse (SHÄNtŌŌz'), *n.*, *pl.* **chanteu·ses** (SHÄNtŌŌz'). a woman who sings in nightclubs, etc.

chan·ti·cleer (CHan'təklēr), *n.* a rooster or cock.

Chan·til·ly (SHantil'ē), *n.* See **mousseline.**

chaos theory, a theory, applicable in many areas of science, that a certain order underlies apparently random events.

chap·ar·ral (CHapəral'), *n.* (in the U.S.) a dense thicket, esp. a growth of dwarf, evergreen oaks.

cha·pa·ti (CHəpat'ē), *n.*, *pl.* **cha·pati** (CHəpat'ē), **cha·pa·tis** (CHəpat'ēz), **cha·pa·ties** (CHəpat'ēz). a kind of Indian flat bread made of a dough of flour and water.

chap·book (CHap'bŌŌk,), *n.* a small book containing popular tales, ballads, etc.

cha·peau (SHapō'), *n.*, *pl.* **cha·peaux** (SHapōz'). a hat.

chap·el (CHap'əl), *n.* a printing house or the association of employees belonging to it.

chap·fall·en (CHap'fôlən), *adj.* crestfallen; downcast; dejected.

chap·let (CHap'lit), *n.* **1.** a garland intended to be worn on the head. **2.** a string of beads.

chap·tal·i·za·tion (SHap,təlizā'SHən), *n.* the addition of sugar to wine before or during fermentation in order to increase the alcoholic content. —**chap'tal·ize,** *v.*

char·a·banc (SHar'əbaNG), *n.* a motor coach, esp. an open one, formerly used for sightseeing tours.

char·ac·ter·y (kar'iktərē) *n.* the use of symbols or characters to convey meaning; such symbols collectively.

char·cu·te·rie (SHärkŌŌtərē'), *n.*, *pl.* **char·cu·te·ries** (SHärkŌŌtərēz'). (in France) a butcher's shop specializing in pork.

char·cu·tier (SHärkŌŌtēā'), *n.*, *pl.* **char·cu·tiers** (SHärkŌŌtēāz'). a butcher who specializes in pork.

char·gé d'af·faires (SHä'ZHä dəfe'), *pl.* **char·gés d'af·faires** (SHä'ZHäz dəfe'). an official in charge of an embassy during the ambassador's absence.

char·i·ly (CHer'əlē), *adv.* cautiously; carefully.

cha·ris·ma (kəriz'mə), *n.*, *pl.* **charis·ma·ta** (kəriz'mətə). an outstanding quality in a person that gives him influence and authority over others.

cha·riv·a·ri (SHəriv,ərē'), *n.* a playful, noisy mock serenade of a newly wed couple, accompanied by the banging of pots and pans, etc. Also **shivaree.**

char·la·tan (SHä'lətən), *n.* one who fraudulently claims to have exceptional powers of some kind.

char·la·tan·ism (SHä'lətniz,əm), *n.* the practices of a charlatan. Also **char'la·tan·ry.**

char·nel (CHä'nəl), *n.* a place where dead bodies are kept.

char·nu (SHarnY'). *adj.* (of a wine) full-bodied.

char·rette, char·ette (SHəret'), *n.* an attempt to meet the deadline set for some task by an all-out effort.

char·ta (kä'tə), *n.*, *pl.* **char·tae** (kä'tē). **1.** a piece of paper impregnated with medicine for external use. **2.** Also **char·tu·la** (kä'CHələ). a piece of paper folded to hold powdered medicine.

char·ta·ce·ous (kätä'sēəs), *adj.* resembling paper.

char·tist (CHä'tist), *n.* a stock market official who makes forecasts by means of charts and graphs.

char·treuse (SHätrûz'), *n.* a liqueur, usually pale green or yellow in colour, made by Carthusian monks.

char·tu·lar·y (CHä'tyələrē), *n.* a collection or register of title deeds, etc.

char·vet (SHä'vä), *n.* a soft fabric in silk or rayon.

char·y (CHer'ē), *adj.* cautious; careful; wary; timid; frugal or sparing. —**char'i·ness,** *n.*

Cha·sid (hä'sid), *n.*, *pl.* **Cha·sid·im** (häsid'im). See **Hasid.**

chas·sé (SHas'āy), *n.* **1.** a sliding step in ballet. **2.** (in ballroom dancing) a series of two quick steps and one slow step to four beats. —*v.* **chas·sés, chas·sé·ing, chas·séd. 3.** to perform either of these steps.

chas·seur (SHas'û), *n.* **1.** a unit in the French army trained for rapid deployment. **2.** a liveried attendant, esp. one in huntsman's uniform. —*adj.* **3.** containing or cooked with white wine and mushrooms.

chaste (CHäst), *adj.* pure; not dirtied, either physically or morally; virginal.

chas·ten (CHä'sən), *v.* **1.** to inflict punishment upon; chastise; discipline. **2.** calm; subdue; restrain.

chas·tise (CHastīz'). *v.* to punish or discipline by beating.

chas·u·ble (CHaz'yəbəl), *n.* a sleeveless outer vestment worn by a celebrant of mass.

chate·laine (SHat'lān), *n.* **1.** the mistress of a castle or large country house. **2.** a girdle or clasp for holding a large bunch of keys.

cha·ton (SHatôN'), *n.* an imitation gem made from paste.

cha·toy·ant (SHətoi'ənt), *adj.* 1. having a changing lustre or colour. 2. (of a jewel, etc.) reflecting a single beam of light when cut in a convex form.

chat·tel (CHat'əl), *n.* a movable possession or item of property.

chauf·fer (CHô'fû), *n.* a small, portable stove.

chau·vin·ism (SHŌ'viniz,əm), *n.* excessive or blind patriotism; jingoism. —**chau'vin·ist,** *n.*

cheap-jack (CHēp'jak), *n.* a pedlar, hawker, etc., who sells cheap goods.

ché·chia (SHĀSH'yä), *n.* a close-fitting hat with a tassel, worn in the Middle East.

Ched·dar (CHed'ə), *n.* a hard, smooth cheese, yellow or white in colour.

chee·cha·ko (CHēCHä'kō), *n.* a newcomer; a naive or inexperienced person; a greenhorn.

cheese-par·ing (CHēz'per,ING), *adj.* miserly; mean; parsimonious.

chef-d'oeu·vre (SHedû'vrə), *n.*, *pl.* **chefs-d'oeu·vres** (SHedû'vrə). a masterpiece in literature or art.

chei·li·tis (kīlī'tis), *n.* an inflammation that affects the lips.

che·la (kē'lə), *n.*, *pl.* **che·lae** (kē'lē). a nipper- or pincer-like organ of certain crustaceans.

che·loid (kē'loid), *n.* See **keloid.**

che·lo·ni·an (kilō'nēən). *adj.* relating to or belonging to turtles or tortoises.

chem·ic (kem'ik), *adj.* relating to alchemy.

chemical warfare, warfare using poisonous, nerve, or corrosive gases.

chem·i·cul·ture (kem'ikul,CHə), *n.* hydroponics.

che·mig·ra·phy (kəmig'rəfē), *n.* the making of engravings with the use of chemicals.

chem·i·lum·i·nes·cence (kem,ilōō,mines'-əns), *n.* light produced by chemical reaction at low temperatures. —**chem,i·lu,mi·nes'cent,** *adj.*

che·min de fer (SHəman'dəfeə'), a card game similar to baccarat.

che·mise (SHəmēz'), *n.* a woman's one-piece, loose-fitting undergarment; a loose, straight-hanging dress.

chem·i·sette (SHemizet'), *n.* a woman's garment worn over a low-cut bodice.

chem·o·ki·ne·sis (kem,ōkinē'sis), *n.* an increase in activity in an organism as a result of a chemical substance.

chem·o·pause (kem'əpôz), *n.* the stratum or boundary lying between the chemosphere and the ionosphere.

chem·o·pro·phy·lax·is (kem,ōprō,filak'sis), *n.* prophylaxis by the means of some chemical agent. —**chem,o,phy·lac'tic,** *adj.*

chem·o·re·cep·tion (kem,ōrisep'SHən), *n.* physiological response to a chemical stimulus.

chem·o·re·cep·tor (kem,ōrisep'tə), *n.* any sense organ stimulated by chemical means.

chem·o·re·flex (kem,ōrē'fleks), *n.* a reflex brought about by a chemical stimulus.

chem·o·sphere (kem'əsfē), *n.* a stratum of the atmosphere in which the most intense chemical activity takes place.

chem·o·sur·ger·y (kem,ōsû'jərē), *n.* the use of a chemical agent to effect a result usually obtained by surgery, as the removal of tissue, etc.

chem·o·syn·the·sis (kemōsin'thisis), *n.* the synthesis of organic compounds by means of energy resulting from chemical reactions. —**chem,o·syn·thet'ic,** *adj.*

chem·o·tax·is (kem,ōtak'sis), *n.* the attraction or repulsion to chemical agents shown by a cell or organism. —**chem,o·tac'tic,** *adj.*

chem·o·ther·a·py (kē,mōther'əpē, kemō-ther'əpē), *n.* the use of chemical agents in the treatment of a disease. Also **chem,o·ther·a·peu·tics** (kem,ōther,əpyōō'tiks). —**chem,o·ther·a·peu'tic,** *adj.*

chem·ot·ro·pism (kemōtrə'piz,əm), *n.* growth or movement in plants and other organisms in response to the presence of chemical stimuli.

chem·ur·gy (kem'ûjē), *n.* a branch of applied chemistry which is concerned with the industrial utilization of organic substances derived from farm products.

che·nier (SHin'yə), *n.* a clump of oak trees growing on a hillock in marshy or swampy regions.

che·nille (SHənēl'). *n.* a fabric having a raised pile, used in the manufacture of bedspreads, etc.

cher·chez la femme (SHeshā, l fäm'), *French.* look for the woman (as the cause of trouble, etc.).

che·root (SHərōōt'), *n.* a cigar cut square at each end.

cherry picker, any of various kinds of crane with a jointed boom and fitted with a basket for working in trees, etc.

cher·so·nese (kû'sənēz), *n.* a peninsula.

chert (CHût), *n.* a rock resembling flint and composed of microcrystalline quartz.

cher·vil (CHû'vil), *n.* a herb with aromatic leaves, belonging to the parsley family and used to flavour salads, soups, etc.

che·val glass (SHəval'), a full-length mirror suspended on a frame so that it can be tilted.

cheval screen, a fire screen supported at the ends and mounted on legs.

che·vee (SHəvā'), *n.* 1. a carving on a gem stone, having a figure in relief on a hollowed out background. 2. a smooth gem, the surface of which forms a slight depression.

chev·re (SHəv'rə), *n.* a variety of French cheese made from goat's milk.

chev·rette (sʜəvret'), *n.* a thin variety of kid-skin.

chev·y (ᴄʜᴇᴠ'ē). See **chivy**.

chez (sʜā), *prep. French.* at or to the home of; with; in.

chi·a·ro·scu·ro (kēä,rəsko͞or'ō), *n.* (in painting) the treatment or arrangement of light and shade in a picture in order to create a general effect. Also **chi·a·ro·o·scu·ro** (kēä,roͦoskoͦor'ō).

chi·bouk, chi·bouque (ᴄʜibo͞ok'), *n.* a Turkish tobacco pipe having a long stem.

chi·cane (sʜikān'), *n.* deceit; chicanery.

chi·can·er·y (sʜikā'nərē), *n.* trickery by the use of subterfuge or sophistry; sharp practice.

chi·chi (sʜē'sʜē'), *adj.* elegant or fashionable in an ornate or pretentious manner.

chick·pea (ᴄʜik'pē,), *n.* a plant bearing edible seeds, looking like peas, eaten esp. in S. Europe and Latin America. Also **garbanzo**.

chic·le (ᴄʜik'əl), *n.* a gum obtained from the latex of the sapodilla and used in making chewing gum.

chide (ᴄʜīd), *v.* to reprove, scold, or rebuke; voice disapproval; worry; harass.

chig·oe (ᴄʜig'ō), *n.* a flea of the Caribbean region and Africa, the female of which burrows under the skin of man and animals. Also **chig·ger** (ᴄʜig'ə), **jigger**.

child·bed (ᴄʜīld'bed,), *n.* the condition of a woman in labour.

chil·i·arch (kil'ēäk), *n.* (in ancient Greece and Rome) an officer in charge of a thousand men.

chil·i·asm (kil'ēaz,əm), *n.* the doctrine that Christ will return to reign on earth for a thousand years.

chil·i con car·ne (ᴄʜil'ē kon kä'nē), a Mexican dish made from meat, chillies, sweet peppers, and beans.

chi·me·ra (kīmēr'ə, kimēr'ə), *n.* **1.** a mythological monster commonly shown as having a lion's head, a goat's body, and a serpent's tail. **2.** any imagined horror or morbid fancy. **3.** (in biology) an organism having tissues of genetically different kinds.

chine (ᴄʜīn), *n.* the backbone of an animal.

chi·noi·se·rie (sʜēnwoz,ərē'), *n.* a style of decoration or ornamentation characterized by imitations of supposedly Chinese motifs.

chintz·y (ᴄʜint'sē), *adj.* tawdry; cheap; gaudy.

chirk (ᴄʜûk), *v.* to make a strident or shrill sound.

chi·rog·ra·phy (kīrog'rəfē), *n.* handwriting or penmanship. —**chi,ro·graph'ic,** *adj.*

chi·ro·man·cy (kīr'əman,sē), *n.* divination by examining the lines of the hand.

chi·rop·o·dy (kirop'ədē), *n.* the treatment of corns, bunions, and other foot ailments. —**chi·rop'o·dist,** *n.*

chi·ro·prac·tic (kīrəprak'tik), *n.* a system of treatment involving the manipulation of the spinal column, based on the theory that disease is caused by the malfunction of nerves. —**chi'ro·prac,tor,** *n.*

chirr (ᴄʜû), *v.* to make the trilling sound characteristic of a grasshopper or cricket.

chi-square (kī'skwer,), *n.* (in statistics) the sum of the quotients, the result of dividing the square of the difference between the observed and expected values of a quantity by the expected value.

chi·tin (kī'tin), *n.* a horny, organic substance forming part of the outer integument of some insects and crustaceans.

chit·ter (ᴄʜit'ə), *v.* to chirp or twitter.

chiv·y, chiv·vy (ᴄʜiv'ē), *v.* to chase; run after; annoy; worry; nag; harass. Also **chev·y**.

chlo·ro·phyll (klôr'əfil), *n.* the green colouring substance of plants and leaves associated with the production of carbohydrates by photosynthesis. —**chlo·ro'phyl·lous,** *adj.*

chlo·ro·sis (klôrō'sis), *n.* a diseased condition in plant tissues marked by a tendency to turn yellow.

chlor·prom·a·zine (klôrprom'əzēn), *n.* a drug used to depress the central nervous system and prevent nausea and vomiting.

chok·er (ᴄʜō'kə), *n.* a short necklace that fits tightly round the throat.

cho·le·cal·cif·er·ol (kō,likalsif'ərol), *n.* a form of vitamin D, found in fish-liver oils.

chol·e·cys·ti·tis (kol,isistī'tis), *n.* inflammation of the gall bladder.

chol·e·lith (kol'əli*th*), *n.* a gallstone.

cho·les·ter·ol (kəles'tərol), *n.* a sterol found in egg yolk, meat, and dairy fats, the main ingredient of the plaques which clog arteries, leading to atherosclerosis.

cho·les·ter·ol·ae·mi·a (kəles,tərōlē'mēə), *n.* a condition in which an abnormal amount of cholesterol is present in the blood.

cho·li, cho·lee (ᴄʜō'lē), *n.* a short blouse worn by women in India.

chon·dral (kon'drəl), *adj.* relating to cartilage.

chon·drule (kon'droͦol), *n.* a rounded mass often found in meteoric stones.

choo·ra (ᴄʜoͦor'ə), *n.* a kind of single-edged Indian dagger.

chop·log·ic (ᴄʜop'loj,ik), *n.* an excessively complicated or specious way of reasoning.

cho·ra·gus (kərā'gəs), *n., pl.* **chora·gi** (kərā'jī), **cho·ra·gus·es.** one who officiates at an entertainment, festival, etc. Also **cho·re·gus** (kərē'gəs).

cho·re·a (kôrē'ə), *n.* a nervous disorder characterized by involuntary, spasmodic movements.

cho·re·o·graph (kor'ēəgraf), *v.* to compose choreography for; work as a choreographer.

cho·re·og·ra·pher (kor,ēog'rəfə), *n.* one who creates dance movements for stage dances, esp. ballet.

cho·re·og·ra·phy (kor,ēog'rəfē), *n.* the art of

composing and arranging techniques, movements, etc., for dances, esp. ballet.

chor·i·zo (cHôrē'zō), *n., pl.* **chor·i·zos.** a spicy pork sausage of Spanish or Mexican cuisine.

cho·rog·ra·phy (kərog'rəfē), *n.* the technique of systematically mapping a region or district.

chor·oid coat (kôr'oid), a vascular membrane lining the eyeball. Also **chor·i·oid** (kôr'ēoid).

chor·tle (cHôr'təl), *v.* to laugh or chuckle triumphantly or gleefully.

chouse (cHous), *v.* **1.** to cheat or swindle. —*n.* **2.** a fraud; swindle.

chow-chow (cHou'cHou,), *n.* mixed pickles in mustard sauce.

chre·ma·tis·tic (krē,mətis'tik), *adj.* of or connected with making money. —**chre,ma·tis'tics,** *n.*

chres·tom·a·thy (krestom'əthē), *n.* a selection of excerpts from literary works, esp. in a foreign language. —**chres,to·math'ic,** *adj.*

chrism (kriz'əm), *n.* consecrated oil used in certain sacraments.

Christian Science, a religion based on a particular interpretation of the Scriptures and including the practice of spiritual healing.

Chris·to·cen·tric (krist,ōsen'trik), *adj.* based exclusively on the doctrines of Jesus Christ.

Chris·to·gram (kris'təgram), *n.* a symbolic representation of Christ.

Chris·tol·o·gy (kristol'əjē), *n.* that branch of theology concerned with the nature, person, and work of Jesus Christ.

Chris·toph·a·ny (kristof'ənē), *n.* an appearance of Christ on earth after the Resurrection.

chro·mat·ic (krōmat'ik), *adj.* **1.** relating to colour. **2.** (in music) modifying the normal scale by the use of accidentals.

chro·mat·i·cism (krōmat'isiz,əm), *n.* (in music) the use of chromatic tones.

chro·ma·tic·i·ty (krō,mətis'itē), *n.* the quality of a colour as characterized by its dominant wavelength and its purity considered together.

chro·mat·ics (krōmat'iks), *n.* the science of colours. Also **chro·ma·tol·ogy** (krō,mətol'əjē).

chro·ma·tog·ra·phy (krō,mətog'rəfē), *n.* a method of separating mixtures into their constituent parts through preferential adsorption by a solid such as clay.

chrom·hi·dro·sis (krō,midrō'sis), *n.* the secretion of coloured sweat.

chro·mo·gen (krō'məjən), *n.* a substance, as a microorganism, which produces pigmented compounds when oxidized.

chro·mo·gen·ic (krōməjen'ik), *adj.* producing pigment.

chro·mo·some (krō'məsōm), *n.* any of several thread-shaped bodies found in the nucleus of living cells and carrying the genetic code.

chro·mo·sphere (krō'məsfēr), *n.* **1.** a gaseous envelope surrounding the photosphere of the sun. **2.** a similar envelope surrounding a star. —**chro,mo·spher'ic,** *adj.*

chron·ic (kron'ik), *adj.* perpetual; unceasing, as a chronic headache.

chron·o·bi·ol·o·gy (krō,nəbīol'əjē, kron,əbīol'əjē), *n.* a branch of biology devoted to the study of how time and seasons influence bodily functions.

chron·o·gram (kron'əgram), *n.* an inscription, sentence, etc., in which certain letters express a date or period through their value as Roman numerals.

chron·o·graph (kron'əgräf), *n.* an instrument for recording and measuring the exact moment of an event or very short time intervals.

chro·nom·e·ter (krənom'itə), *n.* an instrument for measuring time with great accuracy.

chron·o·pher (kron'əfə), *n.* an electrical apparatus used to broadcast time signals.

chron·o·scope (kron'əskōp), *n.* an instrument for making precise measurements of very short intervals of time.

chrys·a·lis (kris'əlis), *n.* the pupa of a butterfly.

chrys·el·e·phan·tine (kris,eləfan'tin), *adj.* containing or composed of gold and ivory.

chrys·o·graph (kris'əgräf), *n.* a manuscript written in ink containing gold or silver in powdered form.

chrys·o·prase (kris'əpräz), *n.* a green-coloured chalcedony used in jewellery.

chtho·ni·an (thō'nēən), *adj.* (in mythology) relating to the gods and spirits of the underworld. Also **chtho'nic.**

chuck·a·luck (cHuk'əluk), *n.* a betting game played with three dice.

chuff·y (cHuf'ē), *adj.* boorish; ill-mannered.

chum (cHum), *n.* **1.** bait cut small and thrown into the water to attract fish. —*v.* **2.** to fish by throwing such bait into the water.

Church invisible, the whole of Christianity both in heaven and on earth.

Church militant, those Christians constantly active in the fight against evil.

Church suffering (in Roman Catholic doctrine) the souls of people in purgatory.

Church triumphant, those Christians in heaven who have been victorious in the fight against evil.

Church visible, the whole body of Christian believers on earth.

church·ward·en (cHûcH'wôd,ən), *n.* a tobacco pipe with a long stem.

chu·rin·ga (cHōōriNG'gə), *n., pl.* **chu·rin·ga, chu·rin·gas.** a carved wooden object regarded as sacred by Australian aborigines.

churl (cHûl), *n.* an ill-mannered or surly person.

churl·ish (cHû'lisH), *adj.* unrefined and boorish; surly.

chur·ri·gue·resque (CHŏŏr,ēgəresk'), *adj.* relating to a style of Baroque architecture that flourished in Spain and Spanish America. Also **chur·ri·gue·res·co** (CHŏŏr,ēgeres'kô).

chut·ney (CHut'nē), *n.* a pickle or relish of Indian origin made from fruits, herbs, and spices.

chutz·pa (CHŏŏt'spə, hŏŏt'spə), *n.* gall; audacity; impudence.

chyle (kīl), *n.* lymph containing emulsified fats formed from chyme in the small intestine.

chy·lo·mi·cron (kī,lōmī'kron), *n.* a microscopic fat droplet occurring in blood.

chyme (kīm), *n.* the semiliquid mass of partially digested food formed by gastric secretion.

chypre (shēpr), *French, n.* a fragrance derived from sandalwood.

ci·bo·ri·um (sibôr'ēəm), *n., pl.* **ci·bo·ri·a** (sibôr'ēə). **1.** a vaulted canopy placed over a high altar. **2.** a vessel or chalice for holding Eucharistic bread or wafers.

cic·a·trix (sik'ətriks), *n., pl.* **cic·atri·ces** (sikətrī'sēz). **1.** the scar that forms on a wound which has healed. **2.** a mark left on a stem by a fallen leaf.

cic·a·trize (sik'ətrīz), *v.* to heal by the formation of a cicatrix.

cic·e·ro·ne (sisərō'nē), *n., pl.* **cic·ero·nes, cic·e·ro·ni** (sisərō'nē). a guide who escorts tourists or sightseers.

ci·cis·be·ism (CHē,CHizbā'izəm), *n.* the practice of keeping a cicisbeo.

ci·cis·be·o (CHē,CHēzbe'ô), *n., pl.* **ci·cis·be·i** (CHē,CHēzbe'ē). (formerly in Italy) the escort or lover of a married woman.

ci·de·vant (sēdəvän'), *adj. French.* former; one-time.

cil·i·a (sil'ēə), *n. pl., sing.* **cil·i·um** (sil'ēəm). any minute, hairlike processes, esp. eyelashes.

cil·i·ar·y (sil'ēer,ē), *adj.* relating to a ring of tissue in the eye or to cilia.

cil·ice (sil'is), *n.* a hairshirt.

cin·cho·na (sinkō'nə), *n.* any of several trees whose barks yield quinine and other alkaloids.

cin·chon·ism (sin'kəniz,əm), *n.* an illness due to excessive use of one of the cinchona alkaloids.

cin·cho·nize (sin'kənīz), *v.* to administer quinine to.

cinc·ture (sinGk'CHə), *n.* something which encircles; a girdle or belt.

cin·e, cin·é (sin'ē), *n.* a motion picture.

cin·e·aste (sin'ēast,), *n.* an enthusiast for motion pictures, esp. in their artistic and technical aspects.

cin·e·mat·ics (sin,əmat'iks), *n.* the art or technique of motion-picture making.

cin·é·ma vér·i·té (sin'əmə veratā'), motion pictures that are imitative of real life.

cin·e·ra·di·og·ra·phy (sin,ərā,dēog'rəfē), *n.* the technique of filming motion pictures through a fluoroscope.

cin·e·rar·i·um (sinərer'ēəm), *n., pl.* **cin·e·rar·i·a** (sinərer'ēə). a place where the ashes of the cremated dead are deposited.

cin·e·rar·y (sin'ərer,ē), *adj.* pertaining to or intended for ashes, esp. those of cremated bodies.

cin·er·a·tor (sin'ərā,tə), *n.* an incinerator.

ci·ne·re·ous (sinēr'ēəs), *adj.* **1.** ash-coloured. **2.** resembling or consisting of ashes.

cin·quain (sinGkān'), *n.* a group of five, esp. a five-line poem.

cinque (sinGk), *n.* the number five in cards or dice.

cin·que·cen·tist (CHinG,kwiCHen'tist), *n.* a writer or artist of the cinquecento period.

cin·que·cen·to (CHinG,kwiCHen'tō), *n.* the 16th century, esp. with reference to Italian art or literature.

cinque·foil (sinNGk'foil), *n.* (in architecture) a decorative design consisting of a rounded form divided into five lobes radiating from a common centre.

cir·ca (sû'kə), *prep., adv.* about (used for approximate dates). *Abbr.:* ca., c.

cir·ca·di·an (sûkā'dēən), *adj.* relating to a cycle occurring at about 24-hour intervals.

cir·ci·nate (sû'sināt), *adj.* rounded or ring-shaped.

cir·clet (sû'klit), *n.* a small circle or ring.

cir·cu·i·tous (səkyōō'ətəs), *adj.* roundabout; indirect.

cir·cu·lus (sû'kyələs), *n.* a concentric circle on the scale of a fish showing the growth of the scale.

cir·cum·am·bi·ent (sû,kəmam'bēənt), *adj.* encircling; encompassing.

cir·cum·am·bu·late (sû,kəmam'byəlāt), *v.* to go around; approach indirectly.

cir·cum·ba·sal (sû,kəmbā'səl), *adj.* surrounding or encircling the base.

cir·cum·bend·i·bus (sû,kəmben'dəbəs), *n., pl.* **cir·cum·bend·i·bus·es.** an indirect or roundabout way; circumlocution.

cir·cum·flex (sû'kəmfleks), *adj.* characterized or shown by the mark (ʌ), as used in French and other languages to indicate changes in vowel sound.

cir·cum·flu·ent (səkum'flōōənt), *adj.* flowing around.

cir·cum·flu·ous (səkum'flōōəs), *adj.* **1.** circumfluent. **2.** entirely surrounded by water.

cir·cum·fuse (sû,kəmfyōōz'), *v.* to surround or cover, as with a liquid.

cir·cum·gy·ra·tion (sû,kəmjīrā'sHən), *n.* a circular movement.

cir·cum·ja·cent (sû,kəmjā'sənt), *adj.* surrounding or encircling; lying all around.

cir·cum·lo·cu·tion (sû,kəmlōkyōō'sHən), *n.*

excessive use of words to express an idea; an evasive or roundabout way of speaking.

cir·cum·lu·nar (sû,kəmloo'nə), *adj.* around the moon.

cir·cum·nu·tate (sû,kəmnyoo'tāt), *v.* (of a plant) to grow in an irregular circular movement.

cir·cum·scribe (sû,kəmskrīb', sû'kəmskrīb,), *v.* **1.** to draw a line around. **2.** to delimit or mark off; constrain with limits; confine.

cir·cum·so·lar (sû,kəmsō'lə), *adj.* around the sun.

cir·cum·spect (sû'kəmspekt), *adj.* cautious; discreet; prudent.

cir·cum·val·late (sû,kəmval'āt), *adj.* **1.** encircled by or as if by a rampart. —*v.* **2.** to encircle or surround with or as with a rampart.

cir·cum·vent (sû,kəmvent'), *v.* **1.** to outwit, evade, get the better of. **2.** to avoid or by-pass. —**cir·cum·ven'tion,** *n.*

cir·cum·vo·lu·tion (sû,kəmvəloo'sHən), *n.* **1.** an act or instance of turning or revolving around. **2.** a winding or bending around; sinuosity.

cir·cum·volve (sû,kəmvolv'), *v.* to wind about or around; rotate.

cire per·due (sēə' pûdoo'). See **lost wax process.**

cirque (sûk), *n.* a basin in a mountain forming a circular space like an amphitheatre.

cir·rho·sis (sirō'sis), *n.* a disease of the liver caused by an excess of connective tissue.

cir·ro·cu·mu·lus (sir,ōkyoo'myələs), *n.* a cloud form consisting of small rounded patches at high altitudes.

cir·ro·stra·tus (sir,ōstrā'təs), *n.* a cloud form having the appearance of a thin, whitish veil and found at high altitudes.

cir·rus (sir'əs), *n.* a cloud form consisting of wispy white strips and found at high altitudes.

cis·al·pine (sisal'pīn), *adj.* on this (the Italian) side of the Alps.

cis·at·lan·tic (sis,ətlan'tik), *adj.* on this side of the Atlantic.

ci·se·lé (sēzəlā'), *adj.* (of velvet) having a pattern in relief.

cis·lu·nar (sisloo'nə), *adj.* lying between the earth and the moon.

cis·mon·tane (sismon'tān), *adj.* on this side of the mountains.

cit·ri·cul·ture (sit'rikul,cHə), *n.* the cultivation of citrus fruits.

cit·rine (sit'rin), *n.* **1.** a semiprecious yellow gemstone derived by heating black quartz; false topaz. —*adj.* **2.** resembling the colour of a lemon.

cit·y·scape (sit'ēskāp), *n.* a panoramic or broad view of a large city, as *a cityscape of London.*

civil death, the legal status of a person who has been deprived of civil rights.

civil disobedience, a refusal on moral grounds to obey certain laws or an attempt to influence government policy, characterized by the use of nonviolent techniques.

civil rights, a citizen's rights supported by law, as in the U.S.

clad·ding (klad'ing), *n.* the technique of bonding one metal to another, usually to prevent corrosion.

cla·dis·tics (klədis'tiks), *n.* (in biology) a system of classifying organisms on the basis of shared characteristics. —**clad·ism** (klad'izəm), *n.* —**clad·ist** (klad'ist), *n.*

clair·voy·ance (kleəvoi'əns), *n.* the power of seeing things beyond the natural limits of the senses. —**clair·voy'ant,** *adj., n.*

cla·mant (klā'mənt), *adj.* noisy; urgent; pressing.

clam·jam·fry (klamjam'frē), *n.* (in British dialect) ordinary people collectively; mob; rabble.

clam·or·ous (klam'ərəs), *adj.* noisy. —**clam'·our,** *n.*

clan·des·tine (klandes'tin), *adj.* held or conducted in secrecy; surreptitious.

clang·or (klang'gə, klang'ə), *n.* a resounding clanging sound or series of such sounds.

claque (klak), *n.* a group of persons hired to applaud a theatrical performance, etc. —**cla·queur** (klakû'), *n.*

clas·tic (klas'tik), *adj.* disintegrating into fragments; consisting of detachable pieces; fragmental.

clau·di·cant (klô'dikənt), *adj.* lame; having a limp.

clau·di·ca·tion (klôdikā'sHən), *n.* a limp.

claus·tral (klô'strəl), *adj.* cloisterlike; cloistral.

claus·tro·phil·i·a (klô,strəfil'ēə), *n.* a morbid desire to be confined in a small place.

claus·tro·pho·bi·a (klô,strəfō'bēə), *n.* an abnormal dread of closed or narrow spaces. —**claus'tro·phobe,** *n.*

cla·vate (klā'vāt), *adj.* having the shape of a club.

clav·i·form (klav'ifōəm), *adj.* having the shape of a club; clavate.

cla·vus (klā'vəs), *n., pl.* **cla·vi** (klā'vī). a headache causing intense pain, found in some forms of hysteria.

clear text. See **plain text.**

cleave[1] (klēv), *v.* **cleaved, cleav·ing.** to cling to closely, as an idea, belief, etc.

cleave[2] (klēv), *v.* **cleft, cleaved,** or **clove; cleft, cleaved,** or **cloven; cleaving.** to separate, split, or divide.

clem·en·cy (klem'ənsē), *n.* mercy or forgiveness, esp. in meting out punishment.

clem·ent (klem'ənt), *adj.* mild; gentle; merciful.

clep·sy·dra (klep'sidrə), *n.*, *pl.* **clepsy·dras, clep·sy·drae** (klep'sidrē). an apparatus for measuring the passage of time by the regulated flow of water.

clep·to·bi·o·sis (klep,tōbiō'sis), *n.*, *pl.* **clep·to·bi·o·ses** (klep,tōbiō'sēz). a mode of existence in which one species steals food from another. —**clep·to·bi·ot'ic,** *adj.*

clere·sto·ry (klēr'stôr,ē), *n.* a part of the interior of a building which rises above adjacent rooftops or the ground and is perforated with a series of windows.

cler·i·hew (kler'ihyōō), *n.* a four-line piece of verse having a usually humorous character.

cler·i·sy (kler'isē), *n.* learned or educated people collectively; intelligentsia.

cle·ro·man·cy (klēr'əman,sē), *n.* divination by casting lots.

clev·is (klev'is), *n.* a U-shaped metal fastening, to which a bolt or hook (clevis pin) can be attached.

cli·ché (klē'shā), *n.* a hackneyed, trite, or stereotyped phrase or expression.

cliff-hang·er (klif'hang,ə), *n.* a story, esp. a serial, which depends for its effect on crude melodramatic suspense.

cli·mac·ter·ic (klīmak'tərik), *n.* a period in life leading to decreased sexual activity in men and to menopause in women.

cli·mac·tic (klīmak'tik). *adj.* relating to or forming a climax.

cli·mat·ic (klīmat'ik), *adj.* relating to climate.

cli·ma·tol·o·gy (klī,mətol'əjē), *n.* the study of climates and climatic conditions.

clink·er-built (klingk'kəbilt,), *adj.* (of ships) having boards or planks that overlap. See also **carvel-built.**

cli·nom·e·ter (klīnom'itə), *n.* an instrument for measuring the amount of slope on an inclined plane.

clin·quant (kling'kənt), *adj.* glittering with tinsel.

clique (klēk, klik), *n.* a small, exclusive circle of people, esp. with identical interests; coterie. —**cli'quish,** *adj.*

clith·ral (klith'rəl), *adj.* (of a classical temple) covered by a roof. See also **hypaethral.**

clo·a·ca (klōā'kə), *n.*, *pl.* **clo·a·cae** (klōā'kē). 1. a sewer. 2. the terminal part into which intestinal, urinary, and generative canals open in birds, amphibians, fishes, and mammals. —**clo·a'cal,** *adj.*

cloche (klosh), *n.* 1. a glass cover, usually bell-shaped, placed over plants to protect them from frost. 2. a woman's close-fitting, brimless hat.

cloi·son (klwä'zon), *n.* a thin strip of metal dividing off the coloured areas in cloisonné enamels.

cloi·son·né (klwäzon'ā), *n.* a coloured decoration made of enamels in which the coloured areas are divided off by thin metal strips secured to a metal groundwork.

clois·tered (klois'təd), *adj.* alone; separated from everything else; sheltered away from the world.

clone (klōn), *n.* 1. one or more organisms that are identical in all respects to a single individual from which they were created by asexual reproduction. —*v.* **cloned, clon·ing.** 2. to create clones by asexual reproduction.

clo·qué (klōkā'), *n.* a fabric with a quilted pattern or a raised design in relief. See also **matelassé.**

closed shop, a factory, etc., in which union membership is an essential condition of employment or in which the employer must ask a particular labour union to provide employees. See also **open shop.**

clo·ture (klō'chər), *n.* (in a legislature, esp. in the U.S. Senate) the ending of a debate by calling for a vote or gaining a two thirds majority vote. Also **closure** (klō'zhər).

cloud chamber, an apparatus for determining the paths of ionizing particles.

clowd·er (klou'də), *n.* a group of cats.

cloy (kloi), *v.* to satiate or become distasteful through excess; surfeit.

clyp·e·ate (klip'ēāt), *adj.* having the shape of a rounded shield.

cly·sis (klī'sis), *n.* 1. the giving of an enema. 2. the administration of intravenous solutions in order to provide nourishment, remove pain, etc.

clys·ter (klis'tə), *n.* an enema.

co·ac·tive (kōak'tiv), *adj.* obligatory; compulsory.

co·ad·ju·tant (kōaj'ətənt), *adj.* 1. providing mutual assistance. —*n.* 2. an assistant.

co·ad·ju·tor (kōaj'ətə), *n.* an assistant, esp. to a bishop or other church dignitary.

co·ad·ju·tress (kōaj'ətris), *n.* a female assistant. Also **co·ad·ju·trix** (kōaj 'ətriks).

co·ag·u·late (kōag'yəlāt), *v.* to thicken; congeal; curdle. —**co·ag,u·la'tion,** *n.*

co·a·li·tion (kō,alish'ən), *n.* a joining together, esp. a temporary alliance between political parties.

co·ap·ta·tion (kō,aptā'shən), *n.* a fitting together of separate parts.

co·arc·tate (kōāk'tāt), *adj.* 1. constricted or compressed; crowded. 2. (of a pupa) enclosed in the previous larval skin. —**co,arc'ta'tion,** *n.*

co·ax·i·al (kōak'sēəl), *adj.* having the same axis. Also **co·ax·al** (kōak'səl).

co·cain·ism (kōkā'nizəm), *n.* a morbid condition caused by excessive consumption of cocaine.

coc·coid (kok'oid), *adj.* berry-shaped. See also **bacciform.**

coc·cyx (kok'siks), *n.*, *pl.* **coc·cy·ges** (koksī'- jēz). a small bone forming the base of the spine.

coch·le·a (kok'lēə), *n.* a spiral-shaped cavity of the inner ear.

coch·le·ate (kok'lēāt), *adj.* having the shape of a snail shell.

cock·a·lo·rum (kok,əlôr'əm), *n.* a conceited or pretentious little man.

cock·a·trice (kok'ətris), *n.* a mythical serpent with a deadly glance, hatched by a serpent from a cock's egg.

cock·boat (kok'bōt,), *n.* a small boat, esp. one used as a tender to a larger vessel.

cock·loft (kok'loft,), *n.* a small attic or garret.

cock·ney (kok'nē). *n.*, *pl.* **cock·neys. 1.** a native of the East End district of London. **2.** the dialect spoken there.

co·cotte¹ (kōkot'), *n.* a prostitute.

co·cotte² (kōkot'), *n.* a kind of small, round casserole.

co·dex (kō'deks), *n.*, *pl.* **co·di·ces** (kō'disēz, kod'isēz). a manuscript book of the Scriptures or ancient classics.

cod·i·cil (kod'isil), *n.* a supplement or appendix, esp. a modificatory addition to a will.

cod·i·fy (kod'ifī), *v.* to put (laws, etc.) in the form of a code; arrange systematically.

coe·la·canth (sē'ləkanth), *n.* a primitive form of fish found off the coast of Southern Africa.

coe·lan·a·glyph·ic (silan,əglif'ik), *adj.* (of a sculpture or carving) carried out in cavo-relievo.

coe·li·ac disease, ce·li·ac disease (sē'- lēak), a nutritional disorder in young children marked by poor digestion, diarrhoea, etc.

coe·li·o·scope (sē'lēəskōp), *n.* a device used in medicine for examining body cavities. Also **coe·lo·scope** (sē'ləskōp).

coe·lo·stat (sē'ləstat), *n.* a telescope fitted with an adjustable mirror used to reflect the light of a star, etc., into the telescope. See also **siderostat.**

coe·lot·o·my (səlot'əmē), *n.* See **herniotomy.**

coen·a·cle (sen'əkəl). See **cenacle.**

coe·nes·the·sia, ce·nes·the·sia (sē'nis- thē'zēə), *n.* the general sense of body consciousness derived from the aggregate of organic sensations.

coe·no·bite, ce·no·bite (sē'nōbīt), *n.* a member of a religious group living in a communal life.

co·erce (kōûs'), *v.* to force; compel by force; constrain. **—co·er'cive,** *adj.*

co·e·ta·ne·ous (kōitā'nēəs), *adj.* of the same age; coeval.

co·e·val (kōē'vəl), *adj.* of the same period, age or duration; contemporary.

cof·fle (kof'əl), *n.* a train of men, as convicts, slaves, etc., or animals, fastened together.

coff·ret (kof'rit), *n.* a small chest or coffer.

co·gent (kō'jənt), *adj.* compelling belief; appealing forcibly to reason; convincing. **—co'gen·cy,** *n.*

cog·i·tate (koj'itāt), *v.* to meditate intently; reflect; ponder. **—cog,i·ta'tion,** *n.* **—cog'i·ta,tive,** *adj.*

co·gi·to, er·go sum (kō'gitō eə'gō sōōm'), *Latin.* I think, therefore I am (a fundamental principle of Cartesian philosophy).

cog·nate (kog'nāt), *n.* **1.** a kinsman whose relationship is traceable through both males and females. **—adj. 2.** related through a common source, as the words *shirt* and *skirt*. See also **agnate. —cog·na'tion,** *n.*

cog·ni·tion (kognisʜ'ən), *n.* the faculty of perception or knowing; the product of such a faculty.

cog·ni·tive (kog'nitiv), *adj.* relating to or characterizing the various ways that knowledge is acquired.

cog·ni·zant (kog'nizənt), *adj.* aware (of); informed (about).

cog·no·men (kognō'mən), *n.*, *pl.* **cog·no·mens, cog·nom·i·na** (kognom'ənə). **1.** a family name or surname. **2.** a distinguishing name, as a nickname.

co·gno·scen·ti (kon,yəsʜen'tē), *n. pl.*, *sing.* **co·gno·scen·te** (kon,yəsʜen'tē). those who are well informed or have superior knowledge in a particular subject, esp. fine arts or literature.

cog·nos·ci·ble (kognos'əbəl), *adj.* capable of being known.

cog·nos·ci·tive (kognos'itiv), *adj.* having the capacity or ability to know.

co·her·ent (kōhĕr'ənt), *adj.* fitting together; connected and consistent in a logical way, as an argument. **—co·here',** *v.* **—co·her'ence,** *n.*

coherent radiation, radiation with definite phase relationships at different positions in a cross section of the energy beam.

cois·trel (koi'strəl), *n.* a rascal or scoundrel.

co·jo·nes (kōkʜō'nes), *Spanish*, *n.* **1.** testicles. **2.** masculine courage; pluck or valour.

col·i·co·bi·o·sis (kol,əkōbīō'sis), *n.*, *pl.* **col·a·co·bi·o·ses** (kol,əkōbīō'sēz). a mode of communal living among insects in which one species subsists parasitically upon another.

col·i·form bacillus (kol'ifôəm), any of several varieties of bacillus found in the large intestine of man and animals.

co·li·tis (kəlī'tis), *n.* inflammation of the colon.

col·lage (kəläzʜ'), *n.* an artistic composition produced by pasteing various materials as newspaper cuttings, old photographs, pieces of advertisements, etc., onto a surface.

col·la·gen (kol'əjən), *n.* a protein found in connective tissue and bones which produces gelatin and glue after prolonged boiling in water.

col·la·tion (kolā'sʜən), *n.* a snack; light meal.

col·lec·ta·ne·a (kol,ektā'nēə), *n. pl.* collected writings; a miscellany or anthology.

col·lec·tiv·ism (kəlek'təviz,əm), *n.* the theory of collective control over a country's means of production and distribution.

col·let (kol'it), *n.* a metal band or collar; a flange in which a gem is set.

col·li·gate (kol'igāt), *v.* to bind or fasten together.

col·li·mate (kol'imāt), *v.* to bring into alignment; make parallel.

col·lo·cate (kol'əkāt), *v.* to arrange in proper order; set side by side.

col·lo·ca·tion (kol,əkā'sHən), *n.* proper arrangement, esp. of words in a sentence.

col·lo·cu·tor (kol'əkyoo,tə), *n.* one who is engaged in dialogue with another.

col·lo·qui·al (kəlō'kwēəl), *adj.* characteristic of everyday speech or familiar conversation.

col·lo·qui·um (kəlō'kwēəm), *n.*, *pl.* **col·lo·qui·ums**, **co·lo·qui·a** (kəlō'kwēə). a conference, esp. an informal one.

col·lo·quy (kol'əkwē), *n.* a dialogue or conversation.

col·lo·type (kol'ətīp), *n.* a photo-mechanical process of making prints from a gelatin-coated plate.

col·lude (kəlood'), *v.* to cooperate together as a result of a secret agreement, esp. for a dishonest purpose. —**col·lu·sion** (kəloo'zHən), *n.* —**col·lu·sive** (kəloo'siv), *adj.*

col·lu·to·ry (kol'ətôr,ē), *n.* a mouthwash. Also **col·lu·to·ri·um** (kol,ətôr'ēəm).

col·lyr·i·um (kəlēr'ēəm), *n.* an eye lotion or eyewash.

co·lon (kō'lən), *n.* the lower part of the large intestine, extending from the caecum to the rectum.

col·o·nette (kol,ənet'), *n.* a small column.

co·lon·ic (kəlon'ik), *adj.* relating to the colon.

col·o·phon (kol'əfon), *n.* 1. a distinctive mark or symbol used on books by a publisher for identification. 2. a detailed, brief description of the type styles used in a book, usually appearing at the end of the work. See also **logo**.

col·or·im·e·ter (kul,ərim'itə), *n.* an instrument for analysing colours and comparing their intensities. —**color·im'e·try,** *n.*

col·por·tage (kol'pôə,tij), *n.* the business of a colporteur.

col·por·teur (kol'pôətə), *n.* 1. one who peddles books. 2. one who distributes cheap religious books.

col·u·brine (kol'yəbrīn), *adj.* relating to or resembling a snake.

col·um·bar·i·um (kol,əmber'ēəm); *n.*, *pl.* **col·um·bar·i·a** (kol,əmber'ēə). a vault with recesses in the walls for holding funerary urns.

col·um·bar·y (kol'əmber,ē), *n.* a dovecote.

col·um·bine (kol'əmbīn), *adj.* resembling a dove.

co·lum·ni·a·tion (kəlum,nēā'sHən), *n.* 1. the use of columns in a structure. 2. the system of columns used in a structure.

co·ma (kō'mə), *n.* 1. a condition of deep unconsciousness due to injury, disease, etc. 2. the nebulous envelope that surrounds the nucleus of a comet.

co·mate (kō'māt), *adj.* covered with hair; shaggy; tufted.

com·a·tose (kom'ətōs), *adj.* relating to or affected by a coma; lethargic; drowsy.

com·e·do (kom'idō), *n.*, *pl.* **com·edos**, **com·e·do·nes** (kom,idō'nēz). a blackhead or pimple on the skin.

co·mes·ti·ble (kəmes'təbəl), *adj.* 1. edible. —*n.* 2. *Usually pl.* food.

com·i·ty (kom'itē), *n.* civility; a courteous manner of behaviour.

comme ci, comme ça (kum sē' kum sä'), *French.* indifferent; neither good nor bad; so-so.

comme il faut (kum ēl fō'), *French.* in conformity with accepted standards; proper; suitable.

com·mend (kəmend'), *v.* to praise; recommend (someone to another). —**com,men·da'·tion,** *n.*

com·men·sal (kəmen'səl), *adj.* 1. taking meals together. 2. (of organisms, plants, etc.) living with or on another without damage to the other. 3. (of an individual or group) occupying the same area as another individual or group having different standards, etc., but not competing with them.

com·men·su·ra·ble (kəmen'sərəbəl), *adj.* measurable by the same standard; proportionate; having a common measure.

com·men·su·rate (kəmen'sərit), *adj.* of equal extent; in accordance with; in proportion to.

com·mère (kom'âr), *n.* a female compere.

com·mi·nate (kom'ināt), *v.* to threaten with divine vengeance. —**com,mi·na'tion,** *n.*

com·mi·nute (kom'inyoot), *v.* to crush to a powder; pulverize.

com·mis (kom'is, kom'ē), *n.*, *pl.* **com·mis.** 1. an assistant or junior chef or a waiter. 2. a deputy.

com·mis·er·ate (kəmiz'ərāt), *v.* to sympathize with (someone); feel or express sympathy with (another).

com·mis·sure (kom'isyoo͝ə), *n.* a juncture; seams; joint.

com·mon·al·ty (kom'ənəltē), *n.* the common people as distinguished from those in authority, the nobility, etc. Also **com·mon·al·i·ty** (kom,-ənal'itē).

common carrier, an individual or company that undertakes to transport people or goods in return for payment.

Common Market, an economic association

of western European countries created to abolish internal tariffs among its members and to set up a common external tariff.

com·move (kəmōōv'), v. to agitate or move violently.

com·mune (kom'yōōn), n. a tightly organized community of people sharing common interests.

com·mun·ion (kəmyōōn'yən), n. 1. the act of sharing in common. 2. the celebration or receiving of the Eucharist.

com·mu·ni·qué (kəmyōō‚nikā'), n. an official report or bulletin.

com·mun·ism (kom'yəniz‚əm), n. a system of society in which all property is held in common, ownership being vested in the community as a whole or the state. —**com'mun·ist,** n.

com·mu·ta·tion (kom‚yətā'sнən), n. the act of replacing one thing by another; substitution.

com·mu·ta·tive (kəmyōō'tətiv, kom'yətā‚tiv), adj. relating to or permitting exchange or substitution.

co·mose (kō'mōs), adj. covered in hairs; comate.

com·pa·ra·tor (kompar'ətə), n. an instrument for making comparisons of similar things, as lengths, shades of colour, etc.

com·pas·sion·ate (kəmpasн'ənit), adj. feeling or expressing sorrow and sympathy for another's hardship, loss, distress, suffering, etc. —**com·pas'sion,** n.

com·pa·ter·ni·ty (kom‚pətû'nitē), n. the relationship between the godparents of a child or between the godparents and the parents.

com·pa·thy (kom'pəthē), n. the sharing of feelings with others.

com·peer (kəmpēə'), n. one having the same rank; an equal in position, ability, etc.

com·pel·la·tion (kom‚pəlā'sнən), n. the action or manner of addressing somebody; designation.

com·pen·di·ous (kəmpen'dēəs), adj. expressing in brief form the substance of a subject; concise.

com·pen·di·um (kəmpen'dēəm), n., pl. com·pen·di·ums, com·pendi·a (kəmpen'dēə). a comprehensive summary of a subject; an abridgement.

com·pen·sa·to·ry damages (kom'pensā‚-təri, kəmpen'sətərē), damages awarded to a plaintiff to provide compensation for injury suffered. See also **exemplary damages.**

com·pla·cent (kəmplā'sənt), adj. self-satisfied; showing undue regard for one's own merits or advantages. —**com·pla'cen·cy,** n.

com·plai·sant (kəmplā'zənt), adj. obliging, agreeable; eager to please. —**com·plai'sance,** n.

com·pla·nate (kom'plənāt), adj. put into a level position.

com·plect·ed (kəmplek'tid), adj. complexioned.

com·ple·ment (kom'plimənt), v. 1. to supply an element or ingredient that makes something complete or better. —n. 2. the element or ingredient supplied. —**com‚ple·men'ta·ry,** adj.

com·pli·ca·cy (kom'pləkəsē), n. complicated state; complicatedness.

com·plot (kom'plot), n. 1. a conspiracy. —v. 2. to conspire together.

com·ply (kəmpli'), v. **com·plied, com·ply·ing.** to do things in keeping with rules, others' requests or demands, etc., esp. by changing one's behaviour.

com·port (kəmpôət'), v. to behave; conduct oneself.

com·pos·si·ble (kompos'əbəl), adj. consistent with; compatible.

com·po·ta·tion (kom‚pətā'sнən), n. drinking together; convivial drinking.

com·pote (kom'pōt), n. 1. fruit stewed in syrup. 2. a dish or bowl of glass, china, metal, etc., having a base and stem and used for serving fruit, nuts, etc.

com·pre·hen·sive (kom‚prihen'siv), adj. bringing or taking many things, subjects, ideas, etc. together, as *a comprehensive examination, a comprehensive programme of exercise*; thorough and inclusive. —**com‚prehen'sive·ness,** n.

compte ren·du (kôΝt räΝdy'), pl. **comptes rendus** (kôΝt räΝdy'), *French.* a record or account of a transaction, proceedings, etc.

com·pur·ga·tion (kom‚pəgā'sнən), n. (formerly) a legal procedure whereby an accused man is cleared of a charge by the sworn oaths of a number of people.

com·pur·ga·tor (kom'pəgā‚tər), n. one who under oath vouches for the innocence of another.

com·put·er (kəmpyōō'tə), n. an automatic electronic apparatus for performing complex mathematical calculations at high speeds. See also **analogue computer, digital computer.**

co·na·tion (kōnā'sнən), n. mental activity concerned with striving, as desire and conscious volition. —**con'a·tive,** adj.

co·na·tus (kōnā'təs), n., pl. **co·na·tus.** an impulse or a striving.

con·cat·e·nate (konkat'ənāt), v. to link or join together; unite in a series. —**con·cat‚e·na'tion,** n.

con·cede (kənsēd'), v. **con·ced·ed, con·ced·ing.** to yield or give up; cede, as points in a dispute; allow. —**con·ces'sion,** n.

con·cel·e·brate (konsel'əbrāt), v. to take part in a concelebration.

con·cel·e·bra·tion (kənsel‚əbrā'sнən), n. the performance of mass by more than one priest.

con·cen·tre (kənsen'tər), v. to draw towards or converge upon a common centre.

con·cen·tric (kənsen'trik), adj. having a common centre or axis.

con·ces·sion (kənsesн'ən), n. the act of yielding or conceding; the admitting of a point in a dispute, etc.

con·ces·sive (kənses'iv), *adj.* denoting a concession; tending to concede.

con·chol·o·gy (konNGkol'əjē), *n.* the branch of study dealing with mollusc shells.

con·cil·i·ar (kənsil'ēər), *adj.* relating to a council, esp. an ecclesiastical one.

con·cil·i·ate (kənsil'ēāt), *v.* to placate; overcome the hostility of; reconcile. —**con·cil,i·a'·tion,** *n.* —**con·cil'i·a·to,ry,** *adj.*

con·cin·nate (kon'sənāt), *v.* to fit together in a precise, appropriate, or harmonious fashion.

con·cin·nous (kənsin'əs), *adj.* elegant in style; harmonious; fitting.

con·ci·sion (kənsizH'ən), *n.* conciseness; brevity.

con·clave (kon'klāv), *n.* a private discussion; secret assembly.

con·coc·tion (kənkok'sHən), *n.* a mixture, esp. one containing unfamiliar ingredients [literally, 'something boiled; a mélange of ingredients boiled together']

con·com·i·tant (kənkom'itənt), *adj.* accompanying; existing with something else; attendant.

con·cord·ant (kənkôr'dənt), *adj.* harmonious; consistent; agreeing.

con·cor·dat (konkôr'dat), *n.* an official agreement; a compact or covenant.

con·cres·cence (kənkres'əns), *n.* a growing together as of plants or cells.

con·cu·bi·nage (konkyōō'bənij), *n.* the cohabiting of a man and woman who are not legally married. —**con·cu·bi·nar·y** (konkyōō'-bənər,ē), *adj.*

con·cu·bine (konG'kyəbīn), *n.* a woman who cohabits with a man to whom she is not married.

con·cu·pis·cence (kənkyōō'pisəns), *n.* sexual desire; lust. —**con·cu'pis·cent,** *adj.*

con·cur (kənkû'), *v.* **con·curred, con·cur·ring.** to agree; come together; coincide. —**con·cur'·rence,** *n.* —**con·cur'rent,** *adj.*

con·dign (kəndīn', kon'dīn), *adj.* fitting; appropriate; well deserved.

con·dis·ci·ple (kon,disī'pəl), *n.* a fellow student.

con·do·lent (kəndō'lənt), *adj.* showing sympathy or sorrow. —**con·do'lence,** *n.*

con·do·min·i·um (kon,dəmin'ēəm), *n.* (in the U.S. and Canada) an association of owners of flats or dwelling units under individual ownership. See also **cooperative.**

con·duce (kəndyōōs'), *v.* to lead or tend towards; tend to produce a particular result. —**con·du'cive,** *adj.*

con·fab·u·late (kənfab'yəlāt), *v.* **1.** to engage in informal discussion; converse. **2.** to take part in confabulation.

con·fab·u·la·tion (kənfab,yəlā'sHən), *n.* **1.** an informal conversation. **2.** (in psychiatry) filling

a blank in memory with a false memory which is accepted as being correct.

con·fect (kənfekt'), *v.* to prepare from ingredients; make up; put together.

con·fer·va (konfû'və), *n.*, *pl.* **con·fer·vae** (konfû'vē), **con·fer·vas.** any of various filamentous green algae.

con·fig·u·ra·tion (kənfig,yərā'sHən), *n.* the relative arrangement of the elements or parts of something.

con·fi·ture (kon'fityōōə), *n.* preserved fruit.

con·fla·grant (kənflā'grənt), *adj.* on fire; burning; ablaze.

con·fla·tion (kənflā'sHən), *n.* the combining of two texts into one; the resulting new text.

con·flu·ence (kon'flōōəns), *n.* the flowing together of two or more rivers, etc.

con·flu·ent (kon'flōōənt), *adj.* coming or flowing together; uniting into one.

con·gé (kon'zHā), *n.* **1.** a formal leave-taking. **2.** permission to take one's leave. Also **con·gee** (kon'jē).

con·ge·la·tion (kon,jəlā'sHən), *n.* **1.** the process of freezing or congealing. **2.** the result of this.

con·ge·ner (kənjē'nə, kon'jənə), *n.* a member of the same group, family, or class.

con·ge·ni·al (kənjē'nyəl), *adj.* friendly and agreeable; pleasing.

con·gen·i·tal (kənjen'itəl), *adj.* from birth; originating at birth, as contrasted with having been acquired later in life.

con·ge·ries (konjēr'ēz), *n.* a collection; assembly; heap, or pile.

con·glo·bate (konglō'bāt), *adj.* formed into a round mass or ball.

con·glu·ti·nate (kənglōōt'ənāt), *v.* to stick together as with glue; become glued together.

con·gru·ent (konG'grōōənt), *adj.* in agreement; congruous. —**con'gru·ence,** *n.*

con·gru·i·ty (kəngrōō'itē), *n.* the state or quality of being congruous; accord or harmony.

con·gru·ous (konG'grōōəs), *adj.* showing harmony in character, etc., suitable; appropriate; fitting.

co·ni·ol·o·gy (kō,nēol'əjē), *n.* See **koniology.**

con·joint (kənjoint'), *adj.* united; associated; combined.

con·ju·gal (kon'jəgəl), *adj.* relating to marriage or the married state.

con·junct (kənjuNGkt', kon'juNGkt), *adj.* joined closely together; united; joint.

con·junc·ti·va (kon,juNGktī'və), *n.*, *pl.* **con·junc·ti·vas, con·junc·ti·vae** (kon,juNGktī'vē). the mucous membrane lining the inner surface of the eyelids.

con·junc·tive (kənjuNGk'tiv), *adj.* uniting; connective.

con·junc·ture (kənjuNGk'cHər), *n.* a combination of events or circumstances.

con·jur·a·tion (kon,jərā'sHən), *n.* **1.** a spell or trick used in conjuring. **2.** the process of conjuring. **3.** a solemn entreaty.

con·nate (kon'āt), *adj.* inborn or innate; associated in origin.

con·nat·u·ral (kənaCH'ərəl), *adj.* inborn; connected by nature.

con·niv·ent (kənī'vənt), *adj.* converging or touching without being fused, as some insect wings, plant parts, etc.

con·nois·seur (kon,əsû'), *n.* a person who is expert in the fine arts and other areas of taste.

con·no·ta·tion (konətā'sHən), *n.* an implied or associated meaning of a word apart from its explicit sense.

con·note (kənōt'), *v.* to imply or suggest.

co·noid (kō'noid), *adj.* having the shape of a cone.

con·san·guin·e·ous (kon,saNGgwin'ēəs), *adj.* descended from the same ancestor; related by blood.

con·san·guin·i·ty (kon,saNGgwin'itē), *n.* relationship by blood; kinship.

con·script (*v.* kənskript'; *adj.* kon'skript), *v.* **1.** to enrol compulsorily for military service. —*adj.* **2.** enrolled by having been conscripted. —**conscrip'tion,** *n.*

con·se·cu·tion (konsəkyōō'sHən), *n.* sequence; succession.

con·sen·su·al (kənsen'syōōəl), *adj.* **1.** made by or resulting from mutual consent, without formal agreement. **2.** denoting an involuntary movement accompanying a voluntary movement.

con·sen·sus (kənsen'səs), *n., pl.* **con·sen·sus·es.** agreement of feeling or opinion.

con·sen·ta·ne·ous (kon,sentā'nēəs), *adj.* agreeing; in accord. —**con,sen·ta·ne'i·ty,** *n.*

con·sen·tient (kənsen'sHənt), *adj.* characterized by unanimous or harmonious agreement; accordant.

con·sis·to·ry (kənsis'tərē), *n.* a Church tribunal or council.

con·so·ci·ate (kənsō'sHēāt), *v.* to bring into association; associate.

con·so·nance (kon'sənəns), *n.* agreement; harmony; accord.

con·sor·ti·um (kənsôr'tēəm), *n., pl.* **con·sor·ti·a** (kənsôr'tēə). a combination of banking or business companies for the purpose of performing some operation involving large financial resources.

con·spe·cif·ic (kon,spisif'ik), *adj.* of the same species.

con·spec·tus (kənspek'təs), *n.* a synopsis or summary; survey; review.

con·stel·late (kon'stəlāt), *v.* to unite or cluster together, as stars to form a constellation.

con·ster·nate (kon'stənāt), *v.* to dismay; terrify. —**con,ster·na'tion,** *n.*

con·sti·tu·tive (kon'stityōō,tiv), *adj.* **1.** essential; constituent. **2.** having the power to establish, enact, create, etc.

con·stringe (kənstrinj'), *v.* to compress; cause to shrink or contract. —**con·strin'gent,** *adj.*

con·strue (kənstrōō'), *v.* **con·strued, con·stru·ing. 1.** to explain or interpret. **2.** to interpret in a particular way. —**con·stru'al,** *n.*

con·sub·stan·tial (kon,səbstan'sHəl), *adj.* having the same essence or substance.

con·sub·stan·ti·a·tion (kon,səbstan,sHēā'sHən), *n.* the doctrine that the body and blood of Christ are simultaneously present within the bread and wine of the Eucharist.

con·sue·tude (kon'swityōōd), *n.* a custom, esp. one having the force of law; social usage. —**con·sue·tu·di·nar·y** (kon,swityōōd'ənerē), *adj.*

consumer price index, an index based on official statistics showing the change in the cost of goods and services over a specified period. Also **price index.**

con·sum·mate (*v.* kon'səmāt; *adj.* kənsum'it, kon'səmit), *v.,* **con·sum·mated, con·sum·mating. 1.** to make complete or perfect. **2.** to verify a marriage by sexual intercourse. —*adj.* **3.** excellent; perfect of its kind. —**con,sum·ma'tion,** *n.*

con·tan·go (kəntaNG'gō), *n., pl.* **con·tan·gos, con·tan·goes.** (on the London Stock Exchange) an arrangement whereby a buyer of securities pays a fee to the seller in return for deferment of payment until the next settlement day. See also **backwardation.**

con·temn (kəntem'), *v.* to disdain, despise; treat with scorn.

con·ten·tious (kənten'sHəs), *adj.* causing strife; quarrelsome; controversial.

con·ter·mi·nous (kəntû'mənəs), *adj.* having a common boundary; adjacent; bordering.

con·tex·ture (kənteks'CHər), *n.* the arrangement of the parts of a whole; framework; structure

con·tig·u·ous (kəntig'yōōəs), *adj.* in contact; adjoining; touching.

con·ti·nen·tal·i·ty (kon,tənəntal'itē), *n.* the degree to which the climate of a place is influenced by its land mass. See also **oceanity.**

con·tin·u·um (kəntin'yōōəm), *n., pl.* **con·tin·u·a** (kəntin'yōōə). a continuous or uninterrupted sequence, series, or extent.

con·trac·tile (kəntrak'tīl), *adj.* having the power to contract; causing contraction.

con·tra·dic·tious (kon,trədik'sHəs), *adj.* marked by contradiction; disputatious; inclined to contradict.

con·tra·dic·tive (kon,trədik'tiv), *adj.* tending to contradict.

con·tra·dis·tin·guish (kon,trədistiNG'gwisH), *v.* to make distinction by contrast of qualities. —**con,tra·dis·tinc'tion,** *n.*

con·trail (kon'trāl), *n.* a trail of condensed water vapour caused by aircraft, rockets, etc.

con·tra·pose (kon'trəpōz), *v.* to place in contraposition.

con·tra·po·si·tion (kon,trəpəzisн'ən), *n.* a setting in opposition; contrast; antithesis.

con·tra·ri·e·ty (kon,trərī'itē), *n.* the state or quality of being contrary.

con·tra·vene (kon,trəvēn'), *v.* to oppose; act contrary to; be in conflict with. —**con,tra·ven'-tion,** *n.*

con·tre·temps (kon'trətän), *n.*, *pl.* **con·tre-·temps.** an embarrassing situation; unfortunate occurrence.

con·trite (kəntrīt'), *adj.* full of remorse; truly repentant; penitent. —**con·tri·tion** (kəntrisн'ən), *n.*

con·tro·vert (kon'trəvût, kontrəvût'), *v.* to dispute; contest; contradict.

con·tu·ma·cious (kon,tyōōmā'sнəs), *adj.* strongly disobedient; rebellious; stubborn. —**con·tu·ma·cy** (kon'tyōōməsē), *n.*

con·tu·me·ly (kon'tyōōmilē), *n.* insulting behaviour in words or deeds; contemptuous treatment. —**con·tu·me·li·ous** (kon,tyōōmē'lēəs), *adj.*

con·tuse (kəntyōōz'), *v.* to injure (tissue, etc.) without laceration of the skin; bruise.

co·nun·drum (kənun'drəm), *n.* a puzzle, esp. one involving word play.

con·ve·nance (kon'vənäns), *n.* propriety; suitability.

con·ven·tu·al (kənven'tyōōəl), *adj.* relating to or appropriate to a convent or monastic life.

con·ver·sant (kanvû'sant), *adj.* (usually followed by *with*) familiar (with); knowledgeable (about).

con·verse (kon'vûs), *n.* the opposite or contrary (of something referred to), as *He is a bad actor, but I can say the converse of her.*

con·vert·i·plane (kənvû'təplän,), *n.* an aeroplane designed for vertical movement like a helicopter and also level forward flight.

con·vive (kon'viv), *n.* a dining companion; a fellow guest at a meal.

con·viv·ial (kənviv'ēəl), *adj.* relating to, indulging in, or suitable for feasting, eating and drinking, etc.

con·vo·ca·tor (kon'vəkä,tə), *n.* one who calls, arranges, or takes part in a meeting, etc.

con·vo·lut·ed (kon'vəlōō,tid), *adj.* tangled, twisted; intricate, complicated.

con·vo·lu·tion (kon,vəlōō'sнən), *n.* one of the ridges or folds on the brain's surface.

con·volve (kənvolv'), *v.* to roll together; twist round.

co·op·er·a·tive (kōōp'ərətiv), *n.* (in the U.S. and Canada) an apartment house whose tenants each own shares of stock proportionate to the value his apartment bears to the total value of the building. See also **condominium.**

co·opt (kōōpt'), *v.* **1.** to elect to a committee, board, etc., by votes of its members. **2.** to commandeer the services of.

co·pa·cet·ic (kō,pəset'ik), *adj., U.S. slang,* entirely satisfactory; fine; excellent.

cop·ro·lag·ni·a (kop,rəlag'nēə), *n.* sexual excitement induced by faecal matter.

cop·ro·la·li·a (kop,rəlä'lēə), *n.* excessive swearing or use of obscene language.

cop·rol·o·gy (koprol'əjē), *n.* scatology.

cop·roph·a·gous (koprof'əgəs), *adj.* feeding on dung.

cop·ro·phil·i·a (kop,rəfil'ēə), *n.* a morbid interest in faeces.

cop·ro·pho·bi·a (kop,rəfō'bēə), *n.* an obsessive fear of faeces.

coq au vin (kôk ō van'), chicken cooked with red wine, onions, garlic, diced pork, etc.

co·quet (kōket'), *v.* (of a woman) to try to attract the amorous attentions of men; flirt.

co·quette (kōket'), *n.* a woman who tries to gain the attention of men by amorous flirtation.

co·quille (kōkil'), *n.* **1.** a dish, usually of meat or fish, cooked with a sauce, and served on a shell-shaped platter. **2.** the casserole or other utensil used for cooking such dishes.

cor·al·lif·er·ous (kor,əlif'ərəs), *adj.* bearing or producing coral.

cor·al·loid (kor'əloid), *adj.* shaped like coral.

co·ram no·bis (kôr'am nō'bis), a writ designed to rectify an injury caused by a mistake of a court of law.

cor·date (kôə'dät), *adj.* shaped like a heart.

cor·delle (kôədel'), *n.* a rope used for towing barges, etc.

cor·di·form (kôə'dəfôəm), *adj.* having the shape of a heart.

cor·dil·le·ra (kôə'dilyer'ə), *n.* a system of mountain ranges; a mountain chain.

cor·don sa·ni·taire (kôə'dôn sanēteə'), *pl.* **cor·dons sa·ni·taires** (kôə'dôn sanēteə'). a line marking off an area under quarantine.

co·re·spond·ent (kō,rispon'dənt), *n.* one charged with adultery together with the defendant in a divorce case.

co·ri·a·ceous (kō,rēä'sнəs), *adj.* resembling leather.

cor·ne·ous (kôə'nēəs), *adj.* of a horny substance or texture.

cor·nic·u·late (kôənik'yəlät), *adj.* having horn-shaped parts; resembling a small horn.

cor·nu (kôə'nyōō), *n.* a horn or horn-shaped structure.

cor·nut·ed (kôənyōō'tid), *adj.* having horns, like a cuckold; horn-shaped.

cor·ol·lar·y (kərol'ərē), *n.* a natural or inevitable result.

co·ro·na (kərō'nə), *n.*, *pl.* **co·ronas, co·ro·nae** (kərō'nē). a luminous circle of light surrounding the sun or moon.

corona discharge, a discharge occurring at the surface of a conductor, etc., and resulting in ionization of the surrounding atmosphere. Also **cor·po·sant** (kôə'pəzant).

co·ro·na·graph (kərō'nəgräf), *n.* an apparatus for observing the sun's corona.

cor·o·nar·y occlusion (kor'əner,e), obstruction of a coronary artery.

coronary thrombosis, the occlusion of a coronary artery caused by a blood clot.

cor·o·nate (kor'ənāt), *adj.* having a crown or coronet.

cor·o·plast (kor'əplast), *n.* one who sculpts figurines, esp. in terracotta.

cor·po·re·al (kôəpôr'ēəl), *adj.* real, tangible, and physical as contrasted with spiritual or ethereal.

cor·pu·lence (kôə'pyələns), *n.* stoutness of body; obesity; fatness. —**cor'pu·lent,** *adj.*

cor·pus·cle (kôə'pəsəl), *n.* a protoplasmic cell, esp. a blood cell.

cor·pus de·lic·ti (kôə'pəs dilik'tē), the fundamental facts about a crime.

cor·pus ju·ris (kôə'pəs jōor'is), the body of laws of a country, state, etc.

cor·rade (kərād'), *v.* 1. to wear away by abrasion or erosion. 2. to disintegrate as a result of abrasion or erosion. —**cor·ra·sion** (kərā'zHən), *n.*

cor·re·late (kor'əlāt), *v.* to connect and relate things systematically; to establish a relationship between or among things in an orderly manner.

cor·ri·gen·dum (kor,ijen'dəm), *n.*, *pl.* **cor·ri·gen·da** (kor,ijen'də). a note of an error to be corrected in a book.

cor·ri·gi·ble (kor'ijəbəl), *adj.* capable of being corrected; submitting to correction.

cor·rob·o·rant (kərob'ərənt), *adj.* confirming; corroborating.

cor·tège (kôətezH'), *n.* a ceremonial procession, esp. at a funeral.

cor·tex (kôə'teks), *n.*, *pl.* **cor·ti·ces** (kôə'tisēz). 1. the bark of a tree. 2. the protective matter that surrounds the brain.

cor·ti·co·lous (kôətik'ələs), *adj.* (in biology) inhabiting the surface of bark.

cor·ti·co·ster·oid (kôə,tikōster'oid), *n.* any of a class of steroids produced by the adrenal cortex.

co·rus·cant (kərus'kənt), *adj.* flashing; gleaming; sparkling.

cor·us·cate (kor'əskāt), *v.* to sparkle or gleam; glitter.

cor·us·ca·tion (kor,əskā'sHən), *n.* a sparkling or gleaming; a sudden flash of wit.

cor·vine (kôə'vīn), *adj.* relating to or resembling a crow or crow family.

cor·y·ban·tic (korəban'tik), *adj.* wild; unrestrained; frenzied.

cor·y·phée (ko,rifā'), *n.* a leading dancer of a corps de ballet.

cosh·er (kosH'ər), *v.* to spoil or pamper.

cos·me·tol·ogy (koz,mitol'əjē), *n.* the art or technique of using cosmetics.

cos·mic (koz'mik), *adj.* of, relating to, or throughout the entire universe, as cosmic dust.

cos·mog·o·ny (kozmog'ənē), *n.* a theory of the origin of the universe.

cos·mog·ra·phy (kozmog'rəfē), *n.* the science dealing with the constitution and description of the universe. —**cos·mog'ra·pher,** *n.*

cos·mo·line (koz'məlēn), *n.* a kind of grease used for protecting weapons against rust, etc., during storage or shipment.

cos·mol·o·gy (kozmol'əjē), *n.* metaphysics dealing with the origin and structure of the universe and the laws of space and time.

cos·mo·naut (koz'mənôt), *n.* an astronaut. —**cos·mo·nau'tic,** *adj.*

cos·mop·o·lis (kozmop'əlis), *n.* a city composed of cosmopolitan elements.

cos·mo·pol·i·tan (koz,məpol'itən), *adj.* widely distributed or known in the world; characterized as sophisticated and knowledgeable because of global outlook and experience; not narrow or provincial.

cos·mop·o·lite (kozmop'əlīt), *n.* one having a cosmopolitan outlook.

cos·mo·ra·ma (koz,mərä'mə), *n.* a display of pictures from various parts of the world.

cos·mos (koz'məs), *n.* the universe viewed as an ordered system.

Cos·sack (kos'ak), *n.* a member of one of several Slav tribes living in southern Russia and known for their horsemanship.

cos·set (kos'it), *v.* to spoil, pamper, or coddle.

cos·ta (kos'tə), *n.*, *pl.* **cos·tae** (kos'tē). a rib or something resembling a rib. —**cos'tal,** *adj.*

cos·tate (kos'tāt), *adj.* having ribs.

cos·ter·mon·ger (kos'təmuNG,ge), *n.* one who hawks fruit and vegetables.

cos·tive (kos'tiv, kô'stiv), *adj.* constipated.

cos·trel (kos'trəl), *n.* a container made of leather or earthenware and having ears by which it may be suspended.

co·te·rie (kō'tərē), *n.* a small, usually exclusive, group of people with shared tastes, a common viewpoint, etc.

co·thur·nus (kōthû'nəs), *n.* a grave, dignified style of drama or acting.

couch·ant (kou'CHənt), *adj.* lying down.

cou·lisse (kōōlēs'), *n.* a piece of timber with a groove to allow a panel to slide along it.

cou·loir (kōōlwää'), *n.* a gorge on a mountainside.

cou·lomb (kōō'lom), *n.* a unit of electricity

equal to the quantity transferred by one ampere in one second.

coun·ten·ance (koun'tənəns), *n.* **1.** face; mien; appearance. —*v.* **coun·ten·anced, coun·ten·anc·ing. 2.** to allow or tolerate.

coun·ter·in·sur·gen·cy (koun,tərinsû'jən-sē), *n.* the taking of measures against internal subversion or guerrilla warfare. —**coun,ter·in·sur'gent,** *n.*

coun·ter·prod·uc·tive (koun,təprəduk'tiv), *adj.* having a result opposite to that intended.

coun·ter·vail (koun,təvāl'), *v.* **1.** to act against with equivalent power: exert equal force against. **2.** to compensate; provide an equivalent for.

coup de grâce (kōō, də gräs'), *pl.* **coups de grâce** (kōōz, də gräs'). *French.* a death blow, esp. one intended to end the agony of a mortally wounded person.

coup d'é·tat (kōō, dätä'), *pl.* **coups d'é·tat** (kōōz, dätä'). a sudden change of government or regime, esp. by force.

coup de thé·â·tre (kōō, də täā'trə), *pl.* **coups de thé·â·tre** (kōō, də täā'trə). *French.* a sudden change or startling development in a play.

coup d'oeil (kōō, doi'), *pl.* **coups d'oeil** (kōō, doi'). *French.* a brief survey or glance.

cour·te·san, cour·te·zan (kô'tizan), *n.* a prostitute, esp. one with wealthy or high-born clientele.

cour·ti·er (kô'tēə), *n.* an attendant upon a king at court.

cous·cous (kōōs'kōōs), *n.* a North African dish of semolina, meat, and vegetables.

cou·vade (kōōväd'), *n.* a custom among primitive peoples in which, at the time of a baby's birth, the father simulates pregnancy and performs other acts associated with the female role in society.

cov·e·nant (kuv'ənənt), *n.* **1.** a formal agreement between two or more parties to perform some specified action. —*v.* **2.** to enter into a covenant; promise; pledge.

cov·ert (kuv'ət), *adj.* **1.** sheltered; protected. **2.** secret; disguised.

cov·er·ture (kuv'əCHə), *n.* a shelter, cover, or covering; disguise or concealment.

cov·et (kuv'it), *v.* to desire avidly, esp. that which belongs to another. —**cov'et·ous,** *adj.*

cov·ey (kuv'ē), *n.* a flock of partridges or similar birds.

cox·al·gi·a (koksal'jēə), *n.* a pain in the hip.

cox·comb (koks'kōm), *n.* a conceited fop or dandy. —**cox·comb·ry** (koks'kōmrē), *n.*

coze (kōz), *v.* to engage in friendly conversation.

coz·en (kuz'ən), *v.* to defraud, cheat or beguile.

coz·en·age (kuz'ənij), *n.* the practice of deceiving or cozening.

crack·nel (krak'nəl), *n.* a biscuit or cake having a hard and brittle texture.

cram·pon (kram'pon), *n.* **1.** a spiked iron plate worn on shoes to prevent slipping on ice, etc. **2.** a grappling iron used in raising weights.

cra·ni·al (krā'nēəl), *adj.* relating to the skull or cranium.

cra·ni·ate (krā'nēit, krā'nēāt), *adj.* having a cranium.

cra·ni·ol·o·gy (krā,nēol'əjē), *n.* the study of variations in the size and shape of human skulls.

cra·ni·om·e·try (krā,nēom'itrē), *n.* the science of cranial measurement.

cra·ni·o·phore (krā'nēəfôr,), *n.* an apparatus for holding a skull in position while it is being measured.

cra·ni·os·co·py (krā,nēos'kəpē), *n.* examination of the human skull.

cra·ni·ot·o·my (krā,nēot'əmē), *n.* the cutting open of the skull, usually for brain operations.

cra·ni·um (krā'nēəm), *n.* the skull, esp. that part which encloses the brain.

cran·kle (kraNG'kəl), *v.* to turn, wind, or bend.

crap·au·dine door (krapədēn'), a door rotating on pivots.

crap·u·lent (krap'yōōlənt), *adj.* sick as a result of gross overindulgence in food or drink.

crap·u·lous (krap'yōōləs), *adj.* **1.** indulging in excessive eating and drinking. **2.** suffering from the effects of excessive eating and drinking.

cra·que·lure (krak,əlōōə), *n.* hairline cracks in the surfaces of very old paintings.

cra·sis (krā'sis), *n.* constitution; makeup.

crass (kras), *adj.* lacking delicacy or refinement; insensitive; boorish; stupid.

cras·si·tude (kras'ityōōd), *n.* **1.** stupidity or ignorance. **2.** coarseness; grossness.

craunch (krônCH), *v.* to crunch.

cra·ven (krā'vən), *adj.* **1.** cowardly. —*n.* **2.** a cowardly person.

cre·a·tion·ism (krēā'sHaniz,əm), *n.* the doctrine that each soul is created out of nothing by God for each newborn individual. See also **tra·ducianism.**

cre·den·dum (kriden'dəm), *n.*, *pl.* **cre·den·da** (kriden'də). that which must be believed; an article of faith.

cre·dent (krē'dənt), *adj.* trusting; believing.

cred·i·ble (kred'əbəl), *adj.* believable; plausible; trustworthy.

cred·it·a·ble (kred'itəbəl), *adj.* worthy of credit; honourable; estimable, as a creditable job.

cre·du·li·ty (krədyōō'litē), *n.* excessive willingness to believe, esp. with only slight evidence.

cred·u·lous (kred'yōōləs), *adj.* ready to believe on insufficient evidence; gullible; naive.

creese (krēs), *n.* a Malay dagger with a wavy blade. Also **kris.**

crème de la crème (krem' də la krem'), *French.* the very best part of something.

cre·morne bolt (krimôən'), one of a pair of rods attached to full-length windows which slide into sockets at the top and bottom to bolt the window to the frame.

cre·nate (krē'nāt), *adj.* having the edge cut into scallop shapes, as certain leaves.

cre·na·tion (krinā'sHən), *n.* a crenate formation on the edge of a leaf. Also **crena·ture** (kren'-ətyōō,ə).

cren·el, cre·nelle (kren'əl), *n.* any of the recesses alternating with the merlons on a battlement.

cren·el·ate (kren'əlāt), *v.* to provide with crenels. **—cren,el·a'tion,** *n.*

cren·u·late (kren'yōōlāt), *adj.* having tiny crenations.

cren·u·la·tion (kren,yōōlā'sHən), *n.* a minute crenation.

cre·o·lized (krē'əlīzd), *adj.* (of a language) having ceased to be pidgin and become a native language.

cre·oph·a·gous (krēof'əgəs), *adj.* carnivorous; meat-eating.

crep·i·tant (krep'itənt), *adj.* rustling; crackling.

crep·i·tate (krep'itāt), *v.* to make a rustling or crackling sound.

cre·pus·cule (kripus'kyōōl), *n.* twilight. **—cre·pus·cu·lar** (kripus'kyōōlə), *adj.*

cre·scen·do (krisHen'dō), *n., pl.* **cre·scen·dos, cre·scen·di** (krisHen'dē). a gradual increase in loudness, force, etc.

cres·cive (kres'iv), *adj.* growing; increasing.

cres·set (kres'it), *n.* an iron basket containing oil, pitch, etc., and suspended on high for use as a beacon or torch.

crest rail, the carved rail at the top of a settee or chair.

Cre·ta·ceous (kritā'sHəs), *adj.* relating to the last period of the Mesozoic era, characterized by the advent of insects and the extinction of the giant dinosaurs.

cret·in (kret'in), *n.* a stupid, stubborn fool.

cre·tin·ism (krēt'iniz,əm), *n.* a disease caused by extreme thyroid deficiency and marked by deformity and by the stunting of both mental and physical growth.

crew·el·work (krōō'əlwûk,), *n.* embroidery done with worsted yarn.

crib·ble (krib'əl), *v.* to make a crible surface.

cri·blé (krēblā'), *adj.* (of an engraving plate) having a pattern of dots designed to tone down the contrast between solid black areas and areas of type.

crib·ri·form (krib'rifôəm), *adj.* having holes like a sieve.

cri·coid (krī'koid), *adj.* **1.** of or relating to a ring-shaped cartilage forming part of the larynx. **—n. 2.** this cartilage itself.

criminal conversation, adultery.

crim·i·nal·is·tics (krim,ənəlis'tiks), *n.* the science of crime detection.

criminal syndicalism, the advocacy of terrorism as a means of achieving political and economic reforms.

crim·i·nate (krim'ināt), *v.* **1.** to accuse of a crime. **2.** to incriminate. **3.** to condemn. **—crim'-i·na,tive,** *adj.*

crim·i·nol·o·gy (krim,inol'əjē), *n.* the scientific study of crime and criminals.

crine (krin), *n.* hair.

cri·no·gen·ic (krīnōjen'ik), *adj.* tending to produce secretions.

cri·nose (krī'nōs), *adj.* hairy.

cri·o·sphinx (krī'əsfiNGks), *n., pl.* **cri·o·sphinx·es, cri·o·sphin·ges** (krī'əsfin,jēz). a sphinx having a ram's head.

cris·pate (kris'pāt), *adj.* curled; wrinkled.

cris·pa·tion (krispā'sHən), *n.* the act or process of curling or of being curled.

cris·sum (kris'əm), *n.* the area around the cloacal vent, underneath the tail of a bird. **—cris'sal,** *adj.*

cris·tate (kris'tāt), *adj.* crested.

cri·ter·i·on (krītēr'ēən), *n., pl.* **criter·i·a** (krītēr'-ēə). a standard or set of standards against which other things are evaluated or measured.

crit·ic·as·ter (krit'ikastə), *n.* a critic lacking in ability.

cri·tique (kritēk'), *n.* a critical estimate of some problem, etc.

croft (kroft), *n.* a small plot of land for tillage or pasture. **—croft'er,** *n.*

crois·sant (krwäsäN'), *n., pl.* **croissants** (krwäsäN'). a crescent-shaped roll made of leavened dough or puff paste.

crom·lech (krom'lek), *n.* a circle of upright stones or of flat stones resting on upright ones. See also **dolmen.**

cro·quette (krōket'), *n.* a rissole of minced meat or fish, coated with egg, breadcrumbs, etc., and fried.

cro·sier (krō'zHə), *n.* the pastoral staff of a bishop. Also **cro'zier.**

cross·let (kros'lit), *n.* a small cross, esp. one appearing in a heraldic bearing.

crotch·et (kroCH'it), *n.* **1.** a hook or a device resembling a hook. **2.** a fanciful notion. **—crotch'et·y,** *adj.*

croûte (krōōt), *n.* a crust.

crou·ton (krōō'ton), *n.* a small cube of fried or toasted bread used in soups.

croze (krōz), *n.* a groove at the ends of the staves of a barrel into which the top and bottom parts fit.

cru·ci·ate (krōō'sнẽit), *adj.* shaped like a cross.

cru·ci·fer (krōō'səfə), *n.* one who bears a cross in a religious procession, e*c.

cru·cif·er·ous (krōōsif'ərəs), *adj.* having or bearing a cross.

cru·ci·form (krōō'səfôəm). *adj.* shaped like a cross.

cru·et (krōō'it), *n.* a container for vinegar, oil, etc.

cruis·er·weight (krōō'zəwãt,), *n.* See **light heavyweight.**

cru·ral (krōōr'əl), *adj.* relating to the thigh or leg.

cruse (krōōz), *n.* a small jar or pot for holding liquids.

crus·ta·cean (krustā'sнən), *n.* any of a class of mainly aquatic arthropods including lobsters, shrimps, crabs, etc.

cry·o·gen (krī'əjən), *n.* an agent or substance for producing low temperatures; refrigerant.

cry·ol·o·gy (krīol'əjē), *n.* the scientific study of snow and ice and low-temperature phenomena.

cry·om·e·ter (krīom'itə), *n.* a thermometer for use at low temperatures.

cry·os·co·py (krīos'kəpē), *n.* the determination of the freezing points of liquids or of the lowering of freezing points produced in liquids by dissolved substances.

cry·o·stat (krī'əstat), *n.* an apparatus for maintaining low temperatures.

cry·o·ther·a·py (krī,ō*ther*'əpē), *n.* medical treatment by the inducing of low bodily temperatures. Also **cry·mo·ther·a·py.**

crypt·aes·the·si·a (krip,təsthē'zēə), *n.* extrasensory perception.

crypt·a·nal·y·sis (kript,ənal'əsis), *n.* the science of interpreting or translating codes, secret writings, cryptograms, etc. Also **cryp·to·a·nal'y·sis.**

cryp·to·clas·tic (krip,tōklas'tik), *adj.* composed of minute fragments.

cryp·to·gram (krip'tōgram), *n.* a message in code.

cryp·to·graph (krip'tägröf), *n.* **1.** a cryptogram. **2.** a method or system of secret writing.

cryp·tog·ra·phy (kriptog'rəfē), *n.* the study of secret codes. See also **plain text.**

cryp·tol·o·gy (kriptol'əjē), *n.* the science of cryptanalysis and cryptography.

cryp·tom·e·ter (kriptom'itə), *n.* a device for examining the surface underneath a coat of paint.

cryp·to·nym (krip'tənim), *n.* a secret name.

cryp·ton·y·mous (kripton'əməs), *adj.* anonymous.

cryp·to·phyte (krip'təfīt), *n.* a plant whose reproductive organs are formed underground.

cryp·to·por·ti·cus (kriptōpôə'təkəs), *n.* an enclosed passage with lights on one side.

crys·tal·log·ra·phy (kris,təlog'rəfē), *n.* the science dealing with the structure and forms of crystals. —**crys,tal·lo·graph'ic,** *adj.*

cte·noid (tē'noid), *adj.* having a rough edge; pectinate.

cua·dril·la (kwädrē'yə), *n.* a group of four assistants to a bullfighter.

cub·age (kyōō'bij), *n.* cubic content.

cu·ba·ture (kyōō'bəcнə), *n.* determination of the cubic contents of a solid.

cu·bic·u·lum (kyōōbik'yələm), *n.. pl.* **cu·bic·u·la** (kyōōbik'yələ). a tomb or burial chamber.

cu·bi·form (kyōō'bəfôəm), *adj.* having the shape of a cube.

Cub·ism (kyōō'bizəm), *n.* an abstract style of painting characterized by attempts to reduce natural forms to their basic geometric shapes.

cu·bit (kyōō'bit), *n.* an ancient measure of length based on the length of the forearm.

cu·boid (kyōō'boid), *adj.* having a shape resembling a cube.

cuck·old (kuk'əld), *n.* **1.** a man whose wife is unfaithful. —*v.* **2.** to make (a man) a cuckold.

cu·cul·ate (kyōō'kəlãt), *adj.* shaped like a hood; hooded.

cu·cu·mi·form (kyōōkyōō'məfôəm), *adj.* having the shape of a cucumber; cylindrical.

cud·dy (kud'ē), *n.* a small cabin on a boat.

cuir·bouil·li (kwērbōōye'), *n. French.* leather which is hardened by soaking in hot water.

cui·sine min·ceur (kwēzēn' mansû'), *French*, *n.* a style of cooking, derived from nouvelle cuisine, that minimizes the use of starchy and fatty ingredients.

culch (kulcн), *n.* the mass of material, as stones, shells, etc., forming an oyster bed.

cul·de·sac (kul'dəsak), *n., pl.* **culs-de-sac** (kulz'dəsak,). **1.** a body cavity or tube, resembling a sac and open only at one end. **2.** a road or passage shut at one end; blind alley; dead-end street.

cu·li·nar·y (kul'inəri), *adj.* relating to cookery or the kitchen.

cul·let (kul'it), *n.* broken glass which can be remelted and used again.

culm (kulm), *n.* **1.** refuse coal; coal dust. **2.** a cheap variety of anthracite.

cul·pa (kul'pə), *n., pl.* **cul·pae** (kul'pē). neglect; sin; guilt.

cul·pa·ble (kul'pəbəl), *adj.* meriting condemnation or censure; blameworthy.

cul·ti·gen (kul'tijən), *n.* a cultivated species of plant whose wild origin is not known.

cul·ti·var (kul'tivä), *n.* a plant which has been originated by cultivation.

cul·trate (kul'trãt), *adj.* having a sharp edge and point, as a leaf.

cultural anthropology, the study of the origins and evolution of human culture.

cultural lag, the relatively slow development of one section of a culture compared with another.

cum·brance (kum'brəns), *n.* a source of trouble; a burden or liability; encumbrance.

cum·brous (kum'brəs), *adj.* burdensome; cumbersome.

cum dividend, including a previously declared dividend. See also **ex dividend.**

cum gra·no sa·lis (kum grä'nō sä'lis), *Latin.* with a grain of salt.

cum lau·de (kum lôdē, kum lou'dā), with honour; with (academic) distinction. See also **magna cum laude, summa cum laude.**

cu·mu·li·form (kyōō'myələfôəm), *adj.* resembling cumulus clouds.

cu·mu·lo·cir·rus (kyōō,myəlōsir'əs), *n., pl.* **cu·mu·lo·cir·rus.** See **cirrocumulus.**

cu·mu·lo·nim·bus (kyōō,myəlōnim'bəs), *n., pl.* **cu·mu·lo·nim·bus.** a cumulus cloud of great depth with a tower- or mountain-shaped summit.

cu·mu·lo·stra·tus (kyōō,myəlōstrā'təs), *n., pl.* **cu·mu·lo·stra·tus.** See **stratocumulus.**

cu·mu·lous (kyōō'myələs), *adj.* resembling a cumulus cloud.

cunc·ta·tion (kuɴɢktā'sʜən), *n.* delay.

cunc·ta·tor (kuɴɢktā'tər), *n.* one who delays or procrastinates.

cu·ne·al (kyōō'nēəl), *adj.* wedge-shaped.

cu·ne·ate (kyōō'nēit, kyōō'nēāt), *adj.* wedge-shaped.

cu·ne·at·ic (kyōō,nēat'ik), *adj.* cuneiform.

cu·ne·i·form (kyōō'nifôəm), *adj.* **1.** wedge-shaped. —*n.* **2.** an ancient form of writing in clay using a wedge-shaped stylus.

cu·nic·u·lus (kyōōnik'yələs), *n., pl.* **cu·nic·u·li** (kyōōnik'yəlī). a small underground passage.

cu·pel (kyōō'pəl), *n.* a shallow porous cup used for separating precious metals from lead.

cu·pid·i·ty (kyōōpid'itē), *n.* a strong or inordinate desire; avarice.

cu·pric (kyōō'prik), *adj.* containing copper.

cu·prif·er·ous (kyōōprif'ərəs), *adj.* yielding or bearing copper.

cup·shake (kəp'sʜāk), *n.* See **windshake.**

cu·pu·late (kyōō'pyəlāt), *adj.* having the shape of a cupule.

cu·pule (kyōō'pyōōl), *n.* a cup-shaped process, as in the acorn.

cu·ra·trix (kyōōrā'triks). *n., pl.* **cura·tri·ces** (kyōōr,ətrī'sez). a woman curator.

cu·ret·tage (kyōōret'ij, kyōōritäzʜ'), *n.* the operation of using a curette.

cu·rette (kyōōret'), *n.* **1.** a small spoon or scooplike instrument for scraping or cleaning body cavities. —*v.* **2.** to scrape with a curette.

curf (kûf), *n.* See **kerf.**

cu·rie (kyōōr'ē), *n.* the unit of measurement of activity of a radioactive substance.

cu·ri·o·sa (kyōōr,ēō'sə), *n.* books dealing with pornographic subjects; erotic literature.

cur·mudg·eon (kûmuj'ən), *n.* a quarrelsome, irritable person who is impatient with others.

cur·ric·u·lum vi·tae (kərik'yələm vē'tī, vī'tī), *pl.* **cur·ric·u·la vi·tae** (kərik'yələ vē'tī, vī'tī). a brief account of one's professional or business career.

cur·rish (kur'isʜ), *adj.* resembling a cur; quarrelsome or contemptible.

cur·so·ry (kû'sərē), *adj.* superficial, ignoring details, as *a cursory examination.*

curt (kût), *adj.* abrupt and impatient in manner to the point of rudeness.

cur·tail (kûtāl'), *v.* to cut short; make brief; abridge. —**cur·tail'ment,** *n.*

curtain shutter. See **focal-plane shutter.**

cur·tate (kû'tāt), *adj.* shortened; curtailed.

cu·rule (kyōōr'ōōl), *adj.* of the highest rank or position.

cur·vet (kûvet'), *v.* to prance, frisk, or caper.

cus·pi·dal (kus'pidəl), *adj.* resembling or having a cusp; cuspidate.

cus·pi·date (kus'pidāt), *adj.* having cusps.

cus·tom·ar·y (kus'təmer,ē, kus'təmri), *n.* a book or code of legal customs. Also **cus·tu·mal** (kus'tyōōməl), *n.*

cus·tom-made (kus'təm mād'), *adj.* made specially to order.

cu·ta·ne·ous (kyōōtā'nēəs), *adj.* relating to or affecting the skin.

cu·tin (kyōō'tin), *n.* a waxy substance forming a layer on the outer epidermal surface of plants.

cu·tin·ize (kyōōt'anīz), *v.* to make into cutin.

cu·tis (kyōō'tis), *n.* the dermis or true skin.

cut·tage (kut'ij), *n.* the propagation of plants from vegetative parts.

cu·vée (kōōvā'), *n.* wine obtained by blending different vintages.

cy·an·e·ous (sīan'ēəs), *adj.* of a deep blue colour.

cy·an·ic (sīan'ik), *adj.* of a bluish colour.

cy·a·nom·e·ter (sī,ənom'itər), *n.* an instrument for measuring the intensity of blue in a sky, etc.

cy·a·no·sis (sī,ənō'sis), *n.* a bluish discoloration of the skin caused by insufficient oxygenation of the blood.

cy·ber·nate (sī'bənāt,), *v.* to control a manufacturing operation or other process by machines, esp. computers. —**cy·ber·na·tion** (sī,bənā'sʜən), *n.*

cy·ber·net·ics (sī,bənet'iks), *n.* the comparative study of communication and control systems in machines, esp. computers, and similar functions in the human nervous system and brain.

cy·ber·punk (sī'bəpuNGk), *n.* **1.** a genre of science fiction set in a nightmarish society controlled by computers and featuring rebellious computer operators or hackers. **2.** a writer of such works.

cy·cle (sī'kəl), *n.* a series of regularly recurrent changes in an electric current.

cy·clo·gen·e·sis (sī,kləjen'isis), *n.* the appearance and development of a cyclone.

cy·cloid (sī'kloid), *adj.* like a circle; circular.

cy·clol·y·sis (sīklol'isis), *n.* the diminution and disappearance of a cyclone.

cy·clom·e·ter (sīklom'itər), *n.* **1.** an instrument for measuring circular arcs. **2.** an instrument for recording the revolutions of a wheel, often used for registering the distance travelled by a wheeled vehicle.

cy·clone (sī'klōn), *n.* a region of low atmospheric pressure surrounded by circular wind motion. See also **anti-cyclone.**

cyclone furnace, a furnace in which is burnt liquid fuel in a revolving column of air.

Cy·clo·pe·an (sīkləpē'ən, sīklō'pēən), *adj.* relating to a method of building using large, irregular, or undressed stones.

cy·clo·ram·a (sīklōrä'mə), *n.* **1.** a panoramic pictorial representation of a landscape, etc., that encircles the spectator as he sits in the centre of a hall, etc. **2.** a curved backcloth, etc., in a theatre designed to give an impression of great distance.

cy·clo·sis (sīklō'sis), *n., pl.* **cy·clo·ses** (sīklō'sēz). the movement of protoplasm inside a cell.

cy·clo·stom·a·tous (sī,klōstōm'ətəs), *adj.* having a circular mouth.

cy·clo·thy·mi·a (sī,klōthī'mēə), *n.* a psychosis marked by alternating moods of depression and elation. —**cy,clo·thy'mi·ac,** *n.*

cy·clo·tron (sī'klətron), *n.* a device for causing electrified particles to move at very high speeds in spiral paths in a strong magnetic field.

cy·e·sis (sīē'sis), *n., pl.* **cy·e·ses** (sīē'sēz). pregnancy.

cyg·net (sig'nit), *n.* a young swan.

cyl·in·droid (sil'indroid), *n.* **1.** a solid shaped like a cylinder. —*adj.* **2.** resembling a cylinder.

cy·maise (sēmez'), *n.* a pewter container for wine with a spout and handle.

cy·ma·ti·um (sīmā'tēəm, sīmā'sHēəm), *n., pl.* **cy·ma·ti·a** (sīmā'tiə, sīmā'sHiə). (in classical architecture) the top moulding of an entablature.

cym·bi·form (sim'bəfôəm), *adj.* shaped like a boat.

cy·mo·graph (sī'məgräf), *n.* See **kymograph.**

cy·mot·ri·chous (sīmo'trəkəs), *adj.* having curly or wavy hair.

Cym·ric (kim'rik), *n.* the Welsh language.

cyn·i·cism (sin'əsiz,əm), *n.* the attitude of a person who doubts sincerity and honest motives in others and behaves selfishly himself, esp. by taking advantage of others' morality and ethical sense.

cy·no·sure (sī'nəsHŌŌr), *n.* **1.** a centre of attention; something that strongly attracts. **2.** something that guides or directs.

Cy·ril·lic (siril'ik), *adj.* relating to the alphabet used for writing Old Church Slavonic and now for Russian and various other languages.

cyr·to·sis (sətō'sis), *n.* curvature of the spine.

cyst (sist), *n.* **1.** a sac in animal tissues. **2.** a sporelike cell in plants enclosing reproductive bodies.

cystic fibrosis (sis'tik fībrō'sis), a hereditary disease affecting the pancreas and lungs, and characterized by an inability to digest and difficulty in breathing.

cyst·oid (sis'toid), *adj.* resembling a cyst.

cys·to·scope (sis'təskōp), *n.* an instrument for examining the bladder.

cys·tos·co·py (sistos'kəpē), *n.* examination of the bladder by using a cystoscope

cy·to·ar·chi·tec·ture (sī,tōär'kitek,CHə), *n.* the structure of cells in a tissue.

cy·to·chem·is·try (sī,tōkem'istrē), *n.* the chemistry of living cells. —**cyto·chem'i·cal,** *adj.*

cy·toc·la·sis (sītok'ləsis), *n.* the destruction of cells. —**cy·to·clas·tic** (sī,tōklas'tik), *adj.*

cy·to·gen·e·sis (sī,tōjen'isis), *n.* the genesis and development of cells.

cy·to·ge·net·ics (sī,tōjənet'iks), *n.* the branch of biology dealing with the study of heredity using the methods of both cytology and genetics.

cy·toid (sī'toid), *adj.* resembling a cell.

cy·to·ki·ne·sis (sī,'tōkinē'sis), *n.* cytoplasmic changes during mitosis, meiosis, and fertilization.

cy·tol·o·gist (sītol'əjist), *n.* one who specializes in cytology.

cy·tol·o·gy (sītol'əjē), *n.* the study of living cells.

cy·tol·y·sis (sītol'isis), *n.* the destruction or dissolution of living cells.

cy·to·meg·a·lo·vi·rus (sī,tōmeg'əlōvī,rəs), *n.* a type of herpes virus that can cause serious disease in immunocompromised individuals and birth defects in children born to mothers infected with the virus during pregnancy.

cy·ton (sīt'ən), *n.* the body of a nerve cell.

cy·to·path·o·gen·ic (sī,tōpath,əjen'ik), *adj.* destructive to cells.

cy·to·pa·thol·o·gy (sī,tōpəthol'əjē), *n.* the study of the diseases of cells.

cy·toph·a·gy (sītof'əjē), *n.* the engulfing of cells by other cells.

cy·to·plasm (sī'tōplaz,əm), *n.* the protoplasm of a cell surrounding the nucleus.

cy·to·plast (sī'tōpläst), *n.* the cytoplasmic contents of a cell.

cy·to·some (sī'tōsōm), *n.* the cytoplasm of a cell.

cy·to·tax·is (sī,tōtak'sis), *n.* the mutual attraction and repulsion of cells.

cy·to·tox·in (sī,tōtok'sin), *n.* a substance in the blood which is harmful to certain cells.

cy·to·trop·ic (sī,tōtrop'ik), *adj.* attracted towards or moving away from cells. —**cy·to·tro·pism** (sī,tōtro'pizəm), *n.*

cy·to·zo·on (sī,təzō'ən), *n., pl.* **cy·to·zo·a** (sī,təzō'ə). a parasite living inside a cell.

czar·e·vitch (zär'əvicн), *n.* See **tsarevitch**.

cza·rev·na (zärev'nə), *n.* See **tsarevna**.

cza·ri·na (zärē'nə), *n.* See **tsarina**.

D

da·cha, dat·cha (da'cнǝ), *n.* (in Russia) a country house.

da·coit, da·koit (dǝkoit'), *n.* (in India and Burma) one of a group of robbers that plunder in bands.

da·coit·y, da·koit·y (dǝkoi'tē), *n.* organized robbery by bands.

dac·ry·a·gogue (dak'rēǝgog), *adj.* causing the secretion of tears.

dac·tyl (dak'tǝl), *n.* a digit, as a finger or toe. —**dac·tyl·ic,** *adj.*

dac·tyl·o·gram (daktil'ǝgram), *n.* a fingerprint.

dac·ty·log·ra·phy (dak,tǝlog'rǝfē), *n.* study of fingerprints for identification.

dac·ty·lol·o·gy (dak,tǝlol'ǝjē), *n.* method of communicating by hand and finger signs.

dac·ty·lo·meg·a·ly (dak,tǝlōmeg'ǝlē), *n.* enlargement of a finger or fingers.

Da·da (dä'dä), *n.* (sometimes *l.c.*) a movement in art and literature of the early 20th century to discredit all previous art by making use of inappropriate materials and unrelated techniques.

dae·dal (dē'dǝl), *adj.* **1.** skilful; cleverly inventive. **2.** intricate; diversified; mazelike.

dae·mon, dai·mon (dē'mǝn), *n.* **1.** a lesser god, as the protector of a place or a man's attendant spirit. **2.** an evil spirit.

dakh·ma (däk'mǝ), *n.* See **tower of silence.**

da·koit (dǝkoit'), *n.* See **dacoit.**

da·koit·y (dǝkoi'tē), *n.* See **dacoity.**

dalles (dalz), *n. pl.* the rapids of a river running down a canyon or gorge. Also **dells.**

dal·li·ance (dal'ēǝns), *n.* amorous behaviour; flirtatious trifling.

dam·a·scene (dam'ǝsēn), *v.* **1.** to ornament steel with wavy lines. —*n.* **2.** steel so ornamented.

D and C, dilation (or dilatation) and curettage; the surgical removal by scraping of tissue from the lining of the uterus.

danse ma·ca·bre (däнs' makä'br), **1.** a symbolic dance leading the dead to the grave. Also **dance of death. 2.** an artist's representation of a symbolic dance leading the dead to the grave. Also **dance of death.**

dap (dap), *v.* to dip into water.

dar·by (dä'bē), *n.* a plasterer's float with two handles.

dark lan·tern (däk lan'tûn), a lantern whose light can be concealed by a shutter.

dar·kle (dä'kǝl), *v.* to be or become dark, gloomy, or indistinct.

dark matter, (in astronomy) matter that is present in the universe but which neither emits nor absorbs electromagnetic radiation.

dark·some (däk'sǝm), *adj.* dark.

dar·tle (dä'tǝl), *v.* to dart back and forth rapidly.

Dar·win·ism (dä'winiz,ǝm), *n.* the theory of evolution proposed by the British naturalist, Charles Darwin (1809–82), which argued that living organisms evolve from ancestral forms by a process of natural selection acting on variations among individuals. See also **Lamarckism, Neo-Darwinism.** —**Dar·win·ian, Dar·win·ist, Dar·win·ite,** *n., adj.* —**Dar·win·is'tic,** *adj.*

da·sein (dä'zīn), *n.* awareness of the circumstances of one's own existence.

dash·pot (dasн'pot,), *n.* a pneumatic or hydraulic pistonlike device for absorbing shocks or reversing the direction of a machine part.

das·tard (das'tûd), *n.* a contemptible coward. —**das'tard·ly,** *adj.*

da·sym·e·ter (dasim'itǝ), *n.* an instrument for measuring gas density.

das·y·phyl·lous (das,ifil'ǝs), *adj.* having hairy leaves.

dat·cha (da'cнǝ), *n.* See **dacha.**

daube (dōb), *n.* a meat and vegetable stew.

dau·er·schlaf (dou'ǝsнläf), *n.* psychiatric treatment by drug-induced sleep.

daughter of Eve, a girl or woman.

dau·phin (dô'fin), *n., pl.* **dauphines** (dô'finz). the title of the eldest son of a King of France.

dau·phin·ess (dô'finis), *n.* the wife of a dauphin. Also **dau·phine** (dô'fēn).

dav·it (dav'it), *n.* any device on a ship or large boat for raising or lowering a small boat.

DDT, dichlorodiphenyltrichloroethane; former insecticide.

dead·fall (ded'fôl,), *n.* a large trap for game in which the prey is struck or crushed by a heavy weight.

dead·ly sins, the sins of pride, covetousness,. lust, anger, gluttony, envy, and sloth. Also **seven deadly sins.**

dead man's control, a device that must be

held down by the driver of a train or other vehicle to control and maintain its motion. Also **dead man's handle, deadman's pedal.**

dead man's hand, (in poker) a hand containing two aces and two eights.

dead reckoning, a method for calculating position using distance and directions run from one's last known position.

de·an·thro·po·mor·phism (dēan͵thrəpə-môə'fizəm), n. the removal of anthropomorphic beliefs from philosophy and religion.

dear text. See **plain text.**

dearth (dûth), n. scarcity or scanty supply; lack.

death instinct, inclination to suicide.

death rate, the number of deaths per thousand of population.

death rattle, a sound often produced in the throat immediately before death, caused by the air forced through mucus.

de·ba·cle (dābä'kəl), n. **1.** a sudden, often ignominious collapse. **2.** the disintegration of ice in a river. See also **embacle.**

de·bauch (dibôcH'), v. to corrupt by excessive sexual pleasures; seduce. —**de·bauch'er·y,** n.

deb·au·chee (debôcHē'), n. one who indulges in excessive sensuality.

de·bil·i·tate (dibil'itāt), v. to weaken.

de·bil·i·ty (dibil'itē), n. state of being physically weak.

deb·o·nair, deb·o·naire, deb·on·naire (debəne'ə), adj. having pleasant manners; gracious; gay.

de·bouch (diboucH'), v. (of a river) to emerge from a narrow valley into a larger one.

de·bouch·ment (diboucH'mənt), n. a mouth or outlet, as of a river or pass. Also **de·bou·chure** (dābōōshōō'ə).

de·bride·ment (dibrēd'mənt), n. removal of dead tissue from a wound by surgery.

de·brief (dēbrēf'), v. to question closely on return from a mission to assess its conduct and results.

de·bug (dēbug'), v. to detect and eliminate errors, esp. from a computer program.

dec·a·gon (dek'əgon), n. a ten-sided plane figure.

dec·a·gram, dek·a·gram (dek'əgram), n. a metric unit of 10 grams, equivalent to 0.3527 ounce avoirdupois.

dec·a·he·dron (dek͵əhē'drən), n. a solid with 10 faces.

de·cal·ci·fy (dēkal'səfī), v. to remove calcareous matter, as from a bone.

de·cal·co·ma·ni·a (dikal͵kəmā'nēə), n. a paper bearing a picture, lettering, or design that may be transferred, usually by wetting it, onto another surface. Also **de·cal** (dikal', dē'kal).

de·ca·les·cence (dē͵kəles'əns), n. the more rapid absorption of heat in a piece of iron as it passes a certain temperature. —**de͵ca·les'cent,** adj.

dec·a·li·tre, dek·a·li·tre (dek'əlē͵te), n. a metric unit of 10 litres, equivalent to 8.8 quarts U.S. dry measure or 2.2 gallons imperial measure.

Dec·a·logue, Dec·a·log (dek'əlog), n. the Ten Commandments. Exodus 20:2-17.

de·cam·er·ous (dikam'ərəs), adj. having 10 parts.

dec·a·me·tre, dek·a·me·tre (dek'əmē͵tə), n. a linear measure of 10 metres.

de·camp (dikamp'), v. to depart hastily; run away.

dec·an (dek'ən), n. one division of ten in a sign of the zodiac.

dec·a·nal (dek'ənəl), adj. pertaining to a dean.

dec·a·pod (dek'əpod), n. **1.** a ten-legged crustacean, as a crab or lobster. **2.** a ten-armed cephalopod, as a cuttlefish.

de·cas·u·al·ize (dēkazH'ōōəlīz), v. to cease or curtail the hiring of temporary personnel.

dec·a·syl·la·ble (dek'əsil͵əbəl), n. a word or verse containing ten syllables. —**dec·a·syl·lab·ic** (dek͵əsilab'ik), adj.

de·cath·lon (dikath'lon), n. an athletic contest involving ten different events with the same participants competing in all.

dec·at·ing (dek'ətiNG), n. an anti-shrinking process for textiles that provides a lustrous finish. Also **dec'a·tiz·ing.**

de·cay (dikā'), v. the disintegration of a radioactive substance in which a nucleus undergoes transformation into one or more different nuclei and simultaneously emits radiation, loses electrons, or undergoes fission. Also **radioactive decay.**

de·ce·dent (disē'dənt), n. (in law) a deceased person.

de·cel·er·ate (dēsel'ərāt), v. to reduce in speed.

de·cel·er·on (dēsel'əron), n. (in aeronautics) an aileron acting as a brake.

de·cen·nial (disen'ēəl), adj. **1.** of or for ten years; occurring every ten years. —n. **2.** an anniversary celebrating this.

de·cen·ni·um (disen'ēəm), n. a period of ten years. Also **de·cen·na·ry** (disen'ərē).

dec·i·bel (des'ibel), n. a unit in which the intensity of a sound wave is measured.

de·cid·u·ous (disij'ōōəs), adj. (of trees, teeth, etc.) dropping off or out after a period of growth.

dec·i·gram (des'igram), n. a metric unit of weight of 1/10th gram, equivalent to 1.543 grains.

dec·ile (des'il), n. a value of a variable that divides its distribution into ten equal sets.

dec·i·li·tre (des'ilētə), n. a metric unit of capacity of 1/10th litre, equivalent to 6.102 cu. in. or 3.381 fl. oz.

de·cil·lion (disil'yən), *n.* a number represented by 1 followed by 33 zeros.

dec·i·mate (des'imāt), *v.* **1.** to destroy a large percentage of. **2.** to reduce by one tenth.

dec·i·metre (des'əmē,tə), *n.* a metric unit of length equal to 1/10th of a metre.

deck·le edge (dek'əl ej), the irregular edge of handmade paper. Also **deck·le.**

de·claim (diklām'), *v.* to make a speech, esp. in a dramatic manner. —**dec·la·ma·tion** (dek,ləmā'-sHən), *n.* —**de·clam·a·to·ry** (diklam'ətôrē), *adj.*

de·clar·ant (dikler'ənt), *n.* one who makes a declaration.

de·clar·a·to·ry judgment (diklar'ətôr,ē), a legal decision limited to declaring the rights of the parties.

dé·clas·sé (dāklasā'), *adj.* having a low-class social status or exhibiting the characteristics of such status, as in appearance, manners, matters of taste, etc.

dec·li·nate (dek'lənāt), *adj.* curving downwards. —**de·cli·na·to·ry** (diklī'nətôr,ē), *adj.*

de·clin·a·ture (diklī'nəcHər), *n.* act of refusal.

dec·li·nom·e·ter (dek,lənom'itə), *n.* an instrument that measures the downwards variation of a magnetic needle from true north or the angular distance of a star or planet from the celestial equator.

de·cliv·ity (dikliv'itē), *n.* a downwards slope (from the observer's point of view). See also **acclivity.** —**de·cli·vous** (diklī'vəs), *adj.* —**de·cliv·i·tous** (dikliv'itəs), *adj.*

de·coct (dikokt'), *v.* to concentrate by boiling down. —**de·coc·tion** (dikok'sHən), *n.*

de·col·late (dikol'āt), *v.* to behead.

dé·colle·tage (dā,koltäzH'), *n.* the neck of a low-cut dress.

dé·colle·té (dā,koltā'), *adj.* (of a dress) cut low at the neck.

de·com·mis·sion (dē,kəmisH'ən), *v.* to remove (equipment) from active service.

de·com·pen·sa·tion (dē,kompənsā'sHən), *n.* the inability of a defective heart to make up for its defect.

de·com·pres·sion sickness (dē,kəm-presH'ən), a condition caused by the formation of nitrogen bubbles in the blood developed in coming from an atmosphere of high pressure to air of ordinary pressure. Also **bends, caisson disease.**

de·con·gest (dē,kənjest'), *v.* to reduce the congestion of.

de·con·ges·tant (dē,kənjes'tənt), *n.* a medicine that relieves congestion.

de·con·ges·tive (dē,kənjes'tiv), *adj.* relieving congestion.

de·con·se·crate (dē,kon'səkrāt), *v.* to secularize.

de·con·struc·tion (dē,kənstruk'sHən), *n.* a literary analytical technique, also applied to film and other media, that seeks to dismantle and examine what its adherents see as the contradictory elements inherent in any text, thereby revealing a profusion of meanings. —**de,con·struc'tion·ist,** *n.*

dec·or·ous (dek'ərəs), *adj.* proper in behaviour, dress, and attitude.

de·cor·ti·cate (dēkôr'təkāt), *v.* to peel; remove the husk or bark from. —**de·cor,ti·ca'tion,** *n.*

de·co·rum (dikôr'əm), *n.* dignified and appropriate demeanour, appearance, etc.

de·cou·page (dā'kōōpäzH'), *n.* decoration with paper cutouts.

de·cree ni·si (dikrē' nī'sī), a legal decree, usually of a divorce, rendering it effective at a future date.

dec·re·ment (dek'rəmənt), *n.* a gradual diminution or the amount so lost.

de·crep·it (dikrep'it), *adj.* weak; enfeebled; worn out by age, as a person, building, etc.

de·crep·i·tate (dikrep'itāt), *v.* to crackle.

de·crep·i·tude (dikrep'ityōōd), *n.* a state of weakness; decrepit condition, esp. from old age.

de·cre·scen·do (de,krisHen'dō), *n.* a gradual decrease in volume.

de·cres·cent (dikres'ənt), *adj.* decreasing; lessening.

de·cre·tal (dikrē'təl), *adj.* pertaining to or embodying a decree.

de·cre·tive (dikrē'tiv), *adj.* of or with the force of a decree.

dec·re·to·ry (dek'ritôr,ē), *adj.* of or in keeping with a decree.

de·cry (dəkrī'), *v.,* **de·cried, de·crying.** to speak or write badly of something; belittle or disparage. —**de·cri'al,** *n.*

de·crypt (dēkript'), *v.* to decode.

de·cu·bi·tus (dikyōō'bitəs), *n.,* pl. **de·cub·i·ti** (dikyōō'bitē). (in medicine) the position a patient assumes in bed.

dec·u·man (dek'yōōmən), *adj.* of great magnitude, as a wave.

de·cum·bent (dikum'bənt), *adj.* prone; recumbent.

dec·u·ple (dek'yōōpəl), *adj.* tenfold.

de·curved (dēkûvd'), *adj.* curving downwards.

de·cus·sate (dikus'āt), *adj.* crossed; intersected.

deem (dēm), *v.* to judge, consider, or estimate; express an opinion about.

deem·ster (dēm'stə), *n.* (on the Isle of Man) a judge.

deer·stalk·er (dē'əstô,kə), *n.* a cloth cap with peaks front and back and flaps for covering the ears.

de·es·ca·late (dē,es'kəlāt), *v.* to lower and

decrease the intensity of, as a war. —**de·es,ca·la'·tion**, *n.*

de·e·sis (dēē'sis), *n., pl.* **de·e·ses** (dēē'sēz). (in Byzantine art) a representation of Christ on a throne attended by St John and the Virgin Mary.

de fac·to (dā fak'tō), *Latin.* **1.** actually existing, though not by legal right. **2.** in reality. See also **de jure.**

de·fal·cate (difal'kāt), *v.* to misappropriate money.

de·fal·ca·tion (dē,falkā'sHən), *n.* the misappropriation of money by a trusted official.

de·fame (difām'), *v.* **de·famed, de·fam·ing.** to say bad things about someone or something. —**def·a·ma·tion** (def,əmā'sHən), *n.*

de·fea·sance (difē'zəns), *n.* (in law) the process of rendering something null and void.

de·fea·si·ble (difē'zəbəl), *adj.* able to be ended or annulled.

de·fend·ant (difen'dənt), *n.* a person against whom a legal suit or charge is being brought in a court of law. See also **plaintiff.**

de·fen·es·tra·tion (dēfen,istrā'sHən), *n.* the throwing of somebody or something out of a window.

def·er·en·tial (def,əren'sHəl), *adj.* respectful; treating with courtesy and regard.

de·fer·vesce (dēfərves'), *v.* to have a fever reduced.

de·fer·ves·cence (dēfərves'əns), *n.* the lessening of fever.

de·fi·bril·late (dēfib'rilāt), *v.* to stop the formation of threadlike fibres in the heart muscles.

de·fi·bril·la·tor (dēfi'brəlā,tə), *n.* a device for defibrillating.

def·i·cit financ·ing (def'isit), a system of governmental finance that allows expenditures to exceed revenues, usually through borrowing.

deficit spend·ing (spen'diNG), a system of governmental finance that allows expenditures in excess of income.

def·i·lade (defəlād'), *n.* protection afforded by any obstacle, as a hill, from enemy fire.

de·fin·i·en·dum (difin,ēen'dəm), *n., pl.* **de·fin·i·en·da** (difin,ēen'də). something to be defined, as a dictionary headword.

de·fin·i·ens (difin'ēənz), *n., pl.* **defin·i·en·tia** (difin,ēen'sHə). something that defines, as a dictionary definition.

de·fin·i·tive (dəfin'itiv), *adj.* authoritative, reliable, and complete, as the works of an author, a text, or a scholarly study.

de·fin·i·tude (difin'ityōōd), *n.* precision; exactness.

def·la·grate (def'ləgrāt), *v.* to burn, esp. with near-explosive force. —**def,la·gra'tion**, *n.*

de·floc·cu·lant (dēflok'yələnt), *n.* a chemical for diluting ceramic slip.

de·floc·cu·late (dēflok'yəlāt), *v.* to disperse compound masses of particles.

def·lo·ra·tion (def,lərā'sHən), *n.* act of depriving a woman of virginity.

de·flow·er (diflou'ər), *v.* to ravish a woman.

de·flux·ion (difluk'sHən), *n.* a fluid discharge, as catarrh.

de·fo·li·ant (dēfō'lēənt), *n.* a chemical that strips the leaves from plants.

de·fo·li·ate (dēfō'lēāt), *v.* to strip the leaves from (a plant or tree). —**de·fo,li·a'tion**, *n.*

deft (deft), *adj.* skilful or clever with one's hands, mind, etc. —**deft'ness**, *n.*

de·funct (difuNGkt'), *adj.* no longer functioning; dead.

de·func·tive (difuNGk'tiv), *adj.* pertaining to dead people.

de·fu·sion (dēfyōō'zHən), *n.* (in psychoanalysis) the distinguishing between the instinct to live and the death instinct.

dé·ga·gé (dāgazHā'), *adj., fem.* **dé·ga·gée.** *French.* free and easy in manner; not emotionally involved.

de·gauss (dēgous'), *v.* to demagnetize (equipment).

de·gla·ci·a·tion (dēglā,sēā'sHən), *n.* the melting of a glacier.

de·glu·ti·tion (dē,glōōtisH'ən), *n.* act of swallowing.

de·gres·sion (digresH'ən), *n.* **1.** a descent. **2.** a decrease in the rate of taxation on incomes below a certain amount. —**de·gres'sive**, *adj.*

de·gust (digust'), *v.* to taste. Also **degus'tate.**

de gus·ti·bus non est dis·pu·tandum (de gōōs'tibōōs nōn est dis,pōōtän'dōōm), *Latin.* there is no (point in) disputing tastes.

de·hisce (dihis'), *v.* to burst open, as a seed pod.

de·his·cence (dihis'əns), *n.* the bursting open of seed pods and discharging of their seeds. —**de·his'cent**, *adj.*

de·i·cide (dē'isīd), *n.* **1.** the killing of a god. **2.** one who kills a god. —**de·i·cid'al**, *adj.*

deic·tic (dīk'tik), *adj.* **1.** (in logic) serving to prove directly. **2.** (in grammar) demonstrating.

de·if·ic (dēif'ik), *adj.* deifying.

de·i·form (de'əfôəm), *adj.* like a god.

de·i·fy (dē'əfī), *v.* to exalt; make a god of; adore and respect as a god. —**de·if·i·ca'tion**, *n.*

deign (dān), *v.* to condescend.

deip·nos·o·phist (dīpnos'əfist), *n.* a good conversationalist.

dé·jà vu (dā'zHa vōō'), one's impression that he has already experienced something when actually it is being encountered for the first time.

de·jec·ta (dijek'tə), *n. pl.* human excrement.

de ju·re (dā jōōr'ē), according to the law; rightfully. See also **de facto.**

dek·a·gram (dek'əgram), *n.* See **decagram.**

dek·a·li·tre (dek'əlētə), *n.* See **decalitre.**

dek·a·me·tre (dek'əmētə), *n.* See **decametre.**

de·lam·i·nate (dēlam'ināt), v. to divide into thin leaves or layers. —**de·lam,i·na'tion,** n.

de·le (dē'lē), v. (in printing) to delete.

de·lec·ta·tion (dē,lektā'sнən), n. delight and enjoyment in something.

del·e·te·ri·ous (del,itēr'ēəs), adj. harmful; noxious.

delft (delft), n. a white and blue earthenware.

del·i (del'ē), n., pl. **del·is** (del'ēz). a delicatessen.

de·lict (dilikt'), n. (in law) an offence.

de·lim·it (dilim'it), v. to fix the boundaries of. Also **de·lim·i·tate** (dilim'itāt).

de·lin·e·ate (dilin'ēāt), v. to describe precisely; portray in words. —**delin'e·a·tor,** n.

del·i·quesce (del,əkwes'), v. to melt; become liquid. —**del,i·ques'cence,** n. —**del,i·ques'cent,** adj.

de·lir·i·urn tre·mens (dilēr'ēəm trē'mənz), delirium caused by chronic alcoholism. Abbr.: **d.t.**

del·i·tes·cent (del,ites'ənt), adj. concealed; hidden away.

dells (delz), n. See **dalles.**

del·phic (del'fik), adj. obscure; ambiguous.

de·lus·ter·ant (dēlus'tərənt), n. a chemical that reduces the lustre on yarn.

dem·a·gogue (dem'əgog), n. a politician who gains and holds power by playing on the passions and prejudices of the people. —**dem·a·gog·ic** (deməgog'ik), adj.

dem·a·gog·u·er·y (dem,əgog'ərē), n. the techniques practised by a demagogue. Also **dem'a·gogu·ism.**

dem·a·gog·y (dem,əgog'ē), n. a group of demagogues.

de·mar·cate (dēmär'kāt), v. to mark out; limit; clearly separate. —**de,mar·ca'tion,** n.

dé·marche (dāmäsн'), n. a manoeuvre or plan for a manoeuvre in the relations with another, esp. in diplomacy.

de·mean (dimēn'), v. 1. to degrade or debase. 2. to behave (oneself). —**de·mean'ing·ly,** adv.

de·mean·our (dimē'nə), n. bearing; conduct; behaviour.

de·men·ti·a (dimen'sнə), n. madness; severe loss of intellectual capacity combined with disintegration of personality.

dementia prae·cox (prē'koks), a mental disease characterized by bizarre behaviour and emotional deterioration; schizophrenia.

de·mer·ger (dēmû'jə), n. the uncoupling of two previously merged companies. —**de·merge',** v.

de·mesne (dimān'), n. the land round an estate, occupied and kept for the owner's sole use.

dem·i·john (dem'ijon), n. a large, narrow-necked bottle with wicker-work woven round it. See also **carboy.**

de·mil·i·ta·rize (dēmil'itərīz), v. to put under civil control.

dem·i·lune (dem'iloon), n. a crescent shape.

dem·i·mon·daine (dem,ēmondān'), n. a woman who has lost her reputation by indiscreet behaviour.

dem·i·monde (dem,ēmond'), n. a woman of dubious social standing.

dem·i·rep (dem'ērep,), n. a woman whose reputation has been compromised.

de·mis·sion (dimisн'ən), n. resignation; abdication.

dem·i·urge (dem'ēûj,), n. 1. the Platonic name for the maker of the world. 2. a superhuman being who is in subordination to the supreme being.

de·moc·ra·cy (dimok'rəsē), n. government by the people; government by the majority.

de·mod·ed (dēmō'did), adj. old-fashioned; out of date.

de·mog·ra·phy (dimog'rəfē), n. the study of population statistics. —**de·mog'ra·pher,** n.

dem·oi·selle (demwäzel'), n. an unmarried girl.

de·mon·e·tize, de·mon·e·tise (dēmon'itīz,), v. 1. to curtail use (of a metal) as a currency standard. 2. to take out of use as a currency. —**de·mon,e·ti·za'tion, de·mon,e·ti·sa'tion,** n.

de·mon·og·ra·phy (dē,mənog'rəfē), n. a study or work about demons.

de·mon·ol·a·ter (dē,mənol'ətə), n. a worshipper of demons.

de·mon·ol·a·try (dē,mənol'ətrē), n. the worship of demons.

de·mon·ol·ogy (dē,mənol'əjē), n. the study of the beliefs held about demons.

de·mos (dē'mos), n. the population viewed as a political unit.

de·mot·ic (dimot'ik), adj. 1. of the people; common. 2. pertaining to the simplified form of ancient Egyptian writing. —n. 3. (D-) the common dialect of Modern Greek. See also **Katharevusa.**

de·mul·cent (dimul'sənt), adj. (of a medical substance) soothing.

de·mul·si·fy (dimul'səfī), v. to separate (an emulsion) into components that cannot recombine to form the same emulsion.

de·mur (dimû'), v. to make difficulties; object; take exception.

de·mur·rage (dimur'ij), n. undue delaying of a ship, as in loading or unloading.

de·mur·rer (dimur'ə), n. an objection.

den·a·ry (den'ərē), adj. containing ten; having ten as the basic of reckoning; decimal.

de·na·tion·al·ize (dēnasн'ənəlīz), v. to remove (an industry) from the control of the government and place it in private hands.

de·nat·ure (dēnā'cнər), v. 1. to destroy the

natural character of. **2.** to add substance to (alcohol) to make it unfit for consumption.·

den·drite (den'drīt), *n.* a treelike pattern on a stone or mineral.

den·drit·ic (dendrit'ik), *adj.* marked like a dendrite; arborescent. Also **den·drit'i·cal.**

den·dro·chro·nol·o·gy (den,drōkrənol'əjē), *n.* the study of the annular rings of trees and their dating.

den·droid (den'droid), *adj.* branching, as a tree. Also **den·droi'dal.**

den·drol·o·gy (dendrol'əjē), *n.* the study of trees.

den·droph·a·gous (dendrof'əgəs), *adj.* feeding on trees.

den·droph·i·lous (dendrof'ələs), *adj.* living in trees.

den·e·ga·tion (den,əgā'sHən), *n.* a denial.

den·gue (deNG'gā), *n.* an infectious tropical disease characterized by severe pains in the joints and muscles. Also **breakbone fever.**

de·ni·er (den'iā, den'yə), *n.* a unit of weight indicating the fineness of silk and synthetic yarns.

den·i·grate (den'əgrāt), *v.* to speak of in a derogatory manner; sneer; criticize.

de·nom·i·nate (dinom'ināt), *v.* to name; designate. —**de·nom,i·na'tion,** *n.* —**de·nom'i·na·tive,** *adj.*

de·no·ta·tion (dē,nōtā'sHən), *n.* the association of ideas that a word conjures up for most people. —**de·no'ta·tive,** *adj.*

de·note (dinōt'), *v.* to indicate; represent by a symbol.

de·noue·ment (dānōō'mäN), *n.* the climax and unravelling of a dramatic or literary plot.

de·nounce (dinouns'), *v.* **de·nounced, de·nounc·ing.** to say or write something bad about another, esp. by revealing some criminal act he has committed.

de no·vo (de nō'vō), *Latin.* again; afresh.

den·sim·e·ter (densim'itə), *n.* an instrument that measures density.

den·tate (den'tāt), *adj.* notched; with toothlike projections.

den·ta·tion (dentā'sHən), *n.* a toothed form.

den·telle (dentel'), *n.* a tooled pattern used to decorate book covers.

den·ti·cle (den'tikəl), *n.* a small tooth; part shaped like a tooth.

den·tic·u·late (dentik'yəlit), *adj.* having many fine teeth, as the edge of a leaf.

den·tic·u·la·tion (dentik,yōōlā'sHən), *n.* a group of denticles.

den·ti·form (den'tifôəm), *adj.* in the shape of a tooth.

den·til (den'til), *n.* one of a continuous pattern of small, square, toothlike projections used in architecture on cornices and mouldings.

den·ti·tion (dentisH'ən), *n.* **1.** the number, arrangement, and kind of teeth. **2.** teething.

den·toid (den'toid), *adj.* like a tooth.

de·nu·mer·a·ble (dinyōō'mərəbəl), *adj.* countable.

de·on·tol·o·gy (dē,ontol'əjē), *n.* the study of duty and ethics. —**de,ontol'o·gist,** *n.*

De·o vo·len·te (dā'ō vōlen'tā), *Latin.* God willing.

de·oxy·ri·bo·nu·cle·ase (dēok,siri,bōnyōō'-klēās,), *n.* an enzyme found in the pancreas. Also **desoxyribonuclease.**

de·ox·y·ri·bo·nu·cle·ic acid (dēok,siri,bōnyōōklē'ik). See **DNA.**

de·paup·er·ate (dipô'pərit), *adj.* poorly developed.

dep·e·ter (dep'itər), *n.* a finish for exterior walls, consisting of mortar into which pebbles are pressed. Also **pebble dash.**

de·pict (dipikt'), *v.* to make a picture of; describe in words as vividly as if a picture had been drawn. —**de·pic'tion,** *n.*

dep·i·late (dep'əlāt), *v.* to remove hair from. —**de·pil'a·to·ry,** *adj., n.*

de·plete (diplēt'), *v.* **de·plet·ed, deplet·ing.** to reduce the quantity of (something); exhaust the supply of. —**de·ple'tion,** *n.*

de·pone (dipōn'), *v.* to declare under oath.

dep·re·cate (dep'rəkāt), *v.* to state one's disapproval of something; criticize adversely. —**dep,re·ca'tion,** *n.* —**dep're·ca·to·ry,** *adj.*

dep·re·date (dep'ridāt), *v.* to plunder; pillage; ravage. —**dep,re·da'tion,** *n.*

depressed area, a region characterized by much unemployment and reduced standards of living.

de·pres·sion (dipresH'ən), *n.* (in meteorology) an area of low atmospheric pressure.

de pro·fun·dis (dā prōfōon'dis), *Latin.* out of the depths.

dep·u·rate (dep'yōōrāt), *v.* to purify; cleanse. —**dep'u·ra,tive,** *adj.*

de·pute (dəpyōōt'), *v.* to appoint as a representative or agent.

de·rac·in·ate (diras'ināt), *v.* to uproot; eradicate.

de·rail·leur (dərāl'yə), *n.* a gear-changing mechanism on a bicycle for transferring the chain from one sprocket wheel to another.

de·re·ism (dērē'izəm), *n.* (in psychology) the tendency to regard life through daydreams and fantasies, with little regard to reality.

de·ride (dirīd'), *v.* to scoff; mock; ridicule.

de·ris·i·ble (diriz'əbəl), *adj.* worthy of being mocked.

de·ri·sion (dirizH'ən), *n.* act of deriding; state of being derided.

de·ri·sive (dirī'siv, dirī'ziv), *adj.* expressing ridicule; mocking.

der·ma (dû'mə), *n.* skin lying below the epidermis.

der·ma·bra·sion (dû,məbrā'zHən), *n.* the surgical removal of scars, etc., by abrasion.

der·ma·therm (dû'məthûm), *n.* an instrument for measuring the temperature of the skin.

der·ma·ti·tis (dû,mətī'tis), *n.* any mild inflammation of the skin.

der·mat·o·glyph·ics (dû,mətōglif'iks), *n. pl.* the patterns and ridges on the skin of the hands and feet.

der·mat·o·graph·i·a (dû,mətəgrä'fēə), *n.* a skin condition in which scratching causes red welts.

der·ma·toid (dû'mətoid), *adj.* skin-like. Also **dermoid.**

der·ma·tol·o·gy (dû,mətol'əjē), *n.* the study of the skin and its diseases. —**der,ma·tol'o·gist,** *n.*

der·ma·to·sis (dû,mətō'sis), *n., pl.* **der·ma·to·ses** (dû,mətō'sēz). a skin disease.

der·nier cri (deə,nyä krē'), *French, n.* the latest fashion.

der·o·gate (der'əgāt), *v.* to detract or lessen as from estimation. —**der,oga'tion,** *n.*

de·rog·a·tive (dirog'ətiv), *adj.* belittling; lessening.

de·rog·a·to·ry (dirog'ətərē, dirog'ətrē), *adj.* disparaging; belittling; detracting from what might be others' views of the value of something. —**der·o·gate,** *v.*

de·scend·er (disen'də), *n.* (in lowercase letters) the part below the body or line. See also **ascender.**

de·scen·sion (disen'sHən), *n.* the part of the zodiac where a planet's influence is weakest.

de·scry (dəskrī'), *v.* **de·scried, de·scry·ing.** to identify or discern (something that is indistinct) by peering at it carefully; distinguish.

de·seam (dēsēm'), *v.* to remove defects, as from ingots.

des·e·crate (des'əkrāt), *v.* **des·e·crated, des·e·crat·ing.** to destroy the holy or sacred nature of (something) by using it or treating it without respect, as in plundering a grave. —**des,e·cra'tion,** *n.*

des·er·tic·o·lous (dez,ətik'ələs), *adj.* growing or living in the desert.

des·ha·bille (dāzəbēl'), *n.* See **dishabille.**

des·ic·cant (des'əkənt), *adj.* having an absorbing or drying effect.

des·ic·cate (des'ikāt), *v.* to dry; dehydrate. —**des'ic·ca,tor,** *n.*

de·sid·er·ate (disid'ərāt), *v.* to wish for; want.

de·sid·er·a·tive (disid'ərā,tiv), *adj.* wanting; desiring.

de·sid·er·a·tum (disid,ərā'təm), *n., pl.* **de·sid·er·a·ta** (disid,ərā'tə). something lacking and required.

des·i·nence (des'ənəns), *n.* termination, as the last syllable of a word.

des·mi·tis (desmī'tis), *n.* inflammation of a ligament.

des·moid (des'moid), *adj.* like a ligament.

des·o·late (des'əlit), *adj.* **1.** lonely; isolated. **2.** barren; devastated or ruined; laid to waste. —**des,o·la'tion,** *n.*

des·ox·y·ri·bo·nu·cle·ase (desok,sirī,bōnyōō'klēas,), *n.* See **deoxyribonuclease.**

des·ox·y·ri·bo·nu·cle·ic acid (desok'sērī,-bōnyōōklē'ik). See **DNA.**

des·pit·e·ous (despit'ēəs), *adj.* spiteful, malicious, or contemptuous.

de·spoil (dispoil'), *v.* to plunder; rob; strip of possessions.

de·spo·li·a·tion (dispō,lēā'sHən), *n.* act of plunder or despoiling.

de·spond (dispond'), *v.* to lose heart; become dejected.

des·pot (des'pot), *n.* a tyrannical, oppressive ruler; autocrat; dictator. —**de·spot'ic,** *adj.* —**des'potism,** *n.*

des·qua·mate (des'kwəmāt), *v.* (of skin) to peel off as scales, as in certain diseases.

de·ster·i·lize (dēster'əlīz), *v.* to use money or a commodity previously unused.

de·struct (distrukt'), *adj.* constructed so as to destroy itself.

des·ue·tude (des'wityōōd, disyōō'ityōōd), *n.* state of disuse. —**des·ue·tu'di·nous,** *adj.*

des·ul·to·ry (des'əltərē, des'əltrē), *adj.* disconnected; casual; unmethodical.

de·su·per·heat·er (dēsōō'pəhē,tə), *n.* an apparatus, as in a boiler, for controlling and lowering the temperature of superheated steam.

de·tec·ta·phone (ditek'təfōn), *n.* a hidden device for listening in on telephone conversations

de·tent (ditent'), *n.* a device for keeping one part of a machine in a certain position.

de·ter (ditû'), *v.* **de·terred, de·ter·ring.** to influence or stop (someone) from doing something. —**de·ter'rent,** *n.*

de·terge (ditûj'), *v.* to clean, as a wound.

de·ter·gen·cy (ditû'jənsē), *n.* cleansing power.

de·ter·gent (ditû'jənt), *n.* a synthetic cleansing agent with strong emulsifying and cleansing powers.

de·ter·sive (ditû'siv), *adj.* **1.** cleansing. —*n.* **2.** a cleansing agent or medicine.

de·tox·i·cate (dētok'səkāt), *v.* to rid of poison. —**de·tox,i·ca'tion,** *n.*

de·tox·i·fy (dētok'səfī), *v.* to free from poison. —**de·tox,i·fi·ca'tion,** *n.*

det·ri·ment (det'rəmənt), *n.* harm, damage, or injury. —**det,ri·men'tal,** *adj.*

de·tri·tal (ditrī'əl), *adj.* consisting of debris or detritus.

de·tri·tion (ditrisH'ən), *n.* a wearing away by abrasion.

de·tri·tiv·or·ous (de,tritiv'ərəs), *adj.* feeding on organic debris, as some insects.

de·tri·tus (ditrī'təs), *n.* any debris or disintegrated material.

de trop (də trō'), *French.* too many; unwanted.

de·trude (ditrōōd'), *n.* to force or thrust down or away. —**de·tru·sion** (ditrōō'zHən), *n.*

de·trun·cate (ditruNG'kāt), *v.* to cut down.

de·tu·mes·cence (dē,tyōōmes'əns), *n.* reduction of a swelling.

de·us ex ma·chi·na (dā'ōos eks ma'kinə), *Latin.* (orig. in classical Greek drama) a god who intervenes and sorts out the entanglements.

De·us vo·bis·cum (dā'ōos vōbis'kum), *Latin.* God be with you.

deu·ter·a·nom·a·ly (dyōō,tərənom'əlē), *n.* a vision defect in which there is a diminished response to green.

deu·ter·an·ope (dyōō'tərənōp), *n.* one with deuteranopia.

deu·ter·a·no·pi·a (dyōō,tərənō'pēə), *n.* a vision defect in which there is a lack of response to green.

deu·ter·og·a·my (dyōōtərog'əmē), *n.* second marriage; digamy. See also **monogamy.**

dev·il·kin (dev'əlkin), *n.* an imp.

dev·il's tat·too (dev'əlz tatōō'), a nervous tapping with the hands or feet.

de·vi·ous (dē'vēəs), *adj.* not straight; crooked, as a road or a person; dishonest, esp. in a stealthy, shifty way.

de·voir (dəvwä'), *n.* **1.** a formal act of respect. **2.** a duty or obligation.

de·vo·lu·tion (dē,vəlōō'sHən), *n.* **1.** the act of passing on from one stage to the next; bequeathal. **2.** biological degeneration.

de·volve (divolv'), *v.* to delegate or transfer (duties, etc.)

dev·o·tee (dev,ōtē', dev,ōtā'), *n.* an enthusiast, aficionado, or fan, as a *devotee of football.*

de·vote·ment (divōt'mənt), *n.* dedication.

dew·lap (dyōō'lap,), *n.* a loose fold of skin under the throat of cattle.

dew·point (dyōō'point,), *n.* the temperature at which dew forms, varying in relation to atmospheric pressure and humidity.

dewpoint spread, the number of degrees between the dewpoint and the temperature of the air.

dex·ter (dek'stər), *adj.* on the right hand side.

dex·ter·ous (dek'strəs), *adj.* skilful, adroit; able to use the hands or to do things cleverly. Also **dex'trous.** —**dex·ter'i·ty,** *n.*

dex·tral (dek'strəl), *adj.* **1.** on the right side. **2.** right-handed.

dex·tro·car·di·a (dek,strōkä'dēə), *n.* a condition in which the heart is on the right side of the chest.

dex·troc·u·lar (dekstrok'yōōlə), *adj.* favouring the right eye rather than the left. See also **sinistrocular.**

dex·tro·ro·ta·to·ry (dek,strōrō'tətrē), *adj.* rotating to the right, as the plane of polarization of light by certain crystals. —**dex,tro·ro·ta'tion,** *n.*

dex·trorse (dek'strôrs), *adj.* (of plants) twisting to the right. See also **sinistrorse.**

dex·tro·sin·is·tral (dek,strōsin'istrəl). *adj.* **1.** extending from right to left. **2.** left-handed, but able to write right-handed.

dhar·ma (dä'mə), *n.* (in Buddhism) natural law or essential quality of the world or of one's own nature.

dhar·na (dä'nə), *n.* (in India) fasting at the doorstep of an offender to exact justice.

di·a·ble·rie (dēä'blərē), *n.* **1.** sorcery; witchcraft. **2.** those things or actions controlled by devils. **3.** demonology; devil-lore. **4.** reckless mischief or daring.

di·ac·o·nal (dīak'ənəl), *adj.* pertaining to a deacon.

di·ac·o·nate (dīak'ənit), *n.* office of deacon.

di·a·crit·ic (dī,əkrit'ik), *n.* a mark or sign used to distinguish sounds or values of the same letter, as a cedilla, etc. Also **diacritical mark.**

di·a·crit·i·cal (dī,əkrit'ikəl), *adj.* distinguishing; distinctive. —**di,a·crit'i·cal·ly,** *adj.*

di·ad·o·cho·ki·ne·si·a (dīad,əkōkinē'zēə), *n.* (in medicine) the ability to perform normally alternating movements of muscles.

di·ad·ro·mous (dīad'rəməs), *adj.* (of certain fish) travelling between salt and fresh water. See also **anadromous, catadromous.**

di·a·graph (dī'əgräf), *n.* an instrument for reproducing scale drawings mechanically.

di·a·lec·tal (dī,əlek'təl), *adj.* of or characteristic of a dialect. Also **di·alec'ti·cal.**

di·a·lec·tic (dī,əlek'tik), *adj.* **1.** pertaining to logical argumentation. —*n.* **2.** the bases of dialectical materialism, as the superiority of mind over matter. Also **di,a·lec'tics.**

dialectical materialism, materialism as developed by Karl Marx.

di·a·lec·tol·o·gy (dī,əlektol'əjē), *n.* the study of dialects.

di·a·log·ic (dī,əloj'ik), *adj.* pertaining to or characteristic of dialogue.

di·a·lo·gism (dīal'əjiz,əm), *n.* (in an imaginary dialogue) the discussion of a subject. —**di·al'o·gist,** *n.*

di·a·mag·net·ic (dī,əmagnet'ik), *adj.* pertaining to a substance, as copper, whose conducting power in a magnetic circuit is less than that of a vacuum and whose induced magnetism is opposite to that of iron. See also **ferromagnetic, paramagnetic.**

di·a·man·tif·er·ous (dī,əmantif'ərəs), *adj.* diamond-bearing; diamond-producing.

di·a·mor·phine (dī,əmôə'fēn), *n.* See **heroin.**

di·a·net·ics (dī,ənet'iks), *n.* the theory that personality behaviour can be explained in terms of an individual's experiences before birth.

di·a·no·et·ic (dī,ənōet'ik), *adj.* pertaining to discursive reasonings.

di·a·noi·a (dī,ənoi'ə), *n.* the faculty used in discursive reasoning.

di·a·pa·son (dī,əpā'zən), *n.* a tune or melody.

di·a·pause (dī'əpôz), *n.* a period of nongrowth during the development of insects.

di·a·pe·de·sis (dī,əpidē'sis), *n.* the normal passage of blood cells into the tissues through capillary walls.

di·a·phane (di'əfān), *n.* a rigid material used to fix tissue for microscopic examination.

di·a·pha·ne·i·ty (dī,əfənē'itē), *n.* the property of being transparent.

di·aph·a·nom·e·ter (dī,əfənom'itə), *n.* an instrument for measuring transparency.

di·aph·a·nous (dīaf'ənəs), *adj.* so thin and light and delicate as to be nearly transparent, as a fabric.

di·a·phone (dī'əfōn), *n.* a foghorn with a low-pitched, penetrating tone.

di·a·pho·re·sis (dī,əfərē'sis), *n.* sweat.

di·a·pho·ret·ic (dī,əfəret'ik), *adj.* producing sweat.

di·aph·y·sis (dīaf'isis), *n., pl.* **diaph·y·ses** (dīaf'isēz). the shaft of a bone.

di·ap·la·sis (dīap'ləsis), *n., pl.* **di·ap·la·ses** (dīap'ləsēz). the setting of bone which has been fractured or dislocated.

di·ar·chy (dī'äkē), *n.* government by two rulers. Also **dinarchy, duarchy, dyarchy.**

di·ar·thro·sis (dī,äthrō'sis), *n., pl.* **di·ar·thro·ses** (dī,äthrō'sēz). articulation of the joints of the body that allow the greatest movement.

di·as·chi·sis (dīas'kisis), *n.* dysfunction of one part of the brain owing to injury in another part.

di·as·po·ra (dīas'pərə), *n.* (in the Old Testament) the dispersion of the Jews after the Babylonian captivity.

di·as·ta·sis (dīas'təsis), *n.* **1.** the parting of bones normally jointed, as in a dislocation. **2.** the period after the dilation of the heart and before the contraction. —**di·a·stat·ic** (dī,əstat'ik), *adj.*

di·as·to·le (dīas'tələ), *n.* the dilation phase of the heart action. See also **systole.** —**di·as·tol·ic** (dī,əstol'ik), *adj.*

di·as·tro·phism (dīas'trəfiz,əm), *n.* the actions that change the earth's crust to produce mountains, etc.

di·ath·e·sis (dīath'isis), *n., pl.* **diath·e·sis** (dīath'isis). susceptibility to a certain disease.

di·a·ton·ic (dī,əton'ik), *adj.* relating to any musical scale comprising five tones and two semitones, as produced by the white keys of a keyboard; not involving sharps or flats. —**di,a·ton'i·cal·ly,** *adv.* —**di·a·ton·i·cism** (dī,əton'isiz,-əm), *n.*

di·a·tribe (dī'ətrīb), *n.* a denunciation; an unpleasant, nasty criticism.

di·ceph·a·lous (dīsef'ələs, dīkef'ələs), *adj.* having two heads.

di·chot·o·mize (dikot'əmīz), *v.* to divide or become divided into two parts.

di·chot·o·my (dīkot'əmē), *n.* a split into two parts, either equally or in order to separate types; division; schism. —**di·chot'o·mous,** *adj.*

dick·er (dik'ə), *n.* a group of ten, especially ten hides.

dick·ey (dik'ē), *n., pl.* **dick·eys** (dik'ēz). a woman's vestlike garment, without sides or sleeves but having a front and collar, for wear under a dress or suit.

Dick test, (in medicine) a test to determine a person's susceptibility or immunity to scarlet fever.

dic·ta·tor·ship (diktā'təsHip), *n.* **1.** a country governed by a dictator. **2.** government by a dictator.

dic·tion (dik'sHən), *n.* the way a person uses language, esp. in choice of words, pronunciation, etc.

dic·tum (dik'təm), *n., pl.* **dic·ta** (dik'tə), **dic·tums.** an expressed opinion of a judge that has no legal force; a maxim.

di·dac·tic (dīdak'tik), *adj.* **1.** intended to instruct. **2.** inclined to give unwanted instruction. **3.** teaching a moral lesson. Also **di·dac'ti·cal.** —**di·dac'ti·cal·ly,** *adv.*

did·di·coy (did'ikoi), *n.* a person who is part Gypsy. Also **did.di.kai** (did'əkī).

did·dle (did'əl), *v.* to cheat or swindle.

di·do (dī'dō), *n., pl.* **di·dos, di·does.** a trick or prank.

did·y·mous (did'əməs), *adj.* paired; twin.

di·e·lec·tric (dīilek'trik), *n.* an electrical insulator; a non-conductor.

di·en·ceph·a·lon (dī,ensef'əlon), *n., pl.* **di·en·ceph·a·lons, di·enceph·a·la** (dī,ensef'ələ). the rear part of the forebrain.

di·er·e·sis (dīer'isis), *n., pl.* **di·er·eses** (dīer'isēz). a symbol consisting of two dots (¨) which, when placed over the second of two vowels, indicates they are to be pronounced separately, as in *coöperate.*

di·es non (dī'ēz non'), *n.* (in law) a day when no legal business is transacted. Also **di·es non ju,rid'i·cus** (jōō,rid'ikus), *Latin,* literally: day which is not juridical.

Dieu et mon droit (dyōō' ā môndrwa'), *French.* God and my right.

dif·fer·en·ti·a (dif,əren'sHēə), *n., pl.* **dif·fer·en-**

·ti·ae (dif,əren'sнēē). the elementary attributes that distinguish one thing from another, as one species from another of the same genus.

dif·fer·en·tial (dif,əren'sнəl), n. an arrangement of gear wheels permitting two or more shafts to rotate at different speeds. Also **differential gear.**

differential calculus, the branch of mathematics dealing with the calculation of the value of the rate of change of a function with respect to constants and variables.

dif·fer·en·ti·ate (dif,əren'sнēāt), v. **dif·fer·en·ti·at·ed, dif·fer·enti·at·ing.** to separate, or distinguish, one thing or set of things from others.

dif·fi·cile (dif,isēl'), adj. difficult; hard to please.

dif·fi·dence (dif'idəns), n. a lack of self-confidence; self-effacement; timidity.

dif·fi·dent (dif'ədənt), adj. shy; timid; self-effacing.

dif·flu·ence (dif'lōōəns) n. a flowing away. —**dif·flu·ent,** adj.

dif·fract (difrakt'), v. **1.** to bend waves, esp. sound waves, around obstacles. **2.** to break up light waves by passing them through an aperture to form patterns of light and dark bands near the edges of the beam. —**dif·frac'tion,** n. —**dif·frac'·tive,** adj.

diffraction grating, a device used for diffracting light to produce its spectrum.

dig·a·my (dig'əmē), n. a second marriage; deuterogamy. See also **monogamy.**

di·ges·tif (dēzнestēf'), n. French. a drink taken after a meal to aid digestion, as brandy.

digital computer, a computer that uses numerical representations to solve mathematical problems. See also **analogue computer, hybrid computer.**

dig·i·tal·is (dijitāl'is), n. a heart stimulant made from the dried leaves of the common foxglove.

dig·i·tate (dij'itāt), adj. (of an animal) having fingers or fingerlike parts. —**dig,i·ta'tion,** n.

dig·i·ti·form (dij'itəfōm), adj. fingerlike.

dig·i·ti·grade (dij'itəgrād), adj. walking on toes, as most four-footed animals. See also **plan·tigrade.**

dig·i·tize (dij'itīz), v. to convert material into a form suitable for processing by a digital computer.

di·glot (dī'glot), adj. fluent in two languages; bilingual.

di·graph (dī'gräf), n. two letters, grouped together, and representing a single sound as *ie* in *sieve, sh* in *shoot,* etc.

di·he·dral (dīhē'drəl), adj. (in mathematics) forming or having two plane faces.

di·lac·er·ate (dilas'ərāt), v. to tear into two parts or into pieces. —**di·lac,er·a'tion,** n.

di·lap·i·dat·ed (dilap'idā,tid), adj. ruined or decayed from lack of use.

dil·a·ta·tion (dilətā'sнən), n. the act of expanding; condition of being widened, swollen, or expanded. Also **di·la·tion** (dīlā'-sнən).

dil·a·to·ry (dil'ətôr,ē), adj. tending to slowness; causing delay; slow.

dil·et·tan·te (dil,itan'tē), n., pl. **dil·et·tan·tes, dil·et·tan·ti** (dil,itan'tē). one who has a superficial and casual interest in a subject; amateur dabbler.

dil·i·gence (dil'ijəns), n. perseverance; earnest persistence in completing what is undertaken.

dil·i·gent (dil'əjənt), adj. hardworking; showing concern that something is done properly and seeing to it.

dil·u·ent (dil'yōōənt), n. a substance used to dilute or thin.

di·lu·vi·al (dilōō'vēəl), adj. pertaining to a flood, esp. the Flood in the Bible. Also **di·lu'vi·an.**

dim·er·ous (dim'ərəs), adj. in two parts.

di·mid·i·ate (dimid'ēāt), adj. divided into halves.

dim·i·nu·tion (diminyōō'sнən), n. the act of diminishing; condition of being diminished; a lessening.

di·min·u·tive (dimin'yōōtiv), adj. small; tiny.

dim·is·so·ry (dim'isərē), adj. giving leave to depart; dismissing.

dim·i·ty (dim'itē), n. a light cotton fabric with a heavier stripe or check woven in it.

di·mor·phism (dīmôə'fizəm), n. the occurrence of two different distinct forms in animals of the same species. —**di·mor'phous,** adj.

din·ar·chy (din'äkē), n. See **diarchy.**

ding·bat (diNG'bat), n. a piece of decorative type, as for printing ornamental borders.

din·gle (diNG'gəl), n. a narrow wooded valley; a deep dell.

di·no·saur (dī'nəsô,ə), n. a reptile of the Mesozoic era, now extinct.

di·o·cese (dī'əsis), n. an ecclesiastical area under a bishop's jurisdiction. —**di·oc·e·san** (dīos'isən), adj.

di·ode (dī'ōd), n. a thermionic valve with an anode and cathode designed with unequal characteristics.

di·oe·cious (dīē'sнəs), adj. having male and female parts on separate plants.

di·oes·trum (dīē'strəm), n. the intervals between the times when female animals are in heat.

Di·on·y·sian (dī,əniz'ēən), adj. pertaining to the Greek wine god, Dionysus, or to his worship; unrestrained; orgiastic. —**Di·o·nys·i·ac** (dīəniz'-ēak), adj.

di·op·tre (dīop'tə), n. a unit of measure of the refractive power of a lens.

di·op·tom·e·ter (dī‚optom'itə), *n.* an instrument for measuring the refraction of the eye.

di·op·trics (dīop'triks), *n.* the branch of optics which deals with the refraction of light. —di·op'tric, *adj.*

di·o·ram·a (dīərä'mə). *n.* a scene painted on a back cloth, given a three-dimensional effect by placing figures, etc., in front.

di·os·mose (dīoz'mōs), *v.* to make a fluid pass through a semipermeable membrane and thus equalize the concentration on both sides.

di·o·tic (dīo'tik), *adj.* involving both ears.

diph·the·ri·a (dipthēr'ēə, difthēr'ēə), *n.* an infectious disease characterized by a false membrane forming in the throat. —diph‚the·rit'ic, *adj.* —diph'the·roid, *adj.*

diph·thong (dif‚thoNG), *n.* a speech sound combining two vowels in one syllable

diph·thong·ize (dif‚thoNGīz), *v.* to pronounce as a diphthong; to become a diphthong.

dip·la·cu·sis (dip‚ləkyōō'sis), *n.*, *pl.* **dip·la·cu·ses** (dip‚ləkyōō'sēz). a condition in which the ears hear with different acuity.

di·ple·gia (dīplē'jə), *n.* paralysis of the same parts on both sides of the body.

dip·loid (dip'loid), *adj.* double.

dip·lo·pho·ni·a (dip‚ləfō'nēə), *n.* a condition in which two sounds of different pitch are produced simultaneously by the voice. Also **di·phoni·a** (dīfō'nēə).

di·plo·pi·a (diplō'pēə), *n.* a vision disorder in which a single object appears as two. See also **haplopia.**

dip·so·ma·ni·a (dip‚səmā'nēə), *n.* an insatiable craving for drink. —dip·so·ma'ni·ac, *n.*

dip·tych (dip'tik), *n.* **1.** a tablet with two leaves hinged vertically used for writing in ancient times. **2.** a wood or metal tablet, similar to this, containing the names of those for whom prayers and Masses are said, with the living on one leaf and the dead on the other.

dire (dīr), *adj.* terrible; dreadful; calamitous.

Di·rec·toire (dērektwär'), *n.* a style of French furnishings of the late 18th century, characterized by Graeco-Roman shapes and Egyptian motifs.

dirge (dûj), *n.* a funeral tune or lament for the dead.

di·rhin·ous (dīrī'nəs), *adj.* with paired nostrils.

dirn·dl (dûrn'dəl), *n.* a woman's dress with a full skirt and close-fitted top.

dis·a·buse (dis‚əbyōōz'), *v.* to undeceive; reveal the truth to.

dis·ad·van·taged (dis‚ədvan'tijd), *adj.* lacking the normal advantages, as of a good home and family.

dis·af·fect (dis‚əfekt'), *v.* to cause (someone) to become disloyal or dissatisfied, esp. by changing his allegiance to or affection for something —dis‚af·fec'tion, *n.*

dis·af·fil·i·ate (dis‚əfil'ēāt), *v.* to sever connections with; dissociate. —dis‚af·fil‚i·a'tion, *n.*

dis·af·for·est (dis‚əfor'ist), *v.* to clear forests; strip.

dis·ap·pro·ba·tion (dis‚aprəbā'sHən), *n.* disapproval.

dis·arm·ing (disä'miNG), *adj.* open and friendly in such a way as to make another person less hostile or suspicious.

dis·ar·tic·u·late (dis‚ätik'yəlāt), *v.* to dislocate, as bones.

dis·a·vow (dis‚əvou'), *v.* to refuse to acknowledge; disclaim; repudiate. —dis‚a·vow'al, *n.*

dis·burse (disbûs'), *v.* to pay out (money); expend; scatter. —disburse'ment, *n.*

dis·calced (diskalst'), *adj.* barefoot.

dis·car·nate (diskä'nit), *adj.* with no physical body or manifestation.

dis·cept (disept'), *v.* to debate; dispute.

dis·cern (disûn'), *v.* to see clearly; perceive; understand or recognize what one is looking at, as *She discerned at once that he liked her.* —dis·cern'ment, *n.*

dis·cerp (disûp'), *v.* to tear apart; divide. —dis·cerp·ti·ble** (disûp'təbəl), *adj.*

dis·cla·ma·tion (dis‚kləmā'sHən), *n.* the act of disclaiming; repudiation; renunciation.

dis·cog·ra·phy (diskog'rəfē), *n.* a complete list of the musical recordings of a composer, performer, or group of performers.

dis·coid (dis'koid), *adj.* in the shape of a discus or disc.

dis·com·bob·u·late (dis‚kəmbob'yəlāt), *v.* to disrupt; upset; confuse.

dis·com·fit (diskum'fit), *v.* **1.** to throw into disorder and confusion. **2.** to defeat completely; rout. **3.** to thwart; foil. —dis·com·fi·ture** (diskum'fiCHə), *n.*

dis·com·mend (dis‚kəmend'), *v.* to disapprove of; deprecate.

dis·com·mode (dis‚kəmōd'), *v.* to inconvenience; trouble; disturb.

dis·con·cert (dis‚kənsût'), *v.* to make (someone) feel uneasy or uncomfortable; confuse; upset.

dis·con·so·late (diskon'səlit), *adj.* so unhappy as to be inconsolable; sad; dejected.

dis·co·phile (dis'kəfīl), *n.* a collector of phonograph records, especially of rare records.

dis·cord (dis'kôəd), *n.* lack of harmony; strife; antagonism; war.

dis·co·theque (dis'kōtek‚), *n.* a nightclub or dance hall where patrons dance to music played on records.

dis·course (dis'kôəs), *v.* **dis·coursed, dis·cours·ing. 1.** to talk about something; converse. —*n.* **2.** conversation; discussion. **3.** a formal written or oral treatment of a subject.

dis·cre·ate (dis,krēāt'), *v.* to destroy; turn to nothing.

dis·creet (diskrēt'), *adj.* careful and tactful about what one says and does, esp. in keeping silent about others' activities, secrets, etc. See also **discrete**. —**dis·cre·tion** (diskresн'ən), *n.*

discrete (diskrēt'), *adj.* distinct; separate; individual. See also **discreet**.

dis·crim·i·nate (diskrim'ināt), *v.* **dis·crim·i·nat·ed, dis·crim·inat·ing. 1.** to see and understand different qualities among things or people and to separate them on the basis of such judgment. **2. discriminate against,** to exercise prejudice against someone or something for one or more characteristics they possess, as *She thought they discriminated against her because she was a woman, but it was because she was rude.* —dis'crim,i·na'tion, *n.*

dis·cur·sive (diskû'siv), *adj.* rambling; without apparent organization.

dis·dain (disdān'), *v.* to look down upon; scorn; despise. —**dis·dain'ful,** *adj.*

dis·em·bogue (dis,imbōg'), *v.* **dis·em·bogues, dis·em·bogu·ing.** (of a river or stream) to flow or pour out from the mouth. —**dis,em·bogue'ment,** *n.*

dis·ha·bille (dis,abēl'), *n.* the state of being incompletely or untidily dressed. Also **des·ha·bille** (dāz,abēl').

dis·in·gen·u·ous (dis,injen'yo͞oəs), *adj.* pretending to be naive, usually in order to gain an advantage; insincere; hypocritical. —**dis,in·gen'uous·ness,** *n.*

dis·in·ter·est·ed (disin'tərəstid), *adj.* unprejudiced; lacking in selfish motive. See also **uninterested.**

dis·jec·ta mem·bra (disjek'tä mem'brä), *Latin.* disjointed members or parts.

dis·junct (disjuNGkt'), *adj.* separated; disjoined. —**dis·junc'tion,** *n.* —**dis·junc'ture,** *n.*

dis·na·ture (disnā'CHə), *v.* to make unnatural; deprive (something) of its true nature.

disorderly house, a brothel.

dis·par·age (dispar'ij), *v.* to speak slightingly of; depreciate.

dis·pa·rate (dis'pərit), *adj.* unlike; dissimilar; essentially different.

dis·par·i·ty (dispar'itē), *n.* inequality; unlikeness; difference.

dis·part (dispät'), *v.* to separate; divide.

dis·pas·sion·ate (dispasн'ənit), *adj.* without bias; calm; free from passion.

dis·pel (dispel'), *v.* **dis·pelled, dispel·ling.** to drive away, or scatter, as fears, clouds, etc.

dis·peo·ple (dispē'pəl), *v.* to depopulate; deprive of people.

dis·perse (dispûs'), *v.* to scatter; spread widely; distribute. —**dis·persion** (dispû'zнən), *n.* —**dis·per'sive,** *adj.*

dis·plume (displo͞om'), *v.* to strip of honours.

dis·port (dispôət'), *v.* to play; divert or amuse oneself.

dis·praise (disprāz'), *v.* to disparage; blame; censure.

dis·pu·ta·tious (dis,pyo͞otā'sнəs), *adj.* quarrelsome; argumentative; contentious.

dis·qui·et (diskwī'it), *n.* **1.** uneasiness; anxiety; restlessness. —*v.* **2.** to disturb; make uneasy or anxious.

dis·qui·e·tude (diskwī'ityo͞od), *n.* anxiety; uneasiness.

dis·qui·si·tion (dis,kwizisн'ən), *n.* a treatise examining and discussing a subject.

dis·rupt (disrupt'), *v.* to disturb the order or calmness of (something or someone), as *The hecklers disrupted the meeting by shouting obscenities.* —**dis·rup'tion,** *n.*

dis·sem·blance (disem'bləns), *n.* **1.** unlikeness. **2.** a pretence; a feigning.

dis·sem·ble (disem'bəl), *v.* to conceal under a false appearance; speak or act hypocritically.

dis·sem·i·nate (disem'ināt), *v.* to scatter; disperse; spread abroad.

dis·sen·sion (disen'sнən), *n.* disagreement; lack of unity; discord.

dis·sent (disent'), *v.* to disagree; withhold consent.

dis·sen·tient (disen'sнənt), *adj.* disagreeing with the opinion of the majority.

dis·sen·tious (disen'sнəs), *adj.* quarrelsome; argumentative.

dis·sep·i·ment (disep'imənt), *n.* a dividing wall or membrane in a plant or animal.

dis·ser·tate (dis'ətāt), *v.* to discuss learnedly.

dis·ser·ta·tion (disətā'sнən), *n.* a treatise on a particular subject, esp. one written as a requirement for a degree.

dis·sev·er (dise'və), *v.* **1.** to break off or become disunited. **2.** to separate; fragment. —**dis·sev'er·ance, dis·sev'er·ment, dis·sev,er·at'·tion,** *n.*

dis·si·dence (dis'idəns), *n.* disagreement; difference of opinion. —**dis'si·dent,** *adj.*

dis·sil·i·ent (disil'ēənt), *adj.* breaking or bursting open.

dis·sim·i·la·tion (disim,ilā'sнən), *n.* the making or becoming unlike. See also **assimilate.**

dis·si·mil·i·tude (dis,imil'ityo͞od), *n.* unlikeness; difference.

dis·sim·u·late (disim'yəlāt), *v.* to disguise or conceal the true nature of; dissemble. —**dis·sim,u·la'tion,** *n.*

dis·si·pate (dis'ipāt), *v.* **1.** to scatter wastefully. **2.** to engage in loose and intemperate pleasures. —**dis,si·pa'tion,** *n.*

dis·so·ci·a·ble (disō'sнəbəl), *adj.* **1.** separable. **2.** not sociable. **3.** irreconcilable.

dis·so·cial (disō'sнəl), *adj.* not sociable.

dis·so·ci·ate (disō'sнēāt), *v.* to cut association with; separate. —**dis·so,ci·a'tion,** *n.*

dis·so·lute (dis'əlōōt), *adj.* given to dissipation; debauched; profligate.

dis·so·lu·tion (dis,əlōō'sHən), *n.* the dissolving or breaking up of a union, organization, or assembly.

dis·so·nance (dis'ənəns), *n.* a discord or harsh sound. **—dis'so·nant**, *adj.*

dis·suade (diswād'), *v.* to persuade against. **—dis·sua·sion** (diswā,zHən), *n.* **—dis·sua'sive**, *adj.*

dis·syl·la·bic (disilab'ik), *adj.* disyllabic.

dis·syl·la·ble (disil'əbəl), *n.* disyllable.

di·stad (dis'tad), *adv.* towards or at the opposite end from the point of attachment.

dis·tal (dis'təl), *adj.* away from the point of attachment as of a limb or appendage.

dis·tel·fink (dis'təlfiNGk), *n.* a bird motif found in Pennsylvania-Dutch art.

dis·tem·per (distem'pə), *n.* a technique in art using glue to bind and achieve a mat surface.

dis·tend (distend'), *v.* to inflate; swell; expand. **—dis·ten'si·ble**, *adj.* **—dis·ten'sile**, *adj.* **—dis·ten'tion**, *n.*

dis·tin·gué (distaNGgā'), *adj.* distinguished in appearance and manner.

dis·train (distrān'), *v.* (in law) to seize goods for payment or settlement of a debt or claim. **—dis·train'a·ble**, *adj.* **—dis·train'ment**, *n.* **—dis·trai'nor, dis·train'er**, *n.*

dis·trait (distrā'), *adj.* absent-minded because of worries, etc.

dis·traught (distrôt'), *adj.* agitated and distracted.

distressed area, an area devastated by a natural disaster, like a flood, and needing outside help in the form of food, medicine, clothing, shelter, and money.

distress flag, any flag or signal flown by a ship showing it to be in distress.

distress frequency, a radio frequency reserved for distress calls, as from ships and aircraft.

distress merchandise, goods sold at a lower than usual price in order to raise money rapidly.

dis·un·ion (disyōōn'yən), *n.* severance of union; lack of unity. **—dis·un'ion·ist**, *n.*

di·syl·lab·ic (dī,silab'ik), *adj.* having two syllables. Also **dissyllabic**.

di·syl·la·ble (dī'silǝbǝl), *n.* a two-syllable word. Also **dissyllable**.

di·the·ism (dī'thēizǝm), *n.* **1.** belief in two gods. **2.** belief in two conflicting principles, one good, one evil.

dith·er (diTH'ə), *n.* **1.** a quivering or trembling. **—v. 2.** to hesitate nervously; vacillate.

dith·y·ram·bic (dith,iram'bik), *adj.* **1.** relating to or in the style of a dithyramb, an ancient Greek choral hymn to Bacchus noted for its

passion and impetuosity. **2.** passionately lyrical or eloquent.

dit·tog·ra·phy (ditog'rǝfē), *n.* repetition in writing or printing, usually in error, of the same word or letter. See also **haplography**.

di·u·re·sis (dī,yōōrē'sis), *n.* excessive discharge of urine.

di·u·ret·ic (dī,yōōret'ik), *adj.* **1.** promoting the increase of discharge of urine, as by medicine. **—n. 2.** a medicine so acting.

di·ur·nal (dīū'nǝl), *adj.* **1.** daily; happening daily. **2.** belonging to the day.

di·va (dē'va), *n., pl.* **di·vas, di·ve** (dē've). a leading female singer; prima donna.

di·va·gate (dī'vǝgāt), *v.* to stray or wander, esp. in speech. **—di,va·ga'tion**, *n.*

di·var·i·cate (dīvar'ǝkāt), *v.* **1.** to branch apart. **—adj. 2.** divergent; spread wide apart.

di·vers (dī'vǝz), *adj.* various; several; sundry.

di·verse (divûs'), *adj.* **1.** dissimilar; unlike; different. **2.** varied; multi-form.

di·ver·si·form (divû'sifôǝm), *adj.* of various shapes; differing in form.

di·vert (divût'), *v.* **1.** to cause (something) to change direction or attitude, as to divert traffic. **2.** entertain or amuse, as to divert the audience with a comic act. **—di·ver'sion**, *n.*

di·ver·tisse·ment (divû'tismǝnt), *n.* an entertainment.

di·ver·tive (divû'tiv), *adj.* entertaining; amusing.

di·vest (dīvest'), *v.* to strip, dispossess, or rid of something.

di·vest·i·ture (dīves'tiCHǝr), *n.* the act of divesting; state of being divested.

div·i·nize, div·i·nise (div'inīz), *v.* to confer divinity on; deify. **—div,i·ni·za'tion, div,i·ni·sa'tion**, *n.*

di·vi·sive (divī'siv), *adj.* causing or showing division; creating discord. **—di·vi'sive·ness**, *n.*

di·vul·gate (divul'gāt), *v.* to publish; make common property.

di·vulse (dīvuls'), *v.* (in surgery) to tear apart, as opposed to cutting. **—di·vul·sion** (dīvul'-sHǝn), *n.*

dix·it (dik'sit), *n.* an utterance, esp. an official promulgation. [Latin for 'he has spoken']

di·zy·got·ic (dī,zīgot'ik), *adj.* formed from two ova, as fraternal twins.

djin·ni (jin'ē), *n., pl.* **djinn** (jin). See **jinni**.

D layer, the lowest region of the ionosphere; from 40-50 to 60-75 miles in altitude.

DMSO, a colourless liquid, dimethyl sulphoxide, used as an antifreeze and for treating headaches, burns, and bruises.

DNA, deoxyribonucleic acid; any of a class of nucleic acids that transfers genetic characteristics.

D.O.A., dead on arrival.

do·cent (dō'sənt), *n*. **1**. a university lecturer. **2**. a museum guide.

doc·ile (dos'īl), *adj*. tame; easy to control. —**do·cil'i·ty**, *n*.

doc·tri·naire (doktrəne'ə), *adj*. dogmatic or fanatical about another's acceptance of one's theories or teaching.

doc·u·dra·ma (dok'yōōdrä,mə), *n*. a film or television programme in the style of a documentary but incorporating the dramatized reconstruction of real events.

do·dec·a·gon (dōdek'əgon), *n*. a plane figure with 12 sides.

do·dec·a·he·dron (dō,dekəhē'drən), *n*. a solid figure with 12 faces.

doge (dōj), *n*. the former chief magistrate of Venice or Genoa.

dog·ger·el (dog'ərəl), *adj*. **1**. (of verse) irregular in metre and comic in content. —*n*. **2**. a comic verse; bad verse.

dog·go (dog'ō), *adv*. in hiding; out of sight.

dog·leg (dog'leg,), *n*. a sharp bend in a route or road.

dog·ma (dog'mə), *n*. a doctrine laid down by an authority, as the Church. —**dog'mat·ism**, *n*. —**dog'ma·tist**, *n*.

dog·ma·tic (dogmat'ik), *adj*. positive of one's position or opinion in a matter; dictatorial in one's certainty; close-minded.

dog·watch (dog'woCH,), *n*. **1**. one of two two-hour watches on board ship, either from 4 pm to 6 pm or from 6 pm to 8 pm. **2**. the time staff stay after a newspaper has gone to press to await any further news developments.

do·lab·ri·form (dōlab'rifôm,), *adj*. (in botany) hatchet-shaped. Also **do·lab·rate** (dōlab'rāt).

dol·ce far nien·te (dōl'CHə fär nyen'te), *Italian*. pleasantly doing nothing; pleasing inactivity.

dol·ce vi·ta (dōl'CHe vē'tä), *Italian*. the good life; life devoted to the pursuit of pleasure.

dol·drums (dol'drəmz), *n*. *pl*. a state of listlessness; inactivity; stagnation.

dole (dōl), *n*. money, food, etc., given by or as by a charity.

dol·i·cho·ce·phal·ic (dol,ikōsifal'ik, dol,ikō-kifal'ik), *adj*. **1**. having a long narrow head. —*n*. **2**. an individual with such a head. Also **dol·i·cho·ceph·a·lous** (dol,ikō'sefələs, dol,ikō'-kefələs). See also **brachycephalic**. —**dol,i·cho·ceph'a·lism, dol,i·cho·ceph'a·ly**, *n*.

dol·lop (dol'əp), *n*. a lump or small unmeasured quantity of something.

doll·y (dol'ē), *adj*. (of a girl) pretty; trendy; modern.

dol·man sleeve (dōl'mən), a sleeve tapering from a wide armhole to a narrow cuff.

dol·men (dol'men), *n*. a prehistoric stone construction consisting of upright stones supporting a horizontal one. See also **cromlech**.

dol·our (dolə), *n*. sorrow; grief. —**dol'or·ous**, *adj*.

dol·o·rim·e·try (dolərim'itrē), *n*. (in medicine) a technique for measuring sensitivity to pain. —**do·lo·rim'eter**, *n*.

dol·o·ro·so (dolərō'sō), *adj*. (used in musical direction) melancholy; plaintive.

do·min·i·cal (dəmin'ikəl), *adj*. **1**. pertaining to Jesus Christ. **2**. pertaining to Sunday.

do·min·i·ca·le (dəmin'əkä'lē), *n*. (formerly) a woman's veil worn at Church.

don·a·tive (don'ətiv), *n*. something given; a gift or donation.

don·jon (dun'jən), *n*. the stronghold of a castle.

don·nish (don'isH), *adj*. pompously academic.

dope sheet, *Slang*. a list giving the names and other information on entries in various horse races.

Dop·pel·gäng·er (dop'əlgaNG,ə), *n*. a ghostly double of a person not yet dead.

Dopp·ler effect (dop'lə), the change in the frequency of a wave resulting from the movement of the source of the wave towards or away from the receiver.

dor·mant (dô'mənt), *adj*. asleep, or as if asleep; completely inactive; torpid. —**dor'man·cy**, *n*.

dor·mer (dô'mə), *n*. a vertical window built out from a sloping roof, usually having a roof of its own. Also **dormer window**.

dor·mi·ent (dô'mēənt), *adj*. sleeping.

dor·sad (dô'sad), *adv*. towards the back, as of a body, or towards the outer surface, as of an organ.

dor·sal (dô'səl), *adj*. pertaining to, near, or on the back, as of an organ or part.

dorse (dôəs), *n*. the back of a document or a book.

DOS (dos), *n*., *Trademark, acronym for* **disc-operating system;** a computer-operating system. Often prefixed, as in *MS-DOS* and *PC-DOS*.

dose equivalent, *n*. a measure, in sieverts, of the probability of a dose of ionizing radiation causing biological changes. It accounts for the energy of the absorbed radiation, the type of radiation (beta particles, X-rays, etc.), and other modifying factors. *Symbol:* **H**.

do·sim·e·ter (dōsim'itə), *n*. an instrument that measures the dosage of x-rays or other radiation. —**do·sim'e·try**, *n*.

dos·sal (dos'əl), *n*. a drape hanging behind an altar or around the chancel. Also **dor'sal**.

dos·ser (dos'ə), *n*. **1**. a pannier or basket carried on the back. **2**. a covering for the back of a throne.

dos·si·er (dos'ēā), *n*. a set of documents concerned with some person or matter.

dot·age (dō'tij), *n*. weakness of mind due to old age.

do·tard (dō'tûd), *n.* a feeble-minded old person.

do·ta·tion (dōtā'SHən), *n.* an endowment or act of endowing.

dot·tle, dot·tel (dot'əl), *n.* the plug of partly burnt tobacco remaining in a pipe after smoking.

double di·ode (dī'ōd). See **duodiode.**

double en·ten·dre (äntän'drə), *pl.* **double en·ten·dres** (äntän'drəz). a word or expression with two ambiguous meanings, one of which is usually slightly risqué.

double in·dem·ni·ty (indem'nitē), a life insurance policy paying double the face value in the event of accidental death.

double jeop·ar·dy (jep'ədē), the trying of a person twice for the same offence.

double standard, a code of principles which bear more heavily on one group of people than on another.

double·think (dub'əlthiNGk,), *v.* to believe in two conflicting versions, ideas, etc., at the same time.

dou·ceur (dōōsû'), *n.* a tip or gratuity.

dough·ty (dou'tē), *adj.* bravely formidable; steadfast; courageous.

dour (dōō'ə), *adj.* stern, severe, or forbidding in appearance and behaviour.

dou·ter (dou'tə), *n.* a candle-snuffer.

dow·a·ger (dou'əjə), *n.* **1.** a title a widow of a titled man assumes to distinguish her from the wife of the heir to his title. **2.** a stately, wealthy, elderly widow.

dow·dy (dou'dē), *adj.* shabby; unfashionable.

down·stage (doun'stāj'), *adv.* **1.** towards the front of a theatrical stage. —*adj.* **2.** of or pertaining to the front of a stage. See also **upstage.**

down·wind (doun'wind'), *adv.* in the same direction as the wind is blowing; with the wind.

dox·ol·ogy (doksol'əjē), *n.* a hymn of praise to God, especially the one starting "Praise God from whom all blessings flow."

dox·y (dok'sē), *n.* opinion or view.

doy·en (doi'ən), *n.* the senior member of a group, society, profession, etc. —**doy·enne** (doien'), *n.*, *fem.*

drab·ble (drab'əl), *v.* to make wet or dirty.

dra·co·ni·an (drākō'nēən), *adj.* harsh; severe; inhuman.

dra·con·ic (drākon'ik), *adj.* dragon-like.

dra·gée (drazHā'), *n.* **1.** a chocolate coated sweet with a liquid centre. **2.** a small, spherical, silver-coloured, edible cake decoration.

drag·o·man (drag'ōmən), *n.*, *pl.* **drag·o·mans, drag·o·men** (drag'ōmən). a guide-interpreter in the East.

dra·goon (drəgōōn'), *v.* to force by harsh measures; coerce.

drag race, a motor race from a standing start, the winner being the one that accelerates the fastest.

drag·ster (drag'stə). *n.* a car prepared for drag races.

drag·strip (drag'strip,), an area, as a straight section of road or aircraft runway, on which drag races are held.

drake (drāk), *n.* a male duck.

dram·a·turge (dram'ətûj), *n.* a playwright. Also **dram·a·tur·gist.**

dram·a·tur·gy (dram'ətûjē), *n.* the art of writing plays.

dras·tic (dras'tik), *adj.* very severe and forceful; more violent than expected, as *We had to take drastic action to prevent his escape.*

drawing account, a bank account used for cash withdrawals.

drawn butter, seasoned melted butter, served on vegetables.

draw runner. See **loper.**

draw slip. See **loper.**

drei·kan·ter (drī'käntə), *n.*, *pl.* **drei·kan·ters, drei·kan·ter.** a three-sided stone or boulder whose faces are formed by wind-blown sand.

dres·sage (drəs'äzH), *n.* the training of a horse in obedience, movement, and bearing.

drift bolt (drift'bōlt,), a bolt or spike for securing heavy timbers together. Also **drift pin.**

drill (dril), *n.* a strong twilled linen or cotton material.

drilling mud, a mudlike substance pumped into an oil well to cool the drilling bit and to flush out the loose cuttings.

drogue (drōg), *n.* a sea anchor consisting of a canvas bag or bucket.

droit (droit), *n.* moral and legal right.

droll (drōl), *adj.* quaintly amusing; whimsical; comic. —**droll·er·y** (drō'lərē), *n.*

drom·os (drom'əs), *n.* **1.** the passage to an ancient subterranean tomb. **2.** (in ancient Greece) a race track.

drone (drōn), *n.* the male honeybee.

drop·out (drop'out,), *n.* a student who never completes his course of studies.

drop shipment, a shipment of goods which, though billed through the retailer or wholesaler, goes directly from the manufacturer to the customer.

drop·sy (drop'sē), *n.* an excessive accumulation of fluid in the cavities or tissues of the body. —**drop'si·cal,** *adj.*

drosh·ky (drosH'kē), *n.* a light, open, four-wheeled carriage used in Russia.

dross (dros), *n.* waste matter or refuse, as from the melting of metals. —**dross'y,** *adj.*

drub (drub), *v.* to beat violently; abuse; flog.

drug·get (drug'it), *n.* a coarse rug made from hair woven with cotton or jute.

drum·beat·er (drum'bē,tə), *n.* one who proclaims the virtues of a movie, product, etc.; publicist.

drum·fire (drum'fī,ə), *n.* heavy gunfire that sounds like the beating of drums.

drupe (drōop), *n.* a fruit, as a cherry or plum, consisting of fleshy pulp surrounding a hard shell which encloses a kernel. —**dru·pa·ceous** (drōōpā'sHəs), *adj.*

dry cell, a type of electric battery or cell with no free fluid.

dry farming, a method of farming without irrigation in areas of low rainfall, by reducing evaporation and making the ground more retentive of moisture.

dry-gulch (drī'gulcH,), *v. SW U.S.* to ambush or betray by a change of attitude.

dry·o·pith·e·cine (drī,ōpith'əsēn,), *n.* any of an extinct group of Old World apes belonging to the subfamily Dryopithecinae, thought to be the ancestors of both man and modern apes.

dry·point (drī'point,), *n.* a copper engraving made with a needle stylus that produces a print with soft, velvety-black lines.

dry rot (drī rot), timber decay caused by fungi, resulting in dry, crumbling wood.

dry sail (drī 'sāl), *v.* to cruise in or possess only a motor-driven boat. —**dry sail·or,** *n.*

dry well, a large concrete cylinder sunk into the earth and surrounded by loose stones, used for the drainage and leaching of waste liquids.

du·ad (dyōō'ad), *n.* a pair.

du·al·ism (dyōō'əliz,əm), *n.* (in philosophy) the theory that there are two principal substances, mind and body. —**du,al·is'tic,** *adj.*

du·al·i·ty (dyōōal'itē), *n.* the state of being dual.

dual personality, a mental disorder in which a person's behaviour exhibits the presence of two different personalities.

du·ar·chy (dyōō'äkē), *n.* See **diarchy.**

du·bi·e·ty (dyōōbī'itē), *n.* doubt; hesitation; doubtfulness.

du·bi·ous (dyōō'bēəs), *adj.* doubtful; subject to question, as dubious honesty.

du·bi·ta·tion (dyōō,bitā'sHən), *n.* doubt.

du·bi·ta·tive (dyōō'bitā,tiv), *adj.* doubting.

duc·tile (duk'til), *adj.* capable of being worked into wire or thin sheets, as certain metals; malleable.

dudg·eon (duj'ən), *n.* a feeling of being offended; angry resentment.

Du·e·cen·to (dōō,əcHen'tō), *n.* the 13th century, esp. Italian art and literature of that period. Also **dugen·to** (dōōjen'tō).

duff (duf), *n.* rotting vegetable matter on a forest floor.

du jour (də ZHōō'ə), *French.* of the day; that being served on this particular day.

dul·cet (dul'sit), *adj.* pleasant; melodious; agreeable; soothing to the ear or eye.

dul·ci·fy (dul'sifī), *v.* to appease; mollify; make agreeable.

du·li·a (dyōō'lēə), *n.* (in Roman Catholicism) the veneration given to saints in their role as God's servants. See also **hyperdulia, latria.**

du·loc·ra·cy (dyōōlok'rəsē), *n.* government by former slaves.

du·lo·sis (dyōōlō'sis), *n.* the enslaving of members of any one colony by ants of a different species.

dum·dum (dum'dum), *n.* a soft-nosed bullet that expands on impact.

dump·ish (dum'pisH), *adj.* dejected; low-spirited; depressed.

dun (dun), *v.* 1. to demand payment of a debt repeatedly. —*adj.* 2. dull greyish-brown.

dun·nage (dun'ij), *n.* 1. personal baggage. 2. poor material stowed round a ship's or railway's cargo to protect it from injury.

du·o·de·cil·lion (dyōō,ōdisil'yən), *n.* a number represented by 1 followed by 39 zeros.

du·o·dec·i·mal (dyōō,ōdes'iməl), *adj.* of the number 12 or of twelfths.

du·o·de·num (dyōō,ōdē'nəm), *n., pl.* **du·o·de·na** (dyōō,ōdē'nə), **du·o·denas.** the first portion of the small intestine nearest the stomach. —**du·o·de'nal,** *adj.*

du·o·di·ode (dyōō,ōdī'ōd), *n.* a radio tube containing two diodes. Also **double diode.**

du·o·logue (dyōō'əlog), *n.* a conversation between two people; a **dramatic dialogue.** See also **monologue.**

du·op·o·ly (dyōōop'əlē), *n.* a condition in the market in which there are two sellers only. See also **monopoly, oligopoly.**

du·op·so·ny (dyōōop'sənē), *n.* a condition in the market in which there are two buyers only. See also **monopsony, oligopsony.**

du·o·tone (dyōō'ətōn,), *n.* 1. a picture in two colours. 2. a printing method enabling a monochrome illustration to be produced in two shades of the same colour from duotypes.

du·o·type (dyōō'ətīp,), *n.* two plates made from the same original, but etched at different angles to produce two intensities when superimposed in printing.

dupe (dyōōp), *n.* 1. a person easily fooled. —*v.* 2. to deceive, fool, or trick.

dup·er·y (dyōō'pərē), *n.* an act or instance of trickery or fooling.

du·pla·tion (dyōōplā'sHən), *n.* a doubling.

du·ple (dyōō'pəl), *adj.* double; two-fold.

du·pli·ca·ture (dyōō'plikācHər), *n.* a doubling over of something, as a membrane.

du·plic·i·ty (dyōōplis'itē), *n.* deceit; hypocrisy; double-dealing.

dur·ance (dyōōr'əns), *n.* a long imprisonment.

dur·bar (dû'bä), *n.* a state reception of an Indian prince or British governor or viceroy.

Dutch (ducH), *adj.* referring to a style of painting in 17th-century Holland, characterized by muted tones and naturalistic colours and depicting landscapes or subjects drawn from contemporary life.

Dutch courage, courage inspired by alcohol.

Dutch oven, a heavy-bottomed utensil used for stews, etc.

du·um·vi·rate (dyōoum'vərit), *n.* an alliance of two men holding together the same office.

du·ve·tine, du·ve·tyne, du·ve·tyn (dōo'-vitēn), *n.* a fabric with a nap, made in a twilled or plain weave of cotton, silk, or wool.

dy·ad (dī'ad), *n.* a couple; pair. —**dy·ad'ic,** *adj.*

dy·ar·chy (dī'äkē), *n.* See **diarchy.**

dy·nam·ic (dīnam'ik), *adj.* characterized by energetic activity; vigorous.

dy·na·mism (dī'nəmiz,əm), *n.* a philosophical theory which explains all phenomena by the action of force. See also **mechanism, vitalism.**

dy·nast (din'ast), *n.* a hereditary ruler.

dys·a·cou·sia, dys·a·cu·sia (dys,əkōo'-zēə), *n.* (in medicine) a condition in which the ear hurts when exposed to noise. Also **dys·a·cous·ma** (dis,əkōoz'mə).

dys·ad·ap·ta·tion (disad,əptā'sHən), *n.* an inability of the iris and retina of an eye to adapt correctly to light. Also **dys·ap·ta'tion.**

dys·aes·the·sia (dis,iəsthē'zēə), *n.* **1.** a faulty sense of touch. **2.** a condition in which any contact with the skin is painful.

dys·an·ag·no·sia (disan,əgnō'zēə), *n.* the inability to understand some words; wordblindness.

dys·ar·thri·a (disä'thrēə), *n.* speech defects as stammering caused by faults in the nerve. —**dys·ar'thric,** *adj.*

dys·bar·ism (dis'bäriz,əm), *n.* a condition caused by two different pressures, the atmospheric pressure outside the body and the pressure of gases within the body.

dys·cra·sia (diskrā'zēə), *n.* a malfunction or unspecified disease of the blood. —**dys·cra'sic, dys·crat·ic** (diskrat'ik), *adj.*

dys·cri·nism (diskrī'nizəm), *n.* a condition caused by defective glandular secretion.

dys·en·ter·y (dis'ənter,ē), *n.* an infectious disease which leads to an inflammation of the lower part of the bowels, resulting in diarrhoea.

dys·er·gia (disû'jēə), *n.* faulty muscular control due to bad conduction of the nerve.

dys·func·tion (disfuNGk'sHən), *n.* abnormal or impaired functioning, as of a bodily organ.

dys·gen·ic (disjen'ik), *adj.* causing degeneration in offspring. Also **cacogenic.** See also **eugenic.**

dys·gno·sia (disnō'zēə), *n.* (in psychiatry) an impairment in intellect.

dys·graph·ia (disgraf'ēə), *n.* the inability to write caused by damage to the brain.

dys·ki·ne·sia (diskinē'zēə), *n.* impairment of the ability to perform muscular movements.

dys·la·li·a (dislā'lēə), *n.* an inability to speak caused by a fault in the speech organs.

dys·lex·i·a (dislek'sēə), *n.* a condition of impaired perception that can cause learning disability.

dys·lo·gia (dislō'jēə), *n.* the inability to express ideas due to a mental disorder.

dys·lo·gis·tic (dislojis'tik), *adj.* not eulogistic or complimentary.

dys·men·orrhoe·a, dys·men·or·rhe·a (dis,menərē'ə), *n.* painful menstruation.

dys·met·ri·a (dismet'rēə), *n.* the inability to get muscles to produce the desired effect because of a fault in the judgment of distances.

dys·mne·sia (disnē'zēə), *n.* a defective or faulty memory.

dys·pa·reu·ni·a (dis,pərōo'nēə), *n.* coitus causing pain. See also **vaginismus.**

dys·pep·sia (dispep'sēə), *n.* chronic indigestion. —**dys·pep'tic, dys·pep'ti·cal,** *adj.*

dys·pha·gia (disfā'jēə), *n.* trouble in swallowing.

dys·pha·sia (disfā'zēə), *n.* inability to speak because of brain damage.

dys·phe·mi·a (disfē'mēə), *n.* a speech disorder caused by neurosis.

dys·pho·ni·a (disfō'nēə), *n.* a speech disturbance. —**dys·phon·ic** (disfon'ik), *adj.*

dys·pho·ri·a (disfôr'ēə), *n.* a state of unease, anxiety, or dissatisfaction. —**dys·phor'ic,** *adj.*

dys·pla·sia (displā'zēə), *n.* an abnormal growth in tissue. —**dys·plas·tic** (displas'tik), *adj.*

dysp·noe·a, dysp·ne·a (dispnē'ə), *n.* laboured breathing.

dys·prax·ia (disprak'sēə), *n.* the inability to coordinate movement.

dys·rhyth·mi·a (disriTH'mēə), *n.* a disorder in rhythm, as of speech, of brain waves recordings, etc.

dys·tel·e·ol·o·gy (dis,teleol'əjē), *n.* a philosophical doctrine that denies a final cause of existence.

dys·thy·mi·a (disthī'mēə), *n.* dejection; despondency.

dys·to·cia (distō'sHə), *n.* (in medicine) difficult birth. —**dys·to'cial,** *adj.*

dys·to·ni·a (distō'nēə), *n.* an abnormal state of tension or firmness of an organ or tissue in the body.

dys·to·pia (distō'pēə), *n.* the opposite of a utopia; a place where everything goes wrong.

dys·tro·phy (dis'trəfē), *n.* any of several conditions characterized by muscular weakening and degeneration. Also **dys·tro·phi·a** (distrō'fēə). —**dys·troph·ic** (distrof'ik), *adj.*

dys·u·ri·a (disyōōr'ēə), *n.* urination that causes pain.

E

ea·gle (ē'gəl), *n.* (in golf) two strokes under par on a hole. See also **birdie, bogey.**

ea·gre, ea·ger (ē'gər, ā'gər), *n.* tidal flood.

Early Christian, a style of early religious architecture, characterized by buildings with plain exteriors and lavishly decorated interiors.

Early Renaissance, a style of art in the 15th century using perspective and geometrically based compositions.

ear·mind·ed (ēə'mīn,did), *adj.* being more aware of or responsive to sound than sight, smell, etc. —**ear'mind·ed·ness,** *n.*

earth science, any science dealing with the earth.

earth·shine (ûth'sʜīn,), *n.* reflected light from the earth illuminating the moon.

earth·y (ûth'ē), *adj.* 1. made of earth or soil. 2. unsophisticated; direct.

ease·ment (ēz'mənt), *n.* (in law) the right held by someone to use the territory of another for a specific purpose, as right of way.

east·er·ling (ē'stəlɪNG), *n.* someone living in a land to the east of another land.

Eastern Church, Byzantine Church. See also **Orthodox Church.**

Eastern Hemisphere, the eastern half of the world, including Asia east of the Ural Mountains, Australia, and Oceania.

eau de vie (ō də vē'), *French.* coarse, unpurified brandy.

é·bauche (ābōsʜ'), *n.* a basic watch movement made without jewels, case, etc.

é·bé·niste (ābänēst'), *n., pl.* **é·bé·nistes** (ābānēst'). *French.* 1. one who works with veneers, inlay, etc. 2. one who works with ebony.

é·bé·nis·te·rie (ābānēstərē'), *n. French.* work done by an ébéniste.

e·bul·lient (ibul'yənt), *adj.* full of enthusiasm. —**e·bul'lience,** *n.* —**eb·ul·li·tion** (eb,əlisʜ'ən), *n.*

e·bur·na·tion (ē,bənā'sʜən), *n.* an abnormal bone condition causing bones to become hard and dense.

e·cau·date (ēkô'dāt), *adj.* without a tail; excaudate.

ec·bol·ic (ekbol'ik), *adj.* 1. accelerating labour or abortion. —*n.* 2. a drug or other substance that accelerates labour or abortion.

ec·ce ho·mo (ek'ē hō'mō), *Latin.* behold the man; words of Pilate when presenting Christ to his accusers.

ec·cen·tric (iksen'trik), *adj.* 1. with the axis not at the centre, as a wheel. —*n.* 2. an instrument for changing circular motion into reciprocating motion.

ec·chy·mo·sis (ek,imō'sis), *n., pl.* **ec·chy·mo·ses** (ek,imō'sēz). discoloration caused by blood, as in a bruise; black-and-blue mark.

ec·cle·si·as·tic (iklē,zēas'tik), *n.* 1. a priest; vicar. —*adj.* 2. ecclesiastical.

ec·cle·si·as·ti·cal (iklē,zēas'tikəl), *adj.* of the Church.

ec·cle·si·ol·a·try (iklēzēol'ətrē), *n.* excessive regard for tradition in religion.

ec·cri·nol·o·gy (ek,rinol'əjē), *n.* a branch of science concerned with the secretory glands.

ec·dem·ic (ekdem'ik), *adj.* (of a disease) originating elsewhere than where it is found, but neither epidemic nor endemic.

ec·dys·i·ast (ekdiz'ēast), *n.* 1. an animal, insect, etc., that sheds its skin or covering, as a snake, caterpillar, etc. 2. a striptease performer.

ec·dy·sis (ek'disis), *n., pl.* **ec·dy·ses** (ek'disēz). the shedding of a skin, etc., as by a snake.

e·ce·sis (isē'sis), *n.* the establishment of a plant in a new region.

ech·i·nate (ek'ināt), *adj.* having bristles; prickly.

e·chi·noid (ikī'noid), *adj.* like a sea urchin.

ech·o·graph (ek'ōgräf,), *n.* an instrument that measures the depth of the ocean by means of sound. —**ech·o·gram** (ek'ōgram,), *n.*

ech·o·la·li·a (ek,ōlā'lēə), *n.* the involuntary repetition of someone else's words immediately after they have been spoken.

ech·o·lo·ca·tion (ek,ōlōkā'sʜən), *n.* the location of objects by natural or artificial means, as by bats, radar, sonar, etc.

ech·o·prax·i·a (ek,ōprak'sēə), *n.* the abnormal copying of another person's actions.

echt

echt (eкʜt), *adj.* German. genuine; real; true.

é·clair·cisse·ment (ākleəsēsmän'), *n., pl.* **é·clair·cisse·ments** (āklersēsmän'). *French.* clarification; explanation.

é·clat (āklä'), *n.* brilliance, as of performance, execution, reputation, etc.

ec·lec·tic (iklek'tik, eklek'tik), *adj.* choosing from many possibilities. —**ec·lec'ti·cism,,** *n.*

e·clip·tic (iklip'tik), *n.* the apparent course of the sun through the sky once a year.

ec·logue (ek'log), *n.* an idyllic poem, often in dialogue.

e·clo·sion (iklō'ZHən), *n.* the hatching of a larva from its egg or the emerging of an insect from its pupa.

e·co·cide (ē'kəsīd,, ek'əsid,), *n.* complete devastation of the natural environment.

e·col·o·gy (ikol'əjē), *n.* the study of the relations between organisms and their surroundings. Also **bionomics, bionomy.**

e·con·o·met·rics (ikon,əmet'riks), *n.* the application of statistical mathematics to actual problems as well as to the proof of theories.

economic determinism, the doctrine that all social phenomena are caused by economic factors.

economic geography, the study of the relationship between economic conditions, etc., and the utilization of raw materials.

economic geology, the study of the industrial uses of raw materials from the earth.

e·con·o·mism (ikon'əmizəm,), *n.* **1.** a theory that considers economics as playing the principal role in society, with most other aspects of culture reduced to economic terms. **2.** the belief that improving material standards should be the main concern of a particular political group or social class.

e·co·spe·cies (ē'kōspē,SHēz, e'kōspē,SHēz, ē'kōspē,sēz, e'kōspē,sēz), *n.* a taxon containing one or several inter-breeding ecotypes.

e·co·sphere (ē'kōsfēr,, e'kōsfē,ə), *n.* a layer of the atmosphere where it is possible to breathe normally.

e·co·sys·tem (ē'kōsis,təm, ek'ōsis,təm), *n.* organisms and their surroundings considered together as a system.

e·co·tone (ē'kətōn, ek'ətōn), *n.* a region of transition from one type of plant community to another, as from savanna to woodland.

e·co·type (ē'kətīp, ek'ətīp), *n.* a race particularly adapted to a certain environment.

é·cra·sé (ākräzā'), *adj.* (of leather) crushed so as to appear grained.

ec·ru (ek'rōō, ā'krōō), *adj.* beige in colour.

ec·stat·ic (ekstat'ik), *adj.* utterly delighted and happy; overjoyed. —**ec'sta·sy,** *n.*

ec·tad (ek'tad), *adv.* outward; out from the inside.

ec·tal (ek'təl), *adj.* outside; exterior.

ec·to·crine (ek'tōkrīn,, ek'tōkrin,), *n.* **1.** a substance discharged by an organism to affect the behaviour of other organisms, either of its own or other species. —*adj.* **2.** describing a gland or secretory tissue that produces such a substance.

ec·tog·e·nous (ektoj'ənəs), *adj.* growing externally, as a parasite, etc. Also **ec,to·gen'ic.**

ec·to·mor·phic (ek,tōmô'fik), *adj.* having a

thin body. See also **endomorphic, mesomorphic.** —**ec'to·morph,** *n.*

ec·to·par·a·site (ek,tōpar'əsīt), *n.* an external parasite. See also **endoparasite.**

ec·to·phyte (ek'tōfit), *n.* an externally parasitic plant. See also **endophyte.**

ec·to·pi·a (ektō'pēə), *n.* a congenital displacement of an organ. See also **entopic.** —**ec·top·ic** (ektop'ik), *adj.*

ec·to·plasm (ek'tōplazəm), *n.* **1.** the outer layer of the cytoplasm of a cell. **2.** (in spiritualism) a substance that allegedly emanates from a medium.

ec·tro·dac·tyl·ism (ek,trōdak'təlizəm), *n.* the congenital absence of part or all of one or more fingers or toes from birth.

ec·type (ek'tīp), *n.* a copy, as opposed to an original. See also **prototype.**

ECU (ā'kyōō), *n.* acronym for European Currency Unit: the currency unit of the European Community.

e·cu·men·i·cal (ē,kyōōmen'ikəl, ek,yōōmen'-ikəl), *adj.* **1.** worldwide; universal. **2.** favouring Christian unity. Also **ec,u·men'ic, oecumenic, oecumenical.** —**e,cu·men'i·cal·ism,, e,cu·men'i·cism,,** *n.* —**e,cu·men'i·cist,,** *n.*

e·cu·men·ism (ikyōō'məniz,əm), *n.* ecumenical doctrines.

ec·ze·ma (ek'səmə), *n.* a skin disease causing inflammation and itching. —**ec·zem·a·tous** (eksem'ətəs), *adj.*

ec·ze·ma·toid (eksē'mətoid), *adj.* like eczema.

e·da·cious (idā'SHəs), *adj.* devouring; consuming.

e·dac·i·ty (idas'itē), *n.* voraciousness; appetite.

e·daph·ic (idaf'ik), *adj.* caused by soil conditions produced by drainage, etc., and not by climate.

ed·a·phon (ed'əfon), *n.* all organisms living in the soil.

ed·dy (ed'ē), *n.* a small whirlpool, or similar condition of air, fog, etc.

e·de·ma (idē'mə), *n., pl.* **e·de·ma·ta** (idē'mətə). See **oedema.**

e·den·tate (ēden'tāt), *adj.* without teeth; toothless.

e·dict (ē'dikt), *n.* a governmental or authoritative decree.

ed·i·fy (ed'əfī), *v.* to instruct; uplift morally. —**ed,i·fi·ca'tion,** *n.* —**e·dif,i·ca'to·ry,** *adj.*

ed·u·ca·ble (ed'yōōkəbəl), *adj.* able to be educated; capable of learning.

ed·u·ca·tion·al·ist (ed,yōōkā'SHənəlist), *n.* a specialist in education. Also **educationist.**

e·duce (idyōōs'), *v.* to bring out; develop.

e·duct (ē'dukt), *n.* the act of bringing out, as something potential; something educed. —**e·duc'tion,** *n.* —**e·duc'tive,** *adj.* —**e·duc'tor,** *n.*

e·dul·co·rate (idul'kərāt), *v.* to purify; remove impurities from.

ef·fa·ble (ef'əbəl), *adj.* able to be expressed.

ef·face (ifās'), *v.* to rub out; destroy.

ef·fec·tor (ifek'tə), *n.* an organ or cell activated by a nerve impulse.

ef·fec·tu·al (ifek'tyŏŏəl), *adj.* producing a desired effect.

ef·fec·tu·ate (ifek'tyŏŏāt,), *v.* to bring about; make happen; cause.

ef·fer·ent (ef'ərənt), *adj.* (in physiology) carrying from or away from, as a nerve carrying an impulse. See also **afferent.**

ef·fete (ifēt'), *adj.* 1. exhausted; depleted. 2. decadent; lax. 3. sterile; barren.

ef·fi·ca·cious (ef,əkā'shəs), *adj.* having the desired effect. —**ef'fi·ca·cy,** *n.*

ef·fig·i·ate (ifij'ēāt,), *v.* to make a statue of.

ef·fleu·rage (efləräzh'), *n.* a gentle stroking used in massage.

ef·flo·resce (efləres'), *v.* to blossom forth. —**ef,flo·res'cence,** *n.* —**ef,flo·res'cent,** *adj.* —**ef,flo·res'cent·ly,** *adv.*

ef·flu·ence (ef'lŏŏəns), *n.* a flowing out. —**ef·flu·ent,** *adj.*

ef·flu·vi·um (eflŏŏ'vēəm), *n., pl.* **ef·flu·vi·a** (eflŏŏ'vēə). a small exhalation of an unpleasant gas.

ef·flux (ef'luks), *n.* an outward flow.

ef·frac·tion (ifrak'shən), *n.* a breaking into by forcible means. —**ef·frac'tor,** *n.*

ef·fron·ter·y (ifrun'tərē), *n.* shameless audacity.

ef·fulge (ifulj'), *v.* to shine brightly. —**ef·ful'gent,** *adj.*

ef·ful·gence (iful'jəns), *n.* a brilliant light; radiance. —**ef·ful'gent,** *adj.*

ef·fuse (ifyŏŏz'), *v.* to pour out; flow forth. —**ef·fu·sion** (ifyŏŏ'zhən), *n.* —**ef·fu'sive,** *adj.*

e·gal·i·tar·i·an (igal,iter'ēən), *adj.* characterized by a belief in human equality.

e·gest (ējest'), *v.* to empty; discharge, as from the body. —**e·ges'tion,** *n.*

e·ges·ta (ējes'tə), *n. pl.* excrement.

egg roll, (in Chinese cooking) a mixture of chopped roast pork, onions, etc., rolled in a casing of egg dough and fried.

eggs Benedict, a dish consisting of ham and poached eggs on toast covered with hollandaise sauce.

é·glo·mi·sé (ā,gləmizā'), *adj.* describing the method of painting the back of glass so that the decorative pattern is visible from the front. Also **e·glo·mi·se'.**

e·go (ē'gō), *n., pl.* **e·gos.** the self; individual essence of a being.

e·go·cen·tric (ē,gōsen'trik), *adj.* seeing the self as the centre of the universe.

e·go·ism (ē'gōiz,əm, eg'ōiz,əm), *n.* utter selfishness. —**e'go·ist,** *n.* —**e,go·is'tic,** *adj.*

e·go·ma·ni·a (ē,gōmā'nēə, eg,ōmā'nēə), *n.* abnormal egoism.

e·go·tism (ē'gətiz,əm, eg'ətizm), *n.* unpleasant self-conceit; boastfulness. —**e'go·tist,** *n.* —**e,go·tis'tic,** *adj.*

e·gre·gious (igrē'jəs, igrē'jēəs), *adj.* outstandingly bad.

e·gress (ē'gres), *n.* 1. an act of leaving a place. 2. the exit. —**e·gres·sion** (igresh'ən), *n.*

Egyptian cotton, cotton with long, silklike fibres.

ei·det·ic (īdet'ik), *adj.* of or pertaining to complete visual memory.

ei·do·lon (īdō'lən), *n., pl.* **ei·do·la, ei·do·lons.** an apparition; a phantom.

ei·dos (ī'dos, ā'dos), *n., pl.* **ei·de** (ī'dē, ā'dē). the essence of a culture.

ein·kan·tor (īn'käntə), *n.* a stone shaped by wind and sand.

eis·e·ge·sis (ī,səjē'sis), *n., pl.* **eis·e·ge·ses** (ī,səjē'sēz). a biased interpretation, especially of Scripture.

eis·tedd·fod (īsted'fəd), *n., pl.* **eis·tedd·fods, eis·tedd·fod·au** (*Welsh* īstedh'vodī). a gathering of Welsh poets and minstrels.

e·jac·u·late (ijak'yəlāt), *v.* 1. to eject semen. 2. speak swiftly and briefly. —**e·jac,u·la'tion,** *n.* —**e·jac'u·la,tor,** *n.* —**e·jac'u·la,to,ry,** *adj.*

e·jec·ta (ijek'tə), *n. pl.* any matter thrown out, as from a volcano.

eke (ēk), *v.* **eked, ek·ing.** *as in* **eke out:** to gain with great difficulty and by very hard work; barely accomplish, as *He eked out a living peddling brushes door-to-door.*

e·kis·tics (ēkis'tiks), *n.* the study of human settlements. —**e·kis'tic, e·kis'ti·cal,** *adj.* —**e·kis·ti·cian** (ē,kistish'ən), *n.*

é·lan (ālän'), *n.* panache; dash.

é·lan vi·tal (ālän vētal'), (in Henri Bergson's philosophy) a force capable of producing growth or change in an organism.

e·las·to·mer (ilas'təmə), *n.* an elastic substance occurring naturally as rubber.

e·late (ilāt'), *v.* to make happy.

E layer, a layer of maximum electron density at a height of between 100 and 120 kilometres from the surface of the earth.

el·dritch, el·drich (el'drich), *adj.* weird; uncanny. Also **elritch.**

electoral college, (in the U.S.) the chosen electors in each state who elect the President and Vice-President.

e·lec·tro·a·cous·tics (ilek,trōəkŏŏ'stiks), *n.* the conversion of acoustical energy into electricity and vice versa. —**e·lec,tro·a·cous'tic,** *adj.*

e·lec·tro·bal·lis·tics (ilek,trōbəlis'tiks), *n.* the measurement of the speed of projectiles with electronic equipment.

e·lec·tro·bi·ol·o·gy (ilek,trōbīol'əjē), *n.* the study of electrical phenomena in plants and animals.

e·lec·tro·car·di·o·gram (ilek,trōkä'dēōgram,), *n.* a graph made by an electrocardiograph.

e·lec·tro·car·di·o·graph (ilek,trōkä'dēōgräf,), *n.* a device for recording heart action.

e·lec·tro·chem·is·try (ilek,trōkem'istrē), *n.* the study of chemical changes caused by electricity and vice versa.

e·lec·tro·co·ag·u·la·tion (ilek,trōkōag,yəlā'sHən), *n.* the hardening of diseased tissue by diathermy.

e·lec·trode (ilek'trōd), *n.* a conductor for leading electricity to or from a nonmetallic conductor, as a vacuum tube.

e·lec·tro·dy·nam·ics (ilek,trōdīnam'iks), *n.* the study of interactions between magnetic, electric, and mechanical phenomena. —**e·lec,-tro·dy·nam'ic,** *adj.*

e·lec·tro·en·ceph·a·lo·gram (ilek,trōensef'ələgram,), *n.* a graph made by an electroencephalograph.

e·lec·tro·en·ceph·a·lo·graph (ilek,trōensef'ələgräf,), *n.* an instrument for recording electric activity in the brain.

e·lec·tro·form (ilek'trəfôm), *v.* to make something by electrically depositing metal on a mould.

e·lec·tro·ki·net·ics (ilek,trōkinet'iks), *n.* the study of electricity in motion. —**e·lec,tro·ki·net'-ic,** *adj.*

e·lec·tro·lier (ilek,trəlēr'), *n.* a chandelier lit by electricity.

e·lec·tro·lu·mi·nes·cence (ilek,trōlŏŏ,mines'əns), *n.* luminescence due to the activation of a dielectric phosphor.

e·lec·trol·y·sis (ilektrol'isis), *n.* 1. the process of passing an electric current through an electrolyte to cause a change in its physical constitution. 2. the burning out of hair follicles, tumours, etc., by an electric current.

e·lec·tro·lyte (ilek'trōlīt), *n.* an electric conductor in which an electric current induces a movement of matter in the form of ions. Also **electrolytic conductor.** —**e·lec·tro·lyt·ic** (ilek,-trōlit'ik), *adj.*

e·lec·tro·mo·tive (ilek,trōmō'tiv), *adj.* tending to cause an electrical flow.

electromotive force, the difference in potential between the terminals of an electrical source, as of a battery. *Abbr.:* **emf.**

e·lec·tro·my·o·gram (ilek,trōmī'əgram), *n.* a graph showing electric currents due to muscular action.

e·lec·tro·my·og·ra·phy (ilek,trōmīog'rəfē), *n.* the making of electromyograms. —**e·lec·tro·my·og'ra·pher,** *n.*

e·lec·tron (ilek'tron), *n.* an elementary particle found in all matter. Also **negatron.**

e·lec·tro·nar·co·sis (ilek,trōnarkō'sis), *n.* electroconvulsive therapy.

electronic music, sounds produced electronically and then combined by the composer. See also **musique concrète.**

e·lec·tron·ics (ilektron'iks), *n.* the science concerned with devices involving the flow of electrons in a semiconductor, vacuum, etc.

electron microscope, an extremely powerful microscope, using beams of electrons to produce a highly enlarged image.

e·lec·tro·phone (ilek'trəfōn,), *n.* any musical instrument using oscillating electric current to produce soɯnds.

e·lec·tro·pho·re·sis (ilek,trōfərē'sis), *n.* the motion of colloidal particles in a fluid caused when electricity is passed through. Also **cataphoresis.**

e·lec·tro·shock (ilek'trōsHok,), *n.* therapy involving the use of electric shocks; electroconvulsive therapy.

e·lec·tro·stat·ics (ilek,trōstat'iks), *n.* the study of electric phenomena not connected with electricity in motion. —**e·lec,tro·stat'ic,** *adj.*

e·lec·tro·sur·ger·y (ilek,trōsur'jərē), *n.* surgery in which electricity is used.

e·lec·tro·tech·nics (ilek,trōtek'niks), *n.* the study of practical applications of electricity.

e·lec·tro·ther·a·peu·tics (ilek,trōther,əpyŏŏ'tiks), *n.* therapy using electricity. Also **e·lec·tro·ther·a·py** (ilek,trōther'əpē).

e·lec·tro·ther·a·pist (ilek,trōther'əpist), *n.* a specialist in electrotherapeutics.

e·lec·tro·ther·mal (ilek,trōthû'məl), *adj.* pertaining to electrically produced heat.

e·lec·tro·ther·mics (ilek,trōthû'miks), *n.* the science concerned with the interchange of heat and electric energy.

e·lec·trot·o·nus (ilektrot'ənəs), *n.* the change in a nerve while electricity is passed through it.

e·lec·tro·type (ilek'trōtīp,), *n.* a copy of a block of type or engraving used in printing, made by electrolytic action in a mould.

e·lec·tu·ar·y (ēlek'tyŏŏəri), *n., pl.* **e·lec·tu·ar·ies.** (in medicine) an orally administered paste containing a drug and honey or syrup; a confection.

el·ee·mos·y·nar·y (el,iēmos'ənerē), *adj.* 1. charitable. 2. provided by charity. 3. supported by charity.

el·e·gi·ac (el,əjī'ak), *adj.* suitable for use as a lamentation.

el·e·gy (el'ijē), *n.* mournful poetry or music, often for the dead.

elementary particle, any entity less complex than an atom. Also **fundamental particle.**

e·len·chus (ileNG'kəs), *n., pl.* **e·len·chi** (ileNG'-kī). 1. a logical refutation. 2. a false refutation.

el·e·phan·ti·a·sis (el,əfəntī'əsis), *n.* a chronic lymphatic disease characterized by gross enlargement of the affected parts, usually the legs.

el·e·phan·tine (el,əfan'tīn), *adj.* clumsy.

e·lic·it (ilis'it), *v.* to draw forth.

e·lide (ilīd'), *v.* 1. to miss out (a sound or group of sounds) in pronunciation. 2. to suppress; ignore.

e·li·sion (ilizH'ən), *n.* the missing out of a sound, etc., in speech.

e·lite, é·lite (ilēt', ālēt'), *n.* a select, aristocratic, or choice group of people.

e·lit·ism (ilē'tizəm, ālē'tizəm), *n.* the belief that only the elite of society should rule. —**e·lit'ist,** *n., adj.*

el·lip·sis (ilip'sis), *n., pl.* **el·lip·ses** (ilip'sēz). the omission of a word or a phrase from a sentence that makes the construction incomplete.

el·lip·ti·cal (ilip'tikəl), *adj.* (of speech or writing) obscure because of its use of ellipsis.

elliptic geometry. See **Riemannian geometry.**

el·o·cu·tion (el,əkyōō'sHən), *n.* 1. the manner in which one speaks, esp. in public. 2. the study of voice control.

e·loign, e·loin (iloin'), *v.* to move away; to keep at a distance.

el·o·quence (el'əkwəns), *n.* the art of speaking well and aptly.

el·o·quent (el'əkwənt), *adj.* characterized by artistic, artful, or persuasive communication, in speech, writing, or effect.

el·ritch (el'riCH), *adj.* See **eldritch.**

el·u·ant, el·u·ent (el'yōōənt), *n.* a liquid used for dissolving.

el·u·ate (el'yōōit), *n.* a liquid solution resulting from dissolving matter.

e·lu·ci·date (ilōō'sidāt,), *v.* to clarify, as by explanation, example, etc. —**e·lu,ci·da'tion,** *n.*

e·lude (ilōōd'), *v.* **e·lud·ed, e·lud·ing.** to avoid; evade; manage to escape from, esp. by cunning.

e·lute (ēlōōt', ilōōt'), *v.* to remove by dissolving.

e·lu·tri·ate (ilōō'trēāt,), *v.* to separate or purify by washing, straining, or suspending in a current of water or air.

e·lu·vi·ate (ilōō'vēāt,), *v.* (of materials) to move through the soil by the action of water. —**e·lu·vi·a'tion,** *n.*

e·lu·vi·um (ilōō'vēəm), *n., pl.* **e·lu·vi·a.** the deposit of soil, etc., resulting from the decomposition of rock; residual soil. —**e·lu'vi·al,** *adj.*

el·ver (el'vər), *n.* a young eel.

el·y·troid (el'itroid), *adj.* like an elytron.

el·y·tron (el'itron), *n., pl.* **el·y·tra** (el'itrə). one of a pair of hardened forewings in insects for protecting the flight wings.

em (em), *n.* a square of any size of type, used as a unit of measurement for anything printed with that size of type.

em·a·nate (em'ənāt,), *v.* to flow out; emit. —**em,a·na'tion,** *n.* —**em'a·na,tive,** *adj.*

e·man·ci·pate (iman'sipāt,), *v.* 1. to free from restraint. 2. (in Roman and Civil Law) to end paternal control over someone. —**e·man,ci·pa'·tion,** *n.* —**e·man'ci·pa,tor,** *n.*

e·mar·gi·nate (imär'jināt,), *adj.* with notches along the edges.

e·mas·cu·late (imas'kyəlāt,), *v.* to make weak or effeminate.

em·ba·cle (embä'kəl), *n.* an agglomeration of broken ice on a river. See also **debacle.**

em·bar·go (embä'gō), *n., pl.* **em·bar·goes.** a government order restricting the movement of merchant ships into or out of its harbours.

em·bay (embā'), *v.* to surround; make into a bay.

em·bo·lism (em'bəliz,əm), *n.* the blocking of a blood vessel by an embolus.

em·bo·lus (em'bələs), *n., pl.* **em·bo·li** (em'-bəlī). undissolved matter lodged in a blood vessel.

em·bon·point (äNbôNpwaN'), *n.* French. obesity.

em·bosk (embosk'), *v.* to conceal with foliage.

em·bou·chure (äm,bōōsHŏŏə'), *n., pl.* **em·bou·chures.** French. 1. a river mouth. 2. the place where a valley opens into a plain. 3. the technique of using the tongue and lips in performing on a wind instrument. 4. the mouthpiece of a wind instrument.

em·bow·er (embou'ə), *v.* to cover with or hide in foliage. Also **imbower.**

em·brac·er·y (embrā'sərē), *n.* (in law) an attempt to sway a judge or jury by bribes or threats. Also **imbracery.** —**em·brace·or** (embrā'-sər), *n.*

em·branch·ment (embränCH'mənt), *n.* a branching out or ramification.

em·bran·gle (embraNG'gəl), *v.* to perplex; confuse. Also **imbrangle.**

em·bro·cate (em'brōkāt,), *v.* to rub with an ointment or lotion. —**em,bro·ca'tion,** *n.*

em·brue (imbrōō'), *v.* See **imbue.**

em·brute (imbrōōt'), *v.* See **imbrute.**

em·bry·ol·o·gy (em,brēol'əjē), *n.* the science concerned with embryos and the study of their growth and development. —**em,bry·ol'o·gist,** *n.* —**em,bry·o·log'i·cal,** *adj.*

em·bry·on·ic (em,brēon'ik), *adj.* like an embryo; undeveloped.

e·mend (imend'), *v.* to edit; remove mistakes. Also **mend.**

e·men·date (ē'məndāt,), *v.* to correct; put right. —**e,men·da'tion,** *n.*

e·mer·i·tus (imer'itəs), *adj.* no longer actively employed, but honourably discharged and kept on the rolls (used esp. of academicians).

em·er·ize (em'ərīz,), *v.* to give lustre to a fabric by rubbing it with emery.

e·mer·sion (imû'zɪɪən), *n.* the reappearance of one heavenly body after its eclipse by another.

e·met·ic (imet'ik), *adj.* **1.** producing vomiting. —*n.* **2.** an emetic agent.

e·mic·tion (imik'sнən), *n.* the passing of urine.

é·mi·gré (em'igrā,), *n.*, *pl.* **é·mi·grés** (em'i-grāz,). *French.* an emigrant, esp. one who flees his native land because of political reasons.

é·min·cé (āмаnsā'), *n. French.* a dish consisting of slices of left-over meat warmed in a sauce.

é·mi·nence grise (āmēnāns grēz'), a person who wields power from behind the scenes and unofficially. [literally, 'grey eminence']

em·i·nent (em'inənt), *adj.* famous; prominent, esp. because a person or thing is better, as an eminent publisher. —**em'i·nence,** *n.*

eminent domain, the power of a state to buy property by compulsory purchase.

em·men·a·gogue (imen'əgog,, imē'nəgog,), *n.* **1.** a drug or agent that promotes menstrual flow. —*adj.* **2.** promoting or assisting menstrual flow.

em·me·tro·pi·a (em,itrō'pēə), *n.* the normal condition of the eye, when rays of light are correctly focused on the retina.

e·mol·lient (imol'yənt), *adj.* **1.** able to soften tissue; soothing to the skin. —*n.* **2.** an emollient medication.

e·mol·u·ment (imol'yəmənt), *n.* payment for a service, as salary.

em·pai·stic (empā'stik), *adj.* decorated with an inlaid, embossed, or stamped design. Also **empestic.**

em·pa·thize (em'pəthīz,), *v.* to communicate; make contact with.

em·pa·thy (em'pəthē), *n.* identification with the feelings, etc., of someone else.

em·pen·nage (empen'ij, äⁿpənäzн'), *n.*, *pl.* **em·pen·nag·es** (empen'ijiz, äⁿpənäzн'). the tail assembly of an aeroplane.

em·per·y (em'pərē), *n.* **1.** an empire. **2.** the land belonging to an emperor.

em·pes·tic (empes'tik), *adj.* See **empaistic.**

em·phy·se·ma (em,fisē'mə), *n.* the abnormal enlargement of an organ owing to air or gas.

em·pir·i·cal (empir'ikəl), *adj.* **1.** discovered by experiment. **2.** depending on observation without the application of theory. —**em·pir'ic,** *n.*

em·pir·i·cism (empir'isiz,əm), *n.* **1.** the empirical method. **2.** (in philosophy) the theory that all knowledge comes from experience. **3.** an overreliance on personal experience to the exclusion of learning.

em·poi·son (empoi'zən), *v.* **1.** to corrupt. **2.** to make bitter.

em·py·e·ma (em,pīē'mə), *n.* pus in a body cavity, esp. in the thorax. Also **pyothorax.**

em·pyr·e·al (empir'ēəl), *adj.* belonging to the highest heaven in ancient cosmology.

em·py·re·an (empir'ēən), *n.* the most exalted of heavenly states.

em·u·late (em'yəlāt,), *v.* to copy the behaviour of another in an attempt at equalling or surpassing him. —**em,u·la'tion,** *n.*

em·u·lous (em'yələs), *adj.* wishing to equal.

e·mul·si·fy (imul'sifī), *v.* to make into an emulsion.

e·mul·sion (imul'sнən), *n.* the suspension of one liquid in another in which it is not soluble.

e·munc·to·ry (imuнcк'tərē), *n.* **1.** an organ of the body that disposes of waste products. —*adj.* **2.** excretory.

en (en), *n.* (in printing) half an em in width.

en·ar·thro·sis (en,äthrō'sis), *n.*, *pl.* **en·ar·thro·ses** (en,äthrō'sēz). a ball-and-socket joint in the body.

e·nate (ē'nāt), *n.* a maternal relative. See also **agnate.**

en·cae·nia (ensē'nyə), *n.* a festival commemorating the founding of a city, etc.

en·car·nal·ize, en·car·nal·ise (inkä'nəl-īz,), *v.* **1.** to invest with bodily form; incarnate. **2.** to make carnal or sensual.

en·car·pus (enkä'pəs), *n.*, *pl.* **en·car·pi** (enkä'-pī). ornamentation in which draperies, weapons, etc., are arranged as a festoon.

en·caus·tic (enkô'stik), *adj.* painted by burning in the colours.

en·ceinte[1] (onsant'), *adj.* pregnant.

en·ceinte[2] (onsant'), *n.* **1.** a fortified boundary surrounding a castle or town. **2.** the area enclosed by such a boundary.

en·ceph·a·lal·gi·a (ensef,əlal'jēə), *n.* headache.

en·ceph·a·las·the·ni·a (ensef,ələsthē'nēə), *n.* mental tiredness owing to emotional stress.

en·ceph·a·li·tis (ensef,əlī'tis), *n.* inflammation of the brain, esp. resulting from a viral disease.

en·ceph·a·lo·gram (ensef'ələgram,), *n.* an X-ray of the brain. Also **encephalograph.**

en·ceph·a·lo·graph (ensef'ələgräf,), *n.* **1.** an electroencephalograph. **2.** an encephalogram.

en·ceph·a·log·ra·phy (ensef,əlog'rəfē), *n.* the making of encephalograms.

en·ceph·a·lo·ma (ensef,əlō'mə), *n.*, *pl.* **en·ceph·a·lo·ma·ta** (ensef,əlō'mətə). a tumour of the brain.

en·ceph·a·lo·my·e·li·tis (ensef,əlōmīəlī'tis), *n.* a disease characterized by inflammation of the spinal cord and the brain. —**en·ceph,a·lo·my,e·lit'ic,** *adj.*

en·ceph·a·lon (ensef'əlon), *n.*, *pl.* **en·ceph·a·la.** the brain.

en·ceph·a·lop·a·thy (ensef,əlop'əthē), *n.* a mental disease of the brain.

en·ceph·a·lo·sis (ensef,əlō'sis), *n.* an organic disease affecting the brain.

en·chase (encнās'), *v.* **1.** to put jewels in a

setting. **2.** to decorate with gems or designs in inlay or embossing.

en·chi·la·da (en'CHilä'də), n. a Mexican dish consisting of a tortiḷḷa filled with highly seasoned meat mixture and covered with a chilli sauce.

en·chi·rid·i·on (en,kīrid'ēən), n., pl. **en·chi·rid·i·ons, en·chi·rid·i·a.** a handbook.

en·cinc·ture (ensiNGk'CHə), v. to encompass with a belt.

en·clave (en'klāv), n. outlying district of one country almost totally surrounded by the territory of another nation. See also **exclave.**

en·co·mi·ast (enkō'mēast), n. a eulogist; a giver of formal praise. —**en·co,mi·as'tic,** adj.

en·co·mi·um (enkō'mēəm), n., pl. **en·co·mi·ums, en·co·mi·a.** a eulogy; ceremonious praise.

en·co·pre·sis (en,kōprē'sis). n. unintentional defecation.

en·crypt (enkript'). v. to put in code.

en·cul·tu·rate (enkul'CHərāt,), v. to adapt to a culture. —**en·cul·tu·ra'tion,** n.

en·cum·ber, in·cum·ber (inkum'bə), v. to cause to slow down; hinder or retard the activity of, esp. by burdening. —**en·cum'brance,** n.

en·cyc·li·cal (ensik'likəl), n. a letter from the pope to all his bishops.

en·dem·ic (endem'ik), adj. native; indigenous. See also **enzootic, epidemic.**

end·er·gon·ic (en,dərgon'ik), adj. noting a biochemical process that needs energy to react. See also **exergonic.**

en·der·mic (endû'mik), adj. taking effect by absorption through the skin.

en·do·car·di·al (en,dōkä'dēəl), adj. in the heart.

en·do·car·di·tis (en,dōkädī'tis), n. inflammation of the endocardium.

en·do·car·di·um (en,dōkä'dēəm), n., pl. **en·do·car·di·a.** the membrane lining the heart.

en·do·cen·tric (en,dōsen'trik), adj. with the same syntactic function as one of its constituents, such as 'cold water', which functions as would 'water'. See also **exocentric.**

en·do·crine (en'dōkrin,, en'dokrin,), adj. **1.** secreting internally, as an endocrine gland. —n. **2.** an internal secretion. See also **exocrine.**

endocrine gland, any gland secreting substances into the blood.

en·do·cri·nol·o·gy (en,dōkrīnol'əjē, en,dōkrinol'əjē), n. the science of endocrine glands.

en·do·cri·nop·a·thy (en,dōkrinop'əthē), n. a disease caused by the improper function of an endocrine gland.

en·do·crin·o·ther·a·py (en,dōkrin,ōther'əpē), n. the treating of disease with hormones from endocrine glands.

en·do·don·tics (en,dōdon'tiks), n. a branch of dentistry concerned with diseases of the dental pulp. —**en,do·don'tist,** n.

en·do·er·gic (en,dōū'jik), adj. pertaining to a chemical reaction involving the absorption of energy. See also **exoergic.**

en·dog·a·my (endog'əmē), n. marriage within a social group. See also **exogamy.**

en·do·lith·ic (en,dōlith'ik), adj. living embedded in rock surfaces.

en·do·lymph (en'dōlimf), n. a fluid in the labyrinth of the ear.

en·do·morph·ic (en,dōmô'fik), adj. having a relatively heavily built body. See also **ectomorphic, mesomorphic.** —**en'do·morph,,** n.

en·do·par·a·site (en,dōpar'əsīt), n. an internal parasite. See also **ectoparasite.**

en·do·pha·sia (en,dōfā'ziə), n. internalized, inaudible speech. See also **exophasia.**

en·do·phyte (en'dəfīt,), n. an internally parasitic plant. See also **ectophyte.**

end organ, one of several specialized structures found at the ends of nerve fibres, etc.

en·dor·phin (endô'fin), n. any of a class of substances, including enkephalins, that are produced in the nervous system and exhibit pain-relieving properties similar to the opiate drugs such as morphine.

en·do·scope (en'dəskōp,), n. a small, cylindrical instrument used for examining the interior of a bodily organ.

en·do·skel·e·ton (en,dōskel'itən), n. the internal skeleton. See also **exoskeleton.**

en·dos·mo·sis (en,dosmō'sis), n. the movement of a substance from an area of lesser concentration to an area of greater concentration. See also **exosmosis.**

en·do·ther·mic (en,dōthû'mik), adj. pertaining to a chemical change involving the absorption of heat. See also **exothermic.**

en·e·ma (en'əmə), n. the injection of fluid into the rectum.

en·er·gu·men (en,əgyoō'mən), n. **1.** someone possessed by an evil spirit. **2.** a fanatic.

en·er·vate (en'əvāt,), v. to make weak.

en fa·mille (äN famē'), French. in the family.

en·fant per·du (äNfäN pedy'), pl. **en·fants per·dus** (äNfäN perdy'). French. a suicide squad.

en·fant ter·ri·ble (äNfäN terē'bl), pl. **en·fants ter·ri·bles** (äNfäN terē'bl). French. a child who causes embarrassment because of his behaviour.

en·fleu·rage (äNflûräzH'), n. a method of making perfume by exposing oil to the scent of flowers.

en·ga·gé (äNgazHā'), adj. French. committed; involved. See also **dégagé.**

en·gen·der (enjen'də), v. to cause; bring about.

en·glut (englut'), v. to gulp down; swallow.

en·gorge (engôj'), v. **1.** to swallow at great speed. **2.** to fill or distend with blood.

en·grail (engrāl'), v. to decorate the edge with curved indentations.

en·gross (engrōs'), v. **1.** to take all the attention of. **2.** to copy clearly and in a formal manner, as a public record.

en·gulf (engulf'), v. to overwhelm by surrounding or swallowing up.

en·hance (enhans'), v. **en·hanced, en·hanc·ing.** to improve; raise the value or importance of, as *Her reputation was enhanced by the success of the play.*

e·nig·ma (ənig'mə), n., pl. **e·nig·mas, e·nig·ma·ta** (ənig'mətə). something that cannot be explained.

en·ig·mat·ic (en,igmat'ik), adj. like an enigma, or puzzle; puzzling; difficult to understand.

en·join (enjoin'), v. **1.** to give an order; command. **2.** to proscribe.

en·keph·a·lin (enkef'əlin), **en·ceph·a·lin** (ensef'əlin), n. either of two substances produced in the brain that have pain-relieving properties similar to morphine. See **endorphin.**

en masse (än mas'), *French.* all together.

en·ne·ad (en'ēad,), n. a group of nine.

en·ne·a·gon (en'ēəgon,), n. nonagon.

en·ne·a·he·dron (en,ēəhē'dron), n., pl. **en·ne·a·he·dra** (en,ēəhē'drə). a solid shape with nine surfaces.

en·nui (änwē'), n. weariness; indifference; boredom.

e·nol·o·gy (ēnol'əjē), n. See oenology.

e·nor·mi·ty (inô'mitē), n. awfulness; horribleness.

e·no·sis (inō'sis, ēnō'sis), n. political union, esp. that of Greece and Cyprus.

e·nounce (inouns'), v. **1.** to declare. **2.** to enunciate.

en rap·port (än rapô'), *French.* in close relation with; in agreement with.

en·san·guine (ensaNG'gwin), v. to stain with blood.

en·sconce (inskons'), v. to make snug and safe.

en·si·form (en'səfôm,), adj. sword shaped.

en·si·lage (en'səlij), n. fodder stored in a silo.

en·sor·cell (ensôr'səl), v. to put a spell on.

en·sue (insyoo'), v. **en·sued, en·su·ing.** to follow, either in a natural sequence or as the result of something.

en suite (än swēt'), *French.* in a series.

en·tab·la·ture (entab'ləchə), n. the part of a classical temple between the columns and the eaves; a modern imitation of it.

en·ta·ble·ment (entā'bəlmənt), n. a platform over the dado of a pedestal.

en·ta·sis (en'təsis), n. a convex outline given to a column, etc., to make it appear straight.

en·tel·e·chy (entel'əkē), n. an actualization or manifestation as contrasted with a possibility or potentiality. **—en,te·lech'i·al,** adj.

en·tente (äntänt'), n., pl. **en·tentes** (äntänt'). an agreement between nations on a common international policy.

entente cor·diale (kôdyäl') *French.* amicable understanding, as between two nations.

en·ter·al·gia (en,təral'jə), n. intestinal pain.

en·ter·ic (enter'ik), adj. of or pertaining to the digestive tract; intestinal. Also **en·ter·al** (en'-tərəl).

enteric fever, typhoid.

en·ter·i·tis (en,tərī'tis), n. intestinal inflammation.

en·ter·ol·o·gy (en,tərol'əjē), n. a branch of medicine concerned with the intestines.

en·ter·on (en'təron), n., pl. **en·ter·a** (en'tərə). the alimentary canal.

en·ter·or·rhex·is (en,tərərek'sis), n. an intestinal rupture.

en·thal·py (en'thəlpē, enthal'pē), n. (in thermodynamics) a property of a system equal to the sum of its internal energy and the product of its pressure and volume. *Symbol: H.* Also called: heat content.

en·thet·ic (inthet'ik), adj. brought in from outside, as a disease introduced by inoculation.

en·thral (inthrôl'), v. to capture the mind or attention of; captivate; charm. **—en·thral'ment,** n.

en·tice (intīs'), v. **en·ticed, en·tic·ing.** to lure, tempt, or attract. **—en·tice'ment,** n.

en·to·mog·e·nous (en,təmoj'ənəs), adj. (of a fungus) living parasitically in or on insects.

en·to·mol·o·gy (en,təmol'əjē), n. the study of insects.

en·to·moph·a·gous (en,təmof'əgəs), adj. insect-eating; insectivorous.

en·to·moph·i·lous (en,təmof'ələs), adj. pollinated by insects, as a plant.

en·top·ic (entop'ik), adj. (of a bodily organ) in the normal place. See also **ectopic.**

en·tour·age (än'tooräzh), n. servants; attendants.

en·to·zo·a (en,tōzō'ə), n. pl., sing. **en·to·zo·on** (entəzō'on). animals living parasitically inside another animal. **—en,to·zo'ic,** adj.

en·treat (intrēt'), v. to beg of (someone), as *He entreated me to keep his secret.* **—en·treat'y,** n.

en·tre·cote (äntrəkōt'), n., pl. **en·tre·cotes** (äntrəkōt'). a cut of steak from between the ribs.

en·trée (än'trā), n. **1.** the act of entering. **2.** means of entrance or access. **3.** any food, esp. any food except a roast served as the main course of a meal.

en·tre·mets (än'trəmā), n., pl. **en·tre·mets. 1.** a side dish between principal courses. **2.** a dessert course.

en·tre nous (äntrə noō'), *French.* secretly; just between the two of us.

en·tre·pre·neur (än,trəprənû'), *n.* an organizer of an enterprise, esp. one that has some financial risk attached. —**en,tre·pre·neur'ship**, *n.*

en·tre·sol (on,trəsol'), *n.* the mezzanine floor.

en·tro·py (en'trəpē), *n.* **1.** the probability of the frequency of occurrence of an event. **2.** similarity; lack of differentiation.

en·try·ism (en'trēizəm), *n.* a strategy whereby members of a political group join an existing organization in order to change its aims and policies, rather than establish their own organization or party. —**en'try·ist**, *n.*, *adj.*

e·nu·cle·ate (inyōō'klēāt,), *v.* **1.** to take away the nucleus of. **2.** to remove the outer covering of (a kernel, tumour, etc.). —*adj.* **3.** without a nucleus.

e·nun·ciate (inun'sēāt,), *v.* to say clearly; proclaim. —**e·nun,ci·a'tion**, *n.*

en·ure (inyoōr'), *v.* See **inure.**

en·u·re·sis (en,yərē'sis), *n.* unintentional urination; incontinence.

en·vi·rons (invī'rənz), *n. pl.* the neighbourhood or area close by.

en·vis·age (inviz'ij), *v.* to picture (something) in the mind; visualize; imagine. See also **envision.**

en·vi·sion (envizH'ən), *v. U.S.* envisage; to create a vision or picture of mentally.

en·zo·ot·ic (en,zōot'ik), *adj.* (of diseases) peculiar to animals in a particular area or region. See also **endemic, epidemic.**

en·zyme (en'zīm), *n.* any organic substance capable of changing other organic substances by acting as a catalyst. —**en,zy·mat'ic**, *adj.*

en·zy·mol·o·gy (en,zīmol'əjē), *n.* the science of enzymes.

E·o·cene (ē'əsēn), *adj.* noting an epoch occurring from 40,000,000 to 60,000,000 years ago, characterized by early forms of all modern animals, including man.

e·o·hip·pus (ē,ōhip'əs), *n.* a horse of the Eocene period.

e·o·lith (ē'əlith), *n.* a flint shaped by natural forces and probably used as a tool by early man. —**e,o·lith'ic**, *adj.*

e·on (ē'on), *n.* See **aeon.**

e·on·ism (ē'əniz,əm), *n.* the wearing of female clothes and adoption of feminine attitudes by a man.

e·pact (ē'pakt), *n.* the difference in length between a lunar year and a solar year.

e·pan·o·dos (ipan'ədos), *n.* the repetition of words or ideas in reverse order.

e·pei·ric (ipī'rik), *adj.* reaching in land, as part of the sea.

ep·ei·rog·e·ny (ep,īroj'ənē), *n.* the vertical tilting of the earth's crust.

e·pergne (ipûn'), *n.* an often elaborate centrepiece for a dinner table.

e·phem·er·a (ifem'ərə), *n., pl.* **e·phem·er·as, e·phem·er·ae** (ifem,ərē). something lasting only a short time. —**e·phem,er·al'i·ty**, *n.*

e·phem·er·al (ifem'ərəl), *adj.* lasting but a short time; insubstantial; temporary; flimsy.

e·phem·er·is (ifem'əris), *n., pl.* **e·phe·mer·i·des** (ef,əmer'idēz). a table showing the position of a heavenly body on regular, recurring dates.

e·phem·er·on (ifem'əron), *n., pl.* **e·phem·er·a** (ifem'ərə), **e·phem·er·ons.** something that lives only a short time.

ep·i·cene (ep'isēn), *adj.* **1.** reflecting both male and female characteristics. **2.** weak; feeble. **3.** effeminate. —**ep,i·cen'ism**, *n.*

ep·i·cen·tre (ep,isen'tə), *n.* the point directly above the centre of an earthquake.

ep·i·con·ti·nen·tal (epi,ikon,tənen'təl), *adj.* in or on a continent.

ep·i·cri·sis, *n.* **1.** (ipik'risis), a critical study. **2.** (ep'ikrī,sis), a minor crisis following a major crisis.

ep·i·crit·ic (epikrit'ik), *adj.* pertaining to the ability to respond to small variations in temperature or pain. See also **protopathic.**

ep·i·cure (ep'ikyoōə), *n.* a person of fastidious tastes, esp. in eating and drinking.

e·pi·cu·re·an (ep,ikyoōrē'ən), *adj.* **1.** of luxurious habits, esp. in connection with food and drink. **2.** befitting an epicure.

Ep·i·cu·re·an·ism (ep,ikyoōre'əniz,əm), *n.* the hedonistic philosophy expounded by Epicurus, in which pleasure is the highest goal attainable.

ep·i·dem·ic (ep,idem'ik), *adj.* affecting many people at the same time, as a disease carried from person to person in an area where it is not usually found. See also **endemic, enzootic.**

ep·i·de·mi·ol·o·gy (ep,idē,mēol'əjē), *n.* the study of epidemic diseases. —**ep,i·de,mi·ol'o·gist**, *n.*

ep·i·der·mis (ep,idû'mis), *n.* the outer layer of skin. —**ep,i·der'moid**, *adj.*

ep·i·di·a·scope (ep,idī'əskōp,), *n.* an instrument for projecting the enlarged image of an opaque object.

ep·i·gam·ic (epigam'ik), *adj.* attractive to the opposite sex during the mating season, as plumage of certain birds.

ep·i·gas·tric (epigas'trik), *adj.* pertaining to the epigastrium.

ep·i·gas·tri·um (epigas'trēəm), *n., pl.* **ep·i·gas·tri·a** (epigas'trēə). that part of the abdomen situated above the stomach.

ep·i·ge·al (ep,ijē'əl), *adj.* (of insects) living near the ground, as on low plants.

ep·i·gene (ep'ijēn), *adj.* (in geology) originating on the surface of the earth. See also **hypogene.**

ep·i·gen·e·sis (ep,ijen'isis), *n.* the theory that embryonic development depends on an undifferentiated structure becoming successively more differentiated. See also **preformation.**

e·pig·e·nous (ipij'inəs), *adj.* (of fungi) growing on the surface, as of leaves.

ep·i·ge·ous (ep,ijē'əs), *adj.* (of plants) growing near the ground.

ep·i·gone (ep'igōn), *n.* a disciple of a famous writer, etc., not famous in his own right. Also **ep·i·gon** (ep'igon).

ep·i·gram (ep'igram,), *n.* a cryptic, witty, or pointed remark. —**ep·i·gram·mat'ic,** *adj.* —**ep·i·gram'ma·tist,** *n.*

ep·i·graph (ep'igräf, ep'igraf), *n.* 1. an inscription on a monument, etc. 2. a quotation at the beginning of a work. —**ep,i·graph'ic,** *adj.*

e·pig·ra·phy (ipig'rəfē), *n.* 1. the study of inscriptions. 2. inscriptions in general; graffiti. —**e·pig'ra·phist, e·pig'ra·pher,** *n.*

ep·i·late (ep'ilāt), *v.* to remove hair from.

ep·i·lep·sy (ep'ilep,sē), *n.* a nervous illness characterized by convulsions and ending in loss of consciousness. See also **grand mal, petit mal.** —**ep,i·lep'tic,** *n., adj.*

ep·i·lim·ni·on (ep,ilim'nēon), *n., pl.* **ep·i·lim·ni·a** (ep,ilim'nēə). a layer of water above the thermocline in some lakes. See also **hypolimnion.**

ep·i·lith·ic (ep,ilith'ik), *adj.* (of plants) growing on stones.

ep·i·logue (ep'ilog,), *n.* a conclusion added to a novel, play, etc.

ep·i·mor·pho·sis (ep,imô'fō'sis), *n.* (in segmented animals) the development of segmentation before hatching.

ep·i·nas·ty (ep'inastē), *n.* excessive growth on the top surface of a leaf causing a plant to bend downwards.

ep·i·neph·rine (ep,inef'rin, ep,inef'rēn), *n.* a U.S. name for adrenaline.

ep·i·neu·ri·um (ep,inyoor'ēəm), *n., pl.* **ep·i·neu·ri·a** (ep,inyoor'ēə). the sheath of tissue protecting the trunk of a nerve.

ep·i·o·nych·i·um (ep,ēōnik'ēəm), *n.* See **eponychium.**

ep·i·pas·tic (ep,ipas'tik), *adj.* suitable as a dusting powder.

E·piph·a·ny (ipif'ənē), *n.* 1. a Christian feast, on January 6, to commemorate the appearance of Christ to the Magi. 2. (e-) the sudden realization of the essential meaning of something. 3. (e-) the symbolic representation of such a realization.

ep·i·phe·nom·e·nal·ism (ep,ēfənom'inəliz,-əm), *n.* the belief that consciousness is a secondary phenomenon and is not able to affect physiological processes.

ep·i·phe·nom·e·non (ep,ēfənom'ənon), *n.* a secondary complication during the course of an illness.

ep·i·phloe·dal (epəflē'dl), *adj.* growing on the bark of a tree. Also **ep·i·phloe'dic.**

ep·i·pho·ne·ma (ep,ifōnē'mə), *n., pl.* **ep·i·pho·ne·mas, ep·i·pho·ne·mae** (ep,ifōnē'mē). a summary of what has been said before.

e·piph·o·ra (ipif'ərə), *n.* an overflow of tears due to a blockage or to excessive secretion.

ep·i·phragm (ep'ifram), *n.* a secretion which a snail in dry weather uses to seal its shell and thus prevent drying out.

ep·i·phy·lax·is (epifilak'sis), *n.* the boosting of bodily defences against disease.

ep·i·phyte (ep'ifīt,), *n.* a plant growing on another but not feeding parasitically on it.

ep·i·phy·tot·ic (ep,ifītot'ik), *adj.* (of a disease) destroying many plants in a given area at one time.

e·pis·co·pa·cy (ipis'kəpəsē), *n.* 1. the government of the Church by bishops. 2. the office of a bishop.

e·pis·co·pal (ipis'kəpəl), *adj.* 1. of a bishop or bishops. 2. (E-) indicating all or part of the Anglican Church.

e·pis·co·pal·ism (ipis'kəpəliz,əm), *n.* the vesting of ecclesiastical authority in the episcopal order as a whole and not in any individual.

e·pis·co·pize (ipis'kəpīz), *v.* to create a bishop of.

e·pis·co·tist·er, e·pis·ko·tist·er (ipis'kətistə), *n.* a solid disc with a segment missing, thus allowing the passage of flashes of light when rotated in front of a light source.

ep·i·spas·tic (ep,ispas'tik), *adj.* causing a blister.

e·pis·ta·sis (ipis'təsis), *n., pl.* **e·pis·ta·ses** (ipis'təsēz). 1. (in genetics) the interaction between nonallelic genes. 2. (in medicine) blockage of a discharge.

ep·i·stax·is (ep,istak'sis), *n.* a nosebleed.

ep·i·ste·mic (ep,istē'mik), *adj.* pertaining to knowledge.

e·pis·te·mol·o·gy (ipis,təmol'əjē), *n.* a branch of philosophy concerned with human knowledge and its limitations.

e·pis·to·lar·y (ipis'tələr,ē), *adj.* carried on in letters, as *epistolary orders.*

e·pis·to·lize (ipis'təlīz), *v.* to write a letter to (someone).

e·pis·to·log·ra·phy (ipis,təlog'rəfē), *n.* the art of letter writing.

e·pit·a·sis (ipit'əsis), *n.* (in ancient drama) the portion in which the main action develops. See also **catastasis, catastrophe, protasis.**

ep·i·tha·la·mi·on (ep,ithəlā'mēən), *n., pl.* **ep·i·tha·la·mi·a** (ep,ithəlā'mēə). a poem or song to celebrate a marriage. Also **ep,i·tha·la'mi·um.**

ep·i·the·li·o·ma (ep,ithē,lēō'mə), *n., pl.* **ep·i·the·li·o·ma·ta** (ep,ithē,lēō'mətə), **ep·i·the·li·o·mas.** a cancer of the cells that line blood vessels, etc.

ep·i·the·li·um (ep,ithē'lēəm), *n., pl.* **ep·i·the·li·ums, ep·i·the·li·a.** any protective tissue, as the epidermis. —**ep,i·the'li·al**, *adj.* —**ep,i·the'li·oid**, *adj.*

ep·i·the·li·za·tion (ep,ithē,līzā'sHən), *n.* the forming of epithelium.

ep·i·thet (ep'ithet,), *n.* a word or phrase ascribing an attribute to someone or something, as *Ivan the Terrible.*

e·pit·o·me (ipit'əmē), *n.* a summary.

e·pit·o·mize (ipit'əmīz), *v.* to be typical of; typify.

ep·i·zo·on (ep,izō'ən), *n.*, *pl.* **ep·i·zo·a** (ep,-izō'ə). an external parasite. —**ep,i·zo'ic**, *adj.*

ep·i·zo·ot·ic (ep,izōot'ik), *adj.* (of a disease) prevalent amongst animals for a short time.

ep·i·zo·o·ty (ep,izō'ətē), *n.* an epizootic disease.

e plu·ri·bus unum (ē' plōōr'əbəs ōō'nəm), *Latin.* one out of the many: the motto of the U.S.

ep·och (ēp'ok), *n.* any of several divisions of a geological period.

ep·o·nych·i·um (ep,ənik'ēəm), *n.* a layer of skin that covers the nails of a fetus and that becomes the cuticle after birth. Also **epionych·ium**.

ep·o·nym (ep'ənim), *n.* a real or fictitious person whose name becomes the name of a tribe, nation, process, product, etc. —**ep·on·y·mous** (ipon'əməs), *adj.*

ep·on·y·my (ipon'əmē), *n.* the making of names from eponyms.

ep·ox·y (ipok'sē), *n.* any substance, esp. a powerful cement, made by polymerization from certain chemicals. Also **epoxy resin**.

ep·u·ra·tion (ep,yərā'sHən), *n.* a purge, as of officials suspected of treachery.

eq·ua·ble (ek'wəbəl), *adj.* uniform; unvarying.

e·qual·i·tar·i·an (ikwol,iter'ēən), *adj.* pertaining to the doctrine that all men are equal.

e·qua·nim·i·ty (ē,kwənim'itē), *n.* calmness; composure; serenity. —**e·quan·i·mous** (ikwan'-iməs), *adj.*

eq·uer·ry (ek'wərē), *n.* an officer in charge of the horses of a royal household.

e·qui·dis·tant (ē,kwidis'tənt), *adj.* at equal distances from.

e·qui·form (ē'kwifôm,), *adj.* with the same shape or serving the same purpose. Also **e·qui·form'al**.

e·qui·lat·er·al (ē,kwilat'ərəl), *adj.* with all sides of equal length.

e·quil·i·brant (ikwil'ibrənt), *n.* a force or forces that counterbalance.

e·quil·i·brate (ikwil'ibrāt), *v.* to balance; to cause to balance equally.

e·quil·i·brist (ikwil'ibrist), *n.* someone skilled at balancing, as a tightrope performer.

e·qui·noc·tial (ē,kwinok'sHəl), *adj.* pertaining to the equal length of day and night.

e·qui·nox (ē'kwinoks,), *n.* the time when night and day are of equal length everywhere, occurring about March 21 and September 22. See also **solstice**.

eq·ui·page (ek'wipij), *n.* **1.** a horse drawn carriage. **2.** all of the equipment or furnishings, as of a home or military unit, considered together.

e·qui·poise (ek'wipoiz), *n.* an equality of force or weight; balance.

e·qui·pol·lent (ē,kwipol'ənt), *adj.* equally effective in force or meaning; equivalent.

e·qui·pon·der·ance (ē,kwipon'dərəns), *n.* equality of weight.

e·qui·pon·der·ate (ē,kwipon'dərāt,), *v.* to counterbalance; equal in importance.

e·qui·po·tent (ē,kwipō'tənt), *adj.* equally powerful.

e·qui·prob·a·ble (ē,kwiprob'əbəl), *adj.* equally probable.

e·qui·ro·tal (ē,kwirō'təl), *adj.* with wheels of equal size.

eq·ui·ta·ble (ek'witəbəl), *adj.* fair; just.

eq·ui·ta·tion (ek,witā'sHən), *n.* the art or act of horseback riding.

e·quiv·o·cal (ikwiv'əkəl), *adj.* ambiguous; with various meanings, as *an equivocal reply.*

e·quiv·o·cate (ikwiv'əkāt,), *v.* to speak in a deliberately vague manner. —**e·quiv,o·ca'tion**, *n.*

eq·ui·voque, eq·ui·voke (ek'wivōk,), *n.* an ambiguous phrase or amusing play on words.

e·ra·di·ate (irā'dēāt,), *v.* to radiate. —**e·ra,di·a'tion**, *n.*

er·e·mite (er'imīt), *n.* a hermit.

er·e·moph·i·lous (er,imof'ələs), *adj.* inhabiting a desert.

er·e·mo·phyte (er'əmōfīt,), *n.* a desert plant.

er·e·thism (er'əthiz,əm), *n.* an excessive stimulation of any organ or tissue.

erg[1] (ûg), *n.* a unit for measuring energy or work.

erg[2] (ûg), *n.* any large expanse of sand, as a desert.

er·gate (û'gāt), *n.* a worker ant.

er·go (û'gō, er'gō), *conj., adv.* therefore; hence, as *The person I despise arrived; ergo, I left.*

er·go·graph (û'gəgräf,, û'gōgraf), *n.* a device for recording the amount of work done when a muscle contracts.

er·go·nom·ics (û,gənom'iks), *n.* the science of making the job fit the worker; study of men at work; biotechnology.

er·gos·ter·ol (ûgos'tərōl), *n.* a substance, found in yeast, that is converted into vitamin D when subjected to ultraviolet light.

er·i·ce·tic·o·lous (er,isətik'ələs), *adj.* living in or on a heath.

er·is·tic (eris'tik), *adj.* controversial. Also **er·is'ti·cal**.

erl·king (ûl'kiNG), *n.* a mischievous spirit.

erne, ern (ûn), *n.* a sea eagle.

e·rod·ent (irō'dənt), *adj.* erosive; causing erosion.

e·rog·e·nous (iroj'ənəs), *adj.* sensitive to sexual stimulation.

e·rose (irōs'), *adj.* uneven, as from the effects of erosion.

e·rot·ic (irot'ik), *adj.* of, relating to, or arousing sexual desire; giving sexual pleasure. —**e·rot'i·cism,,** *n.*

e·rot·o·gen·e·sis (irot,ōjen'isis), *n.* the stimulation of erotic impulses. —**e·ro·to·gen'ic,** *adj.*

e·ro·to·ma·ni·a (irot,ōmā'nēə), *n.* an abnormally powerful sexual desire.

err (û), *v.* to be wrong; to make a mistake.

er·rat·ic (irat'ik), *adj.* **1.** eccentric; unusual. **2.** without aim; with no fixed course.

er·rhine (er'īn, er'in), *adj.* **1.** made to be sniffed into the nose. **2.** causing discharges from the nose.

er·satz (eə'zats, û'zats), *adj.* artificial; used as a substitute for a superior, usually natural, product.

er·u·bes·cent (ər,ōōbes'ənt), *adj.* becoming red.

e·ru·ci·form (irōō'sifōm), *adj.* like a caterpillar.

e·ruct (irukt'), *v.* to belch. Also **e·ruc·tate** (iruk'tāt).

er·u·dite (er'ōōdīt,), *adj.* learned; well-versed in many scholarly and intellectual matters. —**er,u·di'tion,** *n.*

e·rum·pent (irum'pənt), *adj.* bursting out or from.

er·y·sip·e·las (er,isip'ələs), *n.* an infectious disease causing inflammation of the skin.

er·y·the·ma (er,ithē'mə), *n.* a condition in which the skin is abnormally red.

e·ryth·rism (irith'rizəm), *n.* an unusual redness, as of hair.

e·ryth·ro·cyte (irith'rōsīt,), *n.* a red blood cell, carrying oxygen to tissue and taking carbon dioxide away.

e·ryth·ro·cy·tom·e·ter (irith,rōsītom'itə), *n.* an instrument for counting red blood cells.

e·ryth·ro·my·cin (irith,rōmī'sin), *n.* an antibiotic.

e·ryth·ro·pho·bi·a (irith,rōfō'bēə), *n.* an abnormal fear of anything red, or of blushing.

e·ryth·ro·poi·e·sis (irith,rōpoiē'sis), *n.* the production of erythrocytes.

e·ryth·ro·poi·e·tin (irith,rōpoiē'tin), *n.* a substance that stimulates production of red blood cells in bone marrow.

es·ca·lade (es,kəlād'), *n.* the climbing up by means of ladders.

es·ca·late (es'kəlāt), *v.* **1.** to intensify, as a war.

2. to rise or descend, as on an escalator. —**es,ca·la'tion,** *n.*

es·carp (iskäp'), *n.* the inner slope of a ditch; any steep slope.

es·carp·ment (iskäp'mənt), *n.* a ridge of high land like a cliff.

es·char (es'kä), *n.* a scab, esp. one formed from a burn.

es·cha·rot·ic (es,kərot'ik), *adj.* causing an eschar; caustic.

es·cha·tol·o·gy (es,kətol'əjē), *n.* any doctrine dealing with future or final matters, such as death. —**es,chatol'o·gist,** *n.*

es·cheat (esChēt'), *n.* the reversion of property to the state or crown when no legal heir or inheritor exists.

es·chew (esChōō'), *v.* to avoid; shun.

es·cri·toire (es,kritwä'), *n.* a writing desk.

es·crow (es'krō), *n.* a written agreement lodged with a third person and handed over when certain conditions have been fulfilled.

es·cu·lent (es'kyələnt), *adj.* edible.

es·cutch·eon (eskuCH'ən), *n.* a shield that bears a coat of arms.

es·ne (ez'nē), *n.* (in Anglo-Saxon England) a labourer.

e·soph·a·ge·al (ēsof,əjē'əl), *adj.* See **oesophageal.**

e·soph·a·gus (ēsof'əgəs), *n.*, *pl.* **e·soph·a·gi** (ēsof'əji). See **oesophagus.**

es·o·ter·ic (es,ōter'ik), *adj.* intended for or intelligible to only the initiated few.

es·o·ter·i·ca (es,ōter'ikə), *n. pl.* things meant only for the initiated few.

es·pal·ier (espal'yə), *n.* **1.** a flat trellis on which plants, esp. fruit trees, are grown. —*v.* **2.** to train on an espalier.

es·per·ance (es'pərəns), *n.* hope.

es·pi·al (espī'əl), *n.* the act of spying; an observing.

es·pla·nade (es,plənād'), *n.* any public spaces, esp. one for the public to walk or drive on.

es·pous·al (espou'zəl), *n.* the taking up of a cause.

es·pouse (ispouz'), *v.* **es·poused, espous·ing.** to adopt or take as one's own, as a cause, wife, etc. —**es·pous'al,** *n.*

es·pres·so (espres'ō), *n.* coffee made by forcing boiling water through ground coffee beans under pressure.

es·prit (esprē'), *n.* sharp intelligence or spirit.

esprit de corps (də kô'), a feeling of common interest uniting a group of people.

esprit d'es·ca·lier (des,kälyä'), a clever remark or reply that is not thought of at the appropriate moment; an afterthought. [French 'wit of the staircase' (as one is leaving)]

e·squa·mate (ĕskwā'māt), *adj.* without scales.

Es·tab·lish·ment (estab'lisнmənt), *n.* the existing authority in an institution or state.

es·ta·fette (es,təfet'), *n.* a courier on horseback.

es·ta·mi·net (es,tamēnā'), *n., pl.* **es·ta·mi·nets** (estamēne'). *French.* a small café.

es·the·sia (ĕsthē'ziə), *n.* See **aesthesia**.

es·the·sis (ĕsthē'sis), *n.* See **aesthesis**.

es·thete (ĕs,thĕt), *n.* See **aesthete**.

es·thet·ic (ĕsthet'ik), *adj.* See **aesthetic**.

es·ti·ma·ble (es'timəbəl), *adj.* worthy of respect.

es·ti·val (ĕstī'vəl, es'tivəl), *adj.* See **aestival**.

es·ti·vate (ĕs'tivāt,, es'tivāt), *v.* See **aestivate**.

es·to·ca·da (es,təkä'də), *n.* a sword thrust intended to kill the bull in bullfighting.

es·trade (esträd'), *n.* a low platform.

es·tray (esträ'), *n.* something which has gone astray.

es·treat (estrēt'), *n.* a copy of all or part of a written record.

es·tro·gen (ē'strəjən, ĕs'trəjən), *n.* See **oestrogen**.

es·trus (ē'strəs), *n.* See **oestrus**.

es·tu·a·rine (es'tyŏŏərīn, es'снŏŏrīn), *adj.* formed in, found in, or pertaining to estuaries.

es·tu·ar·y (es'tyŏŏrē, es'tjŏŏərē, es'снŏŏrē), *n.* an area at a rivermouth where the current of the river meets the tide of the sea.

e·su·ri·ent (isyŏŏr'ēənt), *adj.* greedy; voracious.

é·ta·gère (ātazнeə'), *n., pl.* **é·ta·gères** (ātazнeə'). *French.* open shelves used for storing bric-a-brac.

et·a·mine (et'əmēn), *n.* light, loosely woven cloth of cotton or similar fabric.

et·a·oin shrd·lu (et'ēoin sнûd'lŏŏ), letters produced from the first two vertical rows of keys on the left of a Linotype machine and used as a temporary marker.

e·the·re·al (ithēr'ēəl), *adj.* **1.** delicate; tenuous. **2.** celestial; spiritual.

eth·ic (eth'ik), *n.* moral values characterizing a culture or tribe.

eth·i·cal (eth'ikəl), *adj.* (of drugs) sold only when prescribed.

eth·narch (eth'näk), *n.* a ruler, as of a tribe or nation.

eth·nar·chy (eth'näkē), *n.* the government or rule of an ethnarch.

eth·nic (eth'nik), *adj.* concerning or characteristic of a group of people who share linguistic, religious, racial, or cultural traits or customs.

eth·no·cen·trism (eth,nōsen'trizəm), *n.* a feeling that one's own group is superior to any other.

eth·noc·ra·cy (ethnok'rəsē), *n.* rule by a certain ethnic group.

eth·nog·e·ny (ethnoj'ənē), *n.* the study of the origin of distinctive groups or tribes.

eth·nog·ra·phy (ethnog'rəfē), *n.* a study of characteristics of races of men and their cultures.

eth·no·lin·guis·tics (eth,nōliNGgwis'tiks), *n.* the study of language within a culture and of its effect on the culture.

eth·nol·o·gy (ethnol'əjē), *n.* the study of the origins, development, etc., of the races of mankind.

eth·no·mu·si·col·o·gy (eth,nōmyŏŏ,zikol'əjē), *n.* the study of primitive music and its cultural background.

e·thol·o·gy (ithol'əjē), *n.* the study of animal behaviour in relation to habitat.

e·thos (ē,thos), *n.* the basic characteristics of a culture.

e·ti·o·late (ē'tēəlāt), *v.* to make (plants) white by denying light.

e·ti·ol·o·gy (ē,tēol'əjē), *n.* See **aetiology**.

et·y·mol·o·gize (et,imol'əjīz), *v.* to trace (a word) historically.

et·y·mol·o·gy (et,imol'əjē), *n.* the study of the derivation and history of a word.

et·y·mon (et'imon), *n., pl.* **et·y·mons**, **et·y·ma** (et'imə). a linguistic form giving rise to another form historically, as Latin *luna*, 'moon,' is the etymon of English *lunar*.

Eu·clid·e·an geometry (yŏŏklid'ēən), geometry based on Euclid's theory, esp. the postulate that only one line may be drawn through a given point parallel to a given line. See also **hyperbolic geometry, Riemannian geometry**.

eu·de·mon, eu·dae·mon (yŏŏdē'mən), *n.* a beneficial demon.

eu·de·mo·ni·a, eu·dae·mo·ni·a (yŏŏ,dēmō'nēə), *n.* happiness. —**eu·de·mon·ic, eu·dae·mon·ic** (yŏŏ,dimon'ik), *adj.*

eu·de·mon·ics, eu·dae·mon·ics (yŏŏ,dimon'iks), *n.* the art of being happy.

eu·de·mon·ism, eu·dae·mon·ism (yŏŏdē'məniz,əm), *n.* the theory that correct actions produce happiness. —**eu·de'mon·ist, eu·dae'mon·ist,** *n.*

eu·gen·ic (yŏŏjen'ik), *adj.* connected with improving the type of offspring produced. See also **dysgenic**.

eu·gen·ics (yŏŏjen'iks), *n.* the science of improving the human race by careful choice of parents. —**eu·gen'ic**, *adj.* —**eu·gen'i·cist,** *n.*

eu·gon·ic (yŏŏgon'ik), *adj.* (of bacteria) living on artificial foodstuffs.

eu·he·mer·ism (yŏŏhē'məriz,əm), *n.* the theory that the mythologies of various gods came from the stories of dead heroes.

eu·lo·gize (yŏŏ'ləjīz), *v.* to praise highly; extol.

eu·lo·gy (yŏŏ'ləjē), *n., pl.* **eu·lo·gies**. a speech

or writing showing high praise for someone or something. Also **eu·lo·gi·um** (yōōlō'jēəm). —**eu·lo·gis'tic,** *adj.* —**eu'lo·gist,** *n.*

eu·no·my (yōō'nəmē), *n.* good order owing to just government and just laws.

eu·pep·sia (yōōpep'sēə), *n.* normal, good digestion. Also **eu'pep·sy.** See also **dyspepsia.**

eu·phe·mism (yōō'fəmiz,əm), *n.* a mild expression to replace an ugly or hurtful one, as *gone to rest* for *died.* —**eu,phe·mist'ic,** *adj.*

eu·pho·nize (yōō'fənīz), *v.* to render pleasing to the ear.

eu·pho·ny (yōō'fənē), *n.* harmonious and pleasant-sounding combinations of words, music, etc. —**eu·pho'ni·ous,** *adj.*

eu·pho·ri·a (yōōfôr'ēə), *n.* a feeling of well-being and pleasure with everything about one, esp. for no accountable reason; vacuous good cheer. —**eu·phor'ic,** *adj.*

eu·phu·ism (yōō'fyōōiz,əm), *n.* an ornate style of language or writing.

eu·plas·tic (yōōplas'tik), *adj.* able to be made into organized tissue.

eup·noe·a, eup·ne·a (yōōpnē'ə), *n.* normal breathing. See also **dyspnoea.**

eu·po·tam·ic (yōō,pətam'ik), *adj.* inhabiting fresh water.

eu·rhyth·mics, eu·ryth·mics (yōōriTH'miks), *n.* an interpretation of musical rhythms by body movements. —**eu·rhyth'mic, eu·ryth'-mic,** *adj.*

eu·rhyth·my, eu·ryth·my (yōōriTH'mē), *n.* a rhythmical motion.

eu·ri·pus (yōōrī'pəs), *n., pl.* **eu·ri·pi** (yōōrī'pī). a strait, esp. with a strong current.

Eu·ro·dol·lars (yōōr'ōdol,əz), *n. pl.* U.S. dollars used as international money in European banks.

European plan, a hotel plan in which the fixed daily charge covers only lodging and service. See also **American plan.**

eu·ry·cho·ric (yōōrikôr'ik), *adj.* widely distributed, as of a plant or animal. See also **stenochoric.**

eu·ry·ha·line (yōōr,ihā'līn), *adj.* capable of existing in an environment where the salinity varies greatly. See also **stenohaline.**

eu·ryph·a·gous (yōōrif'agəs), *adj.* able to live on a wide range of foodstuffs. See also **stenophagous.**

eu·ry·ther·mal (yōōr,ithûr'məl), *adj.* capable of withstanding great temperature variations. See also **stenothermal.**

eu·ry·ther·mo·phil·ic (yōōr,ithû,mōfil'ik), *adj.* (of bacteria) multiplying at temperatures up to 60°C.

eu·ry·top·ic (yōōr,itop'ik), *adj.* capable of withstanding wide variationsin climate, humidity, etc. See also **stenotopic.**

eu·sta·cy (yōō'stəsē), *n.* a change of sea level throughout the world.

eu·tha·na·sia (yōō,thənā'ziə), *n.* the killing of an incurably ill person. Also **mercy killing.**

eu·then·ics (yōōthen'iks), *n.* a science concerned with improving human conditions by improving their surroundings.

eu·ther·mic (yōōthû'mik), *adj.* producing heat.

eu·to·ci·a (yōōtō'sHə), *n.* normal childbirth.

eu·troph·ic (yōōtrof'ik, yōōtrōf'ik), *adj.* **1.** being in a condition of healthy development. **2.** (of lakes) supporting many nutrients inducing dense plant growth. —**eu'tro·phy,** *n.*

e·vag·i·nate (ivaj'ənāt,), *v.* (of a tubular organ) to turn inside out.

ev·a·nesce (ev,ənes'), *v.* to fade slowly. —**ev,a·nes'cent,** *adj.*

e·van·gel·i·cal (ē,vanjel'ikəl), *adj.* being ardently enthusiastic about a cause. Also **e,van·gel'ic.** —**e,van·gel'i·cal·ly,** *adv.*

e·van·ge·lism (ivan'jəliz,əm), *n.* the dissemination of the gospel; activity of a missionary. —**e·van'ge·list,** *n.*

é·va·sé (āvāzā'), *adj.* wider at the top, as a vase.

e·vec·tion (ivek'sHən), *n.* a recurring irregularity in the motion of the moon owing to the attraction of the sun.

e·ven·tu·ate (iven'cHōōāt), *v.* **e·ven·tu·at·ed, e·ven·tu·at·ing.** to happen, esp. as a result of another occurrence.

ever-normal granary, *U.S.* surplus farm produce bought by the state, both to stabilize prices and to guard against shortages.

e·ver·si·ble (ivû'səbəl), *adj.* able to be everted, or turned inside out.

e·vert (ivût'), *v.* to turn to the outside, or inside out. —**e·ver'sion,** *n.*

e·ver·tor (ivû'tə), *n.* a muscle by which a part or parts are turned towards the outside.

ev·i·ta·ble (ev'itəbəl), *adj.* that can be avoided or missed.

ev·o·ca·ble (ev'əkəbəl), *adj.* that can be evoked or drawn forth.

ev·o·ca·tion (ev,əkā'sHən), *n.* the process of summoning forth; calling forth; bringing to mind.

e·voc·a·tive (ivok'ətiv), *adj.* producing, recalling, or causing someone to recall a memory, emotion, sentiment, etc., as *a perfume evocative of my happy days with Farfarella.*

e·volve (ivolv'), *v.* **1.** to develop slowly as by evolution; come slowly into being. **2.** to give off, as a vapour.

e·vul·sion (ivul'sHən), *n.* the act of pulling out; extracting; ripping out by force.

ev·zone (ev'zōn), *n.* an infantryman of a crack corps in the Greek army.

ex·ac·er·bate (igzas'əbāt,, iksas'əbāt,), *v.* to intensify the irritation or virulence of.

ex·ac·tion (igzak'sнən), *n.* extortion.

ex·an·i·mate (igzan'imit, igzan'imāt,), *adj.* **1.** lifeless; dead. **2.** disheartened.

ex·a·rate (ek'sərāt), *adj.* (of a pupa) with free wings, antennae, and legs. See also **obtect.**

ex·as·per·ate (igzäs'pərāt,), *v.* **ex·as·per·at·ed, ex·as·per·at·ing.** to frustrate and annoy extremely.

ex·cau·date (ekskô'dāt), *adj.* without a tail; ecaudate.

ex·cerpt (eksûpt'), *v.* **1.** to take out a part of a document, film, etc., for use either as a shortened version or for another purpose. —*n.* (ek'sûpt) **2.** a part taken out of a document, film, etc.

ex·cerp·ta (ek,sûp'tə), *n. pl.* extracts from or summaries of a longer work.

excess-profits tax, *U.S.* a tax on profits made beyond the average return on capital.

ex·cide (iksīd'), *v.* to cut out.

ex·cip·i·ent (iksip'ēənt), *n.* an inactive, adhesive substance used to bind together the constituents of pills, etc.

ex·cise (iksīz'), *v.* to cut out.

ex·ci·to·mo·tor (iksī,təmō'tə), *adj.* causing increased motor activity. Also **ex·ci·to·mo·tor·y** (iksī,təmō'tərē).

ex·ci·tor (iksī'tə), *n.* a nerve that, when stimulated, causes greater action.

ex·claus·tra·tion (eks,klôstrā'sнən), *n.* the re-entry of a nun or monk to the secular world following release from her or his vows.

ex·clave (eks'klāv), *n.* a part of a country totally surrounded by the territory of another nation. See also **enclave.**

ex·clo·sure (iksklō'zнə), *n.* an area defended by fences, etc., against all intruders.

ex·cog·i·tate (ekskoj'itāt), *v.* to think out; study carefully to understand completely.

ex·com·mu·ni·cate (ekskəmyōō'nikāt), *v.* to deny (someone) the sacraments of the Church. —**ex,com·mu,ni·ca'tion,** *n.*

ex·co·ri·ate (ikskôr'ēāt), *v.* to take the skin from; peel. —**ex·co,ri·a'tion,** *n.*

ex·cor·ti·cate (ekskôr'tikāt), *v.* to husk; peel the bark from.

ex·cul·pate (eks'kulpāt), *v.* to free from blame.

ex·cur·sive (ikskû'siv), *adj.* digressive in speech.

ex·cur·sus (ekskû'səs), *n., pl.* **ex·cur·sus·es, ex·cur·sus.** **1.** a detailed discussion of something in a book. **2.** a written digression.

ex·curved (eks'kûvd), *adj.* curving outward; convex. Also **ex'cur·vate.**

ex dividend, not including the recently declared dividend. See also **cum dividend.**

ex·e·cra·ble (ek'səkrəbəl), *adj.* horrible; detestable; accursed.

ex·e·crate (ek'səkrāt), *v.* **1.** to hate; detest; loathe. **2.** to damn; curse. —**ex,e·cra'tion,** *n.*

ex·e·ge·sis (ek,sijē'sis), *n., pl.* **ex·e·ge·ses** (ek,sijē'sēz). a critical explanation, esp. of the Scriptures. —**ex,e·get'ic,** *adj.*

exemplary damages, damages awarded in excess of fair compensation to punish a plaintiff for reckless behaviour. See also **compensatory damages.**

ex·em·plum (igzem'pləm), *n., pl.* **ex·em·pla** (igzem'plə). a story illustrating a moral point.

ex·en·ter·ate (eksen'tərāt), *v.* to disembowel.

ex·e·qua·tur (ek,sikwä'tə), *n.* written permission given to a consul by the state where he is resident authorizing him to carry on his functions.

ex·e·quy (ek'səkwē). *n.* obsequy; funeral ceremony.

ex·er·gon·ic (ek,sûgon'ik), *adj.* noting a biochemical process that frees energy during reaction. See also **endergonic.**

ex fa·ci·e (eks fā'sнēē), *Latin.* (of a document in law) presumably; apparently; on the face of it.

ex fac·to (eks fäk'tō), *Latin.* according to fact.

ex·haust·ing (igzôs'tiNG), *adj.* tiring; making one extremely tired, as from boredom, hard work, etc.

ex·haust·ive (igzôs'tiv), *adj.* complete; making something complete; thorough, as *An exhaustive search of the file showed nothing.*

ex·hort (igzôt'), *v.* to urge; admonish. —**ex,hor·ta'tion,** *n.* —**ex·hor'ta·tive,** *adj.*

ex·hume (ekshyōōm', igzyōōm'), *v.* to dig up, esp. a body, from the earth.

ex·i·gen·cy (ek'sijənsē, igzij'ənsē), *n.* **1.** a state of emergency; urgency or strong necessity. **2.** (usually pl.) the needs or demands arising as a result of a particular circumstance, as *exigencies of travel.*

ex·i·gent, ex·i·geant (ek'sijənt), *adj.* urgent; pressing.

ex·i·gi·ble (ek'sijəbəl), *adj.* demandable; capable of being exacted.

ex·i·gu·ous (igzig'yōōəs), *adj.* small; scanty; slender.

ex·im·i·ous (egzim'ēəs), *adj.* outstanding; eminent.

ex·is·ten·tial·ism (eg,zisten'sнəliz,əm), *n.* the theory that man forms his essence from his deeds. —**ex,is·ten'tial·ist,** *n., adj.*

existential psychology, a psychology based only on existent data.

ex·o·cen·tric (ek,sōsen'trik), *adj.* with a syntactic function different from that of any of its constituents, as 'in the house' which has a different function from the noun 'house.' See also **endocentric.**

ex·o·crine (ek'sōkrīn,), *adj.* secreting externally. See also **endocrine.**

exocrine gland, any gland secreting externally.

ex·o·don·tics (ek,sōdon'tiks), *n.* a branch of

dentistry concerned with the extraction of teeth. **—ex,o·don'tist,** *n.*

ex·o·dus (ek'sədəs), *n.* **1.** a leaving; migration. **2.** (E-) the migration of the Israelites from Egypt, led by Moses.

ex·o·er·gic (ek,sōû'jik), *adj.* (in chemistry) denoting a reaction in which energy is liberated. See also **endoergic.**

ex of·fi·ci·o (eks əfisн'ēō), in the capacity of one holding an official position.

ex·og·a·my (eksog'əmē), *n.* marriage outside a specified group. See also **endogamy.**

ex·og·e·nous (eksoj'ənəs), *adj.* with an external origin.

ex·on (eks'on), *n.* a segment of a gene that is expressed; i.e. one that codes for (part of) the gene product or itself regulates expression of the gene. Compare **intron.**

ex·on·er·ate (igzon'ərāt,), *v.* to free from blame; rid (someone) of the burden of responsibility, esp. for a bad or illegal action.

ex·o·path·ic (eksōpaтн'ik), *adj.* (of a disease) externally caused.

ex·o·pha·sia (eks,sōfā'zēə), *n.* normal, voiced speech. See also **endophasia.**

ex·o·ra·ble (ek'sərəbəl), *adj.* able to be persuaded.

ex·or·cise (ek'sôəsīz), *v.* to attempt to expel an evil presence by religious ceremonies. **ex'or·cism,,** *n.* **—ex'or·cist,** *n.*

ex·or·di·um (eksô'dēəm), *n.*, *pl.* **ex·or·di·ums,** **ex·or·di·a** (eksô'dēə). a beginning.

ex·o·skel·e·ton (ek,sōskel'itən), *n.* a hard, external covering, as that of an insect, turtle, etc. See also **endoskeleton.**

ex·os·mo·sis (ek,sozmō'sis), *n.* **1.** osmosis from the inside to the outside. **2.** (in osmosis) movement from an area of high density to one of low density. Also **ex,os·mose'.** See also **endosmosis.**

ex·o·sphere (ek'sōsfēə,), *n.* the topmost layer of the atmosphere.

ex·o·ter·ic (ek,sōter'ik), *adj.* appropriate for general dissemination.

ex·o·ter·i·ca (ek,sōter'əkə), *n.* exoteric ideas, etc.

ex·o·ther·mic (ek,sōтнû'mik), *adj.* pertaining to a chemical change involving the giving off of heat. See also **endothermic.**

ex par·te (eks pär'tē), from one side only, as in a dispute.

ex·pa·ti·ate (ikspā'sнēat,, ekspā'sнēāt,), *v.* to enlarge upon.

ex·pec·to·rant (ikspek'tərənt), *adj.* inducing fluid, as saliva or mucus, to flow from the respiratory tract.

ex·pec·to·rate (ikspek'tərāt,), *v.* to spit; to cough up from the lungs. **—ex·pec,to·ra'tion,** *n.*

ex·pe·di·ent (ikspē'dēənt), *adj.* **1.** suitable; advantageous. **—n.** **2.** the means to an end; a

necessary action. **—ex·pe·di·en·tial** (ikspē,dēen'-sнəl), *adj.* **—ex·pe'di·en·cy,** *n.*

ex·ped·i·tate (eksped'itāt,), *v.* to remove the claws or pads of (a hound) to discourage its deer chasing. **—ex·ped,i·ta'tion,** *n.*

ex·pe·dite (eks'pidīt,), *v.* **ex·pe·dit·ed, ex·pe·dit·ing.** to cause (a process or procedure) to move along quickly; hasten, esp. by using efficient or more effective means. **—ex,pe·di'tion,** *n.*

ex·pe·di·tious (ek,spidisн'əs), *adj.* quick; fast; speedy.

ex·pe·ri·en·tial (ikspēr,ēen'sнəl), *adj.* acquired through experience.

ex·per·tise (ek,spûtēz'), *n.* skill; expert knowledge.

ex·pi·ate (ek'spēāt,), *v.* to make amends for. **—ex,pi·a'tion,** *n.*

ex·pla·nate (eks'plənāt,), *adj.* flattened out; spread.

ex·plant (eksplant'), *v.* to put living tissue into a culture medium.

ex·ple·tive (iksplē'tiv), *adj.* **1.** (of words) without real meaning but for emphasis; serving to fill up a sentence. **—n.** **2.** a profane word or oath.

ex·pli·can·dum (ek,splikan'dəm), *n.*, *pl.* **ex·pli·can·da** (ek,splikan'də). something to be explained, as a philosophical term.

ex·pli·cans (eks'pləkanz,), *n.*, *pl.* **ex·pli·can·ti·a** (eks,pləkan'cнēə). the meaning of a term, as in philosophy.

ex·pli·cate (eks'pləkāt,), *v.* to make clear. **—ex,pli·ca'tion,** *n.*

ex·pli·ca·tion de texte (eksplēkäsyôn də tekst'). *pl.* **ex·pli·ca·tions de texte** (eksplēkäsyôn də tekst'). *French.* literary criticism involving analysis with emphasis on language, style, and content to explain the meaning and symbolism of the integrated whole.

ex·plic·it (iksplis'it), *adj.* completely expressed; plainly stated. See also **implicit.**

ex·po·nent (ekspō'nənt), *n.* **1.** one who advocates or champions a cause or idea. **2.** one who explains or interprets. **3.** (in maths) a number or other symbol written as a superscript to an expression to signify the number of times the expression is to be multiplied by itself. Also called: **power, index.** **—adj.** **4.** providing an explanation or interpretation.

ex·po·nen·tial (eks,pōnen'sнəl), *adj.* See **geometric.**

ex·pos·i·tor (ikspoz'itə), *n.* someone who provides an explanation.

ex post fac·to (eks' pōst fak'tō), from or by subsequent action; subsequently.

ex·pos·tu·late (ikspos'tyōōlāt,), *v.* to protest; remonstrate. **—ex·pos·tu·la'tion,** *n.*

ex·pro·pri·ate (eksprō'prēāt,), *v.* to take over, esp. by the state for the public benefit. **—ex·pro,-pri·a'tion,** *n.*

ex·pugn·a·ble (ekspyōō'nəbəl), *adj.* defeatable; conquerable.

ex·punc·tion (ikspuNGK'sHən), *n.* an erasion; an act of expunging.

ex·pur·gate (eks'pəgāt,), *v.* to remove offensive parts from (a book).

ex·san·gui·nate (iksaNG'gwināt,), *v.* to take the blood from.

ex·san·guine (iksaNG'gwin), *adj.* anaemic.

ex·san·guin·ous (iksaNG'gwinəs), *adj.* bloodless; anaemic.

ex·scind (eksind'), *v.* to cut out; destroy.

ex·sect (eksekt'), *v.* to cut out.

ex·sert (eksût'), *v.* to thrust out; project.

ex·sic·cate (ek'sikāt,), *v.* to dry; dehydrate.

ex·tant (ekstant', ek'stənt), *adj.* remaining; still in existence.

ex·tem·po·re (ikstem'pərē), *adv.* **1.** without prior detailed preparation. —*adj.* **2.** (of a speech) delivered from informal notes rather than from a prepared text. See also **impromptu.**

ex·ten·si·fi·ca·tion (eksten,sifikā'sHən), *n.* (in agriculture) the adoption of production systems requiring relatively less capital; the reverse of intensification. —**ex·ten·si·fy,** *v.*

ex·ten·sile (iksten'sīl), *adj.* able to be extended.

ex·ten·sion (iksten'sHən), *n.* (in logic) a class of things that can be covered by one term, as *Hamlet* and *Death of a Salesman* can be classed as *'tragedy'*. Also **extent.** See also **intension.**

ex·ten·som·e·ter (eks,tensom'itə), *n.* a device for measuring extremely small amounts of expansion.

ex·ten·sor (iksten'sə), *n.* a muscle which stretches or straightens part of the body.

ex·ten·u·ate (iksten'yōōāt,), *v.* to show an offence, etc., to be less serious. —**ex·ten·u·a'tion,** *n.*

ex·tern (eks'tûn), *n. U.S.* someone connected with an institution but not living in it. See also **houseman.**

ex·ter·o·cep·tor (ek'stərōsep,tə), *n.* a receptor responsive to outside stimuli. —**ex·ter·o·cep'- tive,** *adj.*

ex·tir·pate (ek'stəpāt), *v.* to uproot; destroy totally. —**ex,tir·pa'tion,** *n.*

ex·tor·tion (ikstô'sHən), *n.* to exact from someone illegally, as by threat, violence, illegal use of authority of an office, etc.

ex·tor·tion·ate (ikstô'sHənit), *adj.* excessive; exorbitant; amounting to extortion.

ex·trac·tive (ekstrak'tiv), *adj.* serving to extract; able to be extracted.

ex·tra·dite (eks'trədīt), *v.* to hand over (a criminal, etc.) to another nation. —**ex'tra·dit,a- ble,** *adj.* —**ex·tra·di·tion** (eks,trədisH'ən), *n.*

ex·tra·ga·lac·tic (ek,strəgəlak'tik), *adj.* beyond the Milky Way.

ex·tra·mar·i·tal (ek,strəmar'itəl), *adj.* pertaining to sexual relations with a person other than one's wife or husband.

ex·tra·mun·dane (ek,strəmun'dān), *adj.* outside the world or the known universe.

ex·tra·mu·ral (ek,strəmyōōr'əl), *adj.* involving members of several schools. See also **intramural.**

ex·tra·phys·i·cal (ek,strəfiz'ikəl), *adj.* not subject to physical laws.

ex·trap·o·late (ikstrap'əlāt,), *v.* to deduce (something unknown) from something known.

ex·tra·pu·ni·tive (ek,strəpyōō'nitiv), *adj.* (in ridding oneself of frustrations) behaving hostilely towards other people or objects. See also **impunitive.**

ex·tra·sen·so·ry (ek,strəsen'sərē), *adj.* beyond normal perception.

ex·tra·sys·to·le (ek,strəsis'təlē), *n.* a premature contraction of the heart interrupting the normal heartbeat. See also **systole.**

ex·tra·ter·res·tri·al (ek,strətəres'trēəl), *adj.* from a place other than the earth.

ex·trav·a·sate (ikstrav'əsāt,), *v.* to force out or pour out, as blood or lava. —**ex·trav·a·sa'tion,** *n.*

ex·tri·cate (eks'trikāt), *v.* **ex·tri·cat·ed, ex·tri·cat·ing.** to manage to remove (something) from a place or a collection of other things, esp. with some difficulty and at the expense of effort, ingenuity, etc., as *They extricated three bodies from the wreckage.*

ex·trin·sic (ekstrin'sik), *adj.* external; coming from outside.

ex·tro·spec·tion (ek,strōspek'sHən), *n.* the observation of externals.

ex·tro·vert (ek'strəvût), *n.* a person concerned with the things and people about him. Also **ex·tra·vert** (ek'strəvût). See also **introvert.**

ex·tru·sile (ikstrōō'sīl), *adj.* able to be extruded.

ex·u·ber·ant (igzyōō'bərənt), *adj.* characterized by unrestrained enthusiasm and joy. —**ex·u'ber·ance,** *n.*

ex·u·date (eks'yōōdāt,), *n.* something exuded.

ex·ude (igzyōōd'), *v.* to seep out slowly in small quantities, as sweat. —**ex,u·da'tion,** *n.*

ex·urb (ek'sûb), *n. U.S.* a relatively small community outside a city's suburbs. —**ex·ur'ban,** *adj.* —**ex·ur'ban·ite,** *n.*

ex·ur·bi·a (eksû'bēə), *n. U.S.* all communities constituting the totality of all exurbs.

ex·u·vi·ae (igzyōō'viē), *n. pl.* any shells or coverings of animals that have been shed.

ex·u·vi·ate (igzyōō'vēāt,), *v.* to shed, as exuviae.

eyre (eə), *n.* a journey in a circuit, as that formerly travelled by circuit justices.

F

Fa·ber·gé (fabəzнā'), *n.* fine gold and enamel ware made in Russia before the Russian Revolution, esp. that designed and made by Peter Carl Fabergé (1846–1920).

Fa·bi·an Society (fā'bēən), a society dedicated to the peaceful spread of socialism.

fab·ri·cant (fab'rikənt), *n.* a manufacturer.

fab·u·list (fab'yəlist), *n.* a liar.

fa·çade (fəsäd', fasäd'), *n.* the front of an impressive building.

fac·et (fas'it), *n.* a polished face of a gemstone; a phase, side, view, or aspect of anything, as an issue.

fa·ce·ti·ae (fəsē'sнiē), *n. pl.* humorous or clever sayings.

fa·ce·tious (fəsē'sнəs), *adj.* witty; amusing; frivolous, as *a facetious remark*.

facial neuralgia. See **tic douloureux.**

fa·ci·es (fā'sнiēz), *n., pl.* **fa·ci·es. 1.** appearance, aspect, or nature of anything. **2.** (in medicine) a facial expression symptomatic of a certain disease or condition.

fac·ile (fas'il), *adj.* dexterous; fluent; moving or acting with ease.

fa·cil·i·tate (fəsil'itāt), *v.* to make easy or easier; to further. —**fa·cil,i·ta'tion**, *n.*

fa·cin·o·rous (fəsin'ərəs), *adj.* excessively wicked.

façonné, faconne (fas'ənā), *adj.* **1.** describing a fabric with the pattern woven in. —*n.* **2.** such a fabric.

fac·tion (fak'sнən), *n.* a united body of persons, esp. a group within a larger group. —**fac'·tion·al**, *adj.* —**fac·tious** (fak'sнəs), *adj.*

fac·ti·tious (faktisн'əs), *adj.* artificial; conventional; affected.

fac·toid (fak'toid), *n.* something that is a piece of questionable information accepted as a fact simply because of its presentation or repetition, esp. in print.

fac·tor (fak'tə), *n.* (in commerce) a commercial organization engaged in financing wholesale or retail sales through the purchase of accounts receivable.

fac·ture (fak'cнə), *n.* the act of making or constructing something.

fac·ul·ta·tive (fak'əltətiv), *adj.* granting a privilege, permission, or faculty.

faille (fīl, fāl), *n.* a soft, ribbed fabric of rayon or silk.

failsafe (fāl'sāf,), *adj.* involving or designating a built-in mechanism or device designed to prevent malfunction or unintentional operation, as in a nuclear-armed aircraft or warning system.

fai·naigue (fənāg'), *v.* to deceive; to finagle or cheat someone.

fai·né·ant (fā'nēənt), *adj.* idle; lazy; indolent.

fair-trade agreement, an agreement under which a retailer undertakes to sell a product at no less than a minimum price set by the manufacturer.

fait ac·com·pli (fet akônplē'), *pl.* **faits ac·com·plis** (fez akônplē'). a thing already done; an accomplished fact, so that argument or discussion are useless.

Fa·lange (fa'lanj), *n.* a Fascist organization that became the official political party of Spain after the Spanish Civil War of 1936–39. —**Fa·lan'gist,** *n.*

fal·cate (fal'kāt), *adj.* curved; sickle-shaped; hooked.

fal·ci·form (fal'sifôm), *adj.* shaped like a sickle; falcate.

fal·la·cy (fal'əsē), *n.* an error; an erroneous, false, or misleading idea, belief, theory, etc. —**fal·la'cious,** *adj.*

fal·lal, fal·lal (fallal'), *n.* a frivolous piece of finery; a useless article of dress.

fal·li·ble (fal'əbəl), *adj.* **1.** (of persons) likely to be mistaken or to err. **2.** likely to be false or inaccurate.

fal·ter (fôl'tə), *v.* to pause or hesitate, esp. from indecision or uncertainty.

fa·ma·cide (fā'məsīd), *n.* (in law) a person who defames the reputation of another; a slanderer.

fam·u·lus (fam'yələs), *n., pl.* **fam·u·li** (fam'yəlī). an assistant, esp. of a medieval sorcerer or scholar.

fan·fa·ron (fan'fəron), *n.* a boaster or braggart.

fan·fa·ron·ade (fan,fərənād'), *n.* boasting talk; bravado; bluster.

Fanny May, *U.S.* nickname for the Federal National Mortgage Association. [from the initials FNMA]

fan·tasm (fan'tazəm), *n.* phantasm.

fan·tast, phan·tast (fan'tast), *n.* a fanciful dreamer; visionary.

far·ad (far'əd), *n.* an electrical unit of capacitance equivalent to one coulomb per volt.

far·ceur (fäsû'), *n. French*. **1.** a writer of farces. **2.** an actor in farces. **3.** a practical joker.

far·ci (färsē'), *adj*. (in cookery) stuffed.

far·i·na·ceous (far,inā'sHəs), *adj*. containing or made from flour or meal.

far·i·nose (far'inōs, far'inōz,), *adj*. resembling farina; mealy.

far·rag·i·nous (fəraj'inəs), *adj*. mixed; heterogeneous.

far·ra·go (fərä'gō), *n., pl*. **far·ra·goes**. a jumbled mixture; hotchpotch; confusion.

far·ri·er (far'ēə), *n*. a man who shoes horses; a blacksmith. —**far'ri·er·y**, *n*.

far·thin·gale (fär'THiNGgāl,), *n*. a hoop or openwork frame worn under a woman's skirt in the 16th and 17th centuries to make it bell out.

fas·ces (fas'ēz), *n*. a bundle of rods bound around an axe with projecting blade, carried before Roman magistrates as a symbol of authority.

fas·ci·a (fāsHēə), *n., pl*. **fas·ci·ae** (fāsH'ēē). any long, flat, vertical surface.

fas·ci·ate (fasH'ēāt,), *adj*. bound with a band, strip, or bandage. Also **fas'ci·at,ed**. —**fas,ci·a'-tion**, *n*.

fas·ci·cle (fas'ikəl), *n*. **1.** a close cluster or tight bundle. **2.** one part of a book being published in instalments. —**fas·cic'u·lar** (fəsik'yələ), *adj*. —**fas·cic'u·late**, *adj*. —**fas·cic,u·la'tion**, *n*.

fas·ci·cule (fas'ikyōōl,), *n*. a fascicle, esp. of a book. Also **fas·cic·u·lus** (fəsik'yələs).

fas·cism (fasH'izəm), *n*. (sometimes **F-**) an authoritarian and aggressively nationalistic dictatorship that forcibly suppresses opposition, completely controls industry and commerce, etc. —**fas'cist**, *n*.

fas·tid·i·ous (fastid'ēəs), *adj*. particular; hard to please; excessively critical.

fas·tig·i·ate (fastij'ēit, fastij'ēāt,), *adj*. tapering to a point. Also **fas·tig'i·at,ed**.

fas·tu·ous (fas'tyōōəs), *adj*. **1.** haughty; overbearing. **2.** ostentatious; pretentious.

fat cat, *U.S. Slang*. an important, wealthy, or influential person.

fath·o·gram (faTH'ōgram,), *n*. a visual representation of sound waves recorded by a sonic depth finder.

fa·tid·ic (fātid'ik), *adj*. pertaining to divination or prophecy; prophetic. Also **fa·tid'i·cal**.

fa·tu·i·tous (fətyōō'itəs), *adj*. foolish; imbecile.

fa·tu·i·ty (fətyōō'itē), *n*. **1.** stupidity; foolishness. **2.** something silly or inane.

fat·u·ous (fat'yōōəs), *adj*. complacently foolish or stupid; silly, as *a fatuous remark*.

fat·wa, fat·wah (fat'wə), *n*. a decree issued by a Muslim religious leader.

fau·cal (fô'kəl), *adj*. **1.** concerning or involving the fauces or opening of the throat. **2.** guttural.

fau·na (fô'nə), *n., pl*. **fau·nas, fau·nae** (fô'nē).

all of the animals, insects, etc., of a particular area, region, continent, planet, etc. See also **flora**.

faute de mieux (fōt də myû'). *French*. for want of anything better.

faux-na·ïf (fōnäēf'), *adj*. **1.** contriving to appear simple or unsophisticated. —*n*. **2.** one who pretends to be unworldly or naive.

faux pas (fō pä'), *pl*. **faux pas**. a blunder, esp. in manners or etiquette; an indiscretion.

fa·ve·o·late (fəvē'əlāt,), *adj*. honeycombed; containing cells.

Fa·vrile glass (fəvrēl'), *Trademark*. a blown glass introduced by Tiffany c. 1890 and used for vases, etc. Also **Tiffany glass**.

fa·vus (fā'vəs), *n., pl*. **fa·vi** (fā'vī). a hexagonal tile or stone for paving.

fawn (fôn), *v*. to pretend to like someone by flattering him, doing him favours, and behaving like a toady, as *Her fans fawned over her, giving her money and gifts*.

faze (fāz), *v*. to cause to feel disturbed, embarrassed, or disconcerted.

fe·al·ty (fē'əltē), *n*. loyalty; fidelity.

fea·si·ble (fē'zəbəl), *adj*. workable; able to be done. —**fea,si·bil'i·ty**, *n*.

feather tract. See pteryla.

feath·er·weight (feTH'əwāt,), *n*. a boxer between bantamweight and lightweight, weighing 126 pounds or less.

feat·ly (fēt'lē), *adv*. **1.** suitably; aptly. **2.** nimbly; adroitly. **3.** neatly; gracefully.

fe·bric·i·ty (fibris'itē), *n*. the state of being feverish.

fe·bric·u·la (fibrik'yələ), *n*. a slight and brief fever.

feb·ri·fa·cient (feb,rifā'sHənt), *adj*. producing fever.

fe·brif·er·ous (fibrif'ərəs), *adj*. producing fever.

fe·brif·ic (fibrif'ik), *adj*. having or producing fever.

feb·ri·fuge (feb'rifyōōj), *adj*. **1.** reducing fever, as a medicine. —*n*. **2.** a fever-reducing agent. **3.** a cooling drink. —**fe·brif·u·gal** (fibrif'yəgəl, feb,-rifyōō'gəl), *adj*.

fe·brile (fē'brīl), *adj*. of or characterized by a fever; feverish.

fe·cit (fā'kit), *v. Latin*. he (or she) made (it); at one time used on works of art after the name of the artist. *Abbr.:* **fe., fec**.

feck·less (fek'lis), *adj*. reckless; inefficient; incompetent; without worth or spirit; indifferent.

fec·u·la (fek'yələ), *n., pl*. **fec·u·lae** (fek'yəlē). faecal matter, esp. of insects; dregs; filth; foul matter. —**fec'u·lent**, *adj*.

fe·cund (fē'kənd, fek'ənd), *adj*. fertile; prolific; fruitful. —**fe·cun'di·ty**, *n*.

fe·cun·date (fē'kəndāt,, fek'əndāt,), *v*. **1.** to

make fruitful. **2.** to fertilize; impregnate; polli-nate.

fed·a·yee (fedä'yē), *n., pl.* **fed·a·yeen** (fədä'-yēn). *Arabic.* an Arab commando.

feign (fān), *v.* to pretend; to make a false show of, as *to feign sleep.*

feist·y (fī'stē), *adj.* quarrelsome; belligerent.

fe·li·cif·ic (fē,lisif'ik), *adj.* producing or tending to produce happiness.

fe·lic·i·tous (filis'itəs), *adj.* appropriate or suit-able; fitting.

fe·lic·i·ty (filis'itē), *n.* bliss; happiness.

fel·lah (fel'ə), *n., pl.* **fel·lahs, fel·la·heen** (fel,-əhēn'). Egyptian peasant or labourer.

fell·mon·ger (fel'muNG,gə, fel'moNG,gə), *n.* a dealer in sheepskins or other animal skins.

fel·loe (fel'ō), *n.* the rim, or portion of the rim, of a spoked wheel. Also **fel'ly.**

fe·lo-de-se (fē,lōdisē', fel,ōdisē'), *n., pl.* **fe·lo-nes-de-se** (fē,lōnēz,disē', fel,ōnēz,disē'). one who commits suicide.

feme (fem), *n.* (in law) a woman or wife.

feme co·vert (kuv'ət), (in law) a married woman.

feme sole (sōl), (in law) an unmarried woman; spinster, widow, or divorcée; a married woman financially independent of her husband.

fem·i·cide (fem'isīd), *n.* the act of killing a woman.

fem·i·nie (fem'ənē), *n.* women collectively; womankind.

femme fa·tale (fem fətal'), *pl.* **femmes fa·tales** (fem fətal'). *French.* an alluring woman, esp. one who leads men to their downfall.

fem·o·ral (fem'ərəl), *adj.* relating to the thigh or thighbone.

fe·mur (fē'mə), *n.* the thighbone.

fe·nes·tra (fines'trə), *n., pl.* **fe·nes·trae** (fines'-trē). a small opening, as in a bone or membrane.

fen·es·tra·tion (fen,istrā'sHən), *n.* the ar-rangement of windows and doors in a building.

fe·ra·cious (fərä'sHəs), *adj.* fruitful; producing abundantly.

fe·ral[1] (fēr'əl, fer'əl), *adj.* wild; undomesti-cated; uncivilized.

fe·ral[2] (fēr'əl), *adj.* fatal; funereal; gloomy.

fe·ri·al (fēr'ēəl), *adj.* pertaining to a holiday.

fe·rine (fēr'īn, fēr'in), *adj.* wild; untamed; feral.

fer·i·ty (fer'itē), *n.* the state of being wild or savage; ferocity.

fer·re·ous (fer'ēəs), *adj.* like, of, or containing iron.

fer·ro·mag·net·ic (fer,ōmagnet'ik), *adj.* per-taining to a material, such as iron, that below a certain temperature can possess magnetization in the absence of any external magnetic field. See also **antiferromagnetic, diamagnetic, per-amagnetic.**

fer·ru·gi·nous (feröö'jinəs), *adj.* containing iron or iron rust; rust-coloured.

fer·u·la·ceous (fer,ōōlä'sHəs), *adj.* like or per-taining to canes or reeds.

fer·vent (fû'vənt), *adj.* having or showing great warmth of feeling; passionate; ardent.

fer·vid (fû'vid), *adj.* passionate; intense; fer-vent.

fer·vour (fû'və), *n.* intense feeling; zeal; ard-our.

fes·tal (fes'təl), *adj.* of or suitable to a joyous occasion or festival.

fes·ti·na len·te (festē'nä len'tē), *Latin.* make haste slowly.

Fest·schrift (fest'sHrift,), *n., pl.* **Fest·schrift·en** (fest'sHrift,ən), **Fest·schrifts.** a collection of arti-cles contributed by the colleagues of a writer or scholar and published in his honour.

fe·tial (fēsHəl), *adj.* relating to declarations of war and peace treaties.

fet·id, foet·id (fet'id, fē'tid), *adj.* stinking; putrid.

fe·tip·a·rous, foe·tip·a·rous (fētip'ərəs), *adj.* bearing young that are not fully developed, as marsupials.

fe·tor, foe·tor (fē'tə, fē'tôə), *n.* a strong, dis-agreeable smell; stench.

fet·tle (fet'l), *n.* condition; state; health.

fet·tu·ci·ne, fet·tuc·ci·ne (*Ital.*), **fet·tu·ci·ni** (fe,tōōcHē'nē), *n.* pasta in the form of slender ribbon-like strips, wider than linguini.

feuil·le·ton (fu'iton,), *n.* a part of a newspaper containing serialized fiction, light or popular pieces of writing, etc.

fey (fā'), *adj.* enchanted or as if enchanted; vaguely detached from everyday reality.

fi·a·cre (fēä'krə), *n., pl.* **fi·a·cres.** a four-wheeled carriage for hire.

fi·as·co (fēas'kō), *n., pl.* **fi·as·cos, fi·as·coes.** an utter failure.

fi·at (fē'at, fī'ət, fī'at), *n.* order; decree; sanction.

fi·bre·glass (fī'bəgläs,), *n.* molten glass pro-cessed into fine filaments, often used in woolly masses as insulating material or pressed and moulded into construction material.

fibre optics, the study of the longitudinal transmission of images through a flexible bun-dle of optical glass fibres.

fi·bri·form (fī'brifôm, fib'rifôm), *adj.* like a fibre.

fi·bril (fī'bril), *n.* a small, threadlike fibre or filament. —**fi·bril·lar** (fī'brilə, fibril'ə), —**fi·bril'-li·form,,** *adj.*

fi·bril·la·tion (fī,brilä'sHən, fib,rilä'sHən), *n.* uncontrolled contractions of muscular fibrils, as in a tic.

fi·bril·lose (fibril'ōs), *adj.* composed of or con-taining fibrils.

fi·brin (fī'brin, fib'rin), *n.* an elastic, fibrous, insoluble protein found in coagulated blood. —**fi'brin·ous**, *adj.*

fi·broid (fī'broid), *adj.* like or consisting of fibres or fibrous tissue.

fi·bro·ma (fībrō'mə), *n., pl.* **fi·bro·ma·ta** (fībrō'mətə), **fi·bro·mas.** a tumour composed largely of fibrous tissue.

fi·bro·pla·sia (fī,brōplā'zēə), *n.* the formation of fibrous tissue. —**fi,bro·plas'tic,** *adj.*

fi·bro·sis (fībrō'sis), *n.* abnormal growth of excess fibroid tissue in an organ. —**fi·brot·ic** (fibrot'ik), *adj.*

fic·tile (fik'tīl), *adj.* that can be moulded; plastic.

fic·tive (fik'tiv), *adj.* invented; fictitious.

fi·du·ci·ar·y (fidoō'sHēərē), *n.* **1.** a person holding property or power of attorney in behalf of another. —*adj.* **2.** descriptive or relating to such a relationship.

FIFO, *Abbr.:* **first-in, first-out.**

Fifth Amendment, an amendment to the U.S. Constitution guaranteeing chiefly that no person be required to testify against himself or be tried twice for the same offence.

fifth column, persons within a country who are in secret sympathy with and prepared to help an enemy. —**fifth-col'umn,** *adj.*

fifth generation *adj.* describing development of computers equipped with artificial intelligence.

fig·ment (fig'mənt), *n.* something made up or imagined; a fantasy.

fig·ur·a·tive (fig'ərətiv), *adj.* relating to something that is imaginary; not literal in meaning; not real, as *'Fifth wheel' is a figurative expression for 'an unnecessary, additional person'.*

fi·lar (fī'lə), *adj.* of, relating to, or having threads.

fi·lasse (filas'), *n.* any of several vegetable fibres, excluding cotton, processed for yarn manufacture.

fi·late (fī'lāt), *adj.* threadlike.

fil·a·ture (fil'əcHə), *n.* a device for the reeling of silk from cocoons.

fil·i·al (fil'ēəl, fil'yəl), *adj.* concerning a son or a daughter, or to a relationship similar to that of a son or a daughter, as *filial duties.*

fil·i·cide (fil'isīd), *n.* the killing of a son or daughter.

fil·i·form (fil'ifôm,, fī'lifôm,), *adj.* having the form of a thread; threadlike.

fil·mog·ra·phy (filmog'rəfi), *n.* a list of films made by a particular director or featuring a particular actor or actress or other film figure.

fi·lose (fī'lōs, fī'lōz), *adj.* threadlike.

fim·bri·ate (fim'brēit, fim'brēāt,), *adj.* having a border of hairs; fringed. Also **fim'bri·at,ed**. —**fim,bri·a'tion,** *n.*

fim·bril·late (fim'brilit, fim'brilāt,), *adj.* having a small fringe or fringelike border.

fi·na·gle (finā'gəl), *v.* to obtain or manoeuvre by trickery; to cheat.

fi·nal·ism (fī'nəliz,əm), *n.* the belief that events are determined by final causes.

fin de siè·cle (faN də sye'kl), *French.* the end of the century.

fi·nesse (fines'), *n.* **1.** subtlety and skill in performance. —*v.* **2.** to manage by finesse.

fi·nes·tra (fines'trə), *n.* an opening, esp. for ventilation in the wall of a tomb.

fin·ger·ling (fiNG'gəliNG), *n.* a small or young fish less than a year old.

fin·i·al (fin'ēəl, fī'nēəl), *n.* an ornamental feature terminating the top of a piece of furniture, as a lamp.

fin·i·cal (fin'ikəl), *adj.* fussy; finicky.

fink (fiNGk), *Slang, esp. U.S. and Canada,* —*n.* **1.** an informer, esp. a police informer. **2.** a strikebreaker; blackleg. **3.** an unpleasant or despicable person. —*v.* **4.** to inform on someone, esp. to the police.

fin·nan had·die (fin'ən had'ē), smoked haddock. Also **fin'nan had'dock.**

fire·damp (fīr'damp,), *n.* a combustible gas, largely methane, formed in coal mines, that is highly explosive when mixed with a certain proportion of air.

fir·kin (fû'kin), *n.* a small wooden tub for butter, lard, etc.

fir·ma·ment (fû'məmənt), *n.* the sky.

firn (fēən), *n.* See **névé.**

firn·i·fi·ca·tion (fû,nifikā'sHən), *n.* the process by which snow changes into névé.

First Amendment, an amendment to the U.S. Constitution guaranteeing freedom from laws respecting establishment of a religion and freedom of worship, of speech, of the press, of assembly, and of the right to petition the government for a redress of grievances.

first-in, first-out, a book-keeping device that assumes items purchased first will be sold first. *Abbr.:* FIFO. See also **last-in, first-out.**

fisc (fisk), *n.* a royal or state treasury.

fishskin disease. See **ichthyosis.**

fis·sile (fis'īl), *adj.* able to be split; fissionable.

fis·sion (fisH'ən), *n.* **1.** a splitting apart; a breaking up into parts. **2.** Also **nuclear fission.** the splitting of heavy atoms into lighter atoms producing atomic energy: the principle of the atom bomb. See also **fusion.**

fis·sip·a·rous (fisip'ərəs), *adj.* reproducing young by fission.

fis·tu·la (fis'tyoōlə), *n.* a narrow tube or duct. —**fis'tu·lous,** *adj.*

fitch·er (ficH'ə), *v.* (in drilling) to clog from accumulation of the substance being drilled.

fix·ate (fik'sāt), *v.* to make or become fixed. —**fix·a'tion,** *n.*

fix·a·tive (fik'sətiv), *n.* a liquid sprayed on something to preserve it by preventing contact with the air.

fl. See **floruit.**

fla·bel·late (fləbel'it, fləbel'āt), *adj.* fan-shaped. Also **fla·bel'li·form,.**

fla·bel·lum (fləbel'əm), *n., pl.* **fla·bel·la** (fləbel'ə). a large fan used in religious ceremonies.

flac·cid (flak'sid, flas'id), *adj.* flabby; limp.

flac·on (flak'ən), *n.* a small flask with a stopper. See also **flagon.**

flag (flag), *n.* See **masthead.**

flag·el·lant (flaj'ələnt, fləjel'ənt), *n.* one who whips himself for religious discipline or sexual stimulation.

flag·el·late (flaj'ilit, flaj'ilāt,), *adj.* producing runners, as the strawberry.

fla·gel·li·form (fləjel'ifôm,), *adj.* long, slender, and tapering; whiplike.

fla·gi·tious (fləjish'əs), *adj.* shamefully wicked; vile; heinous.

fla·gon (flag'ən), *n.* a large vessel for liquids; a large wine bottle. See also **flacon.**

fla·grant (flā'grənt), *adj.* glaringly bad; notorious; outrageous. —**fla'grant·ly,** *adv.*

fla·gran·te de·lic·to (fləgran'tē dilik'tō), (in law) in the act of committing the crime.

flail (flāl), *n.* **1.** a wooden instrument for threshing grain by hand. —*v.* **2.** to strike or beat as with a flail.

flail·ing (flā'liNG), *adj.* (of arms) threshing wildly; waving; swinging.

flam·bé (flämbā'), *adj.* served in a sauce containing liquor set afire to flame. Also **flam·béed.**

flam·beau (flambō'), *n.* a lighted torch.

flame-out, flame·out (flām'out,), *n.* the stopping of combustion in a jet engine. Also **blowout.**

flan (flan), *n.* **1.** an open tart, filled with fruit, custard, cheese, etc. **2.** a sweetened egg custard made in Spain.

flâne·rie (flänrē'), *n.* French. idle strolling; dawdling.

flâ·neur (flänû'), *n.* French. idler; loafer; lounger.

flan·nel (flan'əl), *n.* a soft, loosely woven woollen or cotton material with a slightly napped surface.

flan·nel·board (flan'əlbôd,), *n.* a flannel-covered surface to which flannel cut-outs, such as letters and numbers, adhere, used in schools as a teaching aid.

flan·nel·et, flan·nel·ette (flan,əlet'), *n.* a soft cotton cloth resembling flannel.

flap·doo·dle (flap'dōō,dəl), *n. Slang.* foolish or senseless talk.

flat sour, *U.S. informal.* fermentation that occurs in tinned food after sealing.

flat·u·lent (flat'yələnt), *adj.* producing gas in the stomach or intestines.

fla·tus (flā'təs), *n., pl.* **fla·tus·es.** an accumulation of gas in the stomach or intestines.

flaunt (flônt), *v.* to display oneself conspicuously; to show off ostentatiously.

F layer, the highest layer of the ionosphere where high-frequency radiowaves are reflected back to earth.

flense (flens), *v.* to cut blubber or skin from a whale, seal, etc.

flesh·ly (flesh'lē), *adj.* of the body; carnal; sensual.

flesh·pot (flesh'pot,), *n.* a place providing luxurious bodily comforts and pleasures.

fletch·er (flech'ə), *n.* a person who makes arrows.

fleu·rette (flôret', flûret'), *n.* an ornament formed like a small flower.

fleu·ron (flōō'ron, flûrôn'), *n.* a floral motif used in decoration.

flews (flōōz), *n. pl.* the loose, hanging parts of the upper lip of certain dogs, as bloodhounds.

flex·ile (flek'sīl), *adj.* flexible; pliant.

flex·or (flek'sə), *n.* a muscle that bends a limb or other part of the body.

flex·u·ous (flek'syōōəs), *adj.* winding; full of bends. Also **flex'u·ose.** —**flex,u·os'i·ty,** *n.*

flex·ure (flek'shə), *n.* act of bending; state of being flexed or bent.

flim·flam (flim'flam,), *n.* nonsense; rubbish; humbug.

flin·ders (flin'dəz), *n. pl.* splinters or fragments.

flip·pant (flip'ənt), *adj.* disrespectful; frivolous; lacking in seriousness. —**flip'pan·cy,** *n.*

flitch (flich), *n.* a side of bacon, salted and cured.

floc, flock (flok), *n.* a fine, flufly mass of particles, as in a precipitate.

floc·cil·la·tion (flok,silā'shən), *n.* delirious picking of the bedclothes by a patient. Also **carphology.**

floc·cu·late (flok'yōōlāt,), *v.* to form flocculent masses, as clouds, precipitates,etc.

floc·cule (flok'yōōl), *n.* something resembling a tuft of wool.

floc·cu·lent (flok'yōōlənt), *adj.* like or consisting of small tufts of wool; flaky; fluffy.

floc·cus (flok'əs), *n., pl.* **floc·ci** (flok'sī). a woolly or hairy tuft.

flo·ra (flôr'ə), *n., pl.* **flo·ras, flo·rae** (flôr'ē). all of the plants of a particular area, region, continent, planet, etc. See also **fauna.**

flo·res·cence (flôres'əns), *n.* period of flowering; blossoming. —**flo·res'cent,** *adj.*

flo·ret (flôr'it), *n.* a small flower.

flo·ri·at·ed (flô'rēā,tid), *adj.* decorated with floral ornament.

flo·ri·cul·ture (flō'rikul,CHə), *n.* cultivation of flowering plants, esp. under glass.

flor·id (flor'id), *adj.* **1.** ruddy; rosy. **2.** flowery; elaborately ornamented.

flo·rif·er·ous (flôrif'ərəs), *adj.* bearing flowers; flowering abundantly.

flo·ris·tic (flôris'tik), *adj.* of or having to do with flowers.

flor·u·it (flôr'ōōit), *v.* Latin for 'he or she flourished', used in reference to the year(s) of a person's accomplishments, esp. when birth and death dates are unknown. *Usually abbrev.:* fl.

flout (flout), *v.* to mock; scorn; to show disdain or contempt for.

flow chart, a diagram showing the progress of work in a manufacturing process, a sequence of operations in a computer program, etc.

flow diagram, (in computer technology) a chart showing the general flow of information for solving a problem by a computer.

flow·er·et (flou'ərit), *n.* a small flower; floret.

fluc·tu·ant (fluk'tyōōənt), *adj.* varying; unstable.

fluc·tu·ate (fluk'tyōōāt), *v.* **fluc·tu·at·ed, fluc·tu·at·ing.** to change continually; increase and decrease alternately; vary, as the value of the pound sterling.

flume (flōōm), *n.* a narrow ravine with a stream running through it.

flum·mer·y (flum'ərē), *n.* **1.** any of several dessert dishes made of flour, milk, sugar, and eggs. **2.** meaningless flattery; nonsense.

flu·o·resce (flōō,res'), *v.* to produce or show fluorescence. **—flu·o·res·cent,** *adj.*

flu·o·res·cence (flōō,res'əns), *n.* the emission of light by a substance while it is being acted upon by radiant energy, as light or x-rays. See also **phosphorescence.**

fluor·i·date (flōōr'idāt), *v.* to add fluorides to (a water supply), esp. to strengthen teeth. **—fluor·i·da'tion,** *n.*

fluor·o·scope (flōōr'əskōp), *n.* an instrument for examining internal structures by shadows cast by x-rays on a fluorescent screen. **—fluor·o·scop'ic,** *adj.*

fluo·ro·sis (flôrō'sis), *n.* poisoning due to excessive intake of fluoride, as from treated drinking water.

flu·vi·al (flōō'vēəl), *adj.* of or having to do with a river.

flu·vi·a·tile (flōō'vēətīl), *adj.* of or peculiar to rivers; found in rivers.

flu·vi·o·ma·rine (flōō,vēōmərēn'), *adj.* formed by the combined action of river and sea.

flux (fluks), *n.* **1.** a state of insecurity; continuous change; lack of direction. **2.** a substance used in metal refining that combines with impurities causing them to float off or coagulate. **3.** abnormal discharge of fluid from the bowels.

flux·ion (fluk'sHən), *n.* **1.** the act of flowing. **2.** a flux.

fly·weight (flī'wāt,), *n.* a boxer of the lightest class, weighing 112 pounds or less.

focal length, the distance from the optical centre of a lens to the point where the rays of light passing through it converge. Also **focal distance.**

focal-plane shutter, (in photography) a camera shutter placed directly in front of the film. See also **curtain shutter.**

fo·com·e·ter (fōkom'itə), *n.* an instrument for measuring the focal length of a lens.

foet·id. See fetid.

foe·tip·a·rous. See fetiparous.

foe·tor. See fetor.

fog·bow (fog'bō,), *n.* a phenomenon like a white rainbow, sometimes seen in a fog. Also **mistbow, seadog, white rainbow.**

fog·dog (fog'dog,), *n.* a bright spot sometimes seen in a fog.

fo·gram (fō'grəm), *n.* an old-fashioned or stuffy person. Also **fogrum.**

foi·ble (foi'bəl), *n.* a slight weakness or frailty in character.

foie gras (fwä grä'), the liver of specially fattened geese considered a table delicacy, esp. in paste form (**pâté de foie gras**).

foi·son (foi'zən), *n.* abundance; plenty.

foist (foist), *v.* to palm off; pass fraudulently.

fo·li·a·ture (fō'lēəCHə), *n.* mass of leaves; foliage.

fo·lie de gran·deur (folē' də grändû,), *n.* delusions of grandeur.

fo·li·ic·o·lous (fō,lēik'ələs), *adj.* parasitic on the leaves of plants.

fo·li·if·er·ous (fō,lēif'ərəs), *adj.* leaf-bearing.

fo·li·o·late (fō'lēəlāt,, fōlē'əlāt,, fōlē'əlit), *adj.* having or relating to leaflets.

fo·li·ose (fō'lēōs, fō'lēōz), *adj.* covered with leaves; leafy.

fo·li·um (fō'lēəm), *n., pl.* **fo·li·a** (fō'lēə). a thin layer or stratum.

folk etymology, popular but incorrect notion of the origin of a word, as *Welsh rarebit* from *Welsh rabbit.*

fol·li·cle (fol'ikəl), *n.* a small sac or gland. **—fol·lic'u·lar,** *adj.*

fo·ment (fōment'), *v.* to instigate; incite; stir up (trouble). **—fo,men·ta'tion,** *n.*

fo·mes (fō'mēz), *n., pl.* **fom·i·tes** (fō'mitēz). any agent, as clothing or bedding, capable of absorbing and transmitting germs.

fon·dant (fon'dənt), *n.* a soft, creamy sugar paste.

fon·du (fondyōō'), *n.* (in ballet) a gradual bending of the supporting leg.

fon·due (fondyōō', fon'dyōō), *n.* a dish of Swiss origin in which a food, such as cheese or chocolate, is served melted and kept warm as a dip for other bite-size foods.

font (font), *n. U.S.* fount.

font·al (fon'təl), *adj.* of or coming from a fountain or spring.

foot·le (fōot'əl), *v.* to talk or act in a foolish or trivial way.

foot·ling (fōot'linG), *adj.* trivial; insignificant; foolish; silly, as a *footling remark.*

foo·zle (fōo'zəl), *v.* to spoil by clumsiness; bungle.

fop (fop), *n.* a dandy; a man who is foolishly vain about his clothes, manners, etc. —**fop'per·y,** *n.* —**fop'pish,** *adj.*

for·age (for'ij), *n.* **1.** horse or cattle food; fodder. —*v.* **2.** to search for provisions; hunt; rummage.

fo·ra·men (forā'mən, fərā'mən), *n., pl.* **fo·ram·i·na** (fəram'inə, foram'inə). a small perforation, esp. in a bone or plant ovule.

fo·ram·i·nate (fəram'ināt), *adj.* having many holes or foramina. Also **fo·ram'i·nous.**

for·ay (for'ā), *n.* an incursion or raid, esp. in order to plunder; a sudden attack.

for·bear (fôbe'ə), *v.* **for·bore, for·borne, for·bear·ing.** to hold back; stop, as *I wish she would forbear telling everyone what she thinks.*

force ma·jeure (fôs mazHŌōr'), *pl.* **forces ma·jeures** (fôs mazHŬ'). (in law) an unavoidable event, as an act of God, that may serve as an excuse to abrogate a contract.

for·ci·pate (fô'sipāt), *adj.* like or having the shape of a forceps.

fore·bear (fô'be'ə), *n.* an ancestor.

fore·go (fôgō'), *v.* **fore·went, fore·gone, fore·go·ing.** to go before; precede, as *a foregone conclusion* or *See the foregoing.*

for·el, for·rel (for'əl), *n.* a slipcase for a book.

fo·ren·sic (fəren'sik), *adj.* pertaining to law courts; suited to argumentation; rhetorical.

forensic chemistry, the use of chemical facts in answering questions of law.

forensic medicine, the use of medical facts in answering questions of law; medical jurisprudence.

for·est·ry (for'istrē), *n.* the science of planting and taking care of forests.

for·fend (fôfend'), *v.* to defend or protect.

for·fi·cate (fô'fikit), *adj.* deeply notched or forked, as the tails of some birds.

for·go (fôgō'), *v.* **for·went, for·gone, for·go·ing.** to give up, yield, or sacrifice, as *You will have to forgo sweets if you want to avoid cavities.*

for·lorn (fəlôrn'), *adj.* sad, esp. as a result of feeling alone and deserted; miserable.

for·mic (fô'mik), *adj.* pertaining to ants.

for·mi·car·y (fô'mikərē), *n.* an anthill or ants' nest. Also **for·mi·car'i·um.**

for·mi·ca·tion (fô,mikā'sHən), *n.* a tingling sensation as of insects crawling over the skin.

for·mi·da·ble (fô'midəbəl), *adj.* dreadful; awesome and intimidating in power or magnitude.

for·nic·i·form (fônis'ifôm,), *adj.* in the form of an arched or vaulted structure.

for·sake (fôəsāk'), *v.* **for·sook** (fôəsōok'), **for·sak·en, for·sak·ing.** to leave alone; give up on; desert.

forte (fôt, fôtā), *n.* something at which one is exceptionally good; strong point.

forth·right (fôth'rīt,', *adj.* direct; not beating about the bush.

for·ti·tu·di·nous (fô,tityōod'inəs), *adj.* having patient courage; marked by strength of mind.

for·tu·i·tous (fôtyōo'itəs), *adj.* happening by chance; accidental.

for·tu·i·ty (fôtyōo'itē), *n.* the condition of being fortuitous; an accident or chance.

fos·sa (fos'ə), *n., pl.* **fos·sae** (fos'ē). cavity or pit, as in a bone.

fos·sette (foset'), *n.* a small hollow; a dimple.

fos·sick (fos'ik), *v., Austral.* **1.** to search for gold, esp. in abandoned workings. **2.** to hunt around; rummage. —**fos'sick·er,** *n.*

fos·sil·if·er·ous (fos,ilif'ərəs), *adj.* containing fossils.

fos·so·ri·al (fosô'rēəl), *adj.* burrowing or digging.

fou·droy·ant (fōodroi'ənt), *adj.* dazzling or stunning.

fou·lard (fōoläd'), *n.* a thin material of silk or rayon with printed design.

found·er (foun'də), *v.* to be wrecked, as a ship; sink.

fount (fount), *n.* (in printing) a complete set of type of one particular face and size.

Four Horsemen of the Apocalypse, riders on white, red, black, and pale horses symbolizing pestilence, war, famine, and death.

four·ra·gère (fōor'əzHeə), *n.* an ornamental cord worn on the shoulder of a military uniform.

fourth dimension, time, considered as an added dimension to three spatial dimensions.

fourth estate, journalism or journalists; the press.

fo·ve·a (fō'vēə), *n., pl.* **fo·ve·ae** (fō'viē). a small pit or depression in a bone or other structure. —**fo've·ate,,** *adj.*

fo·ve·o·la (fōvē'ələ), *n., pl.* **fo·ve·o·lae** (fōvē'əlē). a small fovea or pit. —**fo've·o·late,,** *adj.*

foxed (fokst), *adj.* **1.** tricked or deceived. **2.** (of book pages) stained reddish-brown or yellowish.

frac·tal (frak'təl), (in maths) —*n.* **1.** any of a class of irregular shapes generated by repeated subdivision of regular geometrical figures. —*adj.* **2.** of or relating to such a process.

frac·tious (frak'sнəs), *adj.* irritable; cross; rebellious; unruly.

fram·boe·sia, fram·be·sia (frambē'zēə), *n.* yaws.

fran·gi·ble (fran'jibəl), *adj.* breakable; fragile.

fran·gi·pane (fran'jipān,), *n.* **1.** an almond-flavoured cream, used esp. as a pastry filling. **2.** a cake mixture flavoured with ground almonds.

frap·pé (frap'ā), *n.* **1.** a drink, esp. a liqueur, served over crushed ice. —*adj.* **2.** (of a drink) chilled or iced.

frass (fras), *n.* excrement or debris left by insects.

frat·ri·cide (frat'risīd), *n.* the killing of one's own brother.

fraught (frôt), *adj.* filled or involved (with).

free association, (in psychoanalysis) the uninhibited expression of whatever ideas, memories, etc., come to mind, used to uncover and clarify the unconscious processes.

frem·i·tus (frem'itəs), *n., pl.* **frem·i·tus.** a vibration felt in palpation of the chest.

fre·nate (frē'nāt), *adj.* having a frenum or frenulum.

fre·ne·tic (frənet'ik), *adj.* frenzied; frantic.

fren·u·lum (fren'yələm), *n., pl.* **fren·u·la** (fren'-yələ). a small frenum.

fre·num (frē'nəm), *n., pl.* **fre·na** (frē'nə). the fold of skin or membrane that checks the movement of an organ or part, as the fold under the tongue.

fres·co (fres'kō), *n., pl.* **fres·coes, fres·cos.** the technique of painting with watercolours on wet plaster. See also **fresco secco.**

fre·sco sec·co (sek'ō), the technique of painting with watercolours on dry plaster. See also **fresco.**

Fres·nel lens (frānel'), a large lens composed of many small lenses producing a short focal length, used in spotlights, etc.

fret·work (fret'wûk,), *adj.* decorative carving of interlacing parts; openwork.

fri·a·ble (frī'əbəl), *adj.* easily crumbled, as soft plaster, soapstone, etc.

friars' lantern. See **ignis fatuus.**

frib·ble (frib'əl), *v.* to act frivolously; trifle; waste time.

fric·as·see (frik,əsē', frik'əsē, frik'əsā,), *n.* **1.** meat, esp. white meat, stewed with vegetables and served with a thick white sauce. —*v.* **fric·as·sees, fric·as·see·ing, fric·as·seed. 2.** to prepare ingredients for a fricassee.

friction layer. See **surface boundary layer.**

frieze (frēz), *n.* an ornamental band on a building façade, often decorated with sculpture.

frig·i·do·re·cep·tor (frij,idōrisep'tə), *n.* an end organ of a sensory neuron stimulated by cold.

frig·o·rif·ic (frig,ərif'ik), *adj.* making or producing cold.

frip·per·y (frip'ərē), *n.* gaudy or tawdry finery; ostentatious display.

fri·sé (frizā'), *n.* a piled fabric with cut or uncut loops.

fri·sette, fri·zette (frizet'), *n.* a fringe of tightly curled hair, often artificial.

fris·ket (fris'kit), *n.* a thin paper shield used to mask certain areas of a piece of artwork during retouching with an airbrush.

fris·son (frēsôn'), *n.* a shiver or shudder, as from thrill or chill.

fron·des·cence (frondes'əns), *n.* the process or period of coming into leaf. —**fron·des'cent,** *adj.*

front bench, *Brit.* one of two benches near the Speaker where the leaders of the major parties sit in the House of Commons. See also **back bench.**

front money, money advanced to a financier in return for a promise to procure funds for a company.

frot·tage (frotäzн'), *n.* a technique of producing images by rubbing chalk, coloured wax, etc., over paper laid on a surface with a raised design. See also **rubbing.**

frot·teur (frotû'), *n.* one who does frottage.

frowz·y, frouz·y, frows·y (frou'zē), *adj.* **frowz·i·er, frowz·i·est; frouz·i·er, frouz·i·est; frows·i·er, frows·i·est. 1.** having an untidy or slovenly appearance; down at heel. **2.** malodorous; stale. —**frowz'i·ness, frouz'i·ness, frows'i·ness,** *n.*

fruc·tif·er·ous (fruktif'ərəs), *adj.* yielding fruit.

fruc·ti·fi·ca·tion (fruk,tifikā'sнən), *n.* the act of bearing fruit; the fruit of a plant.

fruc·ti·fi·ca·tive (fruk'tifikā,tiv), *adj.* able to yield fruit.

fruc·ti·fy (fruk'tifī), *v.* to become or make fruitful. —**fruc'ti·fi,er,** *n.*

fruc·tose (fruk'tōs, fruk'tōz), *n.* a fruit sugar found in sweet, ripe fruits, nectar, and **honey.**

fruc·tu·ous (fruk'tyōŏəs), *adj.* fruitful; productive; profitable.

fru·gal (frōō'gəl), *adj.* stingy; pennypinching, from either miserliness or poverty. —**fru·gal'i·ty,** *n.*

fru·giv·o·rous (frōōjiv'ərəs), *adj.* fruit-eating.

fru·i·tion (frōōisн'ən), *n.* full realization; fulfilment.

fru·men·ta·ceous (frōō,məntā'sнəs), *adj.* like or having the nature of wheat or other grain.

fru·tes·cent (frōōtes'ənt), *adj.* shrubby or becoming like a shrub.

fru·ti·cose (frōō'tikōs, frōō'tikōz), *adj.* of or like a shrub.

FTSE (fōŏt'sē), *abbrev. for* Financial Times Stock Exchange (Index): any of various share indexes published by the *Financial Times,* esp. the FT-SE 100 Index.

fu·ga·cious (fyo͞oga'sʜəs), *adj.* fleeting; passing quickly away; ephemeral.

fu·gu (fo͞o'go͞o), *n.* a puffer fish, eaten as a delicacy in Japan after the removal of the skin and certain deadly poisonous organs.

ful·crum (fo͞ol'krəm), *n.*, *pl.* **ful·crums, ful·cra** (fo͞ol'krə). the stationary support or pivot on which a lever turns in raising or moving something.

ful·gent (ful'jənt), *adj.* very bright; dazzling; radiant.

ful·gid (ful'jid), *adj.* shining; glittering; flashing.

ful·gu·rant (ful'gyərənt), *adj.* flashing like lightning.

ful·gu·rate (ful'gyərāt,), *v.* to dart like lightning.

ful·gu·rous (ful'gyərəs), *adj.* like or full of lightning.

ful·ham, ful·lam, ful·lom (fo͞ol'əm), *n.* one of a pair of loaded dice.

fu·lig·i·nous (fyo͞olij'inəs), *adj.* full of smoke or soot.

full-fashioned (fo͞ol'fasʜ'ənd), *adj.* knitted to conform to the contours of the body, as sweaters and hosiery.

ful·mi·nant (ful'minənt), *adj.* exploding or occurring suddenly.

ful·mi·nate (ful'mināt,, fo͞ol'mināt,), *v.* **ful·mi·nat·ed, ful·mi·nat·ing.** (*used chiefly with* **against**) to denounce or criticize severely. **—ful,·mi·na'tion,** *n.*

ful·min·ic (fulmin'ik), *adj.* highly unstable or explosive.

ful·mi·nous (ful'minəs), *adj.* of or like thunder and lightning.

ful·some (fo͞ol'səm), *adj.* disgusting; repellent; tastelessly offensive.

ful·vous (ful'vəs), *adj.* tawny; yellowish-brown.

fu·ma·role (fyo͞o'mərōl), *n.* a hole emitting smoke and gases in a volcanic area.

fu·mu·lus (fyo͞o'myələs), *n.*, *pl.* **fu·mu·lus.** a thin layer of clouds or haze.

fu·nam·bu·list (fyo͞onam'byəlist), *n.* a tightrope walker.

func·tion·ar·y (fuɴɢk'sʜənər,ē), *n.* one who performs a certain function; an official.

func·tor (fuɴɢ'tə), *n.* something that performs a particular function.

fun·da·ment (fun'dəmənt), *n.* **1.** the characteristics of a region, as climate, land forms, soils, etc. **2.** the buttocks.

fundamental particle. See **elementary particle.**

fun·dus (fun'dəs), *n.*, *pl.* **fun·di** (fun'dī). the base of an organ, or the part farthest from its opening.

fu·nest (fyo͞onest'), *adj.* portending evil; fatal; sinister.

fun·gi·cide (funɴɢ'gisīd, fun'jisīd), *n.* a substance for killing fungi.

fun·gi·form (fuɴɢ'gifôm,, fun'jifôm,), *adj.* like a fungus in form.

fun·gi·stat (fuɴɢ'gistat,, fun'jistat), *n.* a fungistatic preparation.

fun·gi·stat·ic (fuɴɢ,gistat'ik, fun,jistat'ik), *adj.* of a preparation that stops the growth of a fungus.

fun·gi·tox·ic (fuɴɢ,gitok'sik, fun,jitok'sik), *adj.* poisonous to fungi.

fun·giv·or·ous (fuɴɢgiv'ərəs, funjiv'ərəs), *adj.* fungus-eating.

fun·goid (fuɴɢ'goid), *adj.* like or characteristic of a fungus.

fun·gos·i·ty (fuɴɢgos'itē), *n.* the condition of being fungous.

fun·gous (fuɴɢ'gəs), *adj.* of or caused by fungi; resembling a fungus.

fu·nic·u·lar (fyo͞onik'yələ), *adj.* of, worked by, or hanging from a rope or cable.

fu·nic·u·lus (fyo͞onik'yələs), *n.*, *pl.* **fu·nic·u·li** (fyo͞onik'yəlī). a conducting cord, as an umbilical cord.

fur·be·low (fû'bilō), *n.* a flounce; showy trimmings or finery.

fur·bish (fû'bisʜ), *v.* to brighten up; restore; smarten.

fur·cate (fû'kāt), *adj.* forked; branched.

fur·cu·la (fû'kyələ), *n.*, *pl.* **fur·cu·lae** (fû'kyəlē). the wishbone.

fur·fur (fû'fə), *n.*, *pl.* **fur·fur·es** (fû'fyərēz, fû'fərēz). dandruff; scurf.

fur·fu·ra·ceous (fû,fyərā'sʜəs, fû,fərā'sʜəs), *adj.* of or like bran; covered with dandruff or scurf.

fu·ri·bund (fyo͞or'ibund), *adj.* furious; frenzied.

fur·tive (fû'tiv), *adj.* stealthy; secret; underhandedly concealed.

fu·run·cle (fyo͞or'uɴɢkəl), *n.* a boil.

fu·run·cu·lo·sis (fyo͞oruɴɢ,kyəlō'sis), *n.* a disorder of which furuncles are symptomatic.

fu·sa·role (fyo͞o'zərōl), *n.* a moulding resembling a string of beads.

fus·cous (fus'kəs), *adj.* dusky; brownish-grey.

fu·see (fyo͞ozē'), *n.* a friction match with a large head.

fu·si·form (fyo͞ozifôm,), *adj.* spindle-shaped.

fu·sil (fyo͞o'zil), *n.* made by casting; founded.

fu·sion (fyo͞o'zʜən), *n.* a thermonuclear reaction in which lightweight atomic nuclei join to form nuclei of heavier atoms, with a resultant release of energy; the principle of the hydrogen bomb. Also **nuclear fusion.** See also **fission.**

fus·tian (fus'tēən), *n.* **1.** a thick cotton cloth with a short nap. **2.** bombastic language.

fus·ti·gate (fus'tigāt), *v.* to beat with a stick; cudgel.

fus·ty (fus'tē), *adj.* mouldy; musty; stale-smelling.

fu·su·ma (fyōo'səmä), *n.* a sliding door or partition in a Japanese house.

fu·tile (fyōo'tĭl), *adj.* useless; to no advantage; without result, as *a futile war.* —**fu·til'i·ty,** *n.*

fu·til·i·tar·i·an (fyōotĭl,iter'ēən), *adj.* **1.** of the view that the strivings of humanity are pointless. —*n.* **2.** an adherent of such a view.

future shock, the inability to adapt psychologically to rapid and novel advances and changes, esp. cultural, technological, moral, and social innovations.

fu·tu·ri·ty race (fyōotōor'itē), *U.S.* a horse race in which the contestants are selected long beforehand.

ga·belle (gabel'), *n.* a tax; an excise.

ga·bi·on (gā'bēən), *n.* a wicker cylinder filled with earth or stones used in military fortifications, building dams, etc.

ga·bi·on·ade (gā'bēənād'), *n.* a construction made of or with gabions.

ga·droon (gədrōōn'), *n.* a series of flutings used esp. as an ornamental border on silver dishes.

gaffe (gaf), *n.* a blunder; a tactless remark or action.

gain·say (gān'sā), *v.* **gain·said, gain·say·ing.** to contradict, deny, or speak in opposition to, as *You cannot gainsay the truth of his remarks.*

gait·er (gā'tə), *n.* a cloth or leather covering for the ankle, instep, and lower leg; a spat or spatterdash.

gal (gal), *n.* a unit of acceleration equal to one centimetre per second per second. [after Galileo]

ga·lac·ta·gogue (gəlak'təgog), *adj.* increasing the yield of milk.

ga·lac·tic (gəlak'tik), *adj.* **1.** pertaining to a galaxy. **2.** pertaining to milk.

ga·lac·toid (gəlak'toid), *adj.* milk-like.

ga·lac·to·phore (gəlak'təfô'ə), *n.* a milk-bearing duct.

gal·ac·toph·or·ous (gal,əktof'ərəs), *adj.* secreting milk.

ga·lac·to·poi·et·ic (gəlak,tōpoiet'ik), *adj.* increasing milk secretion.

gal·an·tine (gal'əntēn), *n.* a cold dish of boned fish or meat served in savoury jelly. Also **gal'a·tine.**

gal·ax·y (gal'əksē), *n.* a vast number of stars held together in one system.

ga·le·a (gā'lēə), *n., pl.* **ga·le·ae** (gā'liē). a part, as of a flower, shaped like a helmet.

ga·le·ate (gā'lēāt,), *adj.* having a galea.

ga·le·i·form (gəlē'ifôm,), *adj.* helmet-shaped.

ga·len·i·cal (gālen'ikəl), *n.* **1.** a drug made from herbs or vegetable matter rather than from minerals or chemicals. **2.** an unrefined, crude drug.

gal·i·ma·ti·as (gal,imā'shēəs, galimat'ēəs), *n.* unintelligible talk; nonsense.

gal·li·gas·kins (gal,igas'kins), *n. pl.* leather breeches or leggings.

gal·li·mau·fry (gal,imô'frē), *n.* a jumble or confused medley.

gal·li·na·ceous (gal,inā'shəs), *adj.* like or of the family of birds which includes the domestic fowl.

gal·li·pot (gal'ipot,), *n.* a small ceramic pot for ointments, medicines, etc.

gal·li·vant (gal'ivant,), *v.* to gad gaily about.

gall·stone (gôl'stōn,), *n.* a stonelike concretion in the gall bladder.

gal·lus·es (gal'əsiz), *n. pl.* braces for a pair of trousers.

gal·van·ic (galvan'ik), *adj.* **1.** pertaining to, caused by, or produced by an electric current. **2.** startling; convulsive; shocking.

gal·van·ize (gal'vənīz,), *v.* **1.** to stir into sudden activity; rouse. **2.** to cover with a zinc coating, esp. to prevent rust.

gal·va·nom·e·ter (gal,vənom'ltə), *n.* an instrument for detecting, comparing, and measuring small electric currents.

gal·va·no·tax·is (gal,vənōtak'sis), *n.* movement of an organism in response to an electric current.

gal·va·no·tro·pism (gal,vənot'rəpiz,əm), *n.* tendency of an organism to grow towards or away from an electric current.

gam (gam), *n.* a school of whales.

gam·ba·do (gambā'dō), *n., pl.* **gam·ba·dos, gam·ba·does.** one of a pair of boots or gaiters attached to the saddle instead of stirrups.

gam·bit (gam'bit), *n.* any initial move, esp. in chess, seeking an advantage; a cunning strategy.

gam·boge (gambōj', gambōōzh'), *n.* a yellow or yellow-orange pigment.

gam·brel roof (gam'brəl), a gable roof made up of two surfaces at each side that slope to the ridge at different angles.

gam·e·lan (gam'əlan), *n.* an orchestra consisting of bowed, stringed, and percussion instruments, and flutes, characteristic of southeast Asia.

games·man·ship (gāmz'mənship), *n.* the art of winning games by disconcerting one's opponent.

game·some (gām'səm), *adj.* gay or playful.

gam·ete (gam'ēt), *n.* a reproductive cell which, uniting with another, produces a new organism.

game theory, mathematical theory describing how, on the basis of specific information, competing parties (e.g. business, military) choose strategies to maximize gains and minimize losses. Also called **theory of games.** —**game,-the,or-ret'ic,** adj.

ga·me·to·cyte (gəmē'tōsīt,), n. a cell producing gametes.

gam·e·to·gen·e·sis (gam,itōjen'isis), n. development of gametes.

ga·me·to·phore (gəmē'tōfô,ə), n. a gamete-producing part.

ga·me·to·phyte (gəmē'tōfīt,), n. a plant that reproduces sexually. See also **sporophyte.**

gam·ma·di·on (gamā'dēən), n., pl. **gam·ma·di·a** (gamā'dēə). a figure used in ornamentation formed from the Greek capital letter gamma, as a swastika.

gam·ma glob·u·lin (gam'ə glob'yəlin), a protein in blood plasma containing antibodies effective against measles and poliomyelitis.

gamma rays, rays produced by radio active material.

gam·mon (gam'ən), n. a ham that has been smoked or cured.

gam·o·gen·e·sis (gam,ōjen'isis), n. reproduction by the union of two gametes.

gam·ut (gam'ət), n. the full range; everything one can imagine; the entire scale, as *The actress ran the gamut of emotions from A to B.*

ga·nef (gä'nef), n. U.S. slang. a thief.

gan·gli·a (gaNG'glēə), n. pl. of ganglion.

gan·gli·ate (gaNG'glēāt,), adj. possessing ganglia. Also **gan'gli·on·ate,.**

gan·gli·form (gaNG'glifôm,), adj. in the form of a ganglion.

gan·gli·oid (gaNG'glēoid), adj. like a ganglion.

gan·gli·on (gaNG'glēən), n., pl. **gan·gli·a** (gaNG'glēə), **gan·gli·ons. 1.** a small mass of nerve tissue outside the brain and spinal cord. **2.** a tumour in the sheath of a tendon, as at the wrist. **3.** a centre of activities. —**gan,gli·on'ic,** adj.

gangue (gaNG), n. valueless minerals occurring in a vein or deposit of ore.

gan·is·ter (gan'istə), n. a hard, siliceous rock used to line furnaces.

gan·o·in (gan'ōin), n. a hard, shiny surface on the outer layer of the scales of some fishes.

gan·try (gan'trē), n. a framework of scaffolding, as for erecting vertically launched missiles.

gar·ban·zo (gärban'zō), n. a leguminous plant with edible pealike seeds; chickpea.

garde·robe (gärd'rōb,), n. a wardrobe, or the clothes kept in one; clothespress.

gar·goyl·ism (gär'goiliz,əm), n. a congenital abnormality characterized by grotesque deformities to parts of the body.

gar·ish (ger'isH), adj. cheaply showy; gaudy; tastelessly elaborate.

gar·ner (gä'nə), v. to gather, hoard, and store up.

gar·net (gä'nit), n. a dark red colour.

gar·nish·ee (gä,nisHē'), v. to place (property or money) under garnishment.

gar·nish·ment (gä'nisHmənt), n. a notice to withhold a defendant's money or property subject to a court's direction.

gar·ni·ture (gä'nicHə), n. that which decorates; ornamentation.

gar·rotte (gərot'), n. **1.** an iron collar, wire, or cord used to execute by throttling. **2.** this method of capital punishment. —v. **3.** to throttle or strangle. Also **ga·rote', ga·rotte', gar·rote'.**

gar·ru·li·ty (gəröō'litē), n. the quality of being talkative.

gar·ru·lous (gar'ələs), adj. excessively loquacious; talkative about trivial matters; wordy.

garth (gäth), n. an enclosed yard or courtyard.

gas·con·ade (gas,kənād'), n. bragging; boastful bluster.

gas·tral·gi·a (gastral'jēə), n. violent stomach pain.

gas·tric (gas'trik), adj. of or in the stomach.

gas·tri·tis (gastrī'tis), n. inflammation of the stomach.

gas·tro·en·ter·i·tis (gas,trōen,tərī'tis), n. inflammation of the intestines and stomach.

gas·tro·en·ter·ol·ogy (gas,trōen,tərol'əjē), n. study of the digestive organs.

gas·tro·he·pat·ic (gas,trōhipat'ik), adj. affecting the liver and stomach.

gas·tro·in·tes·ti·nal (gas,trōintes'tinəl), adj. affecting the stomach and intestines.

gas·tro·lith (gas'trəlitH), n. a stone or concretion in the stomach.

gas·trol·o·gy (gastrol'əjē), n. study of the stomach.

gas·tro·nome (gas'trənōm), n. a lover and judge of good food. Also **gas·tron'o·mist.**

gas·tron·o·my (gastron'əmē), n. art and science of good eating.

gas·tro·scope (gas'trəskōp,), n. an instrument for inspecting the interior of the stomach. —**gas·tros,copy** (gastros'kəpē), n.

gat (gat), n. a channel extending inland through shoals, etc.

gat·eau (gat'ō), n., pl. **ga·teaux** (gat'ōz). a decorated cake.

gate·fold (gāt'fōld,), n. a page larger than the book or periodical it is bound in and folded so as not to extend beyond the edges.

gate·leg (gāt'leg,), n. a table having an extra leg which can be swung round to support a drop leaf.

Gat·ling gun (gat'liNG), an early type of machine gun.

gauche (gōsH), adj. clumsy; lacking in social graces; tactless.

gau·che·rie (gōsHərē'), n. a lack of social grace; an act that is awkward or tactless.

gaud (gôd), *n.* a cheap ornament or bit of finery; showy display. —**gaud·er·y,** *adj.*

ga·ze·bo (gəzē'bō), *n.*, *pl.* **ga·ze·bos, ga·ze·boes.** a building such as an ornamental summerhouse.

gaz·pa·cho (gəzpä'сʜō, gaspä'сʜō), *n.* a Spanish vegetable soup served cold.

Ge·brauchs·mu·sik (gəbrouкʜs'mōōzēk,), *n.* music written in a simple manner for performance by amateurs.

ge·füll·te fish (gəfil'tə), minced boned fish, seasoned, shaped into balls, and served cold. Also **ge·fil'te fish.**

ge·gen·schein (gā'gənsʜīn,), *n.* a pale patch of light in the night sky, which is a reflection of sunlight on particles in space.

Gei·ger counter (gī'gə), an instrument used chiefly to measure radioactivity.

ge·la·tion (jelā'sʜən), *n.* the act or process of freezing; making solidly cold.

gel·id (jel'id), *adj.* icy cold; frozen.

ge·mein·schaft (gəmīn'sʜäft), *n.*, *pl.* **ge·mein·schaf·ten** (gəmīn'sʜäftən). **1.** a fellowship of people having similar tastes. **2.** a group with a strong sense of common identity.

gem·el bottle (jem'əl), a pair of cruets coupled together, with the necks curving in opposite directions, used as for oil and vinegar.

gem·eled (jem'əld), *adj.* coupled, as two architectural members.

gem·i·nate (jem'ināt,), *v.* to mate or become paired or doubled. —**gem,i·na'tion,** *n.*

gem·i·ni·flor·ous (jem,ənēflôr'əs), *adj.* with flowers arranged in pairs.

gem·ma·ceous (jemā'sʜəs) *adj.* of or resembling buds.

gem·mate (jem'āt), *adj.* reproducing by budding.

gem·ma·tion (jemā'sʜən), *n.* reproduction by buds. Also **gem,mu·la'tion.**

gem·mif·er·ous (jemif'ərəs), *adj.* having buds.

gem·mi·form (jem'ifôm,), *adj.* having a budlike shape.

gem·mip·a·rous (jemip'ərəs), *adj.* producing or reproducing by buds.

gem·ol·o·gy, gem·mol·o·gy (jemol'əjē), *n.* the science or study of gemstones.

ge·müt·lich (gəmʏt'liкʜ), *adj.* agreeable. Also **ge·muet'lich.**

Ge·müt·lich·keit (gəmʏt'liкʜkīt,), *n.* agreeableness. Also **Ge·muet'lich·keit,.**

ge·nappe (jənap'), *v.* to singe (yarn) to remove loose threads.

ge·ne·al·o·gy (jē,nēal'əjē, jē,nēol'əjē), *n.* a record of the line of descent of an individual, family, etc.

gen·e·arch (jen'eäk), *n.* the head of a family or tribe.

gen·e·col·o·gy (jen,ēkol'əjē), *n.* the study of genetic variation within species in relation to their ecology. —**gen,e·co'log'i·cal,** *adj.*

general semantics, a discipline involving the interrelationships between symbols and human behaviour. See also **semantics.**

ge·ner·ic (jəner'ik), *adj.* referring to all members of a genus or class.

gen·e·sis (jen'isis), *n.* the beginning of anything, esp. its creation or origin.

gene therapy, the application of genetic engineering techniques to alter or replace defective genes in an effort to alleviate or eliminate certain inherited diseases, such as sickle-cell anaemia.

ge·neth·li·ac (jineth'lēak), *adj.* referring to the position of the stars at one's birth.

ge·neth·li·al·o·gy (jəneth,lēol'əjē), *n.* science of calculating the position of the stars, as on a birthday.

genetic engineering, the alteration of genes in the DNA of an individual.

genetic map, a graphic representation of the sequence of genes along a chromosome, often with some indication of the relative distance separating them. —**genetic mapping,** *n.*

ge·net·ics (jinet'iks), *n.* science of heredity.

ge·nic·u·late (jinik'yəlit, jinik'jəlāt), *adj.* **1.** having joints. **2.** bent, as the knee at the knee joint. —**ge·nic·u·la'tion,** *n.*

gen·i·to·u·ri·nar·y (jen,itōyōōr'iner,ē), *adj.* of or pertaining to the urinary and genital organs.

gen·o·cide (jen'ōsīd), *n.* the systematic mass murder of a race or of a religious group.

gen·o·type (jen'ōtīp,), *n.* **1.** the genetic constitution of an organism. **2.** a group sharing a common genetic constitution.

gen·re (zʜän'rə), *n.* a class or kind into which things having a similar style, shape, philosophy, etc., may be classified.

gens (jenz), *n.*, *pl.* **gen·tes** (jen'tēz). a group with a common male ancestor.

gen·ti·lesse (jent'əles,), *n.* good conduct; civility; politeness; as befits one of the gentry.

ge·nu (jen'yōō), *n.*, *pl.* **ge·nu·a** (jen'yōōə). the knee; a kneelike part.

gen·u·flect (jen'yōōflekt), *v.* to bend at the knee as an expression of reverence. —**gen,u·flec'tion,** *n.*

gen·u·pec·tor·al (jen,yōōpek'tərəl), *adj.* pertaining to the knee and chest.

ge·o·cen·tric (jē,ōsen'trik), *adj.* reckoned from the centre of the earth; having the earth as centre.

ge·o·chem·is·try (jē,ōkem'istrē), *n.* the science of the chemistry of the earth.

ge·o·chro·nol·o·gy (jē,ōkrənol'əjē), *n.* the dating of the earth on the basis of geological information.

ge·o·des·ic (jē,ōdes'ik, jē,ōdē'sik), *adj.* pertaining to the geometry of curved surfaces. Also ge,o·des'i·cal.

geodesic dome, a domelike structure, created by R. Buckminster Fuller (1895–1983), made up of linked polygons.

ge·od·e·sy (jēod'isē), n. the science of calculating the measurement of large tracts of land and the dimensions of the earth. Also ge,o·det'-ics. —ge,o·det'ic, adj.

ge·o·dy·nam·ics (jē,ōdīnam'iks), n. the science of the dynamics within the earth.

ge·og·no·sy (jēog'nəsē), n. geology dealing with the earth's water, air, and crust.

ge·oid (jē'oid), n. an imaginary ellipsoid, flattened at the poles, that coincides with sea level.

ge·o·mag·net·ic (jē,ōmagnet'ik), adj. of or pertaining to the earth's magnetism.

ge·o·man·cy (jē'əman,sē), n. divination by means of a handful of earth thrown at random or by means of figures or lines. —ge'o·man,cer, n.

ge·o·med·i·cine (jē,ōmed'isən), n. medicine dealing with the effect of geography on disease.

ge·o·met·ric progression (jē,əmet'rik), a mathematical sequence, as 2, 8, 32, 128, 512, etc., in which each term is obtained by multiplying the preceding by a constant factor. See also **arithmetic progression, harmonic progression.**

ge·o·mor·phic (jē,ōmô'fik), adj. of or pertaining to the form of the surface of the earth.

ge·o·mor·phol·o·gy (jē,ōmôfol'əjē), n. the study of the origins and development of land forms.

ge·o·nav·i·ga·tion (jē,ōnavigā'sHən), n. navigation by terrestrial objects.

ge·oph·a·gy (jēof'əjē), n. the eating of earth or of earthy matter, as clay.

ge·oph·i·lous (jēof'ələs), adj. earthbound, as certain snails.

ge·o·phys·ics (jē,ōfiz'iks), n. the science of the physics of the earth.

ge·o·phyte (je'ōfīt,), n. a plant that buds underground.

ge·o·pol·i·tics (jē,ōpol'itiks), n. the study of politics in relation to geographical factors. —ge·o·po·lit·i·cal (jē,ōpəlit'ikəl), adj. —ge,o·pol,i·ti'cian, n.

ge·o·pon·ics (jē,ōpon'iks), n., construed as sing. the science of agriculture. —ge·o·pon'ic, adj.

Geor·gian (jô'jən), adj. of a style of architecture, art, and design predominant in England for a hundred years from about 1714, during the reigns of George I to George III, typified in buildings and dwellings by a basic construction of brick with white wooden window and door frames and neo-classical porticos.

geor·gic (jô'jik), adj. agricultural.

ge·o·stat·ic (jē,ōstat'ik), adj. of or pertaining to the pressure of earth, as in a mine.

ge·o·stroph·ic (jē,ōstrof'ik), adj. of or pertain-

ing to the pressure in the atmosphere in relation to the Coriolis force.

geosynchronous (jē,ōsiNG'krənəs), adj. having an earth orbit that maintains the same position relative to a point on the earth's surface.

ge·o·syn·cline (jē,ōsin'klīn), n. a part of the earth's crust subject to downward movement.

ge·o·tax·is (jē,ōtak'sis), n. movement of an organism in response to gravitational force.

ge·o·tec·ton·ic (jē,ōtekton'ik), adj. of or pertaining to the structure of the earth's crust.

ge·o·ther·mal (jē,ōthû'məl), adj. of or pertaining to the internal heat of the earth. Also ge,o·ther'mic.

ge·o·trop·ic (jē,ōtrop'ik), adj. of or pertaining to movement with respect to the force of gravity. —ge·o·tro·pism (jēot'rəpiz,əm), n.

ger·a·tol·o·gy (jer,ətol'əjē), n. the study of old age.

ge·rent (jer'ənt), n. a manager.

ger·i·at·rics (jer,ēat'riks), n., construed as sing. 1. the science dealing with the diseases and care of old people. 2. the study of ageing.

ger·mane (jûmān'), adj. relevant; pertinent; appropriate.

ger·mi·cide (jû'misīd), n. a germ killing substance.

ger·mi·nal (jû'minənl), adj. 1. of or like a germ or germ cell. 2. being in an early stage of development; embryonic.

ger·mi·nent (jû'minənt), adj. germinating; growing.

ger·mi·nate (jû'mināt,), v. to begin to develop; start to grow. —ger'mi·na,tive, adj.

ger·o·don·tics (jer,ōdon'tiks), n., construed as sing. dentistry dealing with ageing people. Also ger·o·don·tia (jer,ōdon'sHə).

ger·on·toc·ra·cy (jer,ontok'rəsē), n. government by elders.

ge·ron·to·ge·ous (jəron,təjē'əs), n. belonging to Europe, Asia, or Africa.

ger·on·tol·o·gy (jer,ontol'əjē), n. the scientific study of ageing and of old age.

ger·ry·man·der (jer'ēman,də), v. 1. to manipulate with a gerrymander. —n. 2. reorganization of constituency boundaries, etc., to give one political party an advantage.

ge·sell·schaft (gəzel'sHäft), n., pl. ge·sell·schaf·ten (gəzel'sHäftən). 1. an association of people with a common intellectual, cultural, or business goal. 2. a formal organization usually nontraditional and not sentimental. See also **gemeinschaft.**

ges·so (jes'ō), n. any preparation like plaster used to prepare a surface before painting.

gest (jest), n. 1. bearing; conduct. 2. gesture.

ge·stalt (gəsHtalt'), n., pl. ge·stalts, ge·stal·ten (gəsHtäl'tən). (in psychology) a unified whole that cannot be derived from the sum of its parts.

Gestalt psychology, the theory in psychology that phenomena do not happen through reflexes or sensations.

ges·tate (jes'tāt), v. to be pregnant. —**ges·ta'-tion**, n.

ges·tic·u·late (jestik'yəlāt,), v. to use gestures to emphasize or communicate; to express with gestures. —**ges·tic'u·lar**, adj. —**ges·tic,u·la'tion**, n.

gew·gaw (gyōō'gô), n. a gaudy or useless trinket or trifle.

ghast·ly (gäst'lē), adj. **ghast·li·er, ghast·li·est.** horribly shocking; dreadful, as a ghastly murder.

gib·be·rel·lic acid (jib,ərel'ik), an acid that stimulates plant growth.

gib·bet (jib'it), n. a gallows.

gib·bos·i·ty (gibos'itē), n. the condition of being gibbous.

gib·bous (gib'əs), adj. **1.** hump-backed. **2.** (of the moon) between half and full; convex at both edges. Also **gib·bose** (gib'ōs).

gi·ga·cy·cle (jig'əsīkəl, gī'gəsīkəl), n. a billion cycles.

gi·ga·hertz (jig'əhûtz, gī'gəhûtz), n. a billion hertz.

gl·gan·tism (jīgan'tizəm), n. an abnormal growth in size of the whole body or of parts of the body. Also **gi·'ant·ism.**

gi·gan·tom·a·chy (jī,gantom'əkē), **gi·gan·to·ma·chi·a** (jī,gantōmä'kēə), n., pl. **gi·gan·tom·a·chies, gi·gan·to·ma·chi·as. 1.** (in Greek mythology) a war between rebelling giants and the gods of Olympus. **2.** any conflict involving adversaries with giant-like attributes.

gi·ga·sec·ond (jig'əsek,ənd, gī'gəsek,ənd), n. a billion seconds.

gi·got (ZHē'gō, jig'ət), n. **1.** a leg of mutton. **2.** a sleeve puffed out only above the elbows; leg-of-mutton sleeve.

gil·lion (jil'yən), n., Brit. one thousand million; billion.

gim·bals (jim'bəlz, gim'bəlz), n., construed as sing. a device for mounting instruments or equipment on a vessel, aeroplane, etc., so as to allow them to remain in a horizontal position regardless of the angle of the vessel. Also **gim'-bal ring.**

gim·let (gim'lit), n. **1.** a tool with a sharp screw end for boring holes. **2.** a cocktail of gin and lime juice.

gin·ger·bread (jin'jəbred,), n. elaborate ornamentation.

gin·gi·val (jin'jivəl, jinjī'vəl), adj. of the gums.

gin·gi·vi·tis (jin,jivī'təs), n. inflammation of the gums.

gir·a·sol (jir'əsol, jir'əsōl), n. **1.** an opal with a luminous glow. —adj. **2.** (of a stone) bluish-white with red reflections. Also **gir'a·sole.**

gla·brate (glā'brāt, glā'brit), adj. glabrous or becoming glabrous.

gla·bres·cent (glābres'ənt), adj. becoming glabrous.

gla·brous (glā'brəs), adj. bald; hairless; smooth.

gla·cé (glas'ē, glasā', glä'sā), adj. **1.** candied or crystallized. **2.** iced, as a cake. **3.** Chiefly U.S. frozen or frosted.

gla·cial·ist (glā'sēəlist, glā'SHəlist), n. a specialist in the geological phenomena caused by glacial activity.

gla·ci·ate (glā'siāt,), v. to make or become frozen or covered with ice.

gla·ci·ol·o·gy (glās,ēol'əjē, glā,sēol'əjē), n. study of glaciers.

gla·cis (glas'is, glā'sis), n. a gentle slope.

glad·i·ate (glad'ēit), adj. sword-shaped; ensiform; xiphoid.

glair (gle'ə), n. **1.** raw white of egg. **2.** a glaze made of egg white. **3.** any similar viscous substance. —**glair'y**, adj.

glas·nost (glas'nost,), n. a policy of greater openness and candour in public affairs. It is named after such a policy initiated in the 1980s by Mikhail Gorbachov in the former USSR.

glau·co·ma (glôkō'mə, gloukō'mə), n. a disease of the eye leading to loss of vision. —**glau·co'ma·tous**, adj.

glau·cous (glô'kəs), adj. greenish blue.

glean (glēn), v. to gather, esp. to collect what is left after a field has been harvested.

gle·noid (glē'noid), adj. shallow or slightly cupped, as a bone cavity.

glib (glib), adj. **glib·ber, glib·best.** easily talkative, esp. in a hypocritical way.

glis·sade (glisäd', glisād'), n. a skilful descending glide over snow, as on skis.

glit·ter·a·ti (glit,ərätē), n., Inf. the leading members of fashionable society; celebrities.

glo·bate (glō'bāt), adj. globe-shaped.

glo·big·er·i·na ooze (glōbij,ərī'nə), a deposit on the ocean floor consisting mainly of shells.

glo·boid (glō'boid), adj. globular.

glo·bose (glō'bōs), adj. globelike.

glob·u·lar (glob'yələ), adj. spherical. Also **glob'u·lous.**

glob·ule (glob'yōōl), n. a small round body.

glob·u·lif·er·ous (glob,yəlif'ərəs), adj. yielding or having globules.

glo·chid·i·ate (glōkid'ēāt,), adj. barbed at the apex.

glo·chid·i·um (glōkid'ēəm), n., pl. **glo·chid·i·a** (glōkid'ēə). a hair with a barbed tip.

glo·chis (glō'kis), n., pl. **glo·chi·nes** (glōkī'nēz). a barbed hair.

glom·er·ate (glom'ərit), adj. gathered into a compact mass.

glom·er·a·tion (glom,ərä'SHən), n. a glomerate mass; conglomeration.

gloss (glos), *n.* **1.** an explication of term or expression in a text, usually in the form of a note. —*v.* **2.** to interpret by means of a gloss.

glos·sa (glos'ə), *n.* the tongue. —**glos'sal**, *adj.*

glos·se·mat·ics (glos,əmat'iks), *n. used as singular.* the linguistic study of glossemes.

glos·seme (glos'ēm), *n.* the smallest meaningful signal in language, made up of a morpheme and a tagmeme. —**glos·se'mic**, *adj.*

glos·si·tis (glosī'tis), *n.* inflammation of the tongue.

glos·so·la·li·a (glos,əlā'lēə), *n.* **1.** speaking in an incomprehensible and ecstatic manner during religious worship; the gift of tongues. **2.** (in medicine) speaking in an unintelligible manner, as during hypnosis or sleep.

glot·tal (glot'əl), *adj.* of or produced in the glottis.

glot·tic (glot'ik), *adj.* glottal.

glot·tis (glot'is), *n.* the opening between the vocal cords.

glow·er (glou'ə), *v.* to glare at in a sullen or angry way.

gloze (glōz), *v.* to extenuate; explain away.

glu·cose (glōō'kōz, glōō'kōs), *n.* a sugar occurring in many fruits, about one half as sweet as ordinary sugar.

glu·on (glōō'on), *n.* a hypothetical elementary particle proposed as carrying the force that binds quarks together.

glu·tam·ic acid (glōōtam'ik), an amino acid found in meteorites. Also **glu,ta·min'ic acid.**

glu·ten (glōō'tən), *n.* substance remaining when wheat flour is washed to remove the starch. —**glu'te·nous**, *adj.*

glu·ti·nous (glōō'tinəs), *adj.* like glue; sticky.

gly·cine (glī'sēn), *n.* a simple, common amino acid, traces of which have been found in meteorites.

glyph (glif), *n.* a relief carving; hieroglyph.

glyp·tic (glip'tik), *adj.* pertaining to engraving on gems, ivory, etc.

glyp·tics (glip'tiks), *n.* art of engraving on gems, etc.

glyp·to·gr·aph (glip'təgräf,), *n.* an engraved design, as on a gem.

glyp·tog·ra·phy (gliptog'rəfē), *n.* study of engraved gems.

gnath·ic (nath'ik), *adj.* pertaining to the jaw. Also **gnath'al.**

gna·thon·ic (nathon'ik), *adj.* obsequious; toadying.

gnome (nōm), *n.* an aphorism; maxim; pithy saying. —**gno'mic**, *adj.*

gno·mist (nō'mist), *n.* a writer of maxims.

gno·mol·o·gy (nōmol'əjē), *n.* a collection of aphorisms; gnomic writing.

gno·mon (nō'mon), *n.* the part of a sundial that casts the shadow indicating the time.

gnos·tic (nos'tik), *adj.* possessing mystical knowledge; pertaining to knowledge. Also **gnos'ti·cal.**

gno·to·bi·o·sis (nō,tōbīō'sis), *n.* a condition in which germ-free animals have been inoculated with microorganisms of a given type. —**gno·to·bi·ot·ic** (nō,tōbīot'ik), *adj.*

gno·to·bi·ote (nō,tōbī'ōt), *n.* a gnotobiotic animal.

GNP, gross national product.

gob·bet (gob'it), *n.* a morsel, lump, or mass.

gob·ble·dy·gook (gob'əldigōōk,), *n.* nonsense; pompous talk that is empty of meaning and, often, characterized by the use of much jargon. Also **gob'ble·de·gook,.**

go·det (gōdet'), *n.* a triangular piece of fabric added to a garment to give fullness.

goi·tre, goi·ter (goi'tə), *n.* an enlargement of the thyroid gland in the neck. —**goi·trous** (goi'-trəs), *adj.*

golden handcuffs, a special payment, often spread over several years, that induces a valued employee to remain with a particular organization.

golden parachute, a provision in a contract of employment whereby the employee, usually a top executive, receives special severance payments in the event of redundancy.

go·nad (gō'nad), *n.* the organ producing gametes; reproductive gland.

go·nad·o·trope (gōnad'ōtrōp), *n.* a gonadotrophic substance.

go·nad·o·troph·ic (gōnad,ōtrof'ik), *adj.* pertaining to certain substances that affect the ovary or testis.

gon·fa·lon (gon'fələn), *n.* a banner, with streamers, hanging from a crossbar.

go·ni·om·e·ter (gō,nēom'itə), *n.* an instrument for measuring angles.

gon·o·coc·cus (gon,ōkok'əs), *n., pl.* **gon·o·coc·ci** (gon,ōkok'sī). bacteria causing gonorrhoea.

gon·o·cyte (gon'ōsīt), *n.* a germ cell when it is maturing.

gon·or·rhoe·a (gon,ərē'ə), *n.* a contagious inflammation of the urethra or the vagina.

goof·ball (gōōf'bôl,), *n. U.S. slang.* a barbiturate pill.

goo·gol (gōō'gol), *n.* the number 1 followed by 100 zeros.

gore (gôə), *n.* a triangular piece of material added to a garment or sail for extra width.

gor·gon·ize (gô'gənīz), *v.* to hypnotize; turn as to stone.

Gor·gon·zo·la (gôgənzō'lə), *n.* a very strongly flavoured blue-veined Italian cheese.

gor·man·dize (gô'məndīz), *v.* to eat to excess; behave like a glutton.

gos·port (gos'pôt), *n.* a speaking tube allowing communication between parts of an aircraft.

Goth·ic (goth'ik), *adj.* **1.** pertaining to a medieval style of art, music, and architecture, characterized in the last by the use of pointed arches, ribbed vaults, delicate tracery in stonework, and flying buttresses, gargoyles, and grotesquery. **2.** pertaining to a later style of writing characterized by violent events and an atmosphere of decay.

gouache (gwäsн), *n.* a method of painting in watercolours mixed with gum.

gour·mand·ize (gōōə'məndīz,), *v.* to eat well; eat excessively or gluttonously.

gout (gout), *n.* a disease characterized by swellings in the joints, esp. in the big toe, and caused by excess uric acid in the blood.

goût (gōō), *n. French.* style or preference; taste.

gov·ern·ance (guv'ənəns), *n.* control; act of governing.

gra·ben (grä'bən), *n.* a part of the earth that has been pushed downwards. See also **horst.**

gra·di·ent (grä'dēənt), *n.* the angle of ascent or descent of a road, railway, etc.

grad·u·al·ism (grad'yōōəliz,əm) *n.* the method of achieving a goal by gradual steps rather than drastic action.

grad·u·al·ist (grad'yōōəlist,), *n. U.S.* one who advocates a gradual enforcement of desegregation laws (esp. in the Southern states).

graf·fi·ti (grəfē'tē), *n. pl.* writings or drawings, often of an obscene nature, found on the walls of public places such as lavatories.

graft·age (graf'tij), *n.* the inserting of a part of one plant into another to produce a new combined variety.

gral·la·to·ri·al (gral,ətôr'ēəl), *adj.* pertaining to birds that wade, as the herons, cranes, etc.

gram, gramme (gram), *n.* a metric unit of mass equal to 15.432 grains.

gram·a·ry, gram·a·rye (gram'ərē), *n.* the lore of sorcery.

gram·i·niv·o·rous (gram,iniv'ərəs), *adj.* feeding on seeds.

gram·ma·logue (gram'əlog,), *n.* a word shown as a sign or letter, as '&,' which signifies 'and'.

Gram-neg·a·tive (gram,neg'ətiv), *adj.* (of bacteria) not remaining violet when dyed by Gram's method.

Gram-pos·i·tive (gram,poz'itiv), *adj.* (of bacteria) remaining violet when dyed by Gram's method.

Gram's method, a method of staining bacteria treated with a solution of iodine, potassium iodide, and water.

gran·deur (gran'jə), *n.* majestic quality; imposing and impressive splendour, as *the glory that was Greece and the grandeur that was Rome.*

Grand Gui·gnol (gräɴ gēnyôl'), drama with strong overtones of horror.

gran·dil·o·quence (grandil'əkwəns), *n.* a pompous and lofty style of speech. —**gran·dil'o·quent,** *adj.*

gran·di·ose (gran'dēōs), *adj.* grand; imposing; impressive.

grand mal (grän, mal'), epilepsy characterized by loss of consciousness, frothing at the mouth, etc. See also **epilepsy, petit mal.**

gran·drelle (grandrel'), *n.* yarn made by twisting two strands of contrasting colours.

grang·er·ize (grän'jərīz), *v.* **1.** to add illustrations to a book by inserting additional prints, drawings, etc. **2.** to mutilate (books) to get illustrations.

gra·nif·er·ous (granif'ərəs), *adj.* bearing grain.

gra·niv·o·rous (graniv'ərəs), *adj.* feeding on grain.

gran·u·lo·ma (gran,yəlō'mə), *n., pl.* **gran·u·lo·mas, gran·u·lo·ma·ta** (gran,yəlō'mətə). a tumour composed of proud flesh.

gran·u·lo·ma·to·sis (gran,yəlō,mətō'sis), *n.* a condition characterized by many granulomas.

graph·ic (graf'ik), *adj.* unmistakable; clear; written or drawn or as if written or drawn, as *a graphic description.*

graph·ol·o·gy (grafol'əjē), *n.* the analysis of handwriting to determine the writer's personality.

graph·o·mo·tor (graf,əmō'tə), *adj.* pertaining to muscular control in writing.

gra·phon·o·my (grafon'əmē), *n.* the study of different systems of writing.

grap·pa (grap'ə, *Ital.* gräp'pä), *n.* brandy that has not been aged.

grat·i·cule (grat'ikyōōl,), *n.* a grid of lines on a map or chart.

grat·i·nate (grat'ināt,), *v.* to cook food with a topping of browned crumbs and butter or grated cheese.

gra·ti·né (grat,ēnā'), *adj.* gratinated.

gra·tu·i·tous (grətyōō'itəs), *adj.* free; not entailing any payment or other obligation.

gra·tu·i·ty (grətyōō'itē), *n.* a tip or pourboire; money given to a waiter, taxi driver, or other servant in addition to the fees usually charged.

grat·u·lant (grat'yələnt), *adj.* expressing joy and congratulations.

Grau·stark·i·an (groustäk'ēən), *adj.* typically romantic and melodramatic, as the adventures of military and court figures in certain literature, operettas, etc.

gra·va·men (grəvā'mən), *n., pl.* **gra·vam·i·na** (grəvam'inə). the most important part of a legal accusation.

grav·id (grav'id), *adj.* **1.** pregnant. **2.** containing one or more fetuses or eggs: *a gravid uterus.*

gra·vim·e·ter (grəvim'itə), *n.* **1.** an instrument for measuring specific gravity. **2.** an instrument to measure differences in the earth's gravitational field. Also **gravity meter.**

gra·vim·e·try (grəvim'itrē), *n.* the measurement of weight. —**grav,i·met'ric,** *adj.*

gra·vure (grəvyōō'ə), *n.* a method of printing from engraved plates.

great circle, 1. a circle obtained by cutting a sphere by a plane passing through its centre. See also **small circle.** 2. line of shortest distance between two points on the earth's surface.

greater omentum, an omentum joined to the stomach and extending over the small intestine. See also **lesser omentum.**

greenhouse effect, the effect of screening the earth's surface, raising its temperature by short-wave radiant heat without allowing the escape of long-wave radiant heat, produced by gases in the atmosphere, as carbon dioxide.

gre·gar·i·ous (griger'ēəs), *adj.* living in groups or flocks; loving company.

Gre·go·ri·an calendar (grigôr'ēən), the calendar (still in use) introduced by Pope Gregory XIII in the 16th century, calculating a year as having 365 days, and a leap year, which consists of 366 days, as occurring every fourth year excepting those divisible by 400.

gren·a·dine (grenədēn'), *n.* 1. a type of light, loosely woven cloth. 2. a sweet syrup made from pomegranates.

gres·so·ri·al (gresôr'ēəl), *adj.* adapted for walking.

grey eminence, a person who holds power but wields it through another; power behind the throne. [from French *éminence grise*]

grey matter, *n.* 1. (in anatomy) nerve tissue having a relatively dark appearance owing to the preponderance of nerve cell bodies and connective tissue. In the brain, grey matter forms the cerebral cortex. 2. *Informal.* mental ability; brains.

gride (grīd), *v.* 1. to grate or scrape. 2. to cut.

griev·ous (grē'vəs), *adj.* awful; horrible; atrocious. —**griev'ous·ly,** *adv.* —**griev'ous·ness,** *n.*

gri·gri (grē'grē), *n.* a charm or amulet of African origin.

gril·lade (griläd'), *n.* a dish of broiled or grilled meat.

grim·ace (grim'əs, grimās'), *v.* **grim·aced, grim·ac·ing.** 1. to make a face, esp. an unpleasant or distorted one. —*n.* 2. an unpleasant or distorted facial expression.

gri·mal·kin (grimal'kin, grimôl'kin), *n.* a cat, esp. an old female cat.

gri·saille (grizī'), *n.* a painting entirely executed in shades of grey.

gris·e·ous (gris'ēəs), *adj.* grey.

groin (groin), *n.* 1. the meeting point of the belly and thigh. 2. the curved line formed by the intersection of two vaults.

gross national product, the monetary value of all goods and services of one country in one year. *Abbr.:* **GNP.**

ground layer. See surface boundary layer.

ground·speed (ground'spēd,), *n.* the speed of an aircraft in relation to the ground, which is considered as stationary. See also **airspeed.**

ground state, the lowest stable energy level of a system of elementary particles, such as an atom or nucleus.

group therapy, psychiatric treatment in which a group of patients discuss their problems together with a therapist.

grout (grout), *n.* mortar used to fill joints in masonry.

grov·el (grov'əl), *v.* to lower oneself into a humiliating position, as to show respect, to apologize, etc.

gru·el·ling (grōō'əling), *adj.* extremely difficult and exhausting, as *gruelling work,* or *a gruelling four-hour march.*

grum (grum), *adj.* appearing grim, glum, or surly.

grume (grōōm), *n.* clotting blood.

Gru·yère (grōōye'ə), *n.* a firm, lightly flavoured Swiss cheese having small holes.

gu·ber·na·to·ri·al (gyōō,bənətôr'ēəl, gōō,bənətôr'ēəl), *adj.* of or pertaining to a governor.

gudg·eon (guj'ən), *n.* 1. someone easily duped. 2. a bait. 3. a socket for admitting the pintle of a rudder.

guer·don (gû'dn), *n.* 1. a reward. —*v.* 2. to recompense.

gué·rite (gārēt'), *n.* a wicker chair with a hood over the seat.

guile (gīl), *n.* underhand cunning; deceitfulness; duplicity. —**guile'ful,** *adj.* —**guile'less,** *adj.*

guimpe (gimp), *n.* 1. a yoke as of lace or embroidered linen worn to fill the neck of a low-cut dress. 2. stiffly starched cloth that covers the neck and shoulders of habits of nuns of certain orders.

gui·pure (gipyōōr'), *n.* any of various heavy, large-patterned laces.

guise (gīz), *n.* outward appearance; what someone or something looks like.

gu·la (gōō'lə, gyōō'lə), *n.* the upper part of the throat.

gu·lag (gōō'lag), *n.* one of a series of prison camps in the former Soviet Union. [From a Russian acronym for *Main Administration of Corrective Labour Camps.*]

gulch (gulch), *n. U.S.* a ravine, usually deep and narrow, marking the course of a stream.

gul·gul (gul'gul), *n.* a concoction of powdered seashells in oil, used as a protective coat for wooden ships.

gull (gul), *v.* 1. to dupe; fool; trick. —*n.* 2. one who is easily tricked or deceived.

gul·li·ble (gul'əbəl), *adj.* easily fooled; ready to accept anything said or offered; credulous. —**gul,li·bil'i·ty,** *n.*

gu·los·i·ty (gyo͞olos'itē), *n.* greed; gluttony.

gunk·hole (guNGk'hōl,), *v. U.S. nautical.* to sail gently along the coast stopping in quiet anchorages.

gurge (gûj), *n.* a whirlpool.

gur·gi·ta·tion (gû,jitā'sHən), *n.* a surging and eddying as of water.

gu·ru (go͞o'ro͞o, go͞o'ro͞o), *n.* a Hindu teacher of religion, giving personal religious instruction.

gus·set (gus'it), *n.* a triangular piece of material inserted for strengthening or enlarging the original.

gus·ta·tion (gustā'sHən), *n.* act or faculty of tasting.

gus·ta·to·ry (gus'tətəri, gus'tətri), *adj.* pertaining to the sense of taste or tasting.

gut·buck·et (gut'buk,it), *n.* jazz played in early traditional barrelhouse style.

gut·ta (gut'ə), *n., pl.* **gut·tae** (gut'ē). a drop or something like one.

gut·ta-per·cha (gut'əpû'CHə), *n.* a substance obtained from the sap of certain Malayan trees and used for insulating electric wires and dental fillings.

gut·tate (gut'āt), *adj.* resembling or in the form of a drop.

gut·ti·form (gut'ifôm,), *adj.* shaped like a drop.

gut·tle (gut'əl), *v.* to guzzle; eat greedily.

guy·ot (gē'ō), *n.* a flat undersea mountain in the Pacific Ocean.

gym·kha·na (jimkä'nə), *n.* a meeting held for sports enthusiasts, esp. horseriders, to display their skills.

gym·nog·e·nous (jimnoj'ənəs), *adj.* featherless at birth, as certain birds.

gym·no·rhi·nal (jimnōrī'nəl), *adj.* (of a bird) having the nostrils not covered with feathers.

gym·no·sperm (jim'nōspûm,), *n.* a plant with its seeds not enclosed in an ovary. —**gym·no·sper'mous,** *adj*

gym·no·spore (jim'nōspô,ə), *n.* a spore with no protective envelope.

gy·nae·cic (jīnē'sik, gīnē'sik), *adj.* of or pertaining to women.

gyn·ae·coid (jī'nəkoid, gī'nəkoid), *adj.* of or like a woman.

gy·nae·col·ogy (gī,nəkol'əjē), *n.* the study of the functions and diseases of the reproductive organs of women. —**gy,nae·col'o·gist, gy,ne·col'·o·gist,** *n.*

gy·nae·co·mor·phous (gī,nikōmô'fəs), *adj.* having the appearance of a female.

gy·nae·cop·a·thy (gī,nikop'əthē), *n.* a disease peculiar to women.

gy·nae·pho·bi·a (jī,nifō'bēə, gī,nifō'bēə), *n.* a fear of women.

gy·nan·dro·morph (jinan'drōmôf,, jīnan'drōmôf,, gīnan'drōmôf,), *n.* an organism of mixed sex; hermaphrodite; a monoecious individual.

gy·nan·dry (jinan'drē, jīnan'drē, gīnan'drē), *n.* the condition of having both male and female organs in one individual; hermaphroditism. Also **gy·nan'drism.**

gy·nar·chy (jī'nä,kē, gī'nä,kē), *n.* government by a woman or women. Also **gy·nae·coc·ra·cy, gy·ne·coc·ra·cy** (jī,nikok'rəsē, gī,nikok'rəsē).

gy·ni·at·rics (jī,niat'riks, gī,niat'riks), *n.* treatment of diseases peculiar to females. Also **gy·ni'·at·ry.**

gy·noe·ci·um, gy·nae·ce·um, gy·nae·ci·um (jīnē'sēəm, gīnē'sēəm), *n.* the innermost part of a flower, lying within the ring of stamens and comprising one or more carpels. Also **pistil.**

gy·ro·com·pass (jī'rōkum,pəs), *n.* a nonmagnetic navigational compass making use of a gyroscope to indicate true north.

gy·rose (jī'rōs), *adj.* having wavy striations.

gy·ro·vague (jī'rōvāg,), *n.* an itinerant monk of the early church who travelled between monasteries.

gyve (jīv), *n.* **1.** *Usually pl.* a shackle for the leg; fetter. —*v.* **2.** to shackle or fetter by the leg.

ha·bil·i·ments (həbil'imənts), *n. pl.* furniture; decorations; equipment.

ha·bit·u·al (həbicн'ळळəl, həbit'yळळəl), *adj.* resulting from habit; customary.

ha·bit·u·ate (həbicн'ळळāt, həbit'yळळāt), *v.* **ha·bit·u·at·ed, ha·bit·u·at·ing.** to become or make (someone or something else) become used to; accustom, as *The trainer habituated the horse to a bridle by using a hackamore.*

hab·i·tude (hab'ityळळd), *n.* usual condition or state of mind; usual way of acting.

ha·bit·u·é (həbicн,ळळā', həbit'yळळā), *n.* a person who regularly visits a certain place, as a club, bar, etc.

ha·chure (hashळळ'ə), *n.* one of a number of fine parallel lines of shading drawn on a map to indicate the steepness of a slope.

hack·a·more (hak'əmô,ə), *n.* a horse hair or rawhide bridle with a nose-piece, used mainly for breaking colts.

hack·er (hak'ə), *n.* **1.** a person, esp. an amateur, who has become expert in the use of a computer, esp. a microcomputer. **2.** (sometimes) such a person who uses his knowledge to gain access to secret files, to use communications lines without paying, and to engage in other illegal activities.

hack·neyed (hak'nēd), *adj.* trite; over-used; stereotyped, as *a hackneyed phrase.*

hadj (hadj), *n.*, *pl.* **hadj·es.** See **hajj.**

had·ji (haj'ē), *n.*, *pl.* **hadj·is.** See **hajji.**

haec·ce·i·ty (heksē'itē, hēksē'itē), *n.* the quality that gives something its individuality. See also **quiddity.**

hae·ma·chrome (hē'məkrōm,), *n.* the blood's red colouring matter.

hae·mag·glu·ti·nate (hē,məglळळ'tināt,), *v.* (in immunology) to gather in clumps. —**hae,-mag·glu,ti·na'tion,** *n.*

hae·ma·gogue (hē'məgog), *adj.* encouraging a flow of blood. Also **hae·ma·gog·ic** (hē,məgoj'-ik).

hae·mal (hē'məl), *adj.* belonging or pertaining to the blood or blood system. Also **hae'ma·tal.**

hae·ma·nal·y·sis (hē,mənal'isis), *n.* analysis of the blood, particularly its chemical constituents.

haem·a·ther·mal (hē,məthû'məl), *adj.* warm-blooded.

hae·mat·ic (hēmat'ik), *adj.* of or containing blood.

haem·a·tin·ic (hem,ətin'ik, hē,mətin'ik), *n.* **1.** a substance that promotes the production of red blood cells. —*adj.* **2.** promoting the production of red blood cells; enriching the blood.

hae·ma·to·blast (hēmat'ōblast,), *n.* an immature cell, smaller than the corpuscles, found in the blood.

haem·a·to·cele (hem'ətōsēl,, hē'mətōsēl,), *n.* a tumour or haemorrhage containing blood.

haem·a·to·crit (hem'ətōkrit, hēm'ətōkrit), *n.* a machine separating blood cells from plasma by centrifugal force.

haem·a·to·cry·al (hem,ətōkrī'əl, hē,mətō-krīəl), *adj.* cold-blooded. See also **haemather-mal, homoiothermal.**

haem·a·to·cyst (hem'ətōsist,, hē'mətōsist,), *n.* a cyst containing blood.

haem·a·to·cyte (hem'ətōsīt,, hē'mətōsīt,), *n.* See **haemocyte.**

haem·a·to·gen·e·sis (hem,ətōjen'isis, hē,m-ətōjen'isis), *n.* the formation of blood.

haem·a·tog·e·nous (hem,ətoj'ənəs, hē,m-ətoj'ənəs), *adj.* producing blood, originating in the blood, or borne by the blood.

haem·a·tol·o·gy (hem,ətol'əjē, hē,mətol'əjē), *n.* the branch of biology or medicine dealing with the blood and its organs.

haem·a·to·ma (hemətō'mə, hē,mətō'mə), *n.* a tumour or swelling filled with blood.

haem·a·to·phyte (hem'ətōfīt,, hē'mətōfīt,), *n.* a plant parasite that lives in the blood. See also **haematozoon.**

haem·a·to·poi·e·sis (hem,ətōpoiē'sis, hē,m-ətōpoiē'sis), *n.* the production of blood.

haem·a·to·sis (hem,ətō'sis, hē,mətō'sis), *n.* **1.** the production of blood. **2.** the oxygenation of blood in the lungs.

haem·a·to·ther·mal (hem,ətōthû'məl, hē,mətōthû'məl), *adj.* warm-blooded. Also **haemathermal.**

haem·a·to·zo·on (hem,ətōzō'ən, hē,mətōzō'-ən), *n.*, *pl.* **haem·a·to·zo·a** (hem,ətōzō'ə, hē,m-ətōzō'ə). an animal parasite living in the blood. See also **haematophyte.**

hae·ma·tu·ri·a (hem,ətyळळr'ēə, hē,mətyळळr'-ēə), *n.* the presence of blood in the urine.

hae·mo·cyte (hē'mōsīt), *n.* a blood cell. Also **haematocyte.**

hae·mo·cy·tom·e·ter (hē,mōsītom'itə), *n.* an instrument for counting the number of blood cells in a sample.

hae·mo·dy·nam·ics (hē,mōdīnam'iks), *n.* the branch of science studying the dynamics of blood circulation.

hae·mo·flag·el·late (hē,mōflaj'əlāt), *n.* a parasitic flagellate in the blood.

hae·mo·glo·bin (hē'məglō,bin), *n.* the colouring substance of the red blood corpuscles, carrying oxygen to the tissues, present also in reduced form in the blood of the veins and, mixed with oxygen, in that of the arteries.

hae·moid (hē'moid), *adj.* bloodlike.

hae·mol·y·sis (himol'isis), *n.* the dissolution of red blood cells by the release of haemoglobin. —**hae·mo·ly·tic** (hēmōlit'ik), *adj.*

hae·mo·phile (hē'məfil), *n.* a haemophiliac.

hae·mo·phil·i·a (hē,məfil'ēə), *n.* an abnormal blood condition marked by severe bleeding and haemorrhaging from slight wounds and bruises due to improper clotting, and inherited by males only through the mother.

hae·mo·phil·i·ac (hē,məfil'ēak), *n.* a sufferer from haemophilia.

hae·mo·phil·ic (hē,məfil'ik), *adj.* **1.** affected by or pertaining to haemophilia. **2.** (of bacteria) developed in blood or in a blood culture.

hae·mo·pho·bi·a (hē,məfō'bēə), *n.* an abnormal dread of blood.

hae·mop·ty·sis (himop'tisis), *n.* the spitting out of blood or of blood-flecked mucus.

hae·mo·sta·sis (hē,mōsta'sis, hem,ōsta'sis), *n.* **1.** the arrest of bleeding or haemorrhage. **2.** the cutting off of circulation of the blood in a part.

hae·mo·stat (hē'məstat,), *n.* an instrument to stop bleeding.

hae·mo·stat·ic (hē,məstat'ik), *adj.* arresting bleeding; styptic.

hae·mo·ther·a·py (hē,mōther'əpē), *n.* treatment of disease by means of blood or plasma transfusion.

hae·mo·tho·rax (hē,məmōthôr'aks), *n.* a condition characterized by presence of blood in the pleural cavity.

hag·gis (hag'is), *n.* a Scottish dish made of sheep's or calf's heart, lungs, and liver, chopped with suet and oatmeal, and boiled in the stomach of the animal.

hag·i·oc·ra·cy (hag,ēok'rəsē), *n.* government by saints, priests, or others deemed holy.

hag·i·og·ra·pher (hag,ēog'rəfə), *n.* a writer of the lives of saints. Also **hag,i·og'ra·phist.**

hag·i·og·ra·phy (hag,ēog'rəfē), *n.* the writing and study of the lives of saints.

hag·i·ol·a·try (hag,ēol'ətrē), *n.* the worship or veneration of saints.

hag·i·ol·o·gy (hag,ēol'əjē), *n.* a single work or branch of literature describing the lives and legends of saints.

hag·rid·den (hag'rid,ən), *adj.* worried or tormented, as by a hag or witch.

Hague Tribunal, a court of arbitration set up at The Hague, the Netherlands, in 1899 for the peaceful settlement of international disputes.

ha·ha (hä'hä), *n.* a boundary to a garden or park, usually a barrier in the form of a ditch.

haik, haick (hīk, hāk), *n.* an outer garment worn by Arabs, made from a rectangular piece of cloth.

hai·kai (hī'kī), *n.* a form of Japanese verse, originated in 17th-century Japan.

hai·ku (hī'kōō), *n.* a Japanese poem consisting of 17 syllables.

hajj (haj), *n., pl.* **hajj·es.** a pilgrimage to Mecca made at least once by pious Muslims. Also **hadj.**

hajj·ji (haj'ē), *n., pl.* **haj·jis. 1.** a Muslim who has made the pilgrimage to Mecca. **2.** an Eastern Christian who has visited the Holy Sepulchre in Jerusalem. Also **hadji, haji.**

hal·al, hall·al (häläl'), *n.* **1.** meat from animals slaughtered in accordance with Muslim law. —*adj.* **2.** of or relating to such meat. —*v.* **hal·als, hal·al·ling, hal·alled; hall·als, hall·al·ling, hall·alled. 3.** to slaughter animals in this fashion.

ha·la·tion (həlā'sHən), *n.* a bright, halo-like patch or blur on a developed photograph, caused by light reflected through the surface emulsion from the surface of the backing.

ha·la·vah (hal'əvä), *n.* See **halvah.**

hal·cy·on (hal'sēən), *n.* **1.** a mythical bird said to breed at the winter solstice in a nest floating on the sea and to calm the waves; identified with the kingfisher. —*adj.* **2.** calm; peaceful; happy; prosperous.

half·life (häf'līf,), *n., pl.* **half·lives.** (in physics) the time in which one half the atoms in a quantity of radioactive substance disintegrate. Also **half-life period.**

half title, a page in a book bearing the title only, usually placed before the title page. Also **bastard title.**

half·tone (häf'tōn,), *n.* **1.** a process of photoengraving in which tone gradations are reproduced in the form of minute dots by means of a screen placed before the film. **2.** the metal plate thus prepared for letterpress reproduction. **3.** the print obtained from the plate.

half·track (häf'trak,), *n.* a motor vehicle, particularly for military use, equipped with caterpillar treads on the rear driving wheels.

hal·i·dom (hal'idəm), *n.* a holy place or sanctuary, as a chapel or church. Also **hal'i·dome.**

hal·i·to·sis (hal,itō'sis), *n.* foul, offensive breath.

hal·lu·cin·o·gen (həlōō'sinəjen), *n.* a substance, as a drug, that causes hallucinations or fantasies.

hal·lu·ci·no·sis (həlōōsinō'sis), *n.* mental illness, accompanied by and caused by hallucinations.

hal·lux (hal'əks), *n., pl.* **hal·lu·ces** (hal'yəsēz).

the big toe or the innermost digit of the hind foot of a mammal.

hal·o·phile (hal'əfīl,, hä'ləfīl), *n.* a plant or animal favouring an alkaline or salty environment.

hal·o·phyte (hal'əfīt,, ha'ləfīt), *n.* a plant favouring alkaline or salty soil.

hal·vah (hal'vä), *n.* a sweet, sticky, gelatinous form of sweet made of ground sesame seed, honey, and flavouring. Also **halavah, halva.**

ha·mate (hā'māt), *adj.* **1.** equipped with hooks; hook-like. —*n.* **2.** Also **unciform.** the anatomical name for a bone of the carpus with a hook-like process.

ham·mer·toe (ham'ətō,), *n.* a toe permanently deformed by being bent downwards.

ham·u·lus (ham'yələs), *n.*, *pl.* **ham·u·li** (ham'-yəlī). a small hook-like projection as on a bone, bristle, or feather.

han·a·per (han'əpə), *n.* a wicker case or basket formerly used to carry documents.

hand·sel (han'səl), *n.* **1.** a gift or present, bringing good luck, as at the beginning of a new year or a new enterprise. —*v.* **2.** to give a handsel to. Also **han'sel.**

hanging valley, a valley, the lower end of which opens high above a beach or stretch of coast, usually as a result of erosion.

Han·sard (han'säd), *n. Brit.* the published reports of the debates and proceedings of the two Houses of Parliament.

Han·sen's disease (han'sənz), leprosy, so named after the Norwegian physician who discovered the causative bacterium.

ha·pax le·go·me·non (hap'aks ligom'-ənon), *pl.* **hap·ax le·go·me·na** (hap'aks ligom'-ənə). *Greek.* a word or group of words of which there is only one recorded use.

hap·less (hap'lis), *adj.* unfortunate; unlucky.

hap·log·ra·phy (haplog'rəfē), *n.* a copying or printing error by which a letter or group of letters which should be repeated are omitted, as *dention* for *dentition.*

hap·loid (hap'loid), *adj.* (in biology) single.

hap·lol·o·gy (haplol'əjē), *n.* the contraction of a word by elimination of a syllable, as *symbology* for *symbolology.*

hap·lo·pi·a (haplō'pēə), *n.* normal vision. See also **diplopia.**

hap·tics (hap'tiks), *n.* a branch of psychology dealing with the sense of touch.

hap·tom·e·ter (haptom'itə), *n.* a machine that measures the sense of touch.

ha·ra·ki·ri (har,əkir'ē), *n.* a form of suicide, by slitting open the abdomen, practised in Japan, usually after signal disgrace; seppuku. Also **har·ikar·i** (har,ēkä'rē).

har·ass (har'əs, həras'), *v.* to continue to annoy, torment, and disturb.

har·bin·ger (hä'binjə), *n.* a person, thing, or event that foreshadows or presages a coming event, as *The first cuckoo is a harbinger of spring.*

har·bour (hä'bə), *v.* to maintain; keep safe, as *to harbour refugees* or *to harbour a grudge.*

hard copy, computer output in the form of printed matter.

hard goods, *U.S.* nonperishable merchandise, as furniture, cars, and household appliances. See also **soft goods.**

hard-hat (häd'hat,), *n. Chiefly U.S.* a worker in a hazardous location who wears a protective helmet.

hard-pan (häd'pan,), *n.* hard subsoil, as of clay, gravel, or sand; any firm, unbroken ground.

hard sauce, a creamlike blend of butter and sugar, often flavoured, esp. with brandy, whisky, etc., used for pies and puddings.

hard science, any of the physical or biological sciences, such as chemistry, geology, or biology. —**hard scientist,** *n.*

hard sell, a direct, high-pressure method of advertising or selling. See also **soft sell.**

hard·tack (häd'tak,), *n.* a hard biscuit, once a part of navy or army rations. Also **ship biscuit.**

Ha·ri·jan (hur'ijən, har'ijən), *n.* a member of the Hindu social class in India known as outcastes, afforded the lowest status and formerly called untouchables.

harl (häl), *n.* a fibre of flax or hemp.

har·le·quin (hä'likwin), *n.* the leading male actor in old Italian comedy, traditionally masked and wearing multicoloured tights, carrying a magic wand, and given to playing comic tricks.

har·le·quin·ade (hä,likwinād'), *n.* a play or pantomime in which harlequin plays the lead; horseplay.

har·le·quin·esque (hä,likwinesk'), *adj.* in the guise or manner of a harlequin.

har·mon·ic progression (hämon'ik), a series of numbers whose reciprocals are in arithmetic progression, as 1, 1/2, 1/3, 1/4, 1/5. See also **arithmetic progression, geometric progression.**

har·mo·ni·um (hämō'nēəm), *n.* a small keyboard instrument, similar to an organ, the sounds of which are produced by metal reeds set into vibration by air from a foot-operated bellows.

har·ri·dan (har'idən), *n.* a bad-tempered, disreputable old woman; a hag.

har·ri·er (har'ēə), *n.* one of a breed of hound, smaller than a foxhound, used for hunting, esp. hares.

har·ry (har'ē), *v.* **har·ried, har·ry·ing.** to pester; annoy.

ha·sen·pfef·fer, has·sen·pfef·fer (hä'sənfef,ə), *n.* a stew of pickled rabbit meat, usually served with sour cream.

hash·ish (hasH'ēsH), *n*. a narcotic or intoxicant, prepared from cannabis, and drunk, smoked, or chewed. Also **hash'eesh.**

Ha·sid (ha'sid), *n*., *pl*. **Ha·sid·im** (hasid'im). a member of an orthodox Jewish sect, originating in 18th-century Poland, characterized by its blend of mysticism and prayer with joyful singing and dancing. Also **Has'sid, Chas'sid, Chasid.** —**Has'i·dism,** *n*.

has·let (haz'lit), *n*. the edible entrails, heart, liver, etc., of an animal, esp. the pig, formerly roasted on a spit.

has·lock (has'lok), *n*. a coarse type of wool.

has·tate (has'tāt), *adj*. shaped like a spearhead.

hate·mon·ger (hāt'muNG,gə, hāt'moNG,gə), *n*. someone who stirs up hatred or prejudice.

haus·tel·late (hôstel'it, hôstel'āt), *adj*. adapted for sucking, as the mouth parts of certain crustaceans and insects.

haus·tel·lum (hôstel'əm), *n*., *pl*. **haus·tel·la** (hôstel'ə). the sucking organ or proboscis of some crustaceans and insects.

haute cou·ture (ōt koōtyr'), *French*. high fashion, applied particularly to fashionable dressmaking and to the establishments engaged in it.

haute cui·sine (ōt kwēzēn'), *French*. the art of fine cooking and food preparation.

hau·teur (ōtû', hōtû'), *n*. a lofty or haughty manner and bearing.

haut monde (ō mōnd'), *French*. high society. See also **beau monde.**

have·lock (hav'lok), *n*. a cloth covering for a cap, with a flap to protect the back of the neck from the sun.

heart·burn (hät'bûn,), *n*. an uncomfortable burning sensation in the stomach caused by excess acidity. Also **cardialgia.**

heart murmur. See **murmur.**

heat exchanger, an engineering device for cooling and heating fluids simultaneously, or for transferring the heat of one substance to another, as in reclaiming exhaust gases.

heavy water, water in which deuterium has replaced hydrogen atoms, chiefly used to control nuclear reaction in the furnaces of atomic power plants.

heav·y·weight (hev'ēwāt,), *n*. a boxer of any weight fighting in the heaviest class.

heb·do·mad (heb'dəmad,), *n*. **1.** the number seven, or group of seven. **2.** a week.

heb·dom·a·dal (hebdom'ədəl), *adj*. occurring, meeting, or being published every week.

he·be·phre·nia (hē,bəfrē'nēə), *n*. a form of split-personality disorder, allied to puberty, marked by hallucinations and severe emotional disturbance. —**he·be·phren·ic** (hē,bəfren'ik), *adj*.

heb·e·tate (heb'itāt), *v*. **1.** to make or become dull or inert. —*adj*. **2.** (of a plant part) having a blunt or soft point.

he·be·tic (hibet'ik), *adj*. characteristic of or pertaining to puberty.

heb·e·tude (heb'ityoōd), *n*. state of being dull, inert, and listless.

hec·a·tomb (hek'ətoōm,, hek'ətōm,), *n*. a mass slaughter or sacrifice.

hec·to·li·tre, hek·to·li·tre (hek'təlē,tə), *n*. a metric measure of capacity, equivalent to 100 litres or 21.99 imperial gallons.

hec·to·me·tre, hek·to·me·tre (hek'tōmētə), *n*. a metric measurement of length, equalling 100 metres or 328.089 feet.

hec·tor (hek'tə), *v*. to bully; harass.

hec·to·stere, hek·to·stere (hek'təstē,ə), *n*. a metric measurement of capacity, equal to 100 steres.

he·don·ics (hēdon'iks), *n*. (in psychology) the study of pleasurable and nonpleasurable states of mind. —**he·don'ic,** *adj*.

he·don·ism (hē'dəniz,əm, hed'əniz,əm), *n*. **1.** ethical theory or doctrine that the pursuit of pleasure is the highest good. **2.** devotion to pleasure or happiness as a way of life.

he·don·ist (hē'dənist, hēd'ənist), *n*. a person who believes that the most important thing is happiness; one addicted to pleasure.

he·gem·o·ny (higem'ənē, hijem'ənē), *n*. political or economic leadership or dominance by one state over others in a confederacy.

heg·i·ra, hej·i·ra (hej'irə), *n*. a flight or escape from one situation or place to a better one, esp. (**H-**) the flight of Muhammad from Mecca to Medina in A.D. 622, regarded as the beginning of the Muhammadan era. Also **hijra.**

Hei·li·gen·schein (hī'ligənsHīn,), *n*., *pl*. **Hei·li·gen·scheine** (hi'ligənsHī,nə). *German*. a halo; specifically, the circle of light around the shadow cast on wet grass in sunlight by someone's head.

hei·nous (hā'nəs), *adj*. wicked; atrocious; abominable.

heir apparent, *pl*. **heirs apparent.** one who is in line to succeed to a property or title and whose rights are unassailable.

heir presumptive, *pl*. **heirs presumptive.** one who is in line to succeed to a property or title, unless a closer direct heir is subsequently born.

hek·to·li·tre (hek'təlē,tə), *n*. See **hectolitre.**

hek·to·me·tre (hek'təmē,tə), *n*. See **hectometre.**

hek·to·stere (hek'təstēr), *n*. See **hectostere.**

he·li·a·cal (hilī'əkəl), *adj*. near or pertaining to the sun, esp. applied to the appearance of a visible star before sunrise or its disappearance after sunset. Also **he'li·ac.**

hel·i·cal (hel'ikəl), *adj*. of or in the form of a helix.

he·liced (hē'lĭst), *adj.* adorned or decorated with spirals.

hel·i·cline (hel'ĭklīn), *n.* a curving ramp.

hel·i·co·graph (hel'ĭkōgräf,), *n.* an instrument for drawing spirals.

hel·i·coid (hel'ĭkoid), *adj.* coiled or shaped like a spiral.

he·li·o·cen·tric (hē,lēōsen'trĭk), *adj.* **1.** having or depicting the sun as central. **2.** seen or measured as from the centre of the sun.

he·li·o·gram (hē'lēəgram,), *n.* a message signalled by a heliograph.

he·li·o·graph (hē'lēəgräf,), *n.* **1.** an instrument for signalling messages by reflecting sunlight intermittently through a mirror by means of a shutter. **2.** an apparatus for photographing the sun. **3.** an instrument for measuring the intensity of the sun's rays. —*v.* **4.** to signal by heliograph. —**he,li·og'ra·phy,** *n.*

he·li·ol·a·try (hē,lēol'ətrē), *n.* sun worship.

he·li·o·scope (hē'lēəskōp,), *n.* a telescope for observing the sun, with a device to protect the eyes.

he·li·o·stat (hē'lēəstat,), *n.* an apparatus comprising a mirror turned by clockwork, for reflecting the light of the sun in a certain direction.

he·li·o·tax·is (hē,lēōtak'sĭs), *n.* movement of an organism in relation to the light of the sun.

he·li·o·ther·a·py (hē,lēōther'əpē), *n.* treatment of sickness by sunlight.

he·li·o·trope (hē'lēətrōp,, hel'ēətrōp,), *n.* **1.** any plant whose flowers turn to face the sun. **2.** pale reddish lavender. **3.** a surveyor's construction consisting of mirrors that focus sunlight from a distance to a single point for observation and measurement.

he·li·o·trop·ic (hē,lēōtrop'ĭk), *adj.* (of a plant) growing towards the sun or light. —**he,li·ot'ro·pism,,** *n.*

he·lix (hē'lĭks), *n.,* *pl.* **hel·i·ces** (hel'ĭsēz), **he·lix·es.** a spiral.

hel·minth (hel'mĭnth), *n.* a worm, esp. a parasitic one.

hel·min·thi·a·sis (hel,mĭnthī'əsĭs), *n.* a disease caused by the presence of worms in the body.

hel·min·thic (helmĭn'thĭk), *adj.* pertaining to, or caused by, parasitic intestinal worms.

hel·min·thoid (helmĭn'thoid), *adj.* resembling a helminth; wormlike.

hel·min·thol·o·gy (hel,mĭnthol'əjē), *n.* the medical or scientific study of worms, esp. helminths.

hel·ot (hel'ət), *n.* a serf or slave.

hel·ot·ism (hel'ətiz,əm), *n.* condition or system of being a helot or serf.

hel·ot·ry (hel'ətrē), *n.* state of serfdom or slavery.

helve (helv), *n.* the handle of an axe, chisel, hammer, or similar tool.

hema- For words beginning with this prefix, see **haema-**.

hem·er·a·lo·pi·a (hemərəlō'pēə), *n.* an eye condition in which sight is poor or absent in daylight, but adequate or normal at night or by artificial light; day blindness. See also **nyctalopia.**

hem·i·al·gi·a (hem,ēal'jēə), *n.* severe pain confined to only one side of the head or body.

hem·i·a·nop·si·a (hem,ēənop'sēə), *n.* a condition of half or partial blindness, affecting one or both eyes.

hem·i·cra·ni·a (hem,ikrā'nēə), *n.* pain confined to one side of the head; migraine.

hem·i·dem·i·sem·i·qua·ver (hem,ēdem,ēsem,ēkwā'və), *n.* a musical note having one-eighth the length of a quaver; the sixty-fourth part of a semibreve.

hem·i·me·tab·o·lous (hem,ēmitab'ələs), *adj.* (of an insect) incompletely metamorphosing.

hem·i·pa·re·sis (hem,ēpərē'sis), *n.* mild paralysis on one side of the body.

hem·i·ple·gi·a (hemiplē'jēə), *n.* paralysis on one side of the face or body.

he·mo·di·a (himō'dēə), *n.* extreme sensitivity of the teeth.

hen·dec·a·he·dron (hendek,əhē'drən, hendek,əhed'rən), *n.,* *pl.* **hen·dec·a·he·drons, hen·dec·a·he·dra** (hendek,əhē'drə, hendek,əhed'rə). a three-dimensional solid figure with eleven faces.

hen·dec·a·syl·lab·ic (hendek,əsilab'ĭk), *adj.* (of a line of verse) having eleven syllables.

hen·e·quen (hen'əkin), *n.* the sisal fibre of a species of agave, used for making hemp.

hen·o·the·ism (hen'əthēiz,əm), *n.* a system of religion in which any one of several gods is worshipped.

hen·ry (hen'rē), *n.,* *pl.* **hen·ries, hen·rys.** the unit of inductance in which the electromotive force of one volt is produced by a current varying at one ampere per second.

he·or·tol·o·gy (hē,ôtol'əjē), *n.* a branch of study related to religious festivals.

hep·a·rin (hep'ərin), *n.* an anticoagulant used in the treatment of thrombosis, occurring naturally in human tissues and made commercially from the lungs and liver of domestic food animals.

hep·a·rin·ize (hep'əriniz), *v.* to use heparin to prevent blood clotting.

hep·a·ta·tro·phi·a (hep,ətətrō'fēə), *n.* a wasting away of the liver.

he·pat·ic (hipat'ik), *adj.* **1.** relating to, or acting upon, the liver. **2.** liver-coloured, dark brownish-red.

hep·a·ti·tis (hep,ətī'tis), *n.* inflammation of the liver.

hep·a·tos·co·py (hep,ətos'kəpē) *n.* divination by examining the livers of slaughtered animals.

hep·tam·er·ous (heptam'ərəs), *adj.* consisting of seven parts.

hep·tar·chy (hep'täkē), *n.* **1.** government by seven rulers. **2.** seven kingdoms, each with a separate ruler.

hep·ta·syl·la·ble (hep'təsil,əbəl), *n.* a line of verse, or a word, containing seven syllables.

her·ba·ceous (hûbā'sHəs), *adj.* **1.** herblike. **2.** (of a plant) with a soft stem.

her·bage (hû'bij), *n.* herbaceous vegetation, as grass.

her·ba·list (hû'bəlist), *n.* a collector of or dealer in herbs, formerly botanical, now chiefly medicinal.

her·bar·i·um (hûber'ēəm), *n.*, *pl.* **her·bar·i·ums, her·bar·i·a** (hûber'ēə). a systematically arranged collection of dried plants.

herb·i·cide (hûb'isīd), *n.* a chemical preparation for killing plants, particularly weeds.

her·biv·ore (hû'bivô,ə), *n.* a grass or plant-eating mammal, esp. a hoofed mammal. —**her·biv·o·rous** (hûbiv'ərəs), *adj.*

he·red·i·tist (həred'itist,), *n.* one who believes that heredity, rather than environment, is the chief determinant of character.

her·e·si·arch (hirē'zēäk), *n.* a founder or leader of a heretical group.

her·e·si·mach (hirē'zəmak), *n.* one engaged in combating heresy.

her·e·si·og·ra·phy (hirē,zēog'rəfē), *n.* a written work on heresy.

her·e·si·ol·o·gist (hirē,zēol'əjist), *n.* one who studies or writes about heresy.

her·e·si·ol·o·gy (hirē,zēol'əjē), *n.* the study of heresy.

her·e·sy (her'isē), *n.* a religious doctrine or belief opposed to that of the orthodox system. —**her·e·tic** (her'ətik), *n.* —**he·ret·i·cal** (həret'ikəl), *adj.*

her·it·a·ble (her'itəbəl), *adj.* **1.** capable of being inherited. **2.** (in law) passing by inheritance. —**her,it·a·bil'i·ty**, *n.* —**her'it·ab·ly**, *adv.*

her·i·tage (her'itij), *n.* anything to which a person succeeds by right of birth.

herl (hûl), *n.* a barb or fibre of a feather, esp. as used in fly-fishing.

her·maph·ro·dite (hûmaf'rədīt,), *n.* a human being or animal with both male and female sex organs; gynandromorph.

her·maph·ro·dit·ism (hûmaf'rədītiz,əm), *n.* the condition of being a hermaphrodite; gynandry. Also **her·maph'ro·dism,**.

her·me·neu·tic (hû,minyōō'tik), *adj.* pertaining to explanation or interpretation. Also **her,·me·neu'ti·cal.**

her·me·neu·tics (hû,minyōō'tiks), *n.* the science of interpretation, esp. of the Bible.

her·met·ic (hûmet'ik), *adj.* **1.** airtight or

sealed; impervious to external influence. **2.** *often cap.* of or relating to the alchemical and mystical writings attributed to Hermes Trismegistus. **3.** difficult to understand; esoteric. Also **her·met'i·cal.** —**her·met'i·cal·ly,** *adv.*

her·ni·o·plas·ty (hû'nēōpläs,tē), *n.* an operation to treat a hernia.

her·ni·or·rha·phy (hû,nior'əfē), *n.* the treatment of a hernia by suturing.

her·ni·ot·o·my (hû,nēot'əmē), *n.* the treatment of a hernia by incision. Also **celotomy, kelotomy.**

her·pes fa·ci·a·lis (hû'pēz fā'sHēā'lis), a skin inflammation of the face, often affecting the lips. Also **her'pes la·bi·a'lis** (lā,bēā'lis).

herpes sim·plex (sim'pleks), a skin infection marked by the appearance of clusters of vesicles.

herpes zos·ter (zos'tə), an infection affecting the posterior roots of the nerves, commonly called *shingles*.

her·pe·tol·o·gy (hû,pitol'əjē), *n.* a branch of science dealing with reptiles.

Hes·pe·ri·an (hespēr'ēən), *adj.* western; pertaining to the west.

hes·per·id·i·um (hes,pərid'ēəm), *n.*, *pl.* **hes·per·id·i·a** (hes,pərid'ēə). the fruit of a citrus plant, as an orange or lemon.

Hes·per·us (hes'pəris), *n.* the evening star; Venus. Also **Hes'per.**

he·tae·ra, he·tai·ra (hitī'rə, hitēr'ə), *n.*, *pl.* **he·tae·rae, he·tai·rai** (hitī'rē, hitēr'ē). a courtesan; a woman who uses her beauty and charm to further her social ambitions.

he·tae·rism, he·tai·rism (hitī'rizəm, hitēr'izəm), *n.* a social system in which women are regarded as communal property.

het·er·o·cer·cal (het,ərōsû'kəl), *adj.* (of a fish) having an unevenly divided tail. See also **homocercal.**

het·er·o·chro·mat·ic (het,ərōkrōmat'ik), *adj.* having more than one colour. See also **homochromatic.**

het·er·o·chro·mous (het,ərōkrō'məs), *adj.* consisting of different colours.

het·er·och·tho·nous (het,ərok,thənəs), *adj.* not native; foreign. See also **autochthonous.**

het·er·o·clite (het'ərəklīt,), *adj.* irregular; abnormal.

het·er·o·dox (het'ərōdoks,), *adj.* with opinions or doctrines, chiefly religious, not in accordance with established, orthodox belief. —**het'er·o·dox,y,** *n.*

het·er·o·ge·ne·ous (het,ərōjē'nēəs), *adj.* different in kind; made up of different kinds or parts. See also **homogeneous.**

het·er·o·graft (het'ərōgräft), *n.* an organ or tissue taken from a donor of a different species from the recipient.

het·er·og·ra·phy (het,ərog'rəfē), *n.* **1.** different spelling from that in common use. **2.** the use of a letter or group of letters to represent different sounds, as the *c* in *comb* and *city*.

het·er·og·y·nous (het,əroj'ənəs), *adj.* having two different forms of female, one sexual, the other asexual.

het·er·o·ki·ne·sia (het,ərōkinē'zēə), *n.* (in medicine) the performance of movements opposite to those instructed.

het·er·ol·o·gy (het,ərol'əjē), *n.* **1.** abnormality; structural departure from the normal. **2.** the failure of apparently similar organs to correspond, owing to different origins of constituent parts.

het·er·om·er·ous (het,ərom'ərəs), *adj.* having parts which differ in quality or quantity.

het·er·o·mor·phic (het,ərōmô'fik), *adj.* **1.** of dissimilar shape or form; existing in different forms. **2.** undergoing incomplete metamorphosis, as in certain insects.

het·er·on·o·mous (het,əron'əməs), *adj.* **1.** subject to different laws. **2.** (in biology) having different laws of growth.

het·er·on·o·my (het,əron'əmē), *n.* the state of subjection to another's rule or domination.

het·er·o·nym (het'ərōnim), *n.* a word spelled like another, but with an alternative sound and meaning, as *lead* (to guide) and *lead* (a metal). See also **homograph, homonym, homophone.**

het·er·on·y·mous (het,əron'iməs), *adj.* **1.** pertaining to, or having the nature of, a heteronym. **2.** correlated, but having different names, as *husband* and *wife*.

het·er·o·phemy (het'ərōfē,mē), *n.* an inadvertent use of a word or words other than what is meant, as saying *Caesar* when *Cicero* is intended. —**het'er·o·pheme,,** *n.*

het·er·o·pho·ri·a (het,ərōfôr'ēə), *n.* latent strabismus of one eye or both.

het·er·op·tics (het,ərop'tiks), *n.* incorrect or distorted vision.

het·er·o·sex·u·al (het,ərōsek'sнōōəl, het,ərōsek'syōōəl), *adj.* **1.** relating to the opposite sex or both sexes. **2.** pertaining to, or displaying heterosexuality. —*n.* **3.** a heterosexual individual.

het·er·o·sex·u·al·i·ty (het,ərōsek,sнōōal'itē, het,ərōsek,syōōal'itē), *n.* sexual attraction towards the opposite sex.

het·er·o·sis (het,ərō'sis), *n.* (in biology) the tendency of hybrids to surpass their parents in size, growth, or yield.

het·er·o·tax·is (het,ərōtak'sis), *n.* an abnormal arrangement of parts or organs. —**het·er·o·tac'tic,** *adj.*

het·er·o·to·pi·a (het,ərōtō'pēə), *n.* misplacement of an organ, as the formation of tissue where not normally present. Also **het·er·ot'o·py.**

het·er·o·troph (het'ərōtrof), *n.* a microorganism whose energy is derived from a complex organic compound, such as glucose. See also

autotroph. —**het·er·o·troph·ic** (hetərōtrō'fik), *adj.*

het·er·o·zy·go·sis (het,ərōzīgō'sis), *n.* the condition of being a heterozygote.

het·er·o·zy·gote (het,ərōzī'gōt), *n.* a zygote with dissimilar pairs of genes for an inherited characteristic. See also **homozygote.** —**het,er·o·zy'gous,** *adj.*

het·man (het'mən), *n.*, *pl.* **het·mans.** a Cossack leader or commander.

het·man·ate (het'mənāt), *n.* the domain or authority of a hetman. Also **het'man·ship.**

heu·ris·tic (hyōōris'tik), *adj.* **1.** serving to find out. **2.** stimulating a pupil to find out things for himself.

hex·ad (hek'sad), *n.* **1.** six. **2.** a group of six.

hex·a·em·er·on (hek,saem'əron), *n.* **1.** the six days of the Creation. **2.** a written work on this subject. Also **hex·a·hem·er·on** (hek,səhem'əron), **hex·am'er·on.**

hex·a·gram (hek'səgram,), *n.* a six-pointed plane figure, made up of two overlapping equilateral triangles arranged so that the sides of each are mutually parallel to those of the other.

hex·a·he·dron (hek,səhē'dron), *n.*, *pl.* **hex·a·he·drons, hex·a·he·dra** (hek,səhē'drə). a six-faced three-dimensional figure.

hex·am·er·ous (heksam'ərəs), *adj.* having six parts.

hex·an·gu·lar (heksaNG'gyələ), *adj.* having six angles.

hex·a·par·tite (hek,səpär'tīt), *adj.* divided into six parts.

hex·a·pod (hek'səpod,), *n.* **1.** a member of the class *Insecta*; an insect.—*adj.* **2.** having six feet.

hex·ar·chy (hek'säkē), *n.* a group of six states, each with its own ruler.

hex·a·syl·la·ble (hek,səsil'əbəl), *n.* a line of verse or word containing six syllables. —**hex·a·syl·lab·ic** (hek,səsilab'ik), *adj.*

Hex·a·teuch (hek'sətyōōk), *n.* the first six books of the Old Testament.

hi·a·tus (hīā'təs), *n.*, *pl.* **hi·a·tus·es, hi·a·tus.** a break or gap in a written work, series, or course of action.

hi·ba·kush·a (hibä'kōōsнə), *n.*, *pl.* **hi·ba·kush·a, hi·ba·kush·as.** a survivor of the destruction by atomic bombs of Hiroshima and Nagasaki in 1945.

hi·ber·nac·u·lum (hībənak'yələm), *n.*, *pl.* **hi·ber·nac·u·la** (hībənak'yələ). **1.** a protective cover for winter. **2.** Also **hi·ber·na·cle** (hī'bənakəl). winter quarters, esp. of a hibernating animal.

hi·ber·nal (hībû'nl), *adj.* pertaining to or appearing in winter.

hid·ro·poi·e·sis (hid,rōpoiē'sis), *n.* the production of perspiration.

hi·dro·sis (hidrō'sis), *n.* a condition in which

excessive perspiration is secreted, as in some illnesses.

hi·e·mal (hī'əməl), *adj.* pertaining to winter; wintry.

hi·er·ar·chy (hī'ərä,kē), *n.*, *pl.* **hi·er·ar·chies.** an arrangement in which various elements, people, or things, are ranked in a specific way. —hi,er·ar'chi·cal, hi,er·ar'chic, *adj.*

hi·er·at·ic (hī,ərat'ik), *adj.* 1. pertaining to priests or sacred things. 2. pertaining to an ancient Egyptian form of writing abbreviated hieroglyphics, used by priests.

hi·er·oc·ra·cy (hī,ərok'rəsē), *n.* government or rule by priests.

hi·er·o·gram (hī'ərəgram,), *n.* a sacred emblem or symbol.

hi·er·o·gram·mat (hī,ərəgram'it), *n.* a writer of sacred symbols. Also **hi,er·o·gram'mate.**

hi·er·ol·a·try (hī,ərol'ətrē), *n.* worship of saints or sacred things.

hi·er·ol·o·gy (hī,ərol'əjē), *n.* literature or study of sacred things.

hi·er·o·phant (hī'ərəfant), *n.* an interpreter of religious mysteries.

hi·er·ur·gy (hī'ərû,jē), *n.* a holy act or religious observance.

hig·gler (hig'lə), *n.* a travelling dealer; pedlar; huckster.

high·bind·er (hī'bīn,də), *n. U.S.* a confidence trickster; swindler.

high-level language, (in computing) a programming language in which each symbol represents several machine code instructions, making it more intelligible to humans.

high-level waste, radioactive waste producing high and enduring levels of radiation and requiring special containment and treatment for many years.

hij·ra (hij'rə), *n.* See **hegira.**

Hi·na·ya·na (hēnəyä'nə), *n.* one of the two main schools of Buddhism, in which the believer is expected to work out his own salvation. Also **Theravada.** See also **Mahajana, Bodhisattva.**

hin·ny (hin'ē), *n.* the offspring of a female ass or donkey and a stallion.

hip·pi·at·rics (hip,ēat'riks), *n.* a branch of veterinary medicine specializing in horses.

hip·pie (hip'ē), *n.* a person who has chosen informal, unconventional attire, grooming, and lifestyle usually as an expression of nonconformist attitude towards the Establishment.

hip·po·cam·pus (hip,ōkam'pəs), *n.*, *pl.* **hip·po·cam·pi** (hip,ōkam'pī). 1. a mythical sea monster having a tail of a dolphin and two forefeet. 2. a fold, in cross-section resembling the profile of a sea horse, that forms part of the cerebral cortex and extends into a fissure of a cerebral hemisphere.

hip·pol·o·gy (hipol'əjē), *n.* the study of horses.

hip·poph·a·gist (hipof'əjist), *n.* an eater of horseflesh.

hip·po·phile (hip'ōfil), *n.* a lover of horses.

hir·cine (hû'sīn, hû'sīn), *adj.* 1. goatlike. 2. lecherous; lustful.

hir·sute (hû'syōōt), *adj.* shaggy; hairy.

hir·sut·ism (hû'syōōtiz,əm), *n.* extreme hairiness, esp. in women.

hir·tel·lous (hûtel'əs), *adj.* minutely hairy.

hi·ru·di·noid (hiroō'dənoid), *adj.* resembling or pertaining to a leech.

hi·run·dine (hirun'dīn), *adj.* resembling or pertaining to a swallow.

His·pa·nism (his'pəniz,əm), *n.* a Latin American movement dedicated to the spread of Spanish culture and traditions.

his·pid (his'pid), *adj.* rough with stiff bristles or hairs.

his·pid·u·lous (hispid'yələs), *adj.* covered with tiny, stiff hairs.

his·ta·mine (his'təmēn), *n.* a substance found in all animal and plant cells, thought to be responsible for symptoms of certain allergic reactions as asthma, hay fever, hives, etc., causing capillary dilatation, reduction of blood pressure, and contraction of the uterus. Used in pharmacology for diagnosing gastric and circulatory functions. See also **antihistamine.**

his·ti·o·cyte (his'tēəsīt,), *n.* a large blood cell in connective tissue. Also **macrophage.**

his·to·com·pat·i·bil·i·ty (his,tōkəmpat,ibil'itē), *n.* the degree to which a graft from one organism will be tolerated by the immune system of another. —his,to·com·pat'i·ble, *adj.*

his·to·gen·e·sis (his,tōjen'isis), *n.* the production and development of tissues.

his·toid (his'toid), *adj.* resembling tissue, esp. as of a tumour. Also **his·ti·oid** (his'tēoid).

his·tol·o·gy (histol'əjē), *n.* the scientific study of organic tissue. —his·tol'o·gist, *n.*

his·to·mor·phol·o·gy (his,tōmôfol'əjē), *n.* histology.

his·to·pa·thol·o·gy (his,tōpəthol'əjē), *n.* the study and treatment of abnormal or diseased tissue.

his·to·phys·i·ol·o·gy (his,tōfiz,ēol'əjē), *n.* the physiological study of organic tissues.

his·to·ri·at·ed (histôr'ēātid), *adj.* decorated with figures of men or animals, as in an illuminated capital or border of a medieval manuscript.

his·tor·i·cism (histor'isiz,əm), *n.* the theory that all historical events are predetermined, and unaffected by human thought and action.

his·to·ric·i·ty (his,təris'itē), *n.* authenticity substantiated by history.

his·to·ri·og·ra·phy (histôr,ēog'rəfē), *n.* 1. written history considered as a body of material.

2. the techniques and procedures of historical scholarship. —**his·to·ri·og·ra·pher,** *n.*

his·to·tome (his'tətōm,), *n.* an instrument for cutting very small sections of organic tissue for microscopic examination.

his·tot·o·my (histot'əmē), *n.* the cutting into minute sections of pieces of tissue for microscopic examination.

his·tri·on·ics (his,trēon'iks), *n.* **1.** a stage representation. **2.** exaggerated, insincere speech or behaviour. —**his,tri·on'ic,** *adj.* —**his'tri·o·nism,**, *n.*

HIV *Abbr. for* human immunodeficiency virus: the causal agent of AIDS in humans.

hives (hīvz), *n.* any of various forms of skin eruptions, as urticaria.

HLA system, human leucocyte antigen system: a class of cell surface markers (and the genes encoding them) that crucially determine whether a tissue graft from a particular donor will be rejected by a recipient's immune system. See **histocompatibility.**

hoar·y (hôr'ē), *adj.* grey- or white-haired with age.

Hob·bism (hob'iz,m), *n.* the theories of the philosopher and political thinker Thomas Hobbes, esp. the belief in obedience to an absolute sovereign.

hob·ble·de·hoy (hob'əldēhoi,), *n.* an awkward, overgrown boy.

Hob·son-Job·son (hob,sənjob'sən), *n.* the modification of originally foreign words which are assimilated into already familiar sounds.

Hob·son's choice (hob'sənz), a course of action that offers no alternative. [after Thomas Hobson, 16th-17th-century stable owner of Cambridge, who insisted on a client's taking the horse nearest to the door.]

hock (hok), *n.* any white Rhine wine.

Hodg·kin's disease (hoj'kinz), a form of cancer involving the lymph glands and spleen.

ho·dom·e·ter (hōdom'itə), *n.* See **odometer.**

hoe·down (hō'doun,), *n. U.S.* a gathering where folk and square dances are performed to the accompaniment of hillbilly music.

ho·gan (hō'gən), *n.* a Navaho Indian hut, made of earth, mud, and branches.

hog·back (hog'bak,), *n.* a steeply sloped hill-ridge, somewhat in the shape of a hog's back, that resists erosion.

hogs·head (hogz'hed,), *n.* **1.** a large cask for liquids. **2.** a liquid measure equivalent to 52½ imperial gallons.

hoi pol·loi (hoi' pəloi'), the majority; the common people.

Hol·arc·tic (hōlärk'tik), *adj.* belonging or pertaining to the Nearctic and Palaearctic regions.

hole-and-corner (hōl,ənkô'nə), *adj.* **1.** secret; underhand; furtive. **2.** trivial; undistinguished. Also **hole,-in-cor'ner.**

ho·lism (hō'lizəm), *n.* a philosophical theory that holds that natural phenomena are entities, more than a sum of different parts. —**ho·lis·tic,** *adj.*

hol·lan·daise sauce (hol'əndāz), a sauce, used esp. with fish and vegetables, made of egg yolks, butter, and seasoning.

Hol·ler·ith code (hol'ərith), a former system in computer technology for coding data into punch cards, in which letters, numbers, etc., are expressed in code form in a pattern of horizontal lines and vertical columns.

hol·o·caust (hol'əkôst,), *n.* **1.** an immense or complete slaughter or destruction, esp. by fire. **2.** (H-) the Nazi campaign of mass extermination of the Jews.

hol·o·crine (hol'əkrin), *adj.* (of a gland) producing secretion as a result of disintegrating cells.

hol·o·gram (hol'əgram), *n.* a three dimensional image produced by using coherent light to project a photograph originally taken with coherent light. —**ho·log'ra·phy,** *n.*

hol·o·graph (hol'əgräf,), *n.* a document handwritten by the person in whose name it appears. —**hol,o·graph'ic, hol,o·graph'i·cal,** *adj.*

holographic will, a will entirely handwritten by the testator. See also **nuncupative will.**

hol·o·lith (hol'əlith), *n.* a piece of jewellery fashioned from a single stone.

hol·o·me·tab·o·lous (hol,əmitab'ələs), *adj.* (of insects) undergoing incomplete metabolism.

hol·o·phrase (hol'əfrāz,), *n.* a phrase expressed in a single word, as an imperative command.

ho·loph·ra·sis (həlof'rəsis), *n.,* *pl.* **ho·loph·ra·ses** (həlof'rəsēz). the use of a single word to express the ideas contained in a sentence or phrase. —**hol·o·phras·tic** (hol,əfras'tik), *adj.*

hol·o·phyt·ic (hol,əfit'ik), *adj.* (of plants) feeding by means of synthesis of inorganic substances.

hol·o·ser·i·ceous (hol,əsərisн'əs), *adj.* covered with small, silky hairs.

hol·o·type (hol'ətīp,), *n.* the original type specimen used in defining a species.

hol·o·zo·ic (hol,əzō'ik), *adj.* feeding on solid food, as most animals.

ho·ly·stone (hō'lēstōn,), *n.* a soft sandstone for scouring decks of ships.

ho·ma·lo·graph·ic (hom,əlograf'ik), *adj.* See **homolographic.**

home economics, the art and study of homemaking, including cookery, child care, furnishing, and other domestic crafts.

ho·me·op·a·thy, ho·moe·op·a·thy (hō,-mēop'əthē), *n.* the treatment of disease by administering minute doses of drugs normally producing symptoms like those of the disease itself. See also **allopathy.** —**ho,me·o·path'ic, ho,moe·o·path'ic,** *adj.* —**ho,me·op'a-**

·thist, ho‚moe·op'a·thist, ho'me·o·path, ho'moe-
·o·path, *n.*

ho·me·o·pla·sia (hō‚mēōplā'zēə), *n.* the formation of new, healthy tissue, similar to existing
tissue.

ho·me·o·sta·sis, ho·moe·o·sta·sis (hō‚-
mēōstā'sis), *n.* the tendency, esp. in higher animals, to maintain physiological balance despite
disrupting stimuli.

ho·me·o·ther·a·py, ho·moe·o·ther·a·py
(hō‚mēōther'əpē), *n.* the treatment of a disease
by use of an agent similar to that causing the
disease.

ho·me·o·therm (hō'mēōthûm‚), *n.* See
homoiotherm.

ho·me·o·therm·al (hō‚mēōthû'məl), *adj.* See
homoiothermal.

hom·i·let·ic (homilet'ik), *adj.* pertaining to
sermons or homilies.

hom·i·let·ics (homilet'iks), *n.* the art of
preaching.

hom·i·ly (hom'ilē), *n.* a sermon or moral lecture.

hom·i·nid (hom'inid), *n.* a member of the
human family; man and his ancestors.

hom·i·nine (hom'inīn), *adj.* resembling a
man; human.

hom·i·noid (hom'inoid), *n.* a member of the
superfamily that includes the large apes and
humans.

ho·mo·bront (hō'məbront‚), *n.* a line on a
weather map linking points where simultaneous
thunderstorm activity is recorded. Also **iso-
bront.**

ho·mo·cen·tric (hōmōsen'trik), *adj.* having
the same centre; diverging from or converging
on a central point.

ho·mo·cer·cal (hō‚mōsû'kəl), *adj.* (of fish)
having a symmetrical, evenly divided tail. See
also **heterocercal.**

ho·mo·chro·mat·ic (hō‚mōkrōmat'ik), *adj.* of
or relating to one colour. See also **heterochro-
matic.**

ho·mo·chrome (hō'mōkrōm), *adj.* See **homochromatic.**

ho·mo·chro·mous (hō‚məkrō'məs), *adj.*
being of one colour, as a flower head.

homoeo- For words beginning with this prefix, see **homeo-.**

ho·mo·e·rot·i·cism (hō‚mōirot'isiz‚əm), *n.*
sexual arousal by someone of one's own gender.
Also **ho·mo·er·o·tism** (hō‚mōer'ətiz‚əm). **—ho‚-
mo·e·rot'ic,** *adj.*

ho·mo·ge·ne·i·ty (hō‚mōjinē'itē, hom‚ōjinē'-
itē), *n.* the state of being homogeneous; made up
of like parts. Also **ho·mo·ge'ne·ous·ness.**

ho·mo·ge·ne·ous (hōməjē'nēəs, hom‚əjē'-
nēəs), *adj.* similar; of the same kind or nature;
composed of identical parts. See also **heterogeneous.**

ho·mo·gen·e·sis (hō‚mōjen'isis), *n.* of reproduction in which the offspring is like the parent
and develops in the same way. **—ho‚mo·ge·net'-
ic,** *adj.*

ho·mog·e·nize (həmoj'ənīz), *v.* to make
homogeneous; to form by mixing or blending
unlike elements.

ho·mog·e·nous (həmoj'ənəs), *adj.* having the
same structure, owing to a common descent or
origin.

ho·mog·e·ny (həmoj'ənē), *n.* analogy in
structure, because of a common descent or origin.

hom·o·graph (hom'əgraf, hom'əgräf‚), *n.* a
word spelled but not necessarily sounded in the
same way as another, and with a different meaning, as *tear* (to rip), and *tear* (to fill with tears;
cry). See also **heteronym, homonym, homophone.**

ho·moi·o·therm (hōmoi'əthûm‚), *n.* a warm-
blooded animal, with a relatively constant body
temperature. Also **homeotherm, homotherm.**

ho·moi·o·ther·mal (hōmoi‚əthû'məl), *adj.*
warm-blooded; possessing a more or less constant body temperature regardless of environ-
mont. Also **homeothermal, homothermal.** See
also **poikilothermal.**

ho·mol·o·gate (homol'əgāt), *v.* to condone;
assent.

ho·mo·log·i·cal (hō‚məloj'ikəl), *adj.* having
the same relative structure or condition; homologous.

ho·mol·o·gize (həmol'əjīz), *v.* to correspond;
make homologous.

ho·mol·o·gous (hō‚mol'əgəs, homol'əgəs),
adj. corresponding, as the several parts of a
reptile and those of a bird; with a similar relationship, form, or position.

ho·mol·o·graph·ic (hōmol‚əgraf'ik), *adj.*
showing parts with similar proportions. Also
homalographic.

hom·o·logue (hom'əlog), *n.* anything that is
homologous.

ho·mol·o·gy (hōmol'əjē), *n.* condition of
being homologous; identity of relation.

ho·mo·mor·phism (hō‚mōmô'fizəm), *n.* the
state of being correspondent or analogous in
outward form but not in structure. **—ho‚mo-
·mor'phic,** *adj.*

hom·o·nym (hom'ənim), *n.* a word sounding
and spelled like another but with a different
meaning, as *bear* (carry), and *bear* (animal). See
also **heteronym, homograph, homophone.**
—ho·mon·y·mous (həmon'əməs), *adj.* **—ho-
·mon·y·my** (həmon'əmē), *n.*

hom·o·phone (hom'əfōn), *n.* a word that
sounds but is not necessarily spelled the same
as another, and that has a different meaning, as
pair and *pear.* See also **heteronym, homograph,
homonym.**

hom·o·phon·ic (hom‚əfon'ik), *adj.* having the

same sound. Also **ho·moph·o·nous** (həmof'-ənəs). —**ho·moph'o·ny,** *n.*

ho·mop·la·sy (hō'mōpla,si, hom'ōplā,si), *n.* analogy of form or structure, because of a similar environment.

ho·mo·tax·is (hō,mōtak'sis), *n.* similarity of relative position, but not necessarily contemporaneous, as geological strata.

ho·mo·therm (hō'mōthûm,), *n.* See **homoiotherm.**

ho·mo·ther·mal (hō,mōthû'məl), *adj.* See **homoiothermal.**

ho·mo·thet·ic (hōmōthet'ik), *adj.* similarly positioned.

ho·mo·type (hō'mōtīp,), *n.* a part or organ with a similar structure to that of another; homologue. **ho·mo·typ·ic** (hō,mōtip'ik), **ho·mo·typ·i·cal** (hō,mōtip'ikəl), *adj.*

ho·mo·zy·gote (hōmōzī'gōt), *n.* a zygote with the same pairs of genes for an inherited characteristic. See also **heterozygote.** —**ho,mo·zy·go'·sis,** *n.* —**ho,mo·zy'gous,** *adj.*

ho·mun·cu·lus (homuNG'kyələs), *n.,* *pl.* **ho·mun·cu·li** (homuNG'kyəlī). a diminutive man; midget.

hon·cho (hon'CHŌ), *n.,* *pl.* **hon·chos.** *U.S.* a boss.

ho·ni soit qui mal y pense (ônē swa' kē mal ē päNs'), *French.* 'may he be shamed who thinks evil of it'; motto of the English Order of the Garter.

hon·or·and (on'ərand,), *n.* the receiver of an honorary academic degree.

hon·o·rar·i·um (on,ərer'ēəm), *n.,* *pl.* **hon·o·rar·i·ums, hon·o·rar·i·a.** a token payment made for professional services that is generally less than would be charged.

hon·or·if·ic (onərif'ik), *adj.* **1.** doing or conferring honour. —*n.* **2.** a grammatical form in a language used to convey respect.

hoo·doo (hoō'doō), *n.* **1.** bad luck. —*v.* **2.** to bring bad luck to.

hook·ah (hoōk'ə), *n.* a pipe, of oriental origin, with a long tube which draws the smoke through scented water; hubble-bubble. Also **hook'a.**

hoot·en·an·ny (hoō'tənan,ē), *n.* *U.S.* an informal gathering at which folk singing and, sometimes, dancing take place.

ho·ra (hôr'ə), *n.* a traditional round dance, performed in Rumania and Israel.

ho·ral (hôr'əl), *adj.* pertaining to an hour or hours; hourly.

hor·me (hô'mē), *n.* an impulsive effort, directed towards a fixed goal. —**hor'mic,** *adj.*

hormic theory, a theory that all action and behaviour, conscious or unconscious, have a purpose or a specific goal.

hor·mone (hô'mōn), *n.* a substance secreted by the endocrine glands that stimulates the functions of certain vital org.....

horn·book (hôn'boŏk,), *n.* a primer, a book, the alphabet or early reader.

hor·ni·to (hônē'tō), *n.* a low volcanic mound that gives out smoke and vapour.

hor·o·lo·gi·um (hor,əlō'jēəm), *n.,* *pl.* **hor·o·lo·gi·a** (hor,əlō'jēə). a clock tower.

ho·rol·o·gy (horol'əjē), *n.* the science of measuring time or of making clocks and watches. —**hor,o·log'ic,** *adj.* —**ho·rol'o·gist,** *n.*

hor·o·scope (hor'əskōp,), *n.* a chart showing the position of the planets in relation to the signs of the zodiac, used to predict fortunes and future events. **ho·ro·scop·ic** (hor,əskop'ik), *adj.* —**ho·ros·co·py** (horos'kəpē), *n.*

hor·o·tel·ic (hor,ətel'ik), *adj.* noting a rate of evolution normal for certain plants and animals. See also **bradytelic, tachytelic.**

hor·ren·dous (horen'dəs), *adj.* dreadful; horrifyingly frightful.

hor·rent (horənt), *adj.* standing up like bristles; bristly.

hor·rip·i·late (horip'ilāt,), *v.* to produce goose flesh; strike cold with fear. —**hor·rip,i·la'tion,** *n.*

hors d'oeu·vre (ô dûv'), *pl.* **hors d'oeu·vre, hors d'oeu·vres** (ô dûv'). a light savoury dish served as an appetizer; small appetizing delicacies served on toast, etc., with alcoholic drinks.

horse latitudes, the zones of high barometric pressure, with calms and light winds, lying about 30° N and 30° S and forming the edges of the trade-wind belt.

horst (hôst), *n.* a part of the earth's surface that has been forced upwards in relation to adjoining portions. See also **graben.**

hor·ta·tive (hô'tətiv), *adj.* encouraging; exhorting; giving advice; urging.

hor·ta·to·ry (hô'tətəri), *adj.* urging; hortative.

hor·ti·cul·ture (hô'tikul,CHə), *n.* the cultivation of gardens; the growing of flowers, fruits, and vegetables.

hor·tus sic·cus (hô'təs sik'əs), a collection of dried, preserved plants; herbarium.

hos·pice (hos'pis), *n.* **1.** a house of rest for travellers or pilgrims. **2.** a facility that cares for the terminally ill.

hos·tler (os'lə), *n.* a groom or stableman at an inn.

hotch·potch (hoCH'poCH), *n.* **1.** a random or disorderly array: mixture. **2.** a stew or soup with several kinds of vegetables and meat.

hot line, 1. a direct telephone link between heads of state. **2.** any telephone number that can be reached in case of emergency, as *a suicide hot line.*

hot·spur (hot'spû,), *n.* a rash, impetuous person.

hov·er·craft (hov'əkräft), *n.* former tradename for a vehicle capable of travelling across land or water by hovering a few feet above the surface, suspended on a cushion of air provided by large downward-blowing fans.

hoy·den (hoi'dən), *n.* a rude, boisterous girl or woman; a tomboy.

HTLV *Abbr. for* human T-lymphotropic virus: either of two viruses (HTLV-I or HTLV-II) that attack T-lymphocytes in humans, causing leukaemias and other diseases. HTLV-III is the former name for HIV.

hua·ra·che (hwärä'CHē), *n.* a Mexican sandal with the upper of strips of leather.

hu·bris (hyōō'bris), *n.* excessive or insolent pride; arrogance.

Hu·di·bras·tic (hyōō,dəbras'tik), *adj.* mockheroic.

hug·ger·mug·ger (hug'əmug,ə), *n.* **1.** muddle; confusion. **2.** secrecy.

hu·man·ics (hyōōman'iks), *n.* the study of the affairs of mankind.

hu·man·ism (hyōō'mənizəm), *n.* a system of thought or action concentrating particularly on human interests. —**hu'man·ist**, *n.*

hu·ma·num est er·ra·re (hōōmä'nōōm est erä're), *Latin.* to err is human.

humble pie, enforced humiliation.

hu·mec·tant (hyōōmek'tənt), *n.* a substance that helps keep another substance moist.

hu·mer·al (hyōō'mərəl), *adj.* pertaining to the humerus or to the shoulder.

hu·mer·us (hyōō'mərəs), *n., pl.* **hu·mer·i** (hyōō'mərī). the bone in the arm that runs from the elbow to the shoulder.

hu·mid·i·stat (hyōōmid'istat,), *n.* a device for measuring and controlling humidity. Also **hygrostat.**

hu·mour (hyōō'mə), *n.* a fluid or juice of an animal or plant, either natural or morbid.

hu·mor·al (hyōō'mərəl), *adj.* pertaining to a bodily fluid.

hun·dred·weight (hun'dridwät,), *n.* a unit of avoirdupois weight, equivalent to 112 pounds in Britain, 100 pounds in U.S. *Abbr.:* **cwt.**

hunks (huNGks), *n.* **1.** a mean, disagreeable old person. **2.** a miser.

hurst (hûst), *n.* a hillock, wood, or copse.

hus·band (huz'bənd), *v.* to save; conserve.

hus·band·man (huz'bəndmən), *n., pl.* **hus·band·men.** a farmer; one who tends animals or crops.

hus·band·ry (huz'bəndrē), *n.* farming; agriculture; cultivation of edible crops or food animals.

hy·a·line (hī'əlin), *adj.* glassy; crystalline; transparent.

hy·a·lo·gr·aph (hī'əlōgräf,), *n.* a device used in hyalography.

hy·a·log·ra·phy (hī,əlog'rəfē), *n.* the process of writing or engraving on glass.

hy·a·loid (hī'əloid), *n.* glasslike; hyaline.

hy·brid (hī'brid), *n.* **1.** the offspring of two plants or animals of different species. —*adj.* **2.** bred from two different species. —**hy'brid·ism,** *n.*

hybrid computer, a computer using numerical representations or properties of known physical processes to solve appropriate parts of mathematical problems. See also **analogue computer, digital computer.**

hy·brid·o·ma (hī,bridō'mə), *n.* a hybrid cell formed by fusing an immortal tumour cell with, typically, a cell synthesizing a desired protein but of limited lifespan.

hy·drae·mi·a (hīdrē'mēə), *n.* a condition in which there is an excessive amount of water in the blood.

hy·dra·gogue (hī'drəgog), *adj.* tending to expel or causing the expulsion of watery fluid from the body, as from the bowels.

hy·drau·lics (hīdro'liks), *n.* the science dealing with the motive power of water and other liquids. —**hy·drau'lic,** *adj.*

hy·dric (hī'drik), *adj.* **1.** pertaining to or containing hydrogen. **2.** pertaining to, or adapted to wet, moist surroundings.

hy·dro·ceph·a·lus (hī,drōsef'ələs), *n.* a brain disease often occurring in infancy, in which fluid accumulates in the cranium, causing enlargement of the head and mental deterioration. Also **hy,dro·ceph'a·ly.** —**hy·dro·ce·phal·ic** (hī,drōsəfal'ik), *adj.* —**hy,dro·ceph'a·loid,** *adj.*

hy·dro·cor·ti·sone (hī,drōkô'tisōn,) *n.* a natural steroid hormone of the adrenal cortex or a synthetic imitation of it used in the treatment of arthritis and some skin complaints.

hy·dro·dy·nam·ics (hī,drōdīnam'iks), *n.* the branch of physics, including hydrostatics and hydrokinetics, dealing with the forces or dynamics of liquids. Also **hydromechanics.** —**hy,dro·dy·nam'ic,** *adj.*

hy·dro·e·lec·tric (hī,drōilek'trik), *adj.* pertaining to the production of electric energy by means of the motive power of water.

hy·dro·foil (hī'drəfoil,), *n.* a vessel with submerged wings that lift the hull clear of the water when a certain speed has been attained, thus reducing friction and, hence, the motive power normally needed, enabling it to move at great speed.

hy·dro·ge·ol·o·gy (hī,drōjēol'əjē), *n.* the science dealing with the occurrence and nature of water beneath the earth's surface.

hy·dro·graph (hī'drəgraf, hī'drəgräf,), *n.* a chart, in graph form, showing rises and falls or seasonal changes in water level.

hy·drog·ra·phy (hīdrog'rəfē), *n.* the science describing and charting the waters of the earth's surface, including tides and currents and particularly their application to navigation.

hy·dro·kin·e·ter (hīdrəkin'itə), *n.* a device,

using jets of water or steam, for circulating water.

hy·dro·ki·net·ics (hī,drōkinet'iks, hī,drōkīnet'iks), *n.* the branch of hydrodynamics dealing with liquids in motion. —**hy,dro·ki·net'ic**, *adj.*

hy·drol·o·gy (hīdrol'əjē), *n.* the science dealing with the occurrence, movement, and distribution of water over the earth's surface.

hy·dro·mag·net·ics (hī,drōmagnet'iks), *n.* See **magnetohydrodynamics.**

hy·dro·man·cy (hī'drōman,sē), *n.* divination by means of water.

hy·dro·me·chan·ics (hī,drōməkan'iks), *n.* hydrodynamics. —**hy,dro·me·chan'i·cal**, *adj.*

hy·dro·mel (hī'drōmel), *n.* a drink containing honey and water, which, when fermented, is called mead.

hy·drom·e·ter (hīdrom'itə), *n.* an instrument for measuring the specific gravity of liquids, and sometimes of solids.

hy·drop·a·thy (hīdrop'əthē), *n.* treatment of disease by the internal and external application of water.

hy·dro·phil·ic (hī,drōfil'ik), *adj.* having a strong liking for water.

hy·droph·i·lous (hīdrof'ələs), *adj.* pollinated through the medium of water.

hy·dro·phobe (hī'drəfōb,), *n.* an animal or person suffering from hydrophobia.

hy·dro·pho·bi·a (hī,drəfō'bēə), *n.* **1.** an abnormal fear of water. **2.** rabies. —**hy,dro·pho'·bic**, *adj.*

hy·dro·phone (hī'drəfōn,), *n.* an instrument for detecting and pinpointing sources of sounds under water.

hy·dro·phyte (hī'drōfīt,), *n.* an aquatic plant. —**hy·dro·phyt·ic** (hīdrōfit'ik), *adj.*

hy·dro·plane (hī'drəplān,), *n.* an aircraft with floats enabling it to land on or lift off from water; seaplane.

hy·dro·pon·ics (hī,drōpon'iks), *n.* the cultivation of plants without the use of soil, by placing roots in water or liquid solutions.

hy·dro·scope (hī'drəskōp,), *n.* an optical instrument for seeing objects under water.

hy·dro·sphere (hī'drəsfēə,), *n.* the waters of the earth, both in the oceans and the atmosphere.

hy·dro·stat·ics (hīdrōstat'iks), *n.* the branch of hydrodynamics dealing with the pressure and equilibrium of liquids at rest. —**hy,dro·stat'ic**, *adj.*

hy·dro·tax·is (hīdrōtak'sis), *n.* the movement in the direction of or away from water. —**hy,dro·tac'tic**, *adj.*

hy·dro·ther·a·peu·tics (hī,drōther,əpyōō'tiks), *n.* the treatment of disease by use of water.

hy·dro·ther·a·py (hī,drōther'əpē), *n.* the

treatment of disease by the external application of water.

hy·dro·ther·mal (hī,drōthû'məl), *adj.* relating to the action of gases on or below the earth's surface.

hy·dro·tho·rax (hī,drōthôr'aks), *n.* a disease marked by the presence of serous fluid in one or both pleural cavities.

hy·dro·trop·ic (hī,drōtrop'ik), *adj.* (of a plant) turning towards or away from water.

hy·drot·ro·pism (hīdrot'rəpiz,əm), *n.* (of a plant) the tendency to grow or bend under the influence of water.

hy·drous (hī'drəs), *adj.* containing water.

hy·e·tal (hī'itəl), *adj.* relating to rainfall; rainy.

hy·et·o·graph (hī'itəgraf,, hī'itəgräf,), *n.* a chart showing average rainfall.

hy·e·tog·ra·phy (hī,itog'rəfē), *n.* the study of the distribution and volume of rainfall.

hy·giene (hī'jēn), *n.* the system or rules relating to the preservation of health. —**hy·gien·ic** (hī,jēn'ik), *adj.*

hy·gro·gram (hī'grəgram,), *n.* the record kept by a hygrograph.

hy·gro·graph (hī'grəgraf,, hī'grəgräf,), *n.* an instrument for measuring atmospheric humidity automatically.

hy·grom·e·ter (hīgrom'itə), *n.* an instrument for measuring atmospheric humidity.

hy·gro·met·ric (hī,grəmet'rik), *adj.* pertaining to hygrometry.

hy·grom·et·ry (hīgrom'itrē), *n.* the branch of physics studying atmospheric humidity.

hy·gro·phyte (hī'grōfīt,), *n.* a plant flourishing in wet ground.

hy·gro·scope (hī'grəskōp,), *n.* an instrument indicating, though not precisely measuring, the degree of atmospheric humidity. —**hy·gro·scop·ic** (hī,grəskop'ik), *adj.*

hy·gro·stat (hī'grəstat,), *n.* See **humidistat.**

hy·gro·ther·mo·graph (hī,grəthû'məgraf,, hī,grəthû'məgräf,), *n.* a meteorological device for recording temperature and humidity.

hy·lo·mor·phic (hī,ləmô'fik), *adj.* made up of corporeal and spiritual matter.

hy·lo·mor·phism (hī,ləmô'fizəm), *n.* the theory that only matter and material forms have real existence.

hy·loph·a·gous (hīlof'əgəs), *adj.* feeding on wood, as certain larvae; xylophagous.

hy·lo·the·ism (hī,ləthē'izəm), *n.* a philosophical theory relating gods to matter.

hy·lo·trop·ic (hī,lətrop'ik), *adj.* (of a substance) capable of changing form, as in sublimation, evaporation, etc., without changing the proportions of the original constituents.

hy·me·ne·al (hī,mənē'əl), *adj.* pertaining to marriage.

hy·men·o·tome (hīmen'ətōm,), *n.* an instrument for cutting a membrane.

hym·nol·o·gy (himnol'əjē), *n.* the study of hymns.

hy·oid (hī'oid), *adj.* pertaining to the U-shaped bone at the base of the tongue.

hyp·aes·the·sia (hīp,ēsthē'zēə, hipēsthē'-zēə), *n.* a poor sense of pain.

hyp·al·ge·si·a (hīp,aljē'zēə), *n.* diminished sensitivity to pain. See also **hyperalgesia.**

hy·per·a·cid·i·ty (hī,pərəsid'itē), *n.* excessive amount of acid, as in the gastric juice.

hy·per·ac·tive (hīpərak'tiv), *adj.* excessively or abnormally active.

hy·per·a·cu·sis (hī,pərəkyōō'sis), *n.* unusually acute hearing.

hy·per·a·dre·nal·e·mi·a (hī,pərədrē,nəlē'-mēə), *n.* excessively large amount of adrenalin in the blood. Also **hyperepinephrinemia.**

hy·per·a·dren·al·ism (hī,pərədren'əliz,əm), *n.* a metabolic and urine disorder caused by increased secretory activity of the adrenal gland.

hy·per·ae·mi·a (hī,pəē'mēə), *n.* an excessive amount of blood in any portion of the body.

hy·per·aes·the·sia,   hy·per·es·the·si·a (hī,pərēsthē'zēə), *n.* an unusually acute reaction or sensitivity to pain, heat, cold, etc.

hy·per·al·ge·si·a (hī,pəraljē'zēə), *n.* heightened feeling of or reaction to pain. See also **hypalgesia.**

hy·per·an·a·ki·ne·si·a (hī,pəran,əkənē'zēə), *n.* abnormal automatic movement, as of internal organs.

hy·per·a·phi·a (hīpərā'fēə), *n.* abnormal sensitivity to touch.

hy·per·bar·ic (hīpəbar'ik), *adj.* (applied to anaesthetics) having a specific gravity greater than that of the fluid of the brain and spinal cord. See also **hypobaric.**

hy·per·bo·le (hīpū'bəlē), *n.* a deliberately inflated, exaggerated statement, not to be taken literally. —**hy·per·bol·ic** (hīpəbol'ik), *adj.*

hyperbolic   geometry, non-Euclidean geometry with the postulate that two distinct lines may be drawn parallel to a given line through a point not on the line. See also **Riemannian geometry.**

hy·per·bo·lize (hīpū'bəlīz), *v.* to exaggerate or use hyperbole.

hy·per·bo·re·an (hī,pəbôr'ēən), *adj.* pertaining to the extreme north; frigid.

hy·per·cal·cae·mi·a,   hy·per·cal·ce·mi·a (hī,pəkalsē'mēə), *n.* an excessive amount of calcium in the blood.

hy·per·cal·ci·u·ri·a (hī,pəkal,siyōōr'ēə), *n.* an excessive amount of calcium in the urine.

hy·per·cap·ni·a (hī,pəkap'nēə), *n.* an excessive amount of carbon dioxide in the blood.

hy·per·chlo·rae·mi·a,   hy·per·chlo·re·mi·a (hī,pəklôrē'mēə), *n.* an excessive amount of chloride in the blood.

hy·per·chlor·hy·dri·a (hī,pəklôhī'drēə), *n.*

an excessive amount of hydrochloric acid in the stomach.

hy·per·cho·les·ter·ol·ae·mi·a (hī,pəkəles,-tərolē'mēə), *n.* an excessive quantity of cholesterol in the blood. See also **hypocholesteraemia.**

hy·per·cho·les·ter·o·li·a (hī,pəkəles,tərō'-lēə), *n.* an excessive amount of cholesterol in the bile.

hy·per·cho·li·a (hī,pəkō'lēə), *n.* an abnormally large secretion of bile.

hy·per·con·scious (hī,pəkon'sHəs), *adj.* unusually alert or aware.

hy·per·crin·ism (hī,pəkrin'izəm), *n.* a disorder caused by excessive secretion of an endocrine gland.

hy·per·crit·i·cal (hī,pəkrit'ikəl), *adj.* overly critical; carping. —**hy,per·crit'ic,** *n.* —**hy,per·crit'i·cal·ly,** *adv.* —**hy,per·crit'·i·cism,,** *n.*

hy·per·cry·al·ge·si·a (hī,pəkrī,aljē'zēə), *n.* unusual sensitivity to cold.

hy·per·cy·thae·mi·a (hī,pəsīthē'mēə), *n.* an excessive number of red corpuscles in the blood.

hy·per·cy·to·sis (hī,pəsītō'sis), *n.* an excessive number of cells, especially white, in the blood. Also **hyperleucocytosis.**

hy·per·dac·tyl·i·a (hī,pədaktil'ēə), *n.* the presence of extra fingers or toes.

hy·per·du·li·a (hī,pədyōōlē'ə), *n.* the veneration, above all others, of the Virgin Mary, as by some Roman Catholics. See also **dulia, latria.**

hy·per·en·do·crin·ism (hīpəen'dōkrinizm), *n.* an abnormally increased activity in internally secreting organs.

hy·per·ep·i·neph·ri·nae·mi·a (hī,pərep,-inef,rənē'mēə), *n.* See **hyperadrenalaemia.**

hy·per·ep·i·neph·ry (hī,pərep,inef'rē), *n.* an abnormal increase in adrenal secretion.

hy·per·es·the·sia (hī,pərēsthē'zēə), *n.* See **hyperaesthesia.**

hy·per·gly·cae·mi·a,   hy·per·gly·ce·mi·a (hī,pəglīsē'mēə), *n.* an excessive amount of glucose in the blood. See also **hypoglycaemia.**

hy·per·gly·cis·ti·a (hī,pəglīsis'tēə), *n.* an excessive amount of sugar in the tissues.

hy·per·gol·ic (hīpəgo'lik), *adj.* igniting upon contact with a complementary substance, as the constituents of rocket propellants.

hy·per·he·pat·i·a (hī,pəhipat'ēə), *n.* an excessive functioning of the liver.

hy·per·hi·dro·sis (hī,pəhidrō'sis), *n.* excessive perspiration.

hy·per·ka·lae·mi·a (hi,pəkəlē'mēə), *n.* an excessive amount of potassium in the blood.

hy·per·ker·a·to·sis (hī,pəker,ətō'sis), *n.* a thickening of the horny layer of the skin.

hy·per·ki·ne·si·a (hī,pəkinē'zēə, hī,pəkīnē'-zēə), *n.* an excessive involuntary muscular activity; spasm.

hy·per·leu·co·cy·to·sis (hī,pəlōō,kōsītō'sis), *n.* See **hypercytosis.**

hy·per·li·pae·mi·a (hī,pəlipē'mēə), *n.* excessive quantities of fatty substances in the blood.

hy·per·meg·a·so·ma (hī,pəmegāsō'mə), *n.* abnormal, excessive growth; gigantism.

hy·per·met·a·mor·pho·sis (hī,pəmet,əmō'fəsis), *n.*, *pl.* **hy·per·met·a·mor·pho·ses** (hī,pəmet,əmō'fəsēz). an unusual form of metamorphosis in some insects in which two or more successive larval stages occur.

hy·per·met·rope (hīpəmet'rōp), *n.* a person who suffers from hypermetropia. Also **hy'per·ope.**

hy·per·me·tro·pi·a (hī,pəmitrō'pēə), *n.* farsightedness in which the focal point of parallel rays is behind instead of on the retina. Also **hy·per·o·pi·a** (hī,pərō'pēə). See also **myopia, presbyopia.** —**hy·per·me·trop·ic** (hī,pəmitrop'ik), *adj.*

hy·per·mo·til·i·ty (hī,pəmōtil'itē), *n.* excessive movement capacity of the stomach or intestines.

hy·per·na·trae·mi·a (hī,pənətrē'mēə), *n.* an excessive amount of sodium in the blood.

hy·per·os·mi·a (hī,pəroz'mēə), *n.* an unusually acute sense of smell. —**hy·per·os'mic,** *adj.*

hy·per·os·te·og·e·ny (hī,pəros,tēoj'ənē), *n.* exaggerated bone development.

hy·per·os·to·sis (hī,pərostō'sis), *n.* an abnormal increase of bone tissue.

hy·per·o·var·i·a (hī,pərōver'ēə), *n.* unusually early and advanced sexual development in girls, owing to excessive secretion in the ovaries.

hy·per·ox·ae·mi·a (hī,pəroksē'mēə), *n.* excessive acidity of the blood.

hy·per·par·a·site (hī,pəpar'əsīt), *n.* a parasite that feeds on or in another parasite.

hy·per·par·a·thy·roid·ism (hi,pəpar,əthī'roidiz,əm), *n.* an abnormal bone and muscular condition, caused by excessive activity of the parathyroid gland.

hy·per·pha·gi·a (hīpəfā'jēə), *n.* excessive hunger; bulimia.

hy·per·phos·phe·rae·mi·a (hī,pəfos,fərē'mēə), *n.* an excessive quantity of inorganic phosphorous compounds in the blood.

hy·per·phys·i·cal (hī,pəfiz'ikəl), *adj.* above or beyond the physical; supernatural.

hy·per·pi·et·ic (hī,pəpīet'ik), *adj.* pertaining to hypertension.

hy·per·pi·tu·i·ta·rism (hī,pəpityōō'itəriz,əm), *n.* gigantism caused by overactivity of the pituitary gland.

hy·per·pla·sia (hī,pərplā'zHə), *n.* abnormal cell multiplication, causing organic enlargement.

hy·perp·noe·a (hī,pəpnē'ə, hī,pənē'ə,), *n.* excessively rapid or laboured breathing.

hy·per·pot·as·sae·mi·a (hī,pəpot,əsē'mēə),

n. an excessive amount of potassium in the blood; hyperkalaemia.

hy·per·pro·sex·i·a (hī,pəprōsek'sēə), *n.* an obsessive attention to a relatively unimportant stimulus. See also **hypoprosexia.**

hy·per·py·rex·i·a (hī,pəpīrek'sēə), *n.* an abnormally severe fever.

hy·per·se·cre·tion (hī,pəsikrē'sHən), *n.* excessive secretion. See also **hyposecretion.**

hy·per·som·ni·a (hī,pəsom'nēə), *n.* abnormally prolonged sleep. —**hy·per·som'ni·ac,** *adj.*

hy·per·son·ic (hī,pəson'ik), *adj.* pertaining to speeds at least five times that of sound.

hy·per·space (hī'pəspās,), *n.* Euclidean space of more than three dimensions.

hy·per·tel·y (hīpū'təlē), *n.* (in the colouring and structure of plants and animals) excessive imitation without discernible purpose.

hy·per·ten·sion (hī,pəten'sHən), *n.* high blood pressure and the arterial disease caused by it.

hy·per·ten·sive (hī,pəten'siv), *adj.* pertaining to or caused by high blood pressure.

hy·per·text (hī'pətekst,), *n.* a computer database system that allows storage of documents, graphics, and sound so that related items of each type are linked and can easily be accessed together.

hy·per·ther·mi·a (hī,pəthū'mēə), *n.* 1. exceptionally high fever. 2. treatment of disease by inducing fever, as by heat or injection.

hy·per·throm·bin·ae·mi·a (hī,pəthrom,binē'mēə), *n.* an excessive amount of thrombin in the blood.

hy·per·thy·mi·a (hī,pəthī'mēə), *n.* (in psychiatry) a condition characterized by overactivity.

hy·per·thy·roid (hī,pəthī'roid), *adj.* 1. concerning or suffering from hyperthyroidism. 2. of an unrestrained, highly emotional nature.

hy·per·thy·roid·ism (hī,pəthī'roidiz,əm), *n.* hyperactivity of the thyroid gland leading to an increased metabolic rate and protruding eyeballs.

hy·per·ton·ic (hī,pəton'ik), *adj.* (of tissue) having a greater than normal tone.

hy·per·tro·phy (hīpū'trəfē), *n.* abnormal growth or enlargement of apart or organ.

hy·per·ven·ti·la·tion (hī,pəven,tilā'sHən), *n.* abnormally rapid and heavy breathing.

hyp·es·the·sia (hīpēsthē'zēə), *n.* See **hypaesthesia.**

hyp·e·thral (hipē,thrəl), *adj.* wholly or partially open to the sky, as a building. See also **clithral.**

hyp·no·a·nal·y·sis (hip,nōənal'isis), *n.* a method of psychoanalysis in which the patient is examined while under hypnosis.

hyp·no·gen·e·sis (hip,nōjen'isis), *n.* the process of inducing hypnosis.

hyp·no·graph (hip'nōgraf, hip'nōgräf), *n*. a device for measuring bodily activities during sleep.

hyp·noi·dal (hipnoi'dəl), *adj*. (of a state) resembling hypnosis, but not brought about by it.

hyp·nol·o·gy (hipnol'əjē), *n*. the study of the nature and characteristics of sleep.

hyp·no·ther·a·py (hip‚nōther'əpē), *n*. the treatment of disease by hypnotic means.

hyp·not·ic (hipnot'ik), *adj*. 1. sleep-inducing. —*n*. 2. a sedative; a substance inducing sleep.

hy·po·a·cid·i·ty (hī‚pōəsid'itē), *n*. reduced or subnormal acidity, as of gastric juice.

hy·po·a·cu·sis (hī‚pōəkyōō'sis), *n*. a hearing deficiency.

hy·po·a·de·ni·a (hī‚pōədē'nēə), *n*. subnormal glandular activity.

hy·po·al·i·men·ta·tion (hī‚pōal‚imentā'sнən), *n*. insufficient nourishment.

hy·po·al·o·nae·mi·a (hī‚pōal‚ənē'mēə), *n*. an excessively low quantity of salts in the blood.

hy·po·az·o·tu·ri·a (hī‚pōaz‚otyōōr'ēə), *n*. an abnormally small quantity of nitrogenous matter in the urine.

hy·po·bar·ic (hī‚pōbar'ik), *adj*. (of an anaesthetic) having a specific gravity lower than that of the fluid of the brain and spinal cord. See also **hyperbaric**.

hy·po·ba·rop·a·thy (hī‚pōbərop'əthē), *n*. mountain sickness, caused by lowered air pressure and reduced intake of oxygen.

hy·po·cal·cae·mi·a (hī‚pōkalsē'mēə), *n*. a subnormal quantity of calcium in the blood.

hy·po·chlo·rae·mi·a (hī‚pōklôrē'mēə), *n*. an abnormally small quantity of chloride in the blood.

hy·po·chlor·hy·dri·a (hī‚pōklôhī'drēə), *n*. an abnormally low quantity of hydrochloric acid in the gastric secretions.

hy·po·cho·les·ter·ae·mi·a (hī‚pōkəles‚tərē'mēə), *n*. a reduction in the amount of cholesterol in the blood. See also **hypercholesterolaemia**.

hy·po·chon·dri·a (hī‚pəkon'drēə), *n*. a depressed mental and emotional condition owing to an unfounded belief that some serious bodily disease is present. Also **hy·po·chon·dri·a·sis** (hī‚pōkəndrī'əsis).

hy·po·chon·dri·ac (hī‚pəkon'drēak), *n*. 1. a′ person subject to hypochondria, or excessively worried and obsessed by his state of health. —*adj*. 2. of or pertaining to hypochondria.

hy·po·chon·dri·um (hī‚pəkon'drēəm), *n*., *pl*. **hy·po·chon·dri·a** (hī‚pəkon'drēə). each of the two regions of the abdomen referred to as right and left.

hy·po·co·rism (hīpok'əriz‚əm), *n*. a pet name, or adult imitation of baby talk. —**hy·po·co·ris·tic** (hī'pəkôris'tik), *adj*.

hy·po·cri·nism (hī‚pōkrī'nizəm), *n*. a condition caused by an abnormally small glandular secretion.

hy·poc·ri·sy (hipok'rəsē), *n*. the pretence, with a view to popular approval, of possessing virtues and holding principles quite alien to one's true nature.

hyp·o·crite (hip'əkrit), *n*. a person affecting ethical or religious principles and ideals which he does not truly possess. —**hyp‚o·crit'i·cal**, *adj*.

hy·po·cy·to·sis (hi‚pōsītō'sis), *n*. a deficient number of blood cells; cytopenia. See also **hypercytosis**.

hy·po·dy·nam·i·a (hī‚pōdīnam'ēə), *n*. reduced energy or strength.

hy·po·en·do·crin·ism (hī‚pōen'dōkriniz‚əm), *n*. subnormal activity of the internally secreting organs. See also **hyperendocrinism**.

hy·po·gas·tri·um (hī‚pəgas'trēəm), *n*., *pl*. **hy·po·gas·tri·a** (hī‚pəgas'trēə). the lower part of the abdomen. —**hy‚po·gas'tric**, *adj*.

hy·po·ge·al (hī‚pəjē'əl), *adj*. below ground; subterranean.

hy·po·gene (hī'pəjen‚), *adj*. 1. formed below the surface, as rocks. 2. formed by rising water, as mineral deposits. See also **epigene**, **supergene**.

hy·po·ge·ous (hīpəjē'əs), *adj*. hypogeal; underground.

hy·po·ge·um (hī‚pəjē'əm), *n*. a subterranean vault or chamber.

hy·po·geu·si·a (hī‚pōjōō'zēə), *n*. a reduction in sensitivity to taste.

hy·po·glo·bu·li·a (hī‚pōglobyōō'lēə), *n*. subnormal quantity of red cells in the blood.

hy·po·glos·sal (hī‚pəglos'əl), *adj*. situated beneath the tongue.

hy·po·glot·tis (hī‚pəglot'is), *n*. the underside of the tongue.

hy·po·gly·cae·mi·a (hī‚pōglīsē'mēə), *n*. an insufficient quantity of glucose in the blood.

hy·pog·na·thous (hīpog'nəthəs), *adj*. having a long, protruding lower jaw.

hy·po·gon·ad·ism (hī‚pōgō'nadiz‚əm), *n*. a reduced internal secretion of the gonads.

hy·po·he·pat·i·a (hī‚pōhipat'ēə), *n*. subnormal liver function.

hy·po·hi·dro·sis (hī‚pōhidrō'sis), *n*. inability to produce sufficient perspiration.

hy·po·hy·poph·y·sism (hī‚pōhīpof'isiz‚əm), *n*. abnormally reduced activity of the pituitary gland. Also **hypopituitarism**.

hy·poid (hī'poid), *adj*. (of a gear) designed to mesh with another gear with the axes overlapping approximately at right angles rather than intersecting.

hy·po·in·o·sae·mi·a (hī‚pōin‚əsē'mēə), *n*. abnormally reduced formation of fibrin in the blood, causing difficulty in coagulation.

hy·po·ka·lae·mi·a (hī,pōkəlē'mēə), *n.* excessively low quantity of potassium in the blood.

hy·po·ki·ne·si·a (hī,pōkinē'ziə, hī,pōkīnē'-zēə), *n.* subnormal motor activity or mobility.

hy·po·lim·ni·on (hī,pōlim'nēon), *n.*, *pl.* **hy·po·lim·ni·a** (hī,pōlim'nēə). a layer of water below the thermocline in some lakes. See also **epilimnion**.

hy·po·ma·ni·a (hīpōmā'nēə), *n.* (in psychiatry) a mania of not too severe a nature.

hy·pom·ne·sia (hī,pəmnē'zēə), *n.* impaired memory.

hy·po·mo·til·i·ty (hī,pōmotil'itē), *n.* subnormal motility of the stomach and intestines.

hy·po·my·o·to·ni·a (hī,pōmī,ətō'nēə), *n.* abnormally reduced muscular tone.

hy·po·nas·ty (hī'pōnas,tē), *n.* the tendency of certain plants to grow more rapidly on the lower rather than the upper side, causing upward bending.

hy·po·na·trae·mi·a (hī,pōnətrē'mēə), *n.* an excessively low quantity of sodium in the blood.

hy·po·noi·a (hī,pənoi'ə), *n.* dulled or reduced mental activity; hypopsychosis.

hy·po·pha·lan·gism (hī,pōfəlan'jizəm), *n.* fewer than the normal number of bones in a finger or toe.

hy·po·pho·ne·sis (hī,pōfənē'sis), *n.* a sound of less than normal intensity.

hy·po·pho·nia (hī,pəfō'nēə), *n.* an abnormally weak voice owing to a deficiency in the vocal cords.

hy·poph·y·ge (hīpof'ijē), *n.* the section of a column joined to the base or capital. Also **apophyge**.

hy·poph·y·sis (hīpof'isis), *n.*, *pl.* **hy·poph·y·ses** (hīpof'isēz). the pituitary gland.

hy·poph·y·si·tis (hīpof,isī'tis), *n.* inflammation or irritation of the pituitary gland.

hy·po·pi·e·sis (hī,pōpīē'sis), *n.* unusually low arterial blood pressure.

hy·po·pi·tu·i·ta·rism (hī,pōpityōō'itəriz,-əm), *n.* subnormal activity of the pituitary gland. Also **hypohypophysism**.

hy·po·pla·sia (hī,pōplā'zēə), *n.* a serious deficiency of cells or structural constituents.

hy·pop·noe·a (hīpop'nēə), *n.* unusually shallow breathing.

hy·po·po·tas·sae·mi·a (hi,pōpətasē'mēə), *n.* a subnormal quantity of potassium in the blood; hypokalaemia.

hy·po·prax·i·a (hī,pōprak'sēə), *n.* diminished activity; listlessness.

hy·po·pro·sex·i·a (hī,pōprōsek'sēə), *n.* inability to concentrate for more than short periods. See also **hyperprosexia**.

hy·po·pro·tein·ae·mi·a (hī,pōprō,tēnē'-mēə), *n.* a subnormal amount of protein in the blood.

hy·po·pro·tein·o·sis (hī,pōprō,tēnō'sis), *n.* a protein deficiency.

hy·pop·sel·a·phe·si·a (hī,popsel,əfē'zēə), *n.* a deficiency in the sense of touch.

hy·po·psy·cho·sis (hī,pōsīkō'sis), *n.* dulled or diminished mental activity; hyponoia.

hy·pop·ty·al·ism (hīpōtī'əliz,əm), *n.* insufficient salivary secretion.

hy·po·sal·ae·mi·a (hī,pōsalē'mēə), *n.* an abnormally low salt content in the blood,

hy·po·se·cre·tion (hī,pōsikrē'sHən), *n.* a subnormal secretion. See also **hypersecretion**.

hy·po·sen·si·tize (hī,pōsen'sitīz), *v.* to reduce a person's sensitivity; desensitize.

hy·pos·mi·a (hīpoz'mēə), *n.* a deficient sense of smell.

hy·pos·ta·sis (hīpos'təsis), *n.*, *pl.* **hy·pos·ta·ses** (hīpos'təsēz). (in metaphysics) something that supports or underlines.

hy·pos·ta·size (hīpos'təsīz), *v.* to regard as substance or reality; hypostatize.

hy·po·stat·ic (hī,pəstat'ik), *adj.* pertaining to essence or substance; fundamental.

hy·pos·ta·tize (hīpos'tətīz), *v.* to treat as substance or reality; hypostasize.

hy·pos·the·ni·a (hī,posthē'nēə), *n.* serious lack of strength; weakness.

hy·po·ten·sion (hī,pōten'sHən), *n.* diminished or low blood pressure. See also **hypertension**.

hy·po·ten·sive (hī,pōten'siv), *adj.* pertaining to or causing low blood pressure.

hy·pot·e·nuse (hīpot'ənyōōs), *n.* the side of a right-angled triangle opposite the right angle.

hy·po·thal·a·mus (hī,pəthal'əməs), *n.*, *pl.* **hy·po·thal·a·mi** (hī,pəthal'əmī). the part of the forebrain that coordinates the control over temperature, rage, etc.

hy·poth·e·cate (hīpoth'ikāt), *v.* to give or pledge as security, without parting with possession or title.

hy·poth·e·nar (hī,pōthē'nə), *n.* the fleshy portion of the hand at the base of the little finger.

hy·po·ther·mal (hī,pōthû'məl), *adj.* having abnormally low body temperature.

hy·po·ther·mi·a (hī,pōthû'mēə), *n.* the condition of having subnormal body temperature.

hy·poth·e·sis (hīpoth'əsis), *n.*, *pl.* **hy·poth·e·ses** (hīpoth'əsēz). a proposed idea or explanation of how a number of observed phenomena function together to produce a manifest result.

hy·po·thy·roid·ism (hī,pōthī'roidiz,əm), *n.* a disorder, such as goitre, caused by deficient activity of the thyroid gland. See also **hyperthyroidism.** —**hy·po·thy'roid**, *adj.*

hy·po·ton·ic (hī,pəton'ik), *adj.* (of tissue) having subnormal tone.

hy·po·ty·po·sis (hī,pətīpō'sis), *n.* a vivid, lifelike description of a scene or event.

hy·pox·ae·mi·a (hī,poksē'mēə), *n.* a condition brought about by insufficient oxygen in the blood.

hy·pox·i·a (hīpok'sēə), *n.* an insufficient amount of oxygen reaching the body tissues.

hyp·si·ceph·a·ly (hip,sisef'əlē), *n.* a malformation of the head; acrocephaly.

hyp·sog·ra·phy (hipsog'rəfē), *n.* geographic study relating to surveying and mapping the parts of the earth above sea level.

hyp·som·e·ter (hipsom'itə), *n.* an instrument for measuring heights above sea level.

hyp·som·e·try (hipsom'itrē), *n.* the measuring of altitudes.

hys·ter·ec·to·my (his,tərek'təmē), *n.* excision of the womb.

hys·ter·e·sis (his,tərē'sis), *n.* the time lag in the effect of a magnetic force in relation to the force causing it.

hys·ter·o·cat·a·lep·sy (his,tərōkat'əlepsē), *n.* hysteria with symptoms of cataleptic seizure or trance. —**hys,ter·o·cat,a·lep'tic,** *adj.*

hys·ter·o·gen·ic (his,tərəjen'ik), *adj.* producing hysteria.

hys·ter·oid (his'təroid), *adj.* resembling hysteria.

hy·ther·graph (hī'thəgraf,, hī'thəgräf,), *n.* a weather or climate graph indicating the relationship between temperature and humidity.

i·amb (ī'am, ī'amb), *n.* (in poetry) a metric foot consisting of one unstressed followed by one stressed syllable. —**i·am·bic** (īam'bik), *adj.*

iar·o·vize (yä'əvīz), *v.* See **jarovize.**

i·a·tric (īat'rik), *adj.* relating to a doctor or to medicine.

i·at·ro·chem·is·try (īat,rōkem'istrē), *n.* the study and application of chemistry in relation to diseases and their treatment.

i·at·ro·gen·ic (īat,rōjen'ik), *adj.* (of a disorder) resulting from the diagnosis or treatment of a doctor.

ib·i·dem (ib'idəm), *adv. Latin.* in the same place; on the same page, etc. (used to avoid repetition). *Abbr.:* **ibid.**

ice·blink (īs'blinck,), *n.* a luminous appearance near the horizon caused by the reflection of light from an icefield. See also **snowblink.**

ice·fall (īs'fôl,), *n.* a wall of ice over hanging a precipice.

ice foot, a belt or ledge of ice in polar regions attached to the shore.

ice front, the edge of an ice shelf nearest the sea.

ich·nite (ik'nīt), *n.* a fossilized foot print.

ich·nog·ra·phy (iknog'rəfē), *n.* the art of drawing horizontal sections or ground plans.

ich·nol·o·gy (iknol'əjē), *n.* the branch of science dealing with fossil footprints.

i·chor (ī'kô), *n.* a colourless, watery discharge from a wound or sore.

ich·thy·ic (ik'thēik), *adj.* pertaining to fishes.

ich·thy·og·ra·phy (ik,thēog'rəfē), *n.* a written work on fishes.

ich·thy·oid (ik'thēoid), *adj.* fishlike. Also **ich,-thy·oi'dal.**

ich·thy·o·lite (ik'thēəlīt), *n.* a fish in fossil form.

ich·thy·ol·o·gy (ik,thēol'əjē), *n.* the branch of zoology relating to fishes.

ich·thy·oph·a·gy (ik,thēof'əjē), *n.* the practice of eating fish. —**ich,thy·oph'a·gist,** *n.*

ich·thy·o·sis (ik,thēō'sis), *n.* a congenital skin disease characterized by flaking skin. Also **fish skin disease.**

i·con·o·clasm (īkon'əklaz,əm), *n.* the act of destroying or breaking images.

i·con·o·clast (īkon'əklast), *n.* a breaker of images or attacker of traditional doctrines and institutions.

i·con·o·dule (īkon'ədyŏol), *n.* one who worships icons.

i·con·o·du·ly (īkon'ədyŏolē), *n.* the worship of icons.

i·co·nog·ra·phy (ī,kənog'rəfē), *n.* a pictorial or symbolic representation. —**i,con·o·graph'ic,** *adj.*

i·co·nol·a·try (ī,kənol'ətrē), *n.* the worship of images.

i·co·nol·o·gy (ī,kənol'əjē), *n.* the study and analysis of symbols and icons.

i·co·nos·ta·sis (ī,kənos'təsis), *n., pl.* **i·co·nos·ta·ses** (ī,kənos'təsēz). a screen in a Byzantine church, separating the sanctuary from the main body of the building, on which icons are placed. Also **i·con·o·stas** (ī'kənəstəs,).

i·co·sa·he·dron (ī,kəsəhē'drən), *n., pl.* **i·co·sa·he·drons, i·co·sa·he·dra** (ī,kəsəhē'drə). a solid figure with twenty faces.

i·co·si·tet·ra·he·dron (ikō,sitet,rəhē'drən), *n., pl.* **i·co·si·tet·ra·he·drons, i·co·si·tet·ra·he·dra** (ikō,sitet,rəhē'drə). a solid figure with twenty-four faces.

ic·ter·us (ik'tərəs), *n.* jaundice. —**ic·ter'ic,** *adj.*

ic·tus (ik'təs), *n., pl.* **ic·tus·es, ic·tus.** (in medicine) a fit; a stroke, as sunstroke.

id (id), *n.* a term in psychoanalysis for the unconscious part of the mind, the source of primal, instinctive urges.

i·de·a·is·tic (īdē,əis'tik), *adj.* pertaining to ideas.

i·de·al·ism (īdē'əliz,əm), *n.* (in art or literature) the theory and practice of treating a subject in an imaginative rather than realistic manner, by emphasizing certain aspects or features approximating to a standard of absolute perfection. See also **naturalism, realism.**

i·de·ate (ī'dēāt,), *v.* to form ideas; to think; to imagine. —**i,de·a'tion,** *n.* —**i,de·a'tion·al,** *adj.*

i·dée re·çue (ēdā resō̄'), *n., pl.* **i·dées re·çues** (ēdā resō̄'). a widely held opinion or belief.

i·dem (ī'dem, id'em), *pron., adj. Latin.* the same as previously given or stated.

id·e·o·gram (id'ēəgram), *n.* a written symbol directly representing an object or an idea, rather than a phonetic description of it.

id·e·o·graph (id'ēōgraf, id'ēōgräf,), *n.* an ideogram.

id·e·og·ra·phy (id,ēog'rəfē), *n.* the use of ideograms or ideographs.

i·de·o·mo·tor (ī,dēōmō'tə), *adj.* relating to motor activity arising from an idea.

id·i·o·blast (id'ēəblast), *n.* a cell differently constituted to those surrounding it.

id·i·oc·ra·sy (id,ēok'rəsē), *n.* a peculiar, individual mannerism; idiosyncrasy.

id·i·o·dy·nam·ics (id,ēōdīnam'iks), *n.* (in psychology) a belief in the individual's importance in choosing and responding to stimuli. —id,i·o·dy·nam'ic, *adj.*

id·i·o·glos·si·a (id,ēōglos'ēə), *n.* an invented form of speech for private communication by children who are closely related or associated, as twins.

id·i·o·graph (id'ēəgraf, id'ēōgräf), *n.* a private mark or signature; a trademark. See also logotype.

id·i·o·graph·ic (id,ēōgraf'ik), *adj.* (in psychology) pertaining to the separate study of cases or happenings. See also nomothetic.

id·i·o·lect (id'ēəlekt,), *n.* an individual's discrete lexicon, grammar, pronunciation, and pattern of speech. —id,i·o·lect'al, id,i·o·lect'ic, *adj.*

id·i·o·mor·phic (id,ēōmôr'fik), *adj.* having its own proper characteristic form.

id·i·op·a·thy (id,ēop'əthē), *n.* a disease not preceded or caused by any other. —id,i·o·path'-ic, *adj.*

id·i·o·syn·cra·sy (id,ēōsiNG'krəsē), *n.* a habit, mannerism, or temperament peculiar to an individual.

id·i·o·trop·ic (id,ēōtrop'ik), *adj.* introspective; inward-looking.

id·i·ot sa·vant (id'ēət savänt', ēdyô, savän'), *pl.* id·i·ot sa·vants, id·i·ots sa·vants (ēdyô, savän'). a mentally backward person with one special talent, such as art, music, mathematical calculation, etc.

i·dol·a·ter (īdol'ətə), *n.* one who worships idols. Also i'dol·ist. —i·dol'a·trous, *adj.*

i·dol·a·try (īdol'ətrē), *n.* the worship of idols and images.

idols of the cave, errors arising from personal bias or prejudice.

idols of the market place, popular fallacies arising from factors such as language or custom and exploited for commercial reasons.

idols of the theatre, errors caused by perpetuation of traditional beliefs.

idols of the tribe, fallacies related to man's nature and social organization.

i·do·ne·ous (īdō'nēəs), *adj.* apt; fit; suitable.

i·dyl·lic (idil'ik, īdil'ik), *adj.* simple and peaceful; charming and poetic.

ig·ne·ous (ig'nēəs), *adj.* produced by the action of fire or intense heat, as volcanic rock.

ig·nes·cent (ignes'ənt), *adj.* giving off sparks of fire.

ig·nis fat·u·us (ig'nis fat'yōōəs), *n., pl.* ig·nes fat·u·i (ig'nēz fat'yōōī). a phosphorescent light

that hovers or flickers at night over marshy ground, believed to be due to spontaneous combustion of gas from decayed organic matter. Also friars' lantern, will-o'-the-wisp.

ig·no·ble (ignō'bəl), *adj.* of low character; mean; contemptible. —ig,no·bil'i·ty, *n.*

ig·no·min·y (ig'nəminē), *n.* disgrace; infamy; dishonour. —ig,no·min'i·ous, *adj.*

il·e·i·tis (il,ēī'tis), *n.* inflammation of the ileum.

il·e·o·cae·cal (il,ēōsē'kəl), *adj.* pertaining to the ileum and caecum.

il·e·o·co·li·tis (il,ēōkəlī'tis), *n.* inflammation of the mucous membrane of the ileum and colon.

il·e·um (il'ēəm), *n.* the lower portion of the small intestine, from the jejunum to the caecum.

il·e·us (il'ēəs), *n.* painful intestinal obstruction.

il·i·ac (il'ēak), *adj.* pertaining to the ilium.

il·i·um (il'ēəm), *n., pl.* il·i·a (il'ēə). one of the upper bones of the pelvis, part of the hipbone.

il·la·tion (ilā'sHən), *n.* a deduction; inference; conclusion. —il'la·tive, *adj.*

il·lude (ilōod'), *v.* to trick or mislead, as by creating an illusion.

il·lu·mi·na·ti (ilōo,minä'tē), *n. pl.* persons claiming special perception or enlightenment.

il·lu·sion (ilōo'zHən), *n.* an action, object, or idea that leads a person to think it is something else; something that gives a deceptive impression, as an optical illusion.

il·lu·so·ry (ilōo'sərē), *adj.* imagined; not real; false; deceptive.

il·lu·vi·ate (ilōo'vēāt), *v.* to undergo or cause illuviation.

il·lu·vi·a·tion (ilōo,vēā'sHən), *n.* the accumulation in a soil layer of materials that have percolated from another layer.

il·lu·vi·um (ilōo'vēəm), *n., pl.* il·lu·vi·ums, il·lu·via (ilōo'vēə). material built up through illuviation. —il·lu'vi·al, *adj.*

im·age·ry (im'ijrē, im'ijərē), *n.* the creation of mental figures or representations; images collectively.

im·ag·ism (im'əjiz,əm), *n.* the theory and work of early 20th-century poets reacting against romanticism and advocating the use of precise images, new rhythms, and language of everyday speech.

i·ma·go (imä'gō), *n., pl.* i·ma·goes, i·ma·gi·nes (imaj'ənēz). **1.** a fully developed insect. **2.** an idealized image of someone, formed in infancy and maintained unaltered as an adult.

im·bibe (imbīb'), *v.* to absorb liquid; to drink. —im,bi·bi'ti·on, *n.*

im·bow·er (imbou'ə), *v.* to embower.

im·brac·er·y (imbrā'sərē), *n.* See embracery.

im·bran·gle (imbraNG'gəl), *v.* to perplex; entangle; embrangle.

im·bri·cate (im'brikit, im'brikāt,), *adj.* methodical overlapping, as of roof tiles. —im·bri·ca'tion, *n.*

im·bro·glio (imbrōl'yō), *n., pl.* **im·bro·glios.** a state of confusion; a perplexing situation.

im·brue (imbrōō'), *v.* to dye or stain, as with blood. Also **embrue.**

im·brute (imbrōōt'), *v.* to degrade; become brutish.

im·bue (imbyōō'), *v.* **1.** to inspire, as with feelings, opinions, etc. **2.** to impregnate with moisture, colour, etc.

im·mac·u·late (imak'yəlit), *adj.* without a spot or blemish; completely clean.

im·ma·nent (im'ənənt), *adj.* inherent; remaining within.

im·med·i·ca·ble (imed'ikəbəl), *adj.* unable to be healed; incurable.

im·men·su·ra·ble (imen'sнərəbəl), *adj.* immeasurable; incapable of being measured.

im·merge (imûj'), *v.* **1.** to plunge or dip in a liquid. **2.** (in astronomy) to disappear, as the sun below the horizon, the moon or sun in an eclipse, etc.

im·merse (imûs'), *v.* **im·mersed, im·mers·ing. 1.** to put entirely into a liquid. **2.** (figuratively) to be absorbed fully, as *The professor immersed himself in his studies.* —**im·mer'sion,** *n.*

im·mer·sion (imû'sнən, imur'zнən), *n.* (in astronomy) the disappearance of a celestial body behind or in the shadow of another, as in an eclipse. See also **emersion.**

im·mi·nent (im'inənt), *adj.* about to happen; coming about at any moment.

im·mis·ci·ble (imis'ibəl), *adj.* incapable of being mixed.

im·mix (imiks'), *v.* to mix in; mix up; mingle. —**im·mix'ture,** *n.*

im·mo·late (im'ōlāt), *v.* to kill as a sacrifice, esp. by fire. —**im,mo·la'tion,** *n.*

im·mo·tile (imō'tīl), *adj.* incapable of movement.

im·mu·no·com·pe·tence (im,yənokom'pətəns), *n.* the ability of the body to mount an immune response. —**im,mu·no·com'pe·tent,** *adj.*

im·mu·no·de·fi·cien·cy (im,yənōdifisн'ənsē), *n.* deficiency of the immune system making it incapable of a normal immune response. —**im,mu·no·de·fi'cient,** *adj.*

im·mu·no·ge·net·ics (im,yənōjənet'iks), *n.* the branch of immunology relating to immunity as affected by genetic makeup.

im·mu·nol·o·gy (im,yənol'əjē), *n.* the branch of medicine studying animal and human immunity to infection and disease, and the ways of producing such immunity.

im·mu·no·sup·pres·sion (im,yənōsəpresн'ən), *n.* suppression of the immune system by drugs, esp. to prevent rejection of a transplant. —**im,mu·no·sup·pressed',** *adj.*

im·mure (imyōō'ə), *v.* to wall in; enclose within or as within walls.

im·mu·ta·ble (imyōō'təbəl), *adj.* not subject to change; unalterable.

im·pair (impe'ə), *v.* to worsen; make weak or damage, as impaired vision. —**im·pair'ment,** *n.*

im·pa·na·tion (im,pənā'sнən), *n.* the doctrine that the material body of Christ is present in the bread after consecration.

im·passe (ampäs', im'päs, ampäs', impäs'), *n.* a situation from which there is no way out; deadlock.

im·pas·to (impas'tō, impäs'tō), *n.* (in painting) colour laid on in a thick manner.

im·pec·ca·ble (impek'əbəl), *adj.* without a fault; above criticism, as *impeccable taste.* —**im·pec,ca·bil'i·ty,** *n.*

im·pec·cant (impek'ənt), *adj.* faultless; without sin.

im·pe·cu·ni·ous (im,pəkyōō'nēəs), *adj.* being without any money; poor.

im·pede (impēd'), *v.* **im·ped·ed, im·ped·ing.** to slow the movement or growth of by hindrances or obstacles.

im·pe·di·ent (impē'dēənt), *adj.* obstructive; hindering.

im·ped·i·ment (imped'imənt), *n.* anything that slows or stops movement or progress.

im·ped·i·men·ta (imped,imen'tə), *n. pl.* objects that hinder progress, esp. army supplies.

im·ped·i·tive (imped'itiv), *adj.* causing hindrance or obstruction.

im·pel (impel'), *v.* **im·pelled, im·pel·ling.** to move (something) onwards with force or energy.

im·per·a·tive (imper'ətiv), *adj.* demanding; requiring; unavoidable, as *It is imperative that you brush your teeth at least twice a day.*

im·pe·ra·tor (impərä'tô), *n.* an absolute ruler or commander.

im·per·cep·ti·ble (im,pəsep'tibəl), *adj.* not seen, felt, tasted, or heard; not perceived or made aware of, or only very slightly so; barely noticeable, as *an imperceptible movement of the hand.*

im·per·cip·i·ent (impəsip'ēənt), *adj.* not perceiving; lacking perception.

im·per·fo·rate (impû'fərit, impû'fərāt), *adj.* **1.** lacking perforations: *an imperforate sheet of postage stamps.* **2.** (of a body part) lacking the normal opening; occluded. —**im·per,fo·ra'tion,** *n.*

im·pe·ri·ous (impēr'ēəs), *adj.* domineering; dictatorial.

im·pe·ri·um (impēr'ēəm), *n., pl.* **im·pe·ri·a** (impēr'ēə). command; absolute or supreme power.

im·per·ti·nent (impû'tinənt), *adj.* rude; impolite; disrespectful. —**im·per'ti·nence,** *n.*

im·per·tur·ba·ble (im,pûtû'bəbəl), *adj.* not able to be disturbed or agitated; serene.

im·pe·ti·go (im,pitī'gō), *n.* a skin disease characterized by clusters of pustules.

im·pe·trate (im'pitrāt,), v. to obtain by request or entreaty.

im·pet·u·ous (impet'yŏŏəs, impeCH'ŏŏəs), adj. unrestrained; characterized by lack of thought or planning; rash.

im·pe·tus (im'pətəs), n. a driving force that causes something to be done; stimulus.

im·pig·no·rate (impig'nərāt,), v. to pawn; pledge; mortgage.

im·pinge (impinj'), v. **im·pinged, im·ping·ing.** 1. to affect or make an impression on. 2. (impinge on) to trespass or infringe on, as to impinge on one's time. 3. (impinge on, upon, against) to strike; come into contact with, as Sound waves impinge on the ear.

im·pi·ous (im'pēəs), adj. not pious; irreverent.

im·plac·a·ble (implak'əbəl), adj. not to be appeased; irreconcilable; inexorable.

im·plau·si·ble (implô'zəbəl), adj. unbelievable; unreasonable, as an implausible excuse.

im·pli·cate (im'plikāt,), v. to cause to be involved; draw (someone or something) into a situation.

im·pli·ca·tion (im,plikā'sHən), n. a hint or suggestion; something implied, as He resented the implication that he had done anything dishonest.

im·plic·it (implis'it), adj. 1. unquestioning; absolute. 2. implied, rather than plainly stated. See also **explicit.**

im·plode (implōd'), v. to burst inwards. —**im·plo'sion,** n. —**im·plo'sive,** adj.

im·plore (implô'), v. **im·plored, im·plor·ing.** to beg, esp. in a piteous, pathetic way.

im·pol·i·tic (impol'itik), adj. unwise; inexpedient.

im·pon·der·a·ble (impon'dərəbəl), adj. 1. unable to be judged or weighed or otherwise taken into consideration. —n. 2. anything that cannot readily be judged or considered.

im·po·nent (impō'nənt), n. 1. one who imposes. —adj. 2. imposing.

im·por·tune (impô'tyŏŏn), v. to beg, or beseech, energetically, urgently, and persistently. —**im·por·tun·ate** (impô'tyŏŏnit), adj.

im·pre·cate (im'prikāt), v. to curse; invoke evil on a person. —**im·pre·ca'tion,** n.

im·preg·na·ble (impreg'nəbəl), adj. 1. able to withstand an attack; so strong as to defy any attempt at penetration, as an impregnable wall. 2. able to be fertilized, as an ovum; able to be made or to become pregnant —**im·preg,na·bil'·i·ty,** n.

Im·pres·sion·ism (impresH'əniz,əm), n. a 19th-century art movement endeavouring to capture the immediate sensuous impressions, obtained by the use of bold colour and short brush strokes to convey light and shade effects.

im·pri·ma·tur (im,primä'tə, im,primä'tə), n. a licence or mark of approval from an authority.

im·print·ing (imprint'iNG), n. the process by which young animals learn to recognize and identify with adults of their own species, usually their parent(s).

im·pro·bi·ty (imprō'bitē), n. lack of principle; wickedness.

im·promp·tu (impromp'tyŏŏ), adv. 1. without preparation. —adj. 2. (of a speech) delivered without any prior preparation, even notes. See also extempore.

im·pu·dic·i·ty (im,pyŏŏdis'itē), n. lack of shame; immodesty.

im·pugn (impyŏŏn'), v. to assail by argument; call in question or oppose as false.

im·pu·is·sant (impyŏŏ'isənt, impwē'sənt), adj. feeble; powerless.

im·pu·ni·tive (impyŏŏ'nitiv), adj. (in a situation) not condemning anyone, but accompanied by feelings of shame. See also extrapunitive.

im·pu·ni·ty (impyŏŏ'nitē), n. exemption from penalty or punishment.

im·pute (impyŏŏt'), v. to state or maintain that someone has done something bad. —**im,pu·ta'·tion,** n.

im·pu·tres·ci·ble (im,pyŏŏtres'əbəl), adj. not subject to decomposition; incorruptible.

in ab·sen·tia (in absen'tēə, absen'sHə), Latin. in absence.

in·ad·vert·ent (in,ədvû'tənt), adj. unthinking; unintentional. —**in,ad·vert'ence, in,ad·vert'en·cy,** n.

in·am·o·ra·ta (inam,ərä'tə, in,amərä'tə), masc. **in·am·o·ra·to** (inam,ərä'tō, in,amərä'tō), n., pl. **in·am·o·ra·tas,** masc. **in·am·o·ra·tos.** the person whom one loves; object of love.

in·ane (inān'), adj. silly; completely nonsensical.

in·a·ni·tion (in,ənisH'ən), n. 1. a state of weakness and exhaustion resulting from starvation. 2. absence of spiritual, intellectual, or social vigour; lethargy.

in·ap·pe·tence (inap'itəns), n. lack of appetite. Also **in·ap'pe·ten·cy.**

in·au·spi·cious (in,ôspisH'əs), adj. not holding much hope of success; unfavourable.

in·ca·les·cent (in,kələs'ənt), adj. increasing in warmth or heat.

in·can·des·cence (in,kandes'əns), n. the property of glowing at high temperatures.

in·ca·pac·i·tate (in,kəpas'itāt), v. **in·ca·pac·i·tat·ed, in·ca·pac·i·tat·ing.** to cause (someone or something) to stop functioning normally, as by wounding, damaging, removing an essential part, etc.

in·cept (insept'), v. to take in, as of an organism.

in·ces·sant (inses'ənt), adj. nonstop; continuous, as his incessant nagging.

in·cho·ate (inkō'āt, inkō'it), adj. just begun; incomplete; imperfect. —**in,cho·a'tion,** n.

in·cip·i·ent (insip'ēənt), *adj.* beginning; in an early or initial stage.

in·cite (insīt'), *v.* **in·cit·ed, in·cit·ing.** to cause someone to act by exciting him; egg on.

in·cog·ni·to (inkog'nitō, in,kognē'tō), *adv.* not revealing one's true identity, as *She travels incognito.*

in·co·her·ent (in,kōhēr'ənt), *adj.* not holding together, as an argument; not making sense, as *incoherent muttering.*

in·con·dite (inkon'dit, inkon'dīt), *adj.* ill-composed; unpolished.

in·con·gru·ous (inkONG'grōōəs), *adj.* not going or belonging together; unsuitably matched; ridiculously inappropriate. —**in,con·gru'i·ty,** *n.*

in·con·nu (inkənōō', ANkônY'), *n., pl.* **in·con·nus.** an unknown person; novice; stranger.

in·con·ti·nent (inkon'tinənt), *adj.* unable to control natural bodily functions. —**in·con'ti·nence,** *n.*

in·cras·sate (inkras'āt), *v.* to thicken a liquid by adding another substance or by evaporation.

in·cred·u·lous (inkred'yələs, inkrej'ələs), *adj.* unable to believe what one has learned, seen, etc.; unbelieving.

in·cre·ment (in'krimənt), *n.* an increase in quantity or magnitude, esp. by addition.

in·cu·bus (in'kyəbəs), *n., pl.* **in·cu·bi** (in'kyəbī), **in·cu·bus·es.** an evil spirit said to annoy people while asleep, esp. one seeking sexual intercourse with women. See also **succu·bus.**

in·cul·cate (inkul'kāt), *v.* to impress on the mind by constant repetition; to teach forcibly.

in·cul·pate (inkul'pāt), *v.* to accuse; blame. —**in·cul'pa·to·ry,** *adj.*

in·cum·bent (inkum'bənt), *n.* **1.** a person holding an office, performing a function or role, etc. —*adj.* **2.** in office, esp. a public position, as *an incumbent prime minister.* **3. (incumbent on** or **upon),** compulsory; obligatory. —**in·cum'ben·cy,** *n.*

in·cu·nab·u·la (in,kyōōnab'yələ), *n. pl.* books printed before 1500.

in·cur·sion (inkû'sHən, inkû'zHən), *n.* an invasion; a raid; a harmful inroad.

in·cuse (inkyōōz'), *adj.* hammered or stamped in, as an impression on a coin.

in·de·fea·si·ble (in,difē'zəbəl), *adj.* not to be forfeited or annulled.

in·de·fect·i·ble (in,difekt'əbəl), *adj.* unfailing; faultless.

in·de·his·cent (in,dihis'ənt), *adj.* (of plants) not opening when mature.

in·del·i·ble (indel'ibəl), *adj.* not able to be removed or erased, as *an indelible impression* or *indelible ink.*

in·dem·ni·ty (indem'nitē), *n.* protection or insurance against loss; compensation for loss.

in·di·ci·a (indisH'ēə), *n., pl.* **in·di·ci·a, in·di·ci·as.** a marking on an envelope in place of a stamp. —**in·di'cial,** *adj.*

in·dict (indīt'), *v.* to charge or accuse of a crime. —**in·dict'ment,** *n.*

in·dif·fer·ent (indif'rənt, indif'ərənt), *adj.* not caring or concerned, one way or another; uninterested. —**in·dif'fer·ence,** *n.*

in·di·gene (in'dijēn), *n.* a native.

in·dig·e·nous (indij'ənəs), *adj.* originating in or characteristic of a particular country or region.

in·di·gent (in'dijent), *adj.* poor; needy; lacking the necessities of life.

indirect discourse, a written version of a statement, not quoted exactly but altered grammatically so as to be included in a longer sentence. See also **direct discourse.**

in·dis·posed (in,dispōzd'), *adj.* **1.** sick, esp. slightly or temporarily. **2.** unwilling; reluctant, as *Mother was indisposed to help me with my homework.*

in·dite (indīt'), *v.* to compose; put into words; write.

in·do·lence (in'dələns), *n.* laziness; slothfulness; lack of desire or motivation to do anything. —**in'do·lent,** *adj.*

in·duce (indyōōs'), *v.* **in·duced, in·duc·ing.** to persuade, or try to convince, often by offering something in return. —**in·duce'ment,** *n.*

in·dul·gent (indul'jənt), *adj.* showing lenience or tolerance.

in·du·men·tum (in,dyōōmen'təm), *n., pl.* **in·du·men·ta** (in,dyōōmen'tə), **in·du·men·tums.** a thick, hairy covering.

in·du·rate (in'dyōōrāt,), *v.* to harden; to make stubborn. —**in,du·ra'tion,** *n.*

in·ef·fa·ble (inef'əbəl), *adj.* indescribable; unutterable.

in·e·luc·ta·ble (in,iluk'təbəl), *adj.* unavoidable; inescapable.

in·e·nar·ra·ble (in,inar'əbəl), *adj.* unspeakable; incapable of being told or described.

in·er·rant (iner'ənt), *adj.* unerring; free from error.

in·ert (inût'), *adj.* not moving; apparently lifeless; inactive; not acting chemically, as *Argon is an inert gas.*

in·er·tia (inû'sHə), *n.* inaction; inactivity.

inertial guidance (inû'sHəl), a system of automatic guidance in a missile using internal instruments regulated by the direction and magnitude of acceleration of the missile in flight.

in·ex·o·ra·ble (inek'sərəbəl), *adj.* incapable of persuasion by entreaty; unyielding; relentless.

in·ex·pli·ca·ble (in,iksplik'əbəl, inek'splik·kəbəl), *adj.* unexplainable; unexplained. —**in·ex·plic'a·bly,** *adv.*

in·ex·pug·na·ble (in,ikspug'nəbəl), *adj.* incapable of being taken by force; invincible.

in ex·tre·mis (in ikstrē'mis), *Latin.* near death.

in·ex·tri·ca·ble (in,ekstrik'əbəl, ineks'trəkəbəl), *adj.* unable to get out of; not able to unravel or disentangle, as *an inextricable network of ropes* or *an inextricable problem.* —in·ex·tric'a·bly, *adv.*

in·fa·mous (in'fəməs), *adj.* notorious; of very bad reputation.

in·fan·tile paralysis (in,fəntīl'). See **polio-myelitis.**

in·farct (infäkt'), *n.* a portion of dying or dead tissue, caused by curtailed blood supply. —in·farc'tion, *n.*

infectious mononucleosis, glandular fever; a virus disease affecting the white blood cells, not severe but often prolonged.

in fla·gran·te de·lic·to (in fləgran'te delik'-tō), *Latin.* in the very act of committing an offence, specifically a sexual one.

in·flo·res·cence (in,flōres'əns), *n.* the process or condition of blossoming; flowering.

in·flu·ent (in'floŏənt), *n.* an animal or plant that has a profound effect on the other plants and animals in its environment. See also **subin-fluent.**

in·fo·tain·ment (in,fōtān'mənt), *n.* a programme or film designed to inform the audience in an entertaining manner.

in·fra (in'frə), *adv.* below, as in a textual reference. See also **supra.**

in·fra·cos·tal (in,frəkos'təl), *adj.* situated under the ribs.

in·fract (infrakt'), *v.* to break; infringe.

in·fra dig (in'frə dig'), beneath one's dignity; undignified. [*Abbr.* for Latin *infra dignitatem*]

in·fran·gi·ble (infran'jibəl), *adj.* 1. not capable of being broken or fragmented. 2. not capable of being infringed or violated. —in·fran,gi·bil'i·ty,   in·fran'gi·ble·ness,   *n.* —in·fran'gi·bly, *adv.*

in·fun·dib·u·lum (in,fundib'yələm), *n., pl.* in·fun·dib·u·la (in,fundib'yələ). a funnel-shaped part or structure.

in·gem·i·nate (injem'ināt,), *v.* to reiterate; repeat.

in·ge·ni·ous (injēn'yəs, injē'nēəs), *adj.* skilful; inventive and resourceful in doing something. —in·ge'ni·ous·ness, *n.*

in·gen·u·ous (injen'yoŏəs), *adj.* naive; inexperienced; unworldly.

in·gest (injest'), *v.* to take into the body, esp. food.

in·ges·ta (injes'tə), *n. pl.* substances taken in as nourishment.

in·gle·nook (ING'gəlnoŏk,), *n.* a chimney corner.

in·grate (in'grāt), *n.* an ungrateful person.

in·gra·ti·ate (ingrā'sHēāt), *v.* in·gra·ti·ated, in·gra·ti·at·ing. to seek the friendship or regard of another, esp. for personal gain.

in·gra·ves·cent (in,grəves'ənt), *adj.* increasing in severity or gravity, as an illness.

in·gress (in'gres), *n.* the act, right, or means of entering.

in·gui·nal (ING'gwinəl), *adj.* situated in or pertaining to the groin.

in·gur·gi·tate (ingû'jitāt,), *v.* to swallow up greedily.

in·here (inhēr'), *v.* to remain fixed; to belong or exist permanently. —in·her'ence, *n.*

in·her·ent (inhēr'ənt, inher'ənt), *adj.* basic; fundamental; belonging to someone or something as part of its origin or nature; inborn. —in·her'ence, *n.*

in·he·sion (inhē'zHən), *n.* the fact or condition of inhering.

in·hib·it (inhib'it), *v.* to cause (someone) to behave carefully, esp. to avoid doing something freely; stop or hinder (a wish, action, etc.) because it might be misunderstood, undesirable, ill-advised, etc. —in,hi·bi'tion (in,ibisH'ən, in,hibisH'ən), *n.*

in·hume (inhyoŏm'), *v.* to bury.

in·im·i·cal (inim'ikəl), *adj.* hostile; unfriendly.

in·iq·ui·ty (inik'witē), *n.* unfairness; injustice; wickedness. —in·iq'ui·tous, *adj.*

in lo·co pa·ren·tis (in lō'kō pərən'tis), *Latin.* in place of a parent.

inn·age (in'ij), *n. U.S.* the quantity of goods left in a container when received after dispatch. See also **outage.**

in·nate (ināt'), *adj.* 1. inborn; anything that one is born with. 2. completely natural and characteristic, as if inborn.

in·ner·vate (in'ûvāt,), *v.* to furnish with nervous energy; stimulate. —in,ner·va'tion, *n.*

in·nerve (inûv'), *v.* to supply with nervous energy; innervate.

in·noc·u·ous (inok'yoŏəs), *adj.* harmless; not injurious.

in·nom·i·nate (inom'init), *adj.* anonymous; without a name.

innominate bone, the hipbone, as made up of three bones: ilium, ischium, and pubis.

in·nu·en·do (in'yoŏen'dō), *n., pl.* in·nu·en-dos, in·nu·en·does. a sly suggestion or hint that someone has done something wrong or questionable.

in·nu·mer·a·ble (inyoŏ'mərəbəl), *adj.* far too many to be counted.

in·or·di·nate (inô'dinit), *adj.* not controlled, restrained, or inhibited in behaviour or feelings; immoderate.

in·os·cu·late (inos'kyəlāt,), *v.* to join so as to become continuous.

in·qui·e·tude (inkwī'ityoŏd,), *n.* restlessness; disturbance; uneasiness.

in·qui·line (in'kwilīn,), *n.* **1.** an animal that lives in the same abode as an animal of a different species without harming it. —*adj.* **2.** of or relating to an inquiline or its habit. Compare **commensal.** —**in·qui·lin·ism** (in'kwiliniz,əm), **in·qui·lin·i·ty** (in,kwilin'itē), *n.* —**in·qui·lin·ous** (in,kwilī'nəs), *adj.*

in·sa·lu·bri·ous (insəlōō'brēəs), *adj.* detrimental to health; unhealthy.

in·sa·tia·ble (insā'sHəbəl), *adj.* incapable of being satisfied.

in·scru·ta·ble (inskrōō'təbəl), *adj.* mysterious; not readily yielding to examination or investigation; obscure.

in·sec·ti·cide (insek'tisīd), *n.* a preparation used for destroying insects.

in·sec·ti·fuge (insek'tifyōōj), *n.* a preparation used for repelling insects.

in·sec·ti·vore (insek'tivôə), *n.* a plant or animal that feeds on insects. —**in,sec·tiv'o·rous,** *adj.*

in·sec·tol·o·gy (in,sektol'əjē), *n.* the scientific study of insects; entomology.

in·sen·ti·ent (insen'sHēənt), *adj.* without feeling or sensation.

in·sid·i·ous (insid'ēəs), *adj.* treacherous; cunning; designed to entrap or deceive.

in·sight (in'sīt), *n.* the ability to understand something; creative judgment. —**in·sight'ful,** *adj.*

in·sip·id (insip'id), *adj.* flat, bland, and colourless; uninteresting; having no taste, as a substance.

in si·tu (in sit'yōō), *Latin.* in its original place; in position.

in·so·late (in'sōlāt), *v.* to expose to the rays of the sun. —**in,so·la'tion,** *n.*

in·sou·ci·ance (insōō'sēəns), *n.* indifference; lack of concern.

in·sou·ciant (insōō'sēənt), *adj.* not worrying; not anxious or particularly concerned, esp. from a superior or haughty attitude.

in·spis·sate (inspis'āt), *v.* to make dense or thick.

in·stan·ter (instan'tə), *adv.* instantly; urgently.

in·sti·gate (in'stigāt), *v.* **in·sti·gat·ed, in·sti·gat·ing.** to cause to begin, as by urging. —**in,sti·ga'·tion,** *n.*

in·suf·flate (insuf'lāt), *v.* to blow or breathe in.

in·su·lin (in'syəlin), *n.* a hormone secreted in cells of the pancreas, used for the treatment of diabetes.

insulin shock, a collapsed condition owing to a decrease in blood sugar as a result of excessive doses of insulin. Also **insulin reaction.**

in·sur·gen·cy (insû'jənsē), *n.* an insurrection or rebellion.

in·sur·rec·tion (in,sərek'sHən), *n.* an act of revolt or rebellion against an established authority.

in·ta·gli·o (intä'lēō,), *n., pl.* **in·tagl·ios.** a design incised or engraved on a hard surface. See also **cavo-relievo.**

in·tan·gi·ble (intan'jəbəl), *adj.* not touchable; evanescent; immaterial; difficult or impossible to put one's finger on.

in·tar·si·a (intä'sēə), *n.* the art of decorating a surface with inlaid patterns. Also **tarsia.** —**in·tar'sist,** *n.*

in·te·gral (in'tigrəl, integ'rəl), *adj.* essentially belonging to something; basic.

in·teg·u·ment (integ'yəmənt), *n.* a skin; covering; coating. —**in·teg,u·men'ta·ry,** *adj.*

in·tel·lec·tion (in,tilek'sHən), *n.* the action or process of understanding.

in·tel·li·gent·si·a (intel,ijent'sēə), *n. pl.* intellectuals, considered as an educated, influential class, esp. as an élite.

in·ten·sion (inten'sHən), *n.* comprehension; connotation. See also **extension.**

in·ter a·li·a (in'tə ā'lēə, ä'lēə), *Latin.* among other things.

in·ter a·li·os (in'tə ā'lēōs, ä'lēōs), *Latin.* among other persons.

in·ter·ca·lar·y (intû'kələr,ē), *adj.* interposed; intervening.

in·ter·ca·late (intû'kəlāt,), *v.* to interpose; interpolate. —**in·ter,ca·la'tion,** *n.*

in·ter·cen·sal (intəsen'səl), *adj.* of or pertaining to the period between two censuses; happening between two censuses.

in·ter·cos·tal (intəkos'təl), *adj.* relating to muscles or parts situated between the ribs. —**in·ter·cos'tal·ly,** *adv.*

in·ter·dict (in,tədikt', in,tədīt'), *v.* to forbid; prohibit. —**in·ter·dic'tion,** *n.* —**in·ter·dic'tor·y,** *adj.*

in·ter·dig·i·tate (intədij'itāt,), *v.* to interlock, like the fingers of both hands when clasped.

in·ter·fer·om·e·ter (in,təfərom'itə), *n.* an instrument for measuring lengths, distances, etc. by means of the interference properties of two rays of light.

in·ter·im (in'tərim), *n.* the meanwhile or meantime.

in·ter·ja·cent (in,təjā'sənt), *adj.* lying in between; intervening.

in·ter·loc·u·to·ry (in,tələok'yətərē), *adj.* intermediate; not finally decisive.

International Monetary Fund, an organization set up to stabilize world currencies and to help member nations to overcome financial crises.

International Style, a form of architecture, originating in the 1920s, emphasizing geometric shapes and large surfaces, and making much use of glass, steel, and reinforced concrete.

in·ter·ne·cine (in,tənē'sīn), *adj.* mutually destructive; relating to feuds and struggles within a group.

in·ter·o·cep·tor (in,tərōsep'tə), *n.* a receptor which responds to stimuli that originate inside the body.

in·ter·os·cu·late (in,təros'kyəlāt,), *v.* to form a connecting link.

in·ter·pel·la·tion (in,tǝpǝlā'sHǝn), *n.* (in some legislative bodies) the process of demanding statements or explanations from ministers, often leading to a debate and vote of confidence in the government.

in·ter·po·late (intū'pǝlāt,), *v.* to insert or introduce, as a remark into a conversation, new information into existing data, etc. —**in·ter,po·la'tion,** *n.*

in·ter·reg·num (intǝreg'nǝm), *n.*, *pl.* **in·ter·reg·nums, in·ter·reg·na** (intǝreg'nǝ). a period between the end of a reign and the beginning of a new one.

in·ter·stice (intū'stis), *n.* a small or narrow opening between things or parts. —**in,ter·sti'·tial,** *adj.*

in·ter·vene (in,tǝvēn'), *v.* **in·ter·vened, in·ter·ven·ing. 1.** to interrupt; come between two people, as *to intervene in an argument,* or two events, as *the years intervening between his election and his retirement.* **2.** to interfere.

in·tes·tines (intes'tinz), *n. pl.* the lower part of the alimentary canal between the stomach and the anus. —**in·tes'ti·nal,** *adj.*

in·ti·ma (in'timǝ), *n.,* *pl.* **in·ti·mae** (in'timē). the innermost lining of a bodily part or organ, as a vein, etc.

in·time (aΝtēm'), *adj., French.* cosy; intimate.

in·tim·i·date (intim'idāt,), *v.* to make timid; cow; overawe. —**in·tim,i·da'tion,** *n.*

in·ti·mism (in'timiz,ǝm), *n.* a style of painting emphasizing an impressionistic portrayal of domestic scenes. —**in'ti·mist,** *adj.*

in·tort (intôt'), *v.* to twist about a fixed point; curl. —**in·tor'sion,** *n.*

in·trac·ta·ble (intrak'tǝbǝl), *adj.* stubborn; obstinate; unyielding; refusing to change one's mind.

in·tra·mu·ral (in,trǝmyōōr'ǝl), *adj.* involving only the members of one school.

in·tran·si·gent (intran'sijǝnt), *adj.* unyielding; stubborn; uncompromising.

in·tra·u·ter·ine device (in,trǝyōō'tǝrīn), a device, as a loop, placed in the uterus to stop conception. *Abbr.:* **I.U.D.**

in·trav·a·sa·tion (intrav,ǝsā'sHǝn), *n.* the introduction of foreign matter into a blood vessel.

in·trep·id (intrep'id), *adj.* brave; fearless.

in·trin·sic (intrin'sik, intrin'zik), *adj.* essentially belonging to something or someone, as basic nature.

in·tro·mit (in,trǝmit'), *v.* to put or let in; admit; introduce.

in·tron (in'tron), *n.* a stretch of DNA within a

gene that does not contribute code for the gene product. Compare **exon.**

in·tro·vert (in'trǝvût,), *n.* a person primarily concerned with his own feelings, thoughts, and actions. See also **extrovert.**

in·tu·i·tive (intyōō'itiv), *adj.* known by instinct, without learning or experience.

in·tu·mesce (in,tyōōmes'), *v.* to swell; inflate. —**in,tu·mes'cence,** *n.*

in·tus·sus·cept (in,tusǝsept'), *v.* to take in; invaginate. —**in·tus·sus·cep'tion,** *n.*

in·unc·tion (inuΝGk'sHǝn), *n.* the action of anointing.

in·un·date (in'undāt,), *v.* to overwhelm by deluging; swamp.

in·ure (inyōō'ǝ), *v.* to harden; make impervious to or unaffected by hardship, insult, or other cares.

in·u·tile (inyōō'tīl), *adj.* useless; of no service. —**in,u·til'i·ty,** *n.*

in va·cu·o (in vak'yōōō), *Latin.* in a vacuum; isolated; separate.

in·vag·i·nate (invaj'ināt,), *v.* to insert, as into a sheath; to draw back within itself. —**in·vag,i·na'tion,** *n.*

in·vec·tive (invek'tiv), *n.* violent and abusive denunciation or censure.

in·veigh (invā'), *v.* to attack verbally; denounce; rail.

in·vet·er·ate (invet'ǝrit), *adj.* established or settled on an unchanging pattern of behaviour, as *an inveterate drinker.*

in·vid·i·ous (invid'ēǝs), *adj.* causing dislike or resentment; giving offence; hateful or harmful.

in·vig·i·late (invij'ilāt,), *v.* to supervise students at an examination.

in·vin·ci·ble (invin'sǝbǝl), *adj.* undefeatable; that cannot be conquered or surmounted.

in·vi·o·late (invī'ǝlit, invī'ǝlāt), *adj.* not violated; secure from being hurt, damaged, disturbed, or outraged.

in vi·tro (in vē'trō), *Latin.* within an artificial environment, as a laboratory. [Literally 'in glass']

in vi·vo (in vē'vō), *Latin.* (in biology) within a live organism.

in·voke (invōk'), *v.* **in·voked, in·vok·ing.** to call upon (God or some other power) for help; beg. —**in,vo·ca'tion,** *n.*

in·vo·lu·cre (in'vǝlōōkǝ), *n.* a case or covering, esp. a membranous envelope.

in·vo·lut·ed (in'vǝlōō,tid), *adj.* involved; complex; complicated.

i·on·o·pause (īon'ǝpôz,), *n.* the zone between the ionosphere and mesosphere.

i·on·o·sphere (īon'ǝsfē,ǝ), *n.* **1.** the portion of the earth's atmosphere between the stratosphere and exosphere. **2.** E layer.

i·on propulsion (ī'ǝn, ī'on), a proposed form of propulsion for craft in outer space, the motive force being supplied by exhaust consisting of positive ions and negative electrons repelled by electrostatic forces.

i·o·ta (īō'tə), *n.* the tiniest amount or hint of something; scintilla; jot, as *She hasn't an iota of knowledge about brewing beer.*

ip·se dix·it (ip'sē dik'sit), *Latin.* **1.** he himself said it. **2.** an unproved, dogmatic statement.

ip·so fac·to (ip'sō fak'tō), *Latin.* literally; by the fact itself; by that very fact.

i·ra·cund (ī'rəkund), *adj.* angry; passionate.

i·ras·ci·ble (iras'əbəl), *adj.* easily angered; irritable. —**i·ras·ci·bil'i·ty,** *n.*

i·rate (īrāt'), *adj.* angry; furious; enraged.

i·ren·ic (īrē'nik, īren'ik), *adj.* pacific; promoting peace.

ir·i·dol·o·gy (ir,idol'əjē), *n.* the technique of diagnosing disease by examining the iris of the eye. —**ir,i·dol'o·gist,** *n.*

i·ro·ny (ī'rənē), *n.* a way of saying something in which one purposely says the opposite of what one means, as the statement, 'It's nice and warm outside' when the temperature is 20° below zero. —**i·ron'ic, i·ron'i·cal,** *adj.*

ir·ra·tion·al (irasH'ənəl), *adj.* not rational or able to reason sensibly; characterized by a lack of logic or common sense, as *an irrational argument.*

ir·re·cu·sa·ble (ir,ikyōō'zəbəl), *adj.* not to be refused or rejected.

ir·re·den·ta (ir,iden'tə), *n.* a region linked historically, ethnically, or culturally with one nation, but governed by another.

ir·re·den·tist (ir,iden'tist), *n.* a person who actively supports the acquisition by his country of territory that was once or is considered to be part of it and is now part of another country. Also **revanchist.** —**ir,re·den'tism,** *n.*

ir·ref·ra·ga·ble (iref'rəgəbəl), *adj.* not to be refuted or disproved; undeniable.

ir·re·fran·gi·ble (ir,ifranj'əbəl), *adj.* not to be broken; inviolable.

ir·rem·e·a·ble (irem'ēəbəl, irē'mēəbəl), *adj.* permitting no return; irreversible.

ir·rep·a·ra·ble (irep'ərəbəl, irep'rəbəl), *adj.* not repairable; permanently broken, out of order, or damaged. —**ir·rep'a·ra·bly,** *adv.*

ir·re·plev·i·sa·ble (ir,iplev'isəbəl), *adj.* (in law) not capable of being replevied or delivered on sureties.

ir·ro·rate (ir'ərāt), *adj.* marked with minute dots; speckled. Also **ir'ro·rat,ed.**

ir·rupt (irupt'), *v.* to burst or break in violently; to display emotion or activity. —**ir·rup'tion,** *n.* —**ir·rup'tive,** *adj.*

i·sa·go·ge (ī'səgō,jē), *n.* an introduction, as to a work of research. —**i·sa·gog'ic** (ī,səgoj'ik), *adj.*

is·al·lo·bar (īsal'əbär,), *n.* (in meteorology) a line on a weather map linking points with equal pressure changes.

is·al·lo·therm (īsal'əthûm,), *n.* (in meteorology) a line on a weather chart linking points with equal temperature variations over a given period.

is·a·nom·al (ī,sənom'əl). *n.* (in meteorology) a line on a map connecting points with equal anomaly or irregularity of a meteorological quantity.

i·sa·rithm (ī'səriTH,əm), *n.* See **isopleth.**

is·aux·e·sis (ī,sôgzē'sis, ī,sôksē'sis), *n.* (in biology) the growth rate of a part equal to that of the complete organism. See also **bradyauxesis, tachyauxesis.**

is·chae·mi·a, is·che·mi·a (iskē'mēə), *n.* (in medicine) insufficient blood supply to an organ or part. —**is·chae·mic, is·che·mic** (iskem'ik), *adj.*

is·chi·um (is'kēəm) *n., pl.* **is·chi·a. 1.** the lowest of the three parts of the innominate bone. **2.** either of the bones on which the body rests when seated. —**is,chi·at'ic,** *adj.*

Ish·i·ha·ra test (isH,ēhä'rə), a colour-blindness test, developed in Japan, using cards which reveal different patterns to eyes with normal sight and eyes that are colour blind.

islet of Lang·er·hans (laNG'əhans,), one of several masses of cells in the pancreas secreting insulin.

i·so·bar (ī'sōbä,), *n.* (in meteorology) a line on a weather map connecting points with the same barometric pressure at a given time. —**i,so·bar'-ic,** *adj.*

i·so·bath (ī'sōbath,), *n.* a line drawn on a map to connect points of equal depth below the water surface. —**i,so·bath'ic,** *adj.*

i·so·bath·y·therm (ī,sōbath'əthûm,), *n.* a line on a sea chart linking depths with the same temperature.

i·so·bront (ī'sōbront), *n.* See **homobront.**

i·so·ce·phal·ic (ī,sōsəfal'ik), *adj.* (in a painting) having the representation of heads on the same level. Also **i·so·ceph·a·lous** (ī,sōsef'ələs).

i·so·ce·rau·nic (ī,sōsərô'nik), *adj.* (in meteorology) having the same frequency or intensity or simultaneous activity of thunderstorms. Also **isokeraunic.**

i·so·chasm (ī'sōkaz,əm), *n.* a line on a map linking points where auroras occur with equal frequency.

i·so·chro·mat·ic (ī,sōkrōmat'ik), *adj.* having the same colour.

i·soch·ro·nal (īsok'rənəl), *adj.* occupying or happening in an equal amount of time. Also **i·soch'ro·nous.**

i·so·chrone (ī'sōkrōn,), *n.* a line on a map or chart made up of all points displaying some common and simultaneous property. —**i·soch'-ro·nism,,** *n.*

i·soch·ro·ny (īsok'rənē), *n.* the state or condition of occurring simultaneously.

i·soch·ro·ous (īsok'rōəs), *adj.* having the same colour.

i·soc·ra·cy (īsok'rəsē), *n.* a form of government in which all people have equal power.

i·so·dose (ī'sōdōs), *adj.* relating to all points having an equal intensity of radiation in a contaminated area.

i·so·dros·o·therm (ī,sōdros'ōthûm,), *n.* (in meteorology) a line on a weather chart joining places with an equal dew point.

i·so·dy·nam·ic (ī,sōdīnam'ik), *adj.* 1. marked by equal force or intensity. 2. relating to an imaginary line linking points of equal horizontal intensity in the earth's magnetic field.

i·so·ge·o·therm (i,sōjē'ōthûm,), *n.* an imaginary line connecting all points on the earth's surface with the same mean temperature.

i·sog·o·nal (īsog'ənəl), *adj.* having equal angles; isogonic.

isogonal line, a line on a map linking points where the magnetic declination is the same. Also **i'so·gone,**.

i·so·gon·ic (ī,sōgon'ik), *adj.* 1. with equal angles. 2. pertaining to an isogonal line.

i·so·gra·dient (ī,sōgrā'dēənt), *n.* (in meteorology) a line on a weather map joining points with equal horizontal gradients, such as pressure or temperature.

i·so·gram (ī'sōgram), *n.* a line on a map or chart linking points with some common meteorological factor.

i·so·ha·line (ī,sōhā'lēn), *n.* a line on an ocean chart or map linking all points of equal salinity. Also **i,so·hal'sine.**

i·so·hel (ī'sōhel,), *n.* (in meteorology) a line on a weather chart linking points receiving equal amounts of sunshine.

i·so·hume (ī'sōhyōōm,), *n.* (in meteorology) a line on a weather chart joining points of equal relative humidity.

i·so·hy·et (ī,sōhī'ət), *n.* a line on a map connecting points having equal amounts of rainfall over a given period.

i·so·ke·rau·nic (ī,sōkirô'nik), *adj.* See **isoceraunic.**

i·so·mag·net·ic (ī,sōmagnet'ik), *adj.* pertaining to a line on a map connecting points with equal magnetic elements.

i·so·me·tro·pi·a (ī,sōmətrō'pēə), *n.* a condition in which the refraction is the same in either eye.

i·som·e·try (īsom'itrē), *n.* equality of measure.

i·so·morph (ī'sōmôf,), *n.* an organism which has the same shape and appearance as another, but a different ancestry.

i·so·mor·phic (ī,sōmô'fik), *adj.* having the same form or appearance, but different ancestry.

i·so·mor·phism (ī,sōmô'fizəm), *n.* the state of being isomorphic.

i·so·neph (ī'sōnef,), *n.* (in meteorology) a line on a weather map connecting points with equal amounts of cloudiness.

i·son·o·my (īson'əmē), *n.* equality of laws or political rights.

i·so·pach (ī'sōpak,), *n.* a line on a map connecting all points of equal geological thickness.

i·so·pach·ous (ī,sōpak'əs), *adj.* having equal thickness.

i·so·pag (ī'sōpag,), *n.* a line on a map linking all points where winter ice exists at approximately the same time.

i·so·pec·tic (ī,sōpek'tik), *n.* a line on a map joining all points where winter ice begins to form at approximately the same time.

i·so·pi·es·tic (ī'sōpīes'tik), *adj.* of equal pressure.

i·so·pleth (ī'sōpleth,), *n.* a line on a map joining all points with equal numerical values. Also **isarithm.**

i·so·pod (ī'sōpod,), *n.* a crustacean with a flattened body and seven pairs of legs.

i·so·pol·i·ty (ī,sōpol'itē), *n.* equal civic and political rights.

i·so·por (ī'sōpô,ə), *n.* an imaginary line on a map of the earth joining points with equal annual variations in magnetic phenomena.

i·so·pyc·nic (ī,sōpik'nik), *n.* a line on a map linking points having equal water density.

i·sos·ce·les (īsos'əlēz), *adj.* (of a triangle) having only two equal sides.

i·sos·ta·sy (īsos'təsē), *n.* the equilibrium of the earth's crust. —**i,so·stat'ic,** *adj.*

i·so·stere (ī'sōstē,ə), *n.* (in meteorology) a line on a chart or map linking points of equal atmospheric density.

i·so·tac (ī'sōtak,), *n.* a line on a map connecting points where ice begins to melt during spring at approximately the same time.

i·so·tach (ī'sōtak,), *n.* (in meteorology) a line on a weather chart connecting points where the same wind velocities exist.

i·so·ten·i·scope (ī,sōten'iskōp,), *n.* an instrument for measuring vapour pressure.

i·so·there (ī'sōthē,ə), *n.* (in meteorology) a line on a weather map joining points with the same mean summer temperature.

i·so·therm (ī'sōthûm,), *n.* (in meteorology) a line on a weather map linking points with the same temperature.

i·so·ther·mal (ī,sōthû'məl), *adj.* taking place at a constant temperature.

i·so·ther·mo·bath (ī,sōthû'mōbath), *n.* a line on a vertical section of the sea linking all points having equal temperature.

i·so·tim·ic (ī,sōtim'ik), *adj.* possessing an equal quantitative value at a given time.

i·so·tope (ī'sətōp,), *n.* a chemical element having the same character as another but with a different radioactive property or atomic weight. —i·sot·o·py (īsot'əpē), n.

i·so·type (ī'sətīp,), n. a symbol or drawing representing a certain general fact or quantity about the object depicted. —i,so·typ'ic adj.

i·tai·i·tai (ē,tīē'tī), n. a bone-weakening disease caused by the presence of cadmium in the system. [Japanese 'Ouch! Ouch!']

it·er (it'û), n. (in anatomy) a canal or passage.

it·er·ant (it'ərənt), adj. repeating; recurrent.

it·er·ate (it'ərāt,), v. to utter or do repeatedly.

it·er·a·tive (it'ərətiv), adj. repeating; repetitious.

ith·y·phal·lic (ithifal'ik), adj. indecent; obscene.

i·tin·er·ate (ītin'ərāt,), v. to travel from place to place. —i·tin'er·ant, adj., n.

I.U.D., abbrev. for intrauterine device.

J

ja·bot (zHabō'), *n.* a ruffle or arrangement of lace worn at the neck or waist.

jack·leg (jak'leg'), *adj.* **1.** unskilled for one's job. **2.** dishonest in dealings.

jac·o·net (jak'ənet,). *n.* a lightweight cotton material, used for clothing and bandages.

jac·ta·tion (jaktā'sHən), *n.* boasting; showing-off.

jac·u·late (jak'yəlāt,), *v.* to throw (a javelin or spear).

jac·u·lif·er·ous (jak,yəlif'ərəs), *adj.* possessing spines like darts.

jad·ed (jā'did), *adj.* tired or bored from having been used too much; worn out.

ja·pan (jəpan'), *n.* a hard, longlasting black varnish, of Japanese origin, used on wood or other similar materials.

jape (jāp), *v.* **1.** to joke or make fun of. —*n.* **2.** a practical joke or wisecrack.

jar·di·niere (järdinē'ə), *n.* an ornamental container for plants and flowers.

jar·o·vize (yär'əvīz), *v.* to hasten the development of seeds, etc., by some process. Also **iarovize, yarovize.**

jas·pé (jaspā'), *adj.* made to look veined, like jasper.

ja·to (jā'tō), *n.* a takeoff assisted by jet propulsion, esp. one assisted by rockets which are then jettisoned. [from *j(et)-a(ssisted) t(ake)-o(ff)*]

jaun·dice (jôn'dis), *n.* an illness caused by increased bile pigments in the blood, characterized by yellowness of skin. Also **icterus.**

jaun·diced (jôn'dist), *adj.* showing prejudice, often as the result of a personal experience.

jaw·bon·ing (jô'bōn,iNG), *adj. U.S. slang.* using the power and prestige of the government to persuade business and trade unions to moderate their demands in the national interest.

je·june (jijōōn'), *adj.* **1.** (of food) low in nutritive value. **2.** dull; uninteresting. **3.** lacking wisdom; immature.

je·ju·num (jijōō'nəm), *n.* part of the small intestine between the duodenum and the ileum.

je ne sais quoi (zHə nə sā kwä'), *French.* a pleasing and undefinable quality of personality. [Literally 'I know not what' in the sense, 'I cannot put my finger on what it is.']

jeop·ard·y (jep'ədē), *n., pl.* **jeop·ard·ies.** risk of exposure to harm or death.

jer·e·mi·ad (jer,əmī'ad), *n.* a lamentation or mourning.

jet·a·va·tor (jet'əvātə), *n.* an extended exhaust nozzle on a rocket,used to control the direction of the exhaust.

jet engine, an engine that imparts motion to a vehicle, esp. an aeroplane, by thrusting backwards a stream of liquid or air and gases.

jet·ti·son (jet'isən), *v.* to discard (something no longer wanted or needed).

jet·ton (jet'ən), *n.* a stamped counter, used in card-playing, etc.

jeu d'es·prit (zHû desprē'), *pl.* **jeux d'es·prit** (zHû desprē'). *French.* **1.** a joke. **2.** a piece of sharply witty literature.

jeu·nesse do·rée (zHûnes, dôrā'), *n.* fashionable and wealthy young people. [*French* literally: gilded youth]

jig·ger (jig'ə), *n.* See **chigoe.**

jig·ger·y-pok·er·y (jig'ərēpō'kərē), *n.* falseness, deception, or trickery.

ji·had (jihäd'), *n.* a holy war waged by Muslims as a duty, or any such undertaking for a principle or idea. Also **je·had** (jēhäd').

jin·go (jiNG'gō), *n., pl.* **jin·goes.** someone who is patriotic to excess and wishes always to be prepared for war.

jin·go·ism (jiNG'gōiz,əm), *n.* the policy of being prepared for war; aggressive patriotism.

jin·ni (jin'ē), *n., pl.* **jinn** (jin). (in Islamic mythology) a type of spirit, lower than an angel, which can take human or animal form and influence man. Also **djinni.**

job·ber·y (job'ərē), *n.* the practice of securing improper personal reward or advantage from holding public office.

jo·cose (jōkōs'), *adj.* given to humour or joking. —**jo·cos·i·ty** (jōkos'itē), *n.*

joc·u·lar (jok'yələ), *adj.* characterized by joking. —**joc,u·lar'i·ty,** *n.*

joc·und (jok'ənd), *adj.* cheerful; happy. —**jo·cun·di·ty** (jōkun'ditē), *n.*

joie de vi·vre (zHwa də vēvr'), *French.* pleasure at being alive, esp. carefree enjoyment of life.

jo·jo·ba (hōhō'bə), *n.* a North American shrub whose edible seeds contain an oil used in shampoos and cosmetics.

joule (jōōl, joul), *n.* the unit of work or energy equal to work achieved by one newton when it moves one metre in the direction of the force.

jour·ney·man (jû'nēmən), *n.* a person, esp. an artisan, qualified to work at a trade.

jo·vi·al (jō'vēəl), *adj.* cheerfully jolly; good-natured and friendly.

ju·bate (jōō'bāt), *adj.* hairy, as if covered by a mane.

ju·gal (jōō'gəl), *adj.* belonging to the cheek or cheekbone.

ju·gu·late (jug'yəlāt,), *v.* **1.** to check a disease by drastic measures. **2.** to cut the throat of.

Jukes (jōōks), *n. U.S.* pseudonym for an actual family that over several generations exhibited a history of poverty, crime, illness, and social degeneracy. See also **Kallikak.**

junc·ture (juNGkt'CHə), *n.* a particular time, esp. one when an important or specified event took place, as *At that juncture, we left the house;* now, as *At this juncture, we must stop.*

junk bond, a bond issued by a company to finance the takeover of another company by using the value of the target company as security. See **leveraged buyout.**

Ju·ras·sic (jōōras'ik), *adj.* a part of the Mesozoic epoch, 135,000,000 to 180,000,000 years ago, when dinosaurs and conifers were prevalent.

ju·rat (jōōr'at), *n.* a sworn public officer such as a magistrate.

ju·ra·tion (jōōrā'sHən), *n.* the taking or administering of an oath.

ju·ra·to·ry (jōōr'ətərē, jōōr'ətrē), *adj.* constituting, expressed in, or pertaining to an oath.

ju·ris·dic·tion (jōōr,isdik'sHən), *n.* **1.** the authority to administer law. **2.** the extent, range, or territory where such authority is valid and can be exercised.

ju·ris·pru·dence (jōōr,isprōō'dəns), *n.* the science and philosophy of law; a legal system.

juste-mi·lieu (zHystmēlyû'), *n.,* *pl.* **juste-mi·lieux** (zHystmēlyû'). *French.* the midpoint between two extremes.

just-in-time *adj.* of or relating to a manufacturing system in which components are produced as they are required instead of being stockpiled. *Abbr.:* **JIT.**

ju·ve·nes·cent (jōō,vənes'ənt), *adj.* young or becoming young.

ju·ve·nil·ia (jōō,vənil'ēə), *n. pl.* works, esp. literature, produced for or by young people.

jux·ta·pose (juk'stəpōz,), *v.* to put next to each other, esp. for comparison. —**jux·ta·po·si·tion** (juk,stəpəzisH'ən), *n.*

j'y suis, j'y reste (zHē swē' zHē rest'), *French.* here I am, and here I stay.

K

ka·bu·ki (kəbŌŌ'kē), *n.* popular Japanese theatre, based on legend and characterized by a traditional style of acting, elaborate costumes and makeup, stylized music and dancing, and by male actors assuming all roles. See also **No.**

kaf·tan (kaf'tan, kaf'tän), *n.* See **caftan.**

kak·is·toc·ra·cy (kak,istok'rəsē), *n.* government by the worst people in the state.

ka·lif, ka·liph (kā'lif, kal'if), *n.* See **caliph.**

kal·if·ate (kal'əfāt), *n.* See **caliphate.**

Kal·li·kak (kal'əkak), *n. U.S.* pseudonym for an actual family that over several generations exhibited a history of poverty, crime, illness, and social degeneracy. See also **Jukes.**

ka·o·lin, ka·o·line (kā'əlin), *n.* a fine china clay used in making porcelain.

Ka·po·si's sarcoma (kapŌ'sēz), *n.* a type of skin cancer, common among AIDS patients.

kar·ma (kä'mə), *n.* fate; destiny.

kar·y·og·a·my (kar,ēog'əmē), *n.* the fusion of cell nuclei, as in fertilization.

kar·y·o·ki·ne·sis (kar,ēōkinē'sis, kar,ēōkīn'ē·sis), *n.* the series of changes which take place in a cell nucleus in the process of dividing.

kar·y·o·plasm (kar'ēōplaz,əm), *n.* the substance of a cell nucleus.

kar·y·o·type (kar'ēōtīp,), *n.* the sum total of the characteristics of a set of somatic chromosomes.

ka·sha (kä'sнə), *n.* in E. European cookery boiled buckwheat groats.

ka·tab·a·sis (kətab'əsis), *n., pl.* **ka·tab·a·ses** (kətab'əsēz). a military retreat. See also **anabasis.**

kat·a·bat·ic (kat,əbat'ik), *adj.* (of a wind) moving downwards or down a slope or valley. See also **anabatic.**

kat·a·mor·phism (kat,əmô'fizəm), *n.* metamorphism which changes complex minerals to simple minerals. See also **anamorphism.**

kat·a·pla·sia (kat,əplā'zēə), *n.* See **cataplasia.**

kat·a·to·ni·a (kat,ətō'nēə), *n.* See **catatonia.**

Ka·tha·re·vu·sa (kath,ərev'əsə), *n.* the literary form of modern Greek. See also **Demotic.**

ka·thar·sis (kəthär'sis), *n.* See **catharsis.**

keck (kek), *v.* to retch or heave; be nauseated.

kef (kāf), *n.* **1.** a drowsy, dreamy condition produced by narcotics, esp. marijuana. **2.** a hemp preparation smoked to produce such a condition. Also **keef** (kēf), **kif.**

keg·ler (keg'lə), *n.* a person who bowls; a bowler.

ke·loid, che·loid (kē'loid), an excessive growth of scar tissue on the skin surface.

ke·lot·o·my, ce·lot·o·my (kəlot'əmē), *n.* See **herniotomy.**

ken (ken), *n.* what one knows; knowledge; view or awareness.

ker·a·tal·gia (ker,ətal'jə), *n.* pain in the cornea.

ker·a·tin (ker'ətin), *n.* a substance found in horn, hair, nails, etc. Also **ceratin. —ker·at'i·nous,** *adj.*

ker·a·tog·e·nous (ker,ətoj'ənəs), *adj.* causing the growth of horn or horny tissue.

ker·a·toid (ker'ətoid), *adj.* hornlike; horny. Also **ceratoid.**

ker·a·to·sis (ker,ətō'sis), *n., pl.* **ker·a·to·ses** (ker,ətō'sēz). any disease characterized by horny growth; any horny growth.

kerf, curf (kûf), *n.* the cut or channel made by a saw.

ker·sey (kû'zē), *n.* a heavy fabric of wool, similar to beaver, used for overcoats.

Keynes·i·an (kānz'ēən), *adj.* of or relating to John Maynard Keynes (1883–1946), British economist, or to his works or ideas. Keynes advocated government intervention to regulate economic activity and sustain high levels of employment. **—Keynes'i·an·ism,** *n.*

key punch, a machine with a simplified typewriter keyboard, used for punching holes in cards. Also **card punch.**

khan (kän), *n.* a public inn; caravansarai.

kib·ble (kib'əl), *v.* to grind or divide into coarse particles or bits, as in preparing dry dog food.

kib·butz (kibŌŌts'), *n., pl.* **kib·but·zim** (kibŌŌtsēm'). an Israeli collective settlement, esp. agricultural.

kib·itz·er (kib'itsə), *n. U.S.* a giver of unwanted advice; a meddler or busybody.

kick·shaw (kik'sнô), *n.* **1.** a titbit or delicacy. **2.** a trinket or gewgaw.

kid·ney (kid'nē), *n.* disposition or temperament; kind, class, or sort.

kiel·ba·sa (kilbä'sə), *n., pl.* **kiel·ba·sas, kiel·ba·sy** (kilbä'sē). (in Polish cookery) a spicy smoked sausage of beef and pork. Also **kiel·ba·sy** (kilbä'sē).

kif (kif), *n*. See **kef.**

killer cell, a type of white blood cell that can recognize and destroy cancerous or infected host cells as part of the immune response.

kil·o·byte (kil'ōbīt,), *n*. 1000 bytes, the standard measure of computer data. *Abbrev.*: **Kb, K.**

kil·o·cy·cle (kil'ōsī,kəl), *n*. former word for kilohertz.

kil·o·gauss (kil'ōgous,), *n*. a unit equal to 1000 gauss.

kil·o·gram (kil'ōgram,), *n*. a unit of mass and weight equal to 1000 grams (2.2046 lbs.).

kil·o·hertz (kil'ōhûts,), *n*. a unit of frequency equal to 1000 cycles per second.

kil·o·li·tre (kil'ōlē,tə), *n*. 1000 litres; a cubic metre.

kil·o·me·tre (kil'əmē,tə, kilom'itə), *n*. the common measure of distances of 1000 metres (0.621 mile).

kil·o·volt (kil'ōvōlt,), *n*. a unit of force equal to 1000 volts.

kil·o·watt (kil'ōwot,), *n*. a unit of power equal to 1000 watts.

kil·o·watt-hour (kil,ōwot,ou'ə), *n*. a unit rate of consumption of electrical power equal to one kilowatt in one hour.

kin (kin), *n*. relatives; family; kinfolk.

kin·aes·the·sia (kin,isthē'zēə, kīn,isthē'zēə), *n*. the sensation of movement or position of limbs felt through nerves in the muscles, tendons, or joints. Also **kin·aes·the'sis.**

kin·dred (kin'drid), *adj*. related or similar in attitude, origin, etc., as *Peter and I are kindred spirits—we both love sailing.*

kin·e·mat·ics (kin,əmat'iks, kī,nəmat'iks), *n*. the branch of mechanics that deals with motion in the abstract, without reference to the masses or forces involved in it.

ki·ne·sics (kinē'siks, kīnē'ziks), *n*. the study of bodily and facial movements as related to and accompanying communication or speech.

ki·ne·si·ol·o·gy (kinē,sēol'əjē, kīnē,zēol'əjē), *n*. the study of human muscular movements and their relationship to human anatomy and physiology.

ki·net·ic (kinet'ik, kīnet'ik), *adj*. of, resulting from, or characterized by motion.

ki·net·ics (kinet'iks, kīnet'iks), *n*. the branch of mechanics dealing with the relation between the motions of bodies and the forces acting upon them.

kin·e·to·sis (kin,itō'sis, kī,nitō'sis), *n*. illness caused by travel, usually in a vehicle; motion sickness.

kip (kip), *n*. the untanned hide of a young or small animal.

kir·i·gami (kir,igä'mē), *n*. the Japanese art of folding and cutting paper to make decorative shapes and figures. Compare **origami.**

kirsch (kē'əsH), *n*. a colourless, unaged brandy made from cherries.

kish·ke (kisH'kə), *n*. (in Jewish cookery) a beef intestine stuffed with seasoned flour, breadcrumbs, etc., and roasted. Also **stuffed derma.**

kis·met (kiz'met), *n*. fate; destiny. Also **kis,-mat.**

kith (kith), *n*. friends, acquaintances, or neighbours.

kitsch (kicH), *n*. art or writing of popular but shallow appeal; pretentious nonsense.

klep·to·ma·ni·a (klep,tōmā'nēə), *n*. an abnormal, persistent impulse to steal. **—klep,to·ma'·ni·ac,** *n*.

klis·ter (klis'tə), *n*. a wax applied to skis when the snow is particularly wet.

knag·gy (nag'ē), *adj*. knotty; rough.

knar (nä), *n*. a knot in wood.

knave (nāv), *n*. a thoroughly bad person, esp. one who is dishonest; rogue.

knell (nel), *n*. the sound of a bell tolling, as for a funeral.

knish (knisH), *n*. (in Jewish cookery) a thin piece of dough folded over a filling, usually of potato or meat, and baked or fried.

knoll (nōl), *n*. a small elevation; hill, rock, or mound.

knop (nop), *n*. a knob or knoblike decoration.

knosp (nosp), *n*. an ornament in the shape of a bud.

knout (nout), *n*. a Russian whip with leather thongs.

knur (nû), *n*. a hard nob or knot on a tree.

knurl, nurl (nûl), *n*. any of a series of small beads or ridges, as along the edge of a coin.

kob·old (kob'ōld), *n*. (in German folklore) a house-haunting, often mischievous goblin.

koi·ne (koi'nē, koinā'), *n*. a language used in common by speakers of different languages, esp. the language that replaced classical Greek in the time of the Roman Empire; lingua franca.

ko·la (kō'lə), *n*. an extract of the kola nut.

kola nut, a brownish seed, produced by a tropical African and West Indian tree, used as a flavouring agent in cola drinks.

ko·nim·e·ter (kōnim'itə), *n*. a device for measuring the amount of dust in the air.

ko·ni·ol·o·gy, co·ni·ol·o·gy (kō,nēol'əjē), *n*. the study of impurities in the air, such as pollen, dust, etc.

ko·sher (kō'sHə), *adj*. (in Judaism) clean or fit to eat according to the dietary laws.

kour·bash (kōō'əbasH). See **kurbash.**

kow·tow (kou,tou'), *v*. to bow before another, either in genuine respect or hypocritically.

kraal (kräl), *n*. a South African native fenced village, often surrounding a cattle enclosure.

kra·ken (krä'kən), *n.* a legendary sea monster of northern seas.

krep·lach, krep·lech (krep'läkɦ), *n.* (in Jewish cookery) small casings of dough, usually filled with chopped meat, etc., boiled and served in soup.

krieg·spiel (krēg'spēl), *n.* **1.** a game in which pieces representing military units are manoeuvred on maps. **2.** a form of chess in which each player sees only his own pieces, his opponent's moves being told to him by a referee.

kris (krēs), *n.* See **creese.**

krumm·holz (krŏŏm'hōlts), *n.*, *pl.* **krumm-·holz.** a forest of stunted trees near the timber line.

ku·chen (kŏŏ'kɦən), *n.* (in German cookery) a coffee cake made of yeast dough and often including raisins, nuts, etc.

ku·dos (kyŏŏ'dos), *n.* credit; praise; glory.

ku·gel (kŏŏ'gəl), *n.* (in Jewish cookery) a baked puddinglike casserole.

Kul·tur·kreis (kŏŏltŏŏ'əkrīs), *n.*, *pl.* **Kul·tur-·krei·se** (kŏŏltŏŏr'krīzə). *German.* (in anthropology) cultural traits regarded as the nuclei of subsequent cultures.

Kunst·lied (kŏŏnst'lōt,), *n.*, *pl.* **Kunst·lie·der** (kŏŏnst'lē,də). *German.* art song.

kur·bash, kour·bash (kŏŏ'əbasɦ), *n.* a leather whip.

kur·saal (kû'zəl), *n.* **1.** a visitor's public room or building at a health spa. **2.** an amusement park.

kvass, kvas, quass (kväs), *n.* a weakly alcoholic beverage, of E. Europe and Russia, made from cereals and flavoured with fruit, peppermint, etc.

kwash·i·or·kor (kwasɦ,ēô'kôə), *n.* a nutritional disease of infants and children, occurring chiefly in Africa.

kwe·la (kwä'lə, kwel'ə), *n.* a type of popular music, played esp. in southern Africa, that combines African and Western elements in an ensemble traditionally comprising two flutes, two guitars, and a single-stringed bass.

ky·mo·graph (kī'məgraf, kī'məgräf), *n.* **1.** an instrument that measures and records on a graph variations, as of a human pulse. **2.** Also **cymograph.** a device for measuring the oscillations of an aircraft in flight.

ky·pho·sis (kīfō'sis), *n.* a hunched back caused by curvature of the spine.

L

lab·a·rum (lab'ərəm), *n.*, *pl.* **lab·a·ra** (lab'ərə). a banner or standard bearing Christian symbols.

lab·e·fac·tion (lab,ifak'sнən), *n.* a weakening or downfall.

la·bi·al (lā'bēəl), *adj.* pertaining to a lip or liplike part.

la·bi·a ma·jo·ra (lā'bēə məjôr'ə), *pl.*, *sing.* **la·bi·um ma·jus** (lā,bēəm mā'jəs). liplike outer folds of the female external genital organs.

la·bi·a mi·no·ra (lā'bēə minôr'ə), *pl.*, *sing.* **la·bi·um mi·nus** (lā'bēəm mī'nəs). liplike inner folds of the female external genital organs.

la·bile (lā'bil, lā'bīl), *adj.* unstable; liable to change, esp. chemical change.

la·bi·um (lā'bēəm), *n.*, *pl.* **la·bi·a** (lā'bēə). a lip or liplike part.

la·bret (lā'bret), *n.* an ornament inserted in a hole made through the lip.

la·brum (lā'brəm), *n.*, *pl.* **la·bra** (lā'brə). a lip or part resembling a lip.

lab·y·rin·thi·tis (lab,ərinthī'tis), *n.* inflammation of the inner ear. Also **otitis interna.**

lac·co·lith (lak'əlith), *n.* a domed mass of igneous rock formed by lava which, upon rising, forced up overlying strata without rupturing them. Also **lac·co·lite** (lak'əlīt).

lac·er·til·i·an (lasətil'ēən), *adj.* **1.** pertaining to the suborder comprising the lizards; lizard-like. —*n.* **2.** a lizard. Also **la·cer·tian** (ləsû'sнən).

lach·ry·mal (lak'riməl), *adj.* pertaining to tears. Also **lac'ri·mal.**

lach·ry·mose (lak'rimōs), *adj.* given to weeping; tearful.

la·cin·i·ate (ləsin'ēāt), *adj.* deeply lobed, with jagged edges; (of leaves) fringed.

la·con·ic (ləkon'ik), *adj.* brief or concise in speech. Also **la·con'i·cal.**

lac·o·nism (lak'əniz,əm), *n.* brevity of speech. Also **la·con·i·cism** (lakon'isiz,əm).

lac·tal·bu·min (lak,talbyŏŏ'min), *n.* the water-soluble protein contained in milk; in industry it is obtained by evaporating whey and is used in some prepared foods, in adhesives, and in varnishes.

lac·ta·ry (lak'tərē), *adj.* relating to or resembling milk.

lac·tate (lak'tāt), *v.* to produce or secrete milk naturally. —**lac·ta'tion,** *n.*

lac·tes·cent (laktes'ənt), *adj.* milky; secreting a milky juice.

lac·tif·er·ous (laktif'ərəs), *adj.* secreting or bearing milk or milky juice.

lac·to·scope (lak'təskōp,), *n.* an optical instrument for measuring the cream content of milk.

la·cu·na (lakyŏŏ'nə), *n.*, *pl.* **la·cu·nae** (ləkyŏŏ,-nē), **la·cu·nas.** a missing portion; gap; —**la·cu'-nal, la·cu'nar·y,** *adj.*

la·cus·trine (ləkus'trīn), *adj.* relating to a lake.

lae·vo·gy·rate (lēvōjī'rāt), *adj.* laevorotatory.

lae·vo·ro·ta·tion (lē,vōrōtā'sнən), *n.* a turning to the left of the plane of polarization of a ray of polarized light, caused by various chemical substances and solutions.

lae·vo·ro·ta·to·ry (lē,vōrō,tətərē), *adj.* having the property of laevorotation.

laev·u·lose (lev'yəlōs), *n.* a laevorotatory form of glucose; fructose; fruit sugar.

la·gen·i·form (ləjen'ifôm,), *adj.* flask-shaped.

la·gniappe (lanyap'), *n. U.S.* **1.** a tip, or gratuity, esp. something extra. **2.** a gift or extra measure given to a customer.

la·ic (lā'ik), *adj.* nonclerical; lay; secular. Also **la'i·cal.**

la·i·cism (lā'isiz,əm), *n.* secular control of a society; government by nonclerics.

la·i·cize (lā'isīz), *v.* to secularize; put under the control of nonclerics.

lais·sez faire (les,ā fer'ə), *French.* noninterference in the conduct of others.

la·i·ty (lā'itē), *n.* laymen; those not belonging to a particular profession and thus without first-hand knowledge of it.

lal·la·tion (lalā'sнən), *n.* substitution of the sound 'l' for 'r' or mispronunciation of the sound 'l'.

la·lop·a·thy (lalop'əthē), *n.* any speech defect.

lal·o·pho·bi·a (lal,əfō'bēə), *n.* morbid dread of speaking.

lal·o·ple·gi·a (lal,əplē'jēə), *n.* paralysis of the organs of speech except for the tongue.

La·marck·ism (lämä'kiz,əm), *n.* a theory of evolution proposing that changes acquired by an organism during its lifetime are inherited by its offspring. It lacks evidence and has been largely discounted in favour of Darwinism. [Named after J. B. de Monet Lamarck (1744–1829), French naturalist]

la·ma·ser·y (lä'məsərē), *n.*, *pl.* **la·ma·ser·ies.** a monastery of lamas.

La·maze technique (ləmäz'). See **psycho-prophylaxis**.

lamb·da·cism (lam'dəsiz,əm), *n.* (in phonetics) overuse of the sound 'l' or its substitution for the sound 'r'.

lam·bent (lam'bənt), *adj.* **1.** running lightly over or playing on a surface. **2.** softly radiant. **3.** dealing gently and brilliantly with a topic. —**lam'ben·cy,** *n.*

lam·bert (lam'bət), *n.* a unit used in measuring brightness, equal to the brightness of a perfectly diffusing surface radiating or reflecting one lumen per square centimetre.

lam·bre·quin (lam'brikin, lam'bəkin), *n.* **1.** a short curtain covering the top of a door or window or hung from a shelf. **2.** a protective covering of cloth for a helmet.

lame duck, a disabled or ineffective person or thing, esp. an elected official completing his last term of office.

la·mel·la (ləmel'ə), *n.*, *pl.* **la·mellae** (ləmel'ē). **la·mel·las.** a thin plate, scale, or membrane, esp. of bone or tissue. —**la·mel'lar, lam·el·late** (lam'-ilāt, lam'ilit, lamel'āt, lamel'it), *adj.*

la·mel·li·form (ləmel'ifôm,), *adj.* like a lamella in shape; scale-like.

la·mel·lose (ləmel'ōs, lam'ilōs), *adj.* having or composed of lamellae. —**lam·el·los'i·ty,** *n.*

lam·en·ta·ble (lam'əntəbəl), *adj.* regrettable; deplorable. —**lam'en·ta·bly,** *adv.*

lam·i·na (lam'inə), *n.*, *pl.* **lam·i·nae** (lam'inē), **lam·i·nas.** a thin layer or plate. —**lam'i·nar,** *adj.*

lam·i·nose (lam'inōs), *adj.* composed of laminae; laminar. Also **lam'i·nous.**

lam·poon (lampōōn'), *v.* **1.** to satirize or ridicule. *n.* **2.** a satire.

lam·proph·o·ny (lamprof'ənē), *n.* strength and clearness of voice. Also **lam,pro·pho'ni·a.**

la·nate (lä'nāt), *adj.* covered with wool or a woolly substance. Also **lanose.**

lan·ce·o·late (län'sēəlāt, län'sēəlit), *adj.* shaped like a spearhead; narrow and tapering to the apex.

lan·cet (län'sit), *n.* a small, sharply pointed, double-edged, surgical knife.

lan·ci·form (län'sifôm,), *adj.* lanceshaped.

lan·ci·nate (län'sināt,), *v.* to pierce; stab.

land·lop·er (land'lō,pə), *n.* a wanderer; adventurer. Also **land'loup,er.**

lang·lauf (läNG'louf,), *n.* a ski race over undulating open country. —**lang'lau,fer,** *n.*

lan·guet (laNG'gwet), *n.* a small tongue-shaped part.

lan·guid (laNG'gwid), *adj.* sluggish; lacking in energy or spirit.

lan·guish (laNG'gwish), *v.* **1.** to be or become languid. **2.** to suffer weakening conditions, as in prison or sickbed. **3.** to long for or pretend to long for.

lan·guor (laNG'gə), *n.* **1.** weakness; lack of energy or spirit. **2.** mood of tenderness. **3.** stillness. —**lan'guor·ous,** *adj.*

la·ni·ar·y (lan'ēərē), *adj.* (of teeth) shaped for tearing.

la·nif·er·ous (lənif'ərəs), *adj.* woolbearing. Also **la·nig·er·ous** (lənij'ərəs).

lan·o·lin (lan'əlin), *n.* fatty matter extracted from sheep's wool, used in ointments and toiletries. Also **lan'o·line.**

la·nose (lä'nōs, lä'nōz), *adj.* See **lanate.**

la·nu·gi·nose (lənyōō'jinōs), *adj.* covered with lanugo; downy. Also **la·nu'gi·nous.**

la·nu·go (lənyōō'gō), *n.* a covering of soft, downy hairs, esp. that of a newborn baby.

la·od·i·ce·an (lä,ōdisē'ən), *adj.* **1.** indifferent or lukewarm, esp. to religion or politics. —*n.* **2.** *sometimes cap.* one who is indifferent to religion or politics.

la·pac·tic (ləpak'tik), *adj.* aperient; effecting a purge.

lap·ar·o·scope (lap'ərəskōp,), *n.* an instrument consisting of a flexible tube and integral illumination mechanism that is inserted through the body wall to examine the abdominal organs. —**lap·ar·os·copy** (lap,əros'kəpē), *n.*

lap·a·rot·o·my (ləpərot'əmē), *n.* a surgical procedure of cutting the abdominal wall to gain access to the abdominal cavity.

lap·i·dar·y (lap'idərē), *n.* **1.** Also **lap'i·dist.** one who cuts, polishes, and engraves stones. **2.** the art of cutting, polishing, and engraving stones. —*adj.* **3.** relating to stones and their cutting, polishing, and engraving. **4.** distinguished by the sharpness and accuracy belonging to gem cutting.

lap·i·date (lap'idāt,), *v.* to stone to death.

la·pil·lus (ləpil'əs), *n.*, *pl.* **la·pil·li** (ləpil'ī). a small pebble thrown out by a volcano.

lap·pet (lap'it), *n.* **1.** a small flap or loosely hanging piece (of a garment). **2.** a lobe of flesh.

lap·sus lin·guae (lap'səs liNG'gwē), *Latin.* a slip of the tongue.

lap·sus me·mo·ri·ae (lap'səs memôr'iē), *Latin.* a lapse of memory.

lar·ce·ner (lä'sənə), *n.* one who has committed larceny. Also **lar'ce·nist.**

lar·da·ceous (lädä'sHəs), *adj.* lard-like.

large-scale (läj'skäl,), *adj.* large in relation to the original, as of a model, drawing, or other representation. See also **small-scale.**

lar·gess (läjes', läzHes'), *n.* **1.** the free and ample giving of money or gifts. **2.** the money or gifts thus given. Also **lar·gesse'.**

lar·ine (lar'īn, lar'in), *adj.* gull-like.

la·rith·mics (ləriTH'miks), *n.* the study of the relative numbers comprising different groups within a total population.

lar·va (lä'və), *n.*, *pl.* **lar·vae** (lä'vē). an insect between the time it leaves the egg and its metamorphosis into a pupa. —**lar'val,** *adj.*

lar·vi·cide (lä'visīd), *n.* a preparation for killing larvae.

lar·vip·a·rous (lävip'ərəs), *adj.* of or pertaining to a larva-producing creature, as some insects and molluscs.

lar·viv·o·rous (läviv'ərəs), *adj.* of or pertaining to a creature that eats larvae.

la·ryn·ge·al (lərin'jēəl, la,rinjē'əl), *adj.* **1.** relating to or in the larynx. **2.** of a sound formed in the larynx. —*n.* **3.** a sound formed in the larynx. Also **la·ryn·gal** (ləriNG'gəl).

lar·yn·gec·to·my (lar,injek'təmē), *n.* the surgical removal of all or part of the larynx.

lar·yn·gi·tis (lar,injī'tis), *n.* inflammation of the lining of the larynx.

lar·yn·gol·o·gy (lar,iNGgol'əjē), *n.* the field of medicine concerned with diseases of the throat.

la·ryn·go·pha·ryn·ge·al (ləriNG,gōfərin'jēəl), *adj.* relating to or employing the larynx and pharynx.

la·ryn·go·phar·ynx (ləriNG,gōfar'iNGks), *n.,* *pl.* **la·ryn·go·phar·ynges** (ləriNG,gōfərin'jēz), **la·ryn·go·phar·ynx·es.** the lower part of the pharynx, where it passes behind the larynx.

la·ryn·go·scope (ləriNG'gəskōp,), *n.* a medical instrument for inspecting the larynx by means of a mirror.

lar·yn·gos·co·py (lar,iNGgos'kəpē), *n.* medical examination with a laryngoscope.

la·ryn·go·tra·che·al (ləriNG,gōtrā'kēəl), *adj.* relating to the larynx and trachea.

lar·ynx (lar'iNGks), *n.,* *pl.* **la·ryn·ges** (lərin'jēz), **lar·ynx·es.** the cavity, at the top of the windpipe where it joins the pharynx, that contains the vocal cords.

la·sa·gna (ləzän'yə), *n.* a dish of broad strips of pasta cooked with meat and tomatoes and topped with cheese.

las·civ·i·ous (ləsiv'ēəs), *adj.* lustful; wanton.

la·ser (lā'zə), *n.* an optical maser; a maser that amplifies radiation within or near the range of visible light.

lash·ings (lasH'iNGz), *n. pl. Colloquial.* plenty; an abundance.

las·si·tude (las,ityōōd), *n.* weariness; languor; indolence.

last-in, first-out (lastin' fûstout'), a bookkeeping device of entering materials constituting manufacturing costs at their current market price. *Abbr.:* **LIFO.** See also **first-in, first-out.**

la·tah (lä'tə), *n.* a neurotic compulsion to imitate others in speech and action, occurring mainly among Malays. Also **la'ta.**

la·ten·cy (lā'tənsē), *n.* the condition of being latent.

la·tent (lā'tənt), *adj.* existing but not manifest; potential; hidden.

lat·er·al (lat'ərəl), *adj.* of, at, from, or towards a side or sides.

lat·er·al·i·ty (lat,əral'itē), *n.* the preference for using one hand rather than the other.

lat·er·i·tious (lat,ərisH,əs), *adj.* of a brick-red colour. Also **lat·er·i'ceous.**

la·tex (lā'teks), *n., pl.* **lat·i·ces** (lat'isēz), **la·tex·es.** a milky fluid contained by various plants and exuded when they are cut, esp. that of some plants used in industry to make rubber.

lath·y·rism (lath'əriz,əm), *n.* poisoning caused by eating seeds of the Indian pea or other vetch-like members of the genus *Lathyrus.* Symptoms include muscular weakness and paralysis.

lat·i·cif·er·ous (lat,isif'ərəs), *adj.* latex-bearing.

lat·i·tu·di·nar·i·an (lat,ityōō,diner'ēən), *adj.* tolerating widely differing opinions, esp. in matters of religion.

lat·i·tu·di·nous (lat,ityōō'dinəs), *adj.* having latitude; having a liberal breadth of mind.

la·tri·a (lətrī'ə), *n.* (in the Roman Catholic Church) supreme worship to be offered only to God. See also **dulia, hyperdulia.**

lat·ten (lat'ən), *n.* a brasslike alloy of copper, zinc, lead, and tin, formerly used for church utensils.

lat·ti·ci·nio (lat,iCHē'nyō), *n., pl.* **lat·ti·ci·ni** (lat,iCHē'nē). opaque white glass first made in Renaissance Venice, frequently used to decorate clear glass with thin white lines.

laud (lôd), *v.* to praise; express enthusiastic approval of (a person or action). —**laud'a·ble,** *adj.*

lau·re·ate (lôr'ēit), *adj.* **1.** wreathed with laurel as a token of honour. **2.** worthy of honour; distinguished, as *the laureate artist.*

lau·rence (lôr'əns), *n.* miragelike shimmering seen over a hot surface, caused by the refraction of light rays in the lower density of air at the hot surface.

lav·age (lav'ij, lavāzH'), *n.* a washing.

lav·a·liere (lav,əlē'ə), *n.* an ornament worn on a chain round the neck.

lave (lāv), *v.* (in poetic use) to wash; to bathe. —**la·va'tion,** *n.*

la·ver (lā'və), *n.* a basin or font.

lav·ish (lav'isH), *adj.* very generous or luxurious, often to the extreme of being extravagant and wasteful. —**lav'ish·ness,** *n.*

lawn (lôn), *n.* fine, plain-woven material usually of cotton, formerly of linen.

lax (laks), *adj.* not strict or severe, as a result of an easygoing nature, carelessness, or just not caring.

lax·a·tion (laksā'sHən), *n.* a relaxing or loosening.

lay analyst, a psychoanalyst without medical qualification.

laz·ar (laz'ə), *n.* a diseased person, esp. a leper.

laz·a·ret·to (laz,əret'ō), *n.* a hospital for indigent people suffering from contagious diseases, esp. from leprosy.

leach (lēcн), v. 1. to percolate a liquid through some material. 2. to be subjected to the action of percolating liquid, as soil.

Le·bens·raum (lā'bənzroum,), n. extra scope, either territorial or in the way of freedom, claimed by a person or a nation so as to be able to achieve full development.

lech·er (lecн'ə), n. a man who excessively indulges his sexual desires. —**lech'er·ous**, adj. —**lech'er·y**, n.

lec·i·thal (les'ithəl), adj. having a yolk. Also **lec'i·thic**.

lec·tion (lek'sнən), n. one of variant readings of the same passage in a copy or edition of a written work.

lec·tor (lek'tə), n. a lecturer in a university or college.

lee (lē), n. the sheltered side of something; side away from the wind.

lee·ward (lē'wəd, Naut. lōō'wəd) adj. relating to, on, or towards the side away from the wind.

leg·end·ist (lej'əndist), n. a writer or compiler of legends.

leg·end·ize (lej'əndīz), v. to make a legend of, as His admirers legendized his exploits.

leg·er·de·main (lej,ədəmān'), n. 1. dexterity in using the hands to perform conjuring tricks, juggling, and similar feats. 2. trickery; deception.

le·ger·i·ty (ləjer'itē), n. agility of mind or of limb.

leg·man (leg'man,), n. Chiefly U.S. one who does the work requiring travel outside the office, usually for another whose duties prevent his leaving the office.

leg-of-mutton sleeve. See gigot.

lei·o·my·o·ma (lī,ōmīō'mə), n., pl. **lei·o·my·o·mas, lei·o·my·o·ma·ta** (lī,ōmīō'mətə). an abnormal swelling composed of nonstriated muscle tissue.

leish·man·i·a·sis (lēsнmənī'əsis), n. infection by a certain flagellate protozoan.

leis·ter (lē'stə), n. a spear with three or more prongs, used to catch fish.

leit·mo·tif (līt'mōtēf), n. theme associated throughout a musical drama with a particular character, situation, or sentiment.

lem·ma (lem'ə), n., pl. **lem·mas, lem·ma·ta** (lem'ətə). an argument or subject in a literary composition.

len·i·ty (len'itē), n. gentleness; the quality of being soothing. —**len'i·tive**, adj.

len·tic (len'tik), adj. relating to or dwelling in still water. Also **le·nit'ic**.

len·ti·cle (len'tikəl), n. a window in a clock case allowing the movement of the pendulum weight to be seen.

len·tic·u·lar (lentik'yələ), adj. 1. relating to a

lens. 2. lens-shaped, either with two convex surfaces or with one plane and one convex surface.

len·ti·go (lentī'gō), n., pl. **len·tig·i·nes** (lentij'inēz). a freckle. —**len·tig'i·nous, len·tig'i·nose**, adj.

len·toid (len'toid), adj. lens-shaped.

le·o·nine (lē'ənīn), adj. of lions; lion-like.

lep·i·dop·ter·ol·o·gy (lep,idop,tərol'əjē), n. the study of butterflies and moths. Also **lep,i·dop'te·ry**. —**lep,i·dop,te·rol'o·gist, lep,i·dop'ter·ist**, n.

lep·i·dop·ter·ous (lep,idop'tərəs), adj. belonging to or relating to the order of insects comprising butterflies and moths.

lep·o·rid (lep'ərid), adj. of or relating to the family comprising rabbits and hares.

lep·o·rine (lep'ərīn), adj. relating to or resembling a rabbit or hare.

lep·rol·o·gy (leprol'əjē), n. the medical field of study dealing with leprosy and its treatment.

lep·ro·sar·i·um (lep,rəser'ēəm), n., pl. **lep·ro·sar·i·a** (lep,rəser'ēə). a hospital where lepers are treated.

lep·rose (lep'rōs), adj. leprous.

lep·ro·sy (lep'rəsē), n. a mildly infectious bacterial disease giving rise to thickening and ulceration of the skin, excessive or deficient pigmentation, loss of sensation in certain nerve regions, and, in severe cases, deformity and blindness.

lep·rot·ic (leprot'ik), adj. of leprosy; leprous.

lep·rous (lep'rəs), adj. having, of, or like leprosy.

lep·to·dac·ty·lous (lep,tōdak'tələs), adj. slender-toed; having slender toes.

lep·ton (lep'ton), n. 1. (in physics) a type of elementary particle that has no apparent internal structure and interacts by either the electromagnetic interaction or the weak interaction. Examples include electrons and neutrinos. —**lep·ton'ic**, adj. 2. pl. **lep·ta** (lep'tə). a Greek unit of currency worth one hundredth of a drachma.

lep·to·phyl·lous (lep,tōfil'əs), adj. slender-leaved.

lep·to·pro·so·pic (lep,tōprəsō'pik), adj. having a narrow face.

lep·tor·rhine (lep'tərin), adj. having a narrow, prominent nose.

lep·to·some (lep'təsōm), n. a person of long slender build. See also asthenic.

les·bi·an·ism (lez'bēəniz,əm), n. homosexuality in women. —**les'bi·an**, n., adj.

lese majesty (lēz), attack or outrage upon any institution or custom venerated or held in great affection by a large number of people.

le·sion (lē'zнən), n. wound; injury; damage.

lesser omentum, an omentum joined to the

stomach, and supporting the vessels of the liver. See also **omentum, greater omentum.**

les·to·bi·o·sis (les,tōbīō'sis), *n.*, *pl.* **les·to·bi·o·ses** (les,tōbīō'sēz). a form of living distinguished by furtive stealing; as one of the ways that ants order their society, in which two species live side by side and one lives by furtively stealing the food collected by the other. —**les·to·biot·ic** (les,tōbīot'ik), *adj.*

le·thal (lē'thəl), *adj.* deadly, as a lethal blow or lethal gas.

le·thar·gic (lithä'jik), *adj.* relating to or suffering from lethargy.

leth·ar·gy (leth'əjē), *n.* drowsiness; apathy; torpor.

leu·kae·mi·a (lookē'mēə), *n.* an incurable blood disease characterized by excessive production of white cells; cancer of the blood. Also **leu·cae·mi·a** (lōōsē'mēə).

leu·co·cyte (lōō'kəsīt), *n.* a white blood cell. —**leu,ko·cyt'ic,** *adj.*

leu·co·ma (lookō'mə), *n.* a disorder in which the cornea is white and opaque.

leu·co·pe·ni·a (lookōpē'nēə), *n.* a decrease in the number of white cells in the blood.

leu·co·poi·e·sis (lōō,kōpoiē'sis), *n.* the development of white blood cells.

le·va·tor (livā'tə, livā'tōə), *n.*, *pl.* **lev·a·tores** (levətôr'ēz). any muscle used to raise a part of the body.

lev·ee 1. (lev'ē), *n.* an artificial embankment built to prevent flooding. **2.** (lev'ē, levē', lev'ā), *n.* a reception; assembly of visitors.

le·ver·aged buy·out (lē'vərijd), a financial manoeuvre whereby a company raises loans against its own assets and those of its takeover target to finance the takeover of another company. See **junk bond.**

lev·er·et (lev'ərit), *n.* a young hare.

lev·i·gate (lev'igāt), *v.* to reduce to a fine powder or smooth paste. —**lev,i·ga'tion,** *n.*

lev·i·rate (lev'irit), *n.* the custom by which a dead man's brother or next of kin had to marry his widow, practised formerly in parts of America and Asia, and in Biblical Jewry under certain conditions.

lev·i·ty (lev'itē), *n.* frivolity; lack of serious thought; making light of a serious matter.

lex·i·cal (lek'sikəl), *adj.* pertaining to the vocabulary of a language.

lex·i·cog·ra·pher (lek,sikog'rəfə), *n.* a maker or compiler of a dictionary.

lex·i·cog·ra·phy (lek,sikog'rəfē), *n.* the making or compiling of dictionaries.

lex·i·col·o·gy (lek,sikol'əjē), *n.* **1.** the study of words and their meanings and idiomatic usage. **2.** the study of the theory of lexicography and of lexicon. —**lex,i·col'o·gist,** *n.*

lex·i·con (lek'sikən), *n.*, *pl.* **lex·i·ca** (lek'sikə),

lex·i·cons. the vocabulary of a language, individual, or particular group of people.

lex·i·phan·ic (lek,sifan'ik), *adj.* bombastic or pretentious.

lex ta·li·o·nis (leks tal,ēō'nis), *Latin.* the law of retaliation, as an eye for an eye, a tooth for a tooth. Also **talion.**

li·ba·tion (lībā'sHən), *n.* the pouring of a drink, esp. of wine, as an offering to a god.

lib·er·tar·i·an (libəter'ēən), *n.* an advocate of liberty of thought and action.

lib·er·tine (lib'ətēn), *n.* a dissolute, licentious man; one who gives free rein to his sexual or immoral wishes. —**lib'er·tin,age, lib'er·tin·ism,,** *n.*

li·bid·i·nous (libid'inəs), *adj.* lustful; relating to the libido.

li·bi·do (libē'dō), *n.* the sexual drive; the instinctive desire that prompts all human activities.

li·brate (lī'brāt), *v.* to oscillate; swing from side to side. —**li·bra'tion,** *n.*

li·cen·ti·ate (līsen'sHēit), *n.* holder of a certificate of competence awarded by some academic or professional examination board.

li·cen·tious (līsen'sHəs), *adj.* lustful; uncontrolled in sexual indulgence.

li·chen (lī'kən), *n.* a dual plant organism of fungus and alga in symbiosis, forming a grey, yellow, green, or brown crustlike covering where it grows on trees, stones, etc. —**li'chen·oid, li'chen·ous,** *adj.*

lic·it (lis'it), *adj.* lawful; permitted.

lick·er·ish (lik'ərisH), *adj.* lustful; lecherous. Also **liqu'or·ish.**

lick·spit·tle (lik'spitəl), *n.* toady; sycophant. Also **lick'spit,.**

lieb·frau·milch (lēb'froumilk,), *n.* a white wine from West Germany, produced mainly in the province of Hesse.

lied (lēd), *n.*, *pl.* **lied·er** (lēd'ə). a musical form consisting of lyric poems adapted and scored for solo voice and piano accompaniment.

Lie·der·kranz (lē'dəkränts), *n.* tradename of a strong-flavoured, soft-ripening cheese made up in small blocks.

lief (lēf), *adv.* willingly; gladly.

lien, *n.* **1.** (lēn), the legal right to keep possession of another's property until a debt due on it is paid. **2.** (lī'ən) the spleen.

li·en·ec·to·my (lī,ənek'təmē), *n.* the surgical removal of the spleen; splenectomy.

li·en·i·tis (lī,ənī'tis), *n.* inflammation of the spleen.

life style, the integrated way a person's individual taste and style is expressed through the clothes he wears, the furniture and decor of his home, and the social life he leads. Also **lifestyle.**

LIFO (lī'fō). See **last-in, first-out.**

lig·a·ment (lig'əmənt), *n.* a short band of

strong, flexible fibrous tissue holding two bones together at a joint and preventing dislocation. —lig,amen'tous, *adj.*

li·gate (lī'gāt), *v.* to bind with a ligature.

lig·a·ture (lig'əCHə), *n.* 1. a binding up. 2. something used for binding up, esp. a cord or bandage. 3. a character or type combining two or more letters, as 'fi'.

light·er (lī'tə), *n.* a boat, often flat-bottomed, used for loading and unloading ships standing off a wharf and for carrying goods into the harbour or for other short distances.

light·er·age (lī'tərij), *n.* the use of lighters to load and unload ships.

light heavyweight, a boxer of the class intermediate between middleweight and heavyweight, weighing 178 lbs. or less if an amateur, 175 lbs. or less if a professional. Also cruiserweight.

light middleweight, an amateur boxer of the class intermediate between welterweight and middleweight and weighing 156 lbs. or less.

light·some (līt'səm), *adj.* 1. light in movement or spirit. 2. giving out light; brightly illuminated.

light·weight (līt'wāt,), *n.* a boxer of the class intermediate between featherweight and welterweight and weighing 133 lbs. or less if an amateur, 135 lbs. or less if a professional.

light welterweight, an amateur boxer of the class between lightweight and welterweight, weighing 140 lbs. or less.

light-year (līt'yē,ə), *n.* the distance travelled by light in one solar year; used as a unit in measuring stellar distances. See also **parsec.**

lig·ne·ous (lig'nēəs), *adj.* woody.

lig·nic·o·lous (lignik'ələs), *adj.* growing on or in wood.

lig·ni·form (lig'nifôm,), *adj.* woodlike in form.

lig·ni·fy (lig'nifī), *v.* to become or cause to become wood or woody.

lig·nin (lig'nin), *n.* a compound chemical substance formed in the walls of certain plant cells and giving them strength and rigidity; it forms up to 50 percent of the wood in trees.

lig·nite (lig'nīt), *n.* a brown woody coal.

lig·niv·or·ous (ligniv'ərəs), *adj.* wood-eating; feeding on or boring into wood.

lig·u·la (lig'yələ), *n.,* *pl.* **lig·u·lae** (lig'yəlē), **lig·u·las,** a strap-shaped part, esp. a thin membrane at the base of a leaf-blade in grasses. —**lig'u·late,** *adj.*

li·la·ceous (līlā'SHəs), *adj.* of lilac colour.

lil·i·a·ceous (lil,ēā'SHəs), *adj.* 1. relating to the lily; lily-like. 2. belonging to the family of lilies.

lim·a·cine (lim'əsīn, lim'əsin, lī'məsīn, lī'məsin), *adj.* relating to or resembling a slug.

lim·bate (lim'bāt), *adj.* having a different-coloured border, esp. of flowers.

lim·bo (lim'bō), *n.* a supposed place in which forgotten and unwanted things are regarded as being.

li·men (lī'mən), *n.,* *pl.* **li·mens, lim·in·a** (lim'-inə). threshold; limit below which a given stimulus ceases to be perceptible.

li·mes (lī'mēs), *n.,* *pl.* **lim·i·tes** (lim'itēz). a boundary, esp. a fortified boundary of a country.

li·mic·o·line (līmik'əlīn), *adj.* dwelling on the shore.

li·mic·o·lous (līmik'ələs), *adj.* living in mud or in a muddy place.

lim·i·nal (lim'inəl), *adj.* at or relating to the limen.

limn (lim), *v.* to picture in a drawing or in words.

lim·ner (lim'nə), *n.* a painter, esp. of portraits.

lim·net·ic (limnet'ik), *adj.* of or relating to creatures and plants that live in fresh waters.

lim·nol·o·gy (limnol'əjē), *n.* the study of fresh waters and the plants and creatures that live in them. —**lim,no·log'i·cal,** *adj.*

lim·pid (lim'pid), *adj.* clear and transparent, as water, air, eyes, etc.

lim·u·lus (lim'yələs), *n.,* *pl.* **lim·u·li** (lim'yəlī). a horseshoe crab. —**lim'u·loid,** *adj.*

lin·e·a·ments (lin'ēəmənts), *n.* (*sometimes used in singular*) distinctive features or characteristics, esp. of the face.

lin·e·ar accelerator (lin'ēə), a device to propel charged particles in straight lines by alternating electric voltages arranged to give increasing gains of energy to the particles.

lin·e·ate (lin'ēit, lin'ēāt), *adj.* lined; striped.

lin·e·a·tion (lin,ēā'SHən), *n.* the drawing, tracing, or arrangement of lines.

lin·e·o·late (lin'ēəlāt), *adj.* marked with fine lines.

lin·gua (liNG'gwə), *n.,* *pl.* **lin·guae** (liNG'gwē). the tongue. —**lin'gual,** *adj.*

lin·gua fran·ca (liNG'gwə fraNG'kə), *n.,* *pl.* **lin·gua fran·cas, lin·guae fran·cae** (liNG'gwē fran'sē). any language used by various different peoples who have different native languages.

lin·gui·form (liNG'gwifôm,), *adj.* tongue-shaped.

lin·gui·ni (liNGgwē'nē), *n.* long, flat strips of pasta, narrower than fettucine.

lin·guis·tics (liNGgwis'tiks), *n.* the scientific study of language, including its sounds, word forms, grammar, orthography, and historical development.

lin·gu·late (liNG'gyələt), *adj.* tongue-shaped.

lin·sey·wool·sey (lin'zē·wŏŏl'zē), *n.* a fabric with coarse woollen weft and linen or cotton warp. Also **lin'sey.**

lin·tel (lin'təl), *n.* a horizontal support of timber, stone, or concrete across the top of a window- or door-opening.

li·on·ize (lī'ənīz), *v.* to treat a person as a celebrity.

li·pae·mi·a (lipē'mēə), *n.* the presence of excessive fat or fatty substance in the blood. —li·pae' mic, *adj.*

li·pase (lī'pās), *n.* one of a class of enzymes that break down the fat produced by the liver or pancreas.

li·pec·to·my (lipek'təmē), *n.* the surgical removal of a superficial layer of fat.

lip·o·gram (lip'ōgram,), *n.* a written work using only words that do not contain a certain letter or letters of the alphabet. —lip,o·gram·mat'ic, *adj.*

li·pog·ra·phy (lipog'rəfē), *n.* the accidental elimination of some letter, syllable, etc., in writing.

lip·oid (lip'oid), *adj.* fatlike. Also **lip·oid'al.**

li·po·ma (lipō'mə), *n., pl.* **li·po·mas, li·po·ma·ta** (lipō'mətə). a benign tumour composed of fatty tissue.

lip·o·pex·i·a (lip,ōpek'sēə), *n.* the storage of fat in the body. Also **adipopexia, adipopexis.**

li·quate (lī'kwāt), *v.* to separate or purify metals by heating sufficiently to melt out the various constituents.

liq·ue·fa·cient (lik,wifā'sHənt), *n.* that which causes liquefaction.

liq·ue·fac·tion (lik,wifak'sHən), *n.* the act of becoming or making liquid.

li·ques·cent (likwes'ənt), *adj.* becoming liquid. —li·ques'cence, *n.*

liqu·or·ish (lik'ərisH), *adj.* See **lickerish.**

lis·some, lis·som (lis'əm), *adj.* lithe; supple; agile; active.

lis·sot·ri·chous (liso'trikəs), *adj.* straighthaired.

lis·ter·i·o·sis (listēr,iō'sis), *n.* a type of food poisoning caused by the bacterium *Listeria monocytogenes.* It can result in meningitis and, in pregnant women, fetal abnormalities or abortion.

lit·a·ny (lit'ənē), *n.* a lengthy, monotonous narration, as *a litany of complaints.*

li·tchi, li·chee, li·chi, ly·chee (līcHē), *n.* 1. a small fruit with edible pulp that is usually eaten preserved or dried. 2. a Chinese tree, *Litchi chinensis*, grown for these fruits.

lit·er·al·ly (lit'ərəlē), *adv.* exactly as presented; in a word-for-word manner. —**lit'er·al,** *adj.*

lit·er·ate (lit'ərit), *adj.* able to read and write.

lit·e·ra·ti (lit,ərä'tē), *n. pl.* men of letters; intellectuals.

lit·e·ra·tion (lit,ərā'sHən), *adv.* letter for letter; with exact correspondence to an original text.

li·thae·mi·a (lithē'mēə), *n.* an excess of uric acid in the blood. Also **uricacidemia.**

lithe (līTH), *adj.* flexible; supple. Also **lithe'·some.**

li·thi·a·sis (lithī'əsis), *n.* the presence or development in the body of stony solids usually consisting of layers of mineral salts.

lith·ic (lith'ik), *adj.* composed of or relating to stone, esp. the stony solids formed in the body.

li·thog·ra·phy (lithog'rəfē), *n.* a method of printing using a flat plate of metal, formerly stone, on which specially greased or treated portions take up ink and transfer it to paper while the other parts make no impression. —lith'o·graph, *n.* —li·thog'ra·pher, *n.*

lith·oid (lith'oid), *adj.* stonelike.

li·thol·a·pax·y (lithol'əpak,sē), *n.* a surgical operation in which stones are crushed within the organ where they formed and are washed out.

li·thol·o·gy (lithol'əjē), *n.* 1. the study of the nature and composition of stones and rocks. 2. the field of medicine that deals with the stony substance known as calculus which forms in the human body.

lith·o·me·te·or (lithəmē'tēə), *n.* a mass of solid particles suspended in the air, as dust.

lith·o·phile (lith'əfīl,), *adj.* having a tendency to react to rocks in the earth's crust, as a chemical element.

lith·o·sphere (lith'əsfē,ə), *n.* the earth's outer crust.

lith·o·trip·sy (lith'ətrip,sē), *n.* the use of an ultrasonic device to shatter gallstones and kidney stones, allowing them to be excreted naturally.

li·thot·ri·ty (litho'tritē), *n.* a surgical procedure in which a stone that has formed in the bladder is crushed into particles small enough to pass out when the bladder is emptied.

li·thu·ri·a (lithyōōr'ēə), *n.* a condition in which the urine contains an excess of uric acid.

li·ti·gious (litij'əs), *adj.* disposed to argue; given to frequent legal action against others.

li·tre (lē'tə), *n.* a metric unit of measurement equal to 1.7606 imperial pints.

lit·té·ra·teur (lit,ərətû'), *n.* a person of letters; a professional author.

lit·to·ral (lit'ərəl), *adj.* 1. of, on, or near the shore. —*n.* 2. an area lying along the shore.

lit·ur·gy (lit'əjē), *n.* 1. a set form or ritual for public worship. 2. a collection or arrangement of services for public worship. —**li·tur·gi·cal** (litū'jikəl), *adj.*

liv·er·ish (liv'ərisH), *adj.* having a personality that is bilious; unpleasant and disagreeable.

liv·id (liv'id), *adj.* having a leaden, blue-grey discoloration of the flesh, as from bruising or strangulation.

living fossil, an organism, such as the coelacanth, whose features are little changed from an earlier time and which has few or no living close relatives.

load·stone (lōd'stōn,), *n.* See **lodestone.**

loath, loth (lōth, lōTH), *adj.* disinclined; reluctant; unwilling.

loathe (lōTH), v. to regard with disgust; to detest. —**loath·some** (lōTH'səm), adj.

lo·bar (lō'bə), adj. relating to a lobe.

lo·bate (lō'bāt), adj. having or being a lobe.

lo·be·line (lō'bəlēn), n. a chemical substance extracted from lobelia, used as a nicotine substitute in discouraging tobacco smoking because it produces similar physiological reactions.

lo·bot·o·my (lōbot'əmē), n. a surgical incision made in a lobe of the brain to change the behaviour of a person, usually one suffering severe mental illness.

lobster thermidor, cooked lobster flesh in a cream sauce sprinkled with grated cheese and browned on top.

lob·u·late (lob'yəlit), adj. composed of or having small lobes.

lob·ule (lob'yōōl), n. a small lobe.

lob·u·lus (lob'yələs), n., pl. **lob·u·li** (lob'yəlī). (in anatomy) a lobule.

lo·bus (lō'bəs), n., pl. **lo·bi** (lō'bī). (in anatomy) a lobe.

lock·jaw (lok'jô), n. a form of blood poisoning in which the victim is unable to open his jaws. See also **tetanus.**

loc·u·lar (lok'yələ), adj. relating to or having one or more small cavities or compartments.

loc·u·late (lok'yəlāt), adj. having one or more small cavities or compartments.

loc·u·lus (lok'yələs), n., pl. **loc·u·li** (lok'yəlī). a small cavity or compartment.

lo·cus (lō'kəs), n., pl. **lo·ci** (lō'sī). the exact place; locality.

locus clas·si·cus (klas'ikəs), n., pl. **loci clas·si·ci** (klas'isī,, klas'ikī,). 1. the most familiar or authoritative passage on a given topic. 2. the best example; paradigm.

lo·cu·tion (lōkyōō'sHən), n. a particular idiom or turn of phrase.

lode·stone, load·stone (lōd'stōn,), n. a magnetic oxide of iron (magnetite) that acts as a natural magnet in attracting iron.

log·a·graph·i·a (log,əgraf'ēə), n. the inability to express one's ideas in writing.

log·gia (loj'ə, loj'ēə), n. Italian. an arcade or gallery open on one or both sides.

logical positivism, a contemporary philosophical doctrine based on empiricist traditions, characterized by its attempt to show all philosophical problems to be linguistic in nature and to avoid all metaphysical statements, and aiming to provide a comprehensive philosophy of science founded on linguistic analysis.

logic bomb, (in computing) a computer program designed to sabotage the system when activated.

lo·gi·on (log'ēon), n., pl. **lo·gi·a** (log'ēə), **lo·gi·ons.** a traditional saying; adage; proverb.

lo·gis·tics (lojis'tiks), n. (used as sing. or pl.) the military science and practice of moving, accommodating, and providing supplies for troops. —**lo·gis'tic, lo·gis'tic·al,** adj.

lo·go (lō'gō), n., pl. **lo·gos.** a trademark or symbol used as an identifying emblem by a company for itself or a product. Also **lo·go·type** (log'ōtīp,). See also **colophon.**

log·o·gram (log'əgram,), n. a shorthand sign for a word or phrase. Also **log'o·graph,.** —**log,o·graph'ic,** adj.

lo·gog·ra·phy (logog'rəfē), n. a method of recording in longhand in which several people in turn write down a few words.

log·o·griph (log'ōgrif), n. an anagram or anagrammatic word-puzzle, sometimes involving clues in verse.

lo·gom·a·chy (logom'əkē), n. 1. a dispute about words; a controversy turning on a verbal point. 2. a card game in which words are formed with letters shown singly on cards.

log·o·pae·dics (logəpē'diks), n. the study and treatment of speech defects. Also **log,o·pae'di·a.**

log·or·rhoe·a (log,ərē'ə), n. 1. a medical condition in which speech is incoherent. 2. informal. excessive talking; prattle.

lo·gos (lō'gos), n. 1. the word of God incarnate; Christ. 2. (in philosophy) the principles that govern the universe.

log·o·type (log'ōtīp), n. the trademark or emblem of a company. See also **ideograph.**

log·roll (log'rōl), v. U.S. to bring about the passing of legislation by logrolling.

log·roll·ing (log'rōliNG), n. (in U.S. politics) the mutual patronage or support among politicians to achieve their (sometimes unprincipled) purposes.

lon·ga·nim·i·ty (loNG,gənim'itē), n. long-suffering; endurance of hardship.

lon·ge·vous (lonjē'vəs), adj. long-lived.

long·hair (loNG'he,ə), n. an intellectual or person involved with the arts. —**long'haired,,** adj.

lon·gi·corn (lon'jikôn), adj. with long antennae.

long pig, pidgin for human flesh as a food for cannibals.

long·some (loNG'səm), adj. tedious; so long as to cause boredom.

lon·gueur (loNGgû'), n. a tedious stretch, as of time or of a passage in a musical or literary work.

long wave, a radio wave more than 60 metres long. See also **short wave.** See **L wave.**

loo·by (lōō'bē), n. a silly, stupid fellow.

loo·fah, loo·fa (lōō'fə), n. the fibrous contents of the dried pod of a gourdlike plant, used as a hard sponge. Also **luffa, vegetable sponge.**

loo·kum (lōō'kəm), n. a shelter or roof for some equipment.

lop·er (lō'pə), n. one of two supports which comes forward to support a hinged leaf of a desk or table in horizontal position. Also called **draw runner, draw slip.**

loph·o·dont (lŏf'ədont,), *adj.* having transverse ridges on the crowns of the molar teeth.

lo·qua·cious (lōkwā'SHəs), *adj.* talkative; characterized by wordiness.

lo·quac·i·ty (lōkwas'itē), *n.* talkativeness.

lord·ling (lôrd'lING), *n.* a young or unimportant lord; insignificant person behaving in a lordly manner.

lor·gnette (lônyet'), *n.* a pair of spectacles or opera glasses in a rigid frame with a handle.

lor·gnon (lônyôn'), *n.* a pair of glasses or spectacles, esp. in the form of a pince-nez.

lo·ri·ca (lorī'kə), *n.*, *pl.* **lo·ri·cae** (lorī'sē, lorī'kē). **1.** the defensive covering of hard scales, plates, bone, etc., found on some species of animals. **2.** body armour consisting of a breastplate and backplate made of leather or metal; cuirass. —**lor'i·cate**, *adj.*

lor·i·mer (lor'imə), *n.* a maker of metal parts for harnesses and riding equipment.

loss leader, an item sold in a shop at a loss to attract custom.

lost-wax process, a technique for metal casting of sculpture in which a core of clay is covered with wax which in turn is enclosed by the mould made from the artist's work; molten metal is then poured into a hole at the top and replaces the wax, which melts and runs out at the bottom. Also **cire perdue.**

Lo·thar·i·o (lōthä'rēō) a man who charms and deceives women; rake.

lo·toph·a·gi (lətof'əjī), *n. pl.* lotus-eaters.

lo·tus-eat·er (lō'təsē,tə), *n.* **1.** one of the Lotophagi, in ancient Greek legend a people found by Odysseus living in luxurious indolence and dreaminess because of eating the fruit of the lotus plant. **2.** one who leads a life of dreamy indolence.

louche (lōōSH), *adj.* evasive; of disreputable character.

Louis XIII, designating a style in furniture and architecture prevalent in early 17th-century France, characterized by the beginning of a return to classicism from Renaissance freedom and inventiveness. Also **Louis Treize** (trez).

Louis XIV, designating a style in furniture and architecture prevalent in late 17th-century France, characterized by its classical features. Also **Louis Qua·torze** (kətôz').

Louis XV, designating a style in furniture and architecture prevalent in early- and mid-18th century France, characterized by Rococo features. Also **Louis Quinze** (kanz).

Louis XVI, designating a style in furniture and architecture prevalent in late 18th-century France, characterized by classical models with Rococo embellishment. Also **Louis Seize** (sez).

loupe (lōōp), *n.* a magnifying instrument made to fit in the eye socket, used by jewellers and watchmakers.

loup-ga·rou (lōōgarōō'), *n.*, *pl.* **loups-ga·rous** (lōōgarōō'). *French.* a werewolf; lycanthrope.

low·er (lou'ə), *v.* to frown; to look sullen; (of the sky, etc.) be dark and threatening. Also **lour.** —**low'er·y**, *adj.*

lox (loks), *n.* **1.** smoked salmon. **2.** liquid oxygen.

lox·o·dont (lok'sədont,), *adj.* with only shallow depressions between the ridges of the molar teeth.

lox·o·drome (lok'sədrōm,), *n.* (in map projection) a line that cuts all the meridians at a constant angle. Also called **rhumb line.** —**lox,o·drom'ic,** *adj.*

lox·o·drom·ics (lok,sədrom'iks), *n.* navigational technique of following or being guided by loxodromes.

LSD, lysergic acid diethylamide, a drug that produces temporary hallucinations. Also **LSD-25.**

lu·au (lōō'ou), *n.* a Hawaiian feast, usually with Hawaiian entertainment.

lu·bric·i·ty (lōōbris'itē), *n.* **1.** slipperiness; smoothness, as of a surface. **2.** lecherousness; salaciousness.

lu·bri·cous (lōō'brikəs), *adj.* **1.** (of a surface) slippery; smooth; oily. **2.** lecherous; wanton. Also **lu·bri·cious** (lōōbrisH'əs).

lu·cent (lōō'sənt), *adj.* luminous; translucent.

lu·cid (lōō'sid), *adj.* **1.** clear; shining. **2.** clearly expressed and therefore easily understood. —**lu·cid'i·ty,** *n.*

lu·cif·er·ase (lōōsif'ərās), *n.* an enzyme in the luminous organs of fireflies that causes the pigment in them to give off light.

lu·cif·er·in (lōōsif'ərin), *n.* a pigment in the luminous organs of fireflies that gives off light when acted upon by luciferase.

lu·cra·tive (lōō'krətiv), *adj.* yielding profit; money-making.

lucre (lōō'kə), *n.* gain; money.

lu·cu·brate (lōō'kyoobrāt), *v.* to work or study at night.

lu·cu·bra·tion (lōō,kyoobrā'SHən), *n.* **1.** nocturnal study. **2.** (usually *pl.*) literary work of a pedantic character.

lu·cu·lent (lōō'kyoolənt), *adj.* clear; lucid; convincing.

Lu·cul·lan (lōōkul'ən), *adj.* (of a feast or banquet) characterized by lavishness and luxury.

lu·di·crous (lōō'dikrəs), *adj.* laughable, esp. because something is silly or nonsensical, as *a ludicrous hat.*

lu·es (lōō'ēz), *n.* syphilis. —**lu·et·ic** (lōōet'ik), *adj.*

luf·fa (luf'ə), *n.* See **loofah.**

luge (lōōzH, lōōdzH), *n.* a small toboggan ridden by one person lying supine.

lu·gu·bri·ous (lōōgōō'brēəs), *adj.* doleful;

gloomy in manner, tone, etc., esp. in an exaggerated way.

lum·ba·go (lumbā'gō), *n.* pain in the small of the back, often chronic, caused by muscle inflammation.

lum·bar (lum'bə), *adj.* in or having to do with the loins, the area round the lumbar joints of the lower spine.

lum·bo·sa·cral (lum,bōsā'krəl), *adj.* of or relating to the lower joints of the spine; of the lumbar and sacral area.

lum·bri·cal (lum'brikəl), *n.* any of the muscles of the hand and foot that flex the fingers and toes. Also **lum·bri·ca·lis** (lumbrikā'lis).

lum·bri·coid (lum'brikoid), *adj.* of or like an earthworm.

lu·men (lōō'mən), *n.* the measurement of the rate of transmission of light energy, equivalent to the light energy radiated per second per unit solid angle by a point source of one-candle intensity. Abbr.: **lm**.

lu·men·hour (lōō'mənou,ə), *n.* a measurement of light energy equal to that radiated in one hour by a source of one lumen power.

lu·mi·nar·y (lōō'minərē), *n., pl.* **lu·mi·nar·ies**. one whose behaviour and intelligence inspires others; a person famous for his accomplishments.

lu·mi·nes·cence (lōō,mines'əns), *n.* **1.** cold emission of light; light stimulated by any means other than heating to incandescence. **2.** light so emitted. —**lu,mi·nes'cent,** *adj.*

lu·mi·nif·er·ous (lōōminif'ərəs), *adj.* producing or transmitting light.

lu·mi·no·phore, lu·mi·no·phor (lōō'minəfô,), *n.* a molecule or molecular group that radiates light when illuminated.

lum·pec·to·my (lumpek'təmē), *n., pl.* **lum·pec·to·mies**. the surgical removal of a breast tumour and surrounding tissue. Compare **mastectomy**.

lum·pen (lum'pən), *adj.* relating to people deprived of their rights and homes or degraded in status.

lu·nate (lōō'nāt), *adj.* crescent-shaped. Also **lu'nat·ed**.

lu·na·tion (lōōnā'shən), *n.* the time between one new moon and the next.

lune (lōōn), *n.* anything crescent-shaped or half-moon-shaped.

lunes (lōōnz), *n. pl.* attacks of lunacy.

lu·nette (lōōnet'), *n.* a crescent-shaped or semicircular object.

lunge (lunj), *n.* **1.** a long rope for leading and directing a horse during training or exercise. —*v.* **2.** to exercise or train a horse with a lunge. Also **longe**.

lun·gi, lun·gee, lun·gyi (lōōNG'gē), *n.* (in India) a length of cloth used as a loincloth, turban, or scarf.

lu·ni·so·lar (lōō,nisō'lə), *adj.* concerning the mutual relations or joint action of the moon and sun.

lu·ni·tid·al (lōō,nitī'dəl), *adj.* relating to tidal movement governed by the moon.

lu·nu·la (lōō'nyələ), *n., pl.* **lu·nu·lae** (lōō'nyə-lē). a narrow crescent-shaped area, object, etc., as the white area at the bottom of a fingernail. Also **lu'nule**. —**lu'nu·lar,** *adj.*

lu·pine (lōō'pīn), *adj.* relating to or resembling a wolf; savage; predatory.

lu·rid (lōōr'id), *adj.* appealing to baser tastes; designed to thrill; sensationalistic.

lus·trate (lus'trāt), *v.* to purify by performing some ritual to make amends for a wrong, as a sacrifice or ceremonial washing. —**lus·tra'tion,** *n.*

lus·trum (lus'trəm), *n.* **1.** a period of five years. **2.** (in ancient Rome) a purification ceremony, held every five years. —**lus'tral,** *adj.*

lust·y (lus'tē), *adj.* **lust·i·er, lust·i·est**. full of vigour and energetic good health.

lu·sus na·tu·rae (lōō'səs nətōōr'ē), a freak of nature, as a deformed creature or object.

lu·tan·ist (lōō'tənist), *n.* one who plays the lute.

lu·te·ous (lōō'tēəs), *adj.* of a greenish yellow colour.

Lu·tine bell (lōō'tēn), the bell salvaged from H.M.S. Lutine, a wrecked British warship, now hanging in Lloyd's insurance building in London, and rung at announcements concerning ships missing or sunk.

lu·ting (lōō'tiNG), *n.* a general term for several malleable substances used for joining, sealing, or waterproofing objects.

lux (luks), *n., pl.* **lu·ces** (lōō'sēz). a unit for measuring the degree of illumination, equal to the illumination produced on one square metre by one lumen at a perpendicular distance of one metre.

lux·ate (luk'sāt), *v.* (of a joint) to dislocate.

lux·u·ri·ant (lugzHOOr'ēənt), *adj.* profuse; abundant; as of plant growth. —**lux·u'ri·ance,** *n.*

lux·u·ri·ate (lugzHOOr'ēāt,), *v.* to take one's ease in luxury; to abandon oneself to enjoyment.

lux·u·ri·ous (lugzHOOr'ēəs), *adj.* contributing to or full of luxury.

L wave, a shock wave radiating from an earthquake, usually the third major wave. Also **long wave**. See also **P wave, S wave**.

ly·can·thrope (lī'kənthrōp,, līkan'thrōp), *n.* **1.** a person suffering from the form of insanity known as lycanthropy. **2.** a werewolf; a person in folklore who changes into a wolf.

ly·can·thro·py (līkan'thrəpē), *n.* **1.** a form of insanity in which a person imagines himself to be and behaves like a wolf or some other wild beast. **2.** (in folklore) the taking on by a man of the form and nature of a wolf.

ly·cée (lēsā'), *n.* a state secondary school in France.

Lyd·i·an (lid'ēən), *adj.* (of music) softly and voluptuously sweet.

lymph (limf), *n.* a colourless fluid drained from the intercellular spaces in body tissue by lymphatic vessels that return it to the blood.

lym·phad·e·ni·tis (limfad,ənī'tis), *n.* inflammation of lymph glands, owing to an infection spreading along the lymphatics from the body tissue. —**lym·phad,e·nit'ic,** *adj.*

lym·phad·e·no·ma (limfad,ənō'mə), *n., pl.* **lym·phad·e·no·mas, lym·phad·e·no·ma·ta** (limfad,ənō'mətə). a swollen lymph gland.

lym·phan·gi·o·ma (limfan,jēō'mə), *n., pl.* **lym·phan·gi·o·mas, lym·phan·gi·o·ma·ta** (limfan,jēō'mətə). benign growth of new and enlarged lymphatic vessels.

lym·phan·gi·tis (lim,fanjī'tis), *n., pl.* **lym·phan·git·i·des** (lim,fanjit'idēz). inflammation of a lymphatic vessel.

lym·phat·ic (limfat'ik), *adj.* **1.** of, secreting, or carrying lymph. **2.** pale; flabby; sluggish; formerly used of persons thought to have an excess of lymph.

lymph gland, one of the many small masses of tissue in the lymphatic vessels which filter out from the lymph substances and produce lymphocytes. Also **lymphatic gland, lymph node.**

lym·pho·blast (lim'fōbläst,), *n.* an immature white blood cell.

lym·pho·cyte (lim'fōsīt,), *n.* a kind of white blood cell formed in the lymph glands.

lym·pho·cy·to·pe·ni·a (lim,fōsī,tōpē'nēə), *n.* a condition in which the level of lymphocytes in the blood is abnormally low. Also **lymphopenia.** —**lym,pho·cy,to·pen'ic,** *adj.*

lym·pho·cy·to·sis (lim,fōsītō'sis), *n.* a condition in which the blood contains an abnormally large number of lymphocytes.

lym·pho·gran·u·lo·ma (lim,fōgran,yəlō'-mə), *n., pl.* **lym·pho·gran·u·lo·mas, lym·pho·gran·u·lo·ma·ta** (lim,fōgran,yəlō'mətə). one of several disorders distinguished by the formation on the lymph glands of grainlike prominences that develop into broken tissue and ulceration.

lym·phoid (lim'foid), *adj.* resembling lymph.

lym·pho·ma (limfō'mə), *n.* a tumour arising from a cell in a lymph gland.

lym·pho·pe·ni·a (lim,fōpē'nēə), *n.* a condition in which the blood contains an abnormally low number of lymphocytes.

lyn·ce·an (linsē'ən), *adj.* lynxlike, esp. lynx-eyed; keen-sighted.

ly·on·naise (līənāz'), *adj.* (of any dish, esp. potatoes) cooked with pieces of onion.

ly·rate (līə'rit), *adj.* lyre-shaped.

lyse (līs), *v.* to undergo or carry out lysis; to treat with lysins.

ly·ser·gic ac·id di·eth·yl·am·ide (lisû'jik as'id dīethəlämīd). See **LSD.**

ly·sin (lī'sin), *n.* an antibody causing the disintegration of bacterial or other cells.

ly·sis (lī'sis), *n.* **1.** disintegration of bacterial or other cells as a result of the presence of the antibody lysin. **2.** the gradual decline of a fever or other illness.

ly·so·zyme (lī'səzīm), *n.* an enzyme that destroys bacteria and thus serves as an antiseptic, occurring in tears, mucus, white blood cells, egg white, and some plants.

lys·so·pho·bi·a (lis,əfō'bēə), *n.* a morbid dread of going insane.

mac·a·ron·ic (mak,əron'ik), *adj.* (of comic verse) written in Latin mixed with vernacular words given Latin endings.

mac·é·doine (mas,idwän'), *n.* mixed fruit or vegetables, often diced.

mac·er·ate (mas'ərāt), *v.* to make or become soft by soaking.

ma·chic·o·late (məchik'əlāt), *v.* (in a castle or stronghold) to furnish openings in the floor of a gallery or chamber over an entry or passage so that stones or boiling liquid could be dropped on attackers. —**ma·chic'o·lat·ed**, *adj.* —**ma··chic,o·la'tion**, *n.*

mach·i·nate (mak'ināt), *v.* to contrive artfully; to plot; to intrigue.

mach·i·na·tion (mak,inā'sHən), *n.* a secret scheme, esp. an underhanded intrigue; the practice of plotting.

Mach number (mäk), a number indicating the ratio of the velocity of a body to the local speed of sound, thus where a speed of sound is 750 mph and an aircraft travels at 1500 mph the aircraft's Mach number is 2. Also **Mach.**

mack·le (mak'əl), *n.* a blur in printing. Also **mac'ule.**

mac·ra·mé (məkrä'mē), *n.* a cotton fringe knotted to form patterns and used as a trimming.

mac·ro·car·pous (mak'rōkä'pəs), *adj.* producing large fruit.

mac·ro·cli·mate (mak,rōklī'mit), *n.* the climate of a large area, as of a country. See also **microclimate.**

mac·ro·cli·ma·tol·o·gy (mak,rōklī,mətol'əjē), *n.* the study of the climate of a large area. See also **microclimatology.**

mac·ro·cosm (mak'rəkoz,əm), *n.* the whole world; the universe regarded as a whole. See also **microcosm.**

mac·ro·cyst (mak'rōsist,), *n.* a large cyst.

mac·ro·cyte (mak'rōsīt,), *n.* a red blood cell of abnormal size. See also **microcyte.**

mac·ro·dont (mak'rōdont,), *adj.* with teeth of abnormal largeness or length. See also **microdont.**

mac·ro·don·tia (mak,rōdon'sHiə), *n.* a condition in which the teeth are of abnormal largeness or length. Also **megadontia.** See also **microdontia.**

mac·ro·ec·o·nom·ics (mak,rōek,ənom'iks), *n.* the study of the broad, general aspects of an economy as a whole. See also **microeconomics.** —**mac,ro·e,co·nom'ic,** *adj.*

mac·ro·graph (mak'rōgräf,, mak'rōgraf,), *n.* a representation of an object, as a photograph or drawing, that is life size or larger. See also **micrograph.**

ma·crog·ra·phy (məkrog'rəfē), *n.* examination or study of an object with the naked eye. See also **micrography.**

mac·ro·nu·cle·us (mak,rōnyōō'klēəs), *n.* See **micronucleus.**

mac·ro·nu·tri·ent (mak,rōnyōō'trēənt), *n.* a substance (e.g. water, protein, carbohydrate) that is required in relatively large amounts for the normal growth and maintenance of a living organism.

mac·ro·phage (mak'rōfāj), *n.* See **histiocyte.**

mac·ro·phyl·lous (mak,rōfil'əs), *adj.* large-leaved.

mac·ro·phys·ics (mak,rōfiz'iks), *n.* the science of the physical properties of objects sufficiently large to be observed and dealt with directly.

ma·crop·si·a (makrop'sēə), *n.* a condition of the eye which causes objects to be seen larger than life size. Also **megalopsia.** —**mac·rop'tic,** *adj.*

mac·rop·ter·ous (makrop'tərəs), *adj.* having large wings or fins. —**mac·rop'ter·y,** *n.*

mac·ro·scop·ic (mak,rəskop'ik), *adj.* visible to the naked eye.

mac·ro·sto·mi·a (mak,rəstō'mēə), *n.* the condition of having an abnormal extension of one or both corners of the mouth.

mac·ro·struc·ture (mak'rōstruk,cHə), *n.* the general arrangement or pattern of crystals in a metal or alloy as visible, after deep etching, in low magnification or to the naked eye.

ma·cru·ran (məkrōōr'ən), *adj.* of or relating to the suborder comprising lobsters, crayfishes, shrimps, and prawns.

ma·cru·rous (məkrōōr'əs), *adj.* long-tailed.

mac·u·la (mak'yələ), *n., pl.* **mac·u·lae** (mak'yəlē). a spot or blemish, as on the sun, moon, skin, etc.

mac·u·late (mak'yəlāt), *v.* **1.** to mark with spots; to sully. —*adj.* **2.** spotted; stained; sullied. —**mac,u·la'tion,** *n.*

mac·ule (mak'yōōl), *n.* a macula. See **mackle.**

mad cow disease, *n. Inf.* name for bovine spongiform encephalopathy.

mad·ri·lène (mad'rəlen), *n.* tomato-flavoured consommé, served set and chilled, or hot and liquid.

mael·strom (māl'strəm), *n.* a large whirlpool.

mae·nad, me·nad (mē'nad), *n.* a frenzied or shrewish woman.

Ma·gi (mā'jī), *n. pl., sing.* **Ma·gus** (mā'gəs). the three wise men who came bearing gifts for the baby Jesus. [Matt. 2:1-12.]

mag·is·te·ri·al (maj,istēr'ēəl), *adj.* of or like a master; imperious.

mag·is·tral (maj'istrəl), *adj.* (of a medical preparation) specially made up. See also **offici·nal.**

mag·ma (mag'mə), *n., pl.* **mag·mas, mag·ma·ta** (mag'mətə). 1. a soft, pastelike mixture of mineral or organic dust. 2. molten rock still within the earth.

mag·na cum lau·de (mag'nə kōōm lou'dā), *Latin.* with great praise; (in the U.S.) the next to highest of three special grades of honour for above-average graduates. See also **cum laude, summa cum laude.**

mag·nan·i·mous (magnan'iməs), *adj.* generous or forgiving in spirit; above petty spite. —**mag·na·nim·i·ty** (magnənim'itē), *n.*

mag·ne·to (magnē'tō), *n.* a small electric generator using permanent magnets.

mag·ne·to·chem·is·try (magnē,tōkem'istrē), *n.* the branch of science dealing with the relation to each other of magnetic and chemical phenomena.

mag·ne·to·e·lec·tric·i·ty (magnē,tōilektris'itē), *n.* electricity generated by means of permanent magnets and electric conductors. —**mag·ne·to·e·lec'tric,** *adj.*

mag·ne·to·hy·dro·dy·nam·ic (magnē,tōhī,drōdīnam'ik), *adj.* relating to the phenomena occurring when a fluid electric conductor passes through a magnetic field.

mag·ne·to·hy·dro·dy·nam·ics (magnē,tōhī,drōdīnam'iks), *n.* the branch of physics concerned with magnetohydrodynamic phenomena. Also **hydromagnetics.**

mag·ne·tom·e·ter (mag,nitom'itə), *n.* instrument for measuring magnetic force, esp. the earth's magnetism.

mag·ne·to·mo·tive (magnē,tōmō'tiv), *adj.* producing magnetism.

mag·ne·to·op·tics (magnē,tōop'tiks), *n.* the study of the effect of magnetism on light. —**mag·ne·to·op'tic,** *adj.*

mag·ne·to·ther·mo·e·lec·tric·i·ty (magnē,tōthū,mōilektris'itē), *n.* the production of or effect made on thermoelectricity by a magnetic field.

mag·nil·o·quent (magnil'əkwənt), *adj.* grandiose in speech; boastful.

mag·ni·tude (mag'nityōōd',), *n.* the extent, size, or importance of something, either physically or otherwise, as *the magnitude of the building* or *the magnitude of the crime.*

mag·num (mag'nəm), *n.* a large bottle, as of wine, containing about 50 ounces.

mag·num o·pus (mag'nəm ō'pəs), *n.* a great work; the greatest work of a writer, composer, or artist.

ma·hat·ma (məhät'mə, məhat'mə), *n.* (among the Buddhists of India and Tibet) one of a class of persons of extraordinary wisdom and virtue.

Ma·ha·ya·na (mä,həyä'nə), *n.* one of the two divergent schools of Buddhism; Northern Buddhism, the form practised in China, Tibet, Korea, and Japan, which stresses the hope of personal salvation, the duty to save others, and the power of prayer. See also **Bodhisattva, Hinayana.**

mahl·stick (mal'stik,), *n.* a long thin stick with a padded ball at one end held in one hand by a painter as a support for the hand with the brush. Also **maulstick.**

ma·hout (məhout'), *n.* an elephant-driver.

mai·gre (mā'gə), *adj.* without any meat or meat juices in it, as food allowed on days of religious abstinence in Roman Catholic Church.

mail·lot (māyō'), *n.* 1. a one-piece bathing suit. 2. a close-fitting shirt of knitted fabric.

main·line (mān'līn,), *v.* (in slang usage) to inject a narcotic drug directly into a vein.

mai·son·ette (māzənet'), *n.* part of a house let or used separately, with rooms on more than one storey.

ma·jol·i·ca (məjol'ikə), *n.* Italian earthenware with a white enamel glaze decorated with metallic colours.

ma·jus·cule (maj'əskyōōl), *adj.* (of alphabetic letters) capital, large, or uncial. See also **minuscule.**

ma·la·ceous (məlā'sнəs), *adj.* of or relating to the family of plants including the apple, pear, hawthorn, medlar, quince, etc.

mal·a·chite (mal'əkīt), *n.* a dense, bright-green mineral which is brought to a high polish and used in decorative articles.

ma·la·cia (məlā'sнə), *n.* 1. softening of an organ or tissue. 2. abnormal craving for spiced food. —**ma'la·coid, mal·a·cot'ic,** *adj.*

mal·a·col·o·gy (maləkol'əjē), *n.* the scientific study of molluscs.

mal·a·coph·i·lous (mal,əkof'ələs), *adj.* (of a flower) pollinated by snails.

mal·a·cos·tra·can (mal,əkos'trəkən), *adj.* of or relating to the subclass that includes lobsters, shrimps, crabs, etc.

mal·a·droit (mal,ədroit'), *adj.* clumsy; awkward; tactless.

ma·laise (malāz'), *n.* a general feeling of physical discomfort or uneasiness.

mal·a·prop·ism (mal'əpropiz,əm), *n.* an instance or the habit of confusing, with ludicrous results, similar sounding words, as *Illiterate him from your memory.*

mal·ap·ro·pos (mal,aprapō'), *adj.* inappropriate; untimely.

ma·lar (mā'lə), *adj.* relating to the cheek bone.

mal·a·thi·on (malathī'on), *n.* an insecticide used as a substitute for DDT. See also **rotenone.**

mal·e·dict (mal'idikt), *adj.* accursed. —**mal,e··dic'tion,** *n.*

mal·e·fac·tion (mal,əfak'SHən), *n.* an instance of evil-doing; a crime.

mal·e·fac·tor (mal'əfak,tə), *n.* a criminal; an evil-doer. Also (of a woman) **mal'e·fac,tress.**

ma·lef·ic (məlef'ik), *adj.* of evil effect; malign, as *A malefic spirit possessed him.*

ma·lef·i·cence (məlef'isəns), *n.* the doing of evil; harmful character.

ma·lef·i·cent (məlef'isənt), *adj.* harmful; evil.

ma·lev·o·lence (məlev'ələns), *n.* the wishing of ill to others; malice. —**ma·lev'o·lent,** *adj.*

mal·fea·sance (malfē'zəns), *n.* official misconduct; breach of law or public trust by a public official in the course of his duties. See also **misfeasance, nonfeasance.**

mal·ic (mal'ik, mā'lik), *adj.* of or from apples.

mal·ice (mal'is), *n.* bad feeling; hatred; the wish or intent to do evil.

ma·lign (məlīn'), *v.* 1. to speak ill of; to slander. —*adj.* 2. causing evil; malignant.

ma·lig·nant (məlig'nənt), *adj.* 1. feeling or showing intense ill-will; dangerous in effect. 2. deadly; of a form which tends to cause death, esp. of an illness or a tumour. —**ma·lig·ni·ty** (məlig'nitē), *n.*

ma·lin·ger (məliNG'gə), *v.* to pretend to be ill so as to escape duty or work.

mal·le·a·ble (mal'ēəbəl), *adj.* that can be hammered or rolled into another shape without breaking, esp. metal.

mal·le·ate (mal'ēāt), *v.* to hammer into shape, as in metalworking.

mal·le·o·lus (məlē'ələs), *n.*, *pl.* **mal·le·o·li** (məlē'əlī). the hammer-head shaped bone of the ankle. —**mal·le'o·lar,** *adj.*

malm·sey (mäm'zē), *n.* a strong sweet wine formerly made in Greece but now also in Spain, Madeira, and the Azores.

mal·oc·clu·sion (mal,əkloo'zHən), *n.* imperfect meeting of opposing teeth in upper and lower jaws.

mal·prac·tice (mal,prak'tis), *n.* improper, corrupt, illegal, or incompetent performance of duty by a professional person.

Mal·thu·si·an (malthyoo'zēən, malthoo'zēən), *adj.* 1. of or relating to the theory of Thomas Malthus (1766–1834), British economist. He argued that, without voluntary or involuntary restraint, the growth of human populations tends to outstrip the resources available for subsistence, resulting eventually in catastrophic decline in numbers through famine, disease, or war. —*n.* 2. an adherent of Malthus' theory. —**Mal·thu'si·an·ism,,** *n.*

mal·ver·sa·tion (mal,versā'sHən), *n.* corruption in handling public funds or in performing public office.

mam·mec·to·my (məmek'təmē), *n.* See **mastectomy.**

mam·mog·ra·phy (mamog'rəfē), *n.* the use of x-rays or other radiation to visualize the tissues of the breast in the diagnosis of tumours, etc. —**mam·mo·graph** (mam'ōgräf,), **mam·mo··gram** (mam'ōgram,), *n.*

man·a·kin (man'əkin), *n.* 1. any one of the small, songless, brightly coloured passerine birds native to Central and S. America. 2. manikin.

man·ci·ple (man'səpəl), *n.* official who purchases provisions for a college, monastery, etc.

man·da·rin (man'dərin), *n.* an important official who wields great power and influence.

man·date (man'dāt), *n.* 1. an order or command, esp. one given by an electorate exhorting a representative to act on a certain issue. —*v.* 2. to give an order or command.

man·di·ble (man'dəbəl). *n.* the lower jawbone. —**man·dib·u·lar** (mandib'yələ), *adj.* —**man·dib·u·late** (mandib'yəlit, mandib'yəlät), *adj.*

ma·nège (manezH'), *n.* 1. the art of training horses; horsemanship. 2. the movement of a trained horse.

ma·nes (mā'nēz), *n.* the ghost or spirit of a dead person.

ma·net (mä'net). *v.*, *pl.* **ma·nent.** he or she remains (a stage direction indicating that the character named should remain on stage while others leave).

man·ic-de·pres·sive (man,ikdipres'iv), *adj.* suffering from a psychosis in which periods of great excitement, perhaps with violence and delusions, alternate with periods of acute depression.

ma·ni·cot·ti (man,əkot'ē), *n.* an Italian dish of short tubes of pasta stuffed with cheese and cooked in a tomato sauce.

man·i·fest (man'ifest), *adj.* 1. clearly apparent to the eye or the mind. —*v.* 2. to show plainly. —*n.* 3. a list of cargo carried, by land, on ship, or by plane, to be shown to customs officials or other authority at destination.

man·i·form (man'ifôm), *adj.* hand-shaped.

man·i·kin, man·ni·kin (man'ikin), *n.* 1. a dwarf; small person. 2. a mannequin. 3. a model of the human body used in the teaching of various branches of medicine. Also **manakin.**

ma·nism (mā'nizm), *n.* ancestor-worship; attempted communication with the spirits of ancestors.

man·ne·quin (man'əkin), *n.* 1. a person who wears clothes to display them to potential buyers. **2.** a model of a man or woman for displaying clothing, as in shop windows. **3.** a wooden or stuffed model, often adjustable in size, of the human trunk, used by dressmakers and tailors for fitting clothes.

man·ner·ism (man'əriz,əm), *n.* a gesture or other characteristic that is naturally associated with a particular person or group of people, as *the speech mannerisms of people who gesture while talking.*

man·ni·kin (man'əkin), *n.* **1.** manikin. **2.** any of several finches native to Asia, Australia, and the Pacific islands but often kept as pets elsewhere.

ma·nom·e·ter (mənom'itə), *n.* an instrument for measuring the pressure of gases and vapours; a U-shaped tube containing mercury and with one arm a vacuum or open to the air, so that pressure of a gas or vapour forces the mercury to rise, giving a reading on a scale marked on the glass.

man·qué (mäNkā'), *adj. French.* that might have been; failed; unfulfilled.

man·sard (man'säd), *n.* a roof in which each side has two slopes, the lower much steeper than the upper and usually with projecting windows in it.

manse (mans), *n.* the residence of a minister of religion.

man·sue·tude (man'swityŏŏd), *n.* gentleness; meekness, as *to exhibit mansuetude to the aged.*

man·tic (man'tik), *adj.* relating to or with the power of foretelling the future by supernatural means.

man·tra (man'trə), *n.* (in Hinduism and Buddhism) a sacred word, syllable, or other formula chanted or recited as an aid to focus concentration.

ma·nu·bi·al column (mənyŏŏ'bēəl), a triumphal or memorial column, originally one displaying spoils taken from the enemy.

ma·nu·bri·um (mənyŏŏ'brēəm), *n., pl.* **ma·nu·bri·a** (mənyŏŏ'brēə), **ma·nu·bri·ums.** an anatomical feature, as a bone, cell, segment, that resembles a handle.

man·u·mit (man,yŏŏmit'), *v.* to give freedom to; set free, as a slave. —**man·u·mis·sion** (man,-ŏŏyəmisH'ŏŏn), *n.*

ma·quette (maket'), *n.* a small preliminary model or three-dimensional study for a sculpture or an architectural work.

ma·ras·mus (məraz'məs), *n.* a wasting away of the body from unknown cause, mainly in infants.

marc (mäk), *n.* the residue after the juice has been pressed from grapes.

mar·ces·cent (mäses'ənt), *adj.* in the process of withering, as a leaf.

march·pane (mäcH'pan,), *n.* marzipan.

ma·re (mär'ā) *n., pl.* **ma·ri·a** (mär'ēə). any one

of the large, comparatively flat areas on the moon, seen as dark patches from earth and formerly believed to be seas.

ma·re li·be·rum (mä'rä lib'ərəm), *Latin.* a sea open to all nations.

ma·rem·ma (mərem'ə). *n., pl.* **marem·me** (mərem'ē). **1.** a marshland near the coast, esp. in Italy. **2.** the foul gases given off by marshland.

ma·re nos·trum (mä'rä nos'trŏŏm), *Latin.* our sea, esp. the Mediterranean as referred to by the ancient Romans.

mare's nest (me'əznest), *n.* **1.** something thought to be a discovery but actually a delusion or a hoax. **2.** an extreme muddle.

mar·ga·ri·ta·ceous (mä,gəritā'sHəs), *adj.* like mother-of-pearl; pearly.

mar·i·gram (mar'igram), *n.* a record made by a marigraph.

mar·i·graph (mar'igräf, mar'igraf,), *n.* an automatic device for registering the rise and fall of the tide. Also **mar·e·o·graph** (mar'ēəgräf, mar'ēəgraf,).

ma·ri·jua·na (ma,əwä'nə), *n.* the dried leaves of the hemp plant, *Cannabis sativa,* smoked or ingested to induce euphoria.

mar·i·nade (mar,inäd'), *n.* a liquid, usually wine or vinegar, containing herbs, spices, and seasonings, in which meat or fish is soaked before being cooked.

ma·ri·na·ra (mar,inä'ə), *n.* **1.** a highly seasoned Italian tomato sauce. —*adj.* **2.** served with marinara.

mar·i·nate (mar'inät,), *v.* to soak in a marinade.

Mar·i·ol·o·gy, Mar·y·ol·o·gy (mer,ēol'əjē), *n.* the study of the doctrines of the Blessed Virgin Mary. —**Mar·i·ol'o·gist, Mar·y·ol'o·gist,** *n.*

marl (mäl), *n.* a crumbly rock of mud and lime used in broken or powdered form as a soil conditioner on ground deficient in lime.

mar·mite (mä'mīt), *n.* a deep, lidded cooking pot of metal or earthenware, sometimes with legs.

mar·mo·re·al (mämôr'ēəl), *adj.* of or resembling marble.

ma·rou·flage (mär'əfläzH), *n.* a method of sticking canvas to a surface.

mar·plot (mä'plot), *n.* one who spoils a scheme or plan.

marque (mäk), *n.* the brand of a product, esp. of a car.

mar·que·try (mä'kitrē), *n.* decoration of a flat surface. esp. of furniture, by covering it with glued-on, thin, shaped pieces of coloured woods, ivory, etc.

Mar·ra·no (mərä'nō), *n., pl.* **Mar·ra·nos.** a Spanish or Portuguese Jew who, in the late Middle Ages, was or pretended to be converted to Christianity, esp. under threat of death or exile.

mar·ron (mar'ən), *n*. a sweet chestnut, esp. in syrup.

mar·rons gla·cés (mar'ən glas'ā), chestnuts in sweet syrup.

marsh gas, an inflammable gas, mainly of methane, formed by decaying vegetable matter, as in marshes and coal mines.

mar·su·pi·al (mäsōō'pēəl, mäsyōō'pēəl), *n*. any animal of the order comprised of mammals that are very immature at birth and are carried and suckled in the mother's marsupium or pouch until able to fend for themselves, as kangaroos, opossums, etc.

mar·su·pi·um (mäsōō'pēəm, mäsyōō'pēəm), *n., pl.* **mar·su·pi·a** (mäsōō'pēə, mäsyōō'pēə). the pouch on the abdomen of a female marsupial.

mart (mät), *n*. a market, auction room, trading centre. centre.

mar·ti·net (mätinet'), *n*. a strict disciplinarian, esp. a military man.

Marx·ism (mäk'sizəm), *n*. the political philosophy of Karl Marx, set out in *Das Kapital*, that capitalism takes all the benefits of progress to itself, leaving the workers in increasing dependency and that it should be destroyed by a class war that would put all the property and the means of production in the hands of the community. —**Marx'ist**, *n., adj*.

ma·ser (mā'zə), *n*. (acronym of microwave amplification by stimulated emission of radiation) a device used to provide a high, selective amplification of a particular microwave frequency. See also **laser**.

mas·och·is·m (mas'əkiz,əm), *n*. a condition in which sexual or other gratification depends on suffering physical pain and humiliation. See also **sadism**. —**mas,o·chis'tic**, *adj*.

mas·sif (mas'if), *n*. **1**. a compact plateau-like mass of several mountains. **2**. a large upstanding block of old rock that has resisted erosion.

mast (mäst), *n*. fruit of forest trees such as oak and beech, used as food for animals, esp. pigs.

mas·tec·to·my (mastek'təmē), *n*. a surgical removal of a breast. Also **mammectomy**.

mast·head (mäst'hed), *n*. the name of a publication, its owners, its address, and sometimes its staff, appearing in every issue of a newspaper, magazine, or periodical, usually on the editorial page. Also **flag**.

mas·ti·cate (mas'tikāt), *v*. to chew; to grind to a pulp. —**mas'ti·ca·to·ry**, *adj., n*.

mas·to·car·ci·no·ma (mas,tōkä,sinō'mə), *n., pl.* **mas·to·car·ci·no·mas, mas·to·car·ci·no·ma·ta** (mas,tōkä,sinō'mətə). cancer of the breast.

mas·to·don (mas'tədon), *n*. **1**. an extinct genus of large elephant-like mammals with nipple-shaped projections on the crowns of molar teeth, living in the Oligocene and Pliocene epochs. **2**. a person of great size, stature, influence, etc.

mas·toid (mas'toid), *adj*. **1**. breast-shaped or

nipple-shaped. **2**. relating to the nipple-like prominence of the temporal bone behind the ear, which contains air spaces connecting with the ear.

mas·toid·ec·to·my (mast,oidek'təmē), *n*. surgical removal of part of a mastoid, as to drain an infection in one of its air spaces.

mas·toid·i·tis (mast,oidī'tis), *n*. inflammation of the mastoid.

ma·ta·dor (mat'ədō), *n*. the bullfighter of the final stage of a bullfight, who kills the bull.

mat·e·las·sé (matlas'ā). *n*. a heavy embossed fabric.

ma·ter·fa·mil·i·as (mä,təfəmil'ēas,). *n*. the female head of a household or family.

ma·té·ri·el (mətĕr,ēel'), *n*. the stock of materials and equipment used in an undertaking, as arms, ammunition, etc. in a military operation.

ma·tri·arch (mä'trēäk), *n*. a woman head of a family or tribe. See also **patriarch**. —**ma·tri·ar'·chal, ma·tri·ar'chic,** *adj*.

ma·tri·ar·chate (mä'trēä,kit, mä'trēä,kät), *n*. a matriarchal society.

ma·tri·ar·chy (mä'trēä,kē), *n*. a form of social order in which the mother is head of the family and descent and relationship are through the female line.

mat·ri·cide (ma'trisīd, mä'trisīd), *n*. the killing of one's own mother.

ma·tric·u·late (mətrik'yəlāt), *v*. to admit to membership and privileges of a college, university, etc., by enrolling. —**ma·tric'u·lant,** *n*. —**ma·tric·u·la'tion,** *n*.

mat·ri·lat·er·al (mat,rilat'ərəl), *adj*. of a relative on the mother's side of a family. See also **patrilateral**.

mat·ri·lin·e·age (mat,rilin'ēij), *n*. descent through the female line.

mat·ri·lin·e·al (mat,rilin'ēəl), *adj*. of descent, relationship, or inheritance through the female line.

mat·ri·lin·y (mat'rilin,ē), *n*. the tracing of descent through the female line.

mat·ri·lo·cal (mat'rilōkəl), *adj*. of or relating to living with the wife's family or tribe. See also **patrilocal**.

mat·ri·po·tes·tal (mat'rēpōtes,təl), *adj*. of or relating to authority wielded by a mother or a mother's side of a family.

ma·trix (mā'triks, mat'riks), *n., pl.* **ma·tri·ces** (mā'trisēz, ma'trisēz). the cavity, die, or mould in which anything is cast, formed, or developed.

mat·tock (mat'ək), *n*. a farm tool consisting of a long handle with a metal head having a pick on one side and a hoelike blade on the other.

ma·tu·ti·nal (mat,yōōtī'nəl), *adj*. of or in the morning, esp. early morning.

maud·lin (môd'lin), *adj*. weakly sentimental; tearfully emotional; mawkish.

maul·stick (môl'stik,), *n*. mahlstick.

maun·der (môn'də), *v.* to talk or walk in a rambling, confused manner.

maun·dy (môn'dē), *n.* the ceremony of washing the feet of the poor by an eminent person on the Thursday before Easter, in commemoration of Jesus' washing of his disciples' feet, frequently followed by almsgiving. Also **maundy money**, the alms given at a maundy ceremony.

mav·er·ick (mav'ərik), *n.* a person whose behaviour or opinions are different from those of most other people; an independent person who lets his views be known.

maw·ger (mô'gə), *adj. Caribbean.* lean or scrawny.

mawk·ish (mô'kisн), *adj.* given to tearful sentimentality; self-pitying; maudlin.

max·il·la (maksil'ə), *n., pl.* **max·il·lae** (maksil'ē). the upper jawbone of vertebrates. —**max·il'lar·y,** *adj.*

max·im (mak'sim), *n.* a general truth, esp. neatly phrased; a rule of conduct.

max·i·mal·ist (mak'siməlist), *n.* one who advocates direct action without compromise to secure objectives, esp. a socialist who favours immediate revolution to overthrow the capitalist state.

max·i·min (mak'simin), *n.* a strategy used in games to increase to the utmost a player's possible gain. See also **minimax**.

maz·a·rine (maz,ərēn'), *n.* a silver strainer fitting over a plate, used to strain liquid or juices from meats and fish.

ma·zel tov, ma·zal tov (mä'zel tôf), a Hebrew expression of good wishes.

me·a cul·pa (mā'ä kŏŏl'pə), *Latin.* by my own fault; my fault.

mead (mēd), *n.* an alcoholic beverage made from fermented honey and water.

me·an·der (mēan'də), *v.* to wander or wind, as a stream.

mech·an·ism (mek'əniz,əm), *n.* (in philosophy and biology) a process of nature explained or regarded as being explicable as a product of mechanical forces. See also **dynamism, vitalism.** —**mech·a·nis·tic** (mek,ənis'tik), *adj.*

me·cism (mē'siz,əm), *n.* the abnormal length of a part or parts of the body.

me·com·e·ter (məkom'itə), *n.* an instrument for measuring length, esp. a graduated instrument similar to a calliper, for measuring the length of newborn infants.

me·co·ni·um (mikō'nēəm), *n.* the contents of the intestine of a newborn mammal evacuated as the first excrement, composed mainly of bile, mucus, and swallowed amniotic fluid.

mé·dail·lon (mādayôN'), *n. French.* a portion of food, esp. meat, served as a small round thick slice.

me·di·a·tize, me·di·a·tise (mē'dēətīz,), *v.* to annex a state or other territory while permitting the former ruler to retain his title and, possibly, limited powers. —**me,di·a·ti·za'tion, me,di·a·ti·sa'tion,** *n.*

me·dic·a·ment (mədik'əmənt), *n.* a substance used to heal or to alleviate discomfort; a medicine.

med·i·co·chi·rur·gi·cal (med'ikōkīrŭ'jikəl), *adj.* of or relating to medicine and surgery jointly.

me·di·o·cre (mē,dēō'kə), *adj.* not good in quality, but not very bad either; neither here nor there; common, ordinary, as *a mediocre artist.* —**me'di·oc'ri·ty,** *n.*

me·di·us (mē'dēəs), *n., pl.* **me·di·i** (mē'dēī). the middle finger.

me·du·sa (mədyōō'zə), *n., pl.* **me·du·sas, me·du·sae** (mədyōō'zē). a jelly-fish. —**me·du'san,** *adj.*

meet (mēt), *adj.* appropriate, fitting, suitable. —**meet'ly,** *adv.*

meg·a·cit·y (meg'əsit,ē), *n.* a city with a population of 1,000,000 or more.

meg·a·cy·cle (meg'əsīkəl), *n.* former name for megahertz. *Abbr.:* **mc, MC.**

meg·a·don·tia (meg,ədon'sнə), *n.* See **macrodontia.**

meg·a·hertz (meg'əhŭts), *n.* a unit equal to 1,000,000 cycles per second, used in measuring the frequency of electromagnetic waves. *Abbr.:* **MHz.** Also, formerly, **megacycle.**

meg·a·joule (meg'əjŏōl,, meg'əjoul,), *n.* a unit equal to 1,000,000 joules, used in measuring work or energy. *Abbr.:* **MJ.**

meg·a·lith (meg'əlith), *n.* a very large stone used in buildings or as a monument in prehistoric or ancient periods.

meg·a·lo·car·di·a (meg,əlōkä'dēə), *n.* abnormal enlargement of the heart due to the addition of new tissue.

meg·a·lo·ma·ni·a (meg,əlōmä'nēə), *n.* a mental illness characterized by delusions of grandeur. —**meg,a·lo·ma'ni·ac,** *n.*

meg·a·lop·o·lis (meg,əlop'əlis), *n.* a very large city or several cities which merge together to form an extensive urban area. —**meg,a·lo·pol'i·tan,** *adj., n.*

meg·a·lop·si·a (meg,əlop'sēə), *n.* See **macropsia.**

meg·a·me·tre (meg'əmē,tə), *n.* a metric unit of measurement equal to 1,000,000 metres. *Abbr.:* **Mm.**

meg·a·pod (meg'əpod), *adj.* with large feet.

meg·a·therm (meg'əthŭm), *n.* a plant which needs a high temperature and plenty of moisture constantly for growth.

meg·a·ton (meg'ətun), *n.* a measurement of explosive force equal to that of 1,000,000 tons of TNT. *Abbr.:* **MT.**

meg·a·volt (meg'əvōlt), *n.* a unit for measuring electromotive force, equal to 1,000,000 volts. *Abbr.:* **MV.**

meg·a·volt-am·pere (meg'əvolt·am'pēə), *n.* a unit of measurement of electric current equal to 1,000,000 volt-amperes. *Abbr.:* **MVA.**

meg·a·watt (meg'əwot). *n.* a unit of measurement of electric power equal to 1,000,000 watts. *Abbr.:* **MW.**

meg·a·watt-hour (meg'əwotour'), *n.* a unit used to express the rate of expenditure of electric power in terms of megawatts used in one hour. *Abbr.:* **MWh.**

me·gil·lah (məgil'ə), *n. Slang.* a long, detailed relating of events.

meg·ohm (meg'ōm), *n.* a unit for measuring electrical resistance, equal to 1,000,000 ohms. *Abbr.:* **MΩ.**

meg·ohm·me·ter (meg'ōmmē,tə), *n.* an instrument for measuring large electrical resistance.

me·grims (mē'grimz), *n. pl.* low spirits; depression.

mei·o·sis (mīō'sis), *n., pl.* **mei·o·ses** (mīō'sēz). the maturation of gametes when two cell divisions starting in a diploid cell result in the diploid chromosome number becoming reduced to the haploid.

me·lae·na, me·le·na (məlē'nə), *n.* the presence of blood, blackened through partial digestion, in the faeces owing to a haemorrhage in the stomach or small intestine.

mé·lange (mālänzh'), *n. French.* a mixture.

me·lan·ic (məlan'ik), *adj.* relating to melanism; melanotic.

mel·a·nif·er·ous (mel,ənif'ərəs), *adj.* containing melanin.

mel·a·nin (mel'ənin), *n.* a dark brown pigment present in many animals, including man, which in varying concentrations gives the yellow, brown, and black colouring to skin, hair, feathers, etc.

mel·a·nism (mel'əniz,əm). *n.* darkness of colour due to the presence of a large amount of melanin.

mel·a·noch·ro·i (mel,ənok'rōī), *n. pl.* a class of humans characterized by dark smooth hair and pale skin.

mel·a·no·cyte (mel'ənōsīt,), *n.* a cell that contains and produces melanin.

melanocyte-stimulating hormone, a hormone that produces general darkening of the skin by causing dispersal of the melanin in melanocytes.

mel·an·o·derm (mel'ənōdûm,), *n.* a person whose skin is darkly pigmented.

mel·a·noid (mel'ənoid), *adj.* melanin-like, with dark pigmentation.

mel·a·no·ma (mel,ənō'mə), *n., pl.* **mel·a·no·mas, mel·a·no·ma·ta** (mel,ənō'mətə). a tumour of cells containing melanin and thus of dark colour, most frequent on the skin or eye.

mel·a·no·sis (mel,ənō'sis), *n.* an abnormal deposit or development of melanin in the tissues. **—mel·a·not·ic** (mel,ənot'ik), *adj.*

me·le·na (milē'nə), *n.* See **melaena.**

mel·ic (mel'ik), *adj.* **1.** for singing, as *melic* verse. **2.** relating to, to the more elaborate strophic species of Greek lyric poetry, as distinct from iambic and elegaic poetry.

me·li·o·rate (mē'lēərāt,), *v.* to improve. **—mel·io·ra'tion,** *n.*

me·li·o·rism (mē'lēəriz,əm), *n.* the doctrine that the world is or can be improved by human effort.

me·li·o·ri·ty (mē,lēor'itē), *n.* the quality or condition of being better; superiority.

mel·lif·er·ous (məlif'ərəs), *adj.* making or yielding honey.

mel·lif·lu·ous (məlif'lōōəs), *adj.* **1.** sweet and smooth sounding. **2.** flowing with honey; sweetened with or sweet as honey. Also **mel·lif'lu·ent.**

me·men·to (məmen'tō), *n., pl.* **me·men·tos.** something, usually an object, to remember something, someone, or someplace by, as *This matchbox is a memento of my visit to Italy.*

me·mo·ri·ter (məmôr'itə), *adv. Latin.* from memory; by heart.

men·ac·me (mənak'mē), *n.* that period of years in a female life during which menstruation takes place.

me·nad (mē'nad), *n.* See **maenad.**

mé·nage (mānäzh'), *n.* household; management of a household.

mé·nage à trois (mānäzh' a trwä'), *French.* a household consisting of a married couple and the lover of one of them.

men·ar·che (mənä'kē), *n.* the age at which menstruation begins; the first menstruation.

men·da·cious (mendā'shəs), *adj.* untrue; untruthful.

men·dac·i·ty (mendas'itē), *n.* the tendency to tell lies; an instance of telling a lie.

men·di·cant (men'dikənt), *adj.* **1.** living by begging. **—n. 2.** a beggar.

men·dic·i·ty (mendis'itē), *n.* the practice of begging; the condition of being a beggar.

men·hir (men'hēə), *n.* an upright monumental stone of prehistoric date.

me·ni·al (mē'nēəl), *adj.* **1.** relating to or proper to domestic servants; servile; degrading. **—n. 2.** a domestic servant.

me·nin·ges (minin'jēz), *n. pl., sing.* **me·ninx** (mē'ninGks). the three membranes (dura mater, arachnoid, pia mater) enveloping the brain and spinal cord.

men·in·gi·tis (men,injī'tis), *n.* inflammation of the meninges.

me·nin·go·coc·cus (məninG,gōkok'əs), *n., pl.* **me·nin·go·coc·ci** (mə·ninG,gōkok'sī). a bacterium that causes meningitis.

me·nis·cus (mənis'kəs), *n., pl.* **me·nis·ci** (mənis'ī), **me·nis·cus·es.** a crescent-shaped body.

me·nol·o·gy (mənol'əjē), *n.* a calendar of the months.

men·o·pause (men'ōpôz), *n.* the period of female life, usually between the ages of 45 and 50, when menstruation stops.

men·o·pha·ni·a (men,ōfā'nēə), *n.* the first appearance of menstrual discharge during puberty.

men·or·rha·gi·a (men,ərā'jēə), *n.* excessive discharge at menstruation.

me·nos·che·sis (menos'kisis), *n.* temporary suppression of menstruation.

men·o·stax·is (men,əstak'sis), *n.* an abnormally long menstrual period.

men·sal (men'səl), *adj.* 1. monthly. 2. relating to or used at the table.

men·ses (men'sēz), *n., pl.* **men·ses.** the blood and tissue debris discharged from the uterus of female higher primates, usually at monthly intervals.

mens sa·na in cor·po·re sa·no (mens sä'nä in kô'pərē sä'nō), *Latin.* a sound mind in a healthy body.

men·stru·al (men'strŏŏəl), *adj.* 1. relating to menstruation or the menses. 2. monthly.

men·stru·ate (men'strŏŏāt,), *v.* to shed the lining of the womb each month (except during pregnancy) during the fertile period of life in a female higher primate. —**men,stru·a'tion,** *n.* —**men'stru·ous,** *adj.*

men·stru·um (men'strŏŏəm), *n., pl.* **men·stru·ums, men·stru·a** (men'strŏŏə). a solvent.

men·sur·a·ble (men'sərəbəl), *adj.* measurable.

men·su·ral (men'sHərəl), *adj.* of or relating to measure.

men·su·ra·tion (mensHərə'sHən), *n.* the branch of mathematics concerned with measuring lengths, areas, and volumes. —**men'su·ra·tive,** *adj.*

men·tal·ism (men'təliz,əm), *n.* the philosophical doctrine that, in the last analysis, mind or consciousness is the ultimate reality and matter or objects of knowledge only a mode or form of mind and thus without existence except within the mind of the perceiver.

men·ti·cide (men'tisīd), *n.* an organized attempt, as by interrogation, beating, etc., to remove a person's previous opinions and replace them by radically different ones; brainwashing.

me·phit·ic (məfit'ik), *adj.* offensive to the smell; noisome.

me·phi·tis (məfī'tis), *n.* any noxious stench.

me·pro·ba·mate (mep,rōbam'āt), *n.* a pharmacological preparation used as a tranquillizer.

mer·cer·ize (mû'sərīz), *v.* to treat (cotton) with a solution of caustic alkali to give greater strength, a silky lustre, and an increased affinity for dye.

mer·cu·ri·al (mûkyŏŏr'ēəl), *adj.* lively; volatile; changeable.

mercy killing. See euthanasia.

mer·div·or·ous (mûdiv'ərəs), *adj.* dungeating; coprophagous.

mer·e·tri·cious (meritrisH'əs), *adj.* showily attractive; flashy; founded on deception.

me·rid·i·o·nal (mərid'ēənəl), *adj.* southern. See also **septentrional.**

mer·i·sis (mer'isis), *n.* biological growth, esp. growth by cell division. See also **auxesis.**

mer·i·toc·ra·cy (mer,itok'rəsē), *n., pl.* **mer·i·toc·ra·cies.** 1. government by persons selected on merit, i.e. by virtue of their skills and talents rather than patronage or wealth. 2. the members of such a government. 3. a social or educational system based on selection and promotion of the talented.

merle (mûl), *adj.* 1. bluish-grey marked with black. —*n.* 2. (in Scotland) another name for the blackbird.

mer·lon (mû'lən), *n.* the part between two crenels in a battlement.

me·rog·o·ny (mərog'ənē), *n.* the production of an embryo from a fragment of an egg not containing a nucleus.

me·ro·pi·a (mərō'pēə), *n.* dullness or obscuration of sight; partial blindness.

me·sa (mā'sə), *n.* high, rocky tableland with precipitous sides, commonly found in desert regions of SW United States and Mexico.

mé·sal·li·ance (mezəl'ēəns), *n.* marriage with a social inferior; a bad or improper association.

mes·cal (meskal'), *n.* a strong intoxicant distilled from the fermented juice of some species of agave.

mescal buttons, the button-like tops of a genus of cacti, dried and used as an intoxicant; peyote.

mes·ca·line (mes'kəlēn, mes'kəlin), *n.* an alkaloid obtained from mescal buttons, capable of producing hallucinations and occasionally used in medicine; peyote.

mes·en·ter·i·tis (mesen,tərī'tis), *n.* inflammation of the mesentery.

mes·en·ter·y (mes'əntərē), *n.* a fold of the peritoneum that attaches the intestinal canal to the posterior wall of the abdomen and supplies it with blood, lymph, and nerves.

me·shu·ga (məsHŏŏg'ə) *adj. Slang.* crazy.

me·sic (mēz'ik), *adj.* of or adapted to an environment with a balanced moisture supply.

mes·mer·ism (mez'məriz,əm), *n.* hypnotism.

mes·mer·ize (mez'mərīz), *v.* to hypnotize.

mes·o·dont (mes'ōdont), *adj.* with teeth of medium size.

mes·o·do·nt·ism (mesōdon'tizm), *n.* the condition of having teeth of medium size. Also **mes'o·don·ty.**

Mes·o·lith·ic (mesōlith'ik), *adj.* pertaining to

the period between the Stone Age and Neolithic Age.

mes·o·me·te·or·ol·o·gy (mes,ōmē,tēərol'-əjē), *n.* the study of relatively small atmospheric disturbances, such as thunderstorms, and of details of larger disturbances.

mes·o·morph (mes'ōmôf,), *n.* a mesomorphic type of person.

mes·o·mor·phic (mes,ōmô'fik), *adj.* 1. relating to or being in an intermediate state. 2. with or relating to a muscular, sturdy body build in which the structures developed from the middle germ layer of the embryo (muscle, blood, connective tissue, etc.) are prominent. See also **ectomorphic, endomorphic.**

mes·o·phil·ic (mes,ōfil'ik), *adj.* (in bacteriology) thriving in temperatures in the moderate range between 25 degrees C and 40 degrees C. —**mes'o·phile,** *adj., n.*

mes·o·phyte (mes'ōfīt,), *n.* one of the class of plants, including most trees for example, that grow under average conditions of water supply.

mes·o·sphere (mes'ōsfē,ə), *n.* 1. the part of the earth's atmosphere between the ionosphere and the exosphere, distinguished from them by its chemical properties, and extending from about 250-650 miles above the earth's surface. 2. the part of the earth's atmosphere between the stratosphere and the thermosphere, distinguished by decreasing temperature with increasing height, and extending from about 20-50 miles above the earth's surface.

mes·o·tho·rax (mes,ōthôr'aks), *n.,* *pl.* **mes·o·thor·ax·es, mes·o·thor·a·ces** (mes,ōthôr'əsēz). the middle segment of the three segments of an insect's thorax, bearing the second pair of walking legs and, in winged insects, the first pair of wings.

Mes·o·zo·ic (mes,ōzō'ik), *adj.* denoting or belonging to the geological era when the rocks above the Palaeozoic rocks were formed, occurring between 220,000,000 and 70,000,000 years ago, comprising the Triassic, Jurassic, and Cretaceous periods, and characterized by the appearance of flowering plants and the evolution and extinction of dinosaurs.

mes·si·an·ic (mes,ēan'ik), *adj.* of, relating to, or characteristic of a messiah, or one who sets free or saves a people.

mes·ti·zo (mestē'zō), *n.,* *pl.* **mes·ti·zos, mes·ti·zoes.** a person of mixed ancestry.

met·a·bi·o·sis (met,əbīō'sis), *n.* a biological association of different organisms in which one depends on another to prepare the environment in which it can live.

me·tab·o·lism (mətab'əliz,əm), *n.* all the chemical processes which govern a living organism including the building up of nutritive matter into living matter, the breaking down of food materials to release energy, and the maintenance and renewal of all parts of the organism. —**met,·a·bol'ic,** *adj.* —**me·tab'o·lize,** *v.*

met·a·car·pus (met,əkä'pəs), *n.,* *pl.* **met·a·car·pi** (met,əkä'pī). the bones of the hand between the wrist and the fingers or of the corresponding part of the front foot in four-legged creatures.

met·a·chro·ma·tism (met,əkrō'mətiz,əm), *n.* a change of colour, esp. that caused by a change in temperature of a body.

me·tach·ro·nal (mətak'rənəl), *adj.* of or relating to a rhythmic wave, esp. of muscular contraction which passes along ciliated tissue of multilimbed creatures causing the cilia or limbs to beat, giving the appearance of wave motion and bringing about locomotion.

met·a·gal·ax·y (met,əgal'əksē), *n.* the entire galactic system, the Milky Way and all the surrounding galaxies.

met·a·in·fec·tive (met,əinfek'tiv), *adj.* of a medical disorder arising after an infection.

met·a·lan·guage (met'əlaNG,gwij), *n.* a language or set of symbols used for describing or analysing another language or set of symbols.

met·a·lin·guis·tics (met,əliNGgwis'tiks), *n.* the study of the interrelationship of languages and the cultures they refer to.

met·al·log·ra·phy (met,əlog'rəfē), *n.* the minute study and description of the structure and properties of metals and alloys.

me·tal·lo·ther·a·py (mɪətal,ōt̸her'əpē), *n.* medical treatment making use of metals or their salts.

met·al·lur·gy (metal'əjē), *n.* the science of extracting, working, compounding, and establishing the properties of metals and their alloys.

met·a·mor·pho·sis (met,əmô'fəsis), *n.,* *pl.* **met·a·mor·pho·ses** (met,əmô'fəsēz). 1. any complete change in structure, substance, appearance, or character, or the form resulting from such a change. 2. a zoological process of rapid change or successive changes from an immature to a mature state. —**met·a·mor'phic, met·a·mor'phous,** *adj.*

met·a·phor (met'əfə, met'əfô,), *n.* a figure of speech in which a word or phrase is applied to a concept to which it is not literally applicable so as to imply a comparison with the word or phrase applied, as *He swallowed his pride.*

met·a·phrase (met'əfrāz,), *n.* 1. a word for word translation. —*v.* 2. to translate word for word. —**met·a·phrast** (met'əfrast), *n.*

met·a·phys·i·cal (met,əfiz'ikəl), *adj.* 1. (in philosophy) dealing with abstract subjects or first principles. 2. abstruse. 3. designating a group of 17th-century English poets, including Donne, Cowley, Herbert, whose style is intellectual and makes use of ingenious imagery and turns of wit.

met·a·phys·ics (met,əfiz'iks), *n.* the branch of philosophy dealing with first principles, as being, substance, space, time, identity, etc.

met·a·pla·sia (met,əplā'zēə), *n.* the transformation of tissue from one type to another, as in some types of cancer. —**met,a·plas'tic,** adj.

met·a·pol·i·tics (met,əpol'itiks), n. Often derog. political theory, esp. of an abstruse nature.

me·tas·ta·sis (mətas'təsis), n., pl. **me·tas·ta·ses** (mətas'təsēz). the transference of disease from a primary focus to one in another part of the body by blood, lymph, or membranes.

me·tas·ta·size (mətas'təsīz), v. (of disease) to achieve metastasis.

met·a·tar·sus (met,ətä'səs), n., pl. **met·a·tar·si** (metətä'sī). the bones of the foot or hind limb between the ankle bone and the toes. —**met·a·tar'sal,** adj.

met·a·the·o·ry (met'əthē,ərē), n. 1. a theory formulated to investigate another theory or set of theories. 2. the study of the nature, objectives, and methods of philosophy.

met·a·the·ri·an (met,əthēr'ēən), adj. 1. of or relating to the Metatheria, the subclass of mammals containing the marsupials. —n. 2. a member of this subclass.

me·tath·e·sis (mətath'isis), n., pl. **me·tath·e·ses** (mətath'isēz). the transposition of letters or sounds in a word. —**me·tath'e·size,** v.

met·a·tho·rax (met,əthôr'aks), n., pl. **met·a·thor·ax·es, met·a·thor·a·ces** (met,əthôr'əsēz). the hindmost of the three segments of an insect's thorax bearing the third pair of walking legs and, in many winged insects, the second pair of wings.

met·a·troph·ic (met,ətrof'ik), adj. living on decayed organic matter; saprophytic.

mete (mēt), v. mete out; to distribute or deal out in measured portions.

met·em·pir·ics (met,empir'iks), n. the branch of philosophy dealing with things outside experience. —**met,em·pir'i·cal,** adj.

me·tem·psy·cho·sis (met,əmsīkō'sis), n., pl. **me·tem·psy·cho·ses** (met,əmsīkō'sez). the supposed migration of the soul at death to another body, human, or animal.

me·te·or·o·gram (mē,tēôr'əgram,), n. a record made by a meteorograph.

me·te·or·o·graph (mē,tēôr'əgräf, mē,tēôr'ə graf), n. an instrument for making simultaneous records of several meteorological conditions.

me·te·or·ol·o·gy (mē,tēərol'əjē), n. the science and study of atmospheric phenomena, esp. for weather forecasting.

me·te·or·o·path·o·log·ic (mē,tēərōpath,ə loj'ik), adj. relating to the harmful effect of climate on health.

meth·a·done (meth'ədōn), n. a synthetic narcotic used as a long-lasting drug to curb an addict's craving for heroin.

meth·ane (mē'thān), n. a flammable, colourless, odourless gas, formed by the decay of organic matter, which, together with water

vapour, ammonia, and hydrogen, was part of the early atmosphere on earth.

me·thyl·tri·ni·tro·ben·zene (mē,thəltrī,nī,- trōben'zēn, meth,əltrī,nī,trōben'zēn), n. See TNT.

me·tic·u·lous (mətik'yələs), adj. very careful and exacting about details.

mé·tier (met'ēā, mā'tyā), n. 1. trade or profession. 2. occupation or activity in which a person has special ability; forte.

mé·tis (mātēs'), n., sing. and pl. a person of mixed blood, esp. a Canadian of French and Indian blood.

met·o·nym (met'ənim), n. an instance of metonymy.

me·ton·y·my (miton'əmē), n. a rhetorical device in which an attribute or related concept is substituted for the name of the thing meant, as bottle for drink. —**met,o·nym'i·cal,** adj.

me·top·ic (mətop'ik), adj. of or relating to the forehead; frontal.

me·tre (mē'tə), n. the basic metric unit of length, equal to 39.37 inches.

me·tre-kil·o·gram-sec·ond (mēt'əkil'ə gramsek'ənd), adj. relating to the system of units in which the metre, kilogram and second are the principal units of measurement. Abbr.: mks, m.k.s., MKS.

me·trol·o·gy (mitrol'əjē), n. the science or system of weights and measures.

me·tro·nym·ic (met,rənim'ik), adj. derived from the name of the mother or of a female ancestor.

me·trop·o·lis (mətrop'əlis), n. a city, esp. a large one with suburbs; the main city of an area. —**met,ro·pol'i·tan,** adj.

met·tle (met'əl), n. natural vigour; spirit.

met·tle·some (met'əlsəm), adj. brave; courageous; showing spirit, or mettle.

meu·nière (mənye,ə), adj. (of food) shallow-fried in butter and served with the butter mixed with lemon juice and chopped parsley to make a sauce.

mez·za·nine (mez'ənēn,), n. an intermediate floor in a building, esp. a low storey between two other stories.

mez·zo·re·lie·vo (met,sōrilē'vō), n. medium relief; carving in which the projection of the design from the plane is intermediate between high and low relief. Also **mez,zo·ri·lie'vo.**

mez·zo·tint (met'sōtint,), n. a method of engraving on copper or steel by roughening the plate uniformly and then scraping away the roughness to different degrees according to whether shadow, half-light, or light is required.

mho (mō), n., pl. **mhos.** a unit of measurement of electrical conductance equal to the conductance of a conductor in which a one-volt potential difference maintains a current of one ampere.

mi·as·ma (mēaz'mə), *n., pl.* **mi·as·ma·ta** (mē-az'mətə), **mi·as·mas.** the foul-smelling gases given off by marshes, putrid matter, etc. —**mi·as'mal, mi·as·mat'ic, mi·as'mic,** *adj.*

mi·cro·aer·o·phil·ic (mī,krōer,əfil'ik), *adj.* (of organisms) needing only a minute amount of free oxygen to live. —**mi,cro·aer'o·phile,** *n.*

mi·cro·am·me·ter (mī,krōam'mētə), *n.* instrument for measuring very small electric currents in microamperes.

mi·cro·am·pere (mī,krōam'pēə), *n.* a unit of measurement of electric current, equal to one millionth of an ampere. *Abbr.:* μA.

mi·cro·a·nal·y·sis (mī,krōənal'isis), *n., pl.* **mi·cro·a·nal·y·ses** (mī,krōənal'isēz). the chemical analysis of minute amounts of substances.

mi·cro·bal·ance (mī'krōbal,əns), *n.* a device for weighing extremely small amounts of chemical substances.

mi·cro·bar (mī'krōbä,), *n.* a unit of atmospheric pressure equal to one millionth of a bar. *Abbr.:* μb. Also **barye.**

mi·cro·bar·o·gram (mī,krōbär'əgram,), *n.* a record made by a microbarograph.

mi·cro·bar·o·graph (mī,krōbär'əgräf,, mī,-krōbär'əgraf,), *n.* a device used in meteorology for making a continuous graph of minute fluctuations in atmospheric pressure.

mi·crobe (mī'krōb), *n.* a minute organism, esp. one causing disease.

mi·cro·bi·cide (mīkrō'bisīd), *n.* a substance which kills microbes.

mi·cro·bi·ol·o·gy (mī,krōbīol'əjē), *n.* the scientific study of microscopically small organisms.

mi·crob·ism (mī'krōbiz,əm), *n.* infection with disease-producing microbes.

mi·cro·cli·mate (mī'krōklī,mit), *n.* the climate of a small locality, as a cave, a wood, a garden, a hillside, a built-up area. See also **macroclimate.**

mi·cro·cli·ma·tol·o·gy (mī,krōklī,mətol'əjē), *n.* the study of microclimates. See also **macroclimatology.**

mi·cro·con·stit·u·ent (mī,'krōkənstich'ŌŌ-ənt), *n.* a constituent of a metal or alloy that is present in a microscopically small amount.

mi·cro·cop·y (mī'krōōkop,ē), *n.* a very small copy, usually made by photographic reduction, of a printed page or a similar item.

mi·cro·cosm (mī'krōōkoz,əm), *n.* a world in miniature; anything regarded as an epitome of the world. See also **macrocosm.**

mi·cro·cou·lomb (mī'krōkŌŌ'lom), *n.* a unit of measurement of electric charge equal to one millionth of a coulomb. *Abbr.:* μC.

mi·cro·cu·rie (mī'krōkyŌŌr,ē), *n.* a unit of measurement of radioactivity equal to one millionth of a curie. *Abbr.:* μCi.

mi·cro·cyte (mī'krōsīt,), *n.* a minute, or abnor-

mally small, blood cell or corpuscle. See also **macrocyte.**

mi·cro·de·tec·tor (mī,krōditek'tə), *n.* **1.** an instrument for measuring minute quantities or changes. **2.** a sensitive device for measuring or detecting minute quantities of electric current.

mi·cro·dis·sec·tion (mī,krōdisek'shən), *n.* the dissection of material under a microscope.

mi·cro·dis·til·la·tion (mī,krōdis,təlä'shən), *n.* the distillation of extremely small quantities of chemical substances.

mi·cro·dont (mī'krōdont,), *adj.* with teeth of abnormally small size. See also **macrodont.**

mi·cro·don·tia (mī,krōdon'shə), *n.* the condition of being microdont or an instance of the condition. Also **mi,cro·dont'ism, mi'cro·don,ty.** See also **macrodontia.**

mi·cro·dyne (mī'krōdīn), *n.* a unit of measurement of force equal to one millionth of a dyne. *Abbr.:* μdyn.

mi·cro·e·co·nom·ics (mī,krōē'kənom'iks), *n.* economics as applied to specific aspects of an economy, as the investment-profit relationship in a company. See also **macroeconomics.** —**mi,cro·e,co·nom'ic,** *adj.*

mi·cro·e·lec·tron·ics (mī,krōilektron'iks), *n.* the science and technology of using microminiaturized components such as solid-state devices in electronic systems.

mi·cro·e·lec·tro·pho·re·sis (mī,krōilek,trōfərē'sis), *n.* a technique used in chemistry for examining under a microscope the migration of minute surface particles under the influence of an electric field.

mi·cro·en·vi·ron·ment, (mī,krōinvī'ərnmənt), *n.* the conditions prevailing in a small area or surrounding one organism in a community.

mi·cro·far·ad (mī'krōfar,əd), *n.* a unit of measurement of electrical capacity equal to one millionth of a farad. *Abbr.:* μF, μf.

mi·cro·fiche (mī'krōfēsh,), *n.* microfilm images grouped in a sheet for filing.

mi·cro·film (mī'krōfilm,), *n.* very small film bearing miniature photographic reproduction of documents, etc., and projected on a screen for reading.

mi·cro·fos·sil (mī'krōfos,il), *n.* a fossil too small to be studied without a microscope.

mi·cro·gram (mī'krōgram,), *n.* a unit of measurement of mass equal to one millionth of a gram. *Abbr.:* μg.

mi·cro·graph (mī'krōgräf, mī'krōgraf,), *n.* **1.** an instrument for writing or engraving minutely. **2.** a photograph or drawing of an item as seen under a microscope. See also **macrograph.**

mi·crog·ra·phy (mīkrog'rəfē), *n.* **1.** the verbal or graphic representation of extremely small objects. **2.** examination or study of an object under a microscope. See also **macrography.**

mi·cro·groove (mī'krōgrŌŌv,), *n.* an extremely narrow needle groove on a gramophone record, used to increase the number of groves and record more material.

mi·cro·hard·ness (mī'krōhard,nis), *n.* a measurement of the hardness of a metal denoting that it was indented by a slight pressure on one small area.

mi·cro·hen·ry (mī'krōhen,rē), *n.*, *pl.* **mi·cro·hen·ries, mi·cro·hen·rys.** a unit of measurement of electrical inductance equal to one millionth of a henry. *Abbr.:* μH.

mi·crohm (mī'krōm), *n.* a unit of measurement of electrical resistance equal to one millionth of an ohm. *Abbr.:* μΩ.

mi·cro·im·age (mī'krōim,ij), *n.* a photographic reproduction of such small scale that it cannot be seen clearly without a microscope.

mi·cro·inch (mī'krōinCH,), *n.* a unit used in measuring length, equal to one millionth of an inch. *Abbr.:* μin.

mi·cro·in·jec·tion (mī,krōinjek'sHən), *n.* an injection made under a microscope.

mi·cro·lam·bert (mi'krōlam,bət), *n.* a unit used in measuring brightness, equal to one millionth of a lambert. *Abbr.:* μL.

mi·cro·lith (mī'krōlith), *n.* a small flint usually worked to triangular shape for mounting on a handle or shaft and using as a cutting tool or barbed weapon, common in mesolithic and early neolithic times. —mi,cro·lith'ic, *adj.*

mi·cro·li·tre (mi'krōlē'tə), *n.* a metric unit used in measuring capacity, equal to one millionth of a litre. *Abbr.:* μl.

mi·crol·o·gy (mīkrol'əje), *n.* excessive consideration of minute matters.

mi·cro·lux (mī'krəluks,), *n.* a unit used in measuring illumination, equal to one millionth of a lux. *Abbr.:* μlx.

mi·cro·me·te·or·ite (mi,kroəmē'tēərīt), *n.* a minute meteorite, usually less than a millimetre in diameter.

mi·cro·me·te·or·o·gram (mi,krōmē,tēor'əgram,), *n.* a record made by a micrometeorograph.

mi·cro·me·te·or·o·graph (mī,krōmē,tēor'əgräf,, mī,krōmē,tēor'əgraf,), *n.* a small instrument for use in aircraft for making a simultaneous record of various atmospheric conditions, an adapted form of the meteorograph.

mi·cro·me·te·or·ol·o·gy (mī,krōmē,tēərol'əjē), *n.* the study of small atmospheric phenomena and usually only those that occur in a shallow layer of air immediately above the ground.

mi·crom·e·ter (mīkrom'itə), *n.* any of several precision instruments used to measure minute distances and angles.

mi·cro·me·tre (mī'krōmē,tə), *n.* a metric unit of length equal to one millionth of a metre. Formerly called micron. *Abbrev.:* μm.

mi·crom·e·try (mīkrom'itrē), *n.* the taking of measurements with a micrometer.

mi·cro·mho (mī'krōmō), *n.* a unit of measurement of electrical conductance equal to one millionth of a mho. *Abbr.:* μmho.

mi·cro·mi·cro·cu·rie (mī,krōmī,krōkyoor'ē), *n.* a unit used in measuring radioactivity, equal to one millionth of a microcurie. *Abbr.:* μμCi.

mi·cro·mi·cro·far·ad (mī,krōmī,krōfar'əd) *n.* a unit used in measuring electrical capacity, equal to one millionth of a microfarad. *Abbr.:* μμF.

mi·cro·mi·cron (mī'krōmī,kron), *n.*, *pl.* **mi·cro·mi·crons, mi·cro·mi·cra** (mī'krōmī,krə). (formerly) a a metric unit used in measuring length, equal to one millionth of a micron. *Abbr.:* μμ, mu mu.

mi·cro·mil·li·me·tre (mī,krōmil'əmē,tə), *n.* a metric unit used in measuring length, equal to one millionth of a millimetre. *Abbr.:* μmm.

mi·cro·min·i·a·ture (mī,krōmin'ēəCHə), *adj.* of extremely minute size, esp. of small electronic devices using solid-state components.

mi·cro·min·i·a·tur·i·za·tion (mī,krōmin,ēəCHərizā'sHən), *n.* extreme size reduction, esp. the making small of electronic devices by using solid-state components instead of vacuum tubes. —mi·cro·min'i·a·tur·ize, *v.*

mi·cron, mi·kron (mī'kron), *n.*, *pl.* **mi·crons, mi·krons, mi·cra, mi·kra** (mī'krə). **1.** (formerly) a metric unit used in measuring length, equal to one millionth of a metre. See **micrometre.** *Abbr.:* μ, mu. **2.** a colloidal particle with a diameter between .2 and 10 millionths of a metre.

mi·cro·ne·mous (mī,krənē'məs), *adj.* with short filaments.

mi·cro·nu·cle·us (mī,krōnyōō'klēəs), *n.*, *pl.* **mi·cro·nu·cle·i** (mī,krōnyōō'klēī). the smaller of the two kinds of nuclear material present in ciliated organisms, the other kind being the macronucleus. —mi·cro·nu'cle·ate, *adj.*

mi·cro·or·gan·ism (mī,krōō'gəniz,əm), *n.* any of the organisms too small to be seen by the naked eye, as bacteria, viruses, etc.

mi·cro·pa·lae·on·tol·o·gy (mī,krōpā,lēən·tol'əjē), *n.* the scientific study of microfossils.

mi·cro·par·a·site (mī,krōpar'əsīt), *n.* a microorganism which lives in or on another organism from which it gets its food.

mi·cro·pa·thol·o·gy (mī,krōpəthol'əjē), *n.* the scientific study of the microscopic effects of disease on cells and tissue.

mi·cro·phage (mī'krōfāj), *n.* a minute cell that engulfs particles in its surroundings, present particularly in the blood or lymph where it is part of the defence mechanism against bacteria. See also **macrophage.**

mi·cro·phon·ism (mī,krəfō'niz,əm), *n.* a fault in an electronic device whereby the signal being transmitted is interfered with by noise produced by a vibrating component. —**mi,cro·phon'ic,** *adj.* —**mi,cro·phon'ics,** *n.*

mi·cro·pho·to·graph (mī,krōfō'təgräf,, mī,-krōfō'təgraf,), *n.* **1.** microfilm. **2.** a photograph so small that it cannot be seen clearly without being enlarged. **3.** a photomicrograph.

mi·cro·pho·tom·e·ter (mī,krōfōtom'itə), *n.* an instrument for measuring light intensity given out, transmitted, or reflected by minute objects.

mi·cro·phyl·lous (mī,krōfil'əs), *adj.* with very small leaves. See also **macrophyllous.**

mi·cro·phys·ics (mī,krōfiz'iks), *n.* the science of the physical properties of objects too small to be dealt with directly, as atoms, molecules, etc. See also **macrophysics.**

mi·cro·phyte (mi'krōfīt,), *n.* a plant too small to be seen clearly without a microscope.

mi·cro·po·rous (mī,krōpôr'əs), *adj.* consisting of or having microscopic pores.

mi·cro·print (mī'krōprint,), *n.* a print of a microphotograph for reading or viewing under a magnifying glass.

mi·crop·si·a (mīkrop'sēə), *n.* a condition of the eye which causes objects to be seen smaller than life-size. See also **macropsia.**

mi·cro·py·rom·e·ter (mī,krōpīrom'Itə), *n.* an adaptation of an optical pyrometer to deal with minute objects, by means of which temperatures above 55 degrees C are measured according to their degree of incandescence.

mi·cro·read·er (mī'krōrē,də), *n.* a device for projecting microfilm or microphotographic images onto a screen to give sufficient enlargement for them to be seen clearly.

mi·cro·re·pro·duc·tion (mī,krōrē,prəduk'-sHən), *n.* a photographic image too small to be seen clearly without being magnified.

mi·cro·sec·ond (mī'krōsek,ənd), *n.* a unit of measurement of time equal to one millionth of a second. *Abbr.:* μs, μsec.

mi·cro·seism (mī'krəsī,zəm), *n.* a small tremor in the earth's crust recorded by a seismograph and supposed to be caused by an earthquake or a storm at sea.

mi·cro·sie·mens (mī'krōsē,mənz), *n.* a unit of measurement of electrical conductance equal to one millionth of a siemens. *Abbr.:* μS.

mi·cro·spec·tro·pho·tom·e·ter (mī,krōspek,trōfōtom'itə), *n.* an instrument for examining the light given out, transmitted, or reflected by inanimate objects.

mi·cro·stat (mī'krōstat,), *n.* a photographic copy of a negative of a microphotograph.

mi·cro·steth·o·scope (mī,krōsteth'əskōp,), *n.* a stethoscope adapted to pick up and greatly amplify minute sounds.

mi·cro·stom·a·tous (mī,krōstom'ətəs), *adj.* with an extremely small mouth or opening.

mi·cro·struc·ture (mī'krōstruk,cHə), *n.* the size, shape, and detailed arrangement of crystals

in a metal or alloy as seen under a powerful microscope after etching and polishing. See also **macrostructure.**

mi·cro·switch (mī'krōswicH,), *n.* an extremely sensitive switch used in automatically controlled machines.

mi·cro·therm (mī'krōthûm,), *n.* a plant which grows in conditions of minimum heat.

mi·cro·tome (mī'krōtōm,), *n.* a machine for cutting extremely thin slices of tissue, usually frozen or embedded in paraffin wax, for easy examination under a microscope. —**mi'crot'o·my,** *n.*

mi·cro·volt (mī'krōvōlt,), *n.* a unit used in measuring electromotive force, equal to one millionth of a volt. *Abbr.:* μV.

mi·cro·watt (mī'krōwot,), *n.* a unit used in measuring electric power, equal to one millionth of a watt. *Abbr.:* μW.

mi·cro·wave (mī'krōwāv,), *n.* **1.** a very high frequency electromagnetic (radio) wave, usually one with a wavelength less than 20 cm. **2.** Informal for **microwave oven** or **cooker,** a device that cooks food by means of microwaves.

mic·tu·rate (mik'cHərāt), *v.* to urinate, esp. to urinate with uncontrollable frequency. —**mic,-tu·ri'tion,** *n.*

mid·den (mid'ən), *n.* (*usually* **kitchen midden**) an archaeological site of refuse from a prehistoric settlement.

Middle Ages, the period in European history between ancient and modern times, generally applied to the time between the fall of the western Roman Empire in A.D. 476 and the general establishment of the Renaissance about 1450, but sometimes referring to only the part of this period after 1100.

mid·dle·weight (midə'lwāt,), *n..* a boxer of the class intermediate between light middleweight and light heavyweight in amateur boxing, welterweight and light heavyweight in professional boxing, and weighing 167 lbs. or less if an amateur, 160 lbs. or less if a professional.

midge (mij), *v.* any one of many minute kinds of two-winged biting insects.

mid·i·nette (mid,inet'), *n.* a Parisian shop girl or seamstress.

mid·rash (mid'rasH), *n., pl.* **mid·ra·shim** (midrasH'im). **1.** a Jewish commentary on or explanation of a biblical text. **2.** a collection of midrashim, esp. those of the first millennium of the Christian era.

mien (mēn), *n.* a person's appearance, bearing, or manner, esp. as reflective of character, attitude, etc.

mi·gnon (min'yon), *adj.* small and delicately formed. Also (of a woman) **mi·gnonne'.**

mi·graine (mē'grān, mī'grān), *n.* recurrent paroxysmal headache in one side of the head, following nausea and vomiting and sometimes accompanied by visual disturbances.

mi·kron (mī'kron), *n.*, *pl.* **mi·krons, mi·kra** (mī'krə). micron.

mil (mil), *n.* a unit of measurement of length equal to a thousandth of an inch, used in measuring the thickness of wires, sheets of plastic, etc.

mil·a·nese (mil‚ənēz', mil'ənāz‚), *adj.* (of meat) served with pasta, esp. macaroni, that has been topped with a tomato sauce flavoured with finely chopped meat, mushrooms, and grated cheese.

milch (milCH), *adj.* giving milk; kept for milking.

mil·i·ar·i·a (mil‚ēer'ēə), *n.* a skin disease characterized by small red pustules resembling millet seeds erupting around the sweat glands; prickly heat; miliary fever.

mi·lieu (mēlyû'), *n.* environment; surrounding conditions.

mil·i·tate (mil'itāt), *v.* (of facts, evidence, attitudes, etc.) to exert force; influence, as *Their disapproval militated against a speedy settlement.*

milk·sop (milk'sop‚), *n.* an effeminate man or one lacking in spirit.

milk·toast (milk'tōst‚), *adj.* (of a man) easily dominated; completely lacking in assertiveness.

Milky Way, the band of faint diffuse light, visible at night in the sky, composed of many stars too distant to be seen individually with the naked eye.

mill (mil), *n.* a U.S. unit of money equal to a thousandth of a dollar, used in accounting, esp. in calculating property taxes.

mill·dam (mil'dam‚), *n.* a dam across a stream to build up a force of water to operate a mill wheel.

mille-feuille (mēlfoi'), *n.* a sweet dessert of custard or whipped cream filling in a flat, rectangular base and top of flaky puff pastry with fondant and usually flavoured with fruit; *U.S. name* Napoleon.

mil·le·fi·o·ri (mil'əfēôr'ē), *n.* decorative glass made by fusing bundles of different coloured glass rods together and slicing them into discs to give flowerlike pieces which are grouped in clear glass for blowing to a desired form.

mille·fleur (mēlflû'), *adj.* with a flowered background.

mil·le·nar·i·an (mil‚əner'ēən), *adj.* of or relating to the millennium.

mil·le·nar·y (mil'əner‚ē), *adj.* 1. consisting of or relating to a thousand, esp. a thousand years. 2. relating to the millennium.

mil·len·ni·al (milen'ēəl), *adj.* of or relating to a millennium.

mil·len·ni·um (milen'ēəm), *n.*, *pl.* **mil·len·ni·ums, mil·len·ni·a** (milen'ēə). 1. a period of a thousand years. 2. the period of a thousand

years when Christ will reign on earth, as prophesied in the Book of Revelations. 3. a supposedly coming period of general happiness, prosperity, and justice.

mil·les·i·mal (miles'əməl), *adj.* thousandth.

mil·li·am·me·ter (mil‚ēam'mē‚tə), *n.* an instrument for measuring small electric currents in milliamperes.

mil·li·am·pere (mil‚ēam'pēə), *n.* a unit used in measuring electric current, equal to one thousandth of an ampere. *Abbr.:* **mA.**

mil·li·ang·strom (mil‚ēaNG'strəm), *n.* a unit used to express light wavelengths, equal to one thousandth of an angstrom. *Abbr.:* **mÅ.**

mil·li·ard (mil'ēäd), *n.* (in Britain, formerly) one thousand millions, a billion.

mil·li·are (mil'ēe‚ə), *n.* a unit used in measuring area, equal to one thousandth of an are.

mil·li·ar·y (mil'ēer‚ē), *adj.* indicating a mile.

mil·li·bar (mil'ibä‚), *n.* a unit used in measuring atmospheric pressure equal to one thousandth of a bar. *Abbr.:* **mb, mbar.**

mil·li·barn (mil'ibän‚), *n.* a unit used in measuring a nuclear cross-section, equal to one thousandth of a barn. *Abbr.:* **mb.**

mil·li·cou·lomb (mil'ikōō‚lom), *n.* a unit of measurement of electrical charge equal to one thousandth of a coulomb. *Abbr.:* **mC.**

mil·li·cur·ie (mil'ikyōōr‚ē), *n.* a unit of measurement of radioactivity equal to one thousandth of a curie. *Abbr.:* **mCi.**

mil·lier (mēlyā'), *n.* a unit of measurement of weight equal to one thousand kilograms. Also **tonneau.**

mil·li·far·ad (mil'ifar‚əd), *n.* a unit of measurement of electrical capacity equal to one thousandth of a farad. *Abbr.:* **mF.**

mil·li·gal (mil'igal‚), *n.* a unit used in measuring acceleration, equal to one thousandth of a gal. *Abbr.:* **mGal.**

mil·li·gram (mil'igram‚), *n.* a unit used in measuring weight, equal to one thousandth of a gram. *Abbr.:* **mg.**

mil·li·gram-hour (mil‚igram‚our'), *n.* a unit used in measuring doses of radium received by a person undergoing radiotherapy, equal to the amount of radiation received by exposure for one hour to one milligram of radium.

mil·li·hen·ry (mil'ihen‚rē), *n.* a unit used in measuring electrical inductance, equal to one thousandth of a henry. *Abbr.:* **mH.**

mil·li·lam·bert (mil'ilam‚bût), *n.* a unit used in measuring brightness, equal to one thousandth of a lambert. *Abbr.:* **mL.**

mil·li·li·tre (mil'ilē‚tə), *n.* a unit used in measuring capacity, equal to one thousandth of a litre. *Abbr.:* **ml.**

mil·li·lux (mil'iluks‚), *n.* a unit of measurement of illumination, equal to one thousandth of a lux. *Abbr.:* **mlx.**

mil·li·me·tre (mil'imē,tə), *n.* a unit of measurement of length equal to one thousandth of a metre. *Abbr.*: mm.

mil·li·mho (mil'imō,), *n.* a unit used in measuring electrical conductance, equal to one thousandth of a mho. *Abbr.*: mmho.

mil·li·mi·cron (mil'imī,kron), *n.*, *pl.* **mil·li·mi·crons, mil·li·mi·cra** (mil'imī,krə). (formerly) a unit used in measuring length, equal to one thousandth of a micron. *Abbr.*: mμ, mmu.

mil·li·mole (mil'imōl,), *n.* a unit used to express the amount of substance equal to one thousandth of a mole. *Abbr.*: mmol.

mil·line (mil'līn,), *n.* an advertisement consisting of one line of agate-size type across one column appearing in one million copies of a newspaper or magazine.

mil·li·ohm (mil'ēōm,), *n.* a unit used in measuring electrical resistance, equal to one thousandth of an ohm. *Abbr.*: mΩ.

mil·li·poise (mil'ipoiz,), *n.* a unit used in the measurement of viscosity equal to one thousandth of a poise. *Abbr.*: mP.

mil·li·rem (mil'irem,), *n.* a unit used in measuring dosage of radioactivity, equal to one thousandth of a rem. *Abbr.*: mrem.

mil·li·roent·gen (mil'irent,gən), *n.* a unit of measurement of x-ray dosage, equal to one thousandth of a roentgen. *Abbr.*: mR.

mil·li·sec·ond (mil'isek,ənd), *n.* a unit of measurement of time equal to one thousandth of a second. *Abbr.*: ms, msec.

mil·li·sie·mens (mil'isē,mənz), *n.* a unit used in measuring electrical conductance, equal to one thousandth of a siemens. *Abbr.*: mS.

mil·li·volt (mil'ivōlt,), *n.* a unit used in measuring electromotive force, equal to one thousandth of a volt. *Abbr.*: mV.

mil·li·watt (mil'iwot,), *n.* a unit used in measuring electric power, equal to one thousandth of a watt. *Abbr.*: mW.

milque·toast (milk'tōst,), *n.* a milk toast.

milt (milt), *n.* the roe or reproductive gland of male fish.

milt·er (mil'tə), *n.* a male fish during the breeding season.

Mil·town (mil'toun), *n.* trade name of a preparation of the tranquillizing drug meprobamate.

mi·me·sis (mimē'sis), *n.* mimicry in which one species of animal develops for its protection against predators a similar colouring or marking to another species which is protected from predators, by being poisonous for example. —**mi·met·ic** (mimet'ik), *adj.*

mi·na·cious (minā'shəs), *adj.* threatening.

min·a·to·ry (min'ətərē), *adj.* threatening.

min·er·al·o·gy (min,ərol'əjē, min,əral'əjē), *n.* the scientific study of minerals. —**min·er·al'o·gist**, *n.*

min·e·stro·ne (min,əstrō'nē), *n.* a thick Italian soup made with many vegetables, herbs, and pieces of pasta in meat stock, usually served with finely grated Parmesan cheese.

ming (miNG), *n.* the porcelain produced in China during the Ming dynasty (1368–1644), esp. before 1620 by the imperial factory, characterized by fine porcelain bodies decorated with brilliantly coloured underglaze or enamel.

min·gy (min'jē), *adj.* mean; niggardly.

min·i·a·tur·ize (min'ēəCHərīz), *v.* to make a small version; to reduce in size.

min·i·fy (min'əfī), *v.* to make smaller; minimize.

min·i·kin (min'ikin), *n.* a delicate or diminutive person or object.

min·im (min'im), *n.* the smallest unit of fluid measure, equal to one sixtieth of a fluid dram. *Abbr.*: M, min.

min·i·mal (min'iməl), *adj.* being the smallest or of the least possible extent or size, as *minimal talent.*

min·i·ma·lism (min'iməliz,əm), *n.* **1.** Also **minimal art.** a style of abstract painting or sculpture involving simple geometric forms and unassertive tones to create coolly impersonal and unemotional works; it emerged in the 1960s through such artists as Carl Andre and Tony Smith. **2.** a musical style characterized by the gradual evolution of repeated figures, as in the works of Steve Reich and Philip Glass. **3.** any artistic work, design, or style that employs the minimum content to achieve its aims. —**min'i·mal·ist**,, *n.*

min·i·max (min'imaks), *n.* a strategy used in games to reduce to the utmost a player's possible loss. See also **maximin.**

min·i·mus (min'iməs), *n.* **1.** the smallest or least important person or item in a classification. **2.** the little finger or toe.

min·ion (min'yən), *n.* a servile follower or a favourite of a person in power; a minor official.

min·ne·sing·er (min'isiNG,ə), *n.*, *sing.* and *pl.* German lyric poets and songwriters of the 12th to 14th centuries.

min·u·end (min'yŏŏend), *n.* a number or quantity from which another is subtracted. See also **subtrahend.**

mi·nus·cule (min'əskyŏŏl), *adj.* **1.** very small. **2.** of a cursive script developed in the 7th century using small, non-capital letters. See also **majuscule.**

mi·nu·ti·a (mīnyŏŏ'sHēə, minŏŏ'sHēə), *n.* usually in *pl.* **mi·nu·ti·ae** (mīnyŏŏ'sHēī, minŏŏ'sHēī). small details; trivial points.

minx (miNGks), *n.* a pert or flirtatious girl.

Mi·o·cene (mī'əsēn) *adj.* of or relating to the geological epoch (and the rock systems formed during it) that occurred between the Oligocene and Pliocene epochs that lasted from about 25 million to 15 million years ago, and was characterized by the presence of grazing mammals.

mi·o·sis, my·o·sis (mīō'sis) *n., pl.* **mi·o·ses** (mīō'sēz). a medical condition in which the pupil of the eye is abnormally constricted, as by drugs, etc. —**mi·ot·ic** (mīot'ik), *adj.*

mi·ra·bi·le dic·tu (mēra'bilā dik'tōō), *Latin.* wonderful to relate, strange to tell.

mire·poix (mērpwä'), *n.* a garnish of diced vegetables, herbs, seasonings, and chopped ham cooked in butter or with the meat or fish with which it is to be served.

mis·al·li·ance (mis,əlī'əns), *n.* 1. an unsuitable association, esp. marriage. 2. mésalliance.

mis·al·ly (mis,əlī'), *v.* to make a misalliance.

mis·an·dry (mis'əndrē), *n.* hatred of men. —**mis·an'drist**, *n., adj.* —**mis·an'drous**, *adj.*

mis·an·thrope (mis'ənthrōp,, miz'ənthrōp,), *n.* one who hates mankind or shuns company.

mis·an·thro·py (misan,thrəpē, mizan'thrəpē), *n.* hatred, dislike, or avoidance of mankind. —**mis·an·thro'pic**, *adj.*

mis·be·got·ten (mis,bigot'ən), *adj.* illegitimate; ill-conceived.

mis·ce·ge·na·tion (mis,ijənā'sHən), *n.* marriage or cohabitation between couples of different race.

mis·cel·la·ne·a (mis,əlā'nēə), *n. pl.* a miscellany of writings or objects; a random collection.

mis·ci·ble (mis'əbəl), *adj.* capable of being mixed.

mis·cre·ance (mis'krēəns), *n.* a false belief or religious faith.

mis·cre·ant (mis'krēənt), *adj.* 1. depraved; villainous. 2. holding a false belief or religious faith. —**mis'cre·an·cy**, *n.*

mis·de·mean·ant (mis,dimē'nənt), *n.* one who has performed a misdeed or misbehaved.

mise en scène (mēz, än sen'), *French.* the producer's arrangement of all matters relating to the staging of a play, including the acting, sets, costumes, lighting, etc.

mis·fea·sance (misfē'zəns), *n.* the wrongful exercise of lawful authority. See also **malfeasance.** —**mis·fea'sor**, *n.*

mis·giv·ing (misgiv'iNG), *n.* doubt or hesitation, as *I have misgivings about accepting the invitation.*

mis·hap (mis'hap), *n.* an unfortunate occurrence; accident.

mis·no·mer (misnō'mə), *n.* a name wrongly applied.

mis·o·cai·ne·a (mis,ōkī'nēə), *n.* an abnormally strong dislike of all things new.

mi·sog·a·my (misog'əmē), *n.* hatred of marriage. —**mi·sog'a·mist**, *n.*

mi·sog·y·ny (misoj'ənē), *n.* hatred of women. —**mi·sog'y·nist**, *n.*

mi·sol·o·gy (misol'əjē), *n.* strong aversion to reason or reasoning.

mis·o·ne·ism (mis,ōnē'iz,əm), *n.* hatred of newness or change.

mis·o·pae·di·a, mis·o·pe·di·a (mis,ōpē'dēə), *n.* hatred of children, esp. of one's own children.

mis·pri·sion (misprizH'ən), *n.* 1. a wrongful act, esp. by a public official. 2. contempt; disdain.

mis·prize (misprīz'), *v.* to despise; to fail to appreciate rightly.

mist·bow (mist'bō,), *n.* See **fog bow.**

mith·ri·da·tism (mith'ridā,tiz,əm), *n.* the making of a person proof against a poison by dosing with gradually increasing amounts of it.

mith·ri·da·tize (mith'ridā,tīz), *v.* to make a person proof against a poison by dosing with gradually increasing amounts of it.

mit·i·cide (mit'isīd), *n.* a chemical for killing mites.

mit·i·gate (mit'əgāt), *v.* to make or become less intense or severe.

mi·to·sis (mītō'sis), *n.* the usual process of cell division, in which the nucleus splits into two, each chromosome duplicates, and one of each pair of chromosomes groups with one or other nucleus so that two identical cells result.

mi·tral valve (mī'trəl), a valve consisting of two triangular flaps of membrane and located between the atrium and ventricle of the left side of the heart to prevent blood from flowing back into the atrium when the ventricle contracts. Also **bicuspid valve.**

mix·ol·o·gy (miksol'əjē), *n.* (in colloquial humour) the art of preparing cocktails. —**mix·ol'o·gist**, *n.*

mne·me (nē'mē), *n.* that feature of the mind or of an organism which accounts for memory.

mne·mon·ic (nəmon'ik), *adj.* 1. for use in helping to remember something. —*n.* 2. any device, trick, or other means used to aid the memory.

mne·mon·ics (nēmon'iks), *n.* the art of aiding or improving the memory. —**mne·mon'ic**, *adj.*

Mö·bi·us strip (mū'bēəs), a continuous one-sided surface formed from a rectangular strip by twisting one end through a complete turn about the longitudinal axis and joining it to the other end.

mob·oc·ra·cy (mobok'rəsē), *n.* government by a mob.

mock·he·ro·ic (mok'hirō'ik), *adj.* burlesquely imitating heroic style, as in manner, action, literary form.

mo·derne (mōdûn'), *adj. Chiefly U.S.* noting a style of the 1920s and 1930s characterized by linear geometric motifs executed in solid-coloured materials with much use of plastics and enamelware; Art Deco.

mod·i·cum (mod'əkəm), *n.* a small amount; a reasonably modest quantity.

mo·diste (mōdēst'), *n.* a maker or seller of women's fashions, esp. dresses and millinery.

mod·u·lar (moj'ələ, mod'yələ), *adj.* **1.** (of a part) characterized by being of standard shape and size or comprising a fixed pattern of elements for use in or fitting to a complex device or structure. **2.** consisting of two or more standard parts; made up from modular elements.

mod·ule (mod'yōōl), *n.* a measurement that may range from a few inches to several feet selected as the basis in planning or standardizing a building, building components, a range of furniture, etc. —**mod'u·lar,** *adj.*

mo·dus o·pe·ran·di (mō'dəs op,eran'dē), *Latin.* way of working; system of operation.

mo·dus vi·ven·di (mō'dəs viven'dē), way or mode of living.

mo·fette (mōfet'), *n.* an unpleasant-smelling emanation of carbon dioxide, with some oxygen and nitrogen, from a nearly extinct volcano, coming through a small fissure in the earth's crust.

mog·i·la·li·a (mojələ'lēə), *n.* any defect in speech.

mo·go·te (məgō'tē), *n.* a hillock of cavity-riddled limestone left standing between flat valleys.

Mo·hole (mō'hōl), *n.* a hole drilled through the earth's crust, through the Mohorovičić discontinuity, and into the mantle beneath, for geological research into the mantle.

Mo·ho·ri·vi·čič discontinuity (mō'hōrō'-vəcHicH), the boundary between the earth's crust and the mantle below it, distinguished from them in its physical properties, and occurring on average at 22 miles below the continents and 6 miles below the ocean bed.

moi·e·ty (moi'itē), *n.* **1.** a half. **2.** one of two portions or divisions of something.

moil (moil), *v.* **1.** to toil; drudge. —*n.* **2.** hard work; drudgery. **3.** turmoil; confusion.

moi·ré (mwarā'), *adj.* (of fabrics) watered; with a marking that suggests rippling water.

moit (moit), *n.* a foreign body in wool, as a seed, splinter, etc.

mole (mōl), *n.* a very large structure, usually of stone, built in water to act as a pier or breakwater.

molecular film, a layer or film of the thickness of one molecule. Also **monolayer.**

mol·e·cule (mol'ikyōōl), *n.* the smallest particle of a substance that can exist in a free state without losing its chemical identity, consisting of a minute group of atoms, one or more like atoms in the case of chemical elements and two or more different atoms in the case of chemical compounds. —**mo·lec'u·lar,** *adj.*

mol·les·cent (məles'ənt), *adj.* softening, tending to become soft.

mol·li·fy (mol'ifī), *v.* to appease, to calm down.

Mo·lo·tov cocktail (mol'ətof), a homemade fire bomb consisting of a bottle filled with flammable liquid and fitted with a wick which is ignited just before it is thrown so that when the bottle is smashed against its target, the flaming liquid spreads.

mo·men·tous (mōmen'təs), *adj.* significant; meaningful, as an event.

mom·ism (mom'izəm), *n. U.S.* excessive dependence on a mother figure with resulting inhibition of maturity.

mon·a·chal (mon'əkəl), *adj.* monastic.

mon·ad (mon'ad, mō'nad),´*n.* any one-celled organism.

mo·nan·dry (mənan'drē), *n.* the custom or state of having only one husband at a time. See also **polyandry.** —**mo·nandrous,** *adj.*

mon·arch (mon'ək), *n.* **1.** a hereditary sovereign, as a king, emperor, etc. **2.** a supreme ruler. **3.** a large orange butterfly with black and white markings.

mon·ar·chy (mon'əkē), *n.* a government or state in which the actual or titular ruler is a monarch. —**mo·nar'chal, mo·nar'chi·cal,** *adj.*

mon·au·ral (monôr'əl), *adj.* See **monophonic.**

mon·e·tar·ism (mun'itəriz,əm), *n.* the economic theory that tight control of the money supply is the key element in curbing inflation and regulating the economy. —**mon'e·tar·ist,** *n.,* *adj.*

mon·i·to·ry (mon'itərē, mon'itrē), *adj.* **1.** cautioning or reproving. Also **mon·i·to'ri·al.** —*n.,* *pl.* **mon·i·to·ries. 2.** a letter containing a caution or admonition.

mon·go (moNG'gō), *n.* See **mungo.**

mon·gol·ism (moNG'gəliz,m), *n.* a congenital defect in which the subject has a broad, flat skull, high cheekbones, flattened nose, and slanting eyes, and is usually mentally subnormal.

mon·grel·ize (muNG'grəlīz), *v.* to mix, esp. to interbreed, different races, breeds, kinds.

mon·ism (mon'izəm), *n.* a metaphysical theory that there is only one basis of all reality and that mind and matter are not distinct entities. See also **dualism, pluralism.**

mo·ni·tion (mōnisH'ən), *n.* a warning; a caution.

mon·o·car·pic (mon,ōkä'pik), *adj.* (in plants) bearing fruit only once and then dying.

mon·o·chro·mat·ic (mon,ōkrōmat'ik), *adj.* of one colour.

mon·o·chro·ma·tism (mon,ōkrō'mətiz,əm), *n.* a defect of the eye, in which no differences of colour are perceived.

mon·o·chrome (mon'əkrōm,), *n.* a painting or drawing executed in different shades of one colour.

mon·o·clo·nal antibody (mon,ōklō'nəl), *n.* any antibody of a specific desired type produced by a clone of identical cells cultured in the laboratory, widely used in biochemistry and medicine. *Abbr.:* **mAb.**

mon·o·coque (mon'ōkok), *n.* a type of construction of aircraft, boats, cars, etc., in which the fuselage, outer casing, or skin bears all or most of the structural loads.

mo·noc·ra·cy (mōnok'rəsē), *n.* autocracy; government by one person.

mon·o·crat (mon'əkrat,), *n.* a believer in monocracy.

mo·noc·u·lar (monok'yələ), *adj.* 1. one-eyed. 2. of, relating to, or adapted for one eye, as a telescope.

mon·o·cul·ture (mon'ōkul,CHə), *n.* the cultivation of only one kind of crop.

mon·o·dac·ty·lous (mon,ōdak'tiləs), *adj.* with only one finger, toe, or claw.

mo·nod·o·mous (monod'əməs), *adj.* living in a single nest, as ants and wasps. See also **polydomous.**

mon·o·dra·ma (mon'ōdrä,mə), *n.* a dramatic work for performance by a single person.

mon·o·dy (mon'ədē), *n.* a threnody in which one person laments the death of another.

mo·noe·cious (mone'sHəs), *adj.* hermaphroditic; gynandromorphic.

mon·o·fil·a·ment (mon,ōfil'əmənt), *n.* a single, comparatively large filament of a synthetic fibre, as used in a fishing line.

mo·nog·a·my (monog'əmē), *n.* the practice or condition of being married to only one person at a time. See also **polygamy. —mon·o·gam'ic, mo·nog'a·mous,** *adj.* **—mo·nog'a·mist,** *n.*

mon·o·gen·e·sis (mon,ōjen'isis), *n.* the supposed descent of all mankind from one couple. Also **mo·nog'e·ny. —mo·nog'e·nous, mon·o·ge·net'ic,** *adj.*

mon·o·gen·ic (mon,ōjen'ik), *adj.* bearing only male offspring or only female offspring.

mo·nog·e·nism (monoj'əniz,əm), *n.* the theory that all mankind descended from one couple or from one type of ancestor.

mon·o·graph (mon'əgräf,, mon'əgraf,), *n.* a treatise on a single subject or single class of subjects, as on an author or the works of an author.

mo·nog·y·ny (monoj'ənē), *n.* the custom or state of having only one wife at a time. See also **polygyny. —mo·nog'y·nist,** *n.*

mon·o·ki·ni (mon,əki'nē), *n.* a topless bathing suit for women.

mo·nol·a·try (monol'ətrē), *n.* the worship of one god out of a number accepted as existing.

mon·o·lay·er (mon,ōlā'ə), *n.* See **molecular film.**

mon·o·lith (mon'əlith), *n.* 1. a single large piece of stone or similar material. 2. a large political or social structure giving an impression of unbreakable unity. **—mon,o·lith'ic,** *adj.*

mon·o·logue (mon'əlog,), *n.* a long uninterrupted speech or dramatic presentation by one person speaking alone. See also **duologue.**

mo·nol·o·gy (monol'əjē), *n.* the practice or act of a person speaking to himself, discoursing at length, or performing a work or part of a work which is written for a single person speaking alone.

mon·o·ma·ni·a (mon,ōmā'nēə), *n.* an obsessive enthusiasm for a single idea, interest, pursuit, etc.

mo·nom·er·ous (monom'ərəs), *adj.* consisting of a single part.

mon·o·mor·phic (mon,ōmô'fik), *adj.* 1. (of an animal or plant) existing in only one form. 2. of identical or basically like structure.

mon·o·nu·cle·o·sis (mon,ōnyōō,klēō'sis), *n.* 1. a condition in which the blood contains an abnormally large number of monocytes, a type of white blood cell that engulfs foreign particles. 2. informal designation for **infectious mononucleosis.**

mon·o·pet·al·ous (mon,ōpet'ələs), *adj.* with only one petal.

mon·o·pha·gia (mon,ōfā'jə), *n.* the practice of eating or craving only one kind of food, normal in some animals but considered a disorder in humans.

mo·noph·a·gous (mənof'əgəs), *adj.* feeding on one variety of food only. See also **oligophagous.**

mon·o·pho·bi·a (mon,ōfō'bēə), *n.* an abnormal dread of being alone. **—mon·o·pho'bic,** *adj.*

mon·o·phon·ic (mon,ōfon'ik), *adj.* relating to a system of sound reproduction in which a single signal is put out whether one or more signals are put in. Also **monaural.** See also **stereophonic.**

mon·o·phy·let·ic (mon'ōfilet'ik), *adj.* of a biological class whose members are descended from the same ancestral type.

mon·o·phyl·lous (mon,ōfil'əs), *adj.* with a single leaf.

mon·o·ple·gi·a (mon,ōplē'jēə), *n.* paralysis of one part of the body, as of one extremity, muscle, or group of muscles.

mon·o·pode (mon'əpōd), *adj.* one-footed.

mo·nop·o·ly (mənop'əlē), *n.* the exclusive possession of a trading right which makes possible the manipulation of prices. See also **duopoly, oligopoly.**

mon·o·pol·y·lo·gue (mon,ōpol'ilog), *n.* a theatrical piece in which one player takes several parts.

mo·nop·so·ny (mənop'sənē), *n.* a condition in which there is only one buyer in a particular market. See also **duopsony, oligopsony.**

mon·o·rail (mon'ōrāl,), *n.* a railway that runs on a single rail on which the cars balance or from which they hang.

mon·o·rhi·nous (mon,ōrī'nəs), *adj.* having only one nostril, as lampreys, etc.

mon·o·rhyme (mon'ōrīm,), *n.* a poem or

stanza with all the lines rhyming with each other.

mon·o·so·di·um glu·ta·ma·te (mon,ōso'-dēəm glōō'təmāt), a white powder manufactured from salt and molasses and used to intensify the flavouring of meat and vegetable dishes or products. Also **sodium glutamate.** *Abbr.*: MSG.

mon·o·sper·mous (mon,ōspû'məs), *adj.* having only a single seed.

mon·o·sper·my (mon'ōspû,mē), *n.* the fertilizing of an ovum by a single spermatozoon.

mon·o·stich (mon'əstik,), *n.* **1.** a single metrical line. **2.** a poem of one line.

mon·o·stome (mon'əstōm,), *adj.* with one stoma or other mouthlike opening.

mon·o·the·ism (mon'ōthēiz,əm), *n.* the doctrine that there is only one God.

mon·o·tone (mon'ətōn,), *n.* **1.** sounds or speech continuing or repeated in the same pitch. **2.** the lack of any variation in style, as in writing or music. —**mon·o·ton·ic** (mon,əton'ik), *adj.*

mon·o·treme (mon'ōtrēm), *n.* any mammal of a sub-class of primitive egg-layers found in Australasia and comprising only the duck-billed platypus and spiny anteater. —**mon,o·tre'ma·tous,** *adj.*

mon·soon (monsōōn'), *n.* the rainy season that accompanies the SW monsoon wind in southern Asia.

mon·tane (mon'tān), *adj.* of or relating to mountainous country.

mon·teith (montēth'), *n.* a punch bowl, usually of silver, with a notched rim on which punch cups can be hung.

Mon·tes·so·ri method (mon,təsôr'ē), a system of training small children, devised by the Italian educator Maria Montessori (1870–1952), in which the main emphasis is on discovery through exercise of the senses.

mont·gol·fi·er (montgol'fēā), *n.* a balloon raised by heated air.

mon·ti·cule (mon'tikyōōl,), *n.* a small mountain or hill; a mound; a subsidiary cone of a volcano.

moon·calf (mōōn'kälf,), *n.* a congenital mentally defective person.

moot (mōōt), *adj.* debatable; on which opinions differ.

mo·quette (mōket'), *n.* a velvety fabric with a thick pile of wool on a cotton or jute base, used particularly for upholstery.

mo·raine (mərān'), *n.* a mass of rocks, sand, and clay carried along by a glacier.

Mo·ral Re·ar·ma·ment (mor'əl rēä'məmənt), a movement based on the theory that absolute morality in a person's private and public life leads to a better world. Also **Buchmanism.**

mor·ass (məras'), *n.* **1.** a bog or swamp. **2.** any

messy or entangling situation from which it is difficult to extricate oneself.

mor·a·to·ri·um (mor,ətôr'ēəm), *n., pl.* **mor·a·tor·i·a** (mor,ətôr'ēə), **mor·a·tor'i·ums.** a temporary cessation of activity, esp. of hostilities.

mor·bid (mô'bid), *adj.* **1.** given to gloomy ideas of unwholesome mind, suggesting a sick mind. **2.** gruesome, causing dread. —**mor·bid'i·ty,** *n.*

mor·bif·ic (môbif'ik), *adj.* disease-producing. Also **mor·bif·i·cal.**

mor·da·cious (môdā'sHəs), *adj.* given to biting.

mor·dant (mô'dənt), *adj.* (of wit, etc.) biting, sarcastic. —**mor'dan·cy,** *n.*

mo·res (môr'āz), *n. pl.* the generally accepted customs and ways of a society that have grown out of its fundamental beliefs.

mor·ga·nat·ic (mô,gənat'ik), *adj.* of or pertaining to a marriage between a man of high rank and woman of lower rank in which the wife and any children may not lay claim to the husband's rank or property.

mor·i·bund (mor'əbund), *adj.* in a dying state, at the point of death.

mo·rose (mərōs'), *adj.* of gloomy ill-temper, sullenly unsociable.

mor·pheme (mô'fēm), *n.* the smallest element in language to have semantic or grammatical meaning. —**mor·phe'mic,** *adj.*

mor·phe·mics (môfē'miks), *n.* the study of morphemes.

mor·phol·o·gy (môfol'əjē), *n.* the branch of any science, as biology, philology, etc., that deals with form and structure.

mor·ro (mor'ō), *n.* a rounded hill or headland.

mor·ta·del·la (môtədel'ə), *n.* a cooked, smoked sausage of pork, beef, and pork fat with seasonings and garlic.

mor·tif·er·ous (môtif'ərəs), *adj.* fatal; causing death.

mor·ti·fy (mô'təfī), *v.* **1.** to humiliate, to wound a person's feelings. **2.** to become gangrenous. —**mor·ti·fi·ca'tion,** *n.*

mos·chate (mos'kāt), *adj.* with a musky smell.

moss·back (mos'bak,), *n. U.S. informal.* a person of old-fashioned ideas; a person of extremely conservative notions.

mot (mō), *n.* a witty saying or remark.

mote (mōt), *n.* a dust particle.

moth·er-of-pearl (muth,ərəvpûl'), an iridescent hard lining of some shells, as that of the pearl oyster; nacre.

mo·tif (mōtēf'), *n.* a theme, idea, or pattern repeated in a work of art, as in design, painting, music, etc.

mo·tile (mō'tīl), *adj.* capable of motion; in motion.

motion sickness, a feeling of sickness and

nausea resulting from the motion on a ship, car, etc. See also **naupathia.**

mot juste (mō ZHYst'), *French.* an expression or word that conveys precisely the right shade of meaning.

moue (mōō), *n.* a pouting facial expression.

mou·jik (mōōzink'), *n.* muzhik.

mou·lage (mōōläzH'), *n.* a plaster of Paris mould of objects or imprints, as of footprints for identification purposes.

mould·board (mōld'bord), *n.* a large metal plate at the front of a bulldozer, plough, etc., to push ahead loose earth.

mou·lin (mōō'lin), *n.* a circular shaft in a glacier or the bedrock beneath it caused by water formed from ice or snow melting on its surface falling through a crevasse.

mountain sickness, a disorder occurring in the rarefied air at high altitude and characterized by difficulty in breathing, muscular weakness, mental lethargy, headache, and nausea.

mountain wave, steep wavelike air currents that occur when fast-flowing air meets an abruptly rising mountain range.

moun·te·bank (moun'təbaNGk,), *n.* an itinerant seller of quack remedies who attracts buyers by patter and tricks performed on a platform in a public place; any trickster or charlatan.

mousse (mōōs), *n.* a cold dish based on frothy whipped cream or cream and egg white with a sweet or a meaty flavouring set in a mould, sometimes by gelatin.

mousse·line (mōōslēn'), *n.* any dish made light and fluffy by the addition of beaten egg white or whipped cream. Also **chantilly.**

mousseline de soie (də swä'), *French.* a fine, stiff fabric of silk or rayon.

mou·ton·née (mōōtənä'), *adj.* scattered with rounded rocks that have been smoothed and shaped by glacial action. Also **mou·ton·néed'.**

Mo·vie·o·la (mōō,vēō'lə), *n.* the trademark of a motion-picture viewing device for use by one person who can control its movement and speed, used in film editing.

mox·a (mok'sə), *n.* down from the dried leaves of certain plants or some similarly downy substance for forming into a cone or cylinder to be put on the skin and burnt as a counterirritant for gout, etc.

mox·ie (mok'sē), *n. U.S. slang.* verve; nerve; vigorous assertiveness.

mox·i·bus·tion (mok,sibus'CHən), *n.* the technique of treating with moxa.

moz·za·rel·la (mot,sərel'lə), *n.* a mild, soft, white cheese, originally made in Italy.

mu·ced·i·nous (myōōsed'ənəs), *adj.* of or like mould or mildew.

mu·cif·er·ous (myōōsif'ərəs), *adj.* secreting or containing mucus.

mu·cip·a·rous (myōōsip'ərəs), *adj.* muciferous.

mu·coid (myōō'koid), *adj.* mucus-like. Also **mu·coi'dal.**

mu·co·pu·ru·lent (myōō,kōpyōōr'ələnt), *adj.* consisting of or bearing mucus and pus.

mu·cor (myōō'kə), *n.* any fungus that forms a furlike layer on food and dead or dying plants.

mu·co·sa (myōōkō'sə), *n., pl.* **mu·co·sae** (myōōkō'sē). mucous membrane.

mucous membrane, the moist, inner surface lining of hollow organs of the body that provides them with lubrication.

mu·cro (myōō'krō), *n., pl.* **mu·cro·nes** (myōōkrō'nēz). a pointed projection on a botanical or zoological organ, as on a leaf or feather.

mu·cro·nate (myōō'krōnāt), *adj.* having a mucro. Also **mu'cro·nat·ed.**

mu·cus (myōō'kəs), *n.* a slimy fluid secreted by mucous membrane. Also **mu'cous,** *adj.*

mu·dra (mədrä'), *n.* any of the gestures of the hand in the classical dancing of India, each representing a particular feeling.

muen·ster (mun'stə), *n.* a mild, semi-hard, fermented whole milk cheese often flavoured with caraway or anise seed.

mu·ez·zin (mōōez'in), *n.* an official of a mosque who calls the faithful to prayers.

muf·ti (muf'tē), *n.* civilian clothes worn by one who usually wears a uniform or distinguished from uniform.

mug·wump (mug'wump), *n.* **1.** one who acts independently of political parties or affects superiority in political or other issues. **2.** one who cannot decide his views or who takes a neutral view in political or other issues.

mu·ja·hed·din, mu·ja·he·deen, mu·ja·hi·deen (mōō'jəhədēn'), *pl. n.* Muslim guerrillas, esp. the various radical and traditionalist Islamic groups formed in Afghanistan following the military coup of 1978.

mu·jik (mōō'zHik), *n.* muzhik.

muk·luk (muk'luk), *n.* a soft boot worn by Eskimos, usually of seal or reindeer skin and fur-lined.

mu·lat·to (myōōlat'ō, mōōlat'ō), *n.* **1.** a person of mixed White and Negro ancestry, esp. the offspring of White and Negro parents. —*adj.* **2.** having a light-brown colour.

mulch (mulCH), *n.* **1.** a layer of straw, leaves, compost, etc., spread on soil to enrich it, to conserve moisture, or to protect the roots of plants. —*v.* **2.** to apply a mulch.

mulct (mulkt), *v.* **1.** to extort money from. **2.** to exact money or forfeit from as punishment. —*n.* **3.** a fine or other penalty.

mu·le·ta (myōōlet'ə), *n.* a red cloth on a stick used in a bullfight by a matador to entice and divert the bull. See also **capa.**

mul·ey (myōō'lē), *adj.* (of cattle) hornless; polled.

mu·li·eb·ri·ty (myōō,lēeb'ritē), *n.* the characteristics and qualities of women.

mul·lah, mul·la (mul'ə, mōōl'ə), *n.* a Muslim scholar or teacher of religious law, often with the status of a religious leader.

mul·ler (mul'ər), *n.* a machine for grinding.

mul·li·ga·taw·ny (mul,əgətô'nē), *n.* a curry-flavoured soup, originally of the E. Indies.

mul·tan·gu·lar (multaNG'gyələ), *adj.* with many angles.

mul·ti·cel·lu·lar (mul,tisel'yələ), *adj.* consisting of more than one cell.

mul·ti·far·i·ous (mul,tifer'ēəs), *adj.* of many kinds, parts, forms, etc.

mul·ti·fid (mul'tifid), *adj.* divided into many parts or lobes.

mul·ti·flo·rous (mul,tiflô'əs), *adj.* bearing many flowers.

mul·ti·fo·li·ate (mul,tifō'lēit), *adj.* having many leaves or leaflets.

mul·ti·lat·er·al (mul,tilat'ərəl), *adj.* having many sides.

mul·ti·loc·u·lar (mul,tilok'yələ), *adj.* consisting of more than one cell or chamber.

mul·ti·nom·i·nal (mul,tinom'ənəl), *n.* having many names.

mul·ti·nu·cle·ar (mul,tinyōō'klēə), *adj.* having more than one nucleus.

mul·tip·a·ra (multip'ərə), *n.*, *pl.* **mul·tip·a·rae** (multip'ərē) a woman pregnant for the second or further time; a woman who has borne more than one child.

mul·ti·par·tite (mul,tipär'tīt), *adj.* divided into many parts.

mul·ti·ped (mul'tiped,), *adj.* having many feet. Also **mul'ti·pede,**.

multiple sclerosis, a progressive disease of the nervous system in which small areas of the spinal cord and the brain lose their function with resultant speech disturbance and muscular incoordination.

mul·ti·plex (mul'tipleks), *adj.* **1.** manifold; having many elements. **2.** relating to radio, television, telephone, or telegraph equipment able to carry more than one signal at a time. —*n.* **3.** a cinema complex comprising several screens and auditoriums plus other facilities such as bar and restaurant.

mul·ti·pli·cate (mul'tiplikāt,), *adj.* manifold; having many and varied forms or elements.

mul·ti·plic·i·ty (mul,tiplis'itē), *n.* a great number; a great and varied number.

mul·ti·ver·si·ty (mul,tivû'sitē), *n. Chiefly U.S.* a university with several separate campuses.

mul·tiv·o·cal (mul,tivô'kəl), *adj.* having more than one meaning.

mul·tum in par·vo (mōōl'tōōm in pä'vō), *Latin.* a great deal in little space or compass.

mum·mer (mum'ə), *n.* a person wearing a mask or fancy dress at some festive gathering or masquerade. —**mum'mer·y,** *n.*

mun·dane (mundān'), *adj.* relating to the world or universe; worldly; earthly.

mun·di·fy (mun'difī), *v.* to free from noxious matter, as a wound, an ulcer, the blood, etc.

mun·go (muNG'gō), *n.* a cloth or yarn made from heavily felted woollen rags. Also **mongo.**

mu·nif·i·cent (myōōnif'isənt), *adj.* liberal in giving; splendidly generous.

mu·ni·ments (myōō'nimənts), *n. pl.* **1.** the title deeds or other documents held as evidence of ownership of a property. **2.** (formerly) equipment or provisions.

mun·tin (mun'tin), *n. Chiefly U.S.* a bar for holding window panes within the main framework. Also **glazing bar.**

mure (myōō'ə), *v.* to immure; to imprison; to shut up.

mu·rex (myōōr'eks), *n.*, *pl.* **mu·ri·ces** (myōōr'-isēz), **mu·rex·es.** the mollusc common to tropical seas and giving a reddish-purple dye that was used in the ancient world, esp. for the garments of royalty or rulers.

mu·rine (myoor'in, myoor'īn), *adj.* **1.** of or relating to the family Muridae, containing Old World rodents including mice and rats. **2.** of or resembling a rat or mouse. —*n.* **3.** a member of the Muridae.

mu·ri·cate (myōōr'əkāt), *adj.* having or covered with short, pointed projections. Also **mu'ri·cat,ed.**

mur·mur (mû'mə), *n.* an abnormal noise arising within the heart because of alteration of blood flow, esp. such as is caused by faulty valves, and audible through a stethoscope. Also **heart murmur.**

mur·rey (mur'ē), *n.* a deep reddish-purple colour.

mu·sa·ceous (myōōzā'sHəs), *adj.* of or relating to the genus of plants that includes the plantain or banana.

mus·cae vo·li·tan·tes (mus'ē vol,itan'tēz), dark spots that seem to float before the eyes, due to an eye defect, or to debris floating in the vitreous humour.

mus·ca·tel (mus,kətel'), *n.* a strong sweet white wine made from muscat grapes.

mus·cid (mus'id), *adj.* of or relating to the family of insects that includes the common housefly.

mus·cu·la·ture (mus'kyələcHə), *n.* the system or arrangement of muscles in an animal's body or part of a body.

mu·se·ol·o·gy (myōō,zēolə'jē), *n.* the study of the administration and functioning of a museum.

mu·si·col·o·gy (myōō,zikol'əjē), *n.* all aspects of the study of music except performance or composition, as musical theory, historical research, etc. —**mu,si·col'o·gist,** n.

mu·sique con·crète (myzĕk' koNkret'), *French.* music contrived from various sounds, made both by musical instruments and other objects, recorded and often distorted electronically. See also **electronic music.**

mus·keg (mus'keg), n. a waterlogged depression in the sub-arctic zone of Canada, commonly with a ground covering of sphagnum moss and sedge and with a scattering of lakes and stunted trees.

mus·lin (muz'lin), n. a fine cotton fabric usually of plain weave, varying in thickness according to its purpose, as for making into nappies, girls' and ladies' dresses, curtains, sheets, etc.

mus·si·ta·tion (mus,itā'sHən), n. silent imitation of the lip movements made in speech.

mus·te·line (mus'tilīn), adj. of or relating to the family that includes the weasels, badgers, otters, etc.

musth (must), n. a state of dangerous frenzy occurring periodically in male elephants and camels and accompanied by the secretion of an oily fluid from glands above the mouth. Also **must.**

mu·ta·gen (myōō'təjən), n. any substance that can give rise to a mutation.

mu·ta·gen·e·sis (myōō,təjen'isis), n. the origin and process of mutation.

mu·ta·gen·ic (myōō,təjen'ik), n. capable of giving rise to mutation.

mu·tant (myōō'tənt), adj. 1. in the process of mutating. —n. 2. the product of a mutation, as a new type of gene, cell, or organism.

mu·tate (myōō'tāt), v. to change, as in form or character.

mu·ta·tion (myōōtā'sHən), n. 1. the process of changing; a change, as in form or character. 2. a sudden biological change from the parent form owing to the alteration of a chromosome.

mu·ta·tis mu·tan·dis (mōōtā'tis mōōtan'dis), *Latin.* after making the necesary changes.

mu·ti·cous (myōō'təkəs), adj. (in biology) having no pointed defensive projections, as thorns, spines, claws, etc.

mut·ism (myōō'tiz,əm), n. a deliberate or unconscious refusal to reply when questioned, a feature of some mental illnesses.

mu·to·scope (myōō'təskōp,), n. a machine in which a series of sequential pictures on cards is mounted radially on a drum which is rotated to cause the cards to spring up and become visible rapidly in turn through the eyepiece, thus giving the viewer the impression of seeing a motion picture.

mu·tu·al·ism (myōō'CHōōəliz,əm, myōō'-tyōōəliz,əm), n. 1. the principle that mutual dependence within communities and societies is vital for harmony and prosperity. 2. symbiosis. —**mu'tu·al·ist,** n., adj. —**mu,tu·al·is'tic,** adj.

muu·muu (mōō'mōō,), n. a simple straight loose dress, often bright in colour or pattern, originally the garment worn by Hawaiian women.

mu·zhik, mou·jik, mu·jik (mōō'ZHik), n. a Russian peasant.

my·al·gi·a (mīal'jēə), n. pain in the muscles; muscular rheumatism. Also **myoneuralgia.**

my·al·gic encephalomyelitis (mīal'jik), n. an often persistent condition characterized by tiredness and painful muscles following a virus infection. Also called **postviral syndrome.** Abbr.: ME.

my·as·the·ni·a (mī,əsthē'nēə), n. an abnormal weakness in a muscle.

myasthenia gra·vis (grä'vis), a disease of the muscles, characterized by progressive loss of the power to contract, resulting in paralysis if not treated.

my·a·to·ni·a (mī,ətō'nēə), n. abnormally deficient muscle tone.

my·at·ro·phy (mīa'trəfē), n. See **myoatrophy.**

my·col·o·gy (mīkol'əjē), n. the scientific study of fungi, lichens, etc. —**my·col'o·gist,** n.

my·cor·rhi·za, my·co·rhi·za (mī,kərī'zə), n., pl. **my·cor·rhi·zae, my·co·rhi·zae** (mī,kərī'zē), **my·cor·rhi·zas, my·co·rhi·zas.** a beneficial or parasitic association between a fungus and the roots of a plant. —**my,cor·rhi'zal, my,co·rhi'zal,** adj.

my·co·sis (mīkō'sis), n. the presence in a body of any parasitic fungi, as ringworm.

my·co·stat (mī'kōstat,), n. a substance that prevents or represses the growth of fungi on vegetable or animal matter.

my·co·tox·in (mī,kətok'sin), n. any substance produced by a fungus, esp. a mould, that is harmful if ingested.

my·dri·a·sis (midrī'əsis, mīdrī'əsis), n. an abnormal dilatation of the pupil of the eye, resulting from drugs, disease, etc. —**myd·ri·at'-ic,** adj.

my·e·lin (mī'əlin), n. a soft, white, fatty substance forming a sheath around larger nerve fibres.

my·e·li·tis (mī,əlī'tis), n. inflammation of the substance of the spinal cord or of the bone marrow.

my·e·lo·gram (mī'əlōgram,, mīel'ōgram,), n. an x-ray photograph of the spinal cord after introducing a radio-opaque substance into the spinal fluid.

my·e·lo·gra·phy (mī,əlog'rəfē), n. the taking and developing of myelograms.

my·e·loid (mī'əloid), adj. 1. relating to the spinal cord. 2. relating to marrow.

my·ia·sis (mī'əsis), n., pl. **my·ia·ses** (mī'əsēz). any disease caused by larvae of flies infesting body tissues or cavities.

my·lo·hy·oid (mī,lōhī'oid), *adj.* relating to or near the lower jaw and hyoid bone.

my·o·at·ro·phy (mī,ōat'rəfē), *n.* atrophy of muscle tissue. Also **myatrophy.**

my·o·car·di·al in·farc·tion (mī,ōkä'dēəl infäk'sнən), the destruction of part of the heart muscle due to interruption of its blood supply, as in a coronary thrombosis.

my·o·car·di·o·gram (mī,ōkä'dēəgram,), *n.* the record produced by a myocardiograph.

my·o·car·di·o·graph (mī,ōkä'dēəgräf,, mī,ō-kä'dēəgraf,), *n.* an instrument for making a graphic record of the muscular activity of the heart.

my·o·car·di·tis (mī,ōkädī'tis), *n.* inflammation of the heart muscle, as in rheumatic fever.

my·o·car·di·um (mī,ōkä'dēəm), *n.* the muscular substance of the heart.

my·o·clo·ni·a (mī,ōklō'nēə), *n.* a disease characterized by myoclonus.

my·o·clo·nus (mīok'lənəs), *n.* muscle spasm in which violent contractions and relaxations occur in rapid succession.

my·o·cyte (mī'ōsīt,), *n.* a contractile cell, present esp. in sphincters.

my·o·e·de·ma (mī,ōidē'mə), *n.* swelling of a muscle due to an increase in its fluid content, as in inflammation.

my·o·gen·ic (mī,ōjen'ik), *adj.* arising spontaneously in a muscle independently of nervous stimuli.

my·o·glo·bin (mī,ōglō'bin), *n.* a variety of haemoglobin occurring in muscle fibres and differing from blood haemoglobin in carrying more oxygen and in having a smaller molecular weight. Also **my,o·hae'mo·glo,bin.**

my·o·gram (mī'əgram,), *n.* the record made by a myograph.

my·o·graph (mī'əgräf,, mī'əgraf,), *n.* an instrument for making a graphic record of muscular contractions and relaxations.

my·o·hae·mo·glo·bi·nu·ri·a (mī'ōhē,mō-glō,bənyŏor'ēə), *n.* a medical condition in which myoglobin is present in the urine. Also **my,o-,glo,bi,nu'ri·a.**

my·o·kym·i·a (mī,ōkim'ēə), *n.* a twitch in a segment of a muscle.

my·ol·o·gy (mīol'əjē), *n.* the scientific study of muscles.

my·o·ma (mīō'mə), *n.*, *pl.* **my·o·mas, my·o-·ma·ta** (mīō'mətə). a tumour consisting of muscle tissue.

my·o·neu·ral (mī,ōnyŏor'əl), *adj.* of or relating to muscle and nerve.

my·o·neu·ral·gia (mī,ōnyŏoral'jēə), *n.* See **myalgia.**

my·o·neu·ras·the·ni·a (mī,ōnyŏor,əsthē'-nēə), *n.* muscular weakness in conjunction with nervous debility.

my·op·a·thy (mīop'əthē), *n.* any disease or abnormality affecting the muscles.

my·o·pi·a (mīō'pēə), *n.* short-sightedness, a condition of the eye in which the rays from distant objects are brought to a focus before they reach the retina and so produce a blurred image. See also **hypermetropia. —my·op'ic,** *adj.*

my·o·psy·chop·a·thy (mī,ōsīkop'əthē), *n.* a muscle disease or abnormality in association with mental disorder.

my·o·scope (mī'əskōp,), *n.* an instrument for observing the functioning of muscles.

my·o·sis (mīō'sis), *n.* miosis.

my·ot·o·my (mīot'əmē), *n.* surgical incision into a muscle.

my·o·to·ni·a (mī,ətō'nēə), *n.* a disorder characterized by difficulty in relaxation of muscles after voluntary effort, muscular rigidity.

myr·i·ad (mir'ēəd), *n.* **1.** a huge number. **2.** ten thousand.

myr·i·a·gram (mir'ēəgram,), *n.* a unit used in the measurement of weight, equal to 10,000 grams. *Abbr.:* **myg.**

myr·i·a·li·tre (mir'ēəlē,tə), *n.* a unit used in the measurement of capacity, equal to 10,000 litres. *Abbr.:* **myl.**

myr·i·a·me·tre (mir'ēəmē,tə), *n.* a unit used in measuring distance, equal to 10,000 metres. *Abbr.:* **mym.**

myr·i·a·pod (mir'ēəpod,), *n.* a many-legged arthropod of the class comprising centipedes and millipedes.

myr·i·are (mir'ēer,), *n.* a unit used in measuring area, equal to 10,000 ares.

myr·me·col·o·gy (mû,məkol'əjē), *n.* the scientific study of ants.

myr·me·coph·a·gous (mû,məkof'əgəs), *adj.* ant-eating; adapted for feeding on ants or termites, as the long, extensile tongue of anteaters.

myr·me·co·phile (mû'məkōfil,), *n.* an insect of another species living in an ant colony. **—myr,me·coph'i·lous,** *adj.*

myr·mi·don (mû'midon), *n.* one who follows and obeys his master or leader without question or scruple; a hired ruffian.

my·so·phil·i·a (mīs,ōfil'ēə), *n.* a mental abnormality characterized by an attraction to filth and dirt.

my·so·pho·bi·a (mīs,ōfō'bēə), *n.* a mental abnormality characterized by dread of filth or dirt.

mys·ta·gogue (mis'təgog), *n.* an instructor in mystical doctrines; one who instructs persons before they take part in religious mysteries or sacraments.

mys·tique (mistēk'), *n.* an atmosphere of mystery or mysterious power surrounding a profession or pursuit, as *the mystique of medicine* or *the mystique of wine-drinking.*

myth·i·cal (mi*th*'ikəl), *adj.* imaginary; of the nature of a myth. Also **myth'ic.**

myth·o·ma·ni·a (mi*th*,ōmā'nēə), *n.* telling of lies to an abnormal extent.

myth·o·poe·ia (mi*th*,ōpē'ə), *n.* a mythopoeic act, trait, etc.

myth·o·poe·ic (mi*th*,ōpē'ik), *adj.* 1. causing a myth to arise. 2. perceiving the world with a mythological, not scientific, view.

myx·as·the·ni·a (miks,əs*th*ē'nēə), *n.* deficiency in mucus secretion.

myx·oe·de·ma (miks,idē'mə), *n.* a disease characterized by the slowing of mental pro-cesses and increased thickness of skin, associ-ated with a deficiency of thyroid secretion.

myx·o·ma (miksō'mə), *n., pl.* **myx·o·mas, myx·o·ma·ta** (miksō'mətə). a tumour of mucoid tissue.

myx·o·ma·to·sis (mik,səmətō'sis), *n.* 1. the presence of many myxomas. 2. an infectious disease of rabbits, introduced into England and Australia to curb the number of rabbits.

myx·o·neu·ro·sis (mik,sōnyōōrō'sis), *n., pl.* **myx·o·neu·ro·ses** (mik,sōnyōōrō'sēz). a neurosis characterized by excessive secretions of the res-piratory or intestinal mucous membranes.

Na·bi (nä'bē), *n.* a school of late 19th-century French painters who used flat shapes and strong colours in their work. See also **Synthetism.**

na·bob (nā'bob), *n.* a man of great wealth, esp. one who has made his fortune in India or some other eastern country.

na·cre (nā'kə), *n.* mother-of-pearl.

na·cre·ous (nā'krēəs), *adj.* having the appearance of mother-of-pearl.

na·dir (nā'dēə), *n.* a point in the celestial sphere immediately opposite the zenith and vertically downwards from a given position.

nae·vus (nē'vəs), *n.*, *pl.* **nae·vi** (nē'vī). a congenital skin blemish, as a birthmark or mole.

nai·ad (nā'ad), *n.*, *pl.* **nai·ads**, **nai·a·des** (nā'ədēz). a nymph of classical mythology associated with lakes, springs, and rivers.

nain·sook (nān'sook), *n.* a soft cotton fabric used for underwear and babies' clothes.

nais·sance (nā'səns), *n.* the origin or development of an organization, concept, movement, etc.

na·ive (nīēv'), *adj.* unsophisticated because of lack of experience, as a person; resulting from inexperience, as an idea. —**na·ive·té** (nīev'tā), **na·ive'ty** (nīēv'ətē), *n.*

nal·ox·one (nal'oksōn), *n.* a drug administered as an antagonist to narcotic drugs such as heroin.

na·ma·ste (num'əstā), *n.* a customary expression used by Hindus when greeting or saying good-bye.

nan·ism (nan'izəm), *n.* abnormal smallness in build or size; the condition of being a dwarf.

nan·o·cu·rie (nan'ōkyŏor,ē), *n.* a billionth of a curie.

nan·o·far·ad (nan'ōfar,əd), *n.* a billionth of a farad.

nan·o·hen·ry (nan'ōhen,rē), *n.* a billionth of a henry.

nan·oid (nan'oid), *adj.* abnormally small; dwarfish.

nan·o·me·tre (nan'ōmē,tə), *n.* a billionth of a metre.

nan·o·sec·ond (nan'ōsek,ənd), *n.* a billionth of a second.

nan·o·watt (nan'ōwot,), *n.* a billionth of a watt.

Nan·sen bottle (nan'sən), a self-closing receptacle for collecting samples of sea water at great depth.

na·os (nā'os), *n.* a temple.

na·palm (nā'päm), *n.* a jellified, highly inflammable fuel used in the manufacture of incendiary bombs, flame-throwers, etc.

na·pi·form (nā'pəfôm,), *adj.* having the shape of a turnip.

na·po·le·on (nəpō'lēən), *n.* the U.S. name for mille-feuille.

na·prap·a·thy (nəprap'əthē), *n.* treatment of disease by manipulation of the joints or massage based on the theory that illness results from disorders in connective tissue.

nar·cis·sism (nä'sisiz,əm), *n.* **1.** excessive admiration of oneself, self-love. **2.** love of one's own body; erotic stimulus derived from this. —**nar,cis·sis'tic,** *adj.*

nar·co·a·nal·y·sis (nä,kōənal'isis), *n.* the psychological analysis of a patient under the influence of relaxing drugs.

nar·co·di·ag·no·sis (nä,kōdī,əgnō'sis), *n.* diagnosis of psychiatric disorders with the use of drugs.

nar·co·lep·sy (nä'kəlep,sē), *n.* a condition characterized by an overwhelming desire for brief periods of deep sleep.

nar·co·ma (näkō'mə), *n.*, *pl.* **nar·co·mas,** **nar·co·ma·ta** (näkō'mətə). a state of partial unconsciousness resulting from the use of narcotics.

nar·co·ma·ni·a (nä,kōmā'nēə), *n.* **1.** an abnormal desire for drugs to relieve pain, etc. **2.** psychopathy caused by addiction to narcotics.

nar·cose (nä'kōs), *adj.* in a state of partial unconsciousness or stupor.

nar·co·sis (näkō'sis), *n.* a state of unconsciousness or stupor, esp. one produced by drugs, extremes of temperature, etc.

nar·co·syn·the·sis (nä,kōsin'thisis), *n.* treatment of mental disorders by the use of drugs.

nar·co·ther·a·py (nä,kōther'əpē), *n.* treatment of mental illness by the injection of barbiturates into the veins.

nar·cot·ic (näkot'ik), *n.* any of a number of drugs which, when used in moderate quantities, induce unconsciousness, sleep, and insensibility to pain, but in large doses cause stupor or convulsions and may be habit-forming.

nar·co·tism (nä'kətiz,əm), *n.* the habit of taking narcotics regularly; drug addiction.

nar·co·tize (nä'kətīz), v. to stupefy or render insensible by means of a narcotic.

nard (näd), n. an aromatic ointment used in antiquity, supposedly extracted from the spikenard. Also **spikenard**.

nar·es (ner'ēz), n. pl., sing. **nar·is** (ner'is). the nostrils or nasal cavities. —**nar'i·al**, adj.

nar·ghi·le (nä'gəlē), n. a hookah.

nas·cent (nä'sənt), adj. in the process of being created or developed.

na·so·fron·tal (nä,zōfrun'təl), adj. relating to the nose or the frontal bones of the forehead.

na·so·lac·ri·mal (nä,zōlak'rəməl), adj. relating to the nose and the lacrimal ducts and glands.

na·sol·o·gy (nāzol'əjē), n. the study of the nose.

na·so·pal·a·tine (nä,zōpal'ətīn), adj. relating to the nose and the palate.

na·so·phar·ynx (nä,zōfar'iNGks), n., pl. **na·so·phar·yn·ges** (nä,zōfərin'jēz), **na·so·phar·ynx·es**. the upper part of the pharynx, behind the soft palate and continuous with the nasal passages. —**na,so·pha·ryn'geal**, adj.

na·so·scope (nä'zəskōp,), n. a medical instrument for examimng the nasal passages, rhinoscope.

na·tant (nä'tənt), adj. floating in water, swimming.

na·ta·tion (nätā'SHən), n. the action of swimming.

na·ta·tor (nä'tətə), n. one who swims.

na·ta·to·ri·al (nä,tətôr'ēəl), adj. relating to or adapted for swimming.

na·ta·to·ri·um (nä,tətôr'ēəm), n., pl. **na·ta·to·ri·ums**, **na·ta·to·ri·a** (nä,tətôr'ēə). an indoor swimming pool.

na·tes (nä'tēz), n. pl. the buttocks.

na·tiv·i·sm (nä'tiviz,əm), n. 1. a policy of favouring natives over immigrants. 2. a policy of protecting and promoting the culture of indigenous peoples. 3. (in pyschology) the theory that the structure of the mind, and consequently much of an individual's personality and behaviour, are innately determined. —**na'tiv·ist**, n., adj. —**na,tiv·is'tic**, adj.

nat·u·ral·ism (naCH'ərəliz,əm), n. 1. (in literature) a theory advocating a completely realistic and scientifically objective approach to the depiction of life. 2. (in art) the treatment of forms and colours exactly as they are in nature.

natural justice, a conceptual system of rights derived from the behaviour of man in a hypothetical state of nature, affording self-preservation of free and equal individuals. It is embodied in the works of philosophers such as Thomes Hobbes and John Locke.

na·tur·o·path (nä'CHərəpath,), n. one who is a practitioner of naturopathy.

na·tur·op·a·thy (nä,CHərop'əthē), n. the treatment of disease by laying stress on the assistance of the natural healing processes by the use of exercise, heat, etc.

nau·ma·chi·a (nômä'kēə), n., pl. **nau·ma·chi·ae** (nômä'kēē), **nau·ma·chi·as**. a spectacle presented by the ancient Romans depicting a mock naval battle.

nau·path·i·a (nôpath'ēə), n. seasickness. See also **motion sickness**.

nautch (nôCH), n. an Oriental dance characterized by lithe, supple movements. Also **nautch dance**.

na·vette (navet'), n. a gem, as a diamond, cut in the shape of an oval with many faces.

na·vic·u·lar (nəvik'yələ), adj. shaped like a boat; scaphoid. Also **na·vi·cu·lar·e** (nəvik'yələr,ē).

N-bomb. See **neutron bomb**.

Ne·an·der·thal man (nēan'dəthôl,), an extinct species of man inhabiting Europe and western Asia in the Palaeolithic period. —**Ne·an·der·thal·oid** (nēan'dəthôl,oid), adj., n.

neap (nēp), adj. relating to tides of minimum range.

neat[1] (nēt), adj. unmixed, straight, as whisky.

neat[2] (nēt), n., pl. **neat**. a bovine animal.

neb·u·la (neb'yələ), n., pl. **neb·u·lae** (neb'yəlē), **neb·u·las**. 1. a luminous or dark shape in the sky consisting of gases and dust. 2. a star surrounded by a gaseous envelope. 3. a galaxy lying outside the Milky Way.

neb·u·lize, neb·u·lise (neb'yəliīz,), v. to convert to a fine spray. —**neb,u·li·za'tion, neb,u·li·sa'tion**, n. —**neb'u·liz,er, neb'u·lis,er**, n.

neb·u·lose (neb'yəlōs), adj. resembling a cloud in shape. —**neb·u·los'i·ty**, n.

neb·u·lous (neb'yələs), adj. indistinct; hazy; vague.

ne·ces·si·tous (nəses'itəs), adj. needy; in want; poor.

ne·crae·mi·a (nəkrē'mēə), n. a pathological condition characterized by the circulation in the blood stream of a large number of dead erythrocytes.

ne·crol·a·try (nəkrol'ətrē), n. the worship of the dead.

ne·crol·o·gy (nəkrol'əjē), n. an obituary notice, or a collection of them.

nec·ro·man·cy (nek'rəman,sē), n. sorcery; witchcraft. —**nec'ro·man·cer**, n.

nec·ro·mi·me·sis (nek,rōmimē'sis), n. a morbid mental state in which the sufferer believes himself to be dead.

ne·croph·a·gous (nəkrof'əgəs), adj. normally feeding on corpses or carrion.

nec·ro·phil·i·a (nek,rōfil'ēə), n. a morbid sexual attraction for dead bodies. Also **ne·croph'i·lism**.

nec·ro·pho·bi·a (nek,rōfō'bēə), n. a morbid horror of death or of the dead.

ne·crop·o·lis (nəkrop'əlis), *n.* a large cemetery.

nec·rop·sy (nek'ropsē), *n.* a postmortem examination. Also **ne·cros'co·py.**

ne·crose (nekrōs'), *v.* to cause or be affected with necrosis.

ne·cro·sis (nəkrō'sis), *n.* the localized death of a tissue or organ inside a living body.

nec·tar·ous (nek'tərəs), *adj.* **1.** of or relating to nectar. **2.** sweet; pleasing to the taste.

ne·far·i·ous (nifer'ēəs), *adj.* very wicked; evil.

neg·a·tron (neg'ətron), *n.* See **electron.**

neg·li·gi·ble (neg'lijəbəl), *adj.* of relatively little importance or meaning.

ne·gus (nēgəs), *n.* a drink made of wine, hot water, lemon, sugar, and nutmeg.

nek·ton (nek'ton), *n.* the organisms that actively swim in a sea or lake, such as fish and whales. See also **plankton. —nek·ton'ic,** *adj.*

nem·a·tode (nem'ətōd), *n.* an elongated roundworm, cylindrical in shape.

nem·a·tol·o·gy (nem,ətol'əjē), *n.* the scientific study of nematodes.

Nem·bu·tal (nem'byōōtal), *n.* a trade mark for pentobarbitone.

ne·mer·te·an (nimû'tēən), *n.* any of a group of marine worms usually found in mud or sand on seashores.

nem·e·sis (nem'əsis), *n.* **1.** something that cannot be conquered or achieved. **2.** something that serves to punish or defeat a person.

ne·o·clas·si·cal (nē,ōklas'ikəl), *adj.* **1.** relating to the literature of the 17th century which revived and adapted the style of classical antiquity. **2.** relating to a style of art and sculpture, originating in the mid 18th century, which derived its discipline from the style of classical antiquity. Also **ne,o·clas'sic.**

Ne·o·clas·si·cism (nō,ōklas'isiz,əm), *n.* a style of architecture of the late 18th and early 10th conturies which was derived directly from the models of classical antiquity.

Ne·o·Dar·win·ism (nē,ōdä'winiz,əm), *n.* the modern theory of evolution, representing a synthesis of classical Darwinism with contemporary knowledge of genetics. **—Ne,o·Dar·win'·i·an,** *adj., n.*

ne·o·for·ma·tion (nē,ōfōmā'sHən), *n.* a tumour or abnormal growth in a tissue.

Ne·o·gene (nē'əjēn), *adj.* **1.** relating to the latter half of the Tertiary period and including the Pliocene and Miocene. **—n. 2.** the Neogene period. See also **Palaeogene.**

ne·o·lith (nē'əlith,), *n.* a stone tool of the Neolithic period.

Ne·o·lith·ic (nē,əlith'ik), *adj.* relating to the latter part of the Stone Age characterized by the use of polished stone implements. See also **Mesolithic, Palaeolithic.**

ne·ol·o·gism (nēol'əjiz,əm), *n.* a new word, usage, or idiom in a language. Also **ne·ol'o·gy.**

ne·o·my·cin (nē,ōmī'sin), *n.* an antibiotic used against certain infections.

ne·o·nate (nē'ōnāt), *n.* a newborn child. **—ne·o·na'tal,** *adj.*

ne·o·phyte (nē'ōfīt,), *n.* a novice or beginner.

ne·o·plasm (nē'ōplaz,əm), *n.* a new and abnormal growth of tissue.

ne·o·plas·ty (nē'ōplas,tē), *n.* the repairing of damaged tissue, etc., by plastic surgery.

ne·o·prene (nē'ōprēn,), *n.* a synthetic rubber having a high resistance to oils, etc.

Ne·o·Ro·man·ti·cism (nē,ōrōman'tisiz,əm), *n.* any movement in literature, architecture, or the arts that is characterized by a return to a more romantic style.

ne·ot·e·ny (nēot'ənē), *n.* the achievement of sexual maturity during the larval stage.

ne·o·ter·ic (nē,ōter'ik), *adj.* modern; recent.

ne·ot·er·ism (nēot'əriz,əm), *n.* a new word or expression.

ne·o·type (nē'ōtīp,), *n.* a biological specimen that replaces a lost or destroyed holotype.

ne·pen·the (nipen'thē), *n.* anything which brings forgetfulness of sorrow or suffering. **—ne·pen'the·an,** *adj.*

neph·a·nal·y·sis (nef,ənal'isis), *n.* a chart showing cloud patterns, distribution, and precipitation.

neph·e·lom·e·ter (nef,əlom'itə), *n.* an apparatus for determining the density of suspensions by the measurement of scattered light.

neph·o·gram (nef'əgram,), *n.* a photograph of cloud formations.

neph·o·graph (nef'əgräf,, nef'əgraf,), *n.* an apparatus for photographing clouds.

ne·phol·o·gy (nefol'əjē), *n.* the scientific study of clouds.

ne·phom·e·ter (nefom'itə), *n.* an instrument that measures the proportion of sky covered by cloud.

neph·o·scope (nef'əskōp,), *n.* an apparatus that measures the height, direction, and velocity of clouds.

ne·phral·gi·a (nəfral'jēə), *n.* pain in the kidneys.

ne·phrec·to·my (nəfrek'təmē), *n.* the removal of a kidney by surgery.

ne·phrid·i·um (nəfrid'ēəm), *n., pl.* **ne·phrid·i·a** (nəfrid'ēə). the tubular excretory organ characteristic of many invertebrates.

neph·rism (nef'rizəm), *n.* ill health resulting from chronic kidney disease.

ne·phrit·ic (nəfrit'ik), *adj.* relating to or suffering from nephritis.

ne·phri·tis (nəfrī'tis), *n.* inflammation of the kidneys.

ne·phrog·e·nous (nəfroj'ənəs), *adj.* developing in or proceeding from the kidney. Also **neph·ro·gen·ic** (nef,rōjen'ik).

neph·ro·lith (nef'rəli*th*,), *n.* a stone in the kidney.

neph·ro·li·thot·o·my (nef,rōli*th*ot'əmē), *n.* the opening of a kidney to remove a stone.

ne·phrol·o·gy (nəfrol'əjē), *n.* the study of the kidney and its functions.

neph·ro·lyt·ic (nef,rəlit'ik), *adj.* tending to destroy the kidney cells.

neph·ron (nef'ron), *n.* a functional part of the kidney of vertebrates.

ne·phrop·a·thy (nəfrop'ə*th*ē), *n.* a disease which affects the kidneys.

ne·phro·sis (nəfrō'sis), *n.* a degenerative kidney disease of the renal tubules.

ne·phrot·o·my (nəfrot'əmē), *n.* surgical incision into the kidneys, esp. for removing a stone.

neph·ro·tox·ic (nef,rōtok'sik), *adj.* having a toxic effect on the kidney cells.

ne plus ul·tra (nā plōōs ōol'trä), *Latin.* the highest degree; culminating point.

nep·o·tism (nep'ətiz,əm), *n.* favouritism shown towards relatives, esp. by a person in a high position in business, politics, etc.

ne·rit·ic (nərit'ik), *adj.* relating to or forming the belt of shallow waters near land.

nerve block, a technique in anaesthesia in which local anaesthetic is injected around a nerve to abolish sensation in the part of the body supplied by that nerve.

nerve gas, any of various gases that damage the nervous system.

ner·vule (nû'vyōol), *n.* a small nerve found in the wing of insects.

ner·vu·ra·tion (nû,vyərā'sHən), *n.* the arrangement of veins on an insect's wing. Also **ner·vu·la'tion.**

ner·vure (nû'vyōoə), *n.* **1.** one of the veins that help to strengthen the wings of an insect. **2.** a rib, as in a Gothic vault, that resembles this part.

nes·cience (nes'ēəns), *n.* ignorance; lack of knowledge. —**nes'cient,** *adj.*

ness (nes), *n.* a promontory or headland.

neth·er (neTH'ə), *adj.* lying beneath, under or lower, as *the nether regions* or *nether lip.*

neth·er·most (neTH'əmōst,), *adj.* lowest.

ne·tsu·ke (net'skē), *n.* a small, carved object of ivory, wood, etc., used by Japanese as an ornamental fastening for a sash, girdle, etc.

net·tle·some (net'əlsəm,), *adj.* irritating or irritable.

neu·ral (nyōor'əl), *adj.* relating to or concerned with a nerve or the nervous system.

neu·ral·gia (nyōoral'jə), *n.* an acute pain that moves along a nerve.

neu·ral·gi·form (nyōoral'jifôm,), *adj.* resembling neuralgia.

neu·ras·the·ni·a (nyōor'əs*th*ē'nēə), *n.* a state of nervous exhaustion marked by minor physical complaints such as disturbances of the digestive system, headaches, etc. —**neu,ras·then'ic,** *adj.*

neu·rec·to·my (nyōorek'təmē), *n.* the removal by surgery of a nerve or part of a nerve.

neu·ri·lem·ma (nyōor,ilem'ə), *n.* the outer sheath of a nerve fibre.

neu·rite (nyōor'īt), *n.* See **axon.**

neu·ri·tis (nyōorī'tis), *n.* constant pain in a nerve often accompanying paralysis or disturbances in the sense organs.

neu·ro·a·nat·o·my (nyōor,ōənat'əmē), *n.* the anatomy of the nervous system. —**neu,ro·a·nat'-o·mist,** *n.*

neu·ro·em·bry·ol·o·gy (nyōor,'ōem,brēol'-əjē), *n.* the study of the origin and development of the nervous system.

neu·rog·li·a (nyōorog'lēə), *n.* the supporting tissue that binds together the nerve tissue in the brain, spinal cord, etc.

neu·ro·lep·tic (nyōor,ōlep'tik), *adj.* **1.** able to affect the nervous function of the brain, esp. as a tranquillizer. —*n.* **2.** a drug that affects brain activity, esp. a major tranquillizer.

neu·rol·o·gy (nyōorol'əjē), *n.* the study of the nervous system and its diseases. —**neu·rol'o·gist,** *n.*

neu·rol·y·sis (nyōorol'isis), *n.* the disintegration of a nerve or nervous tissue.

neu·ro·ma (nyōorō'mə), *n.*, *pl.* **neu·ro·mas, neu·ro·ma·ta** (nyōorō'mətə). a tumour growing from nerve tissue.

neu·ro·mus·cu·lar (nyōor,ōmus'kyələ), *adj.* relating to both nerves and muscles.

neu·ron (n,ōor'on), *n.* the basic unit of nervous tissue; nerve cell. Also **neu·rone** (nyōor'ōn).

neu·ro·path (nyōor'əpath,), *n.* a person suffering from a nervous disorder.

neu·ro·pa·thol·o·gy (nyōor,ōpəthol'əjē), *n.* the study of the diseases of the nervous system. —**neu·ro·pa·thol'o·gist,** *n.*

neu·rop·a·thy (nyōorop'ə*th*ē), *n.* a disease of the nervous system.

neu·ro·pep·tide (nyōor,ōpep'tīd), *n.* any peptide molecule produced by nerve cells that influences the activity of other cells and tissues in a hormone-like fashion.

neu·ro·phys·i·ol·o·gy (nyōor,ōfiz,ēol'əjē), *n.* the study of the physiology of the nervous system. —**neu,ro·phys,i·ol'o·gist,** *n.*

neu·ro·plasm (nyōor'əplaz,əm), *n.* protoplasm in a nerve cell.

neu·ro·psy·chi·a·try (nyōor,ōsīkī'ətrē), *n.* the study and treatment of mental disorders and diseases of the nervous system. —**neu·ro·psy·chi'a·trist,** *n.*

neu·ro·psy·cho·sis (nyōor,ōsīkō'sis), *n.* insanity associated with disease of the nervous system. —**neu,ro·psy·chot'ic,** *adj.*, *n.*

neu·ro·sis (nyŏŏrō'sis), *n.*, *pl.* **neu·ro·ses** (nyŏŏrō'sēz). a mental disturbance characterized by feelings of anxiety, obsessions, compulsive acts, and minor physical disorders without physical cause. See also **psychoneurosis.**

neu·ro·sur·ger·y (nyŏŏr,ōsû'jərē), *n.* the surgery of the nervous system. —**neu,ro·sur'geon**, *n.*

neu·rot·ic (nyŏŏrot'ik), *adj.* suffering from a neurosis.

neu·rot·o·my (nyŏŏrot'əmē), *n.* the cutting of a nerve to relieve pain, as that caused by neuralgia.

neu·ro·tox·in (nyŏŏr,ōtok'sin), *n.* a poison that attacks nervous tissue. —**neu·ro·tox'ic**, *adj.*

neu·rot·ro·phy (nyŏŏrot'rəfē), *n.* the influence of the nervous system on the nourishment of body tissue. —**neu,ro·troph'ic**, *adj.*

neu·ro·trop·ic (nyŏŏr,ōtrop'ik), *adj.* displaying an affinity for nerve tissue. —**neu·rot·ro·pism** (nyŏŏrot'rəpiz,əm), **neu·rot'ro·py**, *n.*

neus·ton (nyŏŏ'ston), *n.* the mass of minute organisms which float on the surface of a body of water.

neutral spirits, *U.S.* alcohol of 190 proof (95% pure) used for making gin, liqueurs, etc., and for blending with other alcoholic liquors.

neutron bomb, a nuclear bomb which releases neutrons but relatively little blast and causes only a small amount of contamination. Also **N-bomb.**

neu·tro·phil (nyŏŏ'trəfil), **neu·tro·phile** (nyŏŏ'trəfil,), *n.* **1.** a type of white blood cell that stains with neutral dyes. Also **pol·y·morph** (pol'imôf). —*adj.* **2.** (of cells and tissues) readily staining with neutral dyes. Also **neu·tro·phil·ic** (nyŏŏ,trəfil'ik).

neu·tro·sphere (nyŏŏ'trəsfē,ə), *n.* that part of the atmosphere, stretching from the surface of the earth to the ionosphere, which is generally electrically neutral.

né·vé (nāvā'), *n.* granular snow on high mountains that turns into glacial ice. Also **firn.**

new criticism, a method of literary criticism which confines itself to analysis of text excluding all other considerations as irrelevant. See also **explication de texte.**

New Left, a radical left-wing movement that arose in many countries during the 1960s, esp. among students. Its followers espoused Marx and Freud and advocated sweeping political and social change.

new·ton (nyŏŏ'tən), *n.* a unit of force that gives an acceleration of one metre per second to a mass of one kilogram.

new wave, a movement in literature, the arts, etc., that breaks away from traditional ideas and values. See also **nouvelle vague.**

New York cut, *U.S.* a porterhouse steak without the fillet or bone.

nex·us (nek'səs), *n.*, *pl.* **nex·us.** something that joins or connects; link, tie.

ni·a·cin (nī'əsin), *n.* See **nicotinic acid.**

nice·nel·ly·ism (nīs'nel'ēiz,əm), *n.* *U.S* the use of euphemistic expressions; prudery.

nic·o·tin·a·mide (nik,ətin'əmīd), *n.* a colourless crystalline solid forming part of the vitamin-B complex and used in medicine. Also called **ni·a·cin·a·mide** (nī,əsin'əmīd), **nicotinic acid amide.**

nic·o·tine (nik'ətēn), *n.* a poisonous, oily alkaloid obtained from tobacco. —**nic,o·tin'ic**, *adj.*

nicotinic acid, a crystalline acid forming part of the vitamin-B complex, found in fresh meat, etc., and used in the treatment of pellagra. Also **niacin.**

nic·o·tin·ism (nik'ətēniz,əm), *n.* a condition resulting from the excessive use of tobacco.

nic·ti·tate (nik'titāt), *v.* to wink or blink. Also **nic'tate.**

ni·dic·o·lous (nīdik'ələs), *adj.* noting birds that are reared for a time in the nest after hatching.

nid·i·fi·cate (nid'əfəkāt,), *v.* to build a nest. Also **nid'i·fy.**

ni·dif·u·gous (nīdif'yŏŏgəs), *adj.* noting birds that leave the nest soon after hatching.

ni·el·lo (nēel'ō), *n.*, *pl.* **ni·el·li** (nēel'ī). a black metallic alloy of copper, lead, silver, and sulphur used to fill in patterns engraved on other metals.

nier·stein·er (nē'əstī,nə), *n.* a white wine from Nierstein, in the central part of Germany.

nig·gard (nig'əd), *n.* a miserly or stingy person. —**nig'gard·ly**, *adj.*

nig·gle (nig'əl), *v.* to spend too much time over petty details; work ineffectively.

nig·gling (nig'liNG), *adj.* excessively fussy; finicky; petty-minded.

night blindness. See **nyctalopia.**

night·rid·er (nīt'rī,də), *n.* (in the southern U.S.A.) a member of a gang of men who perform acts of violence in order to intimidate or punish.

night·shade (nīt'sHād,), *n.* any of various plants, as the deadly nightshade, yielding a variety of drugs.

ni·gres·cent (nīgres'ənt), *adj.* becoming a blackish colour.

nig·ri·fy (nig'rifī), *v.* to make black.

nig·ri·tude (nig'rityŏŏd), *n.* blackness; complete darkness.

ni·hil·ism (nī'əliz,əm), *n.* **1.** a form of complete scepticism that denies that there can be any objective basis of truth. **2.** the doctrine of a 19th-century Russian revolutionary group advocating the overthrow of the existing social order.

ni·hil·i·ty (nīhil'itē), *n.* nothingness.

nim·bus (nim'bəs), *n.*, *pl.* **nim·bi** (nim'bī), **nim·bus·es.** a cloud or atmosphere about a person or thing; aura.

ni·mi·e·ty (nimī'itē), *n.* excess.

nim·i·ny-pim·i·ny (nim'ənēpim'ənē), *adj.* effeminate; mincing; affected.

niph·a·blep·si·a (nif,əblep'sēə), *n.* See **snow blindness.**

nir·va·na (nē,əvä'nə), *n.* the extinction of desire and suffering and release from the cycle of reincarnation, as sought by Buddhists.

ni·sus (nī'səs), *n., pl.* **ni·sus.** an effort or impulse; striving.

nit (nit), *n.* **1.** the egg of a louse or parasitic insect, esp. one attached to human hair. **2.** a unit of brightness of light equalling one candela per square metre.

nit·id (nit'id), *adj.* bright; shining.

ni·tro·gen narcosis (nī'trəjən), *n.* intoxication caused by breathing nitrogen under increased atmospheric pressure, as in deep sea diving. Also **rapture of the deep.**

ni·trog·e·nous (nītroj'ənəs), *adj.* containing nitrogen.

ni·tro·glyc·er·in (nī,trōglis'ərin), *n.* a liquid high explosive used in making dynamite, in rocket propellants, and medically, in the treatment of angina pectoris.

nit·ty-grit·ty (nit'ēgrit'ē), *n.* the tedious, though essential, details.

ni·val (nī'vəl), *adj.* relating to or growing in snow.

niv·e·ous (niv'eəs), *adj.* having the appearance of snow, snowy.

no·blesse o·blige (nōbles' ōblēzн'), *French.* moral obligations entailed by high rank or wealth.

no·cent (nō'sənt), *adj.* hurtful, harmful.

no·ci·cep·tive (nō,sisep'tiv), *adj.* **1.** of or relating to pain. **2.** of or relating to a behavioural reflex or sensory structure specialized for responding to painful stimuli.

noc·tam·bu·lism (noktam'byōōliz,əm), *n.* sleepwalking. Also **noc·tam,bu·la'tion.**

noc·u·ous (nok'yōōəs), *adj.* harmful; causing damage.

no·dus (nō'dəs), *n., pl.* **no·di** (nō'dī). a complicated situation, complication; difficulty.

no·e·gen·e·sis (nō,ijen'isis), *n.* fresh or first-hand knowledge acquired through the experience of the senses or the intellect.

no·e·sis (nōē'sis), *n.* the activity of the intellect in the process of cognition.

no·et·ic (nōet'ik), *adj.* relating to reason or the mind.

nog·gin (nog'in), *n.* a small mug or cup.

noi·sette (nwäzet'), *adj.* **1.** of or containing hazelnuts. —*n.* **2.** a small round boneless slice of meat, esp. lamb.

noi·some (noi'səm), *adj.* smelly; foul-smelling.

nol·le pros·e·qui (nol'ē pros'əkwī), *Latin.* an entry in a court's record showing that proceedings in a case have been dropped.

no·lo con·ten·de·re (nō'lō kənten'dərē), *Latin.* (chiefly in U.S. law) the pleading of a defendant not admitting or denying guilt, but allowing the court to impose a fine or a sentence nonetheless.

no·ma (nō'mə), *n.* gangrene of the lips and cheeks, found in debilitated people.

nom de guerre (nom də ge'ə), *pl.* **noms de guerre** (nom də ge'ə) *French.* a pseudonym.

nom de plume (nom də plōōm'), *pl.* **noms de plume** (nom də plōōm'). *French.* a pen name.

no·men·cla·ture (nōmen'kləcнə, nō'mənklā,cнə), *n.* a system of names or terms used for purposes of classification.

nom·i·nal (nom'ənəl), *adj.* **1.** in name or form only. **2.** small; insignificant; trifling.

no·mism (nō'miz,əm), *n.* religious conduct which follows certain laws.

nom·o·gram (nom'əgram), *n.* a kind of graph that enables the value of one dependent variable to be read off when the value of two independent variables are known.

no·mog·ra·phy (nomog'rəfē), *n.* **1.** the art of compiling laws. **2.** the art of constructing nomograms to solve closely related problems.

no·mol·o·gy (nomol'əjē), *n.* the science of law.

nom·o·thet·ic (nom,əthet'ik), *adj.* making laws; legislative.

non·age (non'ij), *n.* the period of being a minor in law.

non·a·gon (non'əgon), *n.* a polygon with nine angles and nine sides. Also **enneagon.**

no·na·ry (nō'nərē), *adj.* being nine in number.

non·bel·lig·er·en·cy (non,bəlij'ərənsē), *n.* a policy of a country which supports one of the countries taking part in a war but without openly intervening. —**non,bel·lig'er·ent,** *n., adj.*

nonce (nons), *n.* the immediate moment; the present occasion.

non·cha·lance (non,sнəläns'), *n.* casual unconcern; indifference. —**non·cha·lant',** *adj.*

non com·pos men·tis (non kom'pəs men'-tis), *Latin.* of unsound mind.

none·such (nun'sucн), *n.* a person or thing that has no equal. See also **nonpareil.**

non·fea·sance (nonfē'zəns), *n.* the failure to perform some action which ought to have been done. See also **malfeasance, misfeasance.**

non·fer·rous (nonfer'əs), *adj.* **1.** (of a metal) having no iron. **2.** relating to metals other than iron or steel.

no·nil·lion (nōnil'yən), *n.* **1.** (in Britain, France, and Germany) the number represented by 1 followed by 54 zeros. Also **quin·til'lion. 2.** (in the U.S.A. and Canada) the number represented by the figure 1 followed by 30 zeros. —**no·nil'lianth,** *adj.*

non·ob·stan·te (non obʌtan'tē), *Latin.* notwithstanding.

non·pa·reil (non,pərel'), *adj.* without equal.

non·par·ous (nonpar'əs), *adj.* not having given birth to any children.

non·plus (nonplus'), *v.* to confuse or disconcert, puzzle.

non se·qui·tur (non sek'witōō,ə), *Latin.* a conclusion which does not follow logically from a premise.

non-U (nonyōō'), *adj.* (of speech, behaviour, etc.) not of the upper class.

no·ri·a (nôr'ēə), *n.* an apparatus for raising water, consisting of buckets attached to a wheel.

normal tax, an income tax levied at a fixed rate. See also **surtax**.

nor·ma·tive (nô'mətiv), *adj.* relating to an accepted standard of behaviour, dress, speech, etc.

nor·mo·cyte (nô'məsīt,), *n.* a red blood corpuscle of normal size.

nor·mo·ten·sive (nô,mōten'siv), *adj.* having normal blood pressure.

nos·o·co·mi·al (nos,əkō'mēəl), *adj.* (of a disease) originating in hospital.

nos·o·gen·e·sis (nos,əjen'isis), *n.* the origination and development of a disease. Also **no·sog'·e·ny**.

nos·o·ge·og·ra·phy (nos,ōjēog'rəfē), *n.* the study of diseases with reference to their geographical distribution and causes. Also **nos·och·tho·nog·ra·phy** (nos,okthənog'rəfē).

no·sog·ra·phy (nosog'rəfē), *n.* the description of diseases.

no·sol·o·gy (nosol'əjē), *n.* **1.** the classification of diseases. **2.** the information available on a disease.

nos·o·pho·bi·a (nos,əfō'bēə), *n.* a morbid fear of disease.

nos·tal·gia (nostal'jə), *n.* homesickness; a sentimental yearning for another time or place. —**nos·tal'gic,** *adj.*

nos·tol·o·gy (nostol'əjē), *n.* the branch of medicine dealing with the problems and diseases of old age; gerontology; geriatrics.

nos·to·ma·ni·a (nos,təmā'nēə), *n.* profound homesickness.

nos·trum (nos'trəm), *n.* **1.** a patent medicine. **2.** a remedy, scheme, etc., intended to solve all problems; panacea.

not·a·ble (nō'təbəl), *adj.* worthy of note; important; famous.

no·tor·i·ous (nōtôr'ēəs), *adj.* having a bad reputation; well known for being bad or for having an undesirable characteristic.

no·tum (nō'təm), *n.*, *pl.* **no·ta** (nō'tə). a segmental plate on the back of an insect.

nou·me·non (nōō'mənon), *n.*, *pl.* **nou·me·na** (nōō'mənə). (in philosophy) a thing as its true nature determines it as contrasted with how it may appear to be.

nous (nous), *n.* the intellect; reason.

nou·veau riche (nōō'vō rēsʜ'), *pl.* **nou·veaux riches** (nōō'vō rēsʜ'). *French.* a person who has recently become rich.

nou·veau·té (nōōvōtā'), *n.*, *pl.* **nou·veau·tés** (nōōvōtā'). *French.* a novelty.

nou·velle cui·sine (nōō'vel kwēzēn'), *n.* a style of cooking, developed in France, that accentuates the inherent flavours and textures of natural ingredients, which are presented raw or lightly cooked and without highly flavoured sauces. See also **cuisine minceur.**

nou·velle vague (nōōvel vag'), *pl.* **nou·velles vagues** (nōōvel vag'). *French.* a new movement in an art form, esp. in the cinema. See also **new wave.**

no·va (nō'və), *n.*, *pl.* **no·vae** (nō'vē), **no·vas.** a star that suddenly becomes very bright for a short time and then grows faint again. See also **supernova.**

no·vel·la (nōvel'ə), *n.*, *pl.* **no·vel·las, no·vel·le** (nōvel'ā). a short novel.

no·vem·de·cil·lion (nō,vəmdisil'yən), *n.* **1.** (in Britain and Germany) a number represented by the figure 1 followed by 114 zeros. **2.** (in the U.S.A.) a number represented by the figure 1 followed by 60 zeros.

no·ver·cal (nōvû'kəl), *adj.* relating to or appropriate to a stepmother.

no·vi·ti·ate, no·vi·ci·ate (novisʜ'ēit), *n.* the period or state of being a novice.

nox·ious (nok'sʜəs), *adj.* harmful to health.

no·yade (nwäyäd'), *n.* execution by drowning.

nu·ance (nyōō'äns), *n.* a subtle distinction in colour, meaning, expression, etc.

nub·bin (nub'in), *n.* a small piece or lump; stub.

nu·bi·a (nyōō'bēə), *n.* a kind of knitted head scarf for women.

nu·bile (nyōō'bīl), *adj.* (of a woman) of marriageable age or condition.

nu·bi·lous (nyōō'bələs), *adj.* cloudy, vague, obscure.

nu·cha (nyōō'kə), *n.*, *pl.* **nu·chae** (nyōō'kē). the nape of the neck.

nu·ci·form (nyōō'səfôm,), *adj.* shaped like a nut.

nu·cle·ar (nyōō'klēə), *adj.* **1.** relating to or comprising a nucleus. **2.** relating to the use of atomic weapons.

nuclear fission. See fission.

nuclear fusion. See fusion.

nuclear mag·net·ic res·o·nance (magnet'ik rez'ənəns), *n.* **1.** the phenomenon whereby certain atomic nuclei absorb electromagnetic radiation when subjected to a magnetic field. It is used to determine the chemical composition and structure of substances in the technique called *nuclear magnetic resonance spectroscopy*. **2.** the technique in which the phenomenon is used to obtain images of body tissues and organs for medical diagnosis, employing a *nuclear magnetic resonance scanner. Abbr.:* **NMR**.

nu·cle·ate (nyōō'klēit), *adj.* possessing a nucleus.

nu·cle·ic acid (nyōōklē'ik), any of various complex acids found in all living cells.

nu·cle·o·lat·ed (nyōō'klēōlā'tid), *adj.* having a nucleolus. Also **nu'cle·o·late**.

nu·cle·o·lus (nyōōklē'ōləs), *n., pl.* **nu·cle·o·li** (nyōōklē'ōlī). a body lying within the nucleus of a cell. Also **nu'cle·ole**.

nu·cle·on·ics (nyōō,klēon'iks), *n.* the branch of physical science concerned with the engineering applications of the properties of atomic nuclei.

nu·cle·us (nyōō'klēəs), *n., pl.* **nu·cle·i** (nyōō'-klēī), **nu·cle·us·es.** a central core or point.

nu·di·caul (nyōō'dəkôl,), *adj.* (of plants) having stems without leaves.

nud·nik (nōōd'nik), *n. Slang.* an importunate or tiring person; a nuisance.

nu·ga·to·ry (nyōō'gətərē), *adj.* worthless; ineffective; insignificant.

nul·li·fid·i·an (nul,ifid'ēən), *n.* a person without religious belief.

nul·lip·a·ra (nulip'ərə), *n., pl.* **nul·lip·a·rae** (nulip'ərē). a woman who has never given birth to a child.

nul·li·ty (nul'itē), *n.* the state of being nothing.

nu·men (nyōō'min), *n., pl.* **nu·mi·na** (nyōō'-mənə). a spirit or deity supposed to inhabit a particular object or place. —**nu'mi·nous,** *adj.*

nu·mer·ol·o·gy (nyōō,mərol'əjē), *n.* the study of numbers as a means of predicting the future. —**nu·mer·ol'o·gist,** *n.*

nu·mis·mat·ics (nyōō,'mizmat'iks), *n.* the study of coins and medals. Also **nu·mis·ma·tol·o·gy** (nyōōmiz,mətol'əjē). —**nu·mis'ma·tist, nu·mis·ma·tol'o·gist,** *n.*

num·ma·ry (num'ərē), *adj.* relating to coins or money.

num·mu·lar (num'yōōlə), *adj.* **1.** relating to coins or money. **2.** shaped like a coin.

nunc di·mit·tis (nuNGk' dimit'is), *Latin.* permission to leave.

nun·ci·o (nun'sēō, nun'SHēō), *n., pl.* **nun·ci·os** (nun'SHēōz). an envoy of the pope accredited to the government of a foreign country. See also **apostolic delegate.** —**nun·ci·a·ture** (nun'sēəCHə, nun'SHēəCHə), *n.*

nun·cu·pa·tive (nuNG,kyəpā'tiv), *adj.* (of a will) not written; by word of mouth.

nuque (nyōōk), *n.* the back of the neck.

nu·tant (nyōō'tənt), *adj.* (of plants) drooping.

nu·ta·tion (nyōōtā'sHən), *n.* **1.** the action of nodding. **2.** a periodic oscillation in the axis of the earth.

nyc·ta·lo·pi·a (nik,təlō'pēə), *n.* a condition of the eye in which vision is extremely poor in reduced light, as at night, but normal in daylight. Also **night blindness.**

nyc·ti·trop·ic (nik,titrop'ik), *adj.* (of the leaves of plants) having a tendency to assume at night positions different from those held during the day.

nyc·to·pho·bi·a (nik,təfō'bēə), *n.* a morbid fear of darkness.

nym·pha (nim'fə), *n., pl.* **nym·phae** (nim'fē). one of the inner lips of the vulva.

nym·phae·um (nimfē'əm), *n., pl.* **nym·phae·a** (nimfē'ə). a room, hall, etc., fitted with a fountain and decorated with statues, etc.

nymph·et (nimfet'), *n.* a sexually attractive young girl.

nym·pho·lep·sy (nim'fəlep,sē), *n.* violent emotional longings, esp. for something unattainable. —**nym·pho·lept** (nim'fəlept), *n.*

nym·pho·ma·ni·a (nim,fəmā'nēə), *n.* abnormally strong sexual desire in women. See also **satyriasis, satyromania.**

nys·tag·mus (nistag'məs), *n.* an involuntary spasmodic movement of the eyeball.

nys·ta·tin (nis'tətin), *n.* an antibiotic used especially for treating fungal diseases.

ob·con·i·cal (obkon'ikəl), *adj.* (of a leaf) conical with the pointed end forming the place of attachment. Also **ob·con'ic.**

ob·cor·date (obkô'dāt), *adj.* (of a leaf) heart-shaped, with the pointed end forming the place of attachment.

ob·dur·ate (ob'dyŏŏrit, ob'dyərit), *adj.* stubbornly resisting appeals to emotion; obstinately hard-hearted; stony-hearted. **—ob'du·ra·cy,** *n.*

o·bei·sance (ōbā'səns), *n.* a bodily movement expressing submission, homage, respect, etc.

ob·fus·cate (obfus'kāt), *v.* to render obscure; confuse.

ob·i·ter dic·tum (ō'bitə dik'təm), *pl.* **ob·i·ter dic·ta** (ō'bitər dik'tə), *Latin.* a comment made in passing; incidental remark.

o·bit·u·ar·y (ōbicH'ŏŏər'ē), *n.* a newspaper announcement of a person's death together with short biographical details. Also **o'bit.**

ob·jec·tive (əbjek'tiv), *n.* an aim or purpose, as *Her objective is to be appointed minister.*

objective idealism, a philosophical theory that experience has an existence aside and separate from that of the objects experienced and of the mind of the observer. See also **subjective idealism.**

ob·jet d'art (ôb,zHe dä'), *pl.* **ob·jets d'art** (ôb,zHe dä'). *French.* an article or object of artistic merit.

ob·jur·gate (ob'jəgāt), *v.* to denounce, scold, or upbraid vehemently.

ob·last (ob'läst), *n.,* *pl.* **ob·lasts, ob·las·ti** (ob'lästē). a region or province; an autonomous administrative area.

ob·late (ob'lāt), *adj.* **1.** (of a spheroid) flattened at the poles. **—n. 2.** one dedicated to monastic life, but not under monastic vows. See also **prolate.**

ob·la·tion (oblā'sHən), *n.* an offering made to a deity or for religious or charitable purposes.

o·blique (əblēk'), *adj.* at an angle; not straight or straightforward.

ob·liq·ui·ty (əblik'witē), *n.* deviation from proper moral conduct; immorality; perversity.

ob·li·ves·cence (ob,ləves'əns), *n.* forgetfulness.

ob·liv·i·on (əbliv'ēən), *n.* the condition of being totally forgotten or no longer known. **—ob·liv'i·ous,** *adj.*

ob·lo·quy (ob'ləkwē), *n.* **1.** disgrace resulting from public censure. **2.** blame; condemnatory language; abuse.

ob·o·vate (obō'vāt), *adj.* (of a leaf, etc.) ovate with the narrower end forming the base.

ob·o·void (obō'void), *adj.* (of certain fruits, etc.) ovoid with the narrower end forming the base.

ob·pyr·i·form (obpir'əfôm,), *adj.* shaped like a pear with the narrower end forming the base.

ob·scene (əbsēn', obsēn'), *adj.* abhorrent to feelings of decency or modesty; designed to arouse sexual excitement.

ob·scu·rant·ism (ob,skyŏŏr'əntiz,əm), *n.* opposition to the spread of knowledge and enlightenment; intentional vagueness or obscurity. **—ob·scu'rant,** *n., adj.*

ob·scure (əbskyŏŏ'ə, obskyŏŏ'ə), *adj.* **1.** not easily seen or understood; vague; distant; not known or recognized. **—v. ob·scured, ob·scur·ing. 2.** to make (something) hard to see or understand; hide. **—ob·scur'i·ty,** *n.*

ob·se·crate (ob'sikrāt), *v.* to implore; beg; beseech.

ob·se·quence (ob'sikwəns), *n.* eagerness to please; willing compliance. Also **ob·se·que·ence** (obsē'kwēəns). **—ob'se·quent,** *adj.*

ob·se·quies (ob'səkwēz), *n. pl.* funeral services or rites.

ob·se·qui·ous (obsē'kwēəs), *adj.* excessively deferential or humble; fawning; servile.

ob·se·quy (ob'səkwē), *n., pl.* **ob·se·quies.** *(usually in the pl.)* a funeral ceremony or rite.

ob·so·lesce (ob,səles'), *v.* to be or become obsolescent.

ob·so·les·cent (ob'sələs'ənt), *adj.* in the process of becoming obsolete. **—ob,so·lesce',** *v.* **—ob,so·les'cence,** *n.*

ob·so·lete (ob,səlēt'), *adj.* out of date; no longer in use, as an idea, device, word, etc.

ob·stet·rics (obstet'riks), *n.* the branch of medicine concerned with childbirth. **—ob·stet'·ric,** *adj.* **—ob·ste·tri·cian** (ob,stətrisH'ən), *n.*

ob·sti·nate (ob'stinit), *adj.* stubborn; not easily moved by argument; firm.

ob·sti·pant (ob'stipənt), *n.* something which causes prolonged constipation.

ob·sti·pa·tion (ob,stipā'sHən), *n.* prolonged constipation.

ob·strep·er·ous (obstrep'ərəs), *adj.* noisily unruly; clamorous; turbulent.

ob·stru·ent (ob'strōōənt), *adj.* causing an obstruction.

ob·tect (obtekt'), *adj.* denoting a pupa in which the wings and legs are stuck to the body by a secretion. Also **ob·tect'ed.**

ob·test (obtest'), *v.* 1. to call as witness. 2. to implore or beseech.

ob·trude (obtrōōd'), *v.* to thrust upon; compel to notice; bring forcibly to the attention of. —ob·tru'sion, *n.*

ob·tru·sive (obtrōō'siv), *adj.* forced upon one; intruding.

ob·tund (obtund'), *v.* to make blunt, dull.

ob·tu·rate (ob'tyōōrāt), *v.* to obstruct or stop up; close; block.

ob·tuse (əbtyōōs'), *adj.* 1. lacking sharpness in form; blunt. 2. lacking alertness, mentally sluggish, stupid.

ob·um·brate (obum'brāt), *v.* to cloud over, darken, cast a shadow over. —ob·um'brant, *adj.*

ob·verse (ob'vûs), *n.* the main or chief surface of anything; front.

ob·vert (obvût'), *v.* to turn so as to present a different view, side, or surface. —ob·ver'sion, *n.*

ob·vi·ate (ob'vēāt), *v.* to make unnecessary, avoid, prevent.

ob·vo·lute (ob'vəlōōt), *adj.* turned inward.

Oc·cam's razor, Ock·ham's razor (ok'-əm), the principle that assumptions put forward to explain phenomena should be kept to a minimum.

oc·ci·dent·al (ok,səden'təl), *adj.* of or pertaining to the west, esp. the western hemisphere.

oc·ci·put (ok'səput), *n., pl.* **oc·ci·puts, oc·ci·pi·ta** (oksip'itə). the back part of the skull. —oc·cip'i·tal, *adj.*

oc·clude (əklōōd'), *v.* to stop up, block; shut off. —oc·clu'sion, *n.* —oc·clu'sive, *adj.*

oc·cul·ta·tion (ok,ultā'sнən), *n.* the state of having disappeared from view; disappearance.

o·ce·a·nic·i·ty (ō,sнēənis'itē), *n.* the effect of the sea upon the climate of a particular region. See also **continentality.**

o·ce·a·nog·ra·phy (ō,'sнēənog'rəfē), *n.* the study of the ocean.

oc·el·lat·ed (os'əlā,tid), *adj.* (of a marking) resembling an eye; having an eye-like spot, as a peaoock. Also **oc·el·late** (os'əlāt). —oc,el·la'tion, *n.*

o·cel·lus (ōsel'əs), *n., pl.* **o·cel·li** (ōsel'ī). a simple kind of eye found in invertebrate animals. —o·cel'lar, *adj.*

och·le·sis (oklē'sis), *n.* an illness or disease caused by population congestion, overcrowded living space, etc. —och,le·sit'ic, och·let'ik, *adj.*

och·loc·ra·cy (oklok'rəsē), *n.* mob rule; government by the mob.

och·lo·pho·bi·a (ok,ləfō'bēə), *n.* a morbid fear of crowds.

o·chroid (ō'kroid), *adj.* of the colour of yellow ochre.

oc·re·a (ok'rēə), *n., pl.* **oc·re·ae** (ok'riē). something which forms a sheath. —oc·re·ate (ok'rēit), *adj.*

oc·tad (ok'tad), *n.* a set or series of eight.

oc·ta·he·dron (ok,təhē'drən), *n., pl.* **oc·ta·he·drons, oc·ta·he·dra** (ok,təhē'drə). a three-dimensional figure having eight sides. —oc,ta·he'dral, *adj.*

oc·tam·er·ous (oktam'ərəs), *adj.* having or containing eight parts.

oc·tan (ok'tən), *adj.* (of a fever) recurring every eight days.

oc·tane (ok'tān), *n.* any of several saturated hydrocarbons, some of which are obtained in the refining of petroleum.

octane number, the measure of the anti-knock characteristics of a fuel, esp. petrol.

oc·tant (ok'tənt), *n.* an eighth part of a circle.

oc·tar·chy (ok'täkē), *n.* rule or government by eight persons.

oc·til·lion (oktil'yən), *n.* 1. (in Britain and Germany) the number represented by the figure 1 followed by 48 zeros. 2. (in the U.S.A., Canada, and France) the number represented by the figure 1 followed by 27 zeros.

oc·to·de·cil·lion (oc,tōdisil'yən), *n.* 1. (in Britain and Germany) the numbers represented by the figure 1 followed by 108 zeros. 2. (in the U.S.A. and Canada) the number represented by the figure 1 followed by 57 zeros.

oc·to·ge·nar·i·an (ok,tōjənər'ēən), *adj.* 1. between the ages of 80 and 89. —n. 2. a person of this age.

oc·to·nar·y (ok'tənərē), *adj.* relating to the number 8.

oc·to·pod (ok'təpod), *n.* any member of an order of eight-armed or --legged animals, which includes the octopuses.

oc·to·roon, oc·ta·roon (ok,tərōōn'), *n.* the offspring of White and quadroon parents; i.e. having one-eighth Negro ancestry.

oc·troi (ok'troi), *n.* a tax imposed on certain goods when brought into a city.

oc·tu·ple (ok'tyōōpəl), *adj.* eight times as much or as great.

oc·tup·let (oktyōōp'lit), *n.* a combination, set, or series of eight connected items.

oc·tu·pli·cate (oktyōō'pləkit), *adj.* consisting of eight identical parts or of one original and seven copies.

oc·u·lo·mo·tor (ok'yōōlōmō,tə), *adj.* causing the eyeball to move.

oc·u·lus (ok'yōōləs), *n., pl.* **oc·u·li** (ok'yōōlī). an eye.

o·da·lisque (ō'dəlisk), *n.* a female slave or concubine in a harem.

o·di·ous (ō'dēəs), *adj.* hateful; repugnant; offensive; disgusting.

o·di·um (ō'dēəm), *n.* extreme dislike marked by feelings of loathing or contempt; abhorrence.

o·dom·e·ter (ōdom'itə), *n.* a device for measuring the distance covered by a vehicle: Also **hodometer.**

o·don·tal·gia (ō,dontal'jēə), *n.* toothache.

o·don·ti·a·sis (ō,dontī'əsis), *n.* teething; the cutting of teeth.

o·don·to·blast (ōdon'təblast,), *n.* any of the outer cells lining the tooth cavity, which secrete dentin.

o·don·tog·e·ny (ō,dontoj'ənē), *n.* the growth and development of teeth. Also **o·don·to·gen'e·sis. —o·don,to·gen'ic,** *adj.*

o·don·toid (ōdon'toid), *adj.* having the form of a tooth; like a tooth.

o·don·tol·o·gy (ō,dontol'əjē), *n.* the care of teeth; dentistry.

oe·cu·men·i·cal (ē,kyōōmen'ikəl), *adj.* See ecumenical. Also **oec,u·men'ic.**

oe·de·ma, e·de·ma (idē'mə), *n., pl.* **oe·de·ma·ta, e·de·ma·ta** (idē'mətə). the presence of serous fluid in body cavities or tissue spaces.

oeil·lade (ûyäd'), *n., pl.* **oeil·lades** (ûyäd'). *French.* a coquettish glance; amorous look.

oe·nol·o·gy, e·nol·o·gy (ēnol'əjē), *n.* the science of wine and wine-making. **—oe·nol'o·gist,** *n.*

oe·no·mel (ē'nəmel), *n.* a beverage made of wine and honey.

oer·sted (û'sted), *n.* a unit of magnetic intensity that is equal to the intensity of a magnetic field in a vacuum when experiencing a force of one dyne.

oe·soph·a·ge·al, e·soph·a·ge·al (ēsof,-əjē'əl), *adj.* of or pertaining to the oesophagus.

oesophageal speech, a method of producing sounds without using the larynx.

oe·soph·a·gi·tis (ēsof,əjī'tis), *n.* inflammation of the oesophagus.

oe·soph·a·gus, e·soph·a·gus (ēsof'əgəs), *n., pl.* **oe·soph·a·gi, e·soph·a·gi** (ēsof'əjī). the tubular connection between the mouth and the stomach.

oe·stro·gen, e·stro·gen (ē'strəjən), *n.* any of several female sex hormones that regulate the reproductive cycle. **—oe,stro·gen'ic,** *adj.*

oe·strus, e·strus (ē'strəs), *n.* a period of female sexual heat. **—oe·strous, e·strous** (e'strəs, ē'strəs), *adj.*

oeu·vre (û'vrə), *n., pl.* **oeu·vres** (û'vre). *French.* the work of a writer, artist, etc., considered as a whole, or an individual work.

off·al (of'əl), *n.* **1.** refuse; rubbish; junk. **2.** the waste products of a butchered animal, some of which may be considered edible.

of·fic·i·nal (ofis'inəl), *adj.* (of a drug, etc.) available without need for any special preparation; kept in stock. See also **magistral.**

of·fi·cious (əfisII'əs), *adj.* interfering; meddling; offering unwanted advice or help.

off·print (of'print,), *n.* a reprint by itself of an article originally published with other articles in a journal, magazine, etc.

og·do·ad (og'dōad), *n.* the number eight or any set, series, or group of eight.

ohm (ōm), *n.* a measure of resistance to electric current by the medium (as a wire) through which it passes, such that one volt acts to produce one ampere. See also **ampere, volt. —ohm'ic,** *adj.*

ohm·age (ō'mij), *n.* the resistance in a conductor measured in ohms.

ohm·me·ter (ōm'mē,tə), *n.* a device for measuring or indicating electrical resistance in ohms.

o·le·ag·i·nous (ō,lēaj'ənəs), *adj.* oily or producing oil.

ol·fac·tion (olfak'sHən), *n.* **1.** the act or process of smelling. **2.** the sense of smell.

ol·fac·to·re·cep·tor (olfak,tōrisep'tə), *n.* a sense organ which is sensitive to smell.

ol·fac·to·ry (olfak'tərē), *adj.* relating to the sense of smell.

ol·i·garch (ol'igäk), *n.* a ruler in an oligarchy.

ol·i·gar·chy (ol'igä,kē), *n.* **1.** a government in which a small group, such as a dominant class or faction, exercises effective control. **2.** a country or state ruled in this manner. **—ol·i·gar'chic,** *adj.*

ol·i·go·car·pous (ol,igōkä'pəs), *adj.* bearing or producing only a few fruits; not fruitful.

Ol·i·go·cene (ol'igōsēn), *adj.* relating to a division of the Tertiary epoch between the Eocene and the Miocene, about 25,000,000 to 40,000,000 years ago.

ol·i·go·cy·thae·mi·a (ol,igōsīthē'mēə), *n.* an anaemic condition characterized by loss of corpuscles in the blood.

ol·i·go·don·tia (ol,igōdon'sHə), *n.* an abnormal condition which results in the growth of fewer than the normal number of teeth.

ol·i·goph·a·gous (ol,igof'əgəs), *adj.* eating only a few particular kinds of food. See also **monophagous.**

ol·i·go·phre·ni·a (ol,igōfrē'nēə), *n.* failure of normal mental growth; feeblemindedness.

ol·i·gop·o·ly (ol,igop'əlē), *n.* a market situation in which there are only a few producers or sellers and many buyers. See also **duopoly, monopoly.**

ol·i·gop·so·ny (ol,igop'sənē), *n.* a market situation in which there are only a few buyers and many sellers. See also **duopsony, monopsony.**

ol·i·gu·ri·a (ol,igyōōr'ēə), *n.* lack of urine resulting from reduced secretion. Also **ol·i·gu·re·sis** (ol,igyōōrē'sis).

o·li·o (ō'lēō) *n.* a mixture or combination of miscellaneous elements.

ol·i·va·ceous (ol,ivā'sHəs), *adj.* deep green in colour; olive.

ol·i·va·ry (ol'ivərē), *adj.* having the shape of an olive.

olivary body, either of two olive-shaped bodies in the brain, lying alongside the medulla oblongata.

ol·la po·dri·da (ol'ə pədrē'də), *n.* **1.** a highly seasoned Spanish stew of meat and vegetables. **2.** a miscellany or mixture of diverse elements.

o·lo·ro·so (ol,ərō'sō), *n.* a variety of sweet, dark-coloured sherry.

O·lym·pi·an (əlim'pēən), *adj.* detached; lofty; imposing; greatly superior; regal.

o·ma·sum (ōmā'səm), *n., pl.* **o·ma·sa** (ōmā'sə). the third of the four stomachs of a ruminant. See also **rumen, reticulum, abomasum.**

om·buds·man (om'boodzmən, om'budsmən), *n., pl.* **om·buds·men** (om'boodzmen, om'budzmen). an official empowered to investigate complaints made by private citizens about injustice or abuse on the part of the government or public service.

o·me·ga (ō'migə, ōmā'gə), *n.* the end; ending; the last of a series; final letter of classical Greek alphabet.

o·men·tum (ōmen'təm), *n., pl.* **o·men·ta** (ōmen'tə). a fold in the peritoneum connecting certain viscera. See also **greater omentum, lesser omentum.**

om·i·nous (om'ənəs), *adj.* evil; threatening; likely to cause evil in the future, as *an ominous remark* or *ominous weather.*

om·ni·far·i·ous (om,nifer'ēəs), *adj.* of all varieties or forms.

om·nif·ic (omnif'ik), *adj.* creating or producing everything.

om·nif·i·cent (om,nif'isənt), *adj.* having unlimited creative power; creating all things.

om·nis·cience (omnis'ēəns), *n.* the state of having infinite awareness or insight; unlimited knowledge. —**om·nis'cient,** *adj.*

om·ni·um-gath·er·um (om'nēəmgaTH'ərəm), *n.* a variety or miscellaneous collection of people or things.

om·ni·vore (om'nivô), *n.* a person or animal that is omnivorous.

om·niv·or·ous (omniv'ərəs), *adj.* eating all kinds of food; unrestricted in diet.

om·pha·los (om'fələs), *n.* the navel.

om·pha·lo·skep·sis (om,fəlōskep'sis), *n.* the study of one's navel as part of an exercise in mysticism.

o·nan·ism (ō'nəniz,əm), *n.* (in sexual intercourse) the withdrawal of the penis from the vagina before orgasm.

on·co·gene (oNG'kōjĕn,), *n.* a gene that potentially can transform a normal cell into a cancerous cell.

on·co·gen·ic (oNG,kōjen'ik), *adj.* causing or promoting the formation of tumours, esp. cancerous tumours. Also **on·cog·e·nous** (oNGkoj'ənəs). —**on·co·gen·e·sis** (oNG,kōjen'əsis), **on·co·ge·nic·i·ty** (oNG,kōjənis'itē), *n.*

on·co·sis (oNGkō'sis), *n.* any pathological condition resulting in the growth of tumours.

on·do·gram (on'dəgram,), *n.* a record made on an ondograph.

on·do·graph (on'dōgräf,, on'dōgraf,), *n.* a device for measuring variations in oscillatory movements, as in an alternating current.

on·dom·e·ter (ondom'itə), *n.* a device for measuring the wavelengths of radio waves.

o·nei·ric (ōnī'rik), *adj.* relating to dreams.

o·nei·ro·crit·ic (ōnī,rōkrit'ik), *n.* one who specializes in the interpretation of dreams. —**o·nei,·ro·crit'i·cism,** *n.*

o·nei·ro·man·cy (ōnī'rōman,sē), *n.* divination by the interpretation of dreams.

on·er·ous (ō'nərəs, on'ərəs), *adj.* constituting a burden or hardship; irksome; troublesome.

o·ni·o·ma·ni·a (ō,nēōmā'nēə), *n.* an irrepressible urge to buy things.

on·o·mas·tics (on,əmas'tiks), *n.* the scientific study of the origins of proper names. Also **on·o·ma·tol·o·gy** (on,əmətol'əjē). —**on·o·mas'tic,** *adj.*

on·o·mat·o·poe·ia (on,ōmat,əpē'ə), *n.* the formation of a word by imitation of a sound associated with the thing to be designated.

on·tog·e·ny (ontoj'ənē), *n.* the growth or history of development of a particular organism. Also **on,to·gen'e·sis.** See also **phylogeny.**

ontological argument, a philosophical argument that claims to prove the existence of God by declaring that since existence is a state of perfection and God is the most perfect being conceivable, He must therefore exist, or else a still more perfect being would be possible. Also called **ontological proof.**

on·tol·o·gism (ontol'əjiz,əm), *n.* the theological doctrine which asserts that the human mind immediately perceives God to be the appropriate object of its cognitions.

on·tol·o·gy (ontol'əjē), *n.* a branch of metaphysics concerned with the nature of being.

o·nus (ō'nəs), *n., pl.* **o·nus·es.** a responsibility, obligation, or burden.

o·nych·i·a (ōnik'ēə), *n.* inflammation of the tissue beneath the nail.

on·y·cho·pha·gia (on,əkōfā'jə), *n.* nail-biting, esp. as a characteristic of an emotionally disturbed condition.

o·ol·o·gy, o·öl·o·gy (ōol'əjē), *n.* the study of birds' eggs.

o·o·pho·rec·to·my, o·ö·pho·rec·to·my (ō,əfərek'təmē), *n.* the removal of one or both ovaries; ovariectomy.

o·o·pho·ri·tis, o·ö·pho·ri·tis (ō,əfərī'tis), *n.* inflammation of the ovaries; ovaritis.

o·o·sperm, o·ö·sperm (ō'əspûm), *n.* a fertilized egg.

o·o·the·ca, o·ö·the·ca (ō,əthē'kə), *n., pl.* o·o·the·cae, o·ö·the·cae (ō,əthē'sē). a capsulelike container for the eggs of snails and of certain insects.

o·pac·i·fy (ōpas'əfī), *v.* to make impenetrable to light; render opaque.

o·pa·cim·e·ter (ō,pəsim'itə), *n.* a device for determining the opacity of something.

o·pal·esce (ō,pəles'), *v.* to shine with various colours, as an opal. **—o,pal·es'cent,** *adj.*

op art (op), a form of modern abstract art that makes use of various patterns and materials to create special optical effects.

op. cit. (op' sit'), (in the work already mentioned. [abbr. of Latin *opere citato*]

open shop, an organization in which union membership is not an essential condition of employment although a democratically elected union represents all the employees in negotiations with the management. See also **closed shop.**

o·pen·work (ō'pənwûk,), *n.* work in any material, as stone, wood, lace, etc., that has openings in it as part of its decorative pattern.

op·er·ant (op'ərənt), *adj.* effective; functioning; in operation.

o·per·cu·lum (ōpû'kyoōləm), *n., pl.* o·per·cu·la (ōpur'kyələ), **o·per·cu·lums.** an organ of a plant or animal that acts as a lid or covering.

op·er·on (op'əron,), *n.* (in genetics) a cluster of genes functioning as a unit. It consists of structural genes, whose expression is controlled by promotor and operator genes.

o·phid·i·an (ōfid'ēən), *adj.* relating to or belonging to snakes.

oph·i·ol·a·try (of,ēol'ətrē), *n.* snake worship.

oph·i·ol·o·gy (of,ēol'əjē), *n.* the study of snakes. See also **herpetology.**

oph·thal·mi·a (ofthal'mēə), *n.* inflammation of the eyeball or its mucous membranes. Also **oph·thal·mi·tis** (of,thəlmī'tis).

oph·thal·mic (ofthal'mik), *adj.* relating to or connected with the eye.

oph·thal·mo·dy·na·mom·e·ter (ofthal,-mōdī,nəmom'itə), *n.* an instrument for determimng the blood pressure in the blood vessels of the retina.

oph·thal·mol·o·gy (of,thalmol'əjē), *n.* the branch of medicine concerned with the structure, function, and diseases of the eye. **—oph,-thal·mol'o·gist,** *n.*

oph·thal·mom·e·ter (of,thalmom'itə), *n.* a device for examining the eye, usually in order to ascertain the presence of astigmatism.

oph·thal·mo·ple·gi·a (ofthal,mōplē'jə), *n.* paralysis of the muscles of the eye.

oph·thal·mo·scope (ofthal'məskōp,), *n.* an instrument for examining the inner part of the eye.

oph·thal·mos·co·py (of,thalmos'kəpē), *n.* the art or technique of using an ophthalmoscope.

opiate (ō'pēit), *n.* anything that dulls the mind or soothes emotions.

o·pis·the·nar (əpis'thä,), *n.* the back of the hand.

op·is·thog·na·thous (op,isthog'nəthəs), *adj.* having jaws that recede.

o·pi·um (ō'pēəm), *n.* the dried juice of the poppy, used in medicine to relieve pain, induce sleep, etc.; an addictive narcotic drug, poisonous in large quantities.

op·pi·late (op'əlāt), *v.* to block up; stop up; obstruct.

op·po·nens (əpō'nenz),· *n., pl.* **op·po·nen·tes** (op,ənen'tēz). a muscle of the hand or foot which brings the fingers or toes together in such a way as to form a hollow in the palm or sole.

op·pro·bri·um (əprō'brēəm), *n.* disgrace caused by shameful behaviour; dishonour. **—op·pro'bri·ous,** *adj.*

op·pugn (əpyoōn'), *v.* to attack with argument or criticism; fight against. **—op·pug·nant** (əpug'-nənt), *adj.*

opt (opt), *v.* to decide, choose, or select (usually followed by to and a verb or for and a noun), as *He opted to go* or *I'll opt for the green tie with the pink dots.* **—op'tion,** *n.*

op·ti·cist (op'tisist), *n.* one who is concerned with optics.

op·tics (op'tiks), *n.* the scientific study of the properties and phenomena of light and of vision.

op·tom·e·ter (optom'itə), *n.* a device for determining the extent of defective vision in an eye.

op·tom·e·try (optom'itrē), *n.* the measuring of defects in vision in order to prescribe suitable correctional lenses. **—op·tom'e·trist,** *n.*

op·u·lent (op'yoōlənt), *adj.* representing wealth; abundant. **—op'u·lence,** *n.*

o·pus (ō'pəs), *n., pl.* **o·pus·es,** op·e·ra (op'ərə). a literary work or a musical composition.

o·pus·cule (opus'kyoōl), *n.* a minor or short literary or musical work.

o·rac·u·lar (ōrak'yoōlə), *adj.* relating to or resembling an oracle, making decisions or passing judgments as if possessing special insight or knowledge.

Or·ange·man (or'injmən), *n.* a member of a secret society founded in the north of Ireland in 1795 with the aim of maintaining the political dominance of Protestantism.

or·bic·u·lar (ōbik'yoōlə), *adj.* circular; spherical; rounded. Also **or·bic'u·late.**

or·bi·cu·lar·is (ōbikyoōlar'is), *n., pl.* **or·bi·cu·**

·lar·es (ôbikyōōlar'ēz). a muscle surrounding an opening in the body.

or·chi·dot·o·my (ô,kidot'əmē), n. a surgical incision of the testis. Also or·chot'o·my.

or·chi·ec·to·my (ô,kēek'təmē), n. the surgical excision of one or both testes; castration. Also or·chec'to·my, or,chi·dec'to·my.

or·chi·tis (ôkī'tis), n. an inflamed condition of the testis.

or·deal (ôdēl'), n. an experience characterized by much discomfort and difficulty.

or·di·nal (ô'dənəl), adj. relating to an order or subdivision of plants or animals.

or·di·nand (ô'dinand,), n. a candidate for ordination.

Or·do·vi·cian (ôr,dōvisн'ən), adj. relating to an early period of the Palaeozoic era, between the Cambrian and the Silurian, occurring 440 to 500 million years ago.

o·rec·tic (ôrek'tik), adj. relating to desire.

o·rex·is (ôrek'sis), n. the aspect of mental activity concerned with emotion and desire rather than cognition.

or·gan·die, or·gan·dy (ô'gəndē), n. a very fine cotton fabric used for blouses, dresses, etc.

or·ga·nelle (ô,gənel'), n. a part or structure of a cell that is specialized for a particular function, such as the flagellum in certain motile cells.

or·ga·no·gen·e·sis (ô,gənōjen'isis), n. the origin and development of organs, as those of the body. Also or·ga·nog·e·ny (ôgənoj'ənē).

or·ga·nog·ra·phy (ô,gənog'rəfē), n. the scientific study of the organs of plants or animals.

or·gan·o·lep·tic (ô,gənōlep'tik), adj. 1. able to stimulate the sense organs. 2. of or relating to the characteristics of a substance (e.g. the temperature of the bathwater) that stimulate the sense organs.

or·ga·nol·o·gy (ô,gənol'əjē), n. the study of the form and functions of the organs of animals and plants.

or·gan·o·me·tal·lic (ô,ganōmital'ik), adj. 1. of or relating to an organic chemical compound that contains one or more metal ions. —n. 2. such a compound.

or·ga·no·ther·a·py (ô,gənōther'əpē), n. the treatment of illness by the use of preparations extracted from the organs of animals. Also or·ga·no·ther·a·peu·tics (ô,gənōther,əpyōō'tiks).

or·ga·non (ô'gənon), n. anything that serves as an instrument to facilitate the acquisition of knowledge, esp. a system of rules or body of principles of scientific investigation.

or·gan·za (ôgan'zə), n. a sheer fabric of silk or man-made fibres used as a dress material.

or·gone (ô'gōn), n. the universal substance of sexual energy, postulated by Austrian psychologist Wilhelm Reich (1897–1957).

o·ri·el (ôr'ēəl), n. a bay window projecting out of a wall and supported by a bracket.

o·ri·en·tal (ôr,ēen'təl), adj. designating or pertaining to the east, esp. the Far East. See also austral, boreal, occidental.

or·i·flamme (ôr'iflam), n. a standard or banner, esp. one which serves to rally troops in battle.

o·ri·ga·mi (ôrigä'mē), n. the Japanese art of folding paper so as to achieve a variety of decorative patterns and constructions.

or·nis (ô'nis), n., pl. or·ni·thes (ônī,thēz). the birds of a particular region or environment considered together.

or·nith·ic (ônith'ik), adj. relating to birds; birdlike.

or·ni·thoid (ô'nithoid), adj. like a bird.

or·ni·thol·o·gy (ô,nithol'əjē), n. the scientific study of birds.

or·ni·thop·ter (ônithop'tə), n. an aeroplane which is powered by flapping wings. Also or·thop·ter (ôrthop'tər).

o·rog·e·ny (oroj'ənē), n. the process by which mountains are formed, esp. by folding of the earth's crust.

o·rog·ra·phy (orog'rəfē), n. the branch of geography concerned with mountains. —or·o·met·ric (ôrəmet'rik), adj.

o·rol·o·gy (orol'əjē) n. the scientific study of mountains.

o·rom·e·ter (orom'itə), n. a type of barometer used for measuring the heights of mountains. —or·o·met·ric (or,əmet'rik), adj.

o·rom·e·try (orom'itrē), n. the art or science of measuring the heights of mountains.

o·ro·phar·ynx (ôr,ōfar'inks), n., pl. o·ro·pha·ryn·ges (ôr,ōfərin'jēz), o·ro·phar·ynx·es. the pharynx proper as distinct from the nasopharynx and the laryngeal pharynx.

or·o·tund (or'ōtund,, ôr'ōtund), adj. 1. (of a voice) sounding clear and resonant; strong. 2. pompous; bombastic.

or·phrey (ô'frē), n. elaborately decorated embroidery.

or·rer·y (or'ərē), n. an apparatus for showing the movements of bodies in the solar system.

or·tho·don·tics (ô,thōdon'tiks), n. the branch of dentistry concerned with the correction of irregularities of the teeth. —or,tho·don'tist, n.

Orthodox Church, that part of the Christian Church that combines under the patriarch of Constantinople, including national and local Eastern Churches.

or·tho·e·py, or·tho·ë·py (ôthō'ipē), n. the study of the correct pronunciation of a language.

or·tho·gen·e·sis (ô,thōjen'isis), n. 1. the evolution of a species along a predetermined path. 2. the theory that social evolution in all cultures must pass through equivalent stages, despite differing environmental factors. —**or,tho·ge·net'ic**, *adj.*

or·tho·gen·ic (ô,*th*ōjen'ik), *adj.* relating to the treatment of emotionally disturbed or mentally backward children.

or·thog·na·thous (ôthog'n*ə*th*ə*s), *adj.* having straight jaws so that the face is approximately vertical when seen in profile. Also **or·thog·nath'ic**.

or·thog·o·nal (ôthog'*ə*n*ə*l), *adj.* relating to or containing right angles or perpendiculars.

or·thog·ra·phize (ôthog'r*ə*fīz), *v.* to spell correctly or in accordance with the rules of orthography.

or·thog·ra·phy (ôthog'r*ə*fē), *n.* the correct spelling of words according to established rules or usage. See also **cacography**. —**or·thog'ra·pher**, *n.* —**or,tho·graph'ic**, *adj.*

or·tho·pae·dics, or·tho·pe·dics (ô,*th*əpē'diks), *n.* the branch of surgery concerned with the correction of deformities of the bones, muscles, spinal system, etc. —**or,tho·pe'dic**, *adj.* —**or,tho·pe'dist**, *n.*

or·thop·noe·a, or·thop·ne·a (ôthop'nē*ə*), *n.* difficulty in breathing when lying down.

or·tho·prax·i·a (ô,*th*əprak'sē*ə*), *n.* the correction of bodily deformities.

or·tho·prax·y (ô'thōprak,sē), *n.* correct or orthodox use or practice.

or·tho·psy·chi·a·try (ô,*th*ōsīkī'*ə*trē), *n.* the treatment of mental illness, esp. in young people.

or·thop·ter (ôthop't*ə*), *n.* See **ornithopter**.

or·thop·ter·ous (ôthop't*ə*r*ə*s), *adj.* relating to or belonging to an order of insects having hind wings that fold longitudinally down the back.

or·thop·tic (ôthop'tik), *adj.* relating to or giving normal vision with both eyes.

or·tho·scope (ô,*th*əskōp,), *n.* an instrument for examining the inner part of the eye. —**or,tho·scop'ic**, *adj.*

or·tho·se·lec·tion (ô,*th*ōsilek'sH*ə*n), *n.* a kind of evolution which favours adaptation to environment.

or·tho·sis (ôthō'sis), *n., pl.* **or·tho·ses** (ôthō'sēz). a mechanical device or special fitting used to correct or assist the function of abnormal or diseased limbs, joints, etc.

or·thot·iks (ôthot'iks), *n.* the medical specialty dealing with the design, manufacture, and use of orthoses.

or·tho·trop·ic (ô,*th*ōtrop'ik), *n.* (of plants, etc.) tending to grow more or less vertically. —**or·thot·ro·pism** (ôthot'r*ə*piz,*ə*m), *n.*

os¹ (os), *n., pl.* a bone.

os² (os), *n., pl.* **o·ra** (ō'r*ə*). an opening, orifice, or entrance.

os·cil·lo·gram (*ə*sil'*ə*gram,), *n.* a recording made by an oscillograph or oscilloscope.

os·cil·lo·graph (*ə*sil'*ə*gräf,, *ə*sil'*ə*graf,), *n.* an

instrument for recording electrical oscillations, as the wave forms of alternating currents, etc.

os·cil·lom·e·ter (os,*ə*lom'it*ə*), *n.* a device that records or measures changes in the arterial pulse.

os·cil·lo·scope (*ə*sil'*ə*skōp,), *n.* an instrument that shows, on the screen of a cathode ray tube, electrical changes in a voltage, current, etc.

os·cine (os'īn, os'in), *adj.* of or relating to the Oscines, a suborder containing the majority of songbirds.

os·ci·tant (os'it*ə*nt), *adj.* lazy; drowsy; lacking attention; careless.

os·cu·lant (os'kyōōl*ə*nt) *adj.* sharing certain characteristics in common.

os·cu·lar (os'kyōōl*ə*), *adj.* relating to an osculum or mouth.

os·cu·late (os'kyōōlāt,), *v.* **1.** to kiss or embrace. **2.** to make close contact with. —**os·cu·la'tion**, *n.*

os·cu·lum (os'kyōōl*ə*m), *n., pl.* **os·cu·la** (os'kyōōl*ə*). a small opening or orifice having the shape of a mouth.

os·mics (oz'miks), *n.* the scientific study of the sense of smell.

os·mi·dro·sis (oz,*m*idrō'sis), *n.* the secretion of sweat of bad odour.

os·mom·e·ter (ozmom'it*ə*), *n.* a device used to measure osmotic pressure.

os·mom·e·try (ozmom'itrē), *n.* the measurement of osmotic pressure.

os·mose (oz'mōs, oz'mōz), *v.* to subject to or to be subjected to osmosis. —**os·mot·ic** (ozmot'ik), *adj.*

os·mo·sis (ozmō'sis), *n.* the diffusion of a liquid through a semipermeable membrane until it is in equal concentrations on both sides of the membrane.

os·o·phone (os'*ə*fōn,), *n.* a telephone receiver that transmits vibrations directly to the bones of the head, used by the hard of hearing.

os·se·ous (os'ē*ə*s), *adj.* consisting of bone; bony; bonelike.

Os·si·an·ic (os,ēan'ik), *adj.* given to pompous or pretentious utterances; bombastic.

os·si·cle (os'ik*ə*l), *n.* a small bone.

os·sif·er·ous (osif'*ə*r*ə*s), *adj.* containing bones or fossilized deposits of bones.

os·si·fy (os'*ə*fī), *v.* **1.** to make or become bone or bonelike; change into bone. **2.** to become rigid or fixed in outlook, attitudes, etc. —**os·si·fi·ca'tion**, *n.*

os·su·ar·y (os'yōō*ə*r'ē), *n.* a place where the bones of the dead are deposited. Also **os·su·ar·i·um** (os,yōō*ə*r'ē*ə*m).

os·tec·to·my (ostek't*ə*mē), *n.* the surgical excision of a bone. Also **os·te·ec·to·my** (os,tēek't*ə*mē).

os·te·i·tis (os,tēī'tis), *n.* inflammation of the bone or bone tissue.

os·ten·sive (osten'siv), *adj.* **1.** obviously or clearly showing. **2.** pretended, professed, or seeming.

os·te·o·ar·thri·tis (os,tēōäthrī'tis), *n.* a kind of chronic arthritis causing degeneration of the joints, found mainly in old people. Also **degenerative joint disease.**

os·te·o·blast (os'tēəblast,), *n.* a cell that forms bone.

os·te·oc·la·sis (os,tēok'ləsis), *n.* the deliberate breaking of a bone in order to correct a deformity.

os·te·o·cope (os'tēōkōp,), *n.* acute pain in the bones.

os·te·o·gen·e·sis (os,tēōjen'isis), *n.* the formation of bone.

os·te·oid (os'tēoid), *adj.* having the appearance of bone; bone-like.

os·te·ol·o·gy (os,tēol'əjē), *n.* the branch of anatomy dealing with bones.

os·te·o·ma (os,tēō'mə), *n., pl.* **os·te·o·mas,** **os·te·o·ma·ta** (os,tēō'mətə). a tumour consisting of bony tissue.

os·te·o·ma·la·ci·a (os,tēōmələ'sHēə), *n.* a softening of the bones resulting from a deficiency of vitamin D, calcium, and phosphorus, often leading to severe deformities.

os·te·om·e·try (os,tēom'itrē), *n.* the measurement of bones to enable the comparative study of the proportions of the human body.

os·te·o·my·e·li·tis (os,tēōmī,əlī'tis), *n.* an inflammatory disease of bone tissue.

os·te·o·path (os'tēōpath,), *n.* one who practises osteopathy. Also **os·te·op·a·thist** (os,tēop'-əthist).

os·te·op·a·thy (os,tēop'əthē), *n.* the treatment of disease by massage and manipulation of the bones.

os·te·o·plas·ty (os'tēōplas,tē), *n.* the surgical replacement of bones. —**os·te·o·plas'tic,** *adj.*

os·te·o·por·o·sis (os,tēōpôrō'sis), *n.* a medical condition characterized by porous and brittle bones and due to loss of calcium from the bone matrix. —**os·te·o·po·rot·ic** (os,tēōpôrot'ik), *adj.*

os·ti·ar·y (os'tēər,ē), *n.* one who guards a door; doorkeeper.

os·tra·cize (os'trəsīz), *v.* to separate (a person) from others; banish. —**os'tra·cism,** *n.*

os·tra·con, os·tra·kon (os'trəkon). *n., pl.* **os·tra·ca, os·tra·ka** (os'trəkə). (in ancient Greece) a fragment of pottery, esp. one used as a ballot.

o·tal·gi·a (ōtal'jēə), *n.* earache.

o·tic (ō'tik), *adj.* relating to the ear.

o·ti·ose (ō'tēōs), *adj.* idle; useless; unnecessary.

o·ti·tis in·ter·na (ōtī'tis intû'nə). See **labyrinthitis.**

o·to·hem·i·neur·as·the·ni·a (ō,tōhem,ē-

nyo͞or,əsthē'nēə), *n.* the state of being able to hear with only one ear.

o·to·lith (ō'tōlith), *n.* a calcareous mass which forms in the inner ear of vertebrates.

o·tol·o·gy (ōtol'əjē), *n.* the study of the structure, function, and diseases of the ear.

o·to·neur·as·the·ni·a (ō,tōnyo͞or,əsthē'nēə), *n.* a malfunction of the nervous system caused by disease of the ear.

o·to·plas·ty (ō'tōplas,tē), *n.* plastic surgery of the ear.

o·to·rhi·no·lar·yn·gol·o·gy (ō,tōrī,nōlar,-iNGgol'əjē), *n.* the branch of medicine dealing with the ear, nose, and throat. Also **o,to·lar,yn-·gol'o·gy.**

o·to·scle·ro·sis (ō,tōsklirō'sis), *n.* the growth of new bone around the innermost bones of the middle ear, causing deafness.

Ot·to·man Empire (ot'əmən), the former Turkish empire that existed from 1300 to the end of World War I and was replaced by the Republic of Turkey.

ou·bli·ette (o͞o,blēet'), *n.* a hidden dungeon that can be entered only from above.

oust (oust), *v.* to eject, or put out, as from a place or position.

out·age (ou'tij), *n.* a stopping in the functioning of a machine due to a lack of power.

out-Her·od (out,her'əd), *v.* to surpass or exceed in evil, violence, extravagance, etc.

outing flannel, a lightweight cotton flannel having a short nap.

ou·trance (o͞oträNs'), *n. French.* the extreme limit; utmost extremity.

ou·tré (o͞otrā'), *n. French.* going beyond the limits of what is acceptable, proper, or decent.

out·spo·ken (out,spō'kən), *adj.* frank; not hiding anything; openly direct and honest.

ou·zo (o͞o'zō), *n.* a Greek liqueur flavoured with anise.

o·va (ō'və), *n.* plural of **ovum.**

o·var·i·an (ōver'ēən), *adj.* relating to or involving an ovary.

o·var·i·ec·to·mize (ōver,ēek'təmīz), *v.* to remove one or both ovaries.

o·var·i·ec·to·my (ōver,ēek'təmē), *n.* the removal of one or both ovaries by surgical operation; oophorectomy.

o·var·i·ot·o·my (ōver,ēot'əmē), *n.* the surgical incision or removal of an ovary.

o·va·ri·tis (ō,vərī'tis), *n.* inflammation of the ovaries; oophoritis.

o·va·ry (ō'vərē), *n.* the female reproductive organ producing ova.

o·ver·kill (ō'vəkil,), *n.* the capacity of a country to cause destruction by nuclear weapons in excess of the amount required for victory over an enemy.

o·vert (ōvût'), *adj.* open; unconcealed; public. —**o·vert'ly,** *adv.*

o·ver·ture (ō'vəcHə), *n.* an introductory move; preliminary step.

o·ver·ween·ing (ō,vəwē'niNG), *adj.* presumptuous; conceited; arrogant; excessive.

o·vi·duct (ō'vidukt,), *n.* either of the two tubes which carry ova from the ovary to the outside.

o·vif·er·ous (ōvif'ərəs), *adj.* bearing or producing eggs.

o·vi·form (ō'vifôm,), *adj.* shaped like an egg.

o·vine (ō'vīn), *adj.* relating to or concerned with sheep.

o·vip·a·ra (ōvip'ərə), *n. pl.* animals that lay eggs.

o·vip·a·rous (ōvip'ərəs), *adj.* producing eggs that hatch outside the body of the mother, as birds, some fishes, etc.

o·vi·pos·it (ō,vipoz'it), *v.* to lay eggs by means of an ovipositor.

o·vi·pos·i·tor (ō,vipoz'itə), *n.* (in certain insects and fish) a specialized organ through which eggs are expelled.

o·vi·sac (ō'visak,), *n.* a container or capsule for holding an ovum or ova.

o·void (ō'void), *adj.* having the shape of an egg.

o·vo·vi·vip·a·rous (ō,vōvīvip'ərəs), *adj.* producing eggs that hatch inside the body of the mother.

o·vu·lar (ov'yo͞olə), *adj.* relating to or having the nature of an ovule.

o·vu·late (ov'yo͞olāt,), *v.* to expel or release eggs from an ovule.

o·vule (ov'yo͞ol), *n.* the sac containing the unfertilized female germ cell.

o·vum (ō'vəm), *n., pl.* **o·va** (ō'və). the female reproductive cell of animals or plants.

ox·im·e·ter (oksim'itə), *n.* a device to measure the extent of oxygen saturation of the haemoglobin in a sample quantity of blood.

ox·im·e·try (oksim'itrē), *n.* the measurement of oxygen saturation of the haemoglobin with an oximeter.

Ox·o·ni·an (oksō'nēən), *adj.* relating to or belonging to Oxford, England, or to Oxford University.

ox·y·mo·ron (ok,simôr'on), *n., pl.* **ox·y·mo·ra.** an apparently self-contradictory expression, as *sounds of silence.*

oys·tered (oi'stûd), *adj.* (of furniture) veneered with designs made up of concentric rings.

o·zo·no·sphere (ōzō'nəsfē,ə), *n.* an atmospheric layer, ranging from 8 to 30 miles above the surface of the earth, characterized by a high concentration of ozone.

P

pab·u·lum (pab'yo͞oləm), *n.* food; anything nourishing.

pace (pā'sē, päCH'ā, pä'kā), *prep.* with the permission of; with deference to. (Used as a polite way of noting the disagreement of another, as *I do not, pace the honourable gentleman, believe the government to be riddled with spies.*)

pach·y·derm (pak'idûm), *n.* any thick-skinned nonruminant hoofed quadruped, as the elephant, rhinoceros, etc. —**pach·y·der'ma·tous.** *adj.*

pach·y·lo·sis (pak,ilō'siz), *n.* a medical disorder in which the skin, esp. on the legs, becomes scaly and thickens.

pa·cif·ic (pəsif'ik), *adj.* peaceful; calm.

pad·nag (pad'nag,), *n.* an old, slow horse; a nag.

pa·dro·ne (pədrō'nē), *n., pl.* **pa·dro·nes.** an employer who controls almost totally the lives of his workers, providing them with accommodation and food as well as employment so as to exploit them to the full.

pad·u·a·soy (pad'yo͞oəsoi,), *n.* a smooth, rich silk fabric. See also **peau de soie, poult-de-soie.**

pae·an, pe·an (pē'ən), *n.* a song of praise or triumph.

paed·er·ast (ped'ərast, pē'dərast), *n.* pederast.

paed·er·as·ty (ped'əraste, pē'dərəs,tē), *n.* pederasty.

pae·di·at·rics, pe·di·at·rics (pē,dēat'riks), *n. sing.* the study and treatment of the diseases of children. —**pae,di·a·tri'cian, pe,di·a·tri'cian, pae·di·at'rist, pe·di·at'rist,** *n.*

pae·do·bap·tism, pe·do·bap·tism (pē,-dōbap'tizəm), *n.* the act or practice of baptizing young children or infants. —**pae,do·bap'tist, pe,do·bap'tist,** *n.*

pae·do·don·tics (pē,dədon'tiks), *n. sing.* the dental care and treatment of children's teeth. Also **pae,do·don'tia.** —**pae,do·don'tist,** *n.*

pae·do·gen·e·sis (pē,dōjen'isiz), *n.* reproduction by animals in the larval or some other juvenile form, which persists into the adult stage of life, as in the axolotl.

pae·do·phil·i·a (pē,dōfil'ēə), *n.* sexual desire felt by an adult for a child.

pa·el·la (pīel'ə), *n.* a Spanish dish consisting of chicken, rice, saffron, tomatoes, seasonings, stock, and often shellfish, all cooked slowly together until the moisture is absorbed.

pag·i·nate (paj'ināt), *v.* to indicate the order of pages in a book, as by marking each with a number. —**pag,i·na'tion,** *n.*

pail·lette (palyet'), *n.* a small shining decoration, resembling a bead or sequin, sewn onto a dress; a spangle.

pail·lon (päyôN'), *n.* a thin sheet of metal foil used in enamelling and gilding.

paint·er·ly (pān'təlē), *adj.* of a style of painting relying on the use of light and shade, tonal relations, and multiple brush strokes to give a naturalistic impression of shape and outline without using firm outlines that can be observed at close quarters.

pais·ley (pāz'lē), *n.* **1.** a soft woollen fabric with a characteristic brightly coloured and finely detailed pattern woven in, first made in Paisley, Scotland. **2.** Also called **paisley print.** a pattern resembling that of paisley fabric.

pal·a·din (pal'ədin), *n.* a knight errant; a chivalrous champion.

Pa·lae·arc·tic, Pa·le·arc·tic (pā,lēäk'tik), *adj.* of or relating to the geographical area made up of Europe, that part of Asia lying north of the Himalayas, the northern part of the Arabian peninsula, and that part of Africa lying north of the tropic of Cancer.

pa·lae·eth·nol·o·gy (pā,lēethnol'əjē), *n.* the scientific study of the early or primitive human races.

pa·lae·o·bi·ol·o·gy, pa·le·o·bi·ol·o·gy (pā,lēōbīol'əjē), *n.* the scientific study of fossil plants and animals.

pa·lae·o·bot·a·ny, pa·le·o·bot·a·ny (pā,-lēōbot'ənē), *n.* the scientific study of fossil plants.

Pa·lae·o·cene, Pa·le·o·cene (pā'lēəsēn), *adj.* relating to or denoting a geological epoch of the Tertiary period of the Cenozoic era, lasting from 70,000,000 years ago to 60,000,000 years ago and characterized by the development of birds and mammals. See also **Tertiary, Neocene.**

pa·lae·o·cli·ma·tol·o·gy, pa·le·o·cli·ma·tol·o·gy (pā,lēōklī,mətol'əjē), *n.* the scientific study of the climates of past geological periods.

pa·lae·o·e·col·o·gy, pa·le·o·e·col·o·gy (pā,lēōikol'əjē), *n.* the branch of ecology dealing with past geological periods.

pa·lae·o·en·to·mol·o·gy, pa·le·o·en·to·mol·o·gy (pā,lēōen,təmol'əjē), *n.* the scientific study of fossil insects.

Pa·lae·o·gene, Pa·le·o·gene (pā'lēəjēn), *adj.* relating to or denoting the earlier part of the Tertiary period of the Cenozoic era of geological time, divided into the Palaeocene, Eocene, and Oligocene epochs, and lasting from 70,000,000 years ago to 25,000,000 years ago. See also **Neogene.**

pa·lae·o·ge·og·ra·phy, pa·le·o·ge·og·ra·phy (pā,lēōjēog'rəfē), *n.* the science of reconstructing or representing the geographical features of the earth as they existed in the various periods of geological time.

pa·lae·o·ge·ol·o·gy (pā,lēōjēol'əjē), *n.* the scientific representation of the geological conditions prevailing in the various periods of geological time.

pa·lae·og·ra·phy (pā,lēog'rəfē), *n.* the study of ancient writing and its forms.

pa·lae·o·lith (pā'lēəlith,), *n.* a chipped stone implement of the early Stone Age.

Pa·lae·o·lith·ic, Pa·le·o·lith·ic (pā,lēōlith'-ik), adj. of or relating to the early Stone Age culture of the Pleistocene epoch, which lasted from c. 500,000 to 10,000 B.C. and was characterized by the use of tools and weapons chipped from stone or bone. See also **Neolithic.**

pa·lae·ol·o·gy, pa·le·ol·o·gy (pā,lēol'əjē), *n.* the study of ancient relics. —**pa·le·o·log'i·cal,** *adj.*

pa·lae·on·tog·ra·phy, pa·le·on·tog·ra·phy (pā,lēontog'rəfē), *n.* the scientific description of extinct animals and plants.

pa·lae·on·tol·o·gy, pa·le·on·tol·o·gy (pā,lēontol'əjē), *n.* the scientific study of the life existing in the various geological periods by means of fossil plants and animals. —**pa,le·on·tol'o·gist,** *n.*

pa·lae·o·pa·thol·o·gy, pa·le·o·pa·thol·o·gy (pā,lēōpəthol'əjē), *n.* the study of disease and other features of medical interest found in fossils of animals and early man.

pa·lae·o·pe·dol·o·gy, pa·le·o·pe·dol·o·gy (pā,lēōpidol'əjē), *n.* the scientific study of the soil conditions of past geological periods.

pa·lae·o·psy·chol·o·gy (pā,lēōsīkol'əjē), *n.* the study of those psychological processes that are thought to have survived from a previous stage in evolution. —**pa·lae·o·psy'chic,** *adj.*

pa·lae·o·trop·i·cal, pa·le·o·trop·i·cal (pā,lēōtrop'ikəl), *adj.* of or relating to the geographical area consisting of the Oriental and Ethiopian regions.

Pa·lae·o·zo·ic, Pa·le·o·zo·ic (pā,lēōzō'ik), *adj.* relating to or denoting the geological era that lasted from 500,000,000 years ago to 220,000,000 years ago and was characterized by the advent of fish, insects, and reptiles.

pa·lae·o·zo·ol·o·gy, pa·le·o·zo·ol·o·gy (pā,lēōzōol'əjē), *n.* the scientific study of fossil animals.

pal·a·tine¹ (pal'ətīn), *adj.* relating to a palace.

pal·a·tine² (pal'ətīn), *adj.* relating to the palate.

pa·lav·er (pəlä'və), *n.* **1.** a lengthy conference, esp. with primitive natives by traders or the like. **2.** idle chatter.

paleo- *For words with this prefix see* **palaeo-.**

pal·frey (pôl'frē), *n.* a horse for ordinary riding, as distinct from riding to war, and esp. for use by women.

pal·imp·sest (pal'impsest), *n.* a parchment or other early writing sheet used for the second time after erasure of the writing originally on it.

pal·in·drome (pal'indrōm), *n.* a word, phrase, line of verse, etc., that reads the same backwards as forwards, as *evil madam, live.*

pal·in·gen·e·sis (pal,injen'isis), *n.* **1.** rebirth; revival. **2.** the type of development in which individuals repeat the features of their ancestral race or group. See also **caenogenesis.**

pal·in·gen·e·sist (pal,injen'isist), *n.* one who believes in the transmigration of souls. Also **pal,in·gen'ist.**

pal·li·ate (pal'ēāt), *v.* to alleviate; to extenuate; to make excuses in attempted mitigation.

pal·li·a·tive (pal'ēətiv), *n.* something that relieves a situation, disease, etc., without solving or curing it; something that hides the worst features of a condition.

pal·lid (pal'id), *adj.* pale; colourless; lacking vitality.

pal·ma·ry (pal'mərē), *adj.* deserving of praise.

pal·mate (pal'māt), *adj.* shaped like an open and spread hand, as certain leaves. —**pal·ma'tion,** *n.*

palm·is·try (pä'mistrē), *n.* fortune-telling based on interpretation of the lines on the palm of the hand.

pal·pa·ble (pal'pəbəl), *adj.* capable of being readily perceived by the senses or the mind; evident.

pal·pate (pal'pāt), *v.* to carry out an examination, esp. medical, by touch. —**pal·pa'tion,** *n.*

pal·pe·bral (pal'pəbrəl), *adj.* relating to the eyelid.

pal·pe·brate (pal'pəbrāt), *adj.* with eyelids.

pal·ter (pôl'tə), *v.* to be insincere in speech or action; to equivocate; to haggle; to trifle.

pa·lu·dal (pəlōō'dəl), *adj.* relating to or caused by marshes.

pal·u·dism (pal'yədiz,əm), *n.* malaria.

pal·y·nol·o·gy (pal,inol'əjē), *n.* the scientific study of fossil and live microscopic plant structures, as spores, pollen grains, etc.

pam·ple·gia (pamplē'jə), *n.* See **panplegia.**

pan·a·ce·a (pan,əsē'ə), *n.* a cure for all ills.

pa·nache (pənᴀsн', panᴀsн'), *n.* **1.** an ornament, as a plume or tassel, esp. on headgear. **2.** a stylish or dashing manner.

pan·at·ro·phy (panat'rəfē), *n.* the wasting

away or other degeneration of a whole structure or body.

pan·car·di·tis (pan,kädī'tis), *n.* inflammation of all parts of the heart.

pan·chro·mat·ic (pan,krōmat'ik), *adj.* reacting to all colours of the spectrum, as a photographic colour film.

pan·cre·as (paNG'krēəs), *n.* a large gland near the stomach secreting digestive juices into the duodenum and insulin into the bloodstream.

pan·cre·a·tec·to·mize (paNG,krēətek'təmīz), *v.* to perform a pancreatectomy.

pan·cre·a·tec·to·my (paNG,krēətek'təmē), *n.* the surgical removal of all or a part of the pancreas.

pan·cre·at·ic juice (paNG,krēat'ik), the digestive juice secreted by the pancreas, consisting of a colourless thick alkaline fluid capable of breaking down protein, fat, and starch by enzyme action.

pan·cre·a·tin (paNG'krēətin), *n.* a substance containing the enzymes, found in pancreatic juice, amylase, lipase, and trypsin, used esp. as an aid to digestion.

pan·cre·a·ti·tis (paNG,krēətī'tis), *n.* inflammation of the pancreas.

pan·cre·a·tot·o·my (paNG,krēətot'əmē), *n.* surgical incision of the pancreas.

pan·dect (pan'dekt), *n.* a comprehensive summary; a digest, as of a code of laws.

pan·dem·ic (pandem'ik), *adj.* distributed or prevalent throughout the world or some large area of it, as a disease; universal.

pan·der (pan'də), *n.* 1. a go-between in secret love affairs; a procurer. 2. one who provides the means for or profits from the vices of others. Also **pan'der·er.**

pan·dic·u·la·tion (pandik,yōōlā'sHən), *n.* the process or act of stretching, esp. as used in medical treatment.

pan·dit (pun'dit), *n.* a highly respected scholar or wise man in India.

pan·dour (pan'dōō,ə), *n.* a ferocious, rapacious soldier.

pan·dow·dy (pandou'dē), *n. U.S.* an apple pie or pudding sweetened with molasses. Also **apple pandowdy.**

pan·du·rate (pan'dyōōrāt), *adj.* fiddle-shaped, as certain leaves. Also **pan·du'ri·form,.**

pan·e·gyr·ic (pan,ijir'ik), *n.* a eulogy; a speech in praise of someone or something. —**pan·e·gyr'-ist,** *n.*

pan·e·gy·rize (pan'ijərīz), *v.* to deliver or write a discourse in praise of a person or thing; to eulogize.

pan·et·to·ne (pan,itō'nē), *n.* an Italian leavened bread containing dried fruits, nuts, etc., eaten on holidays.

pa·niv·o·rous (paniv'ərəs), *adj.* bread-eating; living on bread.

pan·jan·drum (panjan'drəm), *n.* a pompous official; an official who supposes himself to be important.

pan·lo·gism (pan'ləjiz,əm), *n.* the philosophical theory that only the logos, the rational principle, is truly real and the universe is but an act or realization of it.

pan·nic·u·lus (panik'yōōləs), *n., pl.* **pan·nic·u·li** (panik'yōōlī). a layer of tissue, as the layer of fat beneath the skin.

pan·nier (pan'ēə), *n.* 1. a large basket, as for carrying provisions or small items for trade. 2. a frame of oval shape for holding out the skirt of a woman's dress at the hips.

pan·nus (pan'əs), *n.* an abnormal condition of the eye, in which the cornea becomes thickened.

pan·o·ply (pan'əplē), *n.* a complete covering or array, either material or ideal, and especially splendid.

pan·op·tic (panop'tik), *adj.* allowing a view of or taking into consideration all parts or aspects.

pan·ple·gi·a (panplē'jēə), *n.* paralysis of all four limbs; quadriplegia. Also **pamplegia.**

pan·psy·chism (pansī'kizəm), *n.* the philosophical theory that every object has a mind or a psyche. —**pan·psy'chist,** *n.*

pan·soph·ism (pan'səfiz,əm), *n.* a claim to have complete knowledge or wisdom.

pan·so·phy (pan'səfē), *n.* complete knowledge or wisdom.

pan·sper·mi·a (panspū'mēə), *n.* the theory that there are distributed throughout the universe germs or spores capable of developing into living things and that they do develop wherever the conditions are favourable. Also **pan·sper'-ma·tism.**

pan·the·ism (pan'thēiz,əm), *n.* the doctrine that all parts of the universe, esp. nature, are only manifestations of God who is the supreme reality; any doctrine or belief that God is the universe and the universe is God.

pan·to·fle, pan·tof·fle (pantof'əl), *n.* an indoor shoe; a slipper.

pan·to·graph (pan'təgräf,, pan'təgraf,), *n.* 1. an instrument for copying plans or the like in any given scale. 2. a device for carrying electric current from an overhead cable to a vehicle such as a trolley car.

pan·tol·o·gy (pantol'əjē), *n.* a survey or systematic review of all fields of human knowledge.

pan·trop·ic (pantrop'ik), *adj.* affecting or drawn towards many kinds of body tissue.

pan·trop·i·cal (pantrop'ikəl), *adj.* (esp. of living things) distributed throughout the tropics.

pan·zer (pan'zər), *adj.* furnished with armour; armoured, as a military unit with tanks or the like.

pap (pap), *n.* 1. soft or semi-liquid food for babies or invalids. 2. any written or spoken material that is weak in content and lacks substance.

pa·pav·er·a·ceous (pəpav,ərā'sHəs), *adj.* of any plant belonging to the poppy family.

pa·per (pā'pə), *n.* corporate and municipal (stocks and) bonds, treasury notes, negotiable notes, etc.; commercial paper.

pap·e·terie (pap'itrē), *n.* a case or box of writing paper and other writing materials.

pap·il·lote (pap'əlōt), *n.* a fringed paper decoration wrapped round the end of a chop or cutlet bone.

pap·ule (pap'yōol), *n.* a small pointed inflamed prominence on the skin.

pap·y·ra·ceous (pap,ərā'sHəs), *adj.* of a paperlike nature; papery.

par·a·bi·o·sis (par,əbīō'sis), *n.* a union of two individuals, often by surgery as an experiment, so that their blood circulations become one continuous process.

par·a·ble (par'əbəl), *n.* a short story conveying a moral or truth by allegory; any statement conveying its meaning indirectly, as by analogy.

par·a·cen·te·sis (par,əsentē'sis), *n., pl.* **par·a·cen·te·ses** (par,əsentē'sēz), the surgical draining of fluid from a body cavity through a hole punctured in its wall. Also **tapping.**

pa·rach·ro·nism (parak'rəniz,əm), *n.* an error in chronology whereby a date later than the correct one is given to an event or the like. See also **anachronism, prochronism.**

par·a·clete (par'əklēt), *n.* one called upon for help or to intercede.

par·a·cu·sis (par,əkyōo'sis), *n.* partial deafness. Also **par·a·cu·sia.**

par·a·digm (par'ədīm), *n.* an example; a model to use as a standard.

par·aes·the·sia, par·es·the·sia (par,isthē'zHə), *n.* a form of interference with sensation in which numbness, tingling, prickling, etc., are felt, as in cases of injury to peripheral nerves, etc.

par·a·geu·sia (par,əgyōo'zHə), *n.* a psychiatric disorder in which the sense of taste is disordered and subject to hallucinations.

par·a·go·ge (par,əgō'jē), *n.* the incorrect adding of a sound or sounds to the end of a word, as *coolth* for *cool.*

par·a·gon (par'əgon), *n.* an example or model of excellence in general or or of a particular excellence.

par·a·graph·i·a (par,əgraf'ēə, par,əgrä'fēə), *n.* the mental disorder characterized by the inability to put thoughts into writing or the writing of words or letters different from those intended.

par·ai·son (par'əzon), *n.* See **parison.**

par·a·lan·guage (par'əlaNG,gwij), *n.* elements of speech, such as variations in pitch or stress, that may convey meaning in addition to the word sounds.

par·a·lex·i·a (par,əlek'sēə), *n.* a defect in the ability to read, characterized by the mental transposing of letters or words.

par·a·li·pom·e·na (par,əlipom'ənə), *n. pl.* things added as a supplement after being left out of or dealt with inadequately in the main text.

par·al·lel·e·pi·ped, par·al·lel·o·pi·ped (par,əlel,əpī'pid), *n.* a prism with six faces, each of which is a parallelogram. Also **par,al·lel,e·pi'·pe·don.**

pa·ral·o·gize (pəral'əjīz), *v.* to draw illogical conclusions from a set of facts or assumptions.

paralysis agitans. See **Parkinson's disease.**

par·a·mag·net·ic (par,əmagnet'ik), *adj.* relating to or denoting a substance that possesses magnetization in direct proportion to the strength of the magnetic field in which it is placed. See also **antiferromagnetic, diamagnetic, ferromagnetic.**

par·a·med·i·cal (par,əmed'ikəl), *adj.* having a supplementary or secondary capacity in relation to the medical profession.

par·a·ment (par'əmənt), *n., pl.* **par·a·ments, par·a·men·ta.** a decorative hanging or other ornament for a room.

pa·ram·e·ter (pəram'itə), *n.* something used as a standard against which other things are measured. **—par,a·met'ric,** *adj.*

par·a·mil·i·tar·y (par,əmil'itərē), *adj.* relating to or denoting an organized force ancillary to or taking the place of a regular military force.

par·a·mour (par'əmōo,ə), *n.* a lover, esp. that of a married person.

par·a·na·sal (par,ənā'zəl), *adj.* near the nasal passages.

par·a·noi·a (par,ənoi'ə), *n.* a mental disorder in which the patient suffers delusions and imagines himself persecuted by others. **—par·a·noi'ac, par'a·noid,** *adj.*

par·a·nymph (par'ənimf), *n.* a groomsman or bridesmaid at a wedding ceremony.

par·a·pa·re·sis (par,əparē'sis), *n.* partial paralysis, affecting in particular the legs.

par·aph (par'əf), *n.* an elaborate flourish following a signature, originally to make forgery difficult.

par·a·phil·i·a (par,əfil'ēə), *n.* sexual deviation or perversion.

par·a·phras·tic (par,əfras'tik), *adj.* of the nature of a paraphrase; expressed in different words; reworded, as to make clearer. **—pa·raph'·ra·sis, par'a·phrast,** *n.*

par·a·ple·gi·a (par,əplē'jēə), *n.* paralysis of both legs.

par·a·psy·chol·o·gy (par,əsīkol'əjē), *n.* the scientific study of psychic phenomena, as telepathy, clairvoyance, etc.

par·a·sci·ence (par'əsī,əns), *n.* the study of phenomena that cannot be explained by orthodox science. —**par,a·sci'en·tist**, *n.* —**par,a·sci,-en·tif'ic**, *adj.*

par·a·sit·i·cide (par,əsit'isid), *adj.* **1.** killing parasites of plants or animals. —*n.* **2.** a substance or preparation that kills parasites.

par·a·sit·ol·o·gy (par,əsitol'əjē), *n.* the scientific study of parasites and their effect.

par·a·si·to·sis (par,əsītō'sis), *n.* any abnormal condition caused by parasites.

par·a·su·i·cide (par,əsoō'isīd,), *n.* **1.** an attempt to kill oneself that is not necessarily intended to succeed. **2.** one who performs such an act.

par·a·sym·pa·thet·ic (par,əsim,pəthet'ik), *adj.* relating to one of the two types of nerve in the autonomic nerve system, consisting of nerve fibres and ganglia which leave the central nervous system at the cranial and sacral regions, and working in opposition to the sympathetic nerves as in stimulating peristalsis in the gut, which sympathetic nerves inhibit, and contracting the eye pupil, which sympathetic nerves dilate.

par·a·tax·ic (par,ətak'sik), *adj.* relating to or characterized by emotional or personality conflicts.

par·a·thi·on (par,əthī'on), *n.* a yellowish-brown insecticide related to nerve gas and extremely poisonous to mammals.

par·a·thy·roid (par,əthī'roid), *adj.* close to the thyroid gland.

parathyroid gland, one of four small glands or glandlike masses adjacent to the thyroid gland that produce secretions that control the calcium balance between blood and bones.

par·a·troph·ic (par,ətrof'ik), *adj.* living on live organic matter; parasitic.

par·a·ty·phoid (par,ətī'foid), *n.* an infectious disease similar to but less severe than typhoid fever, caused by a salmonella bacillus and spreading where hygiene is poor. Also **para·typhoid fever.**

par·a·vane (par'əvān,), *n.* an apparatus towed by a ship, consisting of a pair of vanes at the ends of cables and used to cut the moorings of submerged mines so that they rise to the surface to be destroyed.

par·a·vent (par'əvent), *n.* a screen against wind or draughts.

par·buck·le (par'bukəl), *n.* a device for raising and lowering casks and the like, consisting of a rope fastened by its centre at the higher level so that the two ends can be passed round the item to be raised and hauled on or let out from the higher level.

par·ce·nar·y (pär'sənərē), *n.* the joint possession of an undivided inheritance, as land, by two or more heirs.

par·e·gor·ic (par,əgor'ik), *n.* any soothing or pain-killing medical preparation.

par·en·ter·al (paren'tərəl), *adj.* entering the body by a means other than absorption from the intestine, as a drug by injection; not intestinal.

pa·ren·ti·cide (pəren'tisīd), *n.* the act of killing one or both of one's parents.

pa·re·sis (pərē'sis), *n.* partial paralysis or weakening of muscular power affecting movement but not sensation. —**pa·ret'ic,** *adj.,* *n.*

par·es·the·sia (par'isthē'zHə), *n.* paraesthesia.

pa·re·ve (pär'əvə), *adj.* (in Judaism) able to be eaten with both meat and dairy meals because it contains neither meat nor milk, consistent with laws of diet. Also **parve.**

par·get (pär'jit), *n.* any of several kinds of rough plaster, esp. one used for lining chimneys.

parg·ing (pär'jiNG), *n.* a thin plaster or mortar coating used for sealing or smoothing over rough masonry.

pa·ri·ah (pərī'ə), *n.* a social outcast.

par·i·es (per'iēz), *n.,* *pl.* **pa·ri·e·tes** (pərī'itēz). the wall of the body or of any of its hollow organs; a structural wall of a plant.

pa·ri·e·tal (pərī'itəl), *adj.* **1.** relating to or situated near the two bones at the top and sides of the skull. **2.** relating to a paries or to parietes. **3.** relating to or with authority over life within the bounds of a college, university, etc.

pa·ri pas·su (par'ē pas'oō), *Latin.* equally; fairly; without bias.

par·i·son (par'isən), *n.* molten glass in a partially shaped state. Also **paraison.**

Park·in·son's disease (pä'kinsənz), a medical disorder in which there is progressive rigidity of the muscles and tremors. Also **Par'kin·son·ism, paralysis agitans, shaking palsy.**

par·lance (pä'ləns), *n.* idiom; the way of speaking proper to a particular subject, as *legal parlance.*

par·lay (pälā'), *v.* *U.S.* **1.** to bet (winnings from a bet) on another event, snowball a bet; to double-up. —*n.* **2.** a bet consisting of a stake and previous winnings.

par·ley (pä'lē), *n.* a discussion of matters in dispute, esp. one among military leaders to arrange peace terms.

par·lous (pä'ləs), *adj.* difficult to escape from or deal with; perilous.

Par·men·tier (pä,mentyā'), *adj.* of a dish made from or garnished with potato. Also **Par·men·tière'.**

Par·me·san (pä'mizan), *n.* a hard, strongly flavoured, skimmed-milk cheese usually grated to serve with pasta, soup, etc., originally made in Parma, N. Italy. Also **Parmesan cheese.**

par·mi·gia·na (pä,mijä'nə), *adj.* of an Italian

dish containing or garnished with Parmesan cheese. Also **par'mi·gia·no.**

Par·nas·sus (pänas'əs), *n.* **1.** a collection of poems or fine pieces of writing. **2.** poetry or poets considered as a lofty whole.

pa·ro·chi·al (pəro'kēəl), *adj.* of excessively narrow interests or views. —**pa·ro'chi·al·ism,** *n.*

parochial school, a school run and maintained by a religious body.

par·o·don·ti·um (par,ədon'sHēəm), *n., pl.* **par·o·don·tia** (par,ədon'sHēə). See **periodontium.**

par·o·dy (par'ədē), *n., pl.* **par·o·dies. 1.** anything, as a statement, literary or artistic work, etc., that makes fun of something, esp. by exaggerating some of its characteristics. —*v.* **par·o·died, par·o·dy·ing. 2.** to make fun of something.

pa·roe·mi·ol·o·gy (pərē'mēol'əjē), *n.* the study or collecting of proverbs. —**pa·roe·mi·ol'·o·gist,** *n.*

par·o·no·ma·sia (par,ənōmā'zēə), *n.* punning, esp. when considered as a technical rhetorical device. —**par,o·no·mas'tic,** *adj.*

par·o·nych·i·a (par,ənik'ēə), *n.* inflammation of the tissue around a fingernail or toenail, usually through infection, causing pus to form. Also **perionychia.**

par·o·nych·i·um (par,ənik'ēəm), *n., pl.* **par·o·nych·i a.** See **perionychium.**

pa·ro·tic (pərō'tik), *adj.* near the ear.

pa·rot·id (pərot'id), *n.* a salivary gland, in man the largest of three, at the base of and in front of the ear.

par·o·ti·tis (par,ətī'tis), *n.* mumps. Also **pa·rot·i·di'tis.**

par·ox·ysm (par'əksiz,əm), *n.* any fit or outburst, as of action or emotion.

par·pen (pär'pən), *n.* See **perpend.**

par·ri·cide (par'isīd), *n.* the act of murdering one's father. Also **patricide.**

par·sec (pä'sek), *n.* a unit used in astronomy in the measurement of stellar distances, equivalent to 3.26 light-years.

par·see (pä'sē), *n.* an Indian who belongs to the Zoroastrian religion.

par·si·mo·ni·ous (pä,səmō'nēəs), *adj.* extremely stingy and frugal; tight-fisted.

par·si·mo·ny (pä'səmō,nē), *n.* excessive carefulness in using money, food, etc.; stinginess.

par·the·no·car·py (pä,*th*ənōkä'pē), *n.* the formation of fruit without fertilization, as can occur in the banana and pineapple, resulting in seedless but otherwise normal fruits. —**par,the·no·car'pic, par,the·no·car'pous,** *adj.*

par·the·no·gen·e·sis (pä,*th*ənōjen'isis), *n.* development of an individual from an unfertilized ovum, normal in aphids and rotifers and able to be artificially induced in many animals.

par·tic·u·late (pätik'yōolit), *adj.* relating to, consisting of, or of the nature of particles.

par·ti·tive (pa'titiv), *adj.* forming or acting as a partition; serving to separate into parts.

par·tu·ri·ent (pätyōōr'ēənt), *adj.* about to give birth; in labour.

par·tu·ri·fa·cient (pätyōōr,əfä'sHənt), *adj.* bringing on or hastening labour.

par·tu·ri·tion (pä'tyōōrisH'ən), *n.* childbirth; the act of giving birth.

pa·rure (pərōō'ə), *n.* a matched set of jewels, jewellery, or other personal ornaments.

par·ve (pär'və), *n.* See **pareve.**

par·ve·nu (pä'vənyōō), *n.* a person who has lately or suddenly become wealthy or important but has not yet acquired the appropriate social refinements, as in dress, manners, etc.; an upstart.

pas·quil (pas'kwil), *n.* a pasquinade.

pas·quin·ade (pas,kwənäd'), *n.* a lampoon or satire, originally one displayed in a public place.

pas·sé (pasä'), *adj.* out of date; no longer fashionable or current.

passe·ment (pas'mənt), *n.* a trimming for garments, made of thread of gold, silver, silk, etc. Also **pass'a·ment.**

passe·men·terie (pasmen'trē), *n.* a trimming of gold or silver braid, lace, cord, or of beads or the like.

passe-par·tout (pas,pätoo'), *n.* **1.** a decorative mat for framing a picture. **2.** a universal pass or means of entry; a master key.

pas·ser·ine (pas'ərin), *adj.* belonging or relating to the biological order encompassing the birds with feet adapted for perching, having one toe pointing backwards and the other three forwards.

pas·si·ble (pas'ibəl), *adj.* capable of sensation or emotion; with easily roused or influenced feelings.

pas·sim (pas'im), *adv. Latin.* here and there; throughout; everywhere, usually of the occurrences of a particular phrase, allusion, topic, name, etc., in a work or the works of an author when these are too frequent to mention or index separately.

pas·sus (pas'əs), *n., pl.* **pas·sus, pas·sus·es.** one of the major parts or sections into which a literary work of prose or poetry is divided.

pas·ta (pas'tə), *n.* any one or all of the many forms of egg and flour paste, Italian in origin, formed into various sized strips, rolls, tubes, shells, etc., for cooking in boiling water and serving with sauces of meat, tomato, etc.; a dish based on such an egg and flour paste.

paste (pāst), *n.* an unleavened dough made from flour and shortening for use as pie crust, flan cases, and in other pastry dishes.

pas·tic·cio (pastē'cHō), *n., pl.* **pas·tic·ci** (pastē'-cHē). a pastiche.

pas·tiche (pastēsH'), *n.* a musical or literary

work or a painting composed of a mixture of borrowed themes, motifs, etc., from others' work; a piece of music or literature or a painting executed in the style of another, usually well known, composer, writer, or painter; an incongruous mixture of items or themes from various sources.

pas·to·ral (päs'tərəl), *adj.* relating to the country or rural life; having or evoking the virtues, as peacefulness, simplicity, of country life.

pas·to·ral·ism (päs'tərəliz,əm), *n.* the rearing of herds of sheep, cattle, or the like, as the chief activity in the economy of a community.

pas·tose (pastōs'), *adj.* of painting in which the paint is laid on thickly.

pas·tra·mi (pəsträ'mē), *n.* beef, usually shoulder, highly seasoned and smoked or pickled.

pâ·té de foie gras (pat'ā də fwä grä'), *pl.* **pâ·tés de foie gras** (pat'āz də fwä gra'). a paste made from the liver of fatted geese, a prized culinary delicacy.

pa·tel·la (pətel'ə), *n.*, *pl.* **pa·tel·lae** (pətel'ē). the bone forming the kneecap.

pa·tel·li·form (pətel'ifôm,), *adj.* having the shape of a shallow cup or saucer.

pat·ent (pā'tənt, pat'ənt), *adj.* obvious.

pa·ter·fa·mil·i·as (pā,tərfəmil'ēəs), *n.*, *pl.* **pa·ter·fa·mil·i·as·es.** the male head of a household, usually the father.

pa·ter·nal·ism (pətû'nəliz,əm), *n.* the exercise of control over a nation, employees, a social group, etc., in the manner of a father over his children.

pathetic fallacy, the attributing of human emotions or characteristics to inanimate objects or parts of nature, as *the brave snowdrops.*

path·o·bi·ol·o·gy (path,ōbīol'əjē), *n.* the study of abnormal or diseased conditions in living things; pathology.

path·o·cure (path'əkyōō,ə), *n.* the termination of a neurosis occurring in conjunction with the appearance of a physical disease.

path·o·for·mic (pathəfô'mik), *adj.* relating to the symptoms occurring in the initial stages of a disease, esp. of a mental illness.

path·o·gen (path'əjən), *n.* any organism that gives rise to disease. Also **path'o·gene.**

path·o·gen·e·sis (path,əjen'isis), *n.* the origin and mode of development of a disease. Also **pa·thog'e·ny.**

path·o·gen·ic (path,əjen'ik), *adj.* capable of causing disease.

path·o·ge·nic·i·ty (path,ōjənis'itē), *n.* the capacity of an organism for causing disease.

pa·thog·no·my (pəthog'nəmē), *n.* the study of diagnosis, the study of the symptoms and characteristics particular to specific diseases. —**pa·thog,no·mon'ic,** *adj.*

pa·thog·ra·phy (pəthog'rəfē) *n.* a scientific description of a disease and its pathogenesis, often in the form of a published treatise.

path·o·log·i·cal (pathəloj'ikəl), *adj.* **1.** relating to pathology. **2.** resulting from or concerning disease. Also **path·o·log'ic.**

pa·thol·o·gy (pəthol'əjē), *n.* **1.** the scientific study of physical diseases, their causes, symptoms, courses, and treatment. **2.** any unhealthy or abnormal physical condition.

path·o·morph·ism (path,əmô'fizəm), *n.* abnormality in form or structure.

path·o·neu·ro·sis (path,ənyōōrō'sis), *n.* an abnormally excessive preoccupation with a real disease being suffered or with a part of the body affected by disease.

pa·thos (pā,thos), *n.* the quality in any event, work of art, etc., that arouses pity or sorrow.

pa·tho·sis (pathō'sis), *n.* any diseased state or condition.

pat·i·na (pat'ənə), *n.* a filmy layer, usually green, formed on old bronze by oxidation and thought to add to its ornamental value.

pat·ois (pat'wä), *n.*, *pl.* **pat·ois.** a form of speech used by the ordinary people of a particular district and different from the standard form of the language; local dialect; jargon.

pa·tri·arch (pā'trēäk), *n.* the male head of a family or tribe.

pa·tri·ar·chy (pā'trēä,kē), *n.* a form of organization of a community in which the father or male head of the family, tribe, or the like, holds authority, descent is through the male line, and children become members of their father's family or tribe. See also **matriarchy.**

pa·tri·cian (pətrisн'ən), *n.* **1.** a person of aristocratic or other high social rank. —*adj.* **2.** of high social rank; aristocratic; befitting an aristocrat.

pa·tri·ci·ate (pətrisн'ēit), *n.* the aristocracy; the patrician class of society.

pat·ri·cide (pat'risīd), *n.* See **parricide.**

pat·ri·lat·er·al (pat,rilat'ərəl), *adj.* related on the father's side of the family. See also **matrilateral.**

pat·ri·lin·e·age (pat,rilin'ēij), *n.* descent traced through the male line of a family.

pat·ri·lin·e·al (pat,rilin'ēəl), *adj.* inheriting or descending through the male line of a family. Also **pat,ri·lin'e·ar.**

pat·ri·li·ny (pat'rilīn,ē), *n.* the tracing of family descent through the male line.

pat·ri·lo·cal (pat,rilō'kəl), *adj.* living with or situated near the husband's family; relating to such living or situation. Also **virilocal.** See also **matrilocal.**

pat·ri·mo·ny (pat'rimō,nē), *n.* heritage; any inherited trait, quality, etc.

pat·ri·po·tes·tal (pat,ripōtes'təl), *adj.* relating to the authority held by a father or his side of a family.

pa·tris·tic (pətris'tik), *adj.* relating to the fathers of the Christian Church or to their writings or the study of them. Also **pa·tris'ti·cal.**

pa·trol·o·gist (pətrol'əjist), *n.* one who studies or is learned in patrology.

pa·trol·o·gy (pətrol'əjē), *n.* the study of the teachings of the fathers of the Christian Church. Also **patris'tics.**

pat·ro·nym·ic (pat,rənim'ik), *adj.* relating to or denoting a name derived from the father or ancestor in the male line.

pat·sy (pat'sē), *n. Slang, chiefly U.S. and Canada.* a scapegoat; a person blamed for something, often wrongfully.

pat·ten (pat'ən), *n.* a wooden sole held on the foot by a leather strap and often raised from the ground on a metal ring so as to keep the wearer's foot clear of mud, puddles, etc.; any similar footwear designed for the same purpose.

pat·u·lous (pat'yŏŏləs), *adj.* open; spreading, as a tree, etc.

pau·ci·ty (pô'sitē), *n.* smallness of number or of quality; insufficiency.

Pav·lo·vi·an (pavlō'vēən), *adj.* 1. of the Russian physiologist, Ivan Pavlov (1849–1936), or his works, esp. his study of reflex behaviour in dogs. 2. describing a reflex or involuntary reaction, esp. one conditioned by experience.

pav·o·nine (pav'ōnīn), *adj.* relating to or resembling the peacock.

pawl (pôl), *n.* a short bar pivoted at one end to a support and engaging at the other end with a toothed wheel or bar so as to prevent recoil or to allow slight forward movement, as of a rope.

Pax Ro·ma·na (paks' rōmä'nə), harsh peace terms imposed by a powerful nation on nations too weak to dispute them and against their will, esp. the peace enforced on its dominions by the Roman Empire.

pax vo·bis·cum (paks' vōbis'kəm), *Latin.* peace be with you.

peace pipe, a calumet.

pe·an (pē'ən), *n.* See **paean.**

pearl·ized (pû'līzd), *adj.* made to look like mother-of-pearl.

peau de soie (pō' də swä'), a smooth heavy silk or rayon fabric with a soft texture and grained, dull satiny surface on both sides, used for dresses, coats, etc. See also **paduasoy, poult-de-soie.**

pebble dash, a finish to an exterior wall made of mortar into which small pebbles are pressed while it is still wet.

pec·ca·ble (pek'əbəl), *adj.* liable to sin, error, or fault.

pec·ca·dil·lo (pek,ədil'ō), *n., pl.* **pec·ca·dil·loes, pec·ca·dil·los.** a small sin; a minor fault or offence.

pec·cant (pek'ənt), *adj.* guilty of sin; erring morally.

pec·ca·vi (pekä'vē), *n., pl.* **pec·ca·vis.** a confession of having sinned or done wrong. [from Latin, literally, I have sinned.]

Peck·sniff·i·an (peksnif'ēən), *adj.* hypocritically professing to be benevolent or of high morals. [after Mr. Pecksniff in Charles Dickens's *Martin Chuzzlewit.*]

pec·ti·nate (pek'tənāt), *adj.* forming or having close-set toothlike projections; like a comb.

pec·tize (pek'tīz), *v.* to make or become set like a jelly; to gel.

pec·to·ral (pek'tərəl), *adj.* in, on, or relating to the chest.

pec·u·late (pek'yŏŏlāt), *v.* to embezzle; to appropriate fraudulently money or property held or controlled on behalf of another. —**pec,u·la'tion,** *n.* —**pec,u·la'to·ry,** *adj.*

pe·cu·li·um (pikyŏŏ'lēəm), *n.* a private or exclusive possession; private property.

pe·cu·ni·ar·y (pikyŏŏ'nēərē), *adj.* concerning or consisting of money.

ped·a·gogue (ped'əgog), *n.* 1. a teacher, esp. in a school. 2. a pedantic, opinionated person who tries to force others to his views. —**ped'a·gogu·er·y,** *n.*

ped·a·go·gy (ped'əgo,jē), *n.* the art or function of teaching. —**ped,a·go'gi·cal,** *adj.*

ped·ant (ped'ənt), *n.* 1. one who shows off his knowledge excessively. 2. one who adheres strictly to petty rules or details or to theoretical knowledge, ignoring common sense. —**pe·dan'-ti·cism, ped'ant·ry,** *n.*

ped·ate (ped'āt), *adj.* having or resembling a foot or feet.

pe·dat·i·fid (pidat'əfid), *adj.* having palmate divisions with each division cleft to resemble toes, as a leaf; pedately divided.

pe·dat·i·lob·ate (pidat,ilō'bāt), *adj.* having palmate lobes with each lobe cleft to resemble toes, as a leaf; pedately lobed. Also **pe·dat'i·lobed.**

ped·er·ast, paed·er·ast (ped'ərast, pē'-dərast), *n.* a man who has sexual relations with another male, esp. with a boy.

ped·er·as·ty, paed·er·as·ty (ped'ərastē, pē'dərastē), *n.* sexual relations between two males, esp. between a man and a boy.

pe·des·tri·an (pədes'trēən), *adj.* unimaginative, ordinary, dull, prosaic.

pe·di·at·rics (pē,dēat'riks), *n.* paediatrics.

ped·i·cel (ped'isəl), *n.* a small, subordinate, stalklike structure in a plant or animal. —**ped·i·cel'late,** *adj.*

ped·i·cle (ped'ikəl), *n.* a pedicel; a peduncle.

pe·dic·u·lar (pədik'yŏŏlə), *adj.* relating to lice.

pe·dic·u·li·cide (pədik'yŏŏlisīd,), *adj.* having the capacity to kill lice. Also **pe·dic·u·li·ci'dal.**

pe·dic·u·lo·sis (pədik'yŏŏlō'sis), *n.* infestation with lice; the state of being lice-ridden. —**pe·dic'u·lous,** *adj.*

ped·i·form (ped'ifôm,), *adj.* having the form of a foot.

pe·do·bap·tism (pē,dōbap'tizəm), *n.* paedobaptism.

pe·dun·cle (piduNG'kəl), *n.* a stalk, esp. a main supporting stalk, as of a flower, fungus, organ, etc. —**pe·dun·cu·late**, *adj.*

peer (pē'ə), *n.* 1. something or someone equal or equivalent to something else. 2. a nobleman or noblewoman.

peign·oir (pānwä'), *n.* a loose dressing gown worn by women.

pej·o·ra·tion (pejorā'sHən), *n.* a worsening; a lowering of worth; depreciation. See also **melioration**.

pe·jo·ra·tive (pijôr'ətiv), *adj.* depreciatory; disparaging; making lower in worth or quality.

pel·age (pel'ij), *n.* hair, fur, wool, or the like covering the skin of an animal.

pe·lag·ic (pəlaj'ik), *adj.* relating to the open sea or ocean.

pe·lec·y·pod (pəles'əpod,), *n.* any bivalve mollusc, as the oyster, the mussel, etc.

pel·er·ine (pel'ərēn), *n.* a woman's fur or cloth close-fitting cape or tippet, usually waist-length in back and with long ends in front.

Pel·e's hair (pel'āz), threads of glass solidified from ejected volcanic lava. [from Hawaiian *Pele*, goddess of Kilauea volcano.]

Pele's tears, globules of volcanic glass solidified from ejected lava.

pe·lisse (pəlēs'), *n.* 1. a fur-lined or fur-trimmed knee-length coat or cloak for women. 2. an ankle-length, narrow woman's cloak with slit arm-holes.

pel·la·gra (pəlā'grə, pəlag'rə), *n.* a disease caused by the deficiency of nicotinic acid in the diet and leading to skin, digestive, and nervous disorders.

pel·li·cle (pel'ikəl), *n.* a thin skin or film; scum.

pel·lu·cid (piloo'sid), *adj.* transparent; translucent; clear to the sight or mind.

pel·oid (pel'oid), *n.* mud used in medical treatment.

pel·vis (pel'vis), *n.*, *pl.* **pel·vis·es, pel·ves** (pel'vēz). the bony girdle formed by the hip bones and sacrum.

pem·mi·can (pem'ikən), *n.* powdered dried meat mixed with fat and dried fruits and formed into a loaf or small cakes.

pen·chant (pänsHän'), *n.* a leaning towards; an inclination; a strong liking.

pend·ent (pen'dənt), *adj.* hanging; suspended from above.

pe·ne·plain, pe·ne·plane (pē'nəplān), *n.* an area of land made almost level by erosion.

pen·e·tra·li·a (pen,ətrā'lēə), *n. pl.* the innermost parts of a place or thing.

pen·e·trom·e·ter (pen,ətrom'itə), *n.* an instrument to measure the power of penetration

of x-rays and other types of radiation. Also **pen,-e·tram'eter, qualimeter.**

pen·i·cil (pen'isil), *n.* a small bristly tuft, as on a caterpillar.

pen·na (pen'ə), *n.*, *pl.* **pen·nae** (pen'ē). one of the stiff-shafted firm-vaned feathers of a bird appearing on the surface of the plumage and giving the body, wings, and tail their characteristic shape; a contour feather.

pen·na·ceous (pənā'sHəs), *adj.* with the firm texture of a penna.

pen·nate (pen'āt), *adj.* having feathers or wings. Also **pen·nat·ed.**

pen·non (pen'ən), *n.* 1. a long, tapering or swallowtail flag; any flag or banner. 2. a bird's wing or the terminal part of it.

Penn·syl·va·ni·an (pen,səlvā'nēən), *adj. U.S.* relating to or denoting a geological period within the Palaeozoic era (but sometimes considered an epoch within the Carboniferous period), lasting from about 300,000,000 years ago to 270,000,000 years ago and characterized by warm climate, swamps, and the advent of large reptiles.

pen·sile (pen'sil), *adj.* 1. suspended, as some birds' nests. 2. that constructs a hanging nest, used of birds.

pen·ta·cle (pen'təkəl), *n.* See **pentagram.**

pen·tad (pen'tad), *n.* a group of five, as a five-year period; the number five.

pen·ta·dac·tyl (pen,tədak'til), *adj.* with five digits to each hand or foot; with five fingerlike parts.

pen·ta·dec·a·gon (pen,tədek'əgon), *n.* a polygon with fifteen sides and containing fifteen angles.

pen·tag·o·noid (pentag'ənoid), *adj.* five-sided; pentagon-shaped.

pen·ta·gram (pen'təgram,), *n.* a star with five points. Also called **pentacle.**

pen·ta·he·dron (pen,təhē'drən), *n.*, *pl.* **pen·ta·he·drons, pen·ta·he·dra.** a five-faced solid.

pen·tam·er·ous (pentam'ərəs), *adj.* having or divided into five parts.

pen·tap·tych (pen'taptik), *n.* a work of art, as a painting, carving, etc., consisting of five panels hinged side by side, each bearing a part of the whole picture or bearing a separate picture. See also **diptych, polyptych, triptych.**

pen·tar·chy (pen'täkē), *n.* government by a group of five people.

pen·to·bar·bi·tone (pen,təbä'bitōn), *n.* a barbiturate drug used chiefly as a sedative and hypnotic. U.S. name: **pentobarbital.**

pen·tose (pen'tōs), *n.* the name given to a group of sugars resembling glucose but having only five carbon atoms in the molecule.

pe·nul·ti·ma (pinul'timə), *n.* the next to the last syllable of a word. Also **pe'nult.** See also **ultima.**

pe·nul·ti·mate (pinul'timit), *adj.* last but for one; next to last.

pe·num·bra (pinum'brə), *n.*, *pl.* **pe·num·brae** (pinum'brē), **pe·num·bras.** a partial shadow around an area of total shadow, as that around the total shadow of the moon or earth during an eclipse or the area around a sunspot.

pe·nu·ri·ous (pənyŏŏr'ēəs), *adj.* 1. poverty-stricken; poor. 2. stingy; tight-fisted.

pen·u·ry (pen'yərē), *n.* destitution; utter poverty; scarcity; lack.

pe·on (pē'ən, pē'on), *n.* 1. (in Spanish America) a landless farm labourer. 2. (in India and Sri Lanka) an infantryman, messenger, or orderly. 3. any poor person.

pep·lum (pep'ləm), *n.* a short flounce attached to a garment around the waist and sometimes long enough to cover the hips.

pep·sin, pep·sine (pep'sin), *n.* a stomach enzyme that breaks down proteins, manufactured commercially to ferment cheese, for use in digestive aids, etc.

pep·tic (pep'tik), *adj.* relating to or aiding digestion.

pep·tide (pep'tīd), *n.* any of a class of chemical compounds consisting of two or more linked amino acids.

per·ad·ven·ture (pûr,ədven'CHə), *n.* 1. chance or possibility. 2. a conjecture. —*adv.* 3. maybe; perhaps. 4. by chance or at random.

per·cale (pəkāl'), *n.* a plain and close-woven, smooth, plain or printed cotton fabric.

per·ca·line (pûkəlēn'), *n.* a light, shiny-surfaced cotton fabric; usually in a plain colour and used for lining.

per cap·i·ta (pû kap'itə), by the person; for each; a method of dividing the estate of a person who leaves no will, whereby all related equally to the decedent receive equal shares. See also **per stirpes.**

per·ceive (pəsēv'), *v.* **per·ceived, per·ceiv·ing.** to see and understand; detect, as *She perceived from my smile that I meant to be friendly.* —**per·cep'tion,** *n.* —**per·cep'ti·ble,** *adj.*

per·cen·tile (pəsen'tīl), *n.* (in statistics) one of the class of values of a variable that divides the total frequency of a sample or population into 100 equal parts. See also **quantile, quartile.**

per·cept (pû'sept), *n.* the result of, as distinct from the act of, perceiving; the thing perceived.

per·cep·tive (pəsep'tiv), *adj.* quick at sizing something up; accurate at understanding.

per·cip·i·ent (pəsip'ēənt), *adj.* in the act of perceiving; having powers of perception or insight.

per·cuss (pəkus'), *v.* to strike with resulting shaking or shock in the person or thing struck.

per·cu·ta·ne·ous (pû,kyŏŏtā'nēəs), *adj.* (in medicine) performed or effected through the skin, esp. as in the absorption of an ointment.

per·di·tion (pədisH'ən), *n.* utter ruin of the spirit or soul; eternal damnation.

per·du, per·due (pûdyŏŏ'), *adj. French.* hidden; out of sight.

per·dur·a·ble (pədyŏŏr'əbəl), *adj.* permanently durable; everlasting.

per·dure (pədyŏŏr'), *v.* to last forever; to endure permanently.

per·e·gri·nate (per'əgrināt), *v.* to make a journey, esp. on foot. —**per·e·gri·na'tion,** *n.*

per·e·grine (per'əgrin), *adj.* from abroad; alien.

per·emp·to·ry (pəremp'tərē), *adj.* allowing no refusal or argument; dictatorial.

peremptory challenge, an objection to a juror that requires no cause to be shown.

per·e·stroi·ka (per,əstroi'kə), *n.* a policy of political and economic reconstruction, esp. that initiated by Mikhail Gorbachov (1931–) in the former Soviet Union in the 1980s. [*Russian,* literally: reconstruction.]

per·fer·vid (pəfû'vid), *adj.* extremely ardent or intense.

per·fid·i·ous (pəfid'ēəs), *adj.* treacherous; disloyal; characterized by deceit.

per·fi·dy (pû'fidē), *n.* treachery; intentional breaking of faith.

per·func·to·ry (pəfuNGk'tərē), *adj.* performed as routine duty; done superficially or mechanically.

per·fuse (pəfyŏŏz'), *v.* to spread liquid, colour, or the like over something. —**per·fu'sion,** *n.*

per·gel·i·sol (pəjel'isol), *n.* permafrost.

per·go·la (pû'gələ), *n.* an arbour or covered walk of climbing plants growing on horizontal trelliswork held overhead on posts or columns.

per·i·anth (per'ēan*th*), *n.* the calyx and corolla of a flower.

per·i·apt (per'ēapt), *n.* a lucky charm for wearing on the person as a bracelet, etc.; an amulet.

per·i·ar·ter·i·tis (per,ēä,tərī'tis), *n.* inflammation around the outside of an artery.

pe·rib·o·los, pe·rib·o·lus (pərib'ələs), *n.*, *pl.* **pe·rib·o·loi** (pərib'əloi). a wall around sacred ground.

per·i·car·di·al (per,əkä'dēəl), *adj.* relating to the pericardium. Also **per·i·car'di·ac.**

per·i·car·di·tis (per,ikädī'tis), *n.* inflammation of the pericardium.

per·i·car·di·um (per,ikä'dēəm), *n.*, *pl.* **per·i·car·di·a** (perikar'dēə). the thin membrane that encloses the heart.

per·i·carp (per'ikäp), *n.* the vessel containing a ripe seed, as a husk, nut, or berry.

per·i·chon·dri·um (per,ikon'drēəm), *n.*, *pl.* **per·i·chon·dri·a** (per,ikon'drēə). the membrane that covers cartilages, except at joints.

Per·i·cle·an (per,iklē'ən), *adj.* of outstanding intellect, power, and wealth. [after Pericles, c.

490–429 B.C., the leader under whom Athens attained its highest power.]

per·i·co·pe (per'ikōp), *n., pl.* **pe·ric·o·pes, pe·ric·o·pae** (pərik'əpē). a short, selected passage from a book.

per·i·gee (per'ijē), *n.* the point in the orbit of a planet or artificial satellite that is nearest the earth. See also **apogee**.

per·i·he·li·on (per,ihē'lēən), *n., pl.* **per·i·he·li·a** (per,ihē'lēə). that point in the orbit of a heavenly body which is nearest the sun. See also **aphelion**.

per·i·o·don·tics (per,ēōdon'tiks), *n. sing.* the branch of dentistry concerned with the periodontium. Also **per,i·o·don'tia**.

per·i·o·don·tium (per,ēōdon'sHəm), *n., pl.* **per·i·o·don·tia** (per'ēədon'sHə). the gum, tissue, and bone surrounding and holding the teeth. Also **parodontium**.

per·i·o·nych·i·a (per,ēōnik'ēə), *n.* See **paronychia**.

per·i·o·nych·i·um (per,ēōnik'ēəm), *n., pl.* **per·i·o·nych·i·a** (per,ēōnik'ēə). the tissue around a fingernail or toenail. Also **paronychium**.

per·i·o·tic (per,ēō'tik), *adj.* denoting, relating to, or near the bony capsule protecting the inner ear.

per·i·pa·tet·ic (per,ipətet'ik), *adj.* going from place to place; itinerant.

per·i·pe·tei·a, per·i·pe·ti·a (per,ipitī'ə, per,ipitē'ə), *n.* an abrupt or unexpected change in circumstances or reversal of fortune, esp. in a play. Also **pe·rip·e·ty** (pərip'ətē). —**per,i·pe·tei'-an, per,i·pe·ti'an,** *adj.*

pe·riph·er·al (pərif'ərəl), *adj.* **1.** of or relating to the external boundaries of something. **2.** involving or focusing on unimportant or trivial aspects of something that are incidental or superficial to its more essential features. —**pe·riph'er·y,** *n.*

pe·riph·ra·sis (pərif'rəsis), *n., pl.* **pe·riph·ra·ses** (pərif'rəsēz). roundabout speech or an instance of it. —**per,i·phras'tic,** *adj.*

per·i·stal·sis (per,istal'sis), *n., pl.* **per·i·stal·ses** (per,istal'sēz). rhythmic contractions progressing in one direction along a muscular tube, as the intestine, and propelling the contents along it. —**per,i·stal'tic,** *adj.*

per·i·to·ne·um (per,itənē'əm), *n., pl.* **per·i·to·ne·ums, per·i·to·ne·a** (per,itənē'ə). the serous membrane forming the lining of the abdomen and surrounding the viscera.

per·i·to·ni·tis (per,itənī'tis), *n.* inflammation of a part of the peritoneum.

per·i·vis·cer·al (per,ivis'ərəl), *adj.* around or near the viscera.

per·ma·frost (pû'məfrost,), *n.* the permanently frozen condition of soil, subsoil, and bedrock in arctic and subarctic regions. Also **pergelisol**.

per·me·a·ble (pû'mēəbəl), *adj.* capable of

being passed through or pervaded; allowing the passage of fluid.

per·me·ant (pû'mēənt), *adj.* penetrating throughout; pervading.

per·mute (pəmyōōt'), *v.* to alter, esp. a sequence. —**per·mu·ta'tion,** *n.* —**per·mu·ta'tion·al,** *adj.*

per·ni·cious (pənisH'əs), *adj.* harmful; fatal.

per·o·rate (per'ərāt), *v.* to make a speech, often a lengthy one; to make a summing up at the end of a formal speech. —**per,o·ra'tion,** *n.*

per·pend (pû'pənd), *n.* a large stone built into a wall so that it passes through the entire thickness. Also **parpend, per'pent**. Also **through stone**.

per·plex (pəpleks'), *v.* to confuse or puzzle.

per·qui·site (pû'kwizit), *n.* a casual profit, advantage, or fee coming in addition to regular revenue or income. Also **perk**.

per·sev·e·ra·tion (pûsev,ərā'sHən), *n.* (in psychology) the continuation or recurrence of movement, speech, etc., in the absence of the provoking stimulus. —**per·sev·e·rate** (pûsev'-ərāt), *v.*

per·si·flage (pû'sifläzH), *n.* light banter.

per·sist (pəsist'), *v.* to continue despite difficulties or obstacles. —**per·sis'tent,** *adj.*

per·so·na (pəsō'nə), *n., pl.* **per·so·nae** (pəsō'-nē). the character, personality, or image that a person presents to the outside world.

per·so·na·li·a (pû,sənä'lēə), *n. pl.* personal effects; a person's belongings.

per·so·na non gra·ta (pəsō'nə nōn grä'tə), *pl.* **per·so·nae non gratae** (pəsō'nē nōn grä'tē). *Latin.* an unwelcome or unacceptable person.

per·son·ate (pû'sənāt,), *v.* **1.** to impersonate; portray, esp. a character in a play. **2.** (in law) to assume the identity of another person, esp. with criminal intent. —**per,son·a'tion,** *n.* —**per'son·a·tive,** *adj.* —**per'son·a·tor,** *n.*

per·spi·ca·cious (pû,spikā'sHəs), *adj.* having keen insight; discerning. —**per,spi·cac'i·ty,** *n.*

per·spi·cu·i·ty (pûspikyōō'itē), *n.* clarity to the mind; lucidity of expression. —**per·spic'u·ous,** *adj.*

per stir·pes (pû, stû'pēz), *a* method of dividing the estate of a deceased person, whereby if one of the legatees is already dead, his share shall pass to his children. See also **per capita**.

per·ti·na·cious (pû,tənā'sHəs), *adj.* holding firmly, as to an intention or opinion; obstinate. —**per,ti·nac'i·ty,** *n.*

pe·ruse (pərōōz'), *v.* **pe·rused, pe·rus·ing.** to read something, esp. thoroughly. —**pe·ru'sal,** *n.*

per·va·sive (pəvā'siv), *adj.* spread or extended throughout something, as *a pervasive odour in the air.*

per·vi·ca·cious (pû,vəkā'sHəs), *adj.* extremely stubborn; dogged.

per·vi·ous (pû'vōəs), *adj.* allowing entry or passage; accessible, as to reason, etc.

pet·al (pet'əl), *n.* one of the ring of conspicuous, usually brightly coloured parts of a flower immediately within the calyx and surrounding the reproductive organs.

pe·tard (pitäd'), *n.* a small explosive device, as one used formerly to breach a gate, etc.

pet·i·ole (pet'ēōl), *n.* 1. the stalk attaching a leaf to a stem. 2. a stalk-like structure in animals, as that joining the abdominal and thoracic segments of the wasp. —**pet'i·o·late,** *adj.*

pe·tit bour·geois (pet,ē bōō'əzʜwä,), *pl.* **pe·tits bour·geois** (pet,ē bōō'əzʜwä,). a member of the lower middle class.

pe·tite bour·geoi·sie (pətēt' bōō,əzʜwä'zē), the section of the middle class with the least wealth and lowest social standing.

pe·tite mar·mite (pətēt' mä'mīt), a thin meat and vegetable broth, usually served in its cooking pot.

pe·tit mal (pet'ē mal'), a mild form of epilepsy, in which only brief loss of consciousness occurs. See also **grand mal.**

pet·ro·glyph (pet'rəglif), *n.* a prehistoric or primitive carving or drawing on rock. Also **pet'·ro·graph,**.

pe·trol·o·gy (petrol'əjē), *n., pl.* **pe·trol·o·gies.** the study of rocks, including their structure, composition, and formation. —**pe·trol'o·gist,** *n.* —**pet·ro·log·i·cal** (pet,rəloj'ikəl), *adj.* —**pet,ro·log'i·cal·ly,** *adv.*

pet·rous (pet'rəs), *adj.* rocky; hard as stone. Also **pe·tro·sal** (pitrō'səl).

pet·ti·fog (pet'ēfog), *v.* to operate a small, inferior, or rascally law practice.

pet·ti·fog·ger (pet'ēfog,ə), *n.* 1. a lawyer who handles trivial legal matters. 2. a person overly concerned with trivial details. —**pet'ti·fog,ger·y,** *n.*

pet·tish (pet'isʜ), *adj.* peevish; apt to sulk.

pet·u·lant (pet'yōōlənt, pecʜ'ələnt), *adj.* given to or exhibiting sudden irritability; peevish over trifles. —**pet'u·lance,** *n.*

pe·yo·te (pāō'tē), *n.* a cactus of the southwestern U.S. and Mexico, containing the narcotic drug mescaline.

phae·ic (fē'ik), *adj.* (of animals) darkly coloured but lighter than in extreme melanism.

phag·e·dae·na, phag·e·de·na (faj,idē'-nə), *n.* an ulcer causing severe erosion.

phag·o·cyte (fag'əsīt), *n.* a colourless blood cell that engulfs and destroys foreign particles in the blood, as dead cells and bacteria.

phag·o·cy·tol·y·sis (fag,əsītol'isis), *n.* the destruction of phagocytes. Also **pha·gol'y·sis.**

phag·o·cy·to·sis (fag,əsītō'sis), *n.* the ingestion and destruction of foreign particles by phagocytes.

pha·lan·ge·al (fələn'jēəl), *n.* relating to a phalanx or the phalanges.

pha·lanx (fā'laɴks), *n., pl.* **pha·lang·es** (fələn'jēz). any bone in the fingers or toes. Also **phal·ange** (fəl'anj).

phan·tasm (fan'tazəm), *n.* a ghost; an illusion; an illusive likeness or vision of something real. —**phan·tas'mal, phan·tas'mic,** *adj.*

phan·tas·ma·go·ri·a (fan,tazməgôr'ēə), *n.* 1. a shifting sense of real or illusory figures and scenes, as in a dream. 2. a dream-like series of shifting, merging images produced by a magic lantern or the like.

phar·i·sa·ic (far,isā'ik), *adj.* observing the outward forms of religion or accepted behaviour without sincerely believing in the spirit behind them; hypocritical. —**phar'i·sa·ism,** *n.*

phar·i·see (far'isē), *n.* a sanctimonious hypocrite; a self-righteous person.

phar·ma·cog·no·sy (fä,məkog'nəsē), *n.* the study of drugs from plant and animal sources. —**phar,ma·cog'no·sist,** *n.* —**phar·ma·cog·nos·tic** (fä,məkognos'tik), **phar,ma·cog·nos'tic·al,** *adj.*

phar·ma·col·o·gy (fä,məkol'əjē), *n.* the scientific study of the effects of chemical substances on the human body and esp. of the nature and action of those used as drugs to treat disease.

phar·ma·co·poe·ia (fä,məkəpē'ə), *n.* an officially published book listing drugs and giving detailed information on them, as their formulas, uses in medicine, and the like.

phar·ma·co·psy·cho·sis (fä,məkōsīkō'sis), *n.* a psychosis resulting from taking a drug.

pha·ryn·ge·al (far,inje'əl, fərin'jēəl), *adj.* relating to or near the pharynx.

phar·yn·gec·to·my (far,injek'təmē), *n.* the surgical removal of a part or all of the pharynx.

phar·yn·gi·tis (far,inji'tis), *n.* inflammation of the pharynx.

phar·yn·gol·o·gy (far,iɴɢgol'əjē), *n.* the scientific study of the pharynx and diseases that affect it.

pha·ryn·go·scope (fəriɴɢ'gəskōp,), *n.* an apparatus used to carry out a medical examination of the pharynx.

phar·ynx (far'iɴɢks), *n., pl.* **phar·yn·ges** (fərin'jēz), **phar·ynx·es.** the cavity behind the nose and mouth and the muscle and membrane enclosing it, communicating with the nose, mouth, and, at the lower end, the larynx, and partially divided by the soft palate into the upper or nasal section and lower or oral section.

phe·net·ics (finet'iks), *n.* (in biology) a system of classification based on the degree of observable similarity between organisms. —**phe·net'ic,** *adj.* —**phe·net'i·cist,** *n.*

phe·no·bar·bi·tone (fē,nōbä'bitōn), *n.* a drug used chiefly as a sedative and hypnotic. U.S. name **phenobarbital.**

phe·nol·o·gy (finol'əjē), *n.* the scientific

study of the part played by climate in annually recurring natural phenomena, as bird migration, flowering time in plants, etc.

phe·nom·e·non (fənom'ənon), n., pl. **phe·nom·e·na**. a condition, fact, or process that can be seen or sensed. —**phe·nom'e·nal,** adj.

phe·no·type (fē'nətīp,), n. the sum of the characteristics exhibited by an organism resulting from the interaction of inherited genes and environment. See also **genotype.**

pher·o·mone (fer'əmōn), n. any of several hormonelike substances important in animal physiology, that are released into the environment and influence behaviour of other individuals, esp. of the same species. They are important in social integration (e.g. in insects), trail marking, reproduction, etc.

phi·lan·der (filan'də), v. (of a man) to flirt, court, or make love merely for amusement with no serious intention.

phi·lip·pic (filip'ik), n. a speech denouncing a person or thing with bitter invective.

phi·lis·tine (fil'istēn), n. an uncultured person; a person of commonplace interests.

phil·lu·men·ist (filōō'mənist, filyōō'mənist), n. a collector of matchbox labels and match books.

phi·log·y·ny (filoj'ənē), n. love of women; liking for women.

phi·lol·o·gy (filol'əjē), n. the study of written records to establish their meaning, authenticity, etc.

phil·o·pro·gen·i·tive (fil,ōprōjen'itiv), adj. bearing many offspring; relating to or having typically a love of one's own or any children.

phi·los·o·phas·ter (filos'əfäs,tə), n. a pretender to knowledge of philosophy; a person with superficial knowledge of philosophy.

phil·tre (fil'tə), n. a love potion; any magic potion.

phil·trum (fil'trəm), n., pl. **phil·tra** (fil'trə). the hollow running down from the septum dividing the nostrils to the upper lip.

phle·bi·tis (flibī'tis), n. inflammation of the veins.

phleb·o·scle·ro·sis (fleb,ōskliro'sis), n. thickening or hardening of the walls of veins.

phle·bo·throm·bo·sis (fleb,ōthrombō'sis), n. the condition of having a blood clot in a vein, but without inflammation of the wall of the vein. See also **thrombophlebitis.**

phleb·o·tome (fleb'ətōm), n. a surgical instrument for cutting open a vein.

phle·bot·o·my (fləbot'əmē), n. incision into a vein. —**phleb,o·tom'ic,** adj. —**phle·bot'o·mist,** n. —**phle·bot'o·mize,** v.

phleg·mat·ic (flegmat'ik), adj. not easily roused to act or to feel emotion; sluggish.

pho·bi·a (fō'bēə), n. an abnormally excessive fear; an irrationally obsessive aversion or dread.

pho·cine (fō'sīn), adj. relating to seals, esp. the earless or hair seals.

phon (fon), n. a unit used in measuring the apparent loudness of a noise, being, for a given sound, equal in number to the decibel intensity of a pure note at a frequency of 100 cycles per second which has been adjusted until in the opinion of a group of listeners the two sounds are equally loud.

pho·net·ics (fōnet'iks), n. sing. the scientific study of the sounds of spoken language, including their production, classification, transcription, etc.

pho·ni·at·rics (fō,nēat'riks), n. sing. the study and treatment of disorders affecting the voice. Also **pho·ni·a·try** (fōnī'ətrē).

phon·ics (fon'iks), n. sing. a method of teaching reading and writing through phonetics.

phos·phate (fos'fāt), n. a salt or ester of phosphoric acid; an ingredient of some detergents that is not biodegradable and hence causes pollution.

phos·pho·res·cence (fos,fəres'əns), n. the property of shining after exposure to light or other radiation. See also **fluorescence.** —**phos,pho·res'cent,** adj.

phot (fot, fōt), n. a unit used in measuring illumination, equal to one lumen per square centimetre.

pho·tics (fō'tiks), n. sing. the scientific study of light. —**pho'tic,** adj.

pho·tism (fō'tizəm), n. a form of synaesthesia in which a visual sensation is produced by a stimulus to a different sense, as hearing, touch, etc.

pho·to·bath·ic (fō,təbath'ik), adj. relating to that layer of the sea that sunlight can penetrate.

pho·to·bi·ot·ic (fō,tōbīot'ik), adj. requiring light to live or thrive.

pho·to·chem·is·try (fō,tōkem'istrē), n. the scientific study of the chemical effects of light.

pho·to·com·pose (fō,tōkəmpōz'), v. to use a photocomposer. —**pho·to·com·po·si·tion** (fō,-tōkom,pəzisн'ən), n.

pho·to·com·po·ser (fō,tōkəmpō'zər), n. a machine that uses photographic techniques to set up type for printing.

pho·to·gram·me·try (fō,tōgram'itrē), n. the process of mapping and surveying by means of photography.

pho·to·he·li·o·graph (fō,tōhē'lēəgräf,, fō,tō-hē'lēəgraf,), n. a camera combined with a modified telescope, used for taking photographs of the sun. Also **heliograph.**

pho·to·ki·ne·sis (fō,tōkīnē'sis), n. movement of a cell or organism in response to the stimulus of light and varying according to the intensity of the stimulus.

pho·tol·y·sis (fōtol'isis), n. the breakdown of substances due to the presence of light.

pho·to·mac·ro·graph (fō,tōmak'rəgräf,,

fō,tōmak'rəgraf,), *n.* a photograph taken through a microscope capable of only low magnification.

pho·to·me·ter (fōtom'itə), *n.* an optical instrument used to measure light intensity, flux, colour. etc., by comparing light from one source with light from another source of which the characteristics are standardized.

pho·tom·e·try (fōtom'itrē), *n.* the measuring of light intensities; the scientific study, as analysis, comparison, etc., of light intensities. —pho,-to·met'ric, *adj.*

pho·to·mi·cro·graph (fō,tōmī'krəgräf,, fō,-tōmī'krəgraf,), *n.* 1. a photograph taken through a microscope. 2. a less common word for microphotograph.

pho·to·mul·ti·pli·er (fō,tōmul'tiplīər), *n.* a device for greatly amplifying light and other radiation.

pho·ton (fō'ton), *n.* a light quantum; the smallest indivisible quantity of light or other radiant energy; the elementary particle by which such energy is transmitted from a source. See also **quantum.**

pho·top·a·thy (fōtop'əthē), *n.* 1. the movement of a cell or organism in response to the stimulus of light and usually away from it. 2. a disease caused by excessive amounts of light.

pho·to·pe·ri·od·ism (fō,tōpēr'ēədiz,əm), *n.* the response of plants and animals to the relative length of day and night. Also **pho,to·pe,ri·o·dic'i·ty.**

pho·toph·i·lous (fōtof'ələs), *adj.* thriving in light, esp. strong light.

pho·to·pho·bi·a (fō,tōfō'bēə), *n.* an abnormally excessive fear of light.

pho·to·pi·a (fōtō'pēə), *n.* normal, full vision in bright daylight. See also **scotopia.**

pho·to·sphere (fō'təsfē,ə), *n.* the shallow layer of ionized gases forming the visible surface of the sun.

pho·to·syn·the·sis (fō,tōsin'thisis), *n.* the forming of organic compounds using light energy, esp. the forming in plants of carbohydrates from carbon dioxide and water under the stimulus of light and with chlorophyll acting as a catalyst.

pho·to·tax·is (fō,tōtak'sis), *n.* the movement of a cell or organism in response to light and orientated in relation to the direction of the light. Also **pho'to·tax·y.**

pho·to·the·od·o·lite (fō,tōthēod'əlīt), *n.* an instrument for tracking and filming a rocket or missile in flight. See also **theodolite.**

pho·to·ther·a·peu·tics (fō,tōther,əpyōō'-tiks), *n. sing.* the study and use of light rays to treat disease.

pho·to·ther·a·py (fōtōther'əpē), *n.* the treating of disease by light rays.

pho·to·ther·mic (fō,tōthû'mik), *adj.* 1. relating to heat produced by light. 2. relating to both light and heat.

pho·to·troph (fo'totrof), *n.* a microorganism for which light is the energy source.

pho·to·trop·ic (fō,tōtrop'ik), *adj.* exhibiting phototropism.

pho·tot·ro·pism (fō,tōtrō'pizəm, fōtot'rəpiz,-əm), *n.* growth or tendency of an organism, as a plant or sedentary animal, in response to light and oriented according to the direction of the light.

pho·to·vol·ta·ic cell (fō,tōvoltā'ik), an electric cell generating electromotive force through the action of light or other electromagnetic radiation on the junction of two dissimilar materials, which causes a potential difference to be developed between them.

pho·tu·ri·a (fōtyōōr'ēə), *n.* a medical disorder in which phosphorescent urine is passed.

phra·se·ol·o·gy (frā,zēol!'əjē), *n.* 1. the manner of using words and phrases. 2. the selection of words and phrases used in a particular utterance or written work.

phra·try (frā'trē), *n.* a grouping of social units, as clans, within a tribe.

phren·o·gas·tric (fren,ōgas'trik), *adj.* relating to both the diaphragm and the stomach.

phre·nol·o·gy (frinol'əjē), *n.* the study of the external contours of an individual's skull as a supposed indication of his mental capabilities and character.

phro·ne·sis (frōnē'sis), *n.* wisdom in deciding aims and the ways of achieving them.

phthis·ic (tiz'ik), *n.* 1. a disease causing wasting away of the lungs; phthisis. —adj. 2. relating to or characterized by phthisis.

phthi·sis (*thi*'sis), *n.* consumption; pulmonary tuberculosis. —phthi'si·cal, *adj.*

phy·col·o·gy (fīkol'əjē), *n.* the scientific study of algae.

phy·let·ic (fīlet'ik), *adj.* relating to race, species, tribe, or clan; relating to the development or history of such a group.

phyl·loid (fī'loid), *adj.* resembling a leaf.

phy·log·e·ny (fīloj'əne), *n.* the history of the development of a race or of a plant or animal type. Also **phy,lo·gen'e·sis.** See also **ontogeny.**

phy·lum (fī'ləm), *n., pl.* **phy·la.** the first division in biological classification of animals, each consisting of one or more related classes.

phy·ma (fī'mə), *n., pl.* **phy·mas, phy·ma·ta** (fī'mətə). a small skin tumour; a nodule of the skin.

phys·i·at·rics (fiz,ēat'riks), *n. sing. U.S.* 1. the diagnosis and treatment of medical disorders by physical means, as manipulation, massage, application of heat, etc. 2. physiotherapy.

phys·i·at·rist (fiz,ēat'rist), *n. U.S.* a doctor who specializes in physiatrics.

physical anthropology, the scientific study of the evolution and biology of man and closely related species.

physical chemistry, the scientific study, description, and interpretation of the physical and chemical properties of substances.

physical geography, the scientific study, description, and interpretation of the natural features and phenomena of the earth's surface, as land forms, climate, vegetation, etc.

physical science, the scientific study of natural phenomena except those relating to living things, as physics, astronomy, etc.

phys·i·og·no·my (fiz,ēog'nəmē), *n.* **1.** the face, esp. regarded as a reflection of character. **2.** Also called **anthroposcopy.** The art of reading a person's character from his bodily, esp. facial, features.

phys·i·og·ra·phy (fiz,ēog'rəfē), *n.* physical geography.

phys·i·ol·o·gy (fiz,ēol'əjē), *n.* the scientific study of the parts and normal functioning of living things. Also called **bionomy. —phys,i·o·log'i·cal,** *adj.*

phys·i·om·e·try (fiz,ēom'itrē), *n.* the science of measuring the human body's physiological functions.

phys·i·o·path·ol·o·gy (fiz,ēōpəthol'əjē), *n.* the scientific study of abnormalities occurring in physiological functions as a result of disease.

phys·i·o·ther·a·py (fiz,ēōther'əpē), *n.* the treatment of medical disorders by physical means only, as exercise, massage, heat, etc., rather than by drugs. U.S. also **physiatrics.**

phy·sis (fī'sis), *n., pl.* **phy·ses** (fī'sēz). (in Greek philosophy) the single fundamental reality underlying and unifying the seeming diversity of nature and the material from which all objects stem with individual variation in properties or forms to differentiate them; the principle of growth or development in nature; that which develops or results.

phy·to·bi·ol·o·gy (fī,tōbīol'əjē), *n.* the scientific study of plants; botany.

phy·to·cide (fī'tōsīd), *n.* a chemical agent for killing plants.

phy·to·cli·ma·tol·o·gy (fī,tōklī,mətol'əjē), *n.* the study of the local climatic conditions in which individual plants and plant communities live.

phy·to·coe·no·sis (fī,tōsēnō'sis), *n., pl.* **phy·to·coe·no·ses** (fī,tōsēnō'sēz). the entire plant life of any given area.

phy·to·gen·e·sis (fī,tōjen'isis), *n.* the origin and evolution of plants. Also **phy·tog'e·ny. —phy,to·gen'ic,** *adj.*

phy·to·ge·og·ra·phy (fī,tōjēog'rəfē), *n.* plant geography, the scientific study of the range and distribution of plants over the globe on land and in water, both as biological units such as families, species, etc., and as communities such as forest plants, grassland plants, etc., and the summation of results by descriptive analysis and in tables and maps.

phy·tog·ra·phy (fītog'rəfē), *n.* the scientific description of plants; descriptive botany.

phy·to·hor·mone (fī,tōhô'mōn), *n.* any hormone present in plants.

phy·to·pa·thol·o·gy (fī,tōpəthol'əjē), *n.* the scientific study of plant diseases; plant pathology.

phy·toph·a·gous (fītof'əgəs), *adj.* plant eating; herbivorous.

phy·to·plank·ton (fī,təplaNGk'tən), *n.* the plant organisms of plankton. See also **zooplankton.**

phy·to·plasm (fī'təplaz,əm), *n.* plant protoplasm.

phy·to·so·ci·ol·o·gy (fī,tōsō,sēol'əjē), *n.* the study of the relationships of plant communities with their environment and of relationships between plants in a community; the ecology of plant communities.

phy·to·suc·civ·o·rous (fī,tōsəksiv'ərəs), *adj.* feeding on the sap of plants, as some insects.

phy·to·tox·in (fī,tətok'sin), *n.* any poison produced by a plant. **phy·to·tox'ic,** *adj.*

pi·ac·u·lar (pīak'yōōlə), *adj.* amending for sin or wrong; expiatory.

pi·a ma·ter (pī'ə mā'tə), the innermost of the three delicate coverings protecting the brain and spinal cord. See also **dura mater, arachnoid.**

pi·a·nism (pē'əniz,əm), *n.* the technical and artistic skill of a pianist.

pi·broch (pē'brokH), *n.* a dirge or military piece played on the bagpipes.

pi·ca (pī'kə), *n.* an abnormal desire to eat something not usually considered as food, as soil, chalk, etc.

pi·ca·dor (pik'ədô), *n., pl.* **pi·ca·dors.** a mounted assistant to a matador who goads the bull in the earlier stages of a bullfight and weakens it by putting lances in its shoulder muscles.

pic·a·resque (pik,əresk'), *adj.* roguish; relating the adventures of a likeable rogue, as a novel.

pic·a·yune (pik,əyōōn'), *adj.* of small amount or importance; paltry.

pic·e·ous (pis'ēəs), *adj.* relating to or like pitch; inflammable.

Pick·wick·i·an (pikwik'ēən), *adj.* unusual or strange, either by design or by accident, esp. relating to the use of words. [after Charles Dickens's character, Mr Pickwick, in *The Pickwick Papers.*]

pi·co·cu·rie (pī'kōkyōōr,ē), *n.* a unit of radioactivity equal to one million millionth of a curie. *Abbrev.:* **pCi.**

pi·co·far·ad (pī'kōfar,əd), *n.* a unit of electrical capacity equal to a million millionth of a farad. *Abbrev.:* **pF.**

pi·co·me·tre (pī'kōme,tə), *n.* a unit of length in the metric system, equal to a million millionth of a metre; a micromicron. *Abbrev.:* **pm.**

pi·co·sec·ond (pī'kōsek,ənd), *n.* a unit of time

pi·cot (pē'kō), *n.* one of a row of small loops of twisted thread used to decorate embroidery, a ribbon edge, etc.

pi·co·watt (pī'kōwot,), *n.* a unit of electric power equal to a million millionth of a watt. *Abbrev.:* **pW.**

pic·ric acid (pik'rik), a bitter, poisonous acid used principally as an explosive.

pic·to·graph (pik'tōgräf,, pik'tōgraf,), *n.* **1.** a written record using stylized pictorial symbols to stand for the thing depicted, as in some primitive writing; a pictorial graph. **2.** a pictorial symbol. —**pic·tog'ra·phy,** *n.*

pie·bald (pī'bôld), *adj.* **1.** with irregular patches of different colours, esp. black and white. **2.** an animal, esp. a horse, with such colouring.

pièce de ré·sis·tance (pēes' də räzēstäns'), *pl.* **pièces de ré·sis·tance** (pēes' də räzēstäns'). *French.* **1.** the most important dish or course of a meal. **2.** the most important item, as in a series of events, achievements, etc.

pied-à-terre (pyädatä'ə), *n., pl.* **pieds-à-terre** (pyädatä'ə). *French.* a dwelling for staying in for short periods, as a flat for overnight stays in a city.

Pi·er·rette (pēəret'), *n.* the female equivalent of and companion of a Pierrot.

Pi·er·rot (pēərō'), *n.* a male character in French pantomime, with whitened face and loose white costume.

pi·e·tism (pī'itiz,əm), *n.* fervent religious devotion; exaggeratedly pious feeling or behaviour.

pi·e·ty (pī'itē), *n.* a dutifully reverent attitude to God; an earnest and devout fulfilment of religious obligations.

pi·e·zo·e·lec·tric·i·ty (pīē'zōilektris'itē), *n.* electricity generated by pressure on certain nonconducting asymmetric crystals, as quartz.

pi·e·zom·e·ter (pī'ēzom'itə), *n.* any of various kinds of instrument for measuring the pressure of a fluid or the compression caused by a fluid in another substance.

pi·e·zom·e·try (pī'ēzom'itrē), *n.* the measurement of pressure or of capacity for being compressed.

pig·gin (pig'in), *n.* a wooden pail of which the handle is formed by a continuation of one of the staves that form its side.

pi·gno·li·a (pēnyō'lēə), *n.* the edible seed contained in cones of the southern European nut pine.

pi·las·ter (pilas'tə), *n.* a rectangularly sectioned projection running up a wall and made in imitation of a column.

pile (pīl), *n.* the lower of the two dies used in minting coins by hand. See also **trussell.**

pi·le·at·ed (pī'lēä,tid), *adj.* having a feathered crest, as the cockatoo.

pil·fer (pil'fə), *v.* to steal, esp. small items of little value. —**pil'fer·age,** *n.*

pi·lif·er·ous (pīlif'ərəs), *adj.* with hair; bearing or producing hair.

pil·i·form (pil'əfôm), *adj.* like hair or a hair.

pi·lose (pī'lōs), *adj.* with a covering of hair or fur. Also **pi·lous** (pī'ləs).

pil·u·lar (pil'yŏŏlə), *adj.* relating to or like a pill or pills.

pil·ule (pil'yŏŏl), *n.* a small pill.

pi·lus (pī'ləs), *n., pl.* **pi·li** (pī'lī). a hair; a structure resembling a hair.

pi·ma cotton (pē'mə), *U.S.* a kind of Egyptian cotton, used for shirts, ties, etc.

pim·o·la (pimō'lə), *n. U.S.* a stuffed olive, usually one stuffed with sweet red pepper.

pinch·beck (pinCH'bek), *n.* something which is not genuine; a counterfeit; a sham.

pin·e·al (pin'ēəl), *adj.* having the shape of a pine cone.

pineal body, a small conical glandular body situated in the midbrain of all vertebrates with a cranium; of unknown function but thought to secrete a hormone and perhaps to represent a vestigial sense organ.

pin·guid (piNG'gwid), *adj.* oily; fat. —**pin·guid'i·ty,** *n.*

pin·ion (pin'yən), *n.* **1.** the terminal segment of a bird's wing. —*v.* **2.** to remove the pinions of or bind a bird's wings to prevent it from flying.

pin·na (pin'ə), *n., pl.* **pin·nae** (pin'ē), **pin·nas.** a feather; a wing; a part resembling a wing.

pin·nate (pin'āt), *adj.* arranged or made like a feather with similar parts ranged along both sides of a central axis, as the leaf of an ash tree. —**pin·na'tion,** *n.*

pin·nat·i·ped (pinat'əped,), *adj.* of birds with a membranous flap along each side of each toe.

pin·nat·i·sect (pinat'isekt), *adj.* divided in pinnate form, usually of a leaf.

pin·ni·grade (pin'igrād,), *adj.* using flippers or finlike structures to effect movement, as seals.

pin·ni·ped (pin'iped,), *adj.* belonging to the aquatic suborder of carnivores that includes the seals and walruses.

pin·nu·la (pin'yŏŏlə), *n., pl.* **pin·nu·lae** (pin'-yŏŏlē). a pinnule.

pin·nule (pin'yŏŏl), *n.* a part or organ resembling a small wing, as a fin, the barb of a feather, etc. —**pin'nu·late,** *adj.*

pin·tle (pin'təl), *n.* a kind of pin on which something, as a rudder, hinge, etc., turns.

pinx·it (piNGk'sit), *Latin.* (he or she) painted it, formerly used after the artist's name in signing a painting, engraving, etc.

pi·pette (pīpet'), *n.* a glass tube, often graduated and used mainly in chemistry for taking up, usually by being sucked like a drinking straw,

pi·co· **equal to a million millionth of a second.** *Abbrev.:* **ps, psec.**

small quantities of liquid for transferring to another vessel.

pi·quant (pē'kənt), *adj.* with a pleasantly sharp or spicy flavour.

pique (pēk), *v.* to cause resentful irritation or a wound to a person's pride.

pi·rosh·ki (pirosH'kē), *n. pl.* a Russian dish consisting of small pies or turnovers made of yeast dough or puff pastry with a sweet or savoury filling. Also **pi·ro·gen** (pirō'gən).

pis al·ler (pē, zalā'), *French.* the final resort; a makeshift; a course followed because of the lack of any better one.

pis·ca·tor (piskā'tə), *n.* a fisherman.

pis·ca·to·ry (pis' kətərē), *adj.* relating to fishermen or fishing; depending on or addicted to fishing. Also **pis·ca·to'ri·al.**

pis·ci·cul·ture (pis'ikul,cHə), *n.* the farming of fish; the rearing of fish in artificial conditions.

pis·ci·form (pis'əfôm,), *adj.* fish-shaped.

pis·cine (pis'īn), *adj.* relating to or like a fish or fishes.

pis·civ·o·rous (pisiv'ərəs), *adj.* living on fish; fish-eating.

pi·si·form (pī'səfôm,), *adj.* pea-shaped.

pis·til (pis'til), *n.* See **gynoecium.**

pis·tol·o·gy (pistol'əjē), *n.* a branch of theology, concerned with faith.

pitch (picH), *v.* to deviate from a stable course because of oscillation about the vertical axis. See also **yaw.**

pith·y (pith'ē), *adj.* **pith·i·er, pith·i·est.** containing the most important part or parts in a concise, concentrated form, as *a pithy argument.*

pit·tance (pit'əns), *n.* an inadequate salary, wage, or living allowance.

pi·tu·i·tar·y gland (pityōō'itərē), a small ductless endocrine gland at the base of the brain, which secretes hormones that regulate many functions of the body, as growth and hormone production in other endocrine glands, as the thyroid, the gonads, etc. Also **hypophysis.**

pit·u·ri (picH'ərē), *n.* a small Australian tree whose leaves and twigs contain nicotine and are dried by the aborigines to use as a narcotic.

pit·y·roid (pit'əroid), *adj.* scaly; bran-like.

pix·i·lat ed (pik'silā,tid), *adj. Chiefly U.S.* **1.** amusingly prankish; eccentric; crazy. **2.** drunk. Also **pixillated.**

plac·age (plak'ij), *n.* a thin outer layer of material put on the front of a building for decoration or protection and different from the building material it covers.

pla·cate (plā'kāt), *v.* **pla·cat·ed, pla·cat·ing.** to pacify or calm; make peaceful.

pla·ce·bo (pləsē'bō), *n., pl.* **pla·ce·bos, pla·ce·boes.** a substance having no pharmacological effect but given as a medicine either to a patient who insists he needs one or to people acting as

the control in an experiment where another group is given a drug that is being tested.

pla·cen·ta (pləsen'tə), *n.* a structure formed of fetal and maternal tissues, attached to the wall of the uterus, developing with the fetus which is attached to it by the umbilical cord, and acting as a channel through which the fetus is given nourishment and freed of its waste products until parturition, when it is expelled after the fetus. —**pla·cen'tal**, *adj.*

plac·id (plas'id), *adj.* tranquil; calm; peaceful, esp. as the result of not having been disturbed or actively concerned.

plack·et (plak'it), *n.* an opening at the top of a skirt or in another garment to make it easier to put on and take off.

plac·oid (plak'oid), *adj.* plate-shaped.

pla·ga (plā'gə), *n., pl.* **pla·gae** (plā'jē). a stripe, streak, or spot of colour. —**pla'gate**, *adj.*

pla·gia·rism (plā'jəriz,əm), *n.* the act of publishing, without permission, as one's own creation the artistic or other published work of another. —**pla'gia·rist**, *n.* —**pla'gia·rize**, *v.*

pla·gi·o·trop·ic (plā,jēətrop'ik), *adj.* relating to, denoting, or showing growth in a direction away from the vertical to a greater or lesser degree. —**pla,gi·ot'ro·pism**, *n.*

plain text, a message transcribed from code or cipher. Also **clear text.** See also **cryptography.**

plaintiff (plān'tif), *n.* the party who brings a suit in a court of law.

plain·tive (plān'tiv), *adj.* expressing sorrowfulness; mournful.

pla·nate (plā'nat), *adj.* having a level or plane surface; flat-topped.

pla·na·tion (plānā'sHən), *n.* the levelling of a surface by erosion.

planch, planche (plāncH), *n.* a tray for use in an enamelling oven, as one of stone or metal.

plan·e·tes·i·mal (plan,ites'iməl), *n.* one of the innumerable minute bodies which originally revolved around the sun and were joined to form the planets, according to one (discredited) theory of the origin of the solar system.

plan·et·oid (plan'itoid), *n.* an asteroid; one of the many thousands of minor planets in the solar system, mostly in the region between Mars and Jupiter.

plan·e·tol·o·gy (plan,itol'əjē), *n.* the scientific study of the physical features of the planets.

plan·gent (plan'jənt), *adj.* (of a sound) deep, low, and resonant; mournful. —**plan'gen·cy.**

pla·ni·form (plā'nifôm,), *adj.* of flattened form.

pla·nim·e·ter (plənim'itə), *n.* a mechanical device for measuring the area of irregular plane figures.

pla·nim·e·try (plənim'itrē), *n.* the measurement of plane surfaces.

plan·ish (plan'isH), v. to flatten out to a smooth finish by hammering or passing through rollers, as sheet metal, paper, etc.

plan·i·sphere (plan'isfē,ə), n. a device for showing that part of a map of the celestial sphere which is visible at a given time and place; projection or other representation on a plane of a sphere or a part of one.

plank·ter (plaNGk'tə), n. any organism in plankton.

plank·ton (plaNGk'tən), n. all of the mostly minute, drifting or floating organisms in the sea or a stretch of fresh water. See also **phytoplankton, zooplankton.**

pla·no·con·cave (plā,nōkon'kāv), adj. relating to or denoting a lens with one side flat and the other concave.

pla·no·con·vex (plā,nōkon'veks), adj. relating to or denoting a lens with one side flat and the other convex.

pla·no·graph (plā'nōgräf,, plā'nəgraf), v. to print from a flat surface, directly or by offset. —**pla·nog'ra·phy,** n

plan·tar (plan'tə), adj. relating to the sole of the foot.

plan·ti·grade (plan'tigrād,), adj. that uses the whole underside of the foot when walking, as man, bears, etc.

plaque (plak, pläk), n. 1. an ornamental tablet of metal or the like fixed on a wall or set into a piece of wood. 2. the mixture of bacteria and saliva that accumulates in a jellylike deposit on the teeth. 3. a small flat mass, mark, or spot on the skin or other part of the body.

pla·quette (plaket'), n. a small metal panel with a design in relief, often set into the covers of books made in France in the 15th and 16th centuries.

plas·ma (plaz'mə), n. 1. the clear liquid part of blood or lymph in which the other parts are suspended. 2. a highly ionized gas with nearly equal numbers of positive and negative charges. Also **plasm.**

plas·ma·pher·e·sis (plaz,məfer'isis), n., pl. **plas·ma·pher·e·ses** (plaz,məfer'isēz). a medical procedure for obtaining blood plasma by centrifuging blood to separate out the corpuscles which can then be returned to the bloodstream of the donor. Also **plas,ma·phor'e·sis.**

plas·mo·di·um (plazmō'dēəm), n., pl. **plas·mo·di·a** (plazmō'dēə). any parasitic protozoan that causes malaria in man.

plas·mo·ma (plazmō'mə), n., pl. **plas·mo·mas, plas·mo·ma·ta** (plazmō'mətə). a tumour consisting of plasma cells.

plastic bomb, a putty-like, sticky mixture of explosives used as a bomb chiefly by guerrilla fighters and terrorists. Also **plastique** (plɔstēk').

plas·tid (plas'tid), n. any of various minute structures occurring in most plant cells and some animal cells that contain pigment (e.g. chlorophyll), starch, oil, etc.

plas·ti·queur (plastēkû'), n., pl. **plas·ti·queurs** (plastēkû'). French. someone who makes or uses plastic bombs.

plas·tom·e·ter (plastom'itə), n. a device used to measure the plasticity of a substance.

plate·let (plāt'lit), n. a small, oval or round body resembling a plate, esp. such a body in blood.

plat·i·tude (plat'ityōōd), n. a commonplace, dull remark, esp. one delivered as if it were original or significant. —**plat,i·tu'di·nous,** adj. —**plat,i·tu'di·nous·ly,** adv.

Pla·ton·ic (plɔton'ik), adj. 1. relating to or typical of Plato or his philosophy. 2. (usually lower case) free from sensual desire, as platonic love.

Platonic year, the time required for a complete revolution of the equinoxes, about 26,000 years. See also **precession of the equinoxes.**

plat·yr·rhine (plat'irīn), adj. having a broad flat nose in which the nostrils point forwards and are divided by a wide septum.

plau·dits (plô'dits), n. pl. applause; enthusiastic approval of an action or performance.

plau·si·ble (plô'zəbəl), adj. believable; regarded as possible or likely, as a plausible explanation. —**plau,si·bil'i·ty,** n.

pleas·ance (plez'əns), n. a place arranged as a pleasure garden or promenade.

ple·be·ian (pləbē'ən), adj. relating to or belonging to the common people; common; coarse.

pledg·et (plej'it), n. a small wad of lint, absorbent cotton, etc., for putting on a cut, etc.

plein air (plān' e'ə), the open air; broad daylight; out of doors.

plei·o·tax·y (plī'ətak,sē), n. an increase in the usual number of parts, as may occur in a plant. Also **plei,o·tax'is.**

Pleis·to·cene (plī'stəsēn), adj. relating to or denoting the geological epoch immediately preceding the present epoch, forming the earlier part of the Quaternary, originating about one million years ago, and characterized by the Ice Ages and the evolution of early man.

ple·na·ry (plē'nərē), adj. 1. full; complete; absolute; not subject to limitation, as plenary pardon. 2. fully constituted; with all members present, as a plenary assembly.

ple·nip·o·tent (plənip'ətənt), adj. having full powers.

plen·i·po·ten·tiar·y (plen,ipəten'sHərē), n. a person invested with full powers to act on behalf of another, as an ambassador on behalf of his sovereign.

plen·i·tude (plen'ityōōd), n. fullness; sufficiency; abundance.

ple·o·mor·phism (plēəmô'fiz,əm), n. the

state or condition of being polymorphous; polymorphism. Also **ple'o·mor,phy.**

ples·sor (ples'ə), *n.* See **plexor.**

pleth·o·ra (ple*th*'ərə), *n.* an excess; glut; superabundance. —**ple·thor'ic,** *adj.*

pleu·ra (ploor'ə), *n., pl.* **pleu·rae** (ploor'ē). a serous membrane surrounding each lung in mammals and lining the thorax.

pleu·ri·sy (ploor'isē),, *n.* inflammation of the pleura, sometimes with liquid forming between the lung and the thorax.

pleu·ro·dy·ni·a (ploor,ədī'nēə), *n.* pain affecting the chest or side.

pleu·ro·pneu·mo·ni·a (ploor,ōnyoomō'-nēə), *n.* pleurisy and pneumonia combined.

pleus·ton (ploo'stən, ploo'ston), *n.* a mass of organisms (e.g. algae) floating at or near the surface of a body of fresh water. —**pleus·ton'ic,** *adj.*

plex·i·form (plek'səfôm,), *adj.* relating to or like a plexus; intricate.

plex·or (plek'sə), *n.* a small hammer used by doctors to strike or tap for diagnostic purposes. Also **plessor.**

plex·us (plek'səs), *n., pl.* **plex·us·es, plex·us.** a network, as of nerve fibres or blood vessels. —**plex'al,** *adj.*

pli·cate (plī'kāt), *adj.* folded; pleated like a fan. Also **pli'cat·ed, pli·ca'tion,** *n.*

plight (plīt), *n.* a serious situation, filled with danger and hardship.

Pli·o·cene (plī'əsēn), *adj.* relating to or denoting a geological epoch, the last of the Tertiary period, lasting from ten million years ago to one million years ago and characterized by a cooling climate, the formation of mountains, and the advent of larger mammals such as the mastodon.

ploy (ploi), *n.* a manoeuvre or trick to gain an advantage.

plu·mate (ploo'māt), *adj.* like a feather; feathered, as a bristle from which small hairs grow.

plum·ba·go (plumbā'gō), *n., pl.* **plum·ba·gos.** graphite; a form of carbon used for pencil leads, as a solid lubricant, etc.

plum·be·ous (plum'bēəs), *adj.* containing lead; leadlike, esp. in colour.

plum·bif·er·ous (plumbif'ərəs), *adj.* lead-bearing; containing or yielding lead.

plu·mose (ploo'mōs), *adj.* with or like feathers or plumes.

plu·mu·la·ceous (ploom,yoolā'sHəs), *adj.* having a downy texture.

plu·mule (ploom'yool), *n.* a down feather.

plu·mu·lose (ploom'yoolōs), *adj.* with the shape of a down feather or a bud inside a plant embryo.

plu·ral·ism (ploor'əliz,əm), *n.* a philosophical theory that there is more than one basic substance or ultimate principle. See also **dualism, monism.**

plu·toc·ra·cy (plootok'rəsē), *n.* rule by the wealthy; the power of wealth. —**plu'to·crat,** *n.* —**plu,to·crat'ic,** *adj.*

Plu·to·ni·an (plootō'nēən), *adj.* relating to or like Pluto or his kingdom of the lower world; infernal. Also **Plu·ton'ic.**

plu·vi·al (ploo'vēal), *adj.* relating to rain; rainy.

plu·vi·om·e·ter (ploo,vēom'itə), *n.* a rain gauge; an instrument for measuring rainfall.

plu·vi·ous (ploo'vēəs), *adj.* rainy; relating to rain.

pneu·drau·lic (nyoodrô'lik), *adj.* relating to a mechanical device using both pneumatic and hydraulic action.

pneu·ma (nyoo'mə), *n.* the soul; the essential spirit.

pneu·mat·ics (nyoomat'iks), *n. sing.* the science of the mechanical properties of elastic fluids, as air and other gases. Also **pneu,mo·dy·nam'ics.** —**pneu·mat'ic,** *adj.*

pneu·ma·tol·o·gy (nyoo,mətol'əjē), *n.* the theological teaching or belief that beings have a spirit or soul.

pneu·ma·tom·e·ter (nyoo,mətom'itə), *n.* a device used to measure the quantity of air breathed in or out at a single breath, or the force of a single breath in or out.

pneu·ma·to·ther·a·py (nyoo,mətō*th*er'əpē), *n.* the treatment of disease by compressed or rarefied air.

pneu·mo·coc·cus (nyoo,mōkok'əs), *n., pl.* **pneu·mo·coc·ci** (nyoo,mōkok'sī). the bacterium which causes lobar pneumonia, and is also associated with meningitis, pericarditis, etc.

pneu·mo·co·ni·o·sis (nyoo,mōkō,nēō'sis), *n.* a group of diseases in which there is progressive lung damage resulting from the inhalation of abrasive dust during industrial procedures, as silicosis in stonecutters and coalminers. Also **pneu,mo·no·co,ni·o'sis, pneu,mo·no·ko,ni·o'sis.**

pneu·mo·graph (nyoo'məgräf,, nyoo'mə-graf,), *n.* a device used in medicine to make a graphic record of the movements of the thorax during breathing. Also **pneu'ma·to·graph,.**

pneu·mog·ra·phy (nyoomog'rəfē), *n.* the recording of chest movements during breathing.

pneu·mon·ic (n,oomon'ik), *adj.* relating to the lungs.

pneu·mo·no·ul·tra·mi·cro·scop·ic·sil·i·co·vol·ca·no·co·ni·o·sis, pneu·mo·no·ul·tra·mi·cro·scop·ic·sil·i·co·vol·ca·no·ko·ni·o·sis (nyoo'mənoul'trəmī'krəskop'-iksil'ikō'volkä'nokō,nēō'sis), *n.* a lung disease resulting from inhaling very fine particles of siliceous dust.

pneu·mo·tho·rax (nyoo,mōthôr'aks), *n.* the presence of air or another gas between the pleura surrounding the lung and that lining the thorax, an abnormal condition in this pleural cavity causing displacement and sometimes collapse of a lung.

pocket veto, *U.S.* a veto on a bill resulting from the President's failure to sign it within ten days of the adjournment of Congress.

po·co·cu·ran·te (pō,kōkŏŏran'tē), *n.*, *pl.* **po·co·cu·ran·ti** (pō,kōkŏŏran'tē). someone who is careless or shows little concern or interest.

poc·u·li·form (pok'yələfôm,), *adj.* with the shape of a cup.

po·dag·ra (podag'rə), *n.* gout, esp. affecting the feet.

po·dal·gi·a (podal'jə), *n.* pain affecting the foot. Also **pod·o·dyn'i·a.**

po·dal·ic (podal'ik), *adj.* relating to the foot or feet.

po·di·a·try (pōdī'ətrē), *n.* the study and treatment of foot disorders.

pod·sol (pod'sol), *n.* an infertile, very acid forest soil with an ashy grey top layer from which basic salts, as iron, aluminium, etc., have been leached into the well-defined brownish lower layer, found across northern North America, Europe, and Asia. Also **pod'zol.**

po·et·as·ter (pō'itas,tə), *n.* a writer of inferior verse.

pog·a·mog·gan (pog,əmog'ən), *n.* a wooden club with a knob at the head, used as a weapon by the Algonquins and other American Indian peoples.

po·grom (pogrom'), *n.* an organized massacre, esp. of Jews, originally in Russia and Poland.

poi (poi, pō'ē), *n.* a Hawaiian dish of baked taro root pounded and fermented.

poign·ant (poin'yənt), *adj.* affecting sharply, esp. the mind or emotions.

poi·ki·lo·ther·mal (poi,kəlōthû'məl), *adj.* with body temperature varying with that of its surroundings; cold-blooded. See also **homoio·thermal.**

poin·tel, poin·tal (poin'təl), *n.* a mosaic pavement of abstract design.

point·til·lism (pwan'tiliz,əm, poin'tiliz,əm), *n.* a technique of the Neo-Impressionist painters to reproduce the effects of light in a scientific way by juxtaposing spots of primary colours, which merge to give the correct colour impression at a distance.

poise (pwäz, poiz), *n.* a unit used in measuring viscosity, equal to the viscosity of a fluid which requires a force of one centimetre per square centimetre to maintain a difference of one centimetre per second in velocity between two parallel planes one centimetre apart in the fluid and lying in the direction of flow. *Abbr.:* **P.** [named after the French physician Poiseuille (1799–1869).]

po·lar·im·e·ter (pō,lərim'itə), *n.* a device for measuring the quantity of polarized light in light from a particular source.

po·lar·i·scope (pōlar'iskōp,), *n.* a device for measuring or exhibiting the properties of polarized light, for studying the effects of various agencies on light of known polarization, and for inspecting substances under polarized light.

po·lar·i·za·tion (pō,lərīzā'sHən), *n.* **1.** a state in which light rays or other radiations have all the vibrations of one type in the same plane; the production of such a state. **2.** the giving of unity and direction, as to a project. —**po'lar·ize,** *v.*

po·lem·ic (pəlem'ik), *n.* **1.** a controversy or argument, esp. one directed at someone personally. **2.** a person who disputes or argues with another. —*adj.* **3.** involving or relating to argument; disputatious.

po·lem·ics (pəlem'iks), *n. sing.* the art of controversial discussion. —**pol'e·mist, po·lem'i·cist,** *n.*

pol·i·cli·nic (pol,iklin'ik), *n. U.S.* the out-patients department of a hospital.

po·li·o·en·ceph·a·li·tis (pō,lēōensef,əlī'tis), *n.* an acute virus infection causing inflammation of the grey matter in the brain. Also **po,li·en·ceph,a·li'tis.**

po·li·o·en·ceph·a·lo·my·e·li·tis (pō,lēōensef,ōlōmī,əlī'tis), *n.* an acute virus infection causing inflammation of the grey matter of the brain and spinal cord. Also **po,li·en·ceph,a·lo·my,e·li'tis.**

po·li·o·my·e·li·tis (pō,lēōmī,əlī'tis), *n.* an acute virus infection causing inflammation of the grey matter of the spinal cord, sometimes leading to permanent paralysis and deformity. Also called **po'li·o, infantile paralysis.**

Polish sausage. See kielbasa.

pol·i·tesse (pol,ites'), *n.* politeness; refined or courteous behaviour.

pol·i·tic (pol'itik), *adj.* sagacious; expedient; scheming; political.

pol·i·ty (pol'itē), *n.* any given system of civil government, as civil, ecclesiastical, etc.

pol·lard (pol'əd, pol'äd), *n.* a tree whose top has been cut off so as to produce a close round head of young shoots.

pollen count, the amount of pollen in the atmosphere, usually given as the average number of pollen grains collecting in a given time on slides in the open air.

pol·lex (pol'eks), *n.*, *pl.* **pol·li·ces** (pol'isēz). the thumb or the corresponding digit in certain other vertebrates, as mammals and amphibians.

pol·li·ce ver·so (pol,isē vû'sō), *Latin.* thumbs down; with thumbs turned down to indicate failure, as ancient Romans asking for a gladiator to be put to death after a poor performance in a combat.

pol·lic·i·ta·tion (pəlis,itā'sHən), *n. U.S.* an offer made by one party to a lawsuit but not yet accepted by the other.

pol·ter·geist (pōl'təgīst), *n.* a noisy ghost or other spirit supposedly showing its presence by breaking crockery, banging doors, etc.

pol·troon (poltrŏŏn'), *n.* a coward. —**pol·troon'er·y,** *n.*

pol·y·an·dry (pol,ēən'drē), *n.* the practice or fact of a woman's having more than one husband at a time. See also **monandry, polygamy, monogamy, bigamy.** —**pol,y·an'drist,** *n.* —**pol,y·an'drous,** *adj.*

pol·y·ar·chy (pol'ēä,kē), *n.* a government by a group of people, usually more than three.

pol·y·ar·tic·u·lar (pol,ēätik'yōōlə), *adj.* relating to several joints.

pol·y·chro·mat·ic (pol,ēkrōmat'ik), *adj.* many-coloured. Also **pol·y·chro'mic.**

pol·y·chrome (pol'ēkrōm), *adj.* consisting of or decorated with many colours. —**pol'y·chro,·my,** *n.*

pol·y·cy·thae·mi·a, pol·y·cy·the·mi·a (pol,ēsīthē'mēə), *n.* a blood disorder in which red blood cells are present in abnormally large numbers.

pol·y·dac·tyl (pol,ēdak'til), *adj.* with several or many digits.

pol·y·dae·mon·ism, pol·y·demon·ism (pol,ēdē'məniz,əm), *n.* belief in the existence and power of many devils or evil spirits.

pol·y·dip·si·a (pol,ēdip'sēə), *n.* abnormally excessive thirst.

po·lyd·o·mous (pəlid'əməs), *adj.* living as a colony but inhabiting more than one nest, as certain colonies of ants. See also **monodomous.**

pol·y·don·tia (pol,ēdon'sнə), *n.* the condition of having more teeth than is usual.

pol·y·eth·nic (pol,ēeth'nik) *adj.* relating to, consisting of, or inhabited by a people or group of many ethnic origins.

po·lyg·a·my (pəlig'əmē), *n.* the practice or fact of having more than two marriage partners at the same time. See also **bigamy, monogamy, polyandry, monandry.** —**po·lyg'a·mist,** —*n.* **po·lyg'a·mous,** *adj.*

po·lyg·e·nism (pəlij'əniz,əm), *n.* the theory that man is descended from more than one ancestral type.

pol·y·glot (pol'iglot,), *adj.* multilingual; knowing or consisting of several languages.

pol·y·gon (pol'igon), *n.* a figure with more, often many more, than four sides and usually in one plane.

pol·y·graph (pol'igräf,, pol'igraf,), *n.* a lie detector.

po·lyg·y·ny (pəlij'ənē), *n.* the practice or fact of having more than one wife at the same time. See also **monogyny.** —**po·lyg'y·nist,** *n.* —**po·lyg'·y·nous,** *adj.*

pol·y·he·dron (pol,ihē'drən), *n., pl.* **pol·y·he·drons, pol·y·he·dra** (pol,ihē'drə). a many-sided solid, usually one with more than six faces. —**pol,y·he'dral,** *adj.*

pol·y·his·tor (pol,ēhis'tə), *n.* a person learned in a variety of subjects; a great scholar. Also **pol·y·his·tor'ian.**

pol·y·math (pol'ēmath,), *n.* a person who knows a great deal about a great many different subjects.

pol·y·mer (pol'imə), *n.* a large molecule made up of many repeated units. —**pol·y·mer·ic** (pol,·ēmer'ik), *adj.* —**po·lym·er·ism** (pəlim'əriz,əm, pol'ēməriz,əm), *n.*

po·lym·er·ase (pəlim'ərīz), *n.* any enzyme that catalyses the formation of polymers, esp. DNA and RNA.

pol·y·mor·phism (pol,imô'fiz,əm), *n.* the condition or fact of being polymorphous.

pol·y·mor·phous (pol,imô'fəs), *adj.* occurring in any of a number of varied forms, as a species of butterfly some individuals of which mimic other species in their colouring.

po·ly·no·mi·al (pol,inō'mēəl), *adj.* having several or many names.

pol·y·nu·cle·ar (pol,inyōō'klēə), *adj.* with several or many nuclei. Also **pol·y·nu'cle·ate.**

pol·yp (pol'ip), *n.* **1.** (in pathology) a stalk-like outgrowth from a mucous membrane or the skin. **2.** (in zoology) a body in the form of a hollow cylinder with a mouth at one end surrounded by a ring of tentacles, as in some coelenterates. —**pol·y·poid** (pol'ēpoid,), *adj.*

pol·y·pep·tide (pol,ēpep'tīd), *n.* a polymer consisting of large numbers of amino acids joined together, as in proteins.

pol·y·pet·al·ous (pol,ipet'ələs), *adj.* many petalled; having more than one petal; with petals separated from one another.

pol·y·pha·gi·a (pol,ifā'jēə), *n.* an abnormally excessive desire for food; the habit of feeding on a wide variety of foods.

pol·y·phon·ic (pol,ifon'ik), *adj.* having more than one sound or voice, as music, a letter of the alphabet, etc. —**pol'y·phone, po·lyph'o·ny,** *n.*

pol·y·phy·let·ic (pol,ifīlet'ik), *adj.* having been descended from quite different ancestors but now classified biologically in the same phylum.

pol·y·ploid (pol'iploid), *adj.* with three or more times the haploid number of chromosomes.

pol·yp·noe·a, pol·yp·ne·a (pol,ipnē'ə), *n.* panting; rapid breathing.

pol·yp·tych (pol'iptik), *n.* a painting or carving consisting of several panels hinged side by side, each bearing a part of the whole picture or bearing a separate picture. See also **diptych, pentaptych, triptych.**

pol·y·rhythm (pol'ērith,əm), *n.* the use of several different rhythms at the same time in a musical composition.

pol·y·sac·cha·ride (pol,ēsak'ərīd,), *n.* a chemical compound consisting of many repeated sugar units, as in starch, cellulose, etc.

pol·y·se·my (pəlis'əmē), *n.* a variety of meanings or senses. —**po·lys'e·mous,** *adj.*

pol·y·sper·mi·a (pol,ispû'mēə), *n.* the abnormally excessive production of semen.

pol·y·style (pol'ēstīl,), *adj.* having many pillars or columns.

pol·y·sty·rene (pol,istī'rēn), *n.* a stiff plastic foam, used for insulating and packing and for heat-resistant cups.

pol·y·syl·lab·ic (pol,ēsilab'ik), *adj.* of words having three or more syllables; of a written piece or a language characterized by having many such words. Also **pol,y·syl·lab'i·cal.**

pol·y·tech·nic (pol,itek'nik), *adj.* relating to or devoted to scientific, technical, and industrial subjects.

pol·y·the·ism (pol'ithēiz,əm), *n.* the doctrine or belief that there is more than one god.

po·lyt·o·my (pəlit'əmē), *n.* the dividing of something into three or more parts.

pol·y·un·sat·u·rat·ed (pol,ēunsaCH'ərātid), *adj.* relating to or denoting a class of fats, as corn oil, cottonseed oil, etc., whose molecules contain many double bonds unsaturated by hydrogen atoms, a feature associated with a low production of cholesterol in the blood.

pol·y·u·ri·a (pol,ēyōōr'ēə), *n.* the abnormally excessive formation of urine, as in diabetes, etc.

pom·ace (pum'is, pom'is), *n.* the pulp remaining when fruit has been crushed and the juice pressed out, as apple pulp after cider making.

po·ma·ceous (pemā'sHəs), *adj.* relating to or like apples.

po·man·der (pōman'də), *n.* a mixture of sweet-smelling substances, as herbs, petals, etc., in a bag, decorative metal case, etc., formerly carried by someone in front of himself to ward off infection.

pom·e·lo (pom'əlō), *n., pl.* **pom·elos.** *n.* 1. a tree, *Citrus maxima,* grown in oriental regions for its edible fruit resembling a grapefruit. 2. (in the U.S.) another name for grapefruit. See **shad·dock.**

po·mi·cul·ture (pō'mikul'CHə), *n.* fruitgrowing; the raising and tending of fruit crops.

po·mif·er·ous (pōmif'ərəs), *adj.* bearing fruits of or similar to the apple family.

po·mol·o·gy (pōmol'əjē), *n.* the science of fruit-growing.

ponce (pons), *n. Slang.* a pimp.

pon·ceau (ponsō'), *n.* a bright orange-red colour.

pon·der (pon'də), *v.* to think over carefully and at length.

pon·der·ous (pon'dərəs), *adj.* heavy; weighty, esp. in an unwieldy way.

pon·gee (ponjē'), *n.* a soft Chinese or Japanese fabric of wild silk in the natural tan colour and of uneven weave. See also **shantung, tussah.**

pon·iard (pon'yəd), *n.* a slender dagger.

po·no·graph (pō'nəgräf,, pō'nəgraf,), *n.* a medical instrument for making a graphic record of fatigue.

pon·tif·i·cate (pontif'ikāt), *v.* to speak pompously; to act or speak as if infallible.

pont·lev·is (pontlev'is), *n.* a drawbridge; a bridge hinged at one end or in the middle so that it can be drawn up to permit tall shipping to pass beneath or to prevent anyone from crossing.

Pop Art, a style of the 1960s in the fine arts, esp. painting, characteristically using very large images usually from commercial art sources, as comics, advertisements, food wrappings, etc.

pop·in·jay (pop'injā), *n.* a vain, showy, foppish, empty-headed person.

pop·lit·e·al (poplit'ēəl), *adj.* relating to the back of the knee.

pop·ple (pop'əl), *v.* to tumble about; to move irregularly to and fro, as water below a waterfall or when boiling.

pop·u·lous (pop'yōōləs), occupied by a large number of people, as *China is a populous country.*

por·cine (pô'sīn), *adj.* relating to or resembling swine; piglike.

po·rif·er·ous (pərif'ərəs), *adj.* having pores.

po·ri·form (pôr'əfôm,), *adj.* poreshaped.

pork barrel, *U.S. slang.* government money, legislation, or policy promoting local improvements, by distribution of which the local member of the legislature hopes to win votes and influence.

por·rect (pərekt'), *adj.* stretching out horizontally.

por·ta·tive (pô'tətiv), *adj.* portable; capable of or relating to carrying.

porte·co·chere, porte·co·chère (pôt'-kōsHe'ə), *n.* an entrance for vehicles leading through the house to a courtyard; a porch to shelter people stepping into or out of vehicles.

por·tend (pôtend'), *v.* to foreshadow; to give warning of. **—por'tent,** *n.* **—por·ten'tous,** *adj.*

por·ti·co (pô'tikō), *n., pl.* **por·ti·coes, por·ti·cos.** an imposing porch consisting of a roof supported by columns.

por·tiere, por·tière (pôtye,ə), *n.* a curtain hung over a door or instead of a door.

port·man·teau (pôtman'tō), *n., pl.* **port·man·teaus, port·man·teaux** (pôtman'tōz). a suitcase or travelling trunk, esp. one hinged along the back to open into two halves.

por·tray (pôtrā'), *v.* to show in speech, writing, or graphically what someone or something is like in appearance or nature; represent or depict.

po·seur (pōzû'), *n.* a person who affects ideas, a style of living, etc., to impress other people.

pos·i·grade rocket (poz'igrād), a rocket, part of a missile with several stages, that fires in the direction of flight, causing the stages yet to be fired to draw away from stages no longer required.

pos·it (poz'it), v. to put in place; to assume as fact or truth.

pos·i·tron (poz'itron,), n. the antiparticle of the electron.

po·sol·o·gy (pōsol'əjē), n. the branch of pharmacology concerned with finding out what amount of a drug should be prescribed.

pos·set (pos'it), n. a drink made of sweetened hot milk curdled with ale, wine, etc., and usually flavoured with spices.

post·bel·lum (pōst,bel'əm), adj. post-war, esp. after the American Civil War.

post·di·lu·vi·an (pōst,dilōō'vēən), adj. in or of the period after the Flood. See also **antediluvian**.

pos·ter·i·ad (postēr'ēad), adv. towards the posterior of a living creature.

pos·te·ri·or (postēr'ēə), adj. at the rear or hind end. See also **anterior**.

pos·tern (pos'tən), n. a back or side entrance; a private door or gate.

post-Ford·ism (pōst,fōd'izəm), n. a concept of manufacturing in which the large-scale mass-production methods introduced by Henry Ford give way to smaller, more flexible manufacturing plants and assembly units. —**post,-Ford'ist**, adj.

post hoc, er·go prop·ter hoc (pōst, hōk' e'əgō prop'tə hōk'), Latin. it happened after this, therefore it happened because of this; a phrase to point up the error in logic of confusing sequence with consequence.

pos·tiche (postēsH'), adj. relating to an ornament added to a work, as of sculpture, already finished, esp. a superfluous or unsuitable ornament; artificial; false.

pos·ti·cous (postē'kəs), adj. posterior; esp., of flowers, relating to the part nearest the main axis.

pos·til·ion, pos·til·lion (postil'yən), n. the man who rides the horse on the left of the pair, or on the left of the leading pair where four or more are used, drawing a carriage.

post·lude (pōst'lōōd), n. 1. a concluding piece of music, esp. an organ work played at the end of a church service. 2. any act or work that marks a conclusion, as of a war, epoch, etc.

post·mod·ern·ism (pōst,mod'əniz,əm), n. a movement in late-20th-century culture, esp. art and architecture, that rejects dogmatic modernism in favour of more eclectic pluralistic styles incorporating fascination with form and delight in ornamentation. —**post,mod'ern·ist**, n.

post·or·bit·al (pōst,ô'bitəl), adj. lying behind the eye socket.

post·par·tum (pōst,pä'təm), relating to or denoting the period of time immediately following childbirth. Also **post,par'tal**. See also **ante partum**.

post·pran·di·al (pōst,pran'dēəl), adj. after dinner; after a meal.

pos·tre·mo·gen·i·ture (post,rimōjen'icHə), n. the right of inheritance or succession by the last-born son. Also called **ultimogeniture**. See also **primogeniture**.

pos·trorse (pos'trôs), adj. turned or bent backwards.

pos·tu·lant (pos'tyōōlənt), n. 1. a person demanding or applying for something. 2. a candidate, esp. for admission into a religious order.

pos·tu·late (pos'tyōōlāt), v. 1. to ask for or demand. 2. to assume without proof. 3. to assume a fact or principle as a basis for discussion. 4. to lay down as indisputable.

post·vi·ral syndrome (pōst,vir'əl), n. see myalgic encephalomyelitis. Abbr.: **PVS**.

po·ta·ble (pō'təbəl), adj. fit to drink; in a drinkable form.

po·tage (pōtäzH'), n. French. soup.

po·tam·ic (pōtam'ik), adj. relating to rivers.

po·ta·tion (pōtā'sHən), n. drinking, esp. the drinking of alcoholic beverages; a drink, usually alcoholic.

po·ta·to·ry (pō'tətərē), adj. relating to drinking; habitually taking strong drink.

pot·au·feu (potōfû'), n. a French dish consisting of stewed meat and vegetables with the broth from them served separately.

po·ten·ti·ate (pōten'sHēāt), v. to endow with the power or ability to do something; to make more effective; to make possible.

po·ten·ti·om·e·ter (pōten,sHēom'itə), n. an instrument for making accurate measurements of electromotive force or differences in electrical potential by balancing that to be measured against that produced by a current of known voltage.

poth·er (poTH'ə), n. commotion; agitation; fuss.

pot·latch (pot'lacH), n. a festival among American Indian peoples of the N. Pacific coast, with great display of wealth, as by lavish presentation of gifts and competition to outdo all others in destroying one's own belongings to show that one can afford it.

pot liquor, pot·liquor, Chiefly U.S. the liquid in which meat or vegetables have been cooked and containing flavoursome juices from them.

po·tom·e·ter (pōtom'itə), n. a device for measuring the amount of water lost by a plant through transpiration, consisting of a vessel holding a known quantity of water and entirely sealed around the emerging plant so that moisture can leave only through the plant.

pot·pour·ri (pō,pōor'ē), n., pl. **pot·pour·ris** (pō'pōorēz'). 1. a mixture of dried petals, spices, and essential oils, kept in a dish or pierced container for their fragrance. 2. a medley of musical or literary pieces; any mixture of unrelated items.

pot·sherd (pot'sHäd), n. a broken piece of

earthenware, usually one of archaeological interest.

pou·lard, pou·larde (poŏoläd'), *n*. a hen spayed to make it more fleshy, tender, and tasty for the table; a fat hen.

poult (pōlt), *n*. a young fowl or gamebird.

poult-de-soie (poŏodəswä'), *n*. a strong, finely corded silk fabric used for dresses. See also **paduasoy, peau de soie.**

poul·tice (pōl'tis), *n*. **1.** a paste of bread-crumbs, starch, meal, linseed oil, herbs, etc., usually spread between layers of muslin and applied to the skin to soothe inflammation, etc. —*v*. **2.** to apply a poultice.

pour·boire (poŏo,əbwä'), *n*., *pl*. **pourboires** (poŏo,əbwä'). *French.* a tip; a gratuity.

prac·ti·cum (prak'tikəm), *n*. that part of a course of study spent on practical work.

prae·cip·i·ta·ti·o (prēsip,itä'sHēō), *n*. rain, hail, or snow that reaches the earth's surface. See also **virga.**

prae·di·al, pre·di·al (prē'dēəl), *adj*. relating to land that is owned or farmed and to its products; attached to the land, as slaves.

prag·mat·ic (pragmat'ik), *adj*. relating to the practical aspect of any matter. Also **prag·mat'i·cal.** —**prag·'ma·tism, prag'ma·tist,** *n*.

pran·di·al (pran'dēəl), *adj*. relating to dinner or to any meal.

prate (prāt), *v*. to talk too much; to keep up a stream of meaningless chatter.

pra·tique (pratēk'), *n*. a certificate showing that a ship presents no health hazard and therefore permitting it to use a particular port.

prat·tle (prat'əl), *v*. to talk in a childish manner; to utter foolish chatter.

prax·is (prak'sis), *n*., *pl*. **prax·is·es, prax·es** (prak'sēz). the practical application of theory, knowledge, or skill.

Pre·cam·bri·an (prēkam'brēən), *adj*. relating to or denoting the earliest era of geological time, lasting from about 4,500,000,000 years ago to 500,000,000 years ago and characterized by the formation of the earth's crust and supposedly by the appearance of the first forms of life, although no fossils remain.

prec·a·to·ry (prek'ətərē), *adj*. relating to or expressing a request or entreaty; supplicatory. Also **prec'a·tive.**

prec·e·dence (pres'idəns), *n*. getting or coming before in time or position; priority.

prec·e·dent (pres'idənt), *n*. something that took place at an earlier time and used esp. as an example or guide for future action or judgment.

pre·cent' (prēsent'), *v*. to perform the duties of a precentor.

pre·cen·tor (prēsen'tə), *n*. a person appointed to lead the singing in church.

pre·cept (prē'sept), *n*. a command giving a rule of conduct or action; an instruction or

exhortation as to morals or behaviour. —**pre·cep'tive,** *adj*. —**pre·cep'tor,** *n*.

pre·ces·sion (prēsesH'ən), *n*. the motion of a rotation axis when a torque disturbs it so that it describes a cone, as the spindle of a spinning top.

precession of the equinoxes, the slow change in the direction of the earth's axis, owing to gravitational forces, so that the celestial North Pole describes a circle once in 26,000 years and in consequence the equinoxes describe a circle round the ecliptic during the same period. See also **Platonic year.**

pré·cieuse (prāsyû'), *n*., *pl*. **pré·cieus·es** (prāsyûz'). **1.** one of the women who frequented the literary salons of 17th-century Paris and aimed at or affected a refined delicacy of language and taste, usually carried to ridiculous extremes. **2.** any woman with an affected manner, esp. in speech.

pré·cieux (prāsyû'), *adj*. (of a man) too fastidious; affected.

pre·ci·os·i·ty (presH,ēos'itē), *n*. an affected refinement; excessive fastidiousness, esp. in the use of language.

pre·cip·i·tant (prisip'itənt), *adj*. hurried; rushing or falling headlong; rash; abrupt.

pre·cip·i·tate (prisip'itit), *adj*. headlong.

pre·cip·i·tous (prisip'itəs), *adj*. extremely steep; like a precipice.

pré·cis (prā'sē), *n*., *pl*. **pré·cis.** a summary.

pre·ci·sian (prisizH'ən), *n*. a person who strictly observes rules or accepted forms of behaviour.

pre·ci·sive (prisī'siv), *adj*. cutting off, separating, or defining one person or thing from another or others.

pre·clude (priklōōd'), *v*. to prevent or exclude from.

pre·co·cial (prikō'sHəl), *adj*. relating to or denoting birds which at the time of hatching are covered with down and able to move about freely.

pre·co·cious (prikō'sHəs), *adj*. forward or premature in development, esp. of the mind or faculties. —**pre·coc'i·ty,** *n*.

pre·cog·ni·tion (prē,kognisH'ən), *n*. knowledge of an event or state before it comes about.

pre·co·nize (prē'kənīz), *v*. **1.** to proclaim, announce, or extol in public. **2.** to summon by name; to call upon publicly.

pre·con·scious (prēkon'sHəs), *adj*. not in the conscious mind but capable of being readily made conscious, as of ideas, memories, etc.

pre·cur·sor (prikû'sə), *n*. a forerunner; someone or something preceding another, as in office, a building, etc. —**pre·cur'so·ry,** *adj*.

pre·da·cious, pre·da·ceous (pridā'sHəs), *adj*. predatory; grasping; extortionate.

pre·da·tion (pridā'sнən), *n.* the act of preying upon or plundering.

pred·a·tor (pred'ətə), *n.* a person or animal living by or habitually preying upon others. —**pred'a·to·ry**, *adj.*

pre·di·al (prē'dēəl), *adj.* See **praedial.**

pred·i·ca·ble (pred'ikəbəl), *adj.* that can be stated as true or asserted.

pred·i·cant (pred'ikənt), *adj.* **1.** preaching. —*n.* **2.** a preacher.

pred·i·cate (pred'ikāt), *v.* to state as true; to assert as a fact; to proclaim or declare.

pre·di·lec·tion (pred,ilek'sнən), *n.* a liking or preference for; a partiality to.

pre·dis·pose (prē,dispōz'), *v.* to make liable to or inclined to. —**pre·dis,posi'tion,** *n.*

pre·dor·mi·tion (prē'dôrmisн'ən), *n.* the period of semiconsciousness before sleep.

pre·em·i·nent, pre-em·i·nent, pre·ēm·i·nent (prēem'inənt), *adj.* distinguished beyond or excelling all others. —**pre·em'i·nence, pre·em'i·nence, pre·ēm'i·nence,** *n.*

preen gland. See **uropygial gland.**

pre·for·ma·tion (prē,fômā'sнən), *n.* the theory held formerly that a complete individual is contained in the germ and grows to normal size during the embryonic period. See also **epigenesis.**

pre·hen·sile (prihen'sīl), *adj.* adapted for or capable of grasping something or wrapping around something, as a hand, a monkey's tail, etc. —**pre·hen·sion** (prihen'sнən), *n.*

prem·ise (prem'is), *n.* an argument, regarded as true, offered as a basis for drawing a conclusion. Also **prem'iss.**

pre·pos·sess (prē,pəzes'), *v.* to prejudice, usually favourably; to impress favourably beforehand or immediately. —**pre,pos·ses'sion,** *n.*

pre·pos·sess·ing (prē,pəzes'iNG), *adj.* arousing a favourable impression. *adj.*

pre·pos·ter·ous (pripos'tərəs), *adj.* absurd; ridiculous; foolish. —**pre·pos'ter·ous·ness,** *n.*

pre·po·tent (prēpō'tənt), *adj.* powerful above all others; predominant.

pre·pran·di·al (prēpran'dēəl), *adj.* before dinner; before a meal.

pre·req·ui·site (prērek'wizit), *n.* **1.** a requirement before all others. —*adj.* **2.** required before anything else.

pre·rog·a·tive (prirog'ətiv), *n.* a right or privilege exclusive to a particular person, group, office, rank, etc.

pres·age (pres'ij), *v.* **1.** to give or have a forewarning of. **2.** to forecast; to make a prediction. —*n.* **3.** an augury; a portent or forewarning.

pres·by·cu·sis (prez,bikyōō'sis), *n.* deterioration of hearing caused by old age. Also **pres·by·cou'sis, pres·by·a·cu'sia, pres·by·a·cou'sia.**

pres·by·o·pi·a (prez,bēō'pēə), *n.* deteriora-

tion of vision with old age due to the inability to alter the focal length of the lens, with consequent difficulty in seeing near objects. —**pres'by·ope,** *n.*

pre·sci·ence (pres'ēəns, presн'ēəns), *n.* foreknowledge; foresight.

pre·scind (prisind'), *v.* **1.** to isolate or separate mentally, as for special consideration. **2.** to withdraw attention (from).

pre·sen·ti·ment (prizen'timənt), *n.* a foreboding or feeling that something bad is going to happen.

pre·sid·i·o (prisid'ēō), *n., pl.* **presid'i·os.** a garrisoned fort or post.

pre·sid·i·um (prisid'ēəm), *n.* a permanent committee, esp. in communist organizations, exercising the full power of the parent assembly when this is in recess.

pres·ti·dig·i·ta·tion (pres,tidij,itā'sнən), *n.* conjuring; legerdemain.

pre·tence (pri'tens'), *n.* the act or an instance of pretending or making believe; faking; a false show or claim, as *He made a pretence of returning the money, but it never turned up.* —**pre·ten'sion,** *n.*

pre·ten·tious (priten'sнəs), *adj.* showily false; pretending to be something one is not. —**pre·ten'tious·ness,** *n.*

pre·ter·hu·man (prēt,əhyōō'mən), *adj.* beyond what is human; more than human.

preter·i·tion (pret,ərisн'ən), *n.* disregard; omission; an act of omission.

pre·ter·mit (prēt,əmit'), *v.* **1.** to disregard; to leave undone. **2.** to suspend or discontinue for a time.

pre·ter·nat·u·ral (prēt,ənacн'ərəl), *adj.* beyond what is normal; supernatural.

pre·text (prē'tekst), *n.* a false excuse or reason for doing something, as *His claim that he stole her necklace was pure pretext.*

pre·vail (privāl'), *v.* to be better and therefore gain in influence and currency.

prev·a·lent (prev'ələnt), *adj.* more widespread because of general acceptance, power, etc. —**prev'alence,** *n.*

pre·var·i·cate (privar'ikāt), *v.* to make evasive or deliberately misleading statements. —**pre·var'i·ca·tor,** *n.*

pre·ven·ient (privē'nēənt), *adj.* occurring before; previous; anticipating.

pri·ap·ic (prīap'ik, prīā'pik), *adj.* **1.** relating to Priapus, in Greek mythology the god of procreation and fertility. **2.** phallic. Also **pri·a·pe·an** (prī,əpē'ən).

price-earnings ratio, the ratio between the market price of a share and its earnings price index. See **consumer price index.**

prie-dieu (prē,dyû'), *n., pl.* **prie dieus, prie dieux** (prē,dyûz'). a piece of furniture for kneeling on during prayer, resembling a chair with a rest for a book at the top and a long seat for kneeling on.

prig (prig), *n.* a self-righteous person, exaggeratedly proper in conduct, fussy about minor details, and demanding similar behaviour from others. —**prig'gish,** *adj.*

pri·ma·cy (prī'məsē), *n.* the state of being above all others, as in rank, authority, etc.

pri·ma don·na (prē'mə don'ə), *pl.* **pri·ma don·nas. 1.** the principal singer, as in an operatic company. **2.** a temperamental and difficult person.

pri·ma fa·ci·e (prī'mə fa'sнiē), apparent; self-evident.

pri·me·val, pri·mae·val (prīmē'vəl), *adj.* relating to, belonging to, or as if belonging to the first age of the world, as *primeval forests* or *primeval instincts.*

pri·mi·ge·ni·al (prī,mijē'nēəl), *adj.* primitive; primordial. Also **pri,mo·ge'ni·al.**

pri·mip·a·ra (prīmip'ərə), *n., pl.* **pri·mip·a·rae** (prīmip'ərē). a woman who has given birth only once or is giving birth for the first time.

pri·mo·gen·i·tor (prī,mōjen'itə), *n.* the earliest ancestor; an ancestor.

pri·mo·gen·i·ture (prī,mōjen'iснə), *n.* **1.** the right of inheritance or succession by the first-born son. See also **postremogeniture. 2.** the state or fact of being the first-born of the children of the same parents.

pri·mor·di·al (prīmō'dēəl), *adj.* relating to, existing in, or since the beginning; original; initial; primitive.

pri·mor·di·um (prīmō'dēəm), *n., pl.* **pri·mor·di·a** (prīmō'dēə). the earliest recognizable stage of an organ during its development.

principal plane, a plane at right angles to the axis of a lens, mirror, or the like, at which rays parallel to the axis start to converge and rays diverging from a focal point become parallel to the axis.

prin·ci·pate (prin'sipāt), *n.* supreme authority or office.

prin·cip·i·um (prinsip'ēəm), *n., pl.* **prin·cip·i·a** (prinsip'ēə). a principle.

prin·ta·nier (praNtänyā'), *adj.* served with a garnish of diced spring vegetables. Also **prin·ta·nière** (praNtänye'ə).

print-out (print'out,), *n.* the printed material put out by a computer, usually on a continuous, folded strip of paper.

pri·on (prī'on), *n.* a hypothetical infectious agent, known only by its associated protein, that is thought to be the cause of scrapie in sheep, bovine spongiform encephalopathy in cattle, and Creutzfeldt-Jakob disease in humans.

pris·tine (pris'tīn, pris'tēn), *adj.* relating to early or the earliest time; retaining its original form or purity.

priv·a·tive (priv'ətiv), *adj.* denoting or marked by the absence, lack, or taking away of something; causing deprivation.

priv·y (priv'e), *adj.* sharing private or secret knowledge; private; confidential. —**priv'i·ly,** *adv.* —**priv'i·ty,** *n.*

prix fixe (prē, fiks'), *pl.* **prix fixes** (prē, fiks'). a set price for a full-course meal selected from a range of choices on a menu.

pro·ac·tive (prōak'tiv), *adj.* **1.** initiating events rather than reacting to them. **2.** (in psychology) of or relating to a mental process that influences or alters a subsequent process.

prob·a·bil·i·ty (prob,əbil'itē), *n.* (in statistics) the likelihood of something occurring measured by the ratio of actual occurrences to the total of possible occurrences.

pro·ba·tive (prō'bətiv), *adj.* acting or designed as a test; giving proof. Also **pro·ba·to·ry.**

pro·bi·ty (prō'bitē), *n.* honesty; incorruptibility.

pro bo·no pub·li·co (prō bō'nō pub'likō), *Latin.* for the public good; for the benefit of the public.

pro·bos·ci·date (prōbos'idāt), *adj.* having a proboscis.

pro·bos·cid·e·an (prō,bəsid'ēən), *adj.* relating to or like a proboscis. **2.** having a proboscis.

pro·bos·cid·i·form (prō,bəsid'ifôm,), *adj.* proboscis-shaped.

pro·bos·cis (prōbos'is), *n., pl.* **pro·bos·cis·es, pro·bos·ci·des** (prōbos'idez). **1.** any elongated snout or snoutlike part used for feeding, as an elephant's trunk. **2.** a prominent nose.

proc·e·leus·mat·ic (pros,əlōosmat'ik), *adj.* arousing to action or animation; putting life into; encouraging.

pro·cel·lous (prōsel'əs), *adj.* stormy; tempestuous.

pro·ces·sive (prəses'iv), *adj.* going on or forward; proceeding; progressive.

pro·cès-ver·bal (prōsā'vûbäl'), *n., pl.* **pro·cès-ver·baux** (prōsā'vûbō'). minutes; a detailed written report of the proceedings at a meeting, etc.

pro·chro·nism (prō'krəniz,əm), *n.* the assigning through error of a date earlier than the true one to a person, happening, etc. Also **prolepsis.** See also **anachronism, parachronism.**

proc·li·nate (prok'lināt), *adj.* bent or directed forward.

pro·cliv·i·ty (prōkliv'itē), *n.* a natural inclination towards or tendency to.

pro·cras·ti·nate (prōkras'tənāt,), *v.* **pro·cras·ti·nat·ed, pro·cras·ti·nat·ing.** to delay or put off, esp. because of indecision. —**pro·cras'tina'tion,** *n.*

pro·cre·ate (prō'krēāt), *v.* to beget offspring; to generate; to bring into being. —**pro'cre·ant,** *adj.*

Pro·crus·te·an (prōkrus'tēən), *adj.* forcing

conformity by drastic and merciless means. [From *Procrustes*, a highwayman of classical Greek legend who amputated or stretched the limbs of his victims to make them fit his bed.]

pro·cryp·tic (prōkrip'tik), *adj.* giving an animal concealment from its predators. See also **anticryptic.**

proc·tol·o·gy (proktol'ajē), *n.* the study and treatment of disorders of the rectum.

proc·to·scope (prok'taskōp,), *n.* a medical instrument passed through the anus to facilitate inspection of the inside of the rectum.

pro·cum·bent (prōkum'bant), *n.* lying face down; prostrate.

pro·cur·ance (prōkyōōr'ans), *n.* the bringing about of or obtaining of something for another or for oneself.

proc·u·ra·tion (prō,kyōōrā'sHan), *n.* the act of procurance. —**proc'u·ra,tor,** *n.*

pro·cure (prakyōōr'), *v.* **pro·cured, pro·cur·ing.** to obtain; purchase; get; (sometimes) to find customers for a prostitute. —**pro·cure'ment,** *n.*

prod·i·gal (prod'igal), *adj.* recklessly extravagant; wastefully lavish, as of money; agreeably lavish, as with gifts. —**prod,i·gal'i·ty,** *n.*

pro·di·gious (pradij'as), *adj.* extraordinary or amazing by reason of size, force, ability, etc.

prod·i·gy (prod'ijē), *n.* a person, esp. a child, endowed with an extraordinary talent or skill.

pro·drome (prō'drōm), *n.* a warning symptom.

pro·em (prō'em), *n.* a preface; an introduction.

pro·fane (prafān', prōfān'), *adj.* **1.** not sacred; unholy; irreverent, as *profane rites* or *profane language.* —*v.* **2.** to defile; desecrate; violate the holiness of. —**pro·fan·i·ty** (prafan'itē, prōfan'-itē), *n.*

prof·fer (prof'a), *v.* to offer.

pro·fi·lom·e·ter (prō,filom'ita), *n.* an instrument for measuring the roughness of a surface.

prof·li·ga·cy (prof'ligasē), *n.* **1.** shameless immorality. **2.** wild extravagance.

prof·li·gate (prof'ligit), *adj.* **1.** thoroughly immoral; licentious. **2.** wildly extravagant. —*n.* **3.** a profligate person.

prof·lu·ent (prof'lōōant), *adj.* flowing out freely, abundantly, or smoothly.

pro for·ma (prō fô'ma), *Latin.* as a matter of form; done according to or for the sake of form.

pro·found (prafound', prōfound'), *adj.* deep; characterized as having or showing the result of concentration and intelligence, as *She is a profound thinker* or *He wrote a profound paper on relativity.* —**pro·fun·di·ty** (prafun'ditē, prōfun'-ditē), *n.*

pro·fuse (prafyōōs', prōfyōōs'), *adj.* abundant; plentiful. —**pro·fu'si·on,** *n.*

pro·fu·sive (prafyōōsiv, prōfyōō'siv), *adj.* lavish; extravagant; prodigal.

pro·gen·i·tor (prōjen'ita), *n.* **1.** an ancestor,

esp. one responsible for begetting or originating a particular line of descendants. **2.** any forerunner, or precursor, who serves as a model or originator of a descendant person or thing.

prog·eny (proj'anē), *n.* children; offspring; issue; outcome.

pro·ges·ter·one (prōjes' taron), *n.* a female hormone secreted by the ovary, responsible for preparing the reproductive organs for pregnancy, and during pregnancy, when it is also secreted by the placenta, responsible for maintaining the uterus.

prog·na·thous (prog'nathas, prognā'thas), *adj.* with projecting jaw.

prog·nose (prognōs'), *v.* to make a medical prognosis.

prog·no·sis (prognō'sis), *n., pl.* **prog·no·ses** (prognō'sēz). a forecast of the likely progress and result of a disease. —**prog·nos'tic,** *adj.*

prog·nos·ti·cate (prognos'tikāt), *v.* to predict from present signs; to foresee; to foreshadow or betoken. —**prog·nos·ti·ca'tion,** *n.*

pro·gram (prō'gram), *n.* the sequence of detailed instructions fed into a computer in accordance with which it deals with problems given to it. —**pro'gram·mer,** *n.*

pro·jec·tile (prōjek'tīl, proj'iktīl), *n.* a missile or any body projected by force, as from a gun.

pro·jet (prōzнā'), *n.* a project; a draft, as of a treaty.

pro·kar·y·ote, pro·car·y·ote (prōkar'ēot), *n.* any organism, such as a bacterium or blue-green alga, that lacks a distinct nucleus to contain the genetic material. —**pro·kar·y·ot·ic, pro·car·y·ot·ic** (prōkar,ēot'ik), *adj.*

pro·lapse (prōlaps'), *n.* the downward displacement of an organ, as the uterus. Also **pro·lap'sus.**

pro·late (prō'lāt), *adj.* elongated in the direction of the polar diameter, as a spheroid described by an ellipse revolving about its longer axis. See also **oblate.**

pro·leg (prō'leg), *n.* one of the thick, jointless appendages on the abdomen of caterpillars, etc., used as a leg.

pro·le·gom·e·non (prō,lagom'inon), *n., pl.* **pro·le·gom·e·na** (prō,lagom'ina). an introductory passage or discussion; a preface or prologue. —**pro,le·gom'e·nous,** *adj.*

pro·lep·sis (prōlēp'sis), *n., pl.* **prolep·ses** (prōlēp'sēz). See **prochronism.**

pro·le·tar·i·at (prō,later'ēat), *n.* the poorest class in a society, esp. the wage-earning labouring class having little or no property.

pro·li·cide (prō'lisīd), *n.* the killing or the crime of killing one's own or other children.

pro·lif·er·ate (prōlif'arāt), *v.* to spread or increase rapidly.

pro·lif·er·a·tion (prōlif,arā'sHan), *n.* rapid growth or increase.

pro·lif·ic (prōlif'ik), *adj.* producing much; fertile; fruitful.

pro·line (prō'lēn), *n.* an amino acid present in all proteins and also discovered in a meteorite.

pro·lix (prō'liks), *adj.* unnecessarily or tediously wordy.

pro·loc·u·tor (prōlok'yōotə), *n.* a chairman.

pro·lu·sion (prōlōō'ZHən), *n.* an introductory essay or article. —**pro·lu·so·ry** (prōlōō'sərē), *adj.*

Pro·me·the·an (prōmē'thēən), *adj.* creative; daringly original.

prom·ul·gate (prom'əlgāt), *v.* to make public by proclaiming or publishing; to put into force, as a new law, etc.

pro·na·tion (prōnā'SHən), *n.* a movement in which the hand or forearm is turned so that the palm faces downward or backward; the position resulting from such a turn. See also **supination.** —**pro'nate,** *v.*

prone (prōn), *adj.* **1.** lying with the face or front downwards. See also **supine. 2.** likely; probable; exhibiting a willingness to accept an influence either from susceptibility or inclination.

pro·nun·ci·a·men·to (prənun,sēəmen'tō), *n., pl.* **pro·nun·ci·amen·tos.** a proclamation; a manifesto, as of rebels.

pro·pae·deu·tic (prō,pidyōō'tik) *adj.* relating to or like introductory instruction, as to some art or science. Also **pro·pae·deu'ti·cal.**

prop·a·ga·ble (prop'əgəbəl), *adj.* that can be propagated.

pro·pag·u·lum (prōpag'yōōləm), *n., pl.* **pro·pag·u·la** (prōpag'yələ). a propagating part, as a bud. Also **prop·a·gule** (prop'əgyōōl).

pro·pen·si·ty (prōpen'sitē), *n.* an inclination or tendency; proneness.

pro·phage (prō'fāj), *n.* a bacteriophage that exists and reproduces inside its host cell without causing its destruction.

proph·e·cy (prof'əsē), *n., pl.* **proph·e·cies.** fortune telling; a prediction of what will happen.

proph·e·sy (prof'əsī), *v.* **proph·e·sied, proph·e·sy·ing.** to predict (something) for the future.

pro·phy·lac·tic (prō,fəlak'tik), *adj.* preventive; protecting, as against disease.

pro·phy·lax·is (prō,fəlak'sis), *n.* the prevention of disease; a measure designed to prevent a particular disease, as inoculation, etc.

pro·pin·qui·ty (prōpiNG'kwitē), *n.* closeness; nearness; affinity.

pro·pi·ti·ate (prōpisH'ēāt), *v.* to make well disposed towards to win forgiveness or tolerance for. —**pro·pi,ti·a'tion,** *n.* —**pro·pit'i·a·to·ry,** *adj.*

pro·pi·tious (prəpisH'əs), *adj.* favourable, as *propitious conditions for sailing.*

prop·jet engine (prop'jet,). See **turbo·propeller engine.**

pro·pound (prəpound'), *v.* to put forward; to propose, as a plan, a question, etc.

pro·pri·o·cep·tor (prō,prēəsep'tə), *n.* a sense organ which detects position, movement, pain, pressure, and other changes caused by stimuli within the body. —**pro,pri·o·cep'tive,** *adj.*

pro·pri·o mo·tu (prō'priō mō'tōō), *Latin.* of one's own accord; at one's own will or initiative.

prop·ter hoc (prop'tə hok'), *Latin.* because of this.

pro·rogue (prōrōg'), *v.* to postpone; to discontinue for a period.

pro·sa·ic (prōzā'ik), *adj.* dull and boring because it is commonplace.

pro·scribe (prōskrīb'), *v.* to forbid; to denounce as dangerous, etc. —**pro·scrip'tion,** *n.*

pro·sect (prōsekt'), *v.* to dissect for demonstration purposes.

pros·e·lyt·ize (pros'əlitīz), *v.* to convert a person from one opinion, religion, etc., to another. —**pros'e·lyte,** *n.*

pros·o·dem·ic (pros,ōdem'ik), *adj.* relating to or denoting a disease spread by personal contact.

pros·o·dy (pros'ədē), *n.* the study of verse form and poetic metre.

pro·so·po·poe·ia, pro·so·po·pe·ia (pros,-ōpōpē'ə), *n.* the rhetorical device of personifying inanimate things or making imagined or dead people speak or act.

pros·tate (pros'tāt), *adj.* relating to or denoting the prostate gland.

pros·ta·tec·to·my (pros'tətek'təmē), *n.* the surgical removal of a part or all of the prostate gland.

prostate gland, a muscular gland at the base of the bladder in male mammals which contributes substances to semen and through which the urethra passes. Also **pros'tate.**

pros·the·sis (prosthē'sis), *n., pl.* **pros·the·ses** (prosthē'sēz). the attachment of an artificial part or device to the body to replace a missing part, for functional or cosmetic purposes; the part or device so added. Also **proth'e·sis.**

pros·thet·ics (prosthet'iks), *n. sing.* the branch of surgery or dentistry concerned with restoring and maintaining function by supplying artificial replacements for missing parts. —**pros'the·tist,** *n.*

pros·tho·don·tics (pros,thədon'tiks), *n. sing.* dental prosthetics. Also **pros,tho·don'tia.** —**pros,tho·don'tist,** *n.*

prot·a·nom·a·ly (prōt,ənom'əlē), *n.* a sight defect in which the retina has an abnormally weak response to the color red.

prot·a·nope (prō'tənōp), *n.* a person who suffers from protanopia.

pro·ta·no·pi·a (prō,tənō'pēə), *n.* a sight defect in which the retina makes no response to the color red.

prot·a·sis (prot'əsis) *n., pl.* **prot·a·ses** (prot'-əsēz). **1.** the conditional clause, usually beginning with 'if' in a conditional sentence. See also **apodosis. 2.** the introductory part of an ancient drama. See also **catastasis, catastrophe, epitasis.**

pro·te·an (prōtē'ən, prō'tēən), *adj.* able to change form or character easily; variable; versatile.

pro·tec·tion·ism (prətek'sHəniz,əm), *n.* market and price protection accorded domestic producers by measures such as high tariffs and quotas restrictions on imported goods. —**pro· ·tec'tion·ist,** *n.*

pro·tein (prō'tēn), *n.* any of a group of organic compounds of high molecular weight, synthesized by plants and animals; the chief nitrogen-containing compounds in their tissue, consisting of amino acids which are the essential tissue-building elements for animals.

pro·tha·la·mi·on (prō,*th*əlā'mēən), *n., pl.* **pro·tha·la·mi·a** (prō,*th*əlā'mēə). a song or poem written for the occasion of a marriage. See also **epithalamion.**

proth·e·sis (prō*th*'isis), *n.* the adding of a sound or syllable at the beginning of a word, as Spanish *escena, espectador* from Latin *scena, spectator.* See **prosthesis.**

pro·thon·o·tar·y (prō*th*on'ətərē), *n.* the chief official in certain law courts, as the chief clerk, etc.

pro·tho·rax (prō*th*ōr'aks), *n., pl.* **pro·tho·rax· ·es, pro·tho·ra·ces** (prō*th*ōr'əsēz). the front one of the three segments of the thorax of an insect, bearing legs but no wings.

pro·throm·bin (prō*th*rom'bin), *n.* a protein formed in the liver from vitamin K and necessary for normal blood-clotting. Also **thrombogen.**

Pro·tis·ta (prōtis'tə), *n. pl.* all single-celled organisms considered as a group.

pro·to·lan·guage (prō'tōlaNG,gwij), *n.* an ancestral language, esp. one unrecorded and reconstructed by analysis of recorded or living languages. Also called **Ur·sprache** (ōōr'· sHpräkHə).

pro·to·lith·ic (prō,tōli*th*'ik), *adj.* pertaining to or denoting stones used as tools because of their shape but not shaped by the user.

pro·to·mor·phic (prō,tōmō'fik), *adj.* of primitive type or structure.

pro·ton (prō'ton), *n.* the nucleus of a hydrogen atom; the fundamental particle that is a constituent of the nucleus of all atoms, having a positive electrical charge equal in magnitude to that of an electron.

pro·to·path·ic (prō,tōpa*th*'ik), *adj.* relating to or denoting response to pain or temperature. See also **epicritic.**

pro·to·plasm (prō'tōplaz,əm), *n.* a colourless fluid, the substance of which all animal and vegetable cells mainly consist, and thus the

essential matter of all life. —**pro,to·plas'mic,** *adj.*

pro·to·troph·ic (prō,tōtrof'ik), *adj.* (of certain microorganisms) **1.** requiring only inorganic substances for growth. **2.** with no nutritional requirements other than those of the majority of its species.

pro·to·type (prō'tōtīp,), *n.* a thing or person serving as the original or model for or typifying something.

pro·to·zo·an (prō,tōzō'ən), *adj.* belonging to or relating to the phylum comprising single-celled organisms. Also **pro,to·zo'ic.** —**pro,to·zo'- al,** *adj.*

pro·to·zo·ol·o·gy,   pro·to·zo·öl·o·gy (prō'tōzōōl'əjē), *n.* the scientific study of protozoa.

pro·to·zo·on (prō,tōzō'on), *n., pl.* **pro·to·zo·a.** a protozoan organism.

pro·tract (prōtrakt'), *v.* **1.** to make longer in time. **2.** to extend or stick out. **3.** to plot and draw to scale using a protractor, as a diagram, plan, etc. —**pro·trac'tion,** *n.*

pro·tract·ed (prōtrak'tid), *adj.* drawn out; lengthened in time beyond the expected period.

pro·trac·tile (prōtrak'tīl), *adj.* able to be protracted; that can be protracted.

pro·tru·sile (prōtrōō'sīl), *adj.* able to be thrust or extended forward, as a frog's tongue.

pro·tru·sive (prōtrōō'siv), *adj.* that projects forward, sticks out, or bulges.

pro·tu·ber·ate (prōtyōō'bərāt,), *v.* to form a rounded prominence; to bulge.

prov·e·nance (prov'ənəns), *n.* place of origin; source. Also **pro·ve'ni·ence.**

prov·i·dent (prov'idənt), *adj.* managing resources in such a way as to anticipate future needs; foresighted. —**prov'i·dence,** *n.*

pro·vin·cial (prəvinsHəl), *adj.* from or characteristic of the provinces, applied esp. to people who are unsophisticated and naive.

pro·vi·rus (prō'vī,rəs), *n.* an intermediate stage in the infection of a host cell by a retrovirus. —**pro·vi'ral,** *adj.*

pro·vi·so (prəvī'zō, prōvī'zō), *n., pl.* **pro·vi· ·sos, pro·vi·soes.** a condition or stipulation, as a limiting clause in a contract, etc.

pro·vit·a·min (prō,vit'əmin), *n.* a substance that can be converted to a vitamin within the body.

pro·voke (prəvōk', prōvōk'), *v.* **pro·voked, pro·vok·ing.** to cause someone to become angry or to do something he would not do ordinarily. —**prov'o·ca'tion,** *n.*

pro·vo·lo·ne (prō,vəlō'nē), *n.* a light-coloured Italian-style cheese usually packed in the shape of a ball.

prox·i·mal (prok'səməl), *adj.* situated towards the centre or point of attachment, as of a limb. See also **distal.**

prox·i·mate (prok'səmit), *adj.* next or nearest, as in sequence, place, time, etc.; immediately before or after; close. —**prox·im'i·ty**, *n.*

prox·y (prok'sē), *n.* **1.** the power or function of someone authorized to act for another. **2.** a document authorizing someone to act for another.

pru·dent (prōo'dənt), *adj.* careful; exercising careful judgment; cautious. —**pru'dence**, *n.*

pru·i·nose (prōo'ōnōs), *adj.* with a bloom or powdery coating, as a grape, certain species of cacti, etc.

pru·nelle (prōonel'), *n.* **1.** a sweet French liqueur made from plums. **2.** Also **pru·nel'la, pru·nel'lo.** a lightweight twill fabric for women's and children's clothes; a smooth fabric of wool or mixed fibres formerly used for clerical robes, etc.

pru·ri·ent (prōor'ēənt), *adj.* **1.** having, given to, or causing lewd thoughts. **2.** full of changing desires, itching curiosity, or an abnormal craving.

pru·ri·go (prōori'gō), *n.* a skin disease characterized by violently itching papules. —**pru·rig'·i·nous** (prōorij'ənəs), *adj.*

pru·ri·tus (prōori'təs), *n.* an itching sensation or other irritation of the skin.

Prze·wal·ski's horse (psHəväl'skēz). See **tarpan.**

psel·lism (sel'izəm), *n.* stuttering.

pse·phol·o·gy (sifol'əjē), *n.* the study, esp. statistical analysis, of elections.

pseud·e·pig·ra·phy (syōo,dipig'rəfē), *n.* the false attribution of an article, novel, poem, etc., to a certain writer.

pseu·do·a·quat·ic (syōo,dōəkwat'ik), *adj.* native to a wet or moist habitat but not aquatic.

pseu·do·de·men·tia (syōo,dōdimen'sHə), *n.* temporary insanity owing to extreme emotion.

pseu·do·her·maph·ro·dite (syōo,dōhəmaf'rədīt), *n.* an individual whose internal reproductive organs are of one sex but whose external genitals resemble those of the opposite or both sexes.

pseu·do·mo·nas (syōo,dōmō'nəs) *n., pl.* **pseu·do·mon·a·des** (syōo,dōmon'ədēz). any of various species of rod-shaped bacteria, some of which cause diseases in plants and animals.

pseu·do·morph (syōo'dəmôf,), *n.* an irregular form which cannot properly be classified.

pseu·do·nym (syōo'dənim), *n.* a pen name; a name other than one's own used to conceal identity, esp. by an author.

pseu·do·pa·ral·y·sis (syōo,dōpəral'isis), *n.* a state which is not true paralysis but in which a person is unable to move a part of the body because of pain, shock, etc.

pseu·do·phone (syōo'dōfōn), *n.* a device which changes the relationship between the direction of a sound and the receptor so as to produce the illusion that the sound comes from a different place or source.

pseu·do·po·di·um (syōo,dōpō'dēəm), *n., pl.* **pseu·do·po·di·a** (syōo,dōpō'dēə). a temporary protrusion of the protoplasm of a cell, occurring in protozoa, white blood cells, etc., and used in movement, feeding, etc. Also **pseu'do·pod.**

pseu·do·scope (syōo'dōskōp,), *n.* an optical instrument which produces an image in reverse relief by means of two adjustable reflecting prisms. —**pseu·dos'co·py**, *n.*

psi·lan·thro·pism (sīlan'thrəpiz,əm), *n.* the doctrine or belief that Christ was an ordinary human being. Also **psi·lan'thro·py.**

psi·lo·sis (sīlō'sis), *n.* loss of hair; falling hair.

psit·ta·cism (sit'əsiz,əm), *n.* repetitious and meaningless speech; parrotlike speech.

psit·ta·co·sis (sitəkō'sis), *n.* parrot fever; a contagious disease affecting birds, esp. parrots, causing diarrhoea and weight loss, and communicable to man when it also causes fever and bronchial pneumonia.

pso·ri·a·sis (sərī'əsis), *n.* a chronic skin disease causing round red patches covered with white scales. Also **pso'ra.**

psy·chas·the·ni·a (sīkasthē'nēə), *n.* a neurosis marked by anxiety and acute fear.

psy·cha·tax·i·a (sī,kətak'sēə), *n.* inability to concentrate.

psy·che (sī'kē), *n.* the soul, spirit, or mind; the principle of mental and emotional life.

psych·e·del·ic (sī,kədel'ik), *adj.* relating to or denoting a state of heightened mental awareness producing intensified sensual perception and enjoyment and increased creativeness; denoting a drug which produces such an effect, as LSD, mescaline, etc. Also **psy,cho·del'ic.**

psy·cho·ac·tive (sī,kōak'tiv), *adj.* (of a drug) capable of affecting the mind. Also **psy·cho·trop·ic** (sī,kōtrop'ik).

psy·cho·bi·ol·o·gy (sīkōbīol'əjē), *n.* the scientific study of the interrelation of body and mind, as in the nervous system, etc.

psy·cho·di·ag·nos·tics (sī'kōdī'əgnos'tiks), *n. sing.* the study of personality through behaviour and mannerisms, as posture, facial expression, etc. —**psy,chodi,ag·no'sis**, *n.* —**psy,-chodi,ag·nos'tic**, *adj.*

psy·cho·dra·ma (sī'kōdrä,mə), *n.* a method of group psychotherapy in which patients dramatize and act out their various problems in the form of a play.

psy·cho·dy·nam·ics (sīkōdīnam'iks), *n. sing.* the study of personality through examining past and present experiences and the motivation that produced them.

psy·cho·gal·van·ic (sī'kōgalvan'ik), *adj.* relating to electric changes in the body owing to mental or emotional stimuli.

psy·cho·gal·va·nom·e·ter (sī,kōgal,və-

nom'ətə), *n.* a type of galvanometer adapted for measuring psychogalvanic currents.

psy·cho·gen·e·sis (sī'kōjen'isis), *n.* **1.** the origin and development of the psyche. **2.** the origin of any physical or psychological state in the interaction of the conscious and unconscious mind.

psy·cho·gen·ic (sī'kōjen'ik), *adj.* originating in the mind.

psy·cho·graph (sī'kōgräf,, sī'kōgraf,), *n.* a graph showing the relative strengths of a person's various personality traits. —**psy·chog'·ra·pher,** *n.*

psy·cho·lin·guis·tics (sī'kōliNGgwis'tiks), *n. sing.* the study of the interrelation of language and the behavioural pattern of its users.

psy·chol·o·gism (sīkol'əjiz,əm), *n.* the giving of great weight to psychological factors in forming a theory (used as a term of disparagement implying that too much weight has been given to psychological factors).

psy·cho·man·cy (sī'kōman,sē), *n.* communication with or between spirits.

psy·chom·e·try (sī'kom'itrē), *n.* the measurement of mental characteristics. Also **psy·cho·met'rics** (sī,kōmet'riks).

psy·cho·mo·tor (sī,kōmō'tə), *adj.* relating to movement induced by mental processes.

psy·cho·neu·ro·sis (sī,kōnyōōrō'sis), *n.* a functional disorder of the mind in which patients show insight into their condition but have personalities dominated variously by anxiety, depression, obsessions, compulsions, and physical complaints with no evidence of organic disease, all of which are symptoms that can be relieved by psychotherapy without cure of the root cause. —**psy·cho·neu·rot'ic,** *adj.*

psy·cho·path (sī'kōpath,), *n.* a mentally deranged or unstable person; a person with a psychopathic personality. —**psy,cho·path'ic,** *adj.*

psychopathic personality, a personality type characterized by outbursts of violence, antisocial behaviour, inability to form meaningful relationships, and extreme egocentricity.

psy·cho·pa·thist (sīkop'əthist), *n.* one who specializes in treating psychopathy.

psy·cho·pa·thol·o·gy (sī,kōpəthol'əjē), *n.* the study of mental disease.

psy·chop·a·thy (sīkop'əthē), *n.* mental disease, esp. severe disease disturbing the moral sense or character.

psy·cho·phar·ma·col·o·gy (sī,kōfä,məkol'-əjē), *n.* the study of the psychological effects of drugs.

psy·cho·phys·ics (sī'kōfiz'iks), *n. sing.* a field of study within psychology concerned with measuring the relations between the physical aspects of stimuli and the sensations they produce.

psy·cho·phys·i·ol·o·gy (sī'kōfiz'ēol'əjē), *n.*

a field of study within physiology concerned with the relations between physical and mental phenomena. —**psy,cho·phys,i·o·log'i·cal,** *adj.*

psy·cho·pomp (sī'kōpomp,), *n.* someone who conducts the souls of the dead to the next world, as Charon in classical mythology.

psy·cho·pro·phy·lax·is (sī'kōprō'fəlak'sis), *n.* a method of preparing pregnant women for childbirth by their studying the labour process and training in breathing exercises, rhythm, and relaxation. Also **Lamaze technique.**

psy·cho·sex·u·al (sī'kōsek'sHōōəl), *adj.* pertaining to the relationship of mental and sexual phenomena.

psy·cho·sis (sīkō'sis), *n., pl.* **psy·cho·ses** (sīkō'sēz). a severe mental illness which may cause alteration of the entire personality.

psy·cho·so·mat·ic (sī,kōsōmat'ik), *adj.* relating to or denoting a physical disorder caused or greatly influenced by emotional stress.

psychosomatic medicine, the use of psychological techniques and principles in treating physical illness. Also **psy,cho·so·mat'ics.**

psy·cho·sur·ger·y (sī,kōsû'jərē), *n.* the use of brain surgery to treat mental illness.

psy·cho·tech·nics (sī'kōtek'niks), *n. sing.* the use of psychological techniques and theories for controlling human behaviour for practical purposes.

psy·cho·tech·nol·o·gy (sī'kōteknol'əjē), *n.* the study of psychotechnics.

psy·cho·ther·a·peu·tics (sī'kōther'əpyōō'-tiks), *n. sing.* the remedial treatment of disease by psychic influence, as mental suggestion, etc.

psy·cho·ther·a·py (sī'kōther'əpē), *n.* the science or technique of treating mental disorders by psychological methods. —**psy,cho·ther'a·pist,** *n.*

psy·chrom·e·ter (sīkrom'itə), *n.* a device used to measure relative atmospheric humidity, consisting of two thermometers mounted side by side, one of which has its bulb wrapped in material kept moist and open to air so that there is evaporation from the wick and consequent cooling of the bulb; the rate of cooling, which depends on the relative humidity of the air, can then be measured by comparing the readings from the two thermometers.

psy·chrom·e·try (sīkrom'itrē), *n.* the scientific measurement of atmospheric humidity.

psy·chro·phil·ic (sī,krōfil'ik), *adj.* able to grow at a temperature at or near 0 degrees C., esp. of bacteria.

pter·i·dol·o·gy (ter,idol'əjē), *n.* the scientific study of ferns, horsetails, clubmosses, etc.

pter·id·o·phyte (tərid'əfīt,), *n.* any plant of the division that includes ferns, horsetails, clubmosses, etc.

pter·o·car·pous (ter,əkä'pəs), *adj.* having winged fruit, as the sycamore tree.

pte·ryg·i·um (tərij'ēəm), *n., pl.* **pte·ryg·i·ums,**

pte·ryg·i·a (tərıj'ēə). a triangular thickened mass of the membrane that covers the eye, stretching from the inner eye corner to the pupil.

pter·y·goid (ter'igoid), *adj.* winglike.

pter·y·gote (ter'igōt), *adj.* relating to the biological subclass comprising the winged insects. Also **pte·ryg'otous.**

pter·y·la (ter'ilə), *n.*, *pl.* **pter·y·lae** (ter'ilē). any of the feathered portions of the skin of a bird. Also **feathertract.** See also **apterium.**

pter·y·lol·o·gy (ter,ilol'əjē), *n.* the study of pterylosis.

pter·y·lo·sis (ter,ilō'sis), *n.* the distribution of birds' feathers in definite areas on the skin.

pti·lo·sis (tilō'sis), *n.* a disorder characterized by falling out of the eyelashes.

pti·san (tiz'ən), *n.* barley water; a nourishing preparation originally made from water in which barley had been boiled, supposedly of some medicinal benefit.

Ptol·e·ma·ic system (tol,əmā'ik), a conception of the universe elaborated by Ptolemy, in which the earth was thought to be central and stationary, with the sun, moon, and other planets moving around it. [after Ptolemy, Greek astronomer, geographer, and mathematician of the 2nd century A.D.]

pto·maine (tō'mān, tōmān'), *n.* any of a group of basic nitrogenous compounds, as cadaverine, muscarine, etc., some of which are highly poisonous, formed during the putrefaction of plant or animal protein, and having a characteristic appearance and smell.

pto·sis (tō'sis), *n.* the downward displacement of an organ, esp. the upper eyelid.

pty·a·lism (tī'əliz,əm), *n.* the abnormally excessive production of saliva.

pu·bes (pyoo'bēz), *n.*, *sing.* and *pl.* **1.** the lower part of the abdomen. **2.** the hair which appears on this part at puberty. See **pubis.**

pu·bes·cent (pyoobes'ənt), *adj.* **1.** at or reaching the age of puberty. **2.** with a covering of soft, downy hair, as insects, leaves, etc.

pu·bis (pyoo'bis), *n.*, *pl.* **pu·bes** (pyoo'bēz). in man, the projecting part at the lower end of either side of the pelvic girdle, forming its front wall, and the corresponding part in four-legged animals.

pub·li·can (pub'likən), *n.* a person who owns or manages a pub or tavern.

public domain, the legal status of works on which copyright has expired or has never been granted.

puce (pyoos), *adj.* purplish-brown in colour; of the colour of a flea. [from the French word for flea.]

pu·den·cy (pyoo'dənsē), *n.* modesty; sensitivity to feelings of shame; shyness.

pu·den·dum (pyooden'dəm), *n.*, *pl.* **pu·den·da** (pyooden'də). *Usually in pl.* the external genital organs, esp. of the female.

pu·er·ile (pyoo'əril), *adj.* relating to a child; immature; childish; trivial. —**pu,er·il'i·ty,** *n.*

pu·er·il·ism (pyoo'ərəliz,əm), *n.* childish behaviour in an adult.

pu·er·per·al (pyooū'pərəl), *adj.* relating to childbirth or women during childbirth.

puerperal fever, a fever that may occur after childbirth, usually due to infection.

pu·er·pe·ri·um (pyoo,əpēr'ēəm), *n.* the state of a woman during childbirth and the period immediately following when the uterus returns to normal size and lactation begins.

puffer fish, one of several related spiny fishes that are able to inflate themselves into a prickly ball when threatened.

puff pastry, a dough rich in shortening, folded, and rolled many times to make it rise in flaky layers when cooked.

pug·na·cious (pug,nā'sнəs), *adj.* given to fighting, belligerent.

pu·is·sance (pyoo'isəns), *n.* great power, might, or influence. —**pu·is·sant** (pwis'ont, pyoo'isənt, pwis'ənt), *adj.*

puk·ka sa·hib (puk'ə säb, sä'hib), a real gentleman, used as a respectful term of address by Indians to British colonial officials in India.

pul·chri·tude (pul'krityood), *n.* physical beauty. —**pul·chri·tu'di·nous,** *adj.*

pule (pyool), *v.* to cry weakly; to whine in a thin tone.

pul·let (pool'it), *n.* a young hen from the time it begins to lay until its first moult; other domestic fowl in this phase.

pul·lu·late (pul'yoolāt), *v.* to sprout or germinate; to breed or multiply rapidly; to exist in large numbers.

pul·mo·nar·y (pul'mənərē), *adj.* relating to the lungs.

pul·mon·ic (pulmon'ik), *adj.* **1.** pulmonary. **2.** relating to pneumonia.

pul·que (pool'kē), *n.* a Mexican fermented drink made from the sap of certain species of agave.

pul·sa·tile (pul'sətīl), *adj.* throbbing; pulsating; beating, as a pulse, percussion music, etc.

pul·sim·e·ter (pulsim'itə), *n.* an instrument for measuring the strength or rapidity of the pulse.

pul·ver·u·lent (pulver'oolənt, pulver'yoolənt), *adj.* consisting of or covered with dust or powder; crumbling to a fine powder.

pul·vi·nate (pul'vənāt), *adj.* shaped like a cushion.

pun·cheon (pun'cнən), *n.* a heavy rough slab of timber used as a floorboard, or upright as a short support or piece of framing.

punc·tate (punck'tāt), *adj.* marked or studded with dots, points, or depressions. Also **punc'tat·ed.** —**punc·ta'tion,** *n.*

punc·ti·form (puNGk'tifôm,), *adj.* like a dot or point.

punc·til·i·o (puNGktil'ēō), *n., pl.* **punc·til·i·os.** a fine point, as of ceremony, honour, conduct, etc.

punc·til·i·ous (puNGktil'ēəs), *adj.* observing all the punctilios; showing great attention to details.

pun·dit (pun'dit), *n.* an authority or expert on some matter (often used jocularly).

pun·gent (pun'jənt), *adj.* sharply bitter in flavour; biting to the taste or sensibilities. —**pun'·gen·cy,** *n.*

pu·ni·tive (pyōō'nitiv), *adj.* punishing; intended to punish; relating to punishment. Also **pu'ni·to·ry.**

pun·kah (puNG'kə), *n.* a very large cloth fan hung from the ceiling and swung to and fro by machinery or a servant, esp. in India.

pu·pa (pyōō'pə), *n., pl.* **pu·pae** (pyōō'pē), **pu·pas.** an insect in the stage between the larva and the imago when it does not move or feed but develops greatly.

pu·pate (pyōō'pāt), *v.* to become a pupa.

pu·pil·lage, pu·pil·age (pyōō'pilij), *n.* **1.** the state of being a pupil or the time spent as such. **2.** (in Britain) the time served by a newly called barrister as assistant to a member of the bar.

pu·pip·a·rous (pyōōpip'ərəs), *adj.* relating to or denoting insects that bear larvae which are already so far developed that they are ready to pupate.

pur·dah, pur·da (pû'də), *n.* (in India, Pakistan, etc.) a curtain, screen, or veil used or worn to conceal women of rank from men or strangers; the system of so concealing women.

pu·rée (pyōōrā'), *n.* cooked and sieved food, esp. fruit or vegetables.

pur·fle (pû'fəl), *v.* **1.** to edge with a decorative border. **2.** to use miniature architectural forms to decorate a shrine, canopy, etc. —**pur'fling,** *n.*

pur·ga·to·ri·al (pû,gətô'rēəl), *adj.* **1.** serving to cleanse of sin. **2.** of or relating to purgatory.

pur·lieu (pû'lyōō), *n.* **1.** a district or area at the edge of a town, forest, etc. **2.** a place where one has the right to come and go at will and wander freely; a place one habitually frequents; a haunt; one's limits.

pur·loin (pûloin'), *v.* to steal; to take dishonestly.

pur·port (pəpôt', pû'pôt), *v.* **1.** to profess; to intend to seem, usually falsely. —*n.* **2.** the meaning or sense, either apparent or real.

pur·pu·ra (pûpyōōrə), *n.* a disease in which the blood is forced from the blood vessels and diffuses through the surrounding tissue causing purplish spots on the skin.

pur·sang (pyrsäN'), *French.* genuine beyond question; full-blooded. [pure blood]

pur·su·ant (pəsyōō'ənt), *adj.* following; pursuing; in accord with. —**pur·su'ance,** *n.*

pur·sui·vant (pûsē'vənt), *n.* a follower; an attendant.

pur·sy (pû'sē), *adj.* short of breath, esp. from being too fat.

pu·ru·lence (pyoor'ōōləns, pyoor'ōōləns), *n.* the condition of forming, containing, or discharging pus. —**pu'ru·lent,** *adj.*

pu·ru·loid (pyoor'ōoloid, pyoor'yōoloid), *adj.* like pus.

pur·vey (pəvā'), *v.* to supply or provide as a trade, esp. provisions. —**pur·vey'ance,** *n.* —**pur·vey'or,** *n.*

pur·view (pû'vyōō), *n.* the scope or province, as of authority, concern, subject, etc.

pu·sil·la·nim·i·ty (pyōō,silənim'itē), *n.* faintheartedness; lack of spirit; timidity; cowardliness.

pu·sil·lan·i·mous (pyōō,silan'əməs), *adj.* cowardly; not courageous or resolute.

pus·tu·late (pus'tyōōlāt), *adj.* **1.** covered with pustules. —*v.* **2.** to cause to break out in pustules. —**pus'tu·lant,** *adj.*

pus·tule (pus'tyōōl), *n.* a small swelling on the skin containing pus; any pimplelike or blisterlike swelling on the skin. —**pus,tu·la'tion,** *n.* —**pus'tu·lar, pus'tu·lous,** *adj.*

pu·ta·tive (pyōō'tətiv), *adj.* reputed; supposed; generally regarded as.

pu·tre·fac·tion (pyōō,trəfak'sHən), *n.* the act or process of decomposition of living matter by bacteria and fungi with resulting foul-smelling products; rotting.

pu·tres·cent (pyōōtres'ənt), *adj.* in process of putrefaction; becoming rotten.

pu·tres·ci·ble (pyōōtres'əbəl), *adj.* liable to putrefaction.

pu·tri·lage (pyōō'trilij), *n.* matter which has become or is becoming putrid.

Putsch (pōō'tsH), *n. German.* a sudden and speedy uprising or takeover of government.

P wave, the first major shock wave radiating from the centre of an earthquake. Also **primary wave.** See also **L wave, S wave.**

pyc·nom·e·ter (piknom'itə), *n.* an instrument for ascertaining the density of a liquid or solid by comparing it under the same conditions of temperature and pressure with an equal volume of a liquid or solid whose density is known.

py·e·li·tis (pī,əlī'tis), *n.* inflammation of the pelvis or the kidney outlet.

py·e·lo·gram (pī'ələgram,), *n.* an x-ray photograph produced by pyelography. Also **py'e·lo·graph,.**

py·e·log·ra·phy (pī,əlog'rəfē), *n.* the science or technique of photographing the kidneys, renal pelves, and ureters by injecting a radiopaque solution before taking x-ray photographs.

py·e·lo·ne·phri·tis (pī,əlōnəfrī'tis), *n.* inflammation of the kidney and the adjoining part of the urinary tract caused by bacterial infection spread back from the urethra and bladder.

py·e·lo·ne·phro·sis (pī,əlōnəfrō'sis), *n.* any disease affecting the kidney and the area immediately surrounding it.

pyk·nic (pik'nik), *adj.* relating to or denoting a physical type characterized by a short, stocky build, bulky muscles, and often excessive fat. See also **athletic, asthenic, leptosome.**

py·lo·rec·to·my (pī,lōrek'təmē), *n.* surgical removal of the pylorus.

py·lo·rus (pīlôr'əs), *n., pl.* **py·lo·ri** (pīlôr'ī). the small opening leading from the stomach into the duodenum.

py·o·der·ma (pī,ōdû'mə), *n.* any skin disease marked by the formation of pus.

py·o·gen·e·sis (pī,ōjen'isis), *n.* the formation of pus; the process by which pus is formed. —**py·o·gen'ic,** *adj.*

py·oid (pī'oid), *adj.* relating to or like pus.

py·o·ne·phri·tis (pī,ōnəfrī'tis), *n.* inflammation of the kidney associated with discharge of pus.

py·o·per·i·car·di·um (pī,ōper,ikä'dēəm), *n.* the presence of pus in the pericardium.

py·oph·thal·mi·a (pī,ofthal'mēə), *n.* inflammation of the eye with associated discharge of pus. Also **py,oph·thal·mi'tis.**

py·o·pneu·mo·tho·rax (pī,ōnyōō,mōthôr'-aks), *n.* the presence of pus and gas in the cavity between the pleura.

py·or·rhoe·a (pī,ərē'ə), *n.* infection of the gums around the teeth, and in its more severe form the formation of pus between the roots of the teeth and the tissue surrounding the roots leading to loosening and loss of teeth. Also **pyorrhoea al,ve·o·lar'is.**

py·o·sis (pīō'sis), *n.* the formation of pus.

py·o·tho·rax (pī,ōthôr'aks), *n.* an abscess in the cavity between the pleura; empyema.

py·re·thrum (pīrē'thrəm), *n.* the dried flower heads of certain chrysanthemums, used as an insecticide and sometimes to treat certain skin diseases.

py·ret·ic (pīret'ik), *adj.* relating to, affected by, or causing fever.

pyr·e·tol·o·gy (pir,itol'əjē), *n.* the study and treatment of fevers.

pyr·e·to·ther·a·py (pī,rətōther'əpē) *n.* treatment of a disease or disorder by raising the body temperature and by inducing fever or by electric currents, etc.

py·rex·i·a (pīrek'sēə), *n.* fever; raised body temperature.

pyr·he·li·om·e·ter (pīr,hēlēom'itə), *n.* an instrument for measuring the rate at which heat energy is received from the sun by means of the rate of rise in temperature of a black surface exposed to the sun.

pyr·i·form (pir'ifôm,), *adj.* pear-shaped.

py·ro·con·duc·tiv·i·ty (pī,rōkon,duktiv'itē), *n.* electrical conductivity created by applying heat, esp. in solids that are not conductors at lower temperatures.

py·ro·e·lec·tric·i·ty (pī,rōilektris'itē), *n.* an electromagnetic force developed between the opposite faces of certain crystals, as tourmaline, when the crystal is heated. —**py,ro·e·lec'tric,** *adj.*

py·ro·gen (pī'rəjen), *n.* any substance which causes a raised body temperature when it enters the bloodstream of man or an animal. Also **pyro·toxin.** —**py,ro·gen'ic,** *adj.*

py·rog·e·nous (pīroj'ənəs), *adj.* produced by the action of heat, as certain rocks, chemical substances, etc.

py·rog·nos·tics (pī,rəgnos'tiks), *n. pl.* those properties that a mineral exhibits when heated by blowpipe, as fusibility, coloration of the flame, etc.

py·rog·ra·phy (pīrog'rəfē), *n.* the process of making designs with a heated tool, as on wood, leather, etc. Also **py·ro·gra·vure'.**

py·ro·lig·ne·ous (pī,rōlig'nēəs), *adj.* distilled from wood, as, formerly, acetone. Also **py·ro·lig'nic.**

py·rol·y·sis (pīrol'isis), *n.* the decomposition of an organic compound by exposure to extremely high temperature.

py·ro·man·cy (pī'rōman,sē), *n.* divination by fire.

py·ro·ma·ni·a (pi,rōmā'nēə), *n.* a form of madness characterized by the compulsion to set fire to things. —**py,ro·ma'ni·ac,** *n.*

py·ro·met·al·lur·gy (pīrōmətal'əjē') *n.* the process or technique of refining ores by applying heat.

py·ro·met·ric bead (pī,rəmet'rik), a ball of material set in a kiln to show when a certain temperature has been reached by changing colour.

pyrometric cone, a triangular piece of material set in a kiln to show when a certain temperature has been reached by melting or changing shape.

py·ro·pho·bi·a (pī,rəfō'bēə), *n.* an abnormally excessive dread of fire.

py·ro·phor·ic (pī,rəfor'ik), *adj.* capable of igniting on exposure to air.

py·ro·pho·tom·e·ter (pī,rōfōtom'itə), *n.* an instrument for measuring high temperatures by optical or photometric means.

py·ro·sis (pīrō'sis), *n.* heartburn.

py·ro·stat (pī'rōstat,) *n.* a device that triggers an alarm if fire breaks out near it.

py·ro·tech·nics (pī,rōtek'niks), *n. sing.* the art or technique of making fireworks; a display of fireworks or the like. —**py,ro·tech'nic,** *adj.* —**py,ro·tech'nist,** *n.*

py·ro·tox·in (pī,rōtok'sin), *n.* See **pyrogen.**

Pyr·rhic (pir'ik), *adj.* relating to or denoting a costly victory. [after Pyrrhus, the king of Epirus, who in the 3rd century B.C. defeated the Romans but lost most of his army.]

Pyr·rho·nism (pir'əniz,əm), *n.* extreme scepticism. [after Pyrrho, c. 360–270 B.C., Greek philosopher.]

pyth·o·gen·ic (pī,thəjen'ik), *adj.* originating in decomposing matter or filth. Also **py·thog'e·nous.**

py·thon·ic (pīthon'ik), *adj.* oracular; prophetic. [after Pythia, priestess of the Delphic oracle in classical mythology]

py·u·ri·a (pīyo͞or'ēə), *n.* the presence of pus in the urine.

Q clearance, (in the U.S. Atomic Energy Commission) the highest level of security clearance, which gives a person access to all secret information.

Q.E.D. See **quod erat demonstrandum.**

Q-fever (kyōō'fē,və), *n.* a fever characterized by symptoms like those of pneumonia, caused by rickettsiae transmitted to man by insects.

qua (kwā, kwä), *adv.* as; considered as; as being, as *The role of parent qua moral teacher is much diminished.*

quack·sal·ver (kwak'sal,və), *n.* an unqualified person practising medicine; a quack doctor.

quad·ra·ge·nar·i·an (kwod,rəjəner'ēən), *adj.* 1. between 40 and 49 years old. —*n.* 2. a person aged 40 or between 40 and 49.

quad·rant (kwod'rənt), *n.* a quarter of a circle.

quad·rate (kwod'rāt), *adj.* rectangular; square.

quad·ra·ture (kwod'rəCHə), *n.* the process or act of squaring.

quad·rel (kwod'rəl), *n.* a stone or brick that is square.

quad·ren·ni·um (kwodren'ēəm), *n., pl.* **quad·ren·ni·ums, quad·ren·ni·a** (kwodren'ēə). a period of four years. —**quad·ren'ni·al,** *adj.*

quad·ri·cen·ten·ni·al (kwod'risenten'ēəl), *adj.* 1. of or relating to a period of 400 years. —*n.* 2. a period of 400 years; the celebration or anniversary marking such a period.

qua·drille (kwədril'), *n.* a game of cards for four persons.

quad·ril·lion (kwodril'ēən), *n.* 1. (in Britain, France, and Germany) the number represented by the figure 1 followed by 24 zeros. U.S. name: **septillion.** 2. (in the U.S.A. and Canada) the number represented by the figure 1 followed by 15 zeros.

quad·ri·ple·gi·a (kwod,riplē'jēə), *n.* paralysis affecting all four limbs. Also **tetraplegia.** —**quad,ri·pleg'ic,** *n.*

quad·ri·sect (kwod'risekt), *v.* to cut or divide into four, usually equal parts.

quad·riv·i·al (kwodriv'ēəl), *adj.* having four roads which meet in a point.

quad·riv·i·um (kwodriv'ēəm), *n., pl.* **quad·riv·i·a** (kwodriv'ēə). the higher division of the seven liberal arts studied in medieval schools, consisting of arithmetic, geometry, astronomy, and music. See also **trivium.**

quad·roon (kwadrōōn'), *n.* a person who is of one-quarter Negro ancestry; the offspring of a mulatto and a White.

quad·ru·mane (kwod'rōōmān), *n.* an animal that can use all four feet as hands, as the monkey. —**quad·ru'ma·nous,** *adj.*

quad·rum·vi·rate (kwodrum'vərit), *n.* joint rule by four men. See also **triumvirate.**

quad·ru·plex (kwod'rōōpleks), *adj.* fourfold; in four parts; four times as large.

quag·gy (kwag'ē), *adj.* like a marsh or quagmire; boggy.

quag·mire (kwag'mīə), *n.* a bog, esp. one which quakes under the tread.

qua·lim·e·ter (kwəlim'itə), *n.* See **penetrometer.**

qualm (kwäm), *n.* a momentary feeling of apprehension or unease; a pang of conscience. —**qualm'ish,** *adj.*

quan·da·ry (kwon'dərē), *n.* a state of uncertainty as to what action to take; a practical dilemma.

quand même (käN mem'), *French.* even so; nevertheless; all the same.

quan·go (kwaNG'gō), *n., pl.* **quan·gos.** *acronym for* quasi-autonomous non-governmental organization *or rarely* quasi-autonomous national governmental organization.

quan·ti·fy (kwon'tifī), *v.* to express as or determine a quantity.

quan·tile (kwon'tīl), *n.* (in statistics) any value of a variate that divides the total frequency of a sample into equal quantities. See also **percentile, quartile.**

quan·ti·ta·tive (kwon'titā,tiv), *adj.* relating to, measured by, or based on quantity.

quan·tum (kwon'təm), *n., pl.* **quan·ta** (kwon'tə). 1. a quantity; amount. 2. the smallest quantity of radiant energy.

quantum mechanics, the branch of mechanics dealing with systems at the atomic and nuclear levels.

qua·qua·ver·sal (kwä,kwəvû'səl), *adj.* (relating to a rock formation) sloping down in every direction from a tip.

quark (kwäk, kwôk). *n.* any of the three types of particle which some physicists believe are the basis of all matter.

quar·rel (kwor'əl), *n.* a square or rhomboidal pane of glass.

quar·tan (kwô'tən), *adj.* of a fever marked by paroxysms recurring every third (or by inclusive reckoning every fourth) day, as in some kinds of malaria. See also **quintan, sextan, tertian.**

quar·ter·age (kwô'tərij), *n.* the provision or cost of accommodation for troops.

quar·ter·fi·nal (kwô,tǝfi'nəl), *adj.* relating to that round of a sports tournament which precedes the semifinal. —**quar,ter·fi'nal·ist,** *n.*

quarter horse, one of a breed of horses bred to run quarter-mile races.

quar·tic (kwô'tik), *adj.* of or relating to the fourth algebraic degree.

quar·tile (kwô'tīl), *adj.* (in statistics) the value of a variable that divides the distribution of the variable into four groups with equal frequencies. See also **quantile, percentile.**

quar·to (kwô'tō), *n., pl.* **quar·tos.** a book size of approximately 9½ x 12 inches; a size of paper obtained by folding a sheet in half twice.

qua·sar (kwā'zä, kwā'sä), *n.* a celestial object emitting powerful radio energy from a distance of four to ten billion light-years; quasi-stellar radio source.

quash 1. (kwoSH), *v.* to suppress; to put an end to. 2. to annul or set aside as not valid, esp. a legal decision.

qua·si (kwā'zī, kwā'sī, kwaz'ī, kwas'ī, kwā'zī, kwä'zē, kwä'sē), *adj.* seeming; as if; having the semblance of, as a *quasijudicial role.*

qua·ter·nar·y (kwətû'nərē), *adj.* 1. having or consisting of four parts. 2. relating or belonging to the present geological period, which began approximately one million years ago. See also **Neocene.**

qua·ter·nate (kwətû'nit), *adj.* consisting of or in groups of four, as some leaves.

qua·ter·ni·on (kwətû'nēən), *n.* a group or set of four.

quat·re·foil (kat'rəfoil,), *n.* a four-lobed leaf.

quat·tro·cen·to (kwat,rōCHen'tō, kwot,rōCHen'tō), *n.* the 15th century, with reference to the Italian art of that period.

quat·tu·or·de·cil·lion (kwot,ōōôdisil'ēən), *n.* 1. (in Britain and Germany) the number represented by the figure 1 followed by 84 zeros. 2. (in the U.S.A. and Canada) the number represented by the figure 1 followed by 45 zeros.

qua·ver (kwā'və), *v.* to shake; to tremble, esp. a voice or musical note.

quean (kwēn), *n.* an ill-behaved woman; a hussy; a prostitute.

quell (kwel), *v.* to put down or subdue, as an uprising, strong emotion, etc.

que·nelle (kǝnel'), *n.* a dish consisting of pounded meat or fish bound with eggs or breadcrumbs, shaped into a ball, poached or sautéed, and served with a sauce.

quer·cine (kwû'sīn), *adj.* relating to the oak tree.

quer·u·lous (kwer'ōōləs, kwer'yōōləs), *adj.* expressing dissatisfaction; complaining, esp. in a peevish way.

quiche (kēsH), *n.* a dish consisting of an open tart of unsweetened pastry filled with beaten eggs and cream or milk mixed with cheese, bacon, or the like, and baked in the oven.

quid·di·ty (kwid'itē), *n.* 1. the essence of a thing which makes it unique. See also **haecceity.** 2. a trivial distinction in argument; a quibble.

quid·nunc (kwid'nuNGk,), *n.* a newsmonger; a gossip. [from Latin, literally, What now?]

quid pro quo (kwid' prō kwō'), *pl.* **quid pro quos, quids pro quo.** something given in return, as for a favour; tit for tat. [from Latin, literally, What for whom?]

qui·es·cent (kwēes'ənt), *adj.* being at rest; silent; motionless.

qui·et·ism (kwī'ətiz,əm), *n.* a form of religious mysticism, originating in 17th-century Europe, which regards complete passivity and annihilation of will as the route to ultimate spirituality. 2. indifference or passivity to worldly things. —**qui'et·ist,** *adj., n.*

qui·e·tus (kwīē'təs, kwīā'təs), *n., pl.* **qui·e·tus·es.** anything that settles or ends something, as an argument.

quill (kwil), *n.* a hollow stem used as a bobbin on which to wind yarn; any bobbin so used.

qui·na·ry (kwī'nərē), *adj.* relating to the number five; consisting of five.

qui·nate (kwī'nāt), *adj.* in groups of five.

quin·cunx (kwin'kuNGks), *n.* an arrangement of five objects with one at each corner of a square and the other at its centre. —**quin·cun·cial** (kwinkun'sHel), *adj.*

quin·dec·a·gon (kwindek'əgon), *n.* a polygon with 15 angles and 15 sides.

quin·de·cen·ni·al (kwin,disen'ēəl), *adj.* 1. relating to a period of 15 years or to a 15th anniversary. —*n.* 2. a 15th anniversary.

quin·de·cil·lion (kwin,disil'ēən), *n.* 1. (in Britain and Germany) the number represented by the figure 1 followed by 90 zeros. 2. (in the U.S.A. and Canada) the number represented by the figure 1 followed by 48 zeros.

quin·qua·ge·nar·i·an (kwiNG,kwəjənər'ēən), *adj.* 1. between 50 and 59 years old. —*n.* 2. a person aged 50 or between 50 and 59.

quin·quag·e·nar·y (kwiNGkwä'jǝnərē), *n.* a 50th anniversary.

quin·que·fid (kwiNG'kwǝfid), *adj.* split into five parts or lobes.

quin·que·foil (kwiNG'kwǝfoil,), *n.* See **cinquefoil.**

quin·quen·ni·al (kwiNGkwen'ēəl), *adj.* 1. relating to or lasting for five years. —*n.* 2. a five-year period.

quin·quen·ni·um (kwiNGkwen'ēəm), *n., pl.* **quin·quen·ni·ums, quin·quen·ni·a** (kwiNGkwen'ēə). a five-year period. Also **quin·quen'ni·ad.**

quin·que·reme (kwiNG,kwirēm'), *n.* a galley with five banks of oars on each side.

quin·sy (kwin'zē), *n.* an abscess on a tonsil, usually occurring as a complication of tonsillitis.

quin·tal (kwin'təl), *n.* **1.** a unit of weight in the metric system equal to 100 kilograms. **2.** a unit of weight equal to 100 lbs.

quin·tan (kwin'tən), *adj.* of a fever marked by paroxysms occurring every fourth (or by inclusive reckoning every fifth) day. See also **tertian, quartan, sextan.**

quinte·foil (kwint'foil), *n.* See **cinquefoil.**

quin·tes·sence (kwintes'əns), *n.* the purest essence of anything; the most perfect embodiment of something.

quin·tic (kwin'tik), *adj.* (in mathematics) of the fifth degree.

quin·til·lion (kwintil'ēən), *n.* **1.** (in Britain, France, and Germany) the number represented by the figure 1 followed by 30 zeros. U.S. and Canadian name: **nonillion. 2.** (in the U.S.A. and Canada) the number represented by the figure 1 followed by 18 zeros. British name **trillion.**

quire (kwī'ə), *n.* a set of 24 equal-sized sheets of paper.

quirk (kwûk), *n.* a mannerism; a peculiarity of behaviour. **—quirk'y,** *adj.*

quirt (kwût), *n.* a riding whip with a short handle and braided leather lash.

quis·ling (kwiz'liNG), *n.* one who collaborates with an invading enemy; a fifth columnist. [after Major Vidkun Quisling, (1887–1945) who in 1940 aided the German invaders of his native Norway.]

quit·tance (kwit'əns), *n.* **1.** recompense. **2.** release from a debt or obligation.

qui vive (kē viv'), *French.* **1.** who goes there? **2.** on the qui vive, on the alert.

quix·ot·ic (kwiksot'ik), *adj.* extremely romantic or chivalrous; pursuing lofty but impractical ideals. Also **quix·ot'i·cal. —quix'ot·ism,** *n.*

quiz·zi·cal (kwiz'ikəl), *adj.* **1.** odd; amusing. **2.** puzzled; questioning. **3.** mockingly questioning; making fun of.

quod e·rat de·mon·stran·dum (kwod' er'at dem,ənstran'dəm), *Latin.* which was to be demonstrated or proved. *Abbrev.:* **Q.E.D.**

quod·li·bet (kwod'libet,), *n.* a subtle argument, esp. on a theological or scholastic topic.

quod·li·betz (kwod'libets,), *n.* a painted decorative motif, as a playing card, letter of the alphabet, or similar small object, used on ceramics and the like.

quoin (kwoin, koin), *n.* the external angle of a building; the stone or brick forming it; a cornerstone.

quon·dam (kwon'dam), *adj.* former; erstwhile; previous; of earlier times.

quo·rum (kwôr'əm), *n.* the number or percentage of members of any board, society, or the like needed to constitute a valid assembly for transacting business.

quo·tid·i·an (kwōtid'ēən), *adj.* **1.** everyday; ordinary. **2.** occurring daily, as paroxysms of some fevers.

quo·tient (kwō'sHənt), *n.* the result of a division. See also **dividend, divisor.**

R

Rab·e·lai·si·an (rab,ǝlā'zēǝn, rab,ǝlā'zнǝn), *adj.* broadly or coarsely humorous, satirical, etc.

ra·bies (rā'bēz), *n.* a contagious infection causing madness in dogs, cats, and other animals and usually fatal to man if transmitted by the bite of an infected animal.

ra·chi·tis (rǝkī'tis), *n.* rickets.

ra·ci·nage (ras,ināzн'), *n.* the technique of treating leather with acid to produce a decorative effect.

rack-rent, rack rent (rak'rent,), *n.* exorbitant rent whose annual amount is equal, or almost equal, to the value of the property.

rac·on·teur (rak,ontû'), *n.* a person who is good at telling stories; someone given to recounting anecdotes.

ra·dar (rā'dä), *n.* a device for detecting the location and direction of an object, as an aircraft, by reflecting radio waves off it.

rad·i·cal (rad'ikǝl), *adj.* **1.** basic; relating to or dealing with the essential roots of a matter; fundamental, as *a radical departure from a plan.* **2.** characterized by or belonging to a group favouring basic changes in policy, philosophy, government, etc. —*n.* **3.** a person who is in favour of basic changes in policy, philosophy, government, etc., esp. by ejecting those in authority.

rad·i·cel (rad'isǝl), *n.* a tiny root; a rootlet.

rad·i·cle (rad'ikǝl), *n.* a small rootlike structure. —**ra·dic'u·lar,** *adj.*

ra·dic·u·li·tis (radik,yǝlī'tis), *n.* inflammation of the root of a spinal nerve.

ra·dic·u·lose (radik'yǝlōs), *adj.* having many radicels.

ra·di·o·ac·tive (rā,dēōak'tiv), *adj.* relating to, connected with, stemming from, or exhibiting radioactivity.

radioactive decay. See **decay.**

ra·di·o·ac·tiv·i·ty (rā,dēōaktiv'itē), *n.* the spontaneous emission of radiation resulting from the disintegration of atomic nuclei.

ra·di·o·bi·ol·o·gy (rā,dēōbīol'ǝjē), *n.* the branch of biology dealing with the effects of radiation on living organisms.

ra·di·o·car·bon (rā,dēōkä'bǝn), *n.* a radioactive isotope of carbon, esp. carbon 14.

radiocarbon dating, the process and technique by which the age of ancient organic matter is estimated from the radioactivity of its carbon content.

ra·di·o·chem·is·try (rā,dēōkem'istrē), *n.* the branch of chemistry dealing with radioactive phenomena.

radio compass, a direction-finding radio receiver used in determining the bearing of a radio transmitter.

ra·di·o·di·ag·no·sis (rā,dēōdī,ǝgnō'sis), *n.* diagnosis by means of x-rays.

ra·di·o·el·e·ment (rā,dēōel'ǝmǝnt); *n.* a radioactive chemical element.

ra·di·o·gen·ic (rā,dēōjen'ik), *adj.* produced by decay of radioactivity, as certain isotopes.

ra·di·o·gram (rā'dēōgram,), *n.* **1.** (in Britain) a unit containing a radio and a record player. **2.** a telegram sent by radio.

ra·di·o·graph (rā'dēōgräf,, rā'dēōgraf,), *n.* an image produced on a photographic plate by x-rays. —**ra·di·og·ra·phy,** *n.*

ra·di·o·i·so·tope (rā,dēōī'sǝtōp,), *n.* an artificially produced, radioactive isotope.

ra·di·o·lo·ca·tion (rā,dēōlōkā'sнǝn), *n.* the determination of the location and speed of objects by use of radar.

ra·di·ol·o·gy (rā,dēol'ǝjē), *n.* the study of the application of x-rays and other forms of radiant energy to medical diagnosis, therapy, etc. —**ra·di·o·log'i·cal** (rā,dēōloj'ikǝl), *adj.*

ra·di·o·lu·cent (rā,dēōlōō'sǝnt), *adj.* offering little or no resistance to the passage of x-rays or other forms of radiant energy. See also **radiopaque, radiotransparent.**

ra·di·o·lu·mi·nes·cence (rā,dēōlōō,mines'-ǝns, rā,dēōlyōō,mines'ǝns), *n.* luminescence induced by radioactivity.

ra·di·o·me·te·or·o·graph (rā,dēōmē'tēǝrǝgräf, rā,dēōmē'tēǝrǝgraf,), *n.* radiosonde.

ra·di·om·e·ter (rā,dēom'itǝ), *n.* a device consisting of a four-bladed fan mounted on a vertical axis in an evacuated glass bulb, with successively alternate sides of the blades blackened and mirrorlike, used for demonstrating and detecting the presence of radiant energy and of its conversion to mechanical energy.

ra·di·o·mi·crom·e·ter (rā,dēōmīkrom'itǝ), *n.* a device for measuring minute emissions of radiant energy.

ra·di·o·paque (rā,dēōpāk'), *adj.* not allowing the passage of x-rays; visible in x-ray photographs. See also **radiolucent, radiotransparent.**

ra·di·o·phare (rā'dēōfer,), *n.* a navigational beacon that broadcasts a radio signal for use by ships to determine their positions.

ra·di·o·phone (rā'dēōfōn,), *n.* a radiotelephone.

ra·di·o·pho·to·graph (rā,dēōfō'təgräf,, rā,-dēōfō'təgraf,), *n.* a photographic image transmitted by radio. Also **ra'di·o·pho,to, ra,di·o·pho'to·gram,**.

radio range beacon, a radio transmitter designed to transmit signals enabling an aviator to determine his approximate position without a radio compass.

ra·di·os·co·py (rā,dēos'kəpē), *n.* the direct internal examination of opaque objects by the use of x-rays or other forms of radiant energy.

ra·di·o·sen·si·tive (rā,dēōsen'sitiv), *adj.* of or pertaining to organisms or tissue sensitive or susceptible to destruction by x-rays or other forms of radiant energy.

ra·di·o·sonde (rā'dēōsond) *n.* a radio transmitter and meteorological instruments carried to great heights by balloon. Also **radiometeorograph.**

ra·di·o·sur·ger·y (rā,dēōsû'jərē), *n.* the surgical insertion of radioactive substances for therapeutic purposes.

ra·di·o·tech·nol·o·gy (rā,dēōtəknol'əjē), *n.* the application of radiation to industry.

ra·di·o·tel·e·gram (rā,dēōtel'əgram,), *n.* a radiogram (sense 2).

ra·di·o·tel·e·graph (rā,dēōtel'əgräf,, rā,dēōtel'əgraf,), *n.* a telegraph using radiowaves rather than wires or cables. —**ra·di·o·te·leg'ra·phy,** *n.*

ra·di·o·tel·e·phone (rā,dēōtel'əfōn,), *n.* a telephone transmitting speech by radio waves. —**ra·di·ote·leph·o·ny** (rā,dēōtəlef'ənē), *n.*

radio telescope, a radio antenna or an array of antennae designed to receive radio waves from celestial sources.

ra·di·o·ther·a·py (rā,dēōther'əpē), *n.* the treatment of disease by the use of x-rays or other radiant energy.

ra·di·o·therm·y (rā'dēōthû,mē), *n.* (in medicine) a form of treatment using heat generated by high-frequency short-wave electrical currents.

ra·di·o·trac·er (rā,dēōtrā'sə), *n.* a tracer making use of an isotope.

ra·di·o·trans·par·ent (rā,dēōtranspar'ənt), *n.* not opaque to radiation; not seen in x-ray photographs. See also **radiolucent, radiopaque.**

ra·dix (rā'diks), *n., pl.* **ra·di·ces** (rā'disēz, rad'-isēz). a root.

ra·dome (rā'dōm), *n.* a dome-shaped housing for a radar antenna.

raff·ish (raf'isH), *adj.* cheap; tawdry; in bad taste; discreditable.

ra·ga (rä'gə), *n.* any of the traditional melody patterns of Hindu music, with characteristic intervals, rhythms, and embellishments.

ra·gout (ragōō'), *n.* a spicy stew of meat or fish and vegetables.

rail·ler·y (rā'lərē), *n.* banter; good-natured pleasantry.

rai·son d'être (rā'zôN det'rə), *pl.* **raisons d'être** (rā'zônz det'rə). *French.* a reason for existence.

rai·son·né (rāzônā'), *adj. French.* ordered; organized, as *a catalogue raisonné.*

rale (räl, ral), *n.* an abnormal rattling or bubbling sound accompanying breathing, usually indicating a diseased condition of the lungs.

ram·e·kin (ram'əkin), *n.* **1.** a lidless ceramic baking dish for individual service. **2.** any preparation baked and served in a ramekin.

ra·men·tum (rəmen'təm), *n., pl.* **ra·men·ta** (rəmen'tə). a thin shaving or scraping.

ram·i·form (ram'ifôm,), *adj.* branched or branchlike.

ram·i·fy (ram'ifī), *v.* to separate into branches or branchlike divisions. —**ram·i·fi·ca'tion,** *n.*

ra·mose (rā'mōs), *adj.* bearing many branches.

ra·mous (rā'məs), *adj.* **1.** ramose. **2.** branchlike.

ram·pa·geous (rampā'jəs), *adj.* with uncontrolled vigour and energy; raging; unruly.

ram·u·lose (ram'yōōlōs), *adj.* with many small branches. Also **ramulous** (ram'yələs).

ra·mus (rā'məs), *n., pl.* **ra·mi** (rā'mī). a branch or branch-like part, as of a capillary, etc.

ran·cid (ran'sid), *adj.* having a bad smell or taste; spoiled. —**ran·cid'i·ty,** *n.*

ran·cour (raNG'kə), *n.* bitter hatred or resentment; deep spite; malice. —**ran'cor·ous,** *adj.*

rand·y (ran'dē), *adj.* lascivious; lustful; lecherous.

range·find·er (rānj'fīn,də), *n.* an instrument for determining the distance of a target or object from the observer or from a gun, camera, etc.

ran·kle (raNG'kəl), *v.* to continue to cause long-lasting anger, resentment, irritation, etc., within the mind.

rap (rap), *n.* **1.** a style of musical presentation originating in black culture and characterized by a vocal delivery that is more conversational than sung, accompanied by a rhythmical instrumental background. —*v.* **2.** (slang) to discuss informally.

ra·pa·cious (rəpā'sHəs), *adj.* disposed to taking by force; plundering; predacious.

ra·phe (rā'fē), *n., pl.* **ra·phae** (rā'fē). a seamlike joining between two halves of an organ, as of the tongue.

rapport (rapô'), *n.* sympathetic relationship; harmony. See also **en rapport.**

rap·por·teur (rap,ôtû'), *n.* a person charged with preparing reports, esp. of committee work.

rap·proche·ment (raprosH'mäN, rap,rosH-mäN'), *n.* a reconciliation; restoration of good relations.

rapt (rapt), *adj.* absorbed, as in thought; concentrating, as *with rapt attention.*

rap·to·ri·al (raptôr'ēəl), *adj.* **1.** of or like a bird of prey; predacious. **2.** equipped for seizing prey.

rapture of the deep, *n.* See **nitrogen narcosis.**

ra·ra a·vis (rer'ə ā'vis, rä'rə ā'vis), *n.*, *pl.* **rarae aves** (rerē ā·vēz). an unusual or rare person or thing.

rar·e·fy (rer'əfī), *v.* to thin out or make less dense; to refine. —**rar·e·fac'tion,** *n.*

ra·so·ri·al (rəsôr'ēəl), *adj.* characteristically scratching the ground for food, as a chicken.

ras·ter (ras'tə), *n.* the device in a cathode-ray tube that creates a pattern of scanning lines over the area onto which the image is projected.

ra·ti·oc·i·nate (rat,ēos'ināt, rasH,ēō'sināt), *v.* to reason, esp. by using formal logic. —**ra·ti·oc·i·na'tion,** *n.*

rat·ion·al (rasH'ənəl), *adj.* reasonable; characterized by common sense and an even temperament.

ra·tion·ale (rasH,ənäl', rasH,ənal'), *n.* **1.** reasons or principles; the fundamental reasons for something. **2.** the ultimate excuse for a certain action.

rat·ite (rat'īt), *adj.* **1.** describing a flightless running bird, such as the ostrich or kiwi, whose sternum lacks a keel and hence the necessary attachment for flight muscles. —*n.* **2.** such a flightless bird.

rau·cous (rô'kəs), *adj.* (of a sound) harsh; grating; hoarse.

raun·chy (rôn'CHē), *adj. Slang.* **1.** lewd; indecent; lusty. **2.** *Chiefly U.S.* slovenly; of poor appearance; sloppy.

rau·wol·fi·a (rôwo͞ol'fēə), *n.* a medicinal extract from the roots of the rauwolfia tree yielding various alkaloids, esp. reserpine.

rav·en·ing (rav'əninG), *adj.* (of predatory beasts) hungry; rapacious.

ra·vi·gote (rav,igōt'), *n.* a spicy sauce of white wine, vinegar, butter, cream, and mushrooms, usually served hot with meats and poultry.

ra·win·sonde (rā'winsond,), *n.* meteorological observations conducted by means of a radar-tracked radiosonde.

re·al·i·a (rēäl'ēə), *pl. n.* real-life objects or activities used in classroom teaching.

re·al·ism (rē'əliz,əm), *n.* **1.** a style in art that attempts to recreate reality. **2.** (in literature) the representation of the ordinary or mundane aspects of life matter-of-factly, in an attempt to reflect life as it actually is. See also **naturalism.**

re·al·po·li·tik (rāäl'politēk,), *n.* a political policy based on power and its ruthless exercise instead of on moralistic or idealistic grounds.

real time, the actual time used by a computer in solving a problem, the result being required to control a process going on at the same time.

re·ap·por·tion·ment (rē,əpô'sHənmənt), *n.* a

redistribution or change in the proportions, esp. of the proportional representation in a congressional body.

re·a·ta (rēä'tə), *n.* See **riata.**

Ré·au·mur (rā'əmyo͞o,ə), *adj.* of or pertaining to a temperature scale in which 0 represents the freezing point and 80 the boiling point of water at sea level.

re·bar·ba·tive (ribä'bətiv), *adj.* repellent; unattractive; forbidding.

reb·o·ant (reb'ōənt), *adj.* loudly echoing or reverberating.

re·bo·zo, re·bo·so (ribō'zō, ribō'sō), *n.* (in Spain and Latin America) a long scarf worn by women over the head and shoulders. Also **rebosa, riboza.**

re·bus (rē'bəs), *n.*, *pl.* **re·bus·es.** the representation of a word or phrase by pictures, letters, symbols, etc., sometimes used in heraldry to represent a surname. See also **canting arms.**

re·but (ribut'), *v.* **re·but·ted, re·but·ting.** to prove (a person or argument) to be wrong. —**re·but'tal,** *n.*

re·cal·ci·trant (rikal'sitrənt), *adj.* rebelliously stubborn; difficult to manage; disobedient.

re·ca·lesce (rē,kəles'), *v.* to appear to increase temporarily in temperature.

re·cant (rikant'), *v.* to withdraw a statement formally; retract.

re·ca·pit·u·late (rē,kəpicH'o͞olāt, rē,kəpit'-yo͞olāt), *v.* to summarize, in brief form, the results of an activity, discussion, number of events, etc. —**re,ca·pit,u·la'tion,** *n.*

re·cede (risēd), *v.* **re·ced·ed, re·ced·ing.** to move away or withdraw, as *a receding hairline, a train receding in the distance.*

re·cen·sion (risen'sHən), *n.* a revision of a text on the basis of detailed study of the sources used.

re·cep·ti·ble (risep'tibəl), *adj.* appropriate for reception.

re·cep·tor (risep'tə), *n.* a nerve ending or group of nerve endings, specialized for the reception of stimuli.

re·ces·sion (risesH'ən), *n.* a period in a business cycle where economic activity slows, prosperity is halted, and unemployment rises; a minor depression.

re·ces·sive (rises'iv), *adj.* tending to recede or move back.

ré·chauf·fé (rāsHōf'), *n.*, *pl.* **ré·chauf·fés** (rāsHōfā'). a reheated dish of food.

re·cher·ché (rəsHe'əsHā), *adj.* uncommon; choice; rare.

re·cid·i·vate (risid'ivāt), *v.* to relapse, esp. into crime.

re·cid·i·vism (risid'iviz,əm), *n.* habitual relapse, as into crime or antisocial behaviour.

re·cip·i·ence (risip'ēəns), *n.* the act of receiving. —**re·cip'i·ent,** *n.*

re·ci·sion (risiZH'ən), *n.* a rescinding or voiding; cancellation.

reck (rek), *v.* to have care or concern for.

ré·clame (rāklam'), *n.* publicity; notoriety; talent for getting publicity.

rec·li·nate (rek'l,nāt), *adj.* bending downwards, as a leaf or beak.

rec·li·vate (rek'l,vāt), *adj.* shaped like the letter 'S' or 'C'; sigmoid.

rec·luse (riklōōs', rek'lōōs), *n.* a person who prefers to remain alone, in seclusion. —**re·clu'sive,** *adj.*

re·clu·sion (riklōō'zHən), *n.* the state of being a recluse.

re·cog·ni·zance (rikog'nizəns, rikon'izəns), *n.* responsibility for behaviour, esp. under guarantee or obligation of a bond.

re·com·bi·nant DNA (rēkom'binənt), *n.* DNA that contains fragments of other DNA molecules, such as genes from another organism, integrated by a process called recombination, as in genetic engineering.

rec·on·dite (rek'əndīt, rikon'dīt), *adj.* concerning or involved with abstruse or difficult subjects; esoteric; little known, obscure.

rec·re·ant (rek'rēənt), *adj.* **1.** cowardly. **2.** traitorous. —*n.* **3.** a coward. **4.** an apostate or traitor.

rec·re·ment (rek'rəmənt), *n.* a bodily secretion that is reabsorbed, as saliva.

re·crim·i·nate (rikrim'ənāt), *v.* to accuse in turn; revile.

re·crim·i·na·tion (rikrim,inā'sHən), *n.* mutual accusation or reproach; countercharge.

re·cru·desce (rē,krōōdes', rek,rōōdes'), *v.* to break out anew after lying inactive, as a sore. —**re·cru·des'cence,** *n.* —**re·cru·des'cent,** *adj.*

rec·ti·fy (rek'tifī), *v.* **rec·ti·fied, rec·ti·fy·ing.** to make or set right; correct.

rec·ti·lin·e·ar (rek,tilin'ēə), *adj.* **1.** being or moving in a straight line or lines. **2.** characterized by a straight line or lines. Also **rec,ti·lin'e·al.** —**rec,ti·lin·e·ar·ly, rec,ti·lin'e·al·ly,** *adv.*

rec·ti·tude (rek'tityōōd,), *n.* moral or religious uprightness; integrity.

rec·to (rek'tō), *n., pl.* **rec·tos.** a right-hand page of a book, magazine, etc. See also **verso.**

rec·trix (rek'triks), *n., pl.* **rec·trices** (rektrī'sēz). any of the large tail feathers of a bird.

rec·tus (rek'təs), *n., pl.* **rec·ti** (rek'tī). any of various straight muscles, as of the eye, neck, or thigh.

re·cum·bent (rikum'bənt), *adj.* reclining; lying down.

re·cur (rikû'), *v.* **re·curred, re·cur·ring.** to occur or happen again; reoccur. —**re·cur'rence,** *n.* —**re·cur'rent,** *adj.*

re·cur·vate (rikû'vāt), *adj.* recurved; bent back.

re·curve (rikûv'), *v.* to curve or bend backwards.

rec·u·sant (rek'yōōzənt), *n.* **1.** a person who refuses to obey authority —*adj.* **2.** refusing to obey authority.

re·demp·tion (ridemp'sHən), *n.* a redeeming or being redeemed; deliverance. —**re·demp'tive,** *adj.* —**re·demp'to·ry,** *adj.*

red herring, *n. Informal.* **1.** something introduced merely to divert attention from an issue at hand. **2.** *U.S. Finance.* a printed prospectus detailing the terms of issuance of shares of a new corporation or of additional shares, debentures, etc., of an existing one. [So called because its first page contains a rubricated summation.]

red·hi·bi·tion (red,ibisH'ən), *n.* the nullification of a sale because of a defect in the article sold.

red·in·te·grate (redin'təgrāt) *v.* to make whole or perfect again; restore; renew. —**red·in·te·gra'tion,** *n.*

red·i·vi·vus (red,ivī'vəs), *adj.* revived; living again; reborn.

red·o·lent (red'ələnt), *adj.* giving out a pleasing odour; fragrant.

re·doubt (ridout'), *n.* a breastwork built for defence around a prominent point.

re·doubt·a·ble (ridou'təbəl), *adj.* formidable; commanding respect.

re·dress (ridres', rē'dres), *n.* the remedying of a wrong; relief from or reparation for a wrong or injury done.

red tide, a reddish discoloration of sea waters by large numbers of red protozoan flagellates.

re·duct (ridukt'), *n.* a small area partitioned off from a room for the sake of balance with a fireplace, etc.

re·duc·ti·o ad ab·sur·dum (riduk'tēō ad absū'dəm, riduk'sHēō ad absū'dəm), *Latin.* a reduction to an absurdity; the disproof of a proposition by showing its consequences to be impossible or absurd when carried to a logical conclusion.

re·duc·tion·ism (riduk'sHəniz,əm), *n.* the analysis of complex data, processes, or systems in terms of their less complex components; often used disparagingly to denote oversimplification. —**re·duc'tion·ist,** *n., adj.* —**re·duc,tion·ist'-ic,** *adj.*

re·dun·dant (ridun'dənt), *adj.* unnecessary or unnecessarily repeated. —**re·dun'dan·cy,** *n.*

reef·er (rē'fə), *n.* a cigarette containing marijuana, usually hand-rolled.

re·fec·to·ry (rifek'tərē), *n.* a dining hall in a monastery, convent, college, etc.

ref·er·en·dum (ref,ərən'dəm), *n., pl.* **ref·er·en·dums, ref·er·en·da** (ref,ərən'də). the referral to a public vote of a bill or issue before a legislative body.

ref·er·ent (ref'ərənt), *n.* the object, concept, etc., referred to by a term or symbol. —**ref·er·en·tial** (ref,ərən'sHəl), *adj.*

re·flate (riflāt'), *v.* to restore a former price

structure by increasing the amount of currency in circulation. —re·fla'tion, *n.*

re·flet (riflā'), *n.* lustre or iridescence, as on glazed pottery.

re·flex·ol·o·gy (rē,fleksol'əjē), *n.* a practice used in alternative medicine involving massage of so-called reflex points on the feet, said to correspond to specific organs of the body. The massage is claimed to restore a healthy energy flow through a postulated network of channels linking the organs and ending at the reflex points. —re,flex·ol'o·gist, *n.*

ref·lu·ent (ref'lōōənt), *adj.* running out; ebbing, as the tide to the sea.

re·flux (rē'fluks), *n.* a flowing back; ebb.

re·frac·tion (rifrak'SHən), *n.* the bending of rays of light, heat, sound, etc., when passing from one medium to another of different density. —re·fract', *v.* —re·frac'tive, *adj.*

re·frac·to·ry (rifrak'tərē), *adj.* 1. hard to manage; resisting conventional treatment. 2. hard to melt or work, as an ore or metal. —*n.* 3. a heat-resistant material.

re·frain[1] (rifrān'), *n.* a repeated theme in a song or piece of music.

re·frain[2] (rifrān') *v.* (*usually* **refrain from**) to stop doing something or not do it at all.

re·fran·gi·ble (rifran'jibəl), *adj.* that can be refracted, as light rays.

re·frin·gent (rifrin'jənt), *adj.* refracting; refractive.

re·ful·gent (riful'jənt), *adj.* shining; resplendent.

re·fute (rifyōōt'), *v.* to prove a person, argument, opinion, etc., to be wrong; confute. —ref·u·ta·tion (ref,yōōtā'SHən), *n.* —re·fut·a·tive (rifyōō'tətiv), *adj.*

re·gale (rigāl'), *v.* re·galed, re·gal·ing. 1. to please, entertain, or delight by lavishing with good food and drink. 2. to amuse, entertain, as *He regaled us with his tales of hunting in India.*

re·ge·late (rē'jəlāt), *v.* to cause to freeze by regelation.

re·ge·la·tion (rē,jəlā'SHən), *n.* the melting of ice and freezing of water at the same temperature by changing the pressure.

Re·gen·cy (rē'jənsē), *adj.* 1. of or designating the style of architecture prevalent during the period 1811–20 in Britain, characterized by simplicity of appearance and often imitating ancient Greek forms. 2. of or designating the style of furnishings or decoration of the British Regency, similar to French Empire styles and often imitating ancient Greek and Egyptian forms, typically with columns and pilasters, ornamentation with ormolu, the use of marble for flat horizontal surfaces, etc.

reg·i·cide (rej'isīd), *n.* the killing of a monarch.

reg·nal (reg'nəl), *adj.* of or relating to a mon-

arch or reign, esp. the length of a reign reckoned from the date of accession.

re·grate (rigrāt'), *v.* 1. to buy (esp. commodities) with the intention of raising the price and selling at a profit. 2. to sell such items; retail. —re·grat'er, *n.*

re·i·fy (rē'əfī), *v.* to make concrete something abstract; concretize. —re,i·fi·ca'tion, *n.*

re·it·er·ate (rēit'ərāt), *v.* re·it·erat·ed, re·it·er·at·ing. to say (something) again. —re·it,e·ra'tion, *n.* —re·it'er·a·tive, *adj.*

re·jec·ta·men·ta (rijek,təmen'tə), *n. pl.* things rejected as valueless.

re·join·der (rijoin'də), *n.* a response to an answer.

re·ju·ve·nate (rijōō'vənāt), *v.* to make young or youthful once more. Also re·ju've·nize.

re·ju·ve·nes·cent (rijōō,vənes'ənt), *adj.* making or becoming young again.

re·late (rilāt'), *v.* (usually followed by *to*) to establish a sympathetic relationship with a person or thing.

rel·a·tiv·i·ty (rel,ətiv'itē), *n.* the theory of the relative, rather than absolute, character of motion, velocity, mass, etc., and the interdependence of matter, time, and space, as formulated by Albert Einstein.

re·lent (rilent'), *v.* to yield or give up doing something in a determined or harsh manner; ease up. —re·lent'less, *adj.*

rel·e·vant (rel'əvənt), *adj.* appropriate or suitable; pertinent. —rel'e·vance, *n.*

rel·ic (rel'ik), *n.* an object that has survived or been kept because it represents the past, esp. a fragment of something associated with a person much venerated in the history of certain religions.

re·lict (rel'ikt), *n.* someone or something extant or surviving.

re·li·gi·ose (rilij'ēōs), *adj.* being religious; pious; excessively religious. —re·lig·i·os'i·ty, *n.*

rel·i·quar·y (rel'əkwərē), *n.* a small box or receptacle for relics.

re·liq·ui·ae (rilik'wiē,), *pl. n.* the remains of the dead; relics.

re·luc·tance (riluk'təns), *n.* the resistance offered to magnetic flux by a magnetic circuit.

REM *Abbr. for* rapid eye movement: saccadic movement of the eyes that characterizes a particular phase of sleep (*REM sleep*) associated with restlessness and dreaming.

rem (rem), *n.* a unit dose of ionizing radiation whose biological effect is equal to that produced by one roentgen of x-rays. [*r(oentgen) e(quivalent in) m(an)*]

rem·a·nent (rem'ənənt), *adj.* remaining; left over.

re·mex (rē'meks), *n.*, *pl.* rem·i·ges (rem'ijēz). one of the flight feathers of a bird's wing.

rem·i·form (rem'ifôm,), *adj.* oar-shaped.

rem·i·grant (rem'igrənt), *n.* that which or one who returns.

rem·i·ped (rem'iped,), *adj.* having feet adapted for use as oars.

re·miss (rimis'), *adj.* neglectful of an obligation.

re·mis·sion (rimisʜ'ən), *n.* **1.** pardon or absolution, as for sins. **2.** decrease or reduction in power or vigour, as of a disease. **3.** release from an obligation.

re·mis·sive (rimis'iv), *adj.* **1.** decreasing; tending to abate. **2.** pardoning.

re·mon·strate (rem'ənsträt, rimon'strät), *v.* to say or plead in protest, complaint, etc. —**re·mon'strance,** *n.* —**re·mon'strant,** *adj.*

re·morse (rimôs'), *n.* regret; a feeling of sorrow for something that one has done. —**re·morse'ful,** *adj.* —**re·morse'less,** *adj.*

ré·mou·lade (rāmǝlād', rāmǝläd'), *n.* a cold sauce of spices, herbs, chopped pickle, etc., with a mayonnaise base. Also **re·mo·lade'.**

Re·nais·sance (rinā'sǝns), *n.* **1.** the period of European cultural history following the Middle Ages characterized by renewed interest and activity in learning, art, and inquiry, lasting from the 14th to the 17th centuries. —*adj.* **2.** of or designating the style of architecture, furnishing, and decoration developed in Italy in the 15th and 16th centuries, typified by an imitation of classical Roman motifs and an adherence to symmetry and mathematical proportions.

re·nas·cent (rinas'ǝnt, rinā'sǝnt), *adj.* acquiring or showing new life or vigour; being reborn. —**re·nas'cence,** *n.*

ren·coun·ter (renkoun'tǝ), *n.* a conflict or contest of any kind. Also **ren·con·tre** (renkôn'tǝ).

re·nege (rinĕg', rināg', rinĕg'), *v.* **re·neged, re·neg·ing.** to go back on one's word; break a promise.

ren·i·fleur (ren'iflû,), *n.* one who is sexually stimulated or gratified by odours.

ren·i·form (ren'ifôm,), *adj.* kidney-shaped.

re·ni·tent (rinī'tǝnt), *adj.* resisting pressure; opposing stubbornly.

re·nounce (rinouns'), *v.* **re·nounced, re·nounc·ing.** to give up something that one has been awarded, as *to renounce the world championship,* or something that one has been doing, as *to renounce a bad habit.* —**re·nun·ci·a·tion** (rinun'sēā'sʜǝn), *n.*

ren·voi (renvoi'), *n.* **1.** the expulsion of an alien, esp. a diplomat, from a country. **2.** the referral of a jurisdictional dispute involving international law to a law other than the local one.

rep·ar·tee (rep,ätē'), *n.* a conversation characterized by witty, apt, or clever remarks, or the remarks themselves.

re·per·cus·sion (rē,pǝkusʜ'ǝn), *n.* a result or effect of something, esp. after a period of time has passed; rebound, as *The repercussions of his*

arrest for embezzlement are still felt three years later.

rep·er·toire (rep'ǝtwä), *n.* the stock of songs, stories, plays, etc., that an entertainer, theatre, opera company, or raconteur has prepared.

re·pine (ripīn'), *v.* to feel or express discontent or downheartedness.

re·plete (riplēt'), *adj.* **(replete with)** abundantly or fully supplied (with).

rep·li·cate (rep'likit), *adj.* folded back on itself. Also **rep'li·cat,ed.**

rep·li·ca·tion (rep,likā'sʜǝn), *n.* **1.** a reply or answer. **2.** a reply to an answer. **3.** duplication.

re·pos·it (ripoz'it), *v.* **1.** to replace. **2.** to deposit or store.

rep·re·hend (rep,rihend'), *v.* to find fault with; reprimand; rebuke. —**rep,re·hen'sion,** *n.*

rep·re·hen·si·ble (rep,rihen'sibǝl), *adj.* meriting or worthy of rebuke or disapproval.

rep·ro·bate (rep'rǝbāt), *n.* **1.** a depraved or unprincipled person. **2.** a person rejected by God and excluded from salvation. —**rep,ro·ba'tion,** *n.* —**rep'ro·ba·tive,** *adj.*

re·prove (riproŏv'), *v.* **re·proved, reprov·ing.** to scold (someone); tell (someone) that what he has done is without approval. —**re·proof',** *n.*

rep·tant (rep'tǝnt), *adj.* (in biology) creeping, crawling, or trailing along the ground.

re·pu·di·ate (ripyoŏ'dēāt), *v.* to deny the authority of; disown; reject with condemnation; reject with denial. —**re·pu,di·a'tion,** *n.*

re·pugn (ripyoŏn'), *v.* to oppose or resist.

re·pug·nant (ripug'nǝnt), *adj.* disgusting; offensive. —**re·pug'nance,** *n.*

req·ui·es·cat (rek,wēes'kat), *n.* a prayer for the repose of the dead which, in its Latin form, begins *Requiescat in pace....*

re·qui·es·cat in pa·ce (rek,wēes'kat in pä'sĕ, pä'cʜā), *Latin.* may he (or she) rest in peace.

req·ui·site (rek'wizit), *adj.* required or necessary for some purpose.

re·quit·al (rikwī'tǝl), *n.* a return, reward, repayment, etc., for a kindness or service; something as reward, punishment, etc., in return.

rere·dos (rē'ǝdos), *n.* **1.** an ornamental screen or partition wall behind an altar in a church. **2.** the back of a fireplace.

re·scind (risind'), *v.* to revoke, retract, or cancel; to invalidate; repeal.

re·scis·si·ble (risis'ibǝl), *adj.* rescindable.

re·scis·sion (risizʜ'ǝn), *n.* the act of rescinding.

re·scis·so·ry (risis'ǝrē), *adj.* acting or tending to rescind.

re·script (rē'skript), *n.* a written order or answer to a petition presented in writing; any official decree or edict.

res·eau (rezō'), *n., pl.* **res·eaux** (rezōz', rǝzō'), **res·eaus. 1.** a network; a netted or meshed background in lace. **2.** a reticle in a glass plate, used in photographic telescopes to produce a grid on photographs of stars, for purposes of location.

res·er·pine (res'əpīn), *n.* an alkaloid obtained from the root of the rauwolfia tree, used in the treatment of hypertension and as a sedative.

res ges·tae (rās' jes'tē), acts; deeds.

re·sid·u·um (rizid'yŏŏəm, rizij'ōŏəm), *n.*, *pl.* re·sid·u·a (rizid'yŏŏə, rizij'ŏŏə). the residue or remainder.

re·sile (rizīl'), *v.* to spring back; recoil.

re·sil·i·ent (rizil'ēənt) *adj.* elastic; returning to the original shape after being bent, stretched, etc.; recovering readily from illness, adversity, etc. —**re·sil'i·ence**, *n.*

res·in·ate (rez'ināt), *v.* to impregnate or treat with resin.

res·in·if·er·ous (rez,inif'ərəs), *adj.* yielding resin.

res·in·oid (rez'ənoid,), *adj.* like resin.

res·in·ous (rez'inəs), *adj.* containing resin; resembling, pertaining to, or having the characteristics of resin.

res·o·lute (rez'əlŏŏt, rez'əlyŏŏt), *adj.* determined in one's mind; with one's mind made up; firm. —**res,o·lu'tion**, *n.*

re·spect·er (rispek'tə), *n.* a person or thing influenced by social standing, importance, power, etc. (usually in negative constructions) as, *Sickness is no respecter of rank or position.*

res·pi·rom·e·try (res,pirom'itrē), *n.* the science of measurement of respiration.

res·tive (res'tiv), *adj.* nervously uneasy; impatiently restless.

re·su·pine (rēsŏŏ'pīn), *adj.* prone; prostrate; supine.

re·sur·gence (risû'jəns), *n.* the rising again from virtual extinction; revival. —**re·sur'gent**, *adj.*

re·tard·ate (ritä'dāt), *n.* a mentally retarded person.

re·te (rē'tē), *n.*, *pl.* re·ti·a (rē'sHēə). a network, as of nerve fibres.

re·ti·ar·y (rē'sHēərē) *adj.* **1.** using a net. **2.** netlike.

ret·i·cent (ret'isənt), *adj.* keeping things to oneself; not outgoing or open; close-mouthed. —**ret'i·cence**, *n.*

ret·i·cle (ret'ikəl), *n.* a network of fine lines, wires, etc., in the focus of the objective of a telescope. —**re·tic·u·lar** (ritik'yŏŏlə), *adj.* —**re·tic'u·late**, *adj.*, *v.* **re·tic·u·la'tion**, *n.*

re·tic·u·lo·cyte (ritik'yŏŏlōsīt,, ritik'yŏŏləsīt,), *n.* an immature red blood cell.

re·tic·u·lo·en·do·the·li·al (ritik,yŏŏlōen,dōthē'lēəl), *adj.* designating or of the system of macrophages found in certain tissues and organs that help maintain resistance and immunity to infection.

re·tic·u·lum (ritik'yŏŏləm), *n.*, *pl.* **retic·u·la**

(ritik'yŏŏlə). **1.** any system or structure resembling a network. **2.** the second of the four stomachs of a ruminant. See also **rumen, omasum, abomasum.**

re·ti·form (rē'tifôm,), *adj.* netlike in form; reticulate.

ret·i·ni·tis (ret,inī'tis), *n.* inflammation of the retina.

ret·i·no·scope (ret'inəskōp,), *n.* skiascope; a device for determining the refractive power of the eye.

ret·i·nos·co·py (ret,inos'kəpē), *n.* a method of measuring the refraction of an eye by observing the movements of light and shadow on the pupil with a skiascope.

re·tort (ritôt'), *n.* **1.** an abrupt, curt, angry answer. —*v.* **2.** to answer in an unpleasant and short manner.

re·trad (rē'trad), *adv.* to the back; backwards.

re·tral (rē'trəl), *adj.* at, near, or to the back; posterior.

re·trench (ritrenCH'), *v.* to reduce or cut back. —**re·trench'ment**, *n.*

ret·ri·bu·tion (ret,ribyŏŏ'sHən), *n.* revenge; the action of getting even or of getting back at someone for something he has done.

ret·ro·bul·bar (ret,rōbul'bə), *adj.* behind the eyeball.

ret·ro·cede (ret,rōsēd'), *v.* to go back; recede.

ret·ro·ces·sion (ret'rōsesH'ən), *n.* **1.** the act of retroceding. **2.** *U.S.* a restoration, in American Indian reservations, of police power to a federal agency.

ret·ro·gress (ret,rōgres'), *v.* to move backwards; go back to a past, less desirable state or condition. —**ret,ro·gres,sion**, *n.*

ret·ro·len·tal fi·bro·pla·sia (ret,rōlen'təl fī,brōplā'zeə), a disease, resulting in blindness, found in premature infants, caused by abnormal growth of fibrous tissue behind the lens of the eye.

re·trorse (ritrôs'), *adj.* bent or turned backwards.

ret·ro·spec·tive (ret,rōspek'tiv), *adj.* **1.** regarding past events; looking back on earlier experiences or conditions. —*n.* **2.** a show of an artist's earlier works, esp. those that reflect a particular style or period.

ret·rous·sé (rə'trŏŏ'sā), *adj.* turned up, as *a retroussé nose.*

ret·ro·ver·sion (ret,rōvû'zHən), *n.* a turning towards the back; the resulting state or condition.

ret·ro·vi·rus (ret'rōvī,rəs), *n.* any of a family of viruses (the Retroviridae), such as HIV, that have the unique ability to synthesize DNA copies of the RNA that comprises their own genes, enabling them to infiltrate the DNA of their hosts. This process therefore reverses the normal flow of genetic information from DNA to RNA. —**ret,ro·vi'ral**, *adj.*

re·trude (ritrōōd'), v. (in dentistry) to produce retrusion in.

re·tru·sion (ritrōō'zнən), n. displacement of the teeth towards the back of the mouth.

ret·si·na (retsē'nə), n. a white or red wine of Greece flavoured with resin.

re·tuse (rityōōs'), adj. having a blunt or rounded tip with a small notch, as some leaves.

re·vanche (rĭvancн'), n. the policy that moves a defeated nation aggressively to seek restoration of its original territory.

re·van·chist (rivan'cнist), n. See **irredentist**. —**re·van'chism**, n.

rev·e·nant (rev'ənənt), n. one who returns; a ghost.

re·ver·ber·ate (rivû'bərāt), v. **re·ver·ber·at·ed**, **re·ver·ber·at·ing**. to echo and reecho; sound and resound often. —**re·ver·ber·a'tion**, n.

re·vers (rivē'ə), n., pl. **re·vers**. a part of a garment turned back to show the reverse side or facing, as a lapel. Also **re·vere'**.

reverse takeover, the takeover of a larger company by a smaller company.

re·vet (rivet'), v. to face, as the side of a trench or embankment, with masonry, sandbags, etc., for protection.

re·vet·ment (rivet'mənt), n. **1.** a facing of masonry, sandbags, etc., for the protection of a wall or bank of earth. **2.** an ornamental facing of marble, tiles, etc.

re·vile (rivīl'), v. to attack with abusive or contemptuous language.

re·viv·i·fy (riviv'əfī), v. to put new life into; revive.

rev·i·vis·cence (rev,ivis'əns), n. the state of being revived; revival.

rev·o·lute (rev'əlōōt), adj. curled back at the edge, as some leaves.

re·vul·sant (rivul'sənt), adj. **1.** causing revulsion. —n. **2.** a medicinal agent that draws blood from one part of the body to another.

re·vul·sion (rivul'sнən), n. **1.** extreme distaste, repugnance, or loathing. **2.** the lessening of action of a disease in one region of the body by irritation in another. —**re·vul'sive**, adj.

rhab·do·man·cy (rab'dōman,sē), n. divination by rod or wand, esp. in finding underground water; dowsing.

rhab·do·my·o·ma (rab,dōmīō'mə), n., pl. **rhab·do·my·o·ma·ta** (rab,dōmīō'mətə). a tumour composed of striated muscular fibres.

rha·thy·mi·a (rəthī'mēə), n. carefree, indifferent behaviour; lightheartedness.

rhe·mat·ic (rimat'ik), adj. pertaining to word formation; of or derived from a verb.

rhe·ol·o·gy (rēol'əjē), n. the study of the change in flow and form of matter.

rhe·om·e·ter (rēom'itə), n. an instrument for measuring fluid flow, as of circulating blood.

rhe·o·re·cep·tor (rē,ōrisep'tə), n. nerve endings stimulated by water currents.

rhe·o·scope (rē'əskōp,), n. a device for detecting the presence of an electric current.

rhe·o·stat (rē'əstat,), n. a device for varying the resistance of an electric circuit without breaking the circuit, used for regulating the brightness of electric lights, etc.

rhe·o·tax·is (rē,ətak'sis), n. the tendency of an organism to move in response to a current of water.

rhe·ot·ro·pism (rēot'rəpiz,əm), n. the tendency of a plant to respond to the stimulus of a current of water by some change in its direction of growth.

rhet·o·ric (ret'ərik), n. the effective use of language to persuade or impress; a style that aims to arouse emotion.

rhe·tor·i·cal (ritor'ikəl), adj. language used for or concerned with style or effect rather than with content or meaningfulness. —**rhe·tor'i·cally**, adv.

rheum (rōōm), n. **1.** a watery discharge from the mucous membrane. **2.** a cold. —**rheum'y**, adj.

rhex·is (rek'sis), n., pl. **rhex·es** (rek'sēz). a break, as of a blood vessel, organ, etc.

Rh factor, a group of inherited antigens present in the red blood cells of most persons (who are said to be Rh positive), which may cause haemolytic reactions during pregnancy or after transfusion of blood containing this factor into someone lacking it (said to be Rh negative).

rhi·nal (rī'nəl), adj. of the nose; nasal.

rhi·nar·i·um (rīner'ēəm), n., pl. **rhi·nar·i·a** (rīner'ēə). the naked, glandular skin surrounding the nostrils of some mammals.

rhi·nen·ceph·a·lon (rī,nensef'əlon), n. the part of the brain concerned with the sense of smell.

rhi·ni·tis (rīnī'tis), n. inflammation of the nasal mucous membrane.

rhi·noc·e·rot·ic (rīnos,ərot'ik), adj. concerned with or like a rhinoceros.

rhi·nol·o·gy (rīnol'əjē), n. the branch of medicine dealing with the nose and its diseases.

rhi·no·plas·ty (rī'nōplas,tē), n. plastic surgery of the nose.

rhi·nor·rhoe·a, rhi·nor·rhe·a (rī,nōrē'ə), n. an excessive mucous discharge from the nose.

rhi·no·scope (rī'nōskōp,), n. an instrument for examining the internal passages of the nose; nasoscope.

rhi·nos·co·py (rīnos'kəpē), n. the examination of the nasal passages.

rhi·zo·gen·ic (rī,zōjen'ik), adj. producing roots. Also **rhi·zog·e·nous** (rīzoj'ənəs).

rhi·zoid (rī'zoid), adj. rootlike.

rhi·zo·mor·phous (rī,zōmô'fəs), adj. formed like a root; root-shaped. Also **rhi,zo·mor'phoid**.

rhi·zoph·a·gous (rīzof'əgəs), *adj.* normally eating roots.

Rh negative, having or denoting blood that lacks the Rh factor.

rhom·bic (rom'bik), *adj.* of or having the form of a rhombus.

rhom·bo·he·dron (rom,bōhē'drən), *n., pl.* **rhom·bo·he·drons, rhombo·he·dra** (rom,bōhē'-drə). a six-sided three-dimensional figure, each side of which is a rhombus.

rhom·boid (rom'boid), *n.* a parallelogram with oblique angles and only the opposite sides equal.

rhom·bus (rom'bəs), *n., pl.* **rhom·bus·es, rhom·bi** (rom'bī). an equilateral parallelogram with oblique angles.

rhon·chus (roNG'kəs), *n., pl.* **rhonchi** (roNG'kī). a rattling sound in the bronchial tubes caused by a partial bronchial obstruction.

rho·ta·cism (rō'təsiz,əm), *n.* excessive use of the sound 'r' or the substitution of some other sound for it.

Rh positive, having the Rh factor in the blood.

ri·a (rē'ə), *n.* a long, narrow inlet, widening and deepening towards the sea.

ri·ant (rī'ənt), *adj.* laughing; smiling; cheerful.

ri·a·ta (rēä'tə), *n.* a lariat. Also **reata.**

rib·ald (rib'əld) *adj.* coarse or vulgar in speech, language, etc. —**rib'ald·ry,** *n.*

ri·bo·fla·vin (rī,bōflā'vin), *n.* a factor of the vitamin B complex found in milk, eggs, meat, leafy vegetables, etc., used in vitamin preparations, etc. Also **ri,bo·fla'vine.**

ribo·nu·cle·ic acid (rī,bōnyōōklē'ik). See RNA. Also **ribose nucleic acid.**

ri·bose (rī'bōs), *n.* a sugar obtained from RNA.

ri·bo·some (rī'bəsōm,), *n.* any of numerous minute particles consisting of protein and RNA (*ribosomal RNA*) that are the sites of protein synthesis in living cells. —**ri,bo·so'mal,** *adj.*

ri·bo·zo (ribō'zō), *n.* See **rebozo.**

rick·ets (rik'its), *n.* a children's disease of the skeletal system, characterized by a softening and, often, bending of the bones, usually caused by a vitamin D deficiency.

rick·ett·si·a (riket'sēə), *n., pl.* **rick·ett·si·ae** (riket'siē,), **rick·ett·si·as.** any of a group of obligate parasitic microorganisms, usually classified as bacteria in the order Rickettsiales, members of which are responsible for spotted fevers, typhus, and other diseases. —**rick·ett'si·al,** *adj.*

rick·rack, ric·rac (rik'rak), *n.* flat, zigzag braid for trimming clothing, linens, etc.

ri·cot·ta (rikot'ə), *n.* a soft Italian cheese made from whey.

ric·tal bristle (rik'təl), a feather resembling a bristle which grows from the base of a bird's bill.

ric·tus (rik'təs), *n., pl.* **ric·tus, ric·tus·es.** the opening produced by the gaping of the mouth. —**ric'tal,** *adj.*

rid·dle (rid'əl), *v.* **1.** to make many holes in; puncture throughout, as *to riddle with gunshot.* —*n.* **2.** a sieve.

ri·dent (rī'dənt), *adj.* laughing; riant.

Rie·man·ni·an geometry (rēmä'nēən), a form of non-Euclidean geometry in which there are no parallel lines and every pair of straight lines intersects. Also **elliptic geometry.** See also Euclidean geometry, hyperbolic geometry.

ri·fa·ci·men·to (rifä,CHimen'tō), *n., pl.* **ri·fa·ci·men·ti** (rifä,CHimen'tē). an adaptation or reworking, as of a piece of music or literature.

rife (rīf), *adj.* common; universal; found everywhere; filled with.

rig·a·to·ni (rig,ətō'nē), *n.* (in Italian cookery) small, ribbed tubes of pasta, often served stuffed with ground meat, tomatoes, cheese, etc.

rig·or·ism (rig'əriz,əm), *n.* extreme strictness or severity.

rig·or mor·tis (rig'ə mô'tis), the progressive stiffening of the body after death.

ri·mose (rī'mōs), *adj.* full of cracks or chinks. Also **ri·mous** (rī'məs).

rim·ple (rim'pəl), *n.* a wrinkle; rumple; crease.

rin·ceau (raNsō'), *n., pl.* **rin·ceaux** (raNsō'). an ornamental motif of flowers, leaves, or leafy branches.

rin·gent (rin'jənt), *adj.* agape; open.

ri·oj·a (rēō'hə, rēō'KHä, *Sp* ryō'KHä), *n. Spanish.* a red or white wine produced in the Ebro valley in N. Spain.

ri·par·i·an (rīper'ēən, riper'ēən), *adj.* of, adjacent to, or living on the bank of a river or other body of water.

ri·poste (ripost'), *n.* a sharp, often witty response in speech or action. Also **ri·post'.**

rip·rap (rip'rap), *n.* broken stone, usually in flat pieces, used for constructing foundations, embankments, etc.

rip·tide (rip'tīd,), *n.* a tide opposing another tide or current thus causing a violent turbulence.

ris·i·ble (riz'əbəl, rī'zəbəl), *adj.* **1.** able or inclined to laugh. **2.** connected with laughing; laughable. —**ris,i·bil'i·ty,** *n.*

ri·sot·to (rizot'ō, risot'ō), *n.* (in Italian cookery) a rice dish cooked with broth and flavoured with grated cheese, etc.

ris·qué (riskā'), *adj.* close to being improper or indecent, as *a risqué joke.*

ris·sole (ris'ōl), *n.* a ball of minced cooked meat coated in egg and breadcrumbs and fried.

ris·so·lé (ris,ōlā'), *adj.* (in cooking) browned in deep fat.

riv·er·ine (riv'ərīn), *adj.* of, like, or near a river.

ri·viè·re (rivē'ə), *n.* a necklace, often in more than one strand, of diamonds or other precious stones.

RNA, any of the ribose-containing nucleic acids present in the cytoplasm of the cell. Also **ribonucleic acid, ribose nucleic acid.** See also **DNA.**

rob·o·rant (rob'ərənt), *adj.* tending to make stronger.

ro·bust (rōbust'), *adj.* strong, esp. in build and constitution; rugged.

ro·bus·tious (rōbus'СНəs), *adj.* rough; boisterous; coarse.

ro·caille (rokī'), *n.* rock, shell, and foliage forms combined with artificial shapes used for decorative effect in Rococo designs.

rock·a·bil·ly (rok'əbil,ē), *n.* a type of music resulting from a combination of rock-'n'-roll and hillbilly music.

rock-'n'-roll (rok,ənrōl'), *n.* a form of music characterized by a strong and regular beat, evolved in part from blues and folk music.

ro·co·co (rəkō'kō), *n.* **1.** a style of architecture and decoration developed in 18th-century France from the baroque and characterized by elaborate rocaille ornamentation. —*adj.* **2.** of or like a style of painting of this period characterized by smallness of scale, delicacy of colour, and playfulness of theme.

ro·den·ti·cide (rōden'tisīd), *n.* a poison used for killing rodents.

rod·o·mon·tade (rod,əmontäd', rod,əmon-tād'), *n.* arrant, arrogant boasting or braggadocio; ranting, blustering talk.

roent·gen (ront'gən, ront'yən, rent'gən, rent'-yən), *n.* a standard unit of radiation.

roent·gen·o·gram, rönt·gen·o·gram (ront'gənəgram,, ront'yənəgram,, rent'gənəgram, rent'yənəgram,), *n.* (old-fashioned) an x-ray photograph. Also **roent'gen·o·graph,, rönt'gen·o·graph,.**

roent·gen·ol·o·gy (ront,gənol'əjē, ront,yən-ol'əjē, rent,gənol'əjē, rent,yənol'əjē), *n.* the study and use of x-rays in diagnosis and therapy.

roent·gen·om·e·ter (ront,gənom'itə, ront,-yənom'itə, rent,gənom'itə, rent,yənom'itə), *n.* a device for measuring the intensity of x-rays.

roent·gen·o·paque (ront,gənōpāk', ront,-yənōpāk,, rent,gənōpāk,, rent,yənōpāk,), *adj.* radiopaque to x-rays.

roent·gen·o·par·ent (ront,gənōper'ənt, ront,yənōper'ənt, rent,gənōper'ənt, rent,-yənōper'ənt), *adj.* made visible by means of x-rays.

roent·gen·o·scope, rönt·gen·o·scope (ront'gənōskōp,, ront'yənōskōp,, rent'gənō-skōp,, rent'yənōskōp,), *n.* a fluoroscope.

roent·gen·o·ther·a·py (ront,gənōther'əpē, ront,yənōther'əpē, rent,gənōther'əpē, rent,yən-ōther'əpē), *n.* the treatment of disease by x-rays.

rog·a·to·ry (rog'ətərē), *adj.* concerning or denoting the process of asking or querying.

roil (roil), *v.* **1.** to cloud or muddy a liquid by stirring up sediment. **2.** to stir up; agitate; irritate.

roil·y (roi'lē), *adj.* muddy; turbid.

rois·ter (roi'stə), *v.* to boast or swagger; revel boisterously.

ro·man à clef (rōmä'nä klä'), *n., pl.* **ro·mans à clef** (rōmän'zä klä'). a novel in which the characters are real people disguised by fictitious names.

Ro·man·esque (rō,mənesk'), *adj.* designating the European style of architecture from the 9th to the 12th centuries, characterized by thick, load-bearing walls, round arches, the barrel vault, etc.

ron·deau (ron'dō), *n., pl.* **ron·deaux** (ron'dō, ron'dōz). a verse form with ten or thirteen lines and only two rhymes, in which the opening words are repeated as a refrain.

ron·dure (ron'dyŏŏə), *n.* a circle or sphere; roundness.

rönt·gen- See words beginning **roent·gen-.**

rood (rŏŏd), *n.* a crucifix, esp. one in a medieval church set over the entry to the chancel.

roor·back (rŏŏ'əbak), *n. U.S.* a report, usually of damaging effect, distributed for political reasons.

Roque·fort (rok'fō), *n.* a strong cheese veined with a bluish mould, made of sheep's or goat's milk and ripened in caves at Roquefort, in France.

ro·sa·ce·a (rōzā'sнēə), *n.* a form of acne characterized by red lesions on the face.

ro·sar·ium (rōzer'ēəm), *n., pl.* **ro·sar·i·ums, ro·sar·i·a** (rōzer'ēə). a rose garden.

ro·se·o·la (rōzē'ələ), *n.* **1.** a childhood illness marked by the eruption of a rose-coloured rash similar to that of measles. **2.** any rose-coloured rash.

ros·in (roz'in), *n.* the brittle, yellowish to amber residue left after oil has been distilled from turpentine; used for rubbing on violin bows and in making varnish, inks, soaps, etc.

ros·tel·late (ros'təlāt), *adj.* with a rostellum.

ros·tel·lum (rostel'om), *n., pl.* **ros·tel·la** (rostel'ə). a small, beaklike process or part.

ros·trum (ros'trəm), *n., pl.* **ros·tra** (ros'trə), **ros·trums.** any platform, stage, etc., for public speaking; a pulpit. —**ros'tral,** *adj.* —**ros'trate,** *adj.*

ro·ta·tive (rōtā'tiv), *adj.* turning on its own axis; rotating or causing rotation; occurring regularly in succession.

ro·te·none (rō'tənōn), *n.* a substitute for DDT. See also **malathion.**

ro·ti·form (rō'tifōm,), *adj.* shaped like a wheel.

rou·é (rŏŏ'ā), *n.* a dissipated man; debauchee; rake.

rou·lade (rŏŏläd'), *n.* a rolled slice of meat filled with chopped meat and cooked.

rou·leau (rŏŏ'lō), *n., pl.* **rou·leaux, rou·leaus**

(rōō'lōz). a roll of coins stacked in a paper wrapper.

roun·del (roun'dəl), *n.* something round or circular in form, as a disc.

roup (rōōp), *n.* hoarseness; huskiness. —**roup'y,** *adj.*

royal jelly, a nutritious mixture secreted by the pharyngeal glands of worker honeybees, fed to all larvae at first and then only to those chosen to be queens.

rub·bing (rub'ing), *n.* the reproduction of a raised design by laying paper on it and rubbing it with a pencil, crayon, charcoal, or the like. See also **frottage.**

ru·be·fa·cient (rōō,bəfā'sнənt), *adj.* causing redness, as of the skin.

ru·be·fac·tion (rōō,bəfak'sнən), *n.* the act or process of making red, as with a rubefacient.

ru·bel·la (rōōbel'ə), *n.* German measles.

ru·be·o·la (rōōbē'ələ), *n.* 1. measles. 2. (sometimes) German measles.

ru·bi·fy (rōō'bifī), *v.* to make red; redden.

ru·big·i·nous (rōōbij'ənəs), *adj.* rustcoloured; reddish-brown.

ru·bi·ous (rōō'bēəs), *adj.* ruby-coloured; red.

ru·bric (rōō'brik), *n.* 1. a title, heading, or other forematter of a book, legal document, etc., formerly printed in red but now usually set off in a distinctive typeface or in another manner. 2. any set of regulations for behaviour or procedure.

ru·bri·cate (rōō'brikāt), *v.* **ru·bri·cat·ed, ru·bri·cat·ing.** to print a title, heading, or other forematter in red. See also **red herring.**

ruc·tion (ruk'sнən), *n.* a noisy disturbance, quarrel, or uproar.

ru·der·al (rōō'dərəl), *adj.* (of a plant) growing in waste places, in rubbish, or along the wayside, etc.

ru·di·men·ta·ry (rōō,dimen'tərē), *adj.* basic, esp. in a crude way that is original and not elaborate.

rue (rōō), *v.* **rued, ru·ing.** to regret; be sorry about, as *You'll rue the day you defied me!*

ru·fes·cent (rōōfes'ənt), *adj.* having a red tinge; rufous.

ru·fous (rōō'fəs), *adj.* reddish; brownish-red; rust-coloured.

ru·ga (rōō'gə), *n., pl.* **ru·gae** (rōō'jē). a wrinkle, fold, or ridge.

ru·gate (rōō'gāt), *adj.* having wrinkles; rugose.

ru·gose (rōō'gōs), *adj.* wrinkled; ridged; ribbed.

ru·gu·lose (rōō'gyōōlōs), *adj.* having many small wrinkles; finely rugose.

ru·men (rōō'min), *n., pl.* **ru·mi·na** (rōō'minə). the first of the four stomachs of a ruminant. See also **reticulum, omasum, abomasum.**

ru·mi·nant (rōō'minənt), *n.* a hoofed mammal that chews its cud and has four stomachs, as the camel, cow, giraffe, etc.

ru·mi·nate (rōō'mināt), *v.* 1. to chew the cud, as a cow does. 2. to meditate; ponder. —**ru,mi·na'tion,** *n.*

run·ci·ble spoon (run'sibəl), a fork with two broad tines and one sharp tine, for serving hors d'oeuvres.

run·ci·nate (run'sinit), *adj.* irregularly sawtoothed, with the teeth curved back, as some leaves.

run·dle (run'dəl), *n.* 1. a rung of a ladder. 2. a rotating object, as a wheel or the drum of a capstan.

rune (rōōn), *n.* a character from an early medieval Indo-European alphabet. —**ru'nic,** *adj.*

run·nel (run'əl), *n.* a small stream, little brook or rivulet.

ruse (rōōz), *n.* a trick, esp. one leading into a trap.

rusk (rusk), *n.* a piece of sweet, raised bread dried and baked a second time until brown and crisp; zwieback.

rus·tic (rus'tik), *adj.* 1. like someone or something one is likely to find in the country; unsophisticated; crude in style or manner. —*n.* 2. a country bumpkin. —**rus·tic'i·ty,** *n.*

rus·ti·ca·te (rus'tikāt), *v.* 1. to go to or remain in the country. 2. to make or finish (a wall surface) in a rustic style. 3. to send down from a university or college for a given period as punishment. —**rus,ti·ca'tion,** *n.* —**rus·tic'ity,** *n.*

ruth (rōōth), *n.* pity or compassion; sorrow or remorse.

ruth·less (rōōth'lis), *adj.* pitiless; utterly without compassion or sympathy, as a *ruthless tyrant.* —**ruth'less·ness,** *n.*

rut·i·lant (rōō'tilənt), *adj.* glittering or glowing with reddish or golden light.

S

sa·bra (sä'brə), *n.* a native-born Israeli.

sab·u·lous (sab'yo͞oləs), *adj.* sandy; gravelly; gritty.

sac·cad·ic (sakä'dik), *adj.* jerky; twitching.

sac·cate (sak'āt), *adj.* saccular; having a sac.

sac·cha·rif·er·ous (sak,ərif'ərəs), *adj.* bearing sugar.

sac·cha·rim·e·ter (sak,ərim'itə), *n.* an optical instrument for measuring the concentration of sugar in a solution.

sac·cha·rim·e·try (sak,ərim'itrē), *n.* the measuring of sugar concentrations in substances.

sac·cha·rine (sak'ərin), *adj.* excessively or deceitfully sweet in facial expression or in speech.

sac·cha·rize (sak'ərīz), *v.* to convert into sugar.

sac·cha·rom·e·ter (sak,ərom'itə), *n.* a type of hydrometer used to measure the density of sugar solutions.

sac·cu·lar (sak'yo͞olə), *adj.* of saclike form; saccate.

sac·cu·late (sak'yo͞olāt), *adj.* having, or having the form of, a sac or saccule.

sac·cule (sak'yo͞ol), *n.* a small sac.

sac·cu·lus (sak'yo͞oləs), *n., pl.* **sac·cu·li** (sak'-yo͞olī). a saccule.

sac·er·do·tal (sas,ədō'təl), *adj.* of priests or priesthood; priestly.

sac·er·do·tal·ism (sas,ədō'təliz,əm), *n.* the system, practices, or principles underlying the priesthood.

sa·cral (sā'krəl), *adj.* of or relating to the sacrum.

sac·ra·ment (sak'rəmənt), *n.* **1.** the consecrated bread and wine of the Eucharist. **2.** something considered to have sacred or mysterious significance or influence. —**sac,ra·men'tal**, *adj.* —**sac,ra·men'tal·ist**, *n.*

sa·crar·i·um (sakrer'ēəm), *n., pl.* **sa·crar·i·a** (sakrer'ēə). **1.** a sanctuary; the most sacred part of a church, esp. the chancel. **2.** a place near the altar where holy water and similar materials are stored and disposed of; piscina. **3.** a shrine or sanctuary for containing sacred relics in a Roman temple.

sac·ri·lege (sak'rəlij), *n.* the act or an attitude of ignoring or of doing damage to something that is considered sacred. —**sac·ri·le·gious** (sak,rilij'-əs), *adj.*

sac·ris·tan (sak'ristən), *n.* an official keeper of the sacred vessels, etc., of a religious house or church. Also **sac'rist**.

sac·ris·ty (sak'ristē), *n.* the room or building where the sacred vessels and vestments of a church or religious house are kept.

sac·ro·il·i·ac (sak,rōil'ēak), *n.* the joint where the ilium joins the sacrum.

sac·ro·sanct (sak'rōsaNGkt), *adj.* secured by religious sanction against violation; especially sacred.

sac·ro·sci·at·ic (sak,rōsīat'ik), *adj.* relating to the sacrum and the ischium.

sa·crum (sā'krəm, sak'rəm), *n., pl.* **sac·ra** (sā'krə, sak'rə). a composite triangular bone consisting, in man, of five fused vertebrae, forming the posterior wall of the pelvic girdle.

SAD *Abbr. for* seasonal affective disorder: a form of depression associated with the winter months and possibly caused by insufficient exposure to sunlight.

sad·ism (sā'dizəm), *n.* **1.** a sexual perversion in which pleasure is derived from inflicting pain and humiliation. **2.** enjoyment in inflicting cruelty on others. See also **masochism**.

sa·do·mas·o·chism (sā,dōmas'əkiz,əm), *n.* a psychiatric disorder in which both sadism and masochism are exhibited.

sa·gac·i·ty (səgas'itē), *n.* acuteness of mind allied to practical wisdom. —**sa·ga'cious**, *adj.*

sage (sāj), *n.* **1.** a man of great wisdom. —*adj.* **2.** wise; of sound judgment.

sag·it·tal (saj'itəl), *adj.* relating to or resembling an arrow or arrowhead.

sag·it·tate (saj'itāt), *adj.* shaped like an arrowhead.

sa·ke (sak'ē), *n.* a Japanese fermented liquor made from rice.

sa·la·cious (səlā'sHəs), *adj.* lustful; lecherous; obscene.

sal·e·ra·tus (sal,ərā'təs), *n.* baking soda; sodium bicarbonate.

sa·li·ent (sā'lēənt), *adj.* **1.** conspicuous; most noticeable. **2.** jutting out; pointing outwards. —**sa'li·ence, sa'li·en·cy**, *n.*

sa·lif·er·ous (səlif'ərəs), *adj.* salt-bearing, as of rocks.

sal·i·fy (sal'ifī), *v.* to form into or combine with a salt.

sa·li·na (səlī'nə), *n.* a salt lake, spring, marsh, etc.; a saltworks.

sa·line (sā'līn), *adj.* containing, relating to, or resembling common salt.

sal·i·nom·e·ter (sal,inom'itə), *n.* an instrument for determinmg the concentration of salt in a solution. Also **sal·im'e·ter.**

sal·low (sal'ō), *adj.* of a sickly yellow or yellowish-brown colour.

sal·ma·gun·di (sal,məgun'dē), *n.* a mixture, a miscellaneous collection.

sal·mi (sal'mē), *n.* a highly seasoned dish of gamebirds partially roasted and then cut into pieces and stewed in wine and butter. Also **sal·mis** (sal'mē).

sal·mo·nel·la (sal,mənel'ə), *n., pl.* **sal·mo·nel·lae** (sal,mənel'ē). any of the large group of rod-shaped microorganisms of the genus *Salmonella* which cause many forms of enteritis, including food poisoning and typhoid fever, and hog cholera.

sal·pi·con (sal'pikən), *n.* any mixture of finely chopped meat, fish, poultry, or vegetables in a sauce. It is used for filling pastries, etc.

sal·pin·gi·tis (sal,pinjī'tis), *n.* inflammation of a Fallopian tube or Eustachian tube.

sal·pinx (sal'piNGks), *n., pl.* **sal·pin·ges** (salpin'jēz). a trumpet-shaped tube.

sal·tant (sal'tənt), *adj.* leaping; dancing; jumping.

sal·ta·tion (saltā'sHən), *n.* a leaping or jumping; a dancing movement; a sudden movement or change. —**sal·ta·tor·i·al** (sal,tətôr'ēəl), **sal·ta·tor·y** (sal'tətərē), *adj.*

salt·ern (sôl'tən), *n.* a saltworks; a series of pools made for the natural evaporation of sea water so as to produce salt.

sal·ti·grade (sal'tigrād), *adj.* moving by leaps.

salt·pe·tre (sôlt,pē'tə), *n.* a salt-like substance, the naturally occurring form of potassium nitrate, used chiefly in making gunpowder and fireworks. Also called **nitre.**

sa·lu·bri·ous (səlōō'brēəs), *adj.* promoting good health; health-giving.

sal·u·tar·y (sal'yōōtərē) *adj.* promoting good health; producing good effect.

sal·u·tif·er·ous (sal,yōōtif'ərəs), *adj.* salutary.

sam·iz·dat (sam'izdat), *n.* (in the former Soviet Union) an underground network publishing and disseminating dissident writings banned as subversive to the state.

san·a·tive (san'ətiv), *adj.* of or able to bring about healing.

sanc·ti·mo·ni·ous (saNGk,timō'nēəs), *adj.* with false righteousness; hypocritically pious. —**sanc'ti·mo,ny,** *n.*

sanc·tion (saNGk'sHən), *n.* **1.** something operating to enforce a rule of conduct, an oath, etc. **2.** action by states to bring about another state's compliance with an international law or agreement, as by withholding economic aid, reducing

trade, etc. **3.** the confirmation or approval of an action.

sanc·tion·a·tive (saNGk'sHənā,tiv), *adj.* relating to or tending towards sanction.

sanc·ti·tude (saNGk'tityōōd), *n.* saintliness; sacred character.

sanc·tum (saNGk'təm), *n., pl.* **sanc·tums, sanc·ta** (saNGkt'ə). a holy place; a person's private retreat, as a study.

sang·froid (saNGfrwä'), *n.* composure; calmness in face of danger or annoyance.

san·gri·a (saNGgrē'ə), *n.* an iced drink made from diluted red wine mixed with sugar, spices, and sometimes fruit juices.

san·guic·o·lous (saNGgwik'ələs), *adj.* living in the blood.

san·guif·er·ous (saNGgwif'ərəs), *adj.* blood-carrying, as an artery.

san·gui·fi·ca·tion (saNG,gwifikā'sHən), *n.* the formation of blood corpuscles; haematopoiesis.

san·gui·nar·y (saNG'gwinər'ē), *adj.* full of or delighting in bloodshed; bloody; bloodthirsty.

san·guine (saNG'gwin), *adj.* **1.** of cheerful and courageous disposition. **2.** blood-red; of reddish colour.

san·guin·e·ous (saNGgwin'ēəs), *adj.* containing or of the colour of blood. Also **san'gui·nous.**

san·guin·o·lent (saNGgwin'ələnt), *adj.* containing or of the colour of blood. Also **san'gui·nous.**

san·guiv·or·ous (saNGgwiv'ərəs), *adj.* blood-eating; feeding of blood.

sa·ni·es (sā'niēz), *n.* a watery fluid, often of greenish colour, discharged from a wound or open sore. —**sa'ni·ous,** *adj.*

sans-cu·lotte (sanz'kyōōlot'), *n.* a person of extreme republican views; a revolutionary.

sans gêne (sänzhen'), *French.* without regard for conventional forms; free of restraint or embarrassment.

sans sou·ci (sänsōōsē'), *French.* without care; carefree; unconcerned.

sa·phe·nous (səfē'nəs), *adj.* of, relating to, or in the region of a saphenous vein.

saphenous vein, either of two large superficial veins running up the foot, leg, and thigh, one on the inner side and one on the outer side. Also **sa·phe'na.**

sap·id (sap'id), *adj.* tasty; savoury; palatable.

sa·pi·ent (sā'pēənt), *adj.* wise; of fancied wisdom.

sa·pi·en·tial (sā'pēen'sHəl), *adj.* containing or characterized by wisdom.

sap·o·dil·la (sap,ədil'ə), *n.* a large evergreen tree native to tropical America, yielding chicle and bearing edible fruit.

sap·o·na·ceous (sap,ənā'sHəs), *adj.* of, resembling, or containing soap.

sa·pon·i·fy (səpon'ifī), *v.* to convert fat or oil into soap by boiling it with an alkali.

sa·por (sā'pə, sā'pô), *n.* the taste of a substance; that property of a substance that effects the sense of taste; the sensation of taste.

sap·o·rif·ic (sap,ərif'ik), *adj.* giving flavour.

sa·po·rous (sā'pərəs), *adj.* flavoursome; tasty.

Sap·phic (saf'ik), *adj.* **1.** describing a form of lyric poetry, named after the ancient Greek poetess Sappho of Lesbos, in four-line stanzas with caesuras after the fifth syllable of each of the first three lines. **2.** of or relating to Sappho. **3.** lesbian.

sa·pre·mi·a (səprē'mēə), *n.* a type of blood poisoning.

sap·ro·gen·ic (sap'rōjen'ik), *adj.* causing putrefaction.

sa·proph·a·gous (saprof'əgəs), *adj.* feeding on dead or decaying organic matter.

sap·ro·phyte (sap'rōfīt), *n.* any organism living on decayed organic matter. —**sap·ro·phyt'ic,** *adj.*

sar·co·ad·e·no·ma (sä,kōad,ənō,mə), *n.,* *pl.* **sar·co·ad·e·no·mas, sar·co·ad·e·no·ma·ta** (sä,-kōad,ənō'mətə). See **adenosarcoma.**

sar·co·car·ci·no·ma (sä,'kōkä,sinō'mə), *n.,* *pl.* **sar·co·car·ci·no·mas, sar·co·car·ci·no·ma·ta** (sä,kōkä,sinō'mətə). See **carcinosarcoma.**

sar·coid (sä'koid), *n.* **1.** a sarcoma-like growth. **2.** sarcoidosis or one of the lesions caused by it. —*adj.* **3.** fleshy; flesh-like.

sar·coid·o·sis (sä,koidō'sis), *n.* a disease characterized by the appearance of minute grainy, inflamed, ulcerating protuberances in the lungs and liver and less often in the kidneys, bones, eyes, on the skin, etc.

sar·co·lem·ma (sä,kōlem'ə), *n.,* *pl.* **sar·co·lem·mas, sar·co·lem·ma·ta** (sä,kōlem'ətə). the thin sheath of membrane around a muscle fibre.

sar·co·ma (säkō'mə), *n.,* *pl.* **sar·co·mas, sar·co·ma·ta** (säkō'mətə). a variety of malignant growth that arises in bones and in the connective tissues lying beneath the skin and between and around muscles and organs.

sar·co·ma·to·sis (säkō,mətō'sis), *n.* a condition characterized by the development of large numbers of sarcomas throughout the body.

sar·coph·a·gous (säkof'əgəs), *adj.* living on flesh; carnivorous.

sar·coph·a·gus (säkof'əgəs), *n.,* *pl.* **sar·coph·a·gi** (säkof'əjī). **1.** a coffin made of stone, usually with inscriptions, reliefs, etc. **2.** a stone thought by the ancient Greeks to consume the remains of corpses.

sar·co·phile (sä'kōfīl,), *n.* any flesh-eating creature.

sar·cous (sä'kəs), *adj.* composed of or relating to flesh or skeletal muscle.

sar·don·ic (sädon'ik), *adj.* of bitter or scornful character.

sar·men·tose (sämen'tōs), *adj.* (in botany) having runners, as a strawberry. Also **sar·men'·tous.**

sar·men·tum (sämen'təm), *n.,* *pl.* **sar·men·ta** (sämen'tə). a stem put out along the ground from the base of a plant, as in the strawberry. Also **sar'ment.**

sa·ros (ser'os, sā'ros), *n.* the period of years after which eclipses are repeated but are 120° towards the west from the previous series, equivalent to 233 synodic months or 6585.32 days.

sar·tor·i·al (sätōr'ēəl), *adj.* of or relating to dress, esp. to men's clothing.

sa·ti·e·ty (səti'ətē, sā'sHēitē), *n.* the state of having had too much; a surfeit.

sat·is·fice (sat'isfīs,), *v.* to satisfy (conditions or requirements) to the minimum acceptable level. —**sat'is·fi,cer,** *n.*

sa·trap (sat'rap), *n.* a subordinate ruler, esp. one enjoying great luxury or practising tyranny. —**sa'tra·py,** *n.*

sat·u·rate (saCH'ərāt, sat'yŏŏrāt), *v.* **1.** to cause a substance to combine with or dissolve the maximum quantity it can of another substance. **2.** to cause to absorb or hold the maximum possible amount of anything, as electric charge, moisture, etc. **3.** to bomb a target so heavily that defences are powerless and the target is completely destroyed.

sat·u·rat·ed (saCH'ərā,tid, sat'yŏŏrā,tid), *adj.* (of fats) containing no double bonds and so unable to accept any additional atoms of hydrogen; such fats, which are hard at room temperature, raise the level of cholesterol in the blood. See also **monounsaturated, polyunsaturated.**

sat·ur·na·li·a (sat,ənə'lēə, sat,ûnä'lēə), *n.,* *pl.* **sat·ur·na·li·a, sat·ur·na·li·as.** a period or scene of wild revelry.

Sa·tur·ni·an (satû'nēən), *adj.* prosperous and peaceful, as in the supposedly golden age of Saturn's reign.

sat·ur·nine (sat'ənīn), *adj.* **1.** of cold, gloomy, sluggish temperament or of an appearance suggesting such a temperament. **2.** of, suffering from, or resulting from lead poisoning.

sat·y·ri·a·sis (sat,irī'əsis), *n.* abnormally excessive and uncontrollable sexual desire in males. See also **nymphomania.**

sat·y·ro·ma·ni·ac (sat,irōmā'nēak), *n.* a lustful man.

sau·ri·an (sô'rēən), *adj.* **1.** belonging to or relating to a group of reptiles that includes the lizards. **2.** lizard-like.

sau·té (sō'tā, sô'tā), *adj.* **1.** lightly browned by being fried in oil or fat over heat. —*v.* **sau·téed, sau·té·ing. 2.** to cook by frying in a small amount of fat or oil over heat.

sau·toir (sō'twä, sô'twä), *n.* **1.** a chain, scarf, ribbon, etc., fastened around the neck with the ends crossing at the front. **2.** a chain or ribbon bearing a pendant for wearing around the neck.

sauve qui peut (sōv kē pû'), *French.* a disorderly flight in which everyone looks only to his own safety; every man for himself.

sa·van·na (səvan'ə), *n.* a great plain, esp. in subtropical regions, of coarse grasses and scattered trees and having seasonal rainfall.

sa·vant (sav'ənt), *n.* a man of great learning.

save-all (sāv'ôl,), *n.* any device or means for stopping loss or reducing waste.

sa·voir-faire (sav,wäfe'ə), *n.* the quality of seeing and doing the right thing in any situation.

sa·voir-vi·vre (sav'wävē'vrə), *n.* the quality of knowing the ways of and being at home in polite society.

sa·vour (sā'və) *n.* **1.** a distinctive taste, smell, or quality; that part of any substance that affects the sense of taste or smell. —*v.* **2.** to perceive or appreciate the taste or smell of something.

saw·yer (sô'yə), *n.* a man who makes his living by sawing timber.

sax·a·tile (sak'sətil), *adj.* living or growing on rocks or in rocky places.

sax·ic·o·line (saksik'ōlīn), *adj.* living or growing in rocky places. Also **sax·ic'o·lous.**

sca·bi·cide (skā'bisīd), *adj.* of any substance used or able to destroy the parasitic mite that causes scabies.

sca·bies (skā'bēz), *n.* a contagious skin disease caused by a parasitic mite burrowing under the skin, occurring in cattle, sheep, and man.

sca·bi·ous (skā'bēəs), adj. composed of or covered with scabs; relating to or like scabies.

scab·rous (skab'rəs), *adj.* **1.** having a surface covered with tiny projections. **2.** full of difficulties. **3.** obscene; indecent.

sca·lar (skā'lə), *n.* a mathematical quantity that has only magnitude. See also **vector.**

sca·lene (skā'lēn, skālēn'), *adj.* (of a triangle) with no two sides equal.

sca·le·no·he·dron (skālē,nōhē'drən), *n.*, *pl.* sca·le·no·he·drons, sca·le·no·he·dra (skālē,- nōhē'drə). a solid with 8 or 12 faces, each one of which forms a scalene triangle.

scal·pri·form (skal'prifôm,), *adj.* chisel-shaped.

scam (skam), a confidence game; a swindle, often elaborately staged and managed.

scan·dent (skan'dənt), *adj.* of climbing habit, as a plant.

scan·sion (skan'sHən), *n.* **1.** analysis of the metre of a verse. **2.** the metrical structure of a verse.

scan·so·ri·al (skansôr'ēəl), *adj.* (in zoology) adapted for climbing; given to climbing.

scaph·oid (skaf'oid), *adj.* shaped like a boat.

scap·u·lar (skap'yo͞olə), *adj.* of or relating to the shoulders.

scap·u·lo·hu·me·ral (skap,yo͞olōhyo͞o'mə-rəl), *adj.* of or relating to the shoulder blade (scapula) and the bone of the upper arm (humerus).

scarce·ment (skers'mənt), *n.* a ledge or foothold formed in a wall by one portion being set back from the rest.

scar·i·fy (skar'ifī), *v.* to make superficial cuts or scratches; to wound with harsh words. —**scar,i·fi·ca'tion, scar'i·fi·ca,tor,** *n.*

scar·i·ous (sker'ēəs), *adj.* dry, papery, and membranous, as a grass bract.

scar·la·ti·na (skä,lətē'nə), *n.* scarlet fever. —**scar·la·ti'noid,** *adj.*

scarlet fever, a contagious disease caused by streptococci and characterized by a scarlet rash on the skin and in the mouth and throat.

scarp (skäp), *n.* a line of cliffs or steeply sloping ground formed by a fracture and vertical separation in the earth's crust; escarpment.

scathe (skāTH), *v.* **1.** to injure, esp. by fire. **2.** to hurt by invective or satire.

scath·ing (skā'THiNG), *adj.* harshly severe, as criticism.

sca·tol·o·gy (skətol'əjē), *n.* **1.** the study of or excessive interest in excrement or obscenity. **2.** the study of fossil excrement. Also called **coprology.**

sca·to·ma (skətō'mə), *n.*, *pl.* sca·to·mas, sca·to·ma·ta (skətō'mətə). a tumour-like mass of faeces in the rectum or large intestine.

sca·toph·a·gy (skətof'əjē) *n.* the religious practice of or psychiatric disorder characterized by eating excrement. —**sca·toph'a·gous,** *adj.*

sca·tos·co·py (skətos'kəpē), *n.* the medical examination of faeces to diagnose certain conditions.

scat singing, singing, usually in jazz, in which the singer improvises nonsense words to fit the music and also makes sounds in imitation of musical instruments.

scau·per (skô'pə), *n.* an engraving tool with a flattened or hollowed blade. Also **scorper.**

scend, send (send), *v.* scends, scend·ing, scend·ded, sends, send·ing, sent. **1.** (of a vessel) to rise on a large wave. —*n.* **2.** the upward movement of a vessel owing to a wave.

sce·nog·ra·phy (sēnog'rəfē), *n.* the graphic representation of objects following the rules of perspective.

scep·tic (skep'tik), *n.* a person who doubts the truth or validity of something. —**scep'ti·cal,** *adj.*

Scha·den·freu·de (sHä'dənfroi'də), *n.* cynical glee at the misfortune of another.

sche·ma (skē'mə), *n.*, *pl.* sche·ma·ta (skē'mətə, skēmätə). a diagram; an outline; a scheme.

schism (siz,əm), *n.* a separation into opposing groups because of a difference of opinion; a group formed by the separation. —**schis·mat'ic,** *adj.*

schis·to·sis (sHistō'sis), *n.* fibrosis of the lungs owing to prolonged inhalation of slate dust.

schis·to·some (sHis'tōsōm), *n.* a type of

blood-fluke, including the parasite that causes bilharzia.

schis·to·so·mi·a·sis (sʜɪs,tōsōmī'əsis), *n.* any of several serious illnesses caused by infestation with parasitic blood-flukes.

schiz·o·gen·e·sis (skit,sōjen'isis, skizōjen'isis, skī,zōjen'isis), *n.* reproduction by the splitting of cells. —**schiz,o·ge·net'ic, schi·zog'e·nous,** *adj.*

schiz·oid (skit'soid), *adj.* of, resembling, having, or tending towards schizophrenia.

schiz·o·phre·ni·a (skit,sōfrē'nēə), *n.* a severe mental illness, often recurring and sometimes progressive, in which the behaviour becomes withdrawn and out of character, the intellect and emotions deteriorate, and hallucinations may occur. —**schiz,o·phren'ic,** *adj.*

schiz·o·phyte (skit'sōfīt,), *n.* any of a group of plants characterized by reproduction by cell-splitting.

schiz·o·thy·mi·a (skit,sōthī'mēə), *n.* the exhibiting of the features that distinguish schizophrenia but within normal limits.

schle·maz·zle, schle·ma·zel (sʜlamä'zəl), *n. Slang.* a particularly stupid and awkward person.

schle·miel, schle·mihl (sʜləmēl'), *n. Slang.* a poor fool who is always the victim of others.

schlepp (sʜlep), *v. Slang.* to drag about, esp. unnecessarily or burdensomely.

schlie·ren (sʜlēr'ən), *n. pl.* **1.** streaks in a fluid having a density and index of refraction different from that fluid. **2.** streaks of differently coloured or textured rock in an igneous rock.

schlock (sʜlok), *adj. Slang.* cheap and trashy. Also **schlock'y.**

schmaltz (sʜmälts), *n. Slang.* exaggerated, sickly sentimentality. —**schmaltz'y,** *adj.*

schneck·en (sʜnek'ən), *n. pl., sing.* **schnecke.** sweet rolls of snail-like spiral shape made from raised dough mixed with chopped nuts, cinnamon, and butter.

schnor·rer (sʜnôr'ə), *n. Slang.* a beggar; a sponger.

scho·li·ast (skō'lēast), *n.* any of the ancient grammarians who wrote explanatory comments on passages in a classical author's work.

schuss (sʜoōs, sʜoōs), *n. Slang.* **1.** a run directly down the steepest line of a slope with no attempt to control speed. —*v.* **2.** to perform a schuss.

sci·am·a·chy (sīam'əkē), *n.* the act of or an instance of fighting an imaginary foe. Also **sci·om'a·chy.**

sci·at·ic (sīat'ik), *adj.* of, relating to, near, or affecting the ischium or lowest part of the pelvic girdle where it connects with the hip.

sci·at·i·ca (sīat'ikə), *n.* pain and soreness in parts of or near the sciatic nerve, which runs from the pelvis down the back of the leg to the foot.

sci·en·tial (sīen'sʜəl), *adj.* of, relating to, or having knowledge.

sci·en·tism (sī'əntiz,əm), *n.* the belief that the methods applicable to physics and biology are equally appropriate to all other disciplines including the humanities and social sciences.

scil·i·cet (sil'iset), *adv.* namely; that is to say.

scin·tig·ra·phy (sin,tig'rəfē), *n.* (in medicine) a technique for producing an image (*scintigram*) of body tissue by detecting and recording the levels of radiation emitted following administration of a radioactive substance to the patient.

scin·til·la (sintil'ə), *n.* a spark, shred, or minute particle, as *not a scintilla of evidence.*

scin·til·late (sin'tilāt), *v.* to give out sparks; to sparkle; to twinkle. —**scin'til·lant,** *adj.* —**scin,·til·la'tion,** *n.*

sci·o·lism (sī'əlizəm), *n.* superficial knowledge.

sci·o·man·cy (sī'əman,sē), *n.* foretelling the future with the assistance of ghosts. —**sci'o·man,cer,** *n.* —**sci,o·man'tic,** *adj.*

sci·on (sī'ən), *n.* a child, esp. an heir; any offshoot, as a twig.

sci·os·o·phy (sīos'əfē), *n.* knowledge of natural or supernatural phenomena based on astrology, phrenology, or the like.

scir·rhus (sir'əs), *n., pl.* **scir·rhi** (sir'ī), **scir·rhus·es.** a hard, painless tumour; a hard cancer.

scis·sel (sis'əl), *n.* the metal strip from which coin blanks have been cut.

scis·sile (sis'il), *adj.* capable of being cut or split.

scis·sion (sizʜ'ən), *n.* a cutting; a division; a split.

sci·u·roid (sī'yŏoroid, sīyŏor'oid), *adj.* resembling a squirrel's tail.

scle·ra (sklēə'rə), *n.* the tough protective membrane that encloses the eyeball. —**scle·ral** (sklēə'rəl), *adj.*

scle·re·ma (sklirē'mə), *n.* hardening or sclerosis, esp. affecting the skin.

scle·ro·der·ma (sklēr,ōdû'mə), *n.* a disease causing all the layers of skin to harden and become rigid. Also **scle·ri·a·sis** (sklərī'əsis).

scle·ro·der·ma·ti·tis (sklēr,ōdû,mətī'tis), *n.* a disease causing hardening and inflammation of the skin. Also **scle,ro·der·mi'tis.**

scle·ro·der·ma·tous (sklēr,ōdû'mətəs), *adj.* having a covering of hardened tissue such as scales.

scle·rog·e·nous (skliroj'ənəs), *adj.* giving rise to hardened tissue.

scle·roid (sklēr'oid), *adj.* hard or hardened.

scle·ro·ma (sklirō'mə), *n., pl.* **scle·ro·mas, scle·ro·ma·ta** (sklirō'mətə). a tumour-like mass of hardened tissue.

scle·rom·e·ter (sklirom'ətə), *n.* any device for making an accurate measure of the hardness of a substance.

scle·ro·phyl·ly (sklĕrofˈilē), *n.* a normal development in foliage which results in it becoming thickened and hardened. —**scle'ro·phyll,**, *adj., n.*

scle·rosed (sklirŏst'), *adj.* thickened or hardened by sclerosis.

scle·ro·sis (sklirōˈsis), *n., pl.* **scle·ro·ses** (sklirōˈsēz). the replacement of normal tissue by increased fibrous or supporting tissue, with a resulting thickening and hardening leading to loss of function. —**scle·rot'ic,** *adj.*

scle·ro·ti·tis (sklĕr,ətīˈtis), *n.* inflammation of the sclera, the external covering of the eyeball. Also **scle·ri'tis.**

scle·rous (sklĕrˈəs), *adj.* hard; thick; firm; bony.

scoff·law (skofˈlô,), *n. Chiefly U.S.* one who shows contempt for the law in word or deed.

sco·li·o·sis (skō,lēōˈsis), *n.* sideways curvature of the spine.

sco·pol·a·mine (skōpolˈəmēn, skōpolˈəmin), *n.* a drug used chiefly to increase the effect of narcotics in bringing about twilight sleep, as a sedative, and to produce dilatation of the pupil of the eye.

sco·po·phil·i·a (skō,pōfilˈēə), *n.* a psychiatric disorder in which sexual gratification is obtained exclusively by looking at nude bodies, erotic photographs, and the like.

scop·u·late (skopˈyōōlāt), *adj.* broom-like; in the shape of a brush.

scor·bu·tic (skôbyōōˈtik), *adj.* of, relating to, resembling, or affected with scurvy.

score (skôr), *n.* twenty in number, as *She gave him a score of examples.*

scor·per (skôˈpə), *n.* See **scauper.**

scor·pi·oid (skôˈpēoid), *adj.* curved back on itself at the end, like the tail of a scorpion.

scotch (skoCH), *v.* to wound without killing so as to render harmless.

sco·to·ma (skotōˈmə), *n., pl.* **sco·to·mas,** **sco·to·ma·ta** (skotōˈmətə). a loss of sight affecting only part of the visual field; a blind spot.

sco·to·pi·a (skətōˈpēə, skōtōˈpēə), *n.* the ability to see in dim light. See also **photopia.**

scourge (skûj), *n.* **1.** a whip for chastising or torturing; a person or thing administering punishment or harsh criticism. **2.** that which brings about addiction or disaster. —*v.* **3.** to whip.

screed (skrēd), *n.* **1.** a long and tedious letter, essay, discourse, or the like. **2.** a wooden or metal strip for levelling a concrete or similar surface as it is made.

scrim (skrim), *n.* **1.** a thin cotton or linen open-weave fabric resembling fine canvas. **2.** a piece of thin fabric used as a stage drop to appear solid when lit from the front and almost transparent when lit from behind.

scrim·shaw (skrimˈSHÔ), *n.* **1.** the craft of carving or engraving whalebone, ivory, shells,

etc., esp. as practised by sailors. **2.** an article produced in this way, or such articles collectively. —*v.* **3.** to carve or engrave such articles.

scro·bic·u·late (skrēbikˈyəlāt), *adj.* having a furrowed or pitted surface.

scro·fu·la (skrofˈyōōlə), *n.* a name formerly used for a tubercular condition characterized by swelling and degeneration of the lymphatic glands and joints. —**scrof'u·lous,** *adj.*

scru·ple (skrōōˈpəl), *n.* a unit used in measuring very small weights, equal to 20 grains or ⅓rd dram.

scru·ta·ble (skrōōˈtəbəl), *adj.* able to be understood after detailed examination or study.

sculp·sit (skulpˈsit), *Latin.* (this person) carved, sculptured, or engraved (this work).

scum·ble (skumˈbəl), *v.* **1.** to lay a thin coat of opaque or semiopaque colour over parts of a painted area with an almost dry brush to soften the colour or line. —*n.* **2.** an effect so achieved.

scun·ner (skunˈə), *n.* a dislike taken with no reason.

scurf (skûf), *n.* any scaly incrustation on a surface. —**scurf'y,** *adj.*

scur·ri·lous (skurˈiləs), *adj.* grossly or obscenely abusive. —**scur·ril'i·ty,** *n.*

scu·tate (skyōōˈtāt), *adj.* having the form of or furnished with a scute or scutes.

scute (skyōōt), *n.* an oblong or round bony or horny plate or large scale forming a defensive covering in creatures such as crocodiles and turtles.

scu·tel·late (skyōōtelˈāt), *adj.* having the form of or furnished with scutes or scutella. —**scu,tel·la'tion,** *n.*

scu·tel·li·form (skyōōtelˈifôm), *adj.* scutellum-shaped.

scu·tel·lum (skyōōtelˈəm), *n., pl.* **scu·tel·la** (skyōōtelˈə). a small plate, scale, or shield-like part.

scu·ti·form (skyōōˈtifôm,), *adj.* shield-shaped.

scu·tum (skyōōˈtəm), *n., pl.* **scu·ta** (skyōōˈtə). a scute.

scy·phate (sīˈfāt), *adj.* cup-shaped.

scy·phi·form (sīˈfifôm,), *adj.* having the shape of a cup or goblet.

scy·pho·zo·an (sī,fōzōˈən), *n.* any animal of the class comprising the jellyfishes.

scy·phus (sīˈfəs), *n., pl.* **scy·phi** (sīˈfī). a cup-shaped part.

sea·dog (sēˈdog,), *n.* See **fogbow.**

sea eagle, any of various large species of eagle that feed mainly on fish.

sea·mount (sēˈmount,), *n.* an underwater mountain reaching a height of several hundred feet above the sea bed but with its peak well below sea level.

seam·y (sēˈmē), *adj.* **seam·i·er,** **seam·i·est.** nasty; morally base, as *the seamier parts of the city.*

se·ba·ceous (sibā'sнəs), *adj*. relating to, resembling, or of the same nature as tallow or fat; fatty.

se·bif·er·ous (sibif'ərəs), *adj*. containing or secreting fat or fatty matter.

seb·or·rhoe·a (sebərēə), *n*. excessive or otherwise abnormal secretion by the sebaceous glands. —**seb,or·rhoe'ic**, *adj*.

se·cern (sisûn'), *v*. to distinguish or be distinguished in thought.

se·cern·ent (sisû'nənt), *adj*. secreting.

se·clu·sive (siklōō'siv), *adj*. tending to retire into privacy.

sec·o·bar·bi·tone (sek,ōbä'bitōn), *n*. a sedative and hypnotic drug.

secondary boycott, a boycott operated by members of a union against their employer intended to force him to exercise his influence on another employer who is in dispute with members of the same union.

se·cret·a·gogue (sikrēt'əgog), *n*. a substance, such as a hormone or drug, that stimulates or enhances secretion. —**se·cret,a·gog'ic**, *adj*.

se·cre·tive (sē'kritiv, sikrē'tiv), *adj*. tending to hide things from others; stealthy. —**se'cre·tive·ness**, *n*.

se·cre·to·ry (sikrē'tərē), *adj*. relating to or capable of secretion.

sec·tile (sek'tīl), *adj*. that can be cut easily with a knife.

sec·tor·i·al (sektôr'ēəl), *adj*. adapted for cutting, esp. of a carnivore's tooth.

sec·u·lar (sek'yŏŏlə), *adj*. of or relating to the things of this world; lay; temporal, as opposed to sacred, spiritual, and religious. —**sec'u·lar·ism, sec,u·lar'i·ty**, *n*.

sec·u·lar·ize (sek'yŏŏlərīz), *v*. to separate from religious or spiritual controls or connections.

sed·en·tar·y (sed'əntərē), *adj*. sitting; characterized by or requiring a sitting position.

se·de·runt (sidēə'rənt), *n*. **1**. a sitting of an ecclesiastical court, assembly, etc. **2**. the list of persons attending such a sitting.

sed·i·men·tol·o·gy (sed,imentol'əjē), *n*. the scientific study of rocks formed of consolidated sediment.

se·di·tion (sidisн'ən), *n*. any incitement to unlawful action against the authority of government. —**se·di'tious**, *adj*.

sed·u·lous (sed'ŏŏləs, sej'ŏŏləs), *adj*. diligent and persevering; persistently and unremittingly kept up. —**se·du'li·ty**, *n*.

se·gue (seg'wā), *v*. to continue without interruption or blend in with the next part or item, usually of a musical performance.

sei·cen·to (sācнen'tō), *n*. the sixteen hundreds, that is, the 17th century, referring esp. to the art or literature of Italy at that time.

seiche (sāsн), *n*. sudden oscillation in the surface of a lake or other large stretch of water caused occasionally by changes in atmospheric pressure, wind direction, earth tremor, etc.

seism (sī'zəm), *n*. an earthquake. —**seis'mic**, *adj*.

seis·mic·i·ty (sīzmis'itē), *n*. the factors in a given area that relate to earthquakes, including frequency of occurrence, force, distribution, etc.

seis·mism (sīz'miz,əm), *n*. the natural phenomena associated with an earthquake.

seis·mo·gram (sīz'məgram,), *n*. a record made by a seismograph.

seis·mo·graph (sīz'məgräf,, sīz'məgraf,), *n*. an instrument for recording and measuring tremors in the earth's crust.

seis·mog·ra·phy (sīzmog'rəfē), *n*. the recording and measuring of earthquake tremors. —**seis·mog'ra·pher**, *n*.

seis·mol·o·gy (sīzmol'əjē), *n*. the scientific study of earthquakes and the natural phenomena associated with them.

seis·mom·e·ter (sīzmom'itə), *n*. a type of seismograph that measures the actual movement of ground during an earthquake and records the direction, duration, and force of the movement.

seis·mo·scope (sīz'məskōp,), *n*. an instrument that records earthquake activity.

se·le·nod·e·sy (sē,lənod'əsē), *n*. the branch of astronomy concerned with measuring the surface of the moon and its gravitational field.

se·le·no·dont (silē'nədont), *adj*. having crescent-shaped ridges on the crowns of the teeth.

se·le·nog·ra·phy (sē,lənog'rəfē), *n*. the branch of astronomy concerned with the physical geography of the moon and the irregularities of its surface.

sel·e·nol·o·gy (sel,ənol'əjē), *n*. the branch of astronomy concerned with the physical characteristics of the moon and the origin of its surface features.

se·le·no·tro·pism (silē,nōtrō'piz,əm), *n*. a response, such as growth or movement, to the stimulus of moonlight.

self-ef·fac·ing (self'ifā'siNG), *adj*. putting oneself down, esp. because of humility. —**self'-ef·face'ment**, *n*.

sel·vage (sel'vij), *n*. the edge of fabric woven so that the weft will not ravel, and often different from the weave of the rest of the fabric.

se·man·tics (siman'tiks), *n*. **1**. the branch of linguistics concerned with meanings. **2**. See general semantics. —**se·man'tic**, *adj*.

se·ma·si·ol·o·gy (simā,sēol'əjē), *n*. the branch of linguistics concerned with meanings and their changes.

se·mat·ic (simat'ik), *adj*. giving warning to enemies or attracting attention, as the markings of poisonous animals.

sem·a·tol·o·gy (sem,ətol'əjē), *n*. semantics.

sem·i·ab·stract (sem,ēab'strakt), *adj.* relating to or denoting a style of art in which the representation is not naturalistic but the subject remains recognizable.

sem·i·breve (sem'ēbrēv,), *n.* (in musical notation) a whole note; the longest note in general use, equal to half the length of a breve.

sem·i·cen·ten·ni·al (sem,ēsenten'ēəl), *adj.* 1. of or relating to a 50th anniversary. —*n.* 2. a 50th anniversary. Also **sem·i·cen·te·na·ry** (sem,-isentē'nərē).

sem·i·con·duc·tor (sem,ēkənduk'tə, sem'-ēkənduk,tə), *n.* a material, used in integrated circuits, whose conductivity is less than that of a metal and more than that of an insulator.

sem·i·de·tached (sem,ēditacнt'), *adj.* of or relating to a house joined to another by a party wall on one side.

sem·i·di·ur·nal (sem,ēdīū'nəl), *adj.* relating to, consisting of, or taking half a day; occurring once in each 12 hours.

sem·i·fi·nal (sem,ēfīn'əl), *adj.* of or relating to the round preceding the final in a contest whose losers are eliminated. —**sem,i·fi'nal·ist**, *n.*

sem·i·nal (sem'inəl), *adj.* 1. that originates something, as an idea, a style, etc., and influences future development. 2. containing, composed of, or relating to semen.

sem·i·na·tion (sem,inā'sнən), *n.* a sowing of, impregnation with, or spreading of seed.

sem·i·nif·er·ous (sem,inif'ərəs), *adj.* containing, carrying, or producing seed or semen.

sem·i·niv·or·ous (sem,iniv'ərəs), *adj.* seed-eating, as certain birds.

se·mi·ol·o·gy (sē,mēol'əjē), *n.* the study of or a system of signs. Also **se,mei·ol'o·gy.**

se·mi·ot·ic (sē,mēot'ik), *adj.* 1. relating to signs. 2. of or relating to medical symptoms. —*n.* 3. Also **semiotics.** a comprehensive philosophical theory of signs and languages.

sem·i·o·vip·a·rous (sem,iōvip'ərəs), *adj.* bearing partially developed young, as the kangaroo.

sem·i·palm·ate (sem,ipam'āt), *adj.* partially palmate; half-webbed, as the feet of certain birds.

sem·pi·ter·nal (sem,pitū'nəl), *adj.* everlasting; eternal. —**sem,pi·ter'nal·ly**, *adv.* —**sem·pi·ter·ni·ty** (sem,pitū'nitē), *n.*

se·na·ry (sē'nərē), *adj.* of or relating to the number six.

se·nes·cent (sines'ənt), *adj.* ageing; becoming old.

sen·e·schal (sen'isнəl), *n.* a steward in charge of all domestic arrangements and order in a great medieval household.

sen·sate (sen'sāt), *adj.* endowed with or perceived by physical sensation.

sen·si·bil·i·a (sen,sibil'ēə), *n.* that which is able to be sensed.

sen·sil·lum (sensil'əm), *n., pl.* **sen·sil·la** (sensil'ə). a simple sense organ composed of one or a small number of cells at the end of a sensory nerve fibre.

sen·so·ri·mo·tor (sen,sərimō'tə), *adj.* of, having, or relating to both sensory and motor functions or parts; of or relating to motor activity in response to a sensory stimulus.

sen·sor·i·um (sensôr'ēəm), *n., pl.* **sen·so·ri·ums, sen·so·ri·a** (sensôr'ēə). the brain, or a particular part of it, regarded as the seat of all sensation.

sen·so·ry (sen'sərē), *adj.* of or relating to sensation or the senses; of a bodily structure, esp. a nerve, that conveys impulses that cause sensation.

sen·ten·tious (senten'sнəs), *adj.* full of pithily expressed truths; given to self-righteous moralizing.

sen·tience (sen'sнəns, sen'sнēəns, sen'tēəns), *n.* the power of or capacity for perception through the senses. —**sen'tient**, *adj.*

sen·tient (sen'sнənt, sen'sнēənt, sen'tēənt), *adj.* able to use the senses to perceive or feel things, as *a sentient being.*

se·pal (sep'əl, sē'pəl), *n.* one of the small, often green, leaf-like parts covering the buds of certain flowers and forming the outermost ring when the flower has opened.

se·pal·oid (sē'pəloid, sep'əloid), *adj.* like a sepal.

sep·a·ra·trix (sep,ərā'triks), *n., pl.* **sep·a·ra·tri·ces** (sep,ərā'trisēz), **sep·a·ra·trix·es.** something that separates or marks off one part from another, as a line, decimal point, punctuation mark, etc.

sep·sis (sep'sis), *n.* the condition of having, the location of, or the presence of dead and decomposing tissue caused by bacterial infection.

sept (sept), *n.* a group of people who believe themselves to be descended from a common ancestor.

sep·tal (sep'təl), *adj.* of or relating to a septum.

sep·tate (sep'tāt), *adj.* having a septum or septa.

sep·tem·vir (septem'vər), *n., pl.* **sep·tem·virs, sep·tem·vi·ri** (septem'varī). one of a ruling body of seven men. —**sep·tem'vi·ral**, *adj.*

sep·tem·vi·rate (septem'vərit), *n.* a ruling body composed of seven men.

sep·te·nar·y (septē'nərē), *adj.* 1. of, relating to, or based on the number seven. 2. septennial. —*n.* 3. a group or set of seven.

sep·ten·de·cil·lion (sep,tendisil'ēən), *n.* 1. (in Britain, France, and Germany) the number represented by the figure 1 followed by 102 zeros. 2. (in the U.S.A. and Canada) the number represented by the figure 1 followed by 54 zeros.

sep·ten·ni·al (septen'ēəl), *adj.* of, for, or every seven years.

sep·ten·tri·o·nal (septen'trēənəl), *adj.* northern. See also **meridional.**

sept·foil (sept'foil,), *n.* a seven-lobed ornament or decorative motif.

sep·tic (sep'tik), *adj.* relating to, of the nature of, or infected by sepsis.

sep·ti·cae·mi·a (sep,tise'mēə), *n.* the spread of septic matter through the blood; blood poisoning.

sep·til·li·on (septil'ēən), *n.* **1.** (in Britain, France, and Germany) the number represented by the figure 1 followed by 42 zeros. **2.** (in the U.S.A. and Canada) the number represented by the figure 1 followed by 24 zeros. British name: **quadrillion.**

sep·tu·a·ge·nar·i·an (sep,tyōōəjəner'ēən), *adj.* **1.** aged between 70 and 79 years. —*n.* **2.** a person of this age.

sep·tum (sep'təm), *n., pl.* **sep·ta** (sep'tə). a dividing wall, partition, layer, membrane, etc., as between the nostrils, the ventricles of the heart, etc.

sep·ul·chre (sep'əlkə), *n.* a tomb or burial place, esp. one cut in rock or made of stone. —**se·pul'chral,** *adj.*

sep·ul·ture (sep'əlcHə), *n.* burial; the placing of a body in a sepulchre.

se·qua·cious (sikwā'sHəs), *adj.* following smoothly or logically; coherent.

se·que·la (sikwē'lə), *n., pl.* **se·que·lae** (sikwē'lē). any abnormal condition present as a result of some disease.

se·quent (sē'kwənt), *adj.* **1.** following; following logically or as a matter of course. **2.** in continuous succession; consecutive.

se·ques·ter (sikwes'tə), *v.* to put into solitude; to seclude. —**se,ques·tra'tion,** *n.*

se·ques·trec·to·my (sek,westrek'təmē), *n.* the surgical removal of dead splinters or pieces, esp. of bone.

se·ques·trum (sikwes'trəm), *n., pl.* **se·ques·tra** (sikwes'trə). a bone fragment that has died through disease or injury and separated from the normal bone.

se·ra·gli·o (sərä'lyō,), *n., pl.* **se·ra·gli·os. 1.** the harem of a Muslim palace or household. **2.** a sultan's palace. Also **se·rail** (sərī', sərīl', sərāl'), *pl.* **se·rails.**

sere (sē'ə), *n.* the succession of changes in the composition of a plant population from the initial colonization by plants to the final state of vegetation.

se·rein (sərān'), *n.* a fine rain falling after sunset from an apparently cloudless sky.

ser·en·dip·i·ty (ser,əndip'itē), *n.* the faculty of accidentally making fortunate discoveries. —**ser,en·dip'i·tous,** *adj.*

se·rene (sərēn'), *adj.* calm and peaceful. —**se·ren·i·ty** (sər:en'itē), *n.*

se·ri·al·ism (sē'riəliz,əm), *n.* a style of musical composition, originating in the 20th century, that is based thematically on a fixed but arbitrary sequence of notes instead of orthodox keys. —**se'ri·al·ist,** *n.*

se·ri·ate (sēr'it), *adj.* in series.

se·ri·a·tim (sēr,ēa'tim), *adv.* singly in succession; one after another.

se·ri·ceous (sirisH'əs), *adj.* silky; with a covering of silky down. Also **ser'i·cate.**

ser·i·cul·ture (ser'ikul,cHə), *n.* silkworm-breeding to produce raw silk.

ser·i·graph (ser'igräf,, ser'igraf,), *n.* a print made by the silk-screen process.

se·ri·o·com·ic (sē,rēōkom'ik), *adj.* partly serious and partly comic.

ser·o·con·vert (sēr,ōkənvût'), *v.* (of an organism or individual) to produce antibodies in response to the presence in the blood of a particular foreign antigen, such as a virus or bacterium. —**se,ro·con·ver'sion,** *n.*

se·rol·o·gy (sirol'əjē), *n.* the scientific study of the constitution, properties, and functions of blood, esp. of blood serum.

se·ro·mu·cous (sēr'ōmyōō'kəs), *adj.* relating to or consisting of serum and mucus.

ser·o·pos·i·tive (sēr,ōpoz'itiv), *adj.* giving a positive result to serological tests, as with a person undergoing tests for the presence in the blood of antibodies to a particular pathogen, such as a virus.

se·ro·si·tis (sē,rōsī'tis), *n.* inflammation of one of the thin membranes that line certain body cavities and exude a serous fluid.

se·ro·ther·a·py (sēr,ōther'əpē), *n.* medical treatment by injections of a serum from an immune animal or person.

se·ro·ti·nal (sē,rōtī'nəl), *adj.* in or relating to late summer.

ser·o·tine (ser'ətīn), *adj.* late in occurring or achieving full development, esp. of late-flowering plants.

ser·o·to·nin (ser,ətō'nin), *n.* a compound crystalline substance that occurs in the brain, intestines, and platelets, and brings about narrowing of blood vessels and contraction of muscles.

se·rous (sēr'əs), *adj.* **1.** serum-like. **2.** of, containing, producing, or relating to serum.

ser·pi·go (səpī'gō), *n.* any spreading skin disease.

ser·rate (ser'āt), *adj.* having a notched edge like a saw, used esp. of leaves. —**ser·ra'tion,** *n.*

ser·ri·form (ser'ifôm,), *adj.* notched like the edge of a saw.

ser·ru·late (ser'yōōlāt), *adj.* with finely toothed edges. —**ser,ru·la'tion,** *n.*

ser·ry (ser'ē), *v.* to crowd together closely.

se·rum (sēr'əm), *n., pl.* **se·rums, se·ra** (sēr'ə). **1.** the clear yellow fluid that remains when blood has clotted. **2.** such fluid obtained from an animal immune to some disease and used as an antitoxic or therapeutic agent against that disease. **3.** the portion of milk left after removal of butterfat, casein, and albumin, or after cheesemaking.

ser·vi·ette (sû,vēet'), *n.* a table napkin.

ser·vile (sû'vīl), *adj.* **1.** of, relating to, or characteristic of a slave or base person. **2.** characterized by fawning flattery and hypocritical praise. —**ser·vil'i·ty,** *n.*

ser·vo·mech·an·ism (sû'vōmek,əniz,əm), *n.* a closed-cycle electronic control system in which a large-output mechanism is actuated and controlled by a small-input signal, as the movement of a gun turret by a small knob.

ses·qui·cen·ten·ni·al (ses'kwisenten'ēəl), *adj.* relating to or celebrating a 150th anniversary.

ses·qui·pe·da·li·an (ses'kwipidā'lēən), *adj.* given to the use of words containing many syllables.

ses·sile (ses'īl), *adj.* fixed and stationary, as certain animals or cells.

ses·tet (sestet'), *n.* a group of six musical performers; a piece of music for such a group.

se·ta (sē'tə), *n.*, *pl.* **se·tae** (sētē). a bristle or bristle-like process.

se·ta·ceous (sitā'sHəs), *adj.* having or resembling bristles. Also **se·ti·form** (sē'tifôm,).

se·tig·er·ous (sitij'ərəs), *adj.* bearing bristles or bristle-like processes.

se·tose (sē'tōs), *adj.* having or covered with setae.

set·u·la (set'yōōlə), *n.*, *pl.* **set·u·lae** (set'yōōlē). a short, blunt bristle or bristle-like process.

set·u·lose (set'yōōlōs), *adj.* having or covered with setulae.

sève (sev), *n. French.* the distinctive fineness and strength of flavouring of a particular wine.

seven deadly sins. See **deadly sins.**

sev·er (sev'ə), *v.* to cut so as to separate; discontinue, as *to sever a relationship or bond.*

sev·er·al·ty (sev'rəltē), *n.*, *pl.* **sev·er·al·ties.** **1.** (in law) ownership or possession of a property by one person, rather than jointly with others. **2.** property, esp. land, held in this way. **3.** the state or condition of being several.

sex·a·ge·nar·i·an (sek'səjənər'ēən), *adj.* **1.** aged between 60 and 69 years. —*n.* **2.** a person of this age.

sex·ag·e·nar·y (seksaj'ənərē), *adj.* of or relating to or based on the number 60.

sex·a·ges·i·mal (sek,səjes'iməl), *adj.* relating to or based on the number 60.

sex·cen·te·na·ry (sek,sentē'nərē), *adj.* **1.** relating to the number 600 or a period of 600 years; celebrating a 600th anniversary. —*n.* **2.** a 600th anniversary; the celebration of a 600th anniversary.

sex·de·cil·li·on (seks,disil'ēən), *n.* **1.** (in Britain, France, and Germany) the number repre-

sented by the figure 1 followed by 96 zeros. **2.** (in the U.S.A. and Canada) the number represented by the figure 1 followed by 51 zeros.

sex·e·na·ry (seksē'nərē), *adj.* **1.** of or relating to the number 6. **2.** consisting of six parts. **3.** based on the number 6.

sex·en·ni·al (seksen'ēəl), *adj.* of, for, or every 6 years.

sex·ol·o·gy (seksol'əjē), *n.* the scientific study of sexual behaviour.

sex·tan (seks'tən), *adj.* (of a fever) recurring every fifth (or by inclusive reckoning sixth) day. See also **tertian, quartan, quintan.**

sex·til·li·on (sekstil'ēən), *n.* **1.** (in Britain, France, and Germany) the number represented by the figure 1 followed by 36 zeros. **2.** (in the U.S.A. and Canada) the number represented by the figure 1 followed by 21 zeros.

shad·dock (sHad'ək), *n.* the largest citrus fruit, that of the tree *Citrus grandis*, with pale-yellow skin and edible flesh of a lighter colour, esp. the larger, coarser, pear-shaped varieties, the smaller, rounder varieties being known as grapefruit.

shadow cabinet, (in the British Parliament) the appointees made by the leadership of the nonincumbent party to posts of responsibility corresponding to those of the cabinet of the party in power.

sha·green (sHəgrēn'), *n.* **1.** a kind of untanned leather with a rough grainy surface made from the skin of a horse, ass, seal, shark, etc., and often dyed green. **2.** the rough skin of certain sharks, rays, etc., covered with minute hard protuberances and used as an abrasive.

sham·an (sHam'ən, sHā'mən, sHä'mən), *n.* a priest and witch doctor exercising supposed powers over the supernatural in the primitive religion of northern Asia or any similar religion. —**sham'an·ism,** *n.*

shan·dy (sHan'dē), *n.* a drink of mixed beer and lemonade.

shan·dy·gaff (sHan'dēgaf), *n.* a drink of mixed beer and ginger beer.

shan·tung (sHan,tuNG'), *n.* a soft, heavy, usually undyed fabric of thick strands of raw silk; a cotton or rayon imitation of such fabric. See also **pongee.**

shan·ty, chant·ey (sHan'tē), *n.* a song sung by sailors at work.

shash·lik (sHasH'lik, sHäsHlik'), *n.* a dish of cubed, seasoned meat broiled or roasted on a skewer. Also **shish kebab.**

sherd (sHäd), *n.* **1.** a piece of broken earthenware. **2.** a scale or shell. **3.** the hard wing-case of a beetle. Also **shard.**

shib·bo·leth (sHib'ələth), *n.* **1.** a password or favourite phrase of a party or sect. **2.** a word, opinion, style of dress, way of behaving, etc., peculiar to and distinguishing one type or group of persons.

shin·gles (SHING'gəlz), *n.*, *sing.* and *pl.* a virus infection of the nerves of the skin causing a rash of clustering blisters and severe pain. Also **herpes zoster, zoster.**

ship biscuit. See **hardtack.**

shirr (SHû), *v.* **1.** to gather fabric or the like with three or more parallel threads. **2.** to bake, esp. eggs, in a shallow dish.

shish ke·bab (SHiSH, kəbab', SHēSH,). See **shashlik.**

shiv·a·ree (SHi,vərē). See **charivari.**

shock therapy, a method of psychiatric treatment by injecting drugs or administering electric or icepack shocks so as to induce convulsions that are usually followed by coma.

shod·dy (SHod'ē), *adj.* **shod·di·er, shod·di·est.** of bad quality, either in material or workmanship, as *shoddy draperies* or *shoddy carpentry.*

sho·gun (SHō'gōōn), *n.* (in Japan) one of the medieval military commanders who later (till 1867) became hereditary military dictators who treated the emperor as a puppet.

short·com·ing (SHôt'kəm,iNG), *n.* an undesirable characteristic or flaw; a failure to come up to an expected level or standard.

shot-peen (SHot'pēn), *v.* to bombard (steel) with hard steel shot so as to increase its durability.

shrive (SHrīv), *v.* **1.** to assign a penance. **2.** to absolve; to grant absolution.

shun (SHun), *v.* **shunned, shun·ning.** to keep away from; avoid.

shut·tle·cock (SHut'əlkok,), *n.* any idea, object, or person pushed back and forth between opposing parties or sides, as *The refugees' plight became a political shuttlecock.*

shy·lock (SHī'lok), *v. U.S. Slang.* to lend money at exorbitant interest rates.

si·a·lad·e·ni·tis (Sī'əlad'ənī'tis), *n.* inflammation of one or more salivary glands.

si·al·o·gogue (sīal'əgog, sī'aləgog,), *n.* something, as a food or drug, that stimulates the production of saliva. —**si·al·a·gog·ic** (sī,aləgoj'-ik), *adj., n.*

si·a·loid (sī'əloid), *adj.* saliva-like.

si·am·oise (sē'amoz'), *n.* an S-shaped sofa.

sib (sib), *adj.* **1.** related by blood. —*n.* **2.** a blood relative. **3.** a group descended through either the male line only or the female line only.

sib·i·lant (sib'ilənt), *adj.* of or denoting any speech sound with some resemblance to a hiss, as *s, sh, z,* etc.

sib·i·late (sib'ilāt), *v.* to hiss.

sib·ling (sib'liNG), *n.* a brother or sister; any child of the same two parents.

sic·ca·tive (sik'ətiv), *adj.* having drying properties; inducing or encouraging the absorption of moisture.

sickle cell, a red blood corpuscle with an abnormal shape, often like a sickle, because it contains abnormal haemoglobin.

sic tran·sit glor·i·a mun·di (sik tran'sit glôr'ēə mun'dē), *Latin.* thus passes away earthly glory.

side (sīd), *n.* the assumption of superiority; an affected manner; impudence.

side·man (sīd'man,), *n.* one who plays an instrument in a band or orchestra.

si·de·re·al (sīdēr'ēəl), *adj.* of, relating to, or determined by the stars.

sid·er·og·ra·phy (sidərog'rəfē), *n.* the technique or art of making steel engravings.

si·der·o·lite (sī'dərōlīt,), *n.* a meteorite composed of approximately half iron and half stone-like material.

si·der·o·phile (sī'dərōfīl,), *adj.* with an affinity for iron.

si·der·o·scope (sī'dərōskōp,), *n.* a device for finding iron or steel splinters in the eye.

si·der·o·sis (sī,dərō'sis), *n.* a lung disease caused by the inhalation of particles of iron or of some other material.

si·der·o·stat (sī'dərōstat,), *n.* an instrument for keeping the light from a star in a constant direction as viewed through a telescope, by using a mirror and clock mechanism to correct for the earth's rotation. See also **coelostat.**

sie·mens (sē'mənz), *n.* a unit used in measuring electrical conductance, equal to one mho. *Abbrev.:* **S.**

si·en·na (sēen'ə), *n.* earth containing iron or iron rust used as a pigment of either yellowish-brown or reddish-brown colour according to whether it is raw or has been roasted in a furnace.

si·er·ra (sēer'ə), *n.* a continuous range of mountains or high hills with jagged peaks projecting like the teeth of a saw esp. in America or Spain.

sie·vert (sē'vət), *n.* the SI unit of dose equivalent, equal to 1 J kg^{-1}. *Symbol:* **Sv.**

sig·il (sij'il), *n.* a small seal, sometimes one set in a finger ring.

sig·il·late (sij'ilāt), *n.* with stamped decorations or markings suggesting sigil-like impressions.

sig·la (sig'lə), *n.* a list of symbols and special characters used in a book.

sig·ma·tism (sig'mətiz,əm), *n.* a speech defect in which sibilant sounds cannot be pronounced or are mispronounced.

sig·moid (sig'moid), *adj.* crescent- or S-shaped.

sig·nal·ment (sig'nəlmənt), *n.* a description in detail of a person's features for identification, esp. by police.

sig·nif·ics (signif'iks), *n.* semantics.

si·lage (sī'lij), *n.* green fodder for animals preserved without drying in a cylindrical structure above ground or a pit in the ground.

si·li·ceous (silisн'əs), *adj.* containing, composed of, or like silica.

sil·i·cif·er·ous (sil,isif'ərəs) *n.* containing or yielding silica.

si·lic·i·fy (silis'ifī), *v.* to convert or be converted into silica.

sil·i·cle (sil'ikəl), *n.* a short silique.

sil·i·co·sis (sil,ikō'sis), *n.* a chronic lung disease caused by the prolonged inhalation of siliceous rock dust, affecting stonecutters, coal miners, etc.

si·lic·u·lose (silik'yŏolōs), *adj.* bearing or resembling a silicle.

si·lique (silēk'), *n.* a long, pod-like two-valved seed vessel.

sil·i·quose (sil'ikwōs), *adj.* bearing siliques; having the appearance of a silique or silicle. Also **sil·i·quous** (sil'ikwəs).

silkscreen process, a technique for making prints by rolling a squeegee over a tightly stretched screen of silk or similar material so as to force colour through the mesh of portions not previously sized with glue.

sil·la·bub (sil'əbub), *n.* See **syllabub.**

sil·vic·o·lous (silvik'ələs), *adj.* belonging to a woodland habitat; growing in or inhabiting woodland.

sil·vi·cul·ture (sil'vikul,cнə), *n.* forestry; the growing and tending of forest trees.

sim·i·an (sim'ēən), *adj.* of, relating to, resembling, or characteristic of apes and monkeys.

sim·i·le (sim'ilē), *n.* a figure of speech explicitly comparing two apparently unlike things for the purpose of creating a heightened effect of emphasizing a particular feature, as *He ran like the wind.*

si·mil·i·tude (simil'ityŏod), *n.* **1.** likeness, as *their similitude of dress.* **2.** a facsimile; that which bears a likeness to another, as *He is a similitude of his father.* **3.** a guise; a semblance, as *It was given a similitude of legality.* **4.** a simile, comparison, or allegory, as *He illustrated it by similitudes.*

si·mo·ni·ac (simō'nēak), *n.* one who practises simony.

si·mo·ny (sī'mənē), *n.* the act or practice of trading in sacred things.

sim·pat·i·co (simpat'ikō, simpä'tikō), *adj.* agreeable by virtue of being in sympathy with ideas, manner, personality, etc.

sim·plex (sim'pleks), *adj.* simple; consisting of one substance, part, action, etc.

sim·plism (sim'plizəm), *n.* oversimplification; the act or practice of choosing to regard, treat, or seize on only one aspect of something more complex.

sim·plis·tic (simplis'tik), *adj.* characterized by simplism.

sim·u·la·crum (sim,yŏolä'krəm), *n.*, *pl.* **sim·u·la·cra** (sim,yŏolä'krə). a supposed, superficial, or deceptive likeness or semblance.

sim·u·lant (sim'yŏolənt), *adj.* imitating; pretending.

sim·u·late (sim'yŏolāt), *v.* **sim·u·lat·ed, sim·u·lat·ing. 1.** to imitate or make something look or seem like something else, as *to simulate sorrow* or *to simulate a natural process in a laboratory.* **2.** to copy; pretend that something fake is real, as *simulated pearls.*

si·mul·cast (sī'məlkäst,), *n.* a broadcast transmitted on television and radio at the same time.

sin·e·cure (sin'əkyŏo,ə, sī'nəkyŏo,ə), *n.* an office yielding honour or profit but entailing few or no duties.

si·ne di·e (sī'nē dī'ē, sin'ē di'ē), *Latin.* without a day having been set for resumption; indefinitely, as *The meeting was adjourned sine die.*

sin·e qua non (sin,ē kwä non', sē,nē, sē,nā, sī,nē kwä, nōn'), *Latin.* an indispensable requirement; an essential condition, as *His agreement was the sine qua non of the plan's being put into operation.*

sin·gul·tus (siNGul'təs), *n.* a hiccup.

sin·is·ter (sin'istə), *adj.* **1.** threatening; of evil omen or appearance; wicked; unfavourable. **2.** on or relating to the left side.

sin·is·trad (sin'istrad), *adv.* to the left; leftwards; sinistrally.

sin·is·tral (sin'istrəl), *adj.* **1.** of, relating to, or on the left. **2.** left-handed. **—sin,is·tral'i·ty, sin,-is·tra'tion, —sin'is·tral·ly,** *adv.*

sin·is·troc·u·lar (sin,istrok'yŏolə), *adj.* using the left eye rather than the right. See also **dex-trocular. —sin,is·troc,u·lar'i·ty,** *n.*

sin·is·tro·dex·tral (sin'istrōdeks'trəl), *adj.* moving from left to right.

sin·is·tro·gy·ra·tion (sin'istrō'jīrā'sнən), *n.* the turning to the left of the plane of polarization of a ray of polarized light, as caused by certain chemical substances. Also called **levorotation.**

sin·i·strorse (sin'istrôs, sinis'trôs), *adj.* with whorls rising to the left as viewed from inside the spiral, as in certain stems and shells. See also **dextrorse.**

sin·is·trous (sin'istrəs), *adj.* **1.** sinister; unfavourable; disastrous. **2.** sinistral.

sin·u·ate (sin'yŏoāt), *adj.* bending in and out; wavy; sinuous.

sin·u·a·tion (sin'yŏoā'sнən), *n.* waviness; a bend.

sin·u·os·i·ty (sin,yŏoos'itē), *n.* a curve or bend; sinuousness.

sin·u·ous (sin'yŏoəs), *adj.* with many bends or curves. **—sin'u·ous·ness,** *n.*

si·nus (sī'nəs), *n.* **1.** a curving portion; a curved recess. **2.** a bend or curve. **3.** any cavity, recess, or passage in the bone or tissue of the body, as one of the cavities in the bone of the skull connecting with the nostrils.

si·nus·i·tis (sīnəsī'tis), *n.* inflammation of a sinus, usually of those connecting with the nostrils.

sip·id (sip'id), *adj.* with a pleasing taste, flavour, or character.

sip·pet (sip'it), *n.* a small piece; a piece of bread for dipping in gravy, milk, or other liquid food; a crouton.

si·re·ni·an (sīrē'nēən), *n.* any large, aquatic, vegetarian mammal of the order that includes manatees, dugongs, and seacows.

si·ren·ic (sīren'ik), *adj.* of or characteristic of a siren; melodious; irresistibly tempting; dangerously alluring.

si·ri·a·sis (sirī'əsis), *n.* sunstroke.

Sis·y·phe·an (sis,ifē'ən), *adj.* **1.** of or relating to Sisyphus, in Greek mythology a king of Corinth whose punishment in Hades was forever to roll a heavy boulder uphill only for it to roll back to the bottom of the hill each time. **2.** describing any endless and futile task.

si·tol·o·gy (sītol'əjē), *n.* the medical field of study concerned with nutrition and dietetics.

si·to·ma·ni·a (sī,tōmā'nēə), *n.* an abnormal or neurotic craving for food.

si·to·pho·bi·a (sītəfō'bēə), *n.* an abnormal or neurotic aversion to food.

sit·u·a·tion·ism (siCH,ōō̃ā'sHəniz,əm, sit,yōō-ā'sHəniz,əm), *n.* a theory of psychology that behaviour is mainly the result of response to an immediate situation.

si·tus (sī'təs), *n.*, *pl.* **si·tus.** position; the original or proper position.

sitz·krieg (sits'krēg, zits'krēg), *n.* warfare in which action is almost at a standstill and frequently stalemated.

skep (skep), *n.* a wicker or wooden basket or hamper, as frequently used on farms.

skew·bald (skyōō'bōld,), *adj.* **1.** marked with white spots or patches on a background usually of brown, but not black. —*n.* **2.** a skewbald animal, esp. a horse.

ski·a·graph (skī'əgräf,, skī'əgraf,), *n.* a photograph made by the exposure of a sensitive film or plate to x-rays passed through an object; shadowgraph.

ski·a·scope (skī'əskōp,), *n.* an instrument for testing the refractive power of the eye by reflecting light onto it from a mirror and observing the movement of the shadow across the pupil. Also **retinoscope.**

ski·jor·ing (skējôr'iNG, skē'jôr,iNG), *n.* a sport in which a skier is towed, usually by a horse or horse-drawn vehicle.

skim·ble·scam·ble (skim'bəlskam'bəl), *adj.* jumbled; rambling; absurd.

skin·tle (skin'təl), *v.* to build unevenly with bricks and mortar so as to create a picturesque effect.

skip·dent (skip'dent), *n.* an open weave appearance given to a fabric by not fixing some of the warp ends (the precise ones depending on the effect desired) to the loom, so that they are not held taut during the weaving.

skip·pet (skip'it), *n.* a small, round, wooden box to preserve a seal affixed to a document, or to protect sealed documents.

skive (skīv), *v.* to split or pare into layers, esp. leather.

skul·dug·ger·y (skul,dug'ərē), *n.* dishonourable conduct; underhanded or rascally trickery.

skulk (skulk), *v.* **1.** to lurk or avoid observation, esp. with sinister or cowardly motive. **2.** to move stealthily.

slake (slāk), *v.* **1.** to relieve or diminish by satisfying, as thirst, desire, etc. **2.** to cool or freshen, as *She slaked his fevered brow with a cold, damp cloth.*

sla·lom (slä'ləm), *n.* a downhill ski race with a zig-zag course between artificial obstacles such as poles or gates.

slat·tern (slat'ən), *n.* a slut; a slovenly or immoral woman; a prostitute.

slav·er (slav'ə), *v.* to let saliva trickle from the mouth; to slobber.

slav·oc·ra·cy (slāvok'rəsē), *n.* government or domination by slaveholders.

sleave (slēv), *v.* **1.** to separate a thread into filaments. —*n.* **2.** anything ravelled or entangled.

slea·zy (slē'zē), *adj.* of thin or poor texture; flimsy.

sleeping sickness, 1. a disease, often fatal, characterized by fever, weight loss, and extreme lethargy, prevalent in parts of W. and S. Africa and caused by a parasite transmitted by the bite of a tsetse fly; African trypanosomiasis. **2.** a virus disease causing inflammation of the brain accompanied by drowsiness, apathy, muscular degeneration, and impairment of vision; encephalitis lethargica.

slew (slōō), *n.* a great many.

sliv·o·vitz (sliv'əvits, slē'vəvits), *n.* plum brandy, esp. from eastern Europe.

sloe (slō), *n.* the fruit of the blackthorn, small, ovate, bluish black, and with a sour taste.

slough (slou), *n.* **1.** a swamp, a muddy area. **2.** (sluf) an outer layer of skin shed periodically, as by a snake, etc.; layer of dead tissue cast off from the surface of a wound, ulcer, etc. —*v.* (sluf) **3.** to cast off or be cast off, as a slough.

slov·en (sluv'ən), *n.* a person who is habitually slipshod or negligent in appearance, behaviour, or work.

slov·en·ly (sluv'ənlē), *adj.* carelessly sloppy in dress, workmanship, etc.

slub·ber (slub'ə), v. to do hastily and without due care.

slue (slo͞o), v. **slued, slu·ing.** to swing around, esp. wildly.

slum·gul·li·on (slum,gul'ēən), n. **1.** a dish of stewed meat and vegetables. **2.** any weak, watered-down soup or beverage.

slur·ry (slur'ē), n. a suspension consisting of particles of a solid in a liquid, esp. a watery mixture of clay used in ceramic work for decoration, etc.

slur·vi·an (slû'vēən), adj. of or related to slurred speech. —**slur'vi·an·ism,** n.

smack (smak), n. Slang. heroin.

small-scale (smôl'skāl'), adj. small in relation to the original, as of a map, model, or other representation.

smarm·y (smä'mē), adj. **smarm·i·er, smarm·i·est.** fulsomely flattering, ingratiating, or fawning.

smaze (smāz), n. smoke and haze mingled together.

smeg·ma (smeg'mə), n. a thick, sebaceous secretion collecting around the clitoris in females or under the foreskin of the penis in males.

smog (smog), n. a manifestation of air pollution, seen as a haze, esp. in urban areas.

smug (smug), adj. self-satisfied; happy with one's own superiority in many matters. —**smug'ly,** adv. —**smug'ness,** n.

smutch (smuCH), v. **1.** to smudge, dirty, or stain. —n. **2.** a smudge or stain.

snail·ing (snā'liNG), n. a spiralling or circular pattern made on watch or clock parts by means of abrasive discs.

sniff·ish (snif'isH), adj. contemptuous; disdainful.

snol·ly·gos·ter (snol'ēgos,tə), n. Colloquial. a clever, unprincipled person.

snoop·er·scope (sno͞o'pəskōp,), n. a device that allows one to detect objects in the dark by transmitting infrared rays which are reflected if they strike a solid object, received by the device, and formed into an image on a fluorescent screen.

snor·kel (snô'kəl), n. **1.** a funnel-like device on submarines consisting of tubes reaching above the water to take in air and expel foul air and fuel exhaust so that the submarine can remain below water for long periods. **2.** a tube held in the mouth by persons swimming just below the surface of the water and reaching above the water to permit breathing.

snow (snō), n. Colloquial. cocaine or heroin.

snow·bird (snō'bûd,), n. Colloquial. a person addicted to cocaine or heroin.

snow blindness, a dimming of vision, usually temporary, caused by the glare of sun on snow. Also **niphablepsia.**

snow·blink (snō'bliNGk), n. a white brilliance on the bottom of clouds caused by light reflected up from a snow-covered surface. See also **ice-blink.**

snow bunny, a woman who frequents ski resorts in the hope of meeting men.

so·a·ve (sōä'vä), n. a dry, white wine from the district round Verona, Italy.

so·bri·quet (sō'brəkā), n. a nickname. Also **soubriquet.**

Social Democratic party, any of several political parties of continental Europe that advocate a gradual change by democratic processes to socialism or a system approaching it.

social disease, a disease that is spread by close contact of people, esp. a venereal disease.

so·cial·ism (sō'sHəliz,əm), n. the organization of society so that the community as a whole owns and controls all sources of wealth and means of production and distribution.

social pathology, any feature of society which tends to disorganize it or inhibit normal development in its members, as poverty, crime, unemployment, etc.

social science, any of several sciences, or fields of study treated scientifically, concerned with an aspect of society, as politics, economics, anthropology, etc.

so·ci·o·ge·net·ic (sō,sHēōjənet'ik, sō,sēōjənet'ik), adj. relating to or affecting social development.

so·ci·o·gen·ic (sō,sHēōjen'ik, sō,sēōjen'ik), adj. having its origin in or being affected by social factors.

so·ci·ol·o·gism (sō,sHēol'əjiz,əm, sō,sēol'əjiz,əm), n. an interpretation, notion, etc., in the context of social factors and esp. emphasizing social factors to the exclusion of other factors concerned. —**so,ci·ol·o·gis'tic,** adj.

so·ci·om·e·try (sō,sHēom'ətrē, sō,sēom'ətrē), n. the measurement of social attitude by means of preferences expressed by members of the society.

so·ci·o·path (sō'sHēəpath,, sō'sēəpath,), n. one who is hostile to society.

Socratic method, a method of instruction and inquiry in which a series of questions is posed so as to develop a latent idea in a pupil or lead an opponent to make admissions that tend to establish the proposition he opposes.

so·dal·i·ty (sōdal'itē), n. **1.** companionship; comradeship. **2.** a guild, association, or society.

sodium ben·zo·ate (ben'zōāt), a chemical used mainly as a food preservative and also as an antiseptic.

sodium bicarbonate, a chemical used mainly in making baking powder, soft drinks, and sodium salts, and as an antacid and a fire extinguisher.

sodium carbonate, 1. soda ash, a chemical used in making glass, soaps, paper, petroleum, and as a cleanser and bleach. **2.** common washing soda, the decahydrated form of sodium carbonate.

sodium citrate, a chemical used in the manufacture of soft drinks, in photography, and as a blood anticoagulant.

sodium cyc·la·mate (sī'kləmāt), a chemical once used (but now banned in the U.S.) as a sweetening agent, esp. in low-calorie foodstuffs.

sodium fluoride, a chemical used in water fluoridation and for killing insects and rodents.

sodium glutamate. See **monosodium glutamate.**

sod·om·y (sod'əmē), n. unnatural, esp. anal, sexual intercourse with a man, woman, or animal.

sof·frit·to (sôfrē'tō), n. a mixture of hot fat, browned onion or garlic, and sometimes other vegetables or herbs, used in Italian cookery for lightly frying or browning meat, etc., before stewing it.

soft goods, items of purchase that wear out, as furnishing fabrics, carpets, clothes. See also **hard goods.**

soft sell, an advertising or merchandising technique employing subtle or indirect persuasion. See also **hard sell.**

soi-di·sant (swädēzäN'), adj. French. self-styled; alleging oneself to be.

soi·gné (of a male), **soi·gnée** (of a female) (swä'nyā), adj. arranged or performed with care and elegance; well-groomed.

soi·ree, soi·rée (swärā'), n. an evening social gathering, esp. for a particular purpose, as listening to a musical performance, or a talk, or holding a discussion on a specific topic.

so·journ (soj'ûn, suj'ûn), n. **1.** a short stay, as for a holiday. —v. **2.** to remain for a short time.

so·lan·der (səlan'də), n. a container for maps, photographs, and the like, made in the form of a book with the front and an edge hinged for ease of access.

so·lar·ize, so·lar·ise (sō'lərīz,), v. **1.** to expose to sunlight. **2.** (in medicine) to treat by exposure to sunlight or equivalent light source. **3.** to treat a photographic image by exposure to light, esp. to reverse the tones in order to highlight details, enhance outlines. etc. —so,lar·i·za'tion, so,lar·i·sa'tion, n.

solar wind, a mass of protons thrown out from the sun by a solar storm and disturbing the magnetic fields of the planets.

sol·e·cism (sol'əsiz,əm), n. any mistake, breach of propriety, or inconsistency, esp. a grammatical error.

sol·emn (sol'əm), adj. **1.** serious; sober; not cheerful or light-hearted. **2.** characterized by formality, as a ceremony. —so·lem'ni·ty, n.

sol·em·nize, sol·em·nise (sol'əmnīz,), v. **1.** to mark or celebrate with formal ceremony, esp. to celebrate marriage by religious rite. **2.** to make

solemn. —sol,em·ni·za'tion, sol,em·ni·sa'tion, n. —sol'em·niz,er, sol'em·nis,er, n.

sol·fe·ri·no (sol,fərē'nō), n. **1.** a purplish-red colour. —adj. **2.** having such a colour.

so·lic·i·tous (səlis'itəs), adj. anxious; concerned, as for or about the welfare or health of a person. —so·lic'i·tude n.

sol·i·dar·y (sol'idərē), adj. distinguished by or relating to joint or like interests and obligations.

solid-state, relating to or denoting electronic devices, capable of controlling current, that have no moving parts, vacuum gaps, or filaments, as transistors, piezoelectric devices, integrated circuits, etc.

sol·id·un·gu·late (sol,iduNG'gyōōlāt), adj. having an undivided hoof on each foot, as a horse.

sol·i·fid·i·an (sol,ifid'ēən), n. one who believes that salvation can be won by faith alone without performing good works.

so·lil·o·quize (səlil'əkwīz), v. to talk while or as if alone, often done in drama to reveal a character's thoughts.

so·lil·o·quy (səlil'əkwē), n. the act of or an instance of soliloquizing; the words so uttered.

sol·ip·sism (sol'ipsiz,əm), n. a philosophical theory that the self is the only thing that exists or can be proved to exist.

sol·stice (sol'stis), n. the time when the sun is at its farthest distance from the equator, occurring twice a year, once on about June 21 (summer solstice), when it reaches its northernmost point (marked on maps by the Tropic of Cancer), and once on about December 22 (winter solstice), when it reaches its southernmost point (marked on maps by the Tropic of Capricorn). See also **equinox.** —sol·sti'tial, adj.

so·lus (sō'ləs), adj. **1.** (fem. **sola**) on one's own; alone (used, esp. formerly, in stage directions). **2.** denoting an advertisement that is positioned on its own, away from other advertisements. **3.** denoting a retail outlet that sells the products of one company exclusively, such as a burger bar.

sol·ute (sol'yōōt), n. the substance dissolved in any solution.

sol·vent (sol'vənt), adj. **1.** able to pay all one's debts. **2.** having the power to dissolve another substance.

so·ma (sō'mə), n., pl. **so·ma·ta** (sō'mətə), **so·mas.** a body cell as opposed to a germ cell, i.e., one of those cells forming the tissues, organs, etc., of an organism as contrasted to those specialized for reproduction.

so·mat·ic (sōmat'ik), adj. of the body; corporeal; physical.

so·ma·tist (sō'mətist), n. a psychiatrist who believes that all mental illnesses are physical in origin.

so·ma·tol·o·gy (sō,mətol'əjē), n. the scientific study of the physical characteristics of mankind.

so·ma·to·to·ni·a (sō,mətōtō'nēə), *n.* the personality pattern usually associated with the mesomorphic body type, characterized by aggressiveness and physical energy. See also **cerebrotonia, viscerotonia.**

so·ma·to·tro·phin (sō,matōtrō'fin), *n.* growth hormone. Also **so·ma·to·tro·pin** (sō,-matōtrō'pin). —**so,ma·to·tro'phic, so,ma·to·tro'-pic,** *adj.*

so·ma·to·type (sō'mətətīp,, sōmat'ətīp,), *n.* a category of bodily form or physique. See also **ectomorphic, endomorphic, mesomorphic.** —**so,mo·to·typ'ic,** *adj.* —**so,ma·to·typ'i·cal·ly,** *adv.*

som·bre (som'bə), *adj.* gloomy; melancholy; dark and depressing.

som·me·lier (sum'əlyā,), *n.* a wine waiter.

som·nam·bu·late (somnam'byoōlāt), *v.* to walk or carry out other actions while asleep. —**som·nam,bu·la'tion, som·nam'bu·lism,** *n.*

som·ni·fa·cient (som,nifā'sHənt), *adj.* causing sleep.

som·nif·er·ous (somnif'ərəs), *adj.* bringing sleep.

som·nif·ic (somnif'ik), *adj.* causing sleep.

som·nil·o·quy (somnil'əkwē), *n.* the act or habit of speaking in one's sleep.

som·no·lent (som'nələnt), *adj.* sleepy; drowsy. —**som'no·lence,** *n.* —**som'no·lent·ly,** *adj.*

so·nant (sō'nənt), *adj.* having sound; sounding. —**so'nance,** *n.*

so·nar (sō'nä), *n.* **1.** a method of detecting and locating objects under water by picking up the sound waves they transmit or reflect. **2.** the apparatus used for such detection and location.

sonde (sond), *n.* a balloon, rocket, or similar device used for observing atmospheric phenomena.

sone (sōn), *n.* a unit of subjective loudness, equal to the loudness produced by a tone at 40 decibels above a reference tone which has been adjusted to the minimum audible threshold of a group of listeners.

sonic boom, a sharp bang heard on the ground when an aircraft moves overhead at a speed just below or above the speed of sound and caused by the shock wave created.

son·ics (son'iks), *n.* the science dealing with sound in its practical applications.

so·nif·er·ous (sonif'ərəs), *adj.* carrying or making sound.

so·no·rous (son'ərəs, sənôr'əs), *adj.* producing or capable of producing sound, esp. a rich, deep sound. —**so·nor'i·ty,** *n.*

soo·gee (soō'jē), *n.* **1.** a soapy or detergent solution for cleaning decks and paintwork. —*v.* **2.** to clean the decks, bulkheads, etc., of a vessel.

sop (sop), *n.* **1.** a piece of bread or similar solid food dipped or soaked in liquid food. **2.** a pleasing item offered as a distraction or pacifier.

soph·ism (sof'izəm), *n.* a deceptive or fallacious argument or belief. —**soph'ist, soph'ist·er,** *n.* —**soph'ist·ry,** *n.* —**so·phis'tic,** *adj.*

so·phis·ti·cat·ed (səfis'tikā,tid), *adj.* not simple; complex; complicated; of many parts, as a machine or an organization.

soph·o·mor·ic (sof,əmôr'ik), *adj.* childish; immature to the point of silliness, as *a sophomoric prank.*

so·phros·y·ne (səfros'ənē), *n.* self-control; moderation; prudence.

so·por (sō'pə), *n.* an unnatural state of deep sleep or lethargy.

so·po·rif·er·ous (sop,ərif'ərəs), *adj.* bringing sleep.

so·po·rif·ic (sop,ərif'ik), *adj.* producing or tending to produce sleep.

sop·o·rose (sop'ərōs), *adj.* abnormally sleepy; characterized by abnormally deep sleep; comatose.

sor·be·fa·cient (sô,bifā'sHənt), *adj.* **1.** causing or enhancing absorption. —*n.* **2.** a drug or other agent with this property.

sor·did (sô'did), *adj.* dirty and repulsive; low; very bad. —**sor'did·ness,** *n.*

sor·i·cine (sor'isīn,), *adj.* **1.** of or relating to the family Soricidae, which comprises the shrews. **2.** resembling a shrew.

sor·or·ate (sor'ərāt), *n.* marriage of one man with two sisters, either consecutively or concurrently.

so·ror·i·cide (səror'isīd), *n.* one who kills his or her sister.

sor·rel (sor'əl), *n.* a light reddish-brown colour.

sor·ti·lege (sô'tilij), *n.* divination by drawing lots; the drawing of lots for divination.

so·ter·i·ol·o·gy (sōtēr,ēol'əjē), *n.* the branch of theology dealing with salvation, esp. concerning the works of Christ. —**so·ter·i·o·log·ic** (sōtēr,-ēəloj'ik), **so·ter,i·o·log'i·cal,** *adj.*

sot·to vo·ce (sot'ō vō'CHē), in a whisper or undertone; in a quiet voice to avoid being overheard.

sou·bise (soōbēz'), *n.* a white or brown sauce containing puréed onions, served with various meats.

sou·brette (soōbret'), *n.* a vivacious, pert, or coquettish young woman.

souf·fle (soō'fəl), *n.* (in medicine) a low murmur or blowing sound such as is listened for with the aid of a stethoscope.

souf·flé (soōflā'), *n.* a baked dish of a light, fluffy texture owing to the use of beaten egg whites in its preparation.

sough (sou), *v.* to make a sighing, rushing, or rustling sound, as of a wind blowing through trees.

sou·mar·qué (sŏo' mäkä'), *pl.* **sous·mar·qués** (sŏo' mäkä'). something of little or no value.

sound spectrogram, a record made by a sound spectrograph.

sound spectrograph, an electronic device for making a graphic record of the frequency, intensity, duration, and variation of a sound or succession of sounds.

soup·çon (sŏopsôn'), *n. French.* a trace; a flavour; a hint or suspicion.

sou·tache (sŏotashʹ), *n.* narrow, flat, ornamental braid, usually made of mohair, silk, or rayon.

sou·tane (sŏotanʹ), *n.* a cassock.

sou·ter·rain (sŏotərän'), *n.* an underground passage or building; a grotto.

south·paw (south'pô,), *n. Slang.* a left-handed person.

sou·vlak·i·a (sŏovlak'ēə), *n.* (in Greek cuisine) lamb kebabs.

space-time (späs'tīm'), *n.* a philosophical concept of a fusion of space and time regarded as a four-dimensional continuum in which all physical entities exist and can be located.

spa·do (spä'dō), *n., pl.* **spa·do·nes** (spädō'nēz). a castrated man or animal.

spaetz·le (spät'səl), *n.* a dish of small dumplings or threadlike pieces made from a batter of flour, milk, eggs, and salt poured through a coarse colander into boiling water before being drained to serve tossed in butter or in a soup, sauce, or stew.

spall (spôl), *n.* **1.** a splinter or chip, esp. of stone or metal ore. —*v.* **2.** to break or split into small pieces or chips.

spa·nae·mi·a (spənē'mēə), *n.* anaemia.

Spanish fly, powder made from certain brilliant green beetles found abundantly in Spain and used medicinally as a skin irritant, diuretic, and aphrodisiac. Also **cantharides.**

sparge (späj'), *v.* **1.** to sprinkle. —*n.* **2.** a scattering.

sparse (späs), *adj.* thinly spread; scanty, as *sparse hair* or *sparse crops.*

spar·ver (spä'və), *n.* a tent-shaped canopy or curtain over a bed.

spasm (spaz'əm), *n.* a sudden, violent, involuntary contraction of a muscle.

spas·mod·ic (spazmod'ik), *adj.* relating to or similar in nature to a spasm; characterized by spasms.

spas·mo·phil·i·a (spaz,mōfil'ēə), *n.* an abnormal condition in which spasms, convulsions, or tetany are brought on by only a little mechanical or electrical stimulation. —**spas,mo·phil'ic,** *adj.*

spas·tic (spas'tik), *adj.* **1.** relating to, of the same nature as, or characterized by involuntary muscular contractions, esp. the long-continued contractions known as tonic spasms. —*n.* **2.** a person afflicted by such spasms; a person suffering from cerebral palsy.

spastic paralysis, an abnormal condition in which muscles are affected by tonic spasm and alteration in reflexes.

spate (spāt), *n.* a sudden rush or outburst, as of water, words, customers, etc.

spathe (spāth), *n.* a single bract or a pair of bracts, frequently brightly coloured, borne on the same axis as and enveloping a flower spike or cluster. —**spa·tha'ceous, spa'those,** *adj.*

spa·ti·og·ra·phy (spä,shēog'rəfē), *n.* the study of outer space, esp. of phenomena likely to affect missiles and spacecraft.

spat·ter·dash (spat'ədash,), *n.* a long gaiter or legging to protect the clothing on the legs from rain, splashing mud, etc.

spav·ined (spav'ind), *adj.* in a worn-out or broken-down condition.

spay (spā), *v.* to remove the ovaries of a female animal.

spé·cia·li·té de la mai·son (spesyälētä' də la mäzôn'), *French.* a dish for which a restaurant is noted; a restaurant's speciality.

spe·ci·a·tion (spē,shēä'shən), *n.* the origination of a species; the process by which new species originate.

spe·cio (spē'ʒıē), *n.* coined money.

spe·cies (spē'shēz), *n.* a group of things or individuals having some characteristics in common; a sort or kind.

spe·cious (spē'shəs), *adj.* superficially good or right but inwardly false; plausible.

spec·tro·bo·lom·e·ter (spek,trōbəlom'itə), *n.* an instrument combining a spectroscope and a bolometer, used for finding accurately the distribution of radiant energy in a spectrum.

spec·tro·chem·is·try (spek,trōkem'istrē), *n.* the branch of chemistry concerned with analysing substances by means of the light spectra they absorb or produce. —**spec,tro·chem'i·cal,** *adj.*

spec·tro·col·o·rim·e·try (spek,trōkul'ərim'itrē), *n.* the measuring of colour quantities by means of a spectrophotometer.

spec·tro·gram (spek'trōgram,), *n.* a photograph or other representation of a light spectrum.

spec·tro·graph (spek'trōgräf,, spek'trōgraf,), *n.* a device for producing a light spectrum and making a photograph or other representation of it.

spec·tro·he·li·o·gram (spek,trōhē'lēōgram,), *n.* a photograph produced by a spectroheliograph.

spec·tro·he·li·o·graph (spek,trōhē'lēōgräf,, spek,trōhē'lēōgraf,), *n.* a photographic apparatus that can be set so that only light of a certain wavelength reaches the photographic plate, used for making photographs of the sun in a given monochrome so that the details of the sun's surface appear as they would if the sun emitted only that given monochrome.

spec·tro·he·li·o·scope (spek,trōhē'lēō-skōp,), *n.* a spectroheliograph or a form of it that produces a visual instead of photographic image.

spec·trol·o·gy (spektrol'əjē), *n.* the study of ghosts or other apparitions.

spec·trom·e·ter (spektrom'itə), *n.* an optical instrument for producing light spectra and making measurements of them, as of their wavelength, amount of refraction, etc.

spec·tro·mi·cro·scope (spek,trōmī'krəskōp,), *n.* a combined spectroscope and microscope.

spec·tro·pho·to·e·lec·tric (spek,trōfō,tōilek'trik), *adj.* relating to the connection between the wavelength of the radiation striking and the number of electrons set free by a substance during photoelectric effect.

spec·tro·pho·tom·e·ter (spek,trōfōtom'itə), *n.* an instrument for measuring and comparing the light intensity of different parts of a spectrum.

spec·tro·po·lar·im·e·ter (spek,trōpō,lərim'itə), *n.* a combined spectroscope and polarimeter used for measuring the amount by which different solutions cause plane-polarized light of various wavelengths to rotate.

spec·tro·po·lar·i·scope (spek,trōpōlar'iskōp,), *n.* a combined spectroscope and polariscope.

spec·tro·ra·di·om·e·ter (spek,trō'rā,dēom'itə), *n.* a combined spectroscope and radiometer, used for determining the distribution of radiant energy in a light spectrum.

spec·tro·scope (spek'trəskōp,), *n.* an optical instrument for producing and examining visible spectra, i.e., spectra of light and radiation, by passing the light or radiation through a slit, arranging it in parallel rays by means of a collimator, and separating it into its component elements by means of a prism.

spec·tros·co·py (spektros'kəpē), *n.* the science concerned with the use of the spectroscope and with analysing bodies and substances by means of the spectra they produce.

spec·trum (spek'trəm), *n.*, *pl.* **spec·tra** (spek'trə). **1.** the effect produced when electromagnetic radiations are resolved into their component waves which are then arranged according to their wavelength and range. **2.** any part of the entire electromagnetic spectrum, as the audio spectrum, but esp. the spectrum of light, which appears as bands of violet, indigo, blue, green, yellow, orange, and red in order of increasing wavelength.

spec·u·lar (spek'yōōlə), *adj.* of or having the properties of a mirror.

spec·u·late (spek'yōōlāt), *v.* **spec·u·lat·ed, spec·u·lat·ing. 1.** to trade in shares, bonds, property, etc., for gain. **2.** to guess. —**spec,u·la'tion,** *n.*

spec·u·lum (spek'yələm), *n.*, *pl.* **spec·u·la** (spek'yōōlə), **spec·u·lums. 1.** a mirror, usually made of polished metal, esp. one on or in an optical instrument. **2.** a surgical instrument for dilating an inaccessible body cavity or passage to make inspection possible.

speech·i·fy (spēcн'ifī,), *v.* **speech·i·fies, speech·i·fy·ing, speech·i·fied.** to make a speech, esp. at length and tediously. —**speech,i·fi·ca'·tion,** *n.* —**speech'i·fi·er,** *n.*

spe·lae·an, spe·le·an (spilē'ən), *adj.* of, relating to, or living in caves.

spe·le·ol·o·gy, spe·lae·ol·o·gy (spē,lēol'əjē), *n.* the scientific exploration and study of caves. —**spe,le·ol'o·gist,** *n.*

spe·lunk (spiluнɢk'), *v.* to explore caves. —**spe·lun'ker,** *n.*

Spen·ce·ri·an (spensēr'ēən), *adj.* relating to or characteristic of a handwriting style in which the letters are clear, rounded, and slope to the right.

sper·ma·cet·i (spû,məset'ē) *n.* a white, waxy substance obtained from the head of the sperm whale and used mainly in making soap, cosmetics, candles, in glazing fabrics, and as an emollient in certain medical preparations. Also **cetaceum.**

sper·ma·ry (spû'mərē), *n.* an organ for generating sperm; a testis.

sper·mat·ic (spûmat'ik), *adj.* of, relating to, or similar to sperm; seminal. Also **sper'mic.**

sper·mat·o·gen·e·sis (spû,matōjen'isis), *n.* the formation and development of spermatozoa. —**sper,ma·tog'e·nous,** *adj.*

sper·ma·toid (spû'mətoid), *adj.* sperm-like.

sper·ma·tor·rhoe·a (spû,mətərē'ə), *n.* abnormally frequent involuntary ejaculation of semen.

sper·ma·to·zo·on (spû,mətōzō'ən), *n.*, *pl.* **sper·ma·to·zo·a** (spû,mətōzō'ə). one of the mature male reproductive cells in semen, which may fertilize the female's ovum.

sper·mi·o·gen·e·sis (spû,mēōjen'isis), *n.* the final process in the development of spermatozoa from male sperm cells.

sperm oil, a thin, yellow liquid obtained from the sperm whale and used mainly as a lubricant for watches, scientific apparatus, and other intricate light machinery.

sper·mous (spû'məs), *adj.* relating to or having the properties of sperm.

sperm whale, a large whale of warm oceans, having a large cavity in its head containing sperm oil, which is valued in itself and from which spermaceti is obtained. Also **cachalot.**

sphac·e·late (sfas'əlāt), *v.* to become or cause to become affected with sphacelus.

sphac·e·lus (sfas'ələs), *n.* a mass of gangrenous tissue.

sphag·num moss (sfag'nəm), *n.* any of a large number of soft mosses comprising a genus, growing on swamps and bogs and used mainly for surgical dressings, packing of plants and the like, and potting of plants.

sphe·nic (sfē'nik), *adj.* shaped like a wedge. Also **sphe'noid.**

sphe·no·gram (sfē'nəgram,), *n.* any of the wedge-shaped characters in cuneiform writing.

sphe·nog·ra·phy (sfēnog'rəfē), *n.* the art of or study of cuneiform writing.

spher·al (sfēr'əl), *adj.* of, pertaining to, or having the form of a sphere.

spher·ics (sfer'iks), *n.* **1.** the geometry and trigonometry of figures described in or on the surface of a sphere. **2.** a branch of meteorology in which electronic devices are used to study the atmosphere and in particular those aspects relating to weather forecasting.

sphe·rom·e·ter (sfērom'itə), *n.* an instrument used to measure the curvature of spheres and of curved surfaces such as lenses.

spher·ule (sfer'ōōl), *n.* a small sphere or globe.

sphinc·ter (sfiNGk'tə), *n.* a ring of voluntary or involuntary muscle encircling the oriface of a hollow organ or the wall of a tubular organ and able to close or narrow it, as *oral, anal,* or *cardiac sphincter.*

sphra·gis·tic (sfrəjis'tik), *adj.* of or relating to seals or signet rings.

sphra·gis·tics (sfrəjis'tiks), *n.* the study of or knowledge of seals or signet rings.

sphyg·mic (sfig'mik), *adj.* of or relating to the pulse.

sphyg·mo·gram (sfig'mōgram,), *n.* a record made by a sphygmograph.

sphyg·mo·graph (sfig'mōgräf,, sfig'mōgraf,), *n.* an instrument for making a graphic record, as a tracing or diagram, of the strength and rapidity of, and any variations in the arterial pulse.

sphyg·moid (sfig'moid), *adj.* resembling an arterial pulse.

sphyg·mo·ma·nom·e·ter (sfig'mōmənom'-itə), *n.* an instrument used in conjunction with a stethoscope for measuring blood pressure and which consists of a manometer and an inflatable cuff to constrict an artery.

sphyg·mom·e·ter (sfigmom'itə), *n.* an instrument for measuring the strength of the arterial pulse.

spi·cate (spī'kāt), *adj.* with points or spikes, as a plant.

spic·u·late (spik'yōōlāt) *adj.* small and needle-like in shape.

spic·ule (spik'yōōl, spī'kyōōl), *n.* a small, needle-like body, part, process, or the like. Also **spic'u·lum,** *pl.* **spic'u·la.**

spiel (spēl), *n. Colloquial.* a high-flown, extravagant speech or story, esp. to attract people to buy or to attend some performance. —**spiel'er,** *n.*

spike·nard (spīk'näd), *n.* See **nard.**

spile (spīl), *n.* **1.** a wooden peg or plug, esp. for

stopping up an opening. —*v.* **2.** to stop up with a peg or plug.

spil·li·kin (spil'ikin), *n.* a jackstraw; one of a heap of small rods of wood, plastic, etc., used in a game in which the object is to remove each rod without disturbing the rest.

spin doctor, *n.* an aide to a politician or other public figure who briefs the press so that a speech, news item, etc., is interpreted favourably.

spin·drift (spin'drift,), *n.* spray blown along the surface of the sea.

spi·nes·cent (spīnes'ənt), *adj.* with a spiny end; spine-bearing; becoming or being spine-like.

spi·nif·er·ous (spīnif'ərəs), *adj.* bearing or covered with spines.

spin·ner·et (spin'əret,), *n.* an organ of insects such as spiders or a device on a machine making synthetic yarn through which a fine thread is extruded.

spi·nose (spī'nōs), *adj.* bearing, covered with, or armed with spines, thorns, or sharp projections, as a plant or animal; resembling a spine. Also **spi'nous.**

spin·thar·i·scope (spinthar'iskōp,), *n.* an instrument for observing alpha particles by making them visible as flashes on a fluorescent screen.

spi·nule (spī'nyōōl), *n.* a small spine.

spi·ra·cle (spī'rəkəl), *n.* **1.** a hole giving access to air. **2.** openings on the side of an insect's body through which it breathes.

spi·rif·er·ous (spīrif'ərəs), *adj.* having a spire or spiral appendages.

spi·ril·lum (spīril'əm), *n., pl.* **spi·ril·la** (spīril'ə). any of various corkscrew-shaped species of bacteria, several of which cause disease in man.

spir·it·ism (spir'itiz,əm), *n.* a doctrine or practice based on spiritualism.

spiritual incest, sexual intercourse between persons baptized or confirmed together.

spi·ri·tu·el (spir'ityōō,əl, spir'iCHōōəl), *adj.* having or exhibiting refinement and grace in mind, wit, or movement.

spi·ri·tus fru·men·ti (spir'itəs frōōmen'tī), whisky.

spi·ro·chaete (spī'rōkēt), *n.* any of several species of long spiral bacteria, many of which cause disease in man and one of which causes syphilis.

spi·ro·chae·to·sis (spī,rōkētō'sis), *n.* any disease caused by a spirochaete.

spi·ro·graph (spī'rəgräf,, spī'rəgraf,), *n.* an instrument for recording the movements concerned with respiration.

spi·roid (spī'roid), *adj.* nearly spiral; resembling a spiral.

spi·rom·e·ter (spīrom'itə), *n.* an instrument used to measure lung capacity.

spitch·cock (spicн'kok), *n.* an eel split or cut up and grilled or fried.

splanch·nic (splaɴGk'nik), *adj.* of or relating to the viscera.

splanch·nol·o·gy (splaɴGknol'əjē), *n.* the branch of medicine concerned with the viscera.

spleen (splēn), *n.* **1.** a ductless gland, in mammals situated at the left side under the diaphragm, of which the main functions are to form antibodies, to destroy red blood cells at the end of their life, and to store red blood cells. **2.** ill-nature; peevishness.

splen·dent (splen'dənt), *adj.* shining; brilliant; lustrous.

splen·dif·er·ous (splendif'ərəs), *adj. Colloquial.* magnificent; splendid.

sple·nec·to·my (splinek'təmē), *n.* the surgical removal of part or all of the spleen.

sple·net·ic (splinet'ik), *adj.* of, relating to, or affecting the spleen; ill-natured; irritable; spiteful.

splen·ic (splē'nik), *adj.* of, relating to, or affecting the spleen.

sple·ni·tis (splinī'tis), *n.* inflammation of the spleen.

spon·du·lix, spon·du·licks (spondyōō'-liks), *n. Slang.* money.

spon·dy·li·tis (spon,dilī'tis), *n.* a medical disorder in which the vertebrae are inflamed.

spon·gi·form (spun'jifôm,), *adj.* resembling a sponge, as some types of body tissue in certain diseases.

spon·sion (spon'sнən), *n.* a promise, esp. an engagement to act as surety for another person.

spon·son (spon'sən), *n.* a structure projecting from a ship's or other vessel's side, as a gun platform, the edge of a paddle box, a buoyancy tank, or a canoe.

spon·ta·ne·ous (spontā'nēəs), *adj.* characterized by absence of planning or outside influence, as *a spontaneous action* or *a spontaneous gift to charity.*

spoo·ner·ism (spōō'nəriz,əm), *n.* the exchange of the initial sounds of two or more words in an expression, usually by accident, creating a ludicrous result, as *queer dean* for *dear queen.* [From W. A. *Spooner,* English clergyman who became known for such slips]

spoor (spōō'ə), *n.* a track or trail, esp. of a person or animal being pursued or hunted.

spo·rad·ic (spôrad'ik), *adj.* recurring at irregular intervals of time.

spo·ri·cide (spôr'isīd), *n.* a substance or preparation used to kill spores.

spo·rif·er·ous (spôrif'ərəs), *adj.* bearing or capable of bearing spores.

spo·ro·gen·e·sis (spôr,ōjen'isis), *n.* the formation and development of spores.

spo·ro·zo·an (spô,rəzō'ən, spo,rəzō'ən), *n.* **1.** any parasitic protozoan belonging to the class

Sporozoa, such as the malaria parasite *Plasmodium.* —*adj.* **2.** of or relating to the Sporozoa.

Sprach·ge·fühl (sнpräkн'gəfvl,), *n. German.* an instinctive grasp of the spirit of a language, esp. consciousness of what is acceptable usage in the grammar or idiom of a particular language.

spritz·er (sprit'sə), *n.* a drink made from wine and soda water and served chilled in tall glasses.

sprue (sprōō), *n.* a chronic condition in which inability to absorb certain food constituents, esp. fats, leads to diarrhoea and ulceration of the lining of the digestive tract, the condition being caused by malnutrition and occurring most often in the tropics.

spu·mes·cent (spyōōmes'ənt), *adj.* foaming; frothy.

spu·ri·ous (spyōōr'ēəs), *adj.* not genuine; of counterfeit origin; bastard; of illegitimate birth.

spu·tum (spyōō'təm), *n., pl.* **spu·ta** (spyōō'tə). spittle, esp. that mixed with mucus or pus expectorated by persons with diseases of the throat or lungs.

squal·id (skwol'id), *adj.* dirty; filthy; in foul condition, as from neglect or poverty.

squa·ma (skwā'mə), *n., pl.* **squa·mae** (skwā'-mē). a scale or scale-like part, as of skin or bone.

squa·mate (skwā'māt), *adj.* furnished with or covered with squamae. —**squa·ma'tion,** *n.*

squa·mi·form (skwā'mifôm,), *adj.* in the shape of a squama.

squa·mo·sal (skwəmō'səl), *adj.* of or relating to the thin, scale-like portion of skull behind the ear which articulates with the bones of the lower jaw.

squa·mous (skwā'məs), *adj.* covered with, composed of, or resembling squamae.

squa·mu·lose (skwā'myōōlōs), *adj.* having or covered with small squamae.

square mile, a unit used in measuring area, equal to the area contained by a square whose sides each measure one mile. *Abbrev.*: sq. mi., mi^2.

square millimetre, a unit used in measuring area, equal to the area contained by a square whose sides each measure one millimetre. *Abbrev.*: sq. mm., mm^2.

squar·rose (skwer'ōs, skwor'ōs), *adj.* with a rough or rugged surface.

squas·sa·tion (skwosā'sнən), *n.* a form of or device for torture or punishment in former times, in which the victim, with arms bound behind and feet heavily weighted, was jerked up and down on a rope passing under his arms. See also **strappado.**

squeam·ish (skwē'misн), *adj.* easily sickened or shocked by something disgusting, the sight of blood, immoral behaviour, etc. —**squeam'ish·ness,** *n.*

squib (skwib), *n.* **1.** a short, witty composition

or saying. **2.** a short item of news used as a filler in a newspaper.

squint (skwint), *n.* strabismus.

sta·bile (stā'bīl), *adj.* **1.** fixed; stable. —*n.* **2.** a piece of sculpture consisting of immobile pieces attached to supports. See also **mobile**.

stac·ca·to (stəkä'tō), *adj.* sharply disconnected; composed of abruptly disjointed words, notes, movements, or the like.

stac·tom·e·ter (staktom'itə), *n.* an instrument for finding the number of or the weight of individual drops in a volume of liquid. Also **stalagmometer**.

sta·dim·e·ter (stədim'itə), *n.* an instrument for measuring the angle subtended by an object of known height and from it determining the distance of the object from the observer.

sta·di·om·e·ter (stā,dēom'itə), *n.* an instrument that runs a toothed wheel over curves, dashed lines, and the like to measure their length.

stag·fla·tion (stagflā'sHən), *n.* an economic situation characterized by inflation, stagnant or falling output, and unemployment.

stag·ing (stā'jiNG), *n.* scaffolding; a temporary support.

stag·nate (stag'nāt), *v.* **stag·nat·ed, stag·nat·ing.** to become foul, dull, or unimaginative from inactivity, as a pool of water, an unchanging, undeveloping person, etc. —**stag'nant,** *adj.*

staid (stād), *adj.* sedate or steady in character or bearing.

sta·lac·ti·form (stəlak'tifōm,), *adj.* shaped like or similar to a stalactite.

sta·lac·tite (stal'əktīt), *n.* an icicle-like formation of crystalline calcium carbonate built up by the dripping of water through overlying limestone and hanging from the roof or wall of a cave or the like.

sta·lag·mite (stal'əgmīt), *n.* a deposit on the floor of a cave or the like, resembling an inverted stalactite and formed in the same way.

stal·ag·mom·e·ter (stal,əgmom'itə), *n.* See **stactometer**.

stal·wart (stôl'wŭt), *adj.* **1.** steadily strong; stout and sturdy; giving support through dependability and courage. —*n.* **2.** a supportive person; one who can be counted on for strength.

sta·men (stā'mən), *n.* the male reproductive organ of a flowering plant, consisting of the anther which has two lobes each with two pollen sacs, borne at the apex of the slender filament.

stam·inate (stam'ənāt), *adj.* of or denoting a flower with stamens but no pistil, and therefore male.

stam·i·nif·er·ous (stam,inif'ərəs), *adj.* bearing or capable of bearing stamens.

stam·i·no·dy (stam'inō,dē), *n.* the transformation into a stamen of some other part of a flower, as a petal.

stanch (stäncH), *v.* to check the flow, as of blood, from a leak. Also **staunch**.

stanch·less (stäncH'lis), *adj.* unstoppable; incessant.

stan·na·ry (stan'ərē), *n.* a tin-mining area.

stan·num (stan'əm), *n.* tin.

sta·pes (stā'pēz), *n.,* *pl.* **sta·pes, sta·pe·des** (stəpē'dēz). a small stirrup-shaped bone in the middle ear of mammals.

staph·y·lo·coc·cus (staf,ilōkok'əs), *n.,* *pl.* **staph·y·lo·coc·ci** (staf,ilōkok'sī). any of several species of bacteria globular in form and tending to cluster, certain of which cause severe but localized infections in man, as abscesses, carbuncles, etc.

staph·y·lo·ma (staf,ilō'mə), *n.* an abnormal localized bulge on the eyeball from a variety of causes.

staph·y·lor·rha·phy (staf,ilor'əfē), *n.* a surgical operation to join a cleft palate.

Star Chamber, **1.** (in Tudor England) the Privy Council sitting to try civil and criminal cases, especially those affecting Crown interests, until its abolition in 1641 for being arbitrary in its judgments, **2.** any tribunal, committee, or the like whose methods are unfair.

starve·ling (stäv'liNG), *adj.* starving; underfed.

sta·sis (stā'sis), *n.* the state of balance or inactivity brought about by opposing equal forces or powers.

stat·ics (stat'iks), *n.* the branch of physics dealing with the action of forces on bodies at rest. See also **dynamics**.

stat·ism (stā'tizəm), *n.* the belief in or policy of putting the control of economic, political, and other such matters in the hands of the state instead of the individual. —**stat'ist,** *n.*

sta·tis·tics (stətis'tiks), *n.* the branch of study concerned with collecting, classifying, analysing, and interpreting facts, esp. numerical facts.

sta·tive (stā'tiv), *adj.* **1.** (of a verb) expressing a mental or bodily state rather than an action or event, such as *desire* in contrast to *dress*.

stat·o·cyst (stat'ōsist), *n.* an organ of balance present in certain invertebrates such as flatworms and crustaceans and consisting of a sac containing sensory cells and granules of sand, lime, etc., the granules stimulating the cells as the animal moves.

stat·o·lith (stat'ōlith), *n.* **1.** one of the granules present in a statocyst. **2.** a solid inclusion, frequently a starch grain, in a plant cell, free to change position under the influence of gravity and assumed to cause corresponding change in the position of the plant.

sta·tor (stā'tə), *n.* a stationary or fixed part of an electrical machine, esp. of a generator.

stat·u·ar·y (stacH'ōōərē, stat'yōōərē), *n.,* *pl.*

stat·u·ar·ies. 1. statues collectively. **2.** the art of statue making. —*adj.* **3.** of or suitable for statues.

stat·ure (staCH'ə), *n.* the way a person or animal stands; height; position and attitude; status, as *her stature in the community.*

sta·tus quo (stā'təs kwō'), the existing or previous state of affairs. Also **sta'tus in quo'.**

staunch (stônCH), *adj.* **1.** strong, faithful, and reliable; substantial. **2.** a variant spelling of stanch.

stead·fast (sted'fəst, sted'fäst,), *adj.* faithful and reliable; steady.

steady state theory, the theory that the universe is constantly expanding and can continue to do so without limit. See also **big bang theory.**

steal·age (stē'lij), *n.* **1.** stealing. **2.** loss due to stealing.

steamboat Gothic, a style of architecture in the 19th-century United States characterized by elaborate ornamentation around windows and doors and on beams and rails, etc., in imitation of river steamboats.

ste·a·tite (stē'ətīt), *n.* soapstone, a greyish-green or brown variety of talc with a waxy feel, used in cosmetics and as a pigment in ceramics.

ste·a·to·py·gi·a (stē,ətōpij'ēə), *n.* a large deposit of fat on and around the buttocks, esp. of women, as among Hottentots, Bushmen, and other peoples of southern Africa.

ste·a·tor·rhoe·a (stē,ətərē'ə), *n.* the presence of an abnormal amount of fat in the faeces causing diarrhoea with consequent weight loss and due to disease of the pancreas or intestine, to malnutrition, and other causes. Also **ste,ar·rhoe'a.**

steel·yard (stēl'yäd,), *n.* a lever with unequal arms used as a balance, the item to be weighed hanging from the shorter arm and a movable counterpoise being pushed along the calibrated longer arm to give a reading of weight.

steeve (stēv), *n.* **1.** a long deck or boom used to lift and lower cargo into a ship's hold. —*v.* **2.** to pack tightly, as cargo in a ship's hold.

ste·le (stē'lē), *n.*, *pl.* **ste·les, ste·lai** (stē'lī). an upright slab or pillar of stone bearing a sculptured design or inscription used as a gravestone or other marker.

stel·late (stel'āt), *adj.* star-shaped.

stel·lif·er·ous (stelif'ərəs), *adj.* having, esp. many, stars.

stel·li·form (stel'ifôm,), *adj.* star-shaped.

St.-É·mi·li·on (sant,ämē'lēən), *n.* a dry claret from the parish of St. Émilion, Bordeaux, France.

stem turn, a ski turn in which the skier pushes the heel of one ski outwards, so that it glides over the snow at an angle to the direction of movement and points in the direction to be turned to, and then shifts weight and brings the other ski parallel.

sten·o·cho·ric (sten,ōkôr'ik), *adj.* not widely distributed, as of a plant or animal. See also **eurychoric.**

sten·o·graph (sten'əgräf,, sten'əgraf,), *n.* a machine resembling a typewriter for writing in one of various shorthand systems.

sten·o·ha·line (sten,ōhā'līn), *adj.* able to tolerate only a slight variation in the salinity of its environment. See also **euryhaline.**

sten·o·pe·ic (sten,ōpē'ik), *adj.* **1.** having or relating to a narrow slit or other minute opening. —*n.* **2.** an appliance worn over the eyes for keeping out bright sunlight and consisting of a piece of cardboard, metal, wood, or the like with a narrow horizontal slit.

sten·o·pet·al·ous (sten,ōpet'ələs), *adj.* having narrow petals.

sten·oph·a·gous (stinof'əgəs), *adj.* able to live on a narrow range of foodstuffs. See also **euryphagous.**

sten·o·phyl·lous (sten,ōfil'əs), *adj.* narrow-leaved.

ste·nosed (stinōst'), *adj.* exhibiting stenosis; of abnormal narrowness.

ste·no·sis (stinō'sis), *n.* a medical condition of abnormal narrowness of an opening, tube, or vessel, as of an artery, etc.

sten·o·ther·mal (sten,ōthû'məl), *adj.* able to tolerate only a narrow variation in the surrounding temperature. See also **eurythermal.**

sten·o·ther·mo·phile (sten,ōthû'məfīl), *n.* an obligate bacterium growing best at temperatures not lower than 60 degrees C. —**sten,o·thur,mo·phil'ic,** *adj.*

sten·o·top·ic (sten,ōtop'ik), *adj.* able to withstand only narrow variation in environmental conditions, as temperature, humidity, etc. See also **eurytopic.**

sten·o·typ·y (sten,ōtīpē), *n.* shorthand in which the shortened forms of words or groups of words consist of written or typed alphabetic letters, as distinct from phonetic or other symbols.

sten·to·ri·an (stentôr'ēən), *adj.* with a very loud or powerful voice or sound. Also **sten·to'ri·ous.**

steppe (step), *n.* a vast, grassy, largely treeless plain in the temperate zone, as across Eurasia.

ster·co·ra·ceous (stû,kərā'sHəs), *adj.* of, like, or relating to dung or faeces.

ster·co·ric·o·lous (stû,kərik'ələs), *adj.* inhabiting dung.

stere (stē'ə), *n.* a unit of the metric system for solid measures, equal to one cubic metre, and used chiefly in measuring blocks of timber. *Abbrev.:* **s.**

ster·e·og·no·sis (ster,ēognō'sis, stēr,ēognō'sis) *n.* the faculty of recognizing similarities and differences in the size, weight, shape, and texture of objects by touching or lifting them.

ster·e·o·gram (ster'ēəgram,, stēr'ēəgram,,), *n.*

a picture or diagram conveying an impression of the solidity of the object represented.

ster·e·o·graph (ster'ēəgräf,, ster'ēəgraf,, stēr'-ēəgraf,), *n.* one or both of the two pictures required to produce a stereoscopic picture.

ster·e·og·ra·pher (ster,ēog'rəfə, stēr,ēog'-rəfə), *n.* a person who takes stereoscopic photographs.

ster·e·og·ra·phy (ster,ēog'rəfē, stēr,ēog'rəfē), *n.* 1. the art of drawing solid bodies on a plane. 2. a branch of geometry concerned with the construction of regularly defined solids.

ster·e·om·e·try (ster,ēom'itrē, stēr,ēom'itrē), *n.* the measurement of solids; geometry as applied to solids.

ster·e·o·phon·ic (ster,ēəfon'ik, stēr,ēəfon'ik), *adj.* of a system of sound reproduction using more than one microphone or loudspeaker, separately placed, to enhance the realism of the reproduction, used esp. in high-fidelity recordings and for wide-screen motion pictures. See also **monophonic.** —**ster,e·oph'o·ny,** *n.*

ster·e·o·pho·tog·ra·phy (ster,ēōfətog'rəfē, stēr,ēōfətog'rəfē), *n.* the production of stereoscopic photographs.

ster·e·op·sis (ster,ēop'sis, stēr,ēop'sis), *n.* stereoscopic vision.

ster·e·op·ter (ster'ēoptə, stēr'ēoptə), *n.* an opthalmic instrument for measuring the eye's perception of three-dimensionality.

ster·e·op·ti·con (ster,ēop'tikon, stēr,ēop'tikon), *n.* a projector that makes one picture dissolve as the next forms, usually by having two complete lanterns.

ster·e·o·scope (ster'ēəskōp,, stēr'ēəskōp), *n.* an optical instrument for showing two pictures of the same object, made from slightly different points of view, one to one eye and one to the other, producing the effect of a single image with the illusion of three-dimensionality.

ster·e·o·scop·ic (ster,ēəskop'ik, stēr,ēəskop'-ik), *adj.* denoting or relating to three-dimensional vision or any process or device that produces an illusion of three-dimensionality from two-dimensional images.

ster·e·os·co·py (ster,ēos'kəpē, stēr,ēos'kəpē), *n.* three-dimensional vision; the study of the stereoscope.

ster·e·o·tax·is (ster,ēōtak'sis, stēr,ēōtak'sis), *n.* movement of an organism resulting from the stimulus of contact with a solid. See also **thigmotaxis.**

ster·e·ot·o·my (ster,ēot'əmē, stēr,ēot'əmē), *n.* the technique of precision-cutting of solids such as stones.

ster·e·o·type (ster'ēətīp,, stēr'ēətīp,), *n.* 1. a process of making a metal printing plate by taking a papier maché or similar mould of a form of type and then casting the mould in metal. Also **ster'e·o·ty,py.** 2. a plate so made. 3. a hack-

neyed form; something perpetuated in unchanged form.

ster·ling (stû'liNG), *adj.* 1. of or relating to the money of the United Kingdom. 2. having the standard fineness of 92.5 per cent silver and 7.5 per cent copper; formerly the standard fixed by law for silver coin and now used for jewellery, utensils, etc.

sterling bloc, the group of countries, mostly in the British Commonwealth, between which payment is freely made in sterling, for which institutions in the City of London act as bankers, and whose currency value tends to vary directly with that of the pound sterling. Also **sterling area.**

ster·nal (stû'nəl), *adj.* of or relating to the sternum.

ster·no·cos·tal (stû,nōkos'təl), *adj.* of, relating to, or between the sternum and the ribs.

ster·num (stû'nəm), *n., pl.* **ster·na** (stû'nə), **ster·nums.** the breastbone; a bone or series of bones along the middle and ventral side of the chest of vertebrates and having the ribs and shoulder girdle attached to it.

stern·u·ta·tion (stûrn,yōōtā'sHən), *n.* the act of or an instance of sneezing.

stern·u·ta·tor (stûn'yōōtā,tə), *n.* a poison gas causing coughing and irritation of the nose.

stern·u·ta·to·ry (stûn,yōōtā'tərē), *adj.* causing or able to cause sneezing.

ster·oid (stēr'oid, ster'oid), *n.* any of a large group of organic chemical compounds, similar chemically but diverse biologically, having important and specific physiological function, and including bile acids, vitamin D, some sex hormones, some carcinogens, etc.

ster·ol (stēr'ol, ster'ol), *n.* any of a group of unsaturated fat-soluble organic chemical compounds, as cholesterol and ergosterol, present in all animal and plant cells.

ster·tor (stû'tə), *n.* an abnormally heavy rasping sound that accompanies breathing in some illnesses.

ster·to·rous (stû'tərəs), *adj.* accompanied by stertor or snoring.

stet (stet), *v.* to let stand, used as an imperative to a printer to retain a letter, word, passage, etc., cancelled on a manuscript or proof and marked by a row of dots under the part affected.

ste·thom·e·ter (stethom'itə), *n.* an instrument for measuring the movements of the chest walls and abdomen during breathing.

steth·o·scope (steth'əskōp,), *n.* a medical instrument used for listening to sounds in the body, esp. in the chest, and consisting of a piece to be applied to the body, to receive and amplify the sound, connected by rubber tubing to closely fitting ear-pieces. —**steth,o·scop'ic,** *adj.*

sthe·ni·a (sthənī'ə), *n.* a medical condition of abnormal strength or energy.

sthen·ic (*sthen'ik*), *adj.* sturdy or strong in build.

stich (stik), *n.* a line, a verse, or a stanza of poetry. —**stich'ic,** *adj.*

sti·chom·e·try (stikom'itrē), *n.* the practice of setting out prose in lines divided according to the sense and indicating the phrasing.

stig·ma (stig'mə), *n.*, *pl.* **stig·ma·ta** (stig'mətə, stigmä'tə), **stig·mas. 1.** a mark of disgrace; a stain on one's good name; a mark characterizing a defect or disease. **2.** a spot on the skin, esp. one that bleeds spontaneously, as during hysteria. **3.** that part of a pistil, or gynoecium, that receives pollen. **4.** (*pl.*) marks resembling wounds on the crucified body of Christ, said to have developed on the bodies of some saints or other holy people.

stig·mat·ic (stigmat'ik), *adj.* **1.** of or relating to a stigma. **2.** converging to a point, as of light, the effect of lenses, etc.; free of astigmatism.

stig·ma·tism (stig'mətiz,əm), *n.* **1.** the property of converging or causing convergence to a point. **2.** the medical condition of having stigma.

stig·ma·tize (stig'mətīz), *v.* to mark, as with a sign or brand; to mark with or describe in terms of disgrace.

still hunt, a hunt for game by stealth, as by stalking or by ambush from cover.

stil·li·form (stil'ifôm,), *adj.* drop-shaped; spherical.

stim·u·lus (stim'yōōləs), *n.*, *pl.* **stim·u·li** (stim'-yōōlī). something that rouses or spurs on activity of body or mind; something that rouses an organism or tissue to specific activity.

stint (stint), *n.* **1.** an amount of work or the time required to do it, as *She did her stint from 9 to 5 today.* —*v.* **2.** to pinch pennies; be stingy or miserly, as *That company has always stinted on the salaries paid to married women.*

stipe (stīp), *n.* a stalk; a stalk-like part.

sti·pend (stī'pend), *n.* a fixed periodical payment from public funds, as to a teacher, student, public official, or esp. clergyman; a salary.

sti·pen·di·a·ry (stīpen'dēərē), *adj.* **1.** relating to, similar to, receiving, working for, or paid for by a stipend. —*n.* **2.** a person who receives a stipend, esp. as opposed to one who gives services freely.

stip·i·tate (stip'itāt), *adj.* bearing or borne by a stipe.

stip·i·ti·form (stip'itifôm,), *adj.* of stipe-like form.

stir·pi·culture (stû'pikul,CHə), *n.* the raising of special stocks or strains by selective breeding.

stirps (stûps), *n.*, *pl.* **stir·pes** (stû'pēz). a stock; a breed; a family; a line of descent.

stith·y (stiTH'ē), *n.* an anvil; a forge; a smithy.

sti·ver (stī'və), *n.* the smallest value or amount, as *I would not give a stiver for it* or *not a stiver of effort.*

sto·chas·tic (stokas'tik, stəkas'tik), *adj.* of or relating to a process of the science of statistics concerned with the behaviour of systems evolving in time in accordance with probabilistic laws and in particular with the effect of such evolution on random variables in a system.

stock car, a standard production automobile adapted for racing.

stock·pot (stok'pot,), *n.* a pot in which is made and kept a liquid derived from stewed meat, bones, or vegetables and used for soups and sauces.

stodge (stoj), *v.* to eat greedily, to gorge, to stuff, esp. with food.

stodg·y (stoj'ē), *adj.* dull; heavy; too full of facts or details; tedious, as a person, book, style, etc.

sto·i·cal (stō'ikəl), *adj.* impassive; self-controlled; courageous in the face of pain; austere in the face of temptation.

stoi·chi·om·e·try (stoi,kēom'itrē), *n.* the branch of chemistry concerned with the quantitative and other relationships among the elements of a compound substance.

stol·id (stol'id), *adj.* not easily excited; slow to feel or show feeling; unemotional.

sto·ma (stō'mə), *n.*, *pl.* **sto·ma·ta** (stō'mətə), **sto·mas.** a small or simple mouth-like aperture in lower animals and plants, acting as a mouth, pore, or the like.

sto·mat·ic (stōmat'ik), *adj.* relating to the mouth.

sto·ma·ti·tis (stō,mətī'tis), *n.* inflammation of the tissues and mucous membranes of the mouth.

sto·ma·tol·o·gy (stō,mətol'əjē), *n.* the scientific study of the mouth and its diseases.

stone·ware (stōn'we,ə), *n.* a hard, dense kind of pottery made from clay containing or mixed with flint or sand particles.

stope (stōp), *n.* the working face of a mine; any excavation of ore made accessible by shafts and drifts.

stop·ple (stop'əl), *n.* a stopper or plug for a bottle, etc., usually made of the same material as the bottle.

stoup (stoōp), *n.* a container for holy water, usually a stone basin set in the wall near or standing near the door of a church.

stra·bis·mus (strəbiz'məs), *n.* a squint; a visual condition in which one or both eyes are turned from the normal position so that they cannot reach a focus jointly.

stra·bot·o·my (strəbot'əmē), *n.* a surgical operation on one or more eye muscles to correct strabismus.

strafe (strāf), *v.* to attack from aircraft with machine-gun fire.

strait·en (strā'tən), *v.* **1.** to place in difficulty, esp. financial. **2.** to narrow or restrict in income, amount, scope, extent, etc.

stra·min·e·ous (strəmin'ēəs), *adj.* of or like straw; straw-coloured.

strange·ness (strānj'nis), *n.* **1.** the quality or condition of being strange. **2.** (in physics) a property of certain elementary particles that accounts for their unexpectedly slow decay. It is characterized by a quantum number (*strangeness number*). Symbol: **s.**

strap·pa·do (strəpā'dō, strəpä'dō), *n.*, *pl.* **strap·pa·does** (strəpā'dōz, strəpä'dōz). a form of punishment or torture in former times in which the victim was hoisted by a rope, usually by his hands tied behind him, and allowed to fall to the length of the rope, which did not reach the ground and so caused a painful jerk. See also **squassation.**

strass (stras), *n.* a glass-like composition with a high lead content used to make imitation gems.

strat·a·gem (strat'əjəm), *n.* a plan, trick, or device to attain an objective or deceive or gain advantage over an adversary.

stra·te·gic (strətē'jik), *adj.* **1.** (of a military operation) intended to make the enemy incapable of warfare, as a bombing mission to destroy materials, the economy, or morale. **2.** essential to the conduct of warfare, as of particular materials, industries, etc. See also **tactical.**

strat·e·gy (strat'əjē), *n.*, *pl.* **strat·e·gies.** a carefully laid plan, often complicated, for achieving something, as *a sales strategy* or *a battle strategy.*

stra·tig·ra·phy (strətig'rəfē), *n.* the study, description, classification, and interpretation of the order and succession of rock strata; historical geology.

stra·toc·ra·cy (strətok'rəsē), *n.* government by the army.

stra·to·cu·mu·lus (strā,tōkyōō'myōōləs), *n.*, *sing.* and *pl.* a type of heavy cloud lying below 8000 feet and consisting of round grey masses of water vapour in lines, waves, or groups within a continuous sheet.

strat·o·sphere (strat'əsfē,ə), *n.* the region of the atmosphere lying above the tropopause, extending from about 10 miles above the equator and 4 miles above the poles to about 15 miles above the earth, and within which the temperature remains comparatively stable.

stra·tum (strā'təm), *n.*, *pl.* **stra·ta.** a layer; a level, as in the earth, in society, etc.

stra·tus (strā'təs), *n.*, *sing.* and *pl.* a cloud or a class of cloud lying horizontally with a uniform base, heavy and grey in appearance, usually below 8000 feet, and often giving persistent drizzle.

stren·u·ous (stren'yōōəs), *adj.* involving much work and energy; difficult to do because of the strength or stamina required.

strep·i·tous (strep'itəs), *adj.* noisy; noisily rough.

strep·to·coc·cus (strep,tōkok'əs), *n.*, *pl.* **strep·to·coc·ci** (strep,tōkok'sī). any of a group of spherical or oval, chain-forming bacteria causing many common infections, esp. of the throat, with a more generalized effect than is caused by a staphylococcus but less violent at the source of infection, as scarlet fever, tonsillitis, endocarditis, puerperal fever.

strep·to·my·ces (strep,tōmī'sēz), *n.*, *sing.* and *pl.* any of several species of aerobic bacteria which produce antibiotics.

strep·to·my·cin (strep,tōmī'sin), *n.* an antibiotic produced by a mould-like bacterium found in soil and used chiefly as a highly effective treatment for tuberculosis.

stres·sor (stres'ə), *n.* something that causes stress.

streu·sel (strōō'zəl, sHtroi'zəl), *n. Chiefly U.S.* a crumbly mixture of sugar, cinnamon, flour, butter, and chopped nuts used as a topping for cakes, esp. for coffee-cake.

stri·a (strī'ə), *n.*, *pl.* **stri·ae** (strī'ē). a slight ridge, furrow, score, stripe, or similar linear mark, esp. one of several arranged in parallel fashion.

stri·ate (strī'āt), *v.* **1.** to mark with striae. —*adj.* **2.** marked with striae. —**stri·a'tion,** *n.*

strick·le (strik'əl), *n.* a rod for levelling off heaped up grain, etc., in line with the top of a measuring container.

stric·tion (strik'sHən), *n.* the act of pulling tight or constricting.

stric·ture (strik'CHə), *n.* **1.** a comment, esp. one of adverse criticism. **2.** an abnormal narrowing of a passage or tube of the body, as the rectum, urethra.

stri·dent (strī'dənt), *adj.* having or making a harsh or grating sound.

stri·dor (strī'də), *n.* a loud, harsh, grating sound.

strid·u·late (strid'yōōlāt), *v.* to make a shrill grating noise by rubbing together hard parts of the body, as does a grasshopper. —**strid'u·lous,** *adj.*

strig·i·form (strij'ifôm,), *adj.* of, relating to, or belonging to the order consisting of the owls.

stri·gose (strī'gōs), *adj.* bristly or hairy; finely ridged or grooved; with close-set, fine points.

strin·gent (strin'jənt), *adj.* rigorous or binding, as of laws, regulations, etc.; compelling; urgent.

string·piece (strinG'pēs), *n.* a long horizontal timber connecting and supporting parts of a framework.

stro·bic (strō'bik), *adj.* spinning or appearing to spin.

stro·bi·la·ceous (strō,bilā'sHəs), *adj.* cone-like.

stro·bo·scope (strō'bəskōp,), *n.* **1.** a device for studying the motion of a rapidly vibrating or revolving object by illuminating it periodically with a flash of the same frequency as the vibration or revolution, or by revealing it through widely spaced openings on a revolving disc, so that the object appears to slow down or stop. **2.** a photographic device for illuminating a rapidly moving object such as a bullet for a very brief period and synchronizing the illumination with a rapid shutter opening of a camera so as to produce a still photograph; a photograph produced by such a device.

stro·bo·tron (strō'bətron), *n.* a lamp used in a stroboscope to produce a brilliant flash of light in response to a pulsing voltage.

stro·ga·noff (strō'gənof, strog'ənof), *adj.* denoting a way of serving meat, usually beef, cut into thin strips, sautéed with onion and mushroom in butter, and with sour cream stirred into the mixture to form a sauce.

stro·phe (strō'fē), *n.* **1.** a part of an ancient Greek choral ode during which the chorus moved to its left as it sang. **2.** any of the separate sections of a poem that do not have a regularly recurring pattern. —**stro'phic,** *adj.*

struc·tur·al·ism (struk'CHərəliz,əm), *n.* **1.** an approach used in linguistics, anthropology, literature, psychology, and other disciplines that analyses languages, social customs, texts, etc. in terms of basic structures and patterns that, its adherents claim, can be identified in virtually all fields of human activity and culture. **2.** a branch of linguistics concerned with the structure of the phonology, morphology, and syntax of language, rather than its semantic content. —**struc'tur·al·ist,** *n.*

stru·del (strōō'dəl, SHrōō'dəl), *n.* a pastry consisting of a roll of extremely thin flaky pastry filled with a fruit or cheese mixture.

stru·ma (strōō'mə), *n., pl.* **stru·mae** (strōō'mē). **1.** goitre. **2.** a scrofulous swelling. —**stru'mous,** *adj.*

stru·thi·ous (strōō,thēəs), *adj.* like or of the same family as the ostriches.

strych·nine (strik'nēn, strik'nin, strik'nīn), *n.* a poison extracted from certain plants, esp. nux vomica, and having a highly stimulative effect on the nervous system, used mainly as an antidote for poisoning by depressant drugs.

strych·nin·ism (strik'niniz,əm), *n.* a medical condition caused by an overdose, perhaps accumulated, of strychnine.

stuffed derma. See **kishke.**

stul·ti·fy (stul'tifī), *v.* to make foolish; to show up in a ridiculous light; to render futile or worthless.

stum (stum), *n.* **1.** unfermented or incompletely fermented grape juice. **2.** wine to which stum has been added and which has therefore undergone further fermentation.

stump·age (stum'pij), *n. U.S. and Canadian.* standing timber with reference to its value; the right to cut timber standing on another's land.

stu·pa (stōō'pə), *n.* a dome-shaped or pyramidal monument, of earth or other materials, built over relics of or at a place associated with Buddha.

stupe (styōōp), *n.* layers of flannel or similar material soaked in hot water and put on the skin as a counter-irritant.

stu·pe·fa·cient (styōō,pəfā'SHənt), *adj.* causing stupor; stupefying; stunning.

stu·pe·fac·tion (styōō,pəfak'SHən), *n.* the act of producing or the state of being in a stupor. —**stu·pe·fac'tive,** *adj.*

Styg·i·an (stij'ēən), *adj.* depressingly dark and gloomy.

sty·lar (stī'lə), *adj.* like a stylus, pen, needle, or similar pointed instrument.

style (stīl), *n.* (in a flower). See **carpel.**

sty·let (stī'lit), *n.* a slender dagger.

sty·li·form (stī'lifôm,), *adj.* resembling a stylus in shape.

sty·lo·graph (stī'ləgräf,, stī'ləgraf,), *n.* a type of fountain pen with a fine tube forming the writing point. —**sty,lo·graph'ic,** *adj.*

sty·log·ra·phy (stīlog'rəfē), *n.* the art of using a stylus.

sty·loid (stī'loid), *adj.* stylus-like; slender and pointed.

sty·lus (stī'ləs), *n., pl.* **sty·li** (stī'lī), **sty·lus·es.** an ancient writing implement made of metal, bone, or similar material, with one end sharp for cutting letters in a waxed tablet and the other end blunt for obliterating letters and smoothing the wax; any implement similar in form or function.

styp·sis (stip'sis), *n.* the use of or application of a styptic agent or substance.

styp·tic (stip'tik), *adj.* having the property of contracting organic tissue or checking bleeding.

sua·sion (swā'ZHən), *n.* the act of attempting to convince or impel by reason or advice, as opposed to compulsion by force.

sub·al·i·men·ta·tion (subal,imentā'SHən), *n.* See **hypoalimentation.**

sub·al·tern (subôl'tən), *adj.* of lower rank; subordinate.

sub·cla·vate (subklā'vāt), *adj.* nearly or to some degree club-shaped.

sub·clin·i·cal (subklin'ikəl), *adj.* of or relating to a phase of disease during which no symptoms are exhibited. —**sub·clin'i·cal·ly,** *adv.*

sub·con·tig·u·ous (sub,kəntig'yōōəs), *adj.* nearly touching.

sub·crit·i·cal (subkrit'ikəl), *adj.* (in nuclear physics) **1.** denoting a mass of fissile material less than the critical mass; a mass less than that needed to sustain a nuclear chain reaction, as in an atomic bomb. **2.** (of a process, plant, etc.) designed to operate with a subcritical fissile mass: a *subcritical reactor.*

sub·cu·ta·ne·ous (sub,kyōōtā'nēəs), *adj.*

under the skin, as tissue, an injection, or certain parasites.

sub·duct (səbdukt'), v. 1. (in anatomy) to turn or rotate downwards, esp. the eyes. 2. to deduct; subtract; take away. —**sub·duc'tion,** n.

sub·fe·brile (subfē'brīl) adj. slightly fevered.

sub·fusc (subfusk'), adj. dusky; dingy; sombre. Also **sub·fus'cous.**

sub·in·flu·ent (subin'flōoənt), n. a plant or animal that has a subordinate effect on the other animals or plants in its environment. See also **influent.**

sub·ja·cent (subjā'sənt), adj. underlying.

sub·jec·tive (səbjek'tiv), adj. resulting from personal opinion, behaviour, character, etc., esp. without any attempt at fairness or at considering another person, thing, or situation.

subjective idealism, a philosophical theory that all experience consists of ideas that originate in or are distorted in the mind of the observer. See also **objective idealism.**

sub·li·mate (səb'limāt), v. **sub·li·mat·ed, sub·li·mat·ing.** to raise to a higher purpose or rationale an emotion or action originally of a baser nature.

sub·lim·i·nal (sublim'ənəl), adj. below the threshold of consciousness; perceived unconsciously. See also **supraliminal.**

sub·lux·a·tion (sub,luksā'sHən), n. partial dislocation of a joint due to stretching of the ligaments by injury; sprain.

sub·merse (səbmûs'), v. to submerge.

sub·min·i·a·tur·ize (submin'ēəCHərīz), v. to make or design in an extremely small size, as electronic equipment.

sub·mis·sive (səbmis'iv), adj. weakly agreeing to the will or demands of another or others.

sub·orn (səbôn'), v. to bribe or to induce by unlawful or underhand means to commit a crime or misdeed. —**sub,or·na'tion,** n.

sub·poena (səpē'nə, səbpē'nə), n. legally binding summons to appear for the giving of testimony.

sub·rep·tion (səbrep'sHən), n. a misleading or mistaken representation; a conclusion drawn from such representation.

sub·ro·gate (sub'rəgāt), v. to substitute.

sub ro·sa (sub rō'zə), Latin. in confidence; secretly.

sub·se·quent (sub'səkwənt), adj. following; next in order, as The subsequent days were occupied with sunbathing.

sub·se·rous (subsēr'əs), adj. under a serous membrane.

sub·serve (səbsûv'), v. to be instrumental in furthering; to serve as a means toward.

sub·ser·vi·ent (səbsû'vēənt), adj. servile; cringing; obsequious.

sub·side (səbsīd'), v. **sub·sid·ed, sub·sid·ing.** to go or sink downwards, as the ground; reduce in

strength or power, as a temperature. —**sub·sid·ence** (səbsī'dəns, sub'sidəns), n.

sub·sid·i·ar·i·ty (səbsid,iar'ətē), n. the policy that government should be devolved to the level most closely associated with legislation or administration in any given field, whether supranational, national, regional, or local.

sub·sist (səbsist'), v. 1. to have existence. 2. to endure, persist. 3. to live or be sustained at the most basic level: to subsist on maize. 4. (followed by in) to be part of; to be inherent in. 5. (in philosophy) to be logically conceivable; to exist as a concept rather than a fact. —**sub·sis'tent,** adj. —**sub·sis'ter,** n.

sub·stan·ti·ate (səbstan'sHēāt), v. **sub·stan·ti·at·ed, sub·stan·ti·at·ing.** supporting; helping to establish. —**sub·stan,ti·a'tion,** n.

sub·struc·tion (substruk'sHən), n. the foundation or structure acting as foundation of a building or other construction.

sub·sume (səbsyōōm', səbsōōm'), v. to take into or consider as part of a larger whole, as one idea, instance, or principle into a theory, rule, class, etc.

sub·tend (səbtend'), v. to act as, contain in, or define an outline.

sub·ter·fu·ge (sub'təfyōōj), n. an evasion, trick, or device used to avoid or conceal something.

sub·ter·rane (sub,tərān'), n. a cave; a room underground.

sub·tle (sut'əl), adj. 1. not obvious; hidden from easy detection or understanding because it is not obvious, as a subtle odour, or because it was deliberately concealed, as a subtle poem. 2. so delicate or refined that understanding requires great intelligence, exceptional taste, or unusual ability. —**sub'tle·ty,** n.

sub·to·pi·a (subtō'pēə), n. suburban paradise, used ironically of the spread of commonplace houses and narrowly conventional attitudes.

sub·tra·hend (sub'trəhend), n. a number or quantity to be subtracted from another. See also **minuend.**

su·bu·late (sē'byōōlāt), adj. shaped like an awl.

sub·ur·bi·car·i·an (səbû'biker'ēən), adj. near Rome.

sub·vene (səbvēn'), v. to serve as a support or relief.

sub·ven·tion (səbven'sHən), n. 1. a grant of money, esp. by a government, to support or help an enterprise or institution; a subsidy. 2. the supplying of support or help.

sub·ver·sive (səbvû'siv), adj. tending to subvert.

sub·vert (səbvût'), v. to overthrow; to bring about the ruin of; to corrupt.

suc·ce·da·ne·um (suk,sidā'nēəm), n., pl. **suc·ce·da·ne·a** (suk,sidā'nēə). a substitute, frequently an inferior one.

suc·cès de scan·dale (sŏōksä, də skondäl'), *n.*, *pl.* **suc·cès de scan·dale.** something, esp. a play, book, film, etc., that achieves popularity due to its scandalous or controversial nature rather than artistic merit. [*French*, literally, success of scandal]

suc·cès d'es·time (sŏōksä, destēm'), *n.*, *pl.* **suc·cès d'es·time.** something, esp. a dramatic or literary work, that achieves critical success rather than popular acclaim. [*French*, literally, success of esteem]

suc·cès fou (sŏōksä, fŏō'), *n.*, *pl.* **suc·cès fous.** an amazing success. [*French*, literally, mad success]

suc·cinct (səksiNGkt'), *adj.* concise; brief in verbal expression.

suc·cour (suk'ə), *n* **1.** aid or relief in time of need. —*v.* **2.** to give help or relief in tlme of need; to come to the aid of.

suc·cu·bus (suk'yŏōbəs), *n.*, *pl.* **suc·cu·bi** (suk'yŏōbī). a female demon supposed to have sexual intercourse with men while they are asleep. Also **succuba.** See also **incubus.**

suc·cumb (səkum'), *v.* to give way to a superior force, as disease, old age, etc.

suc·cur·sal (səkû'səl), *adj.* subsidiary; subordinate to another, esp. of a religious foundation.

suc·cuss (səkus'), *v.* to shake up. —**suc·cus'·sion,** *n.*

suc·to·ri·al (suktôr'ēəl), *adj.* **1.** designed or adapted for sucking, as the mouthparts of certain insects. **2.** relating to or having suction or suckers.

su·da·to·ri·um (sŏō,dətôr'ēəm), *n.*, *pl.* **su·da·to·ri·a** (sŏō,dətôr'ēə). a room where hot air baths are taken to induce sweating; such a bath.

su·da·to·ry (sŏō'dətərē), *adj.* relating to or inducing sweating.

su·dor·if·er·ous (sŏō,dərif'ərəs), *adj.* containing or secreting sweat.

su·dor·if·ic (sŏō,dərif'ik), *adj.* causing or promoting sweating.

su·dor·ip·a·rous (sŏō,dərip'ərəs), *adj.* producing or secreting sweat.

suf·fice (səfīs'), *v.* to be enough; to meet the needs of.

suf·frage (suf'rij), *n.* the right of voting at elections, esp. political elections.

suf·fra·gist (suf'rəjist), *n.* an advocate of granting voting rights.

suf·fru·tes·cent (suf,rŏōtes'ənt), *adj.* partly or to some degree woody.

suf·fu·mi·gate (səfyŏō'migāt), *v.* to subject to fumes or smoke, esp. from below.

suf·fuse (səfyŏōz'), *v.* to overspread with or as if with a fluid, a colour, light, etc.

sug·gest·i·ble (səgjes'təbəl), *adj.* capable of being influenced or easily influenced by suggestion.

sug·ges·tive (səgjes'tiv), *adj.* that suggests; full of suggestions; evocative; suggesting something indecent.

su·i gen·er·is (sŏō,ī jen'əris), *adj.* unique; one-of-a-kind, as *a sui generis work of art.* [*Latin*, of his, her, or its own kind]

su·i ju·ris (sŏō,ī jŏōr'is), *Latin.* of full age and capacity to manage one's affairs or take legal responsibility.

su·ki·ya·ki (sŏō,kēyä'kē, skēyä'kē), *n.* a Japanese dish of pieces of beef, chicken, or pork, green vegetables, and bean curd, usually flavoured with soy sauce and cooked at the table in a chafing dish.

sul·cate (sul'kāt), *adj.* furrowed; grooved; cleft, as certain plant stems or animal hoofs.

sul·cus (sul'kəs), *n.* a furrow; a groove; a fissure, esp. between brain convolutions.

sul·lage (sul'ij), *n.* sewage; sediment deposited by running water.

sul·len (səl'ən), *adj.* gloomy and unfriendly; antisocial.

sul·ly (sul'ē). *v.* to soil or stain; to pollute or defile.

sul·pha·di·a·zine (sul,fədī'əzēn), *n.* a drug derived from sulphanilamide and used mainly to treat infections caused by pneumococci, staphylococci, streptococci, and gonococci.

sulpha drug. See **sulphonamide.**

sul·pha·mer·a·zine (sul,fəmer'əzēn), *n.* a drug derived from sulphadiazine and used mainly to treat infections caused by meningococci.

sul·pha·nil·a·mide (sul,fənil'əmīd), *n.* a synthetic organic chemical compound used mainly to arrest infections caused by haemolytic bacteria such as staphylococci, gonococci, etc.

sul·pha·pyr·a·zine (sul,fəpēr'əzēn), *n.* a drug derived from sulphonamide and used to treat infections caused by staphylococci or gonococci.

sul·pha·pyr·i·dine (sul,fəpēr'idēn), *n.* a drug derived from sulfanilamide and used chiefly to treat one form of dermatitis but formerly to treat pneumococcal infections.

sulph·ars·phen·a·mine (sulf,äsfen'əmin, sulf,äsfen'əmēn), *n.* a drug formerly used to treat syphllis.

sul·pha·thi·a·zole (sul,fəthī'əzōl), *n.* a drug derived from sulphanilamide and used formerly to treat pneumonia and infections caused by staphylococci but now little used because of its toxic side effects.

sul·phi·sox·a·zole (sul,fisok'səzōl), *n.* a drug derived from sulphanilamide and used mainly to treat infections of the urinary tract.

sul·phon·a·mide (sulfon'əmīd), *n.* any of a certain group of drugs, the first effective antibacterial drugs to be discovered, which have the effect of arresting the development of bacteria and are still widely used to treat various bacterial diseases, infections, burns, wounds, and the like, although partly superseded by antibiotics. Also **sulpha drug.**

sulphur dioxide, a suffocating gas formed when sulphur burns and used mainly as a bleach, a disinfectant, a fumigating agent, in preserving fruit and vegetables, and in the production of sulphuric acid.

sul·try (sǝl'trē), *adj.* **sul·tri·er, sul·tri·est. 1.** very hot and humid. **2.** arousing or suggesting passion, as *a sultry blonde.*

su·mi (soo'mē), *n.* a black ink much used by calligraphers and painters, made by a Japanese method of mixing soot from burnt plants with glue and letting the mixture solidify into cakes or sticks which are then powdered into water to form the ink.

sum·ma cum lau·de (soom'ǝ koom lou'dǝ), with highest praise; (in the U.S.A.) the highest of the three special grades of honour granted to above-average graduates. See also **cum laude, magna cum laude.**

sum·mand (sum'and), *n.* an item to be added in a sum.

sum·ma·ry (sum'ǝrē), *n.* **1.** a brief but comprehensive account of previous statements; résumé —*adj.* **2.** concise; performed with prompt directness; done without formality or due ceremony.

su·mo (soo'mō), *n.* a form of Japanese wrestling, usually between tall, extremely heavy participants, in which the aim is to force the opponent out of the ring or to make him touch the ground with any part other than his feet.

sump (sump), *n.* a pit, well, or other such reservoir for collecting liquid.

sump·tu·ary (sump'CHOOǝrē), *adj.* regulating expenditure or expense.

sump·tu·ous (sump'CHOOǝs), *adj.* costly; splendidly luxurious.

su·per·an·nu·at·ed (soo,pǝan'yooǎ,tid), *adj.* **1.** retired because of old age or infirmity, esp. with a pension. **2.** discarded as too old; outdated.

su·per·bomb (soo'pǝbom,), *n.* a bomb of unusually great destructive power, as a hydrogen bomb.

su·per·cil·i·ous (soo,pǝsil'ēǝs), *adj.* showing haughty contempt.

su·per·con·duc·tiv·i·ty (soo,pǝkon,dǝktiv'itē), *n.* the property possessed by some substances at very low temperatures of having no resistance to the flow of electric current.

su·per·cool (soo,pǝkool'), *v.* to cool a liquid below its freezing point without bringing about its solidification or crystallization.

su·per·e·go (soo,pǝrē'gō), *n.* that part of the mind, part conscious and part unconscious, that mediates between the desires of the ego and social ideals.

su·per·er·o·gate (soo,pǝrer'ǝgāt), *v.* to do

more than is required by duty or circumstances. —**su,per·e·rog'a·to·ry,** *adj.*

su·per·fi·ci·es (soo,pǝfisH'iēz), *n., sing.* and *pl.* the surface; the outside; the outward appearance.

su·per·flu·id (soo,pǝfloo'id), *n.* a fluid that exhibits abnormally low viscosity and frictionless flow (so that it flows easily through small openings or long narrow tubes), and also has extremely high heat conductivity, the only known example being liquid helium at a temperature lower than 2.19 degrees K.

su·per·flu·ous (soopû'flooǝs), *adj.* extra and unnecessary beyond what is needed. —**su·per'flu·ous·ness,** *n.* —**su,per·flu'i·ty,** *n.*

su·per·gene (soo'pǝjēn), *adj.* formed by waters percolating down through rocks, as mineral and ore deposits. See also **hypogene.**

supergiant star, a star of exceptional brightness and enormous size, being more than 10 times greater in diameter than the sun, as Antares.

su·per·graph·ics (soo,pǝgraf'iks), *n. pl.* decorative graphic designs in oversized patterns or panels.

su·per·in·cum·bent (soo,pǝrinkum'bǝnt), *adj.* lying on or overhanging something else.

su·per·ja·cent (soo,pǝjā'sǝnt), *adj.* lying on or above something else.

su·per·max·il·la (soo,pǝmaksil'ǝ), *n., pl.* **su·per·max·il·lae.** the upper jaw.

su·per·mun·dane (soo,pǝmundān'), *adj.* above or superior to earthly or worldly matters.

su·per·nal (soopû'nǝl), *adj.* belonging or relating to a higher state of existence than on earth; heavenly; in or of the skies; celestial; lofty in powers or position.

su·per·no·va (soo,pǝnō'vǝ), *n., pl.* **su·per·no·vae** (soo,pǝnō'vē), **su·per·no·vas.** a nova of extreme brilliance, giving out ten million to a hundred million times more light than the sun, leaving behind some permanent change, as the patch of gas known as the Crab Nebula, and of such rare occurrence that only three have been recorded in our galaxy and about 50 more in other galaxies.

su·per·nu·mer·ar·y (soo,pǝnyoo'mǝrǝrē), *adj.* **1.** in excess of the usual or necessary number; extra. **2.** of or denoting an actor employed in addition to the regular company and appearing on stage but having no lines to speak.

su·per·sat·u·rate (soo,pǝsacH'ǝrāt), *v.* to increase the concentration, as of a solution, a vapour, etc., beyond saturation point.

su·per·sede (soo,pǝsēd'), *v.* **su·per·sed·ed, su·per·sed·ing.** to replace something that is no longer functioning, fashionable, or useful.

su·per·son·ic (soo,pǝson'ik), *adj.* with or at a speed greater than the speed of sound.

su·per·string (soo'pǝstriNG,), *n.* (in physics) a concept applied to the interactions of certain elementary particles in which their behaviour is considered to be analogous to minute loops of string rather than definite points.

su·per·vene (sōō,pəvēn'), v. to occur as something in addition or unrelated to the matter in hand.

su·pi·na·tion (sōō,pinā'sHən), n. the movement of the hand or forearm so that the palm faces forwards or upwards; the position resulting from such a turn. See also **pronation**.

su·pine (sōō'pīn), adj. lying with the face or front upward. See also **prone**.

sup·plant (səplänt'), v. to replace, often by trickery.

sup·ple·to·ry (sup'litəre), adj. added to fill a deficiency; supplementary.

sup·pli·ant (sup'lēənt), n. a person who supplicates.

sup·pli·cate (sup'likat), v. to pray, ask, or beg for humbly. —**sup,pli·ca'tion,** n.

sup·po·si·tious (sup,əzisH'əs), adj. assumed; based on hypothesis or supposition; supposititious.

sup·pos·i·ti·tious (səpoz,itisH'əs), adj. substituted for the real, esp. fraudulently; not genuine.

sup·pu·rate (sup'yōōrāt), v. to produce, secrete, or discharge pus. —**sup,pu·ra'tion,** n. —**sup'pu·ra·tive,** adj.

su·pra (sōō'prə) adv. above, as referring to a previous part of a text. See also **infra**.

su·pra·lim·i·nal (sōō,prəlim'inəl, syōō,prəlim'inəl), adj. above the threshold of consciousness or sensation, thus within normal consciousness. See also **subliminal**.

su·pra·ra·tion·al (sōō,prərasH'ənəl, syōō,-prərasH'ənəl), adj. above or beyond the power of reason or comprehension.

su·ral (syoor'əl), adj. of or relating to the calf of the leg.

sur·cease (sûsēs'), v. to cease; to desist.

sure·ty (sHoor'itē), n. a thing pledged as a security against loss or damage, or for the fulfilment of a promise or debt.

surface-active agent (sû'fisak'tiv ā'jənt), any substance that affects the surface tension or interfacial tension of water or water-based solutions, usually reducing it so that the wetting or spreading capability of the liquid is increased. Also **surfactant**.

surface boundary layer, the thin layer of air immediately above the surface of the earth and usually no more than 300 feet in height. Also **ground layer, friction layer, atmospheric boundary layer.**

sur·fac·tant (sûfak'tənt), n. See **surface-active agent**.

sur·feit (sû'fit), n. an excess.

sur·ly (sû'lē), adj. sur·li·er, sur·li·est. ill-mannered; unpleasantly hostile.

sur·mise (sûmīz'), v. **1.** to form an opinion on

slight evidence; to guess. —n. **2.** a guess; an opinion formed on slight evidence.

sur·rep·ti·tious (sur,əptisH'əs), adj. stealthy; sneaky.

sur·ro·gate (sur'əgāt), n. **1.** a person appointed to act or be deputy for another. —v. **2.** to appoint a deputy or successor.

sur·tax (sû'taks), n. a tax levied in addition to normal tax on incomes above a certain level. See also **normal tax**.

sur·tout (sûtōō'), n. a man's overcoat; a hooded cape for a woman.

sur·veil·lance (sûvā'ləns), n. a close guard or watch, as over a prisoner, suspect premises, or the like. —**sur·veil'lant,** adj.

sus·cep·ti·ble (səsep'təbəl), adj. open to or yielding easily to, esp. as a result of weakness or lack of resistance, as *susceptible to a woman's allure* or *susceptible to disease.* —**sus·cep,ti·bil'·i·ty,** n.

sus·pi·ra·tion (sus,pirā'sHən), n. a heavy sigh.

sus·tain (səstān'), v. to maintain; keep up; keep on (doing something). —**sus'ten·ance,** n.

sus·ten·ta·tion (sus,tentā'sHən), n. the sustaining or maintaining of life or activity; the providing of support, maintenance, or money for upkeep.

sus·ten·tion (səsten'sHən), n. the act of sustaining; the condition of being sustained.

su·sur·rant (syōōsur'ənt), adj. whispering; gently rustling. —**su,sur·ra'tion,** n.

su·sur·rus (syōōsur'əs), n. a whisper; a gentle rustle or murmur. —**su·sur'rous,** adj.

sut·ler (sut'lə), n. a person who follows an army to sell food and other provisions to the soldiers.

sut·tee (sutē', sut'ē), n. **1.** the former Hindu custom of a widow's self-immolation on her husband's funeral pyre. **2.** a woman who cremates herself in this fashion. —**sut·tee·ism** (sutē'iz,əm), n.

su·ze·rain (sōō'zərān), n. a sovereign or state holding political control over another. —**su'ze·rain·ty,** n.

swale (swāl), n. *Chiefly U.S.* a depression in a stretch of land, frequently damper and with coarser vegetation than its surroundings.

sward (swôd), n. the short grass covering a lawn or open land; turf.

swarf (swôf)n. a mass of small pieces and shavings of metal, plastic, or the like, removed by grinding or cutting tools during machining operations.

swarth·y (swô'THē), adj. dark in colour, usually of the complexion. Also **swart**.

swas·ti·ka (swos'tikə), n. a figure consisting of a cross with four equal arms, each arm having an extension at right angles to it and all extensions pointing clockwise or all pointing anti-clockwise, the figure having been universally used since prehistoric times as a symbol and ornament and, with clockwise extensions, as the symbol of the Nazi party in Germany.

swath (swôth), *n.* the area covered by one stroke of a scythe or one passage of a mower.

swathe (swāTH), *v.* to bind or envelop with strips of linen, bandage, rope, or the like.

S wave, secondary wave; the second major shock wave radiating from an earthquake. See also **L wave, P wave.**

sweetheart agreement, *Colloquial.* a contract agreed by collusion between representatives of management and labour to pay union employees low wages.

swindle sheet, *Slang.* an account drawn up of expenses incurred in carrying out one's job and to be repaid in addition to salary; an expense account.

syb·a·rite (sib'ərīt), *n.* a person who practises luxurious and sensuous self-indulgence. —**syb,·a·rit'ic,** *adj.*

syc·o·phan·cy (sik'əfənsē), *n.* excessive flattery and servility to a superior, esp. to hold or gain a position.

syc·o·phant (sik'əfənt), *n.* a person practising or in the habit of practising sycophancy. —**syc,·o·phan'tic,** *adj.*

sy·co·sis (sīkō'sis), *n.* chronic inflammation of the hair follicles, esp. of the beard and moustache, most commonly due to bacterial infection.

syl·la·bar·y (sil'əbərē), *n.* a system of symbols representing syllables and used for writing a particular language, as several ancient West Semitic, Aegean, and Mesopotamian languages, and Japanese.

syl·la·bub (sil'əbub), *n.* a dish of cream or milk whipped with wine, sweetened, and sometimes flavoured, as with lemon. Also **sillabub.**

syl·lo·gism (sil'əjiz,əm), *n.* **1.** (in logic) a form of reasoning in which a conclusion is drawn from two premises which have a term in common, as *All rivers flow to the sea; this is a river; therefore, this flows to the sea.* **2.** a subtle or specious argument. —**syl,lo·gis'tic,** *adj.*

sylph (silf), *n.* a slender, graceful woman.

syl·van (sil'vən), *adj.* of, relating to, or living in woodlands.

syl·vi·cul·ture (sil'vikul,CHə), *n.* See **silviculture.**

sym·bi·ont (sim'bēont), *n.* a symbiotic organism.

sym·bi·o·sis (sim,bēō'sis), *n.,* *pl.* **sym·bi·o·ses** (sim,bēō'sēz). an association of two dissimilar organisms living either attached each to the other or one as tenant of the other, usually when the association benefits both organisms. —**sym,·bi·o'tic,** *adj.*

sym·met·al·lism (simet'əliz,əm), *n.* the use of more than one metal as a monetary standard

with each having its value fixed in relation to the other(s). See also **bimetallism.**

sym·pa·thet·ic (sim,pəthet'ik), *adj.* pertaining to the major part of the motor nerve supply to smooth muscles and glands which consists of nerves and ganglia running from the thoracic and lumbar regions of the spinal cord to all of the skin, the limbs, and the internal organs, in many of which they act antagonistically to parasympathetic nerves, as in stimulating the heartbeat, dilating the pupil of the eye, inhibiting peristalsis in the gut, etc. See also **parasympathetic.**

sym·pa·tho·mi·met·ic (sim,pəthōmimet'ik), *adj.* **1.** (of a drug, etc.) stimulating the sympathetic nervous system or mimicking the effects of such stimulation. —*n.* **2.** a sympathomimetic drug.

sym·pat·ric (simpat'rik), *adj.* from or in the same locality or region, as of biological species.

sym·phy·sis (sim'fisis), *n.,* *pl.* **sym·phy·ses** (sim'fisēz). a fusion of bones or a joint allowing only slight or no movement, as that of the lower jawbone or of the pubis in man.

sym·po·si·arch (simpō'zēāk,), *n.* the director or chairman of a symposium.

sym·po·si·um (simpō'zēəm), *n.,* *pl.* **sym·po·si·ums, sym·po·si·a** (simpō'zēə). a conference where lectures are given or discussions (esp. before an audience) held by several speakers on a particular subject.

symp·to·sis (simptō'sis), *n.* local or general wasting away of the body.

syn·aes·the·si·a (sin,isthē'zēə), *n.* a sensation produced in one part of the body by a stimulus in another part; an effect on one of the senses produced by a stimulus to another, as a mental impression of a particular smell produced by the stimulus of a particular sight.

syn·ar·thro·sis (sin,äthrō'sis), *n.,* *pl.* **syn·ar·thro·ses** (sin,äthrō'sēz). a fixed joint, as of the bones of the skull or the teeth sockets.

sync (siNGk), *n.* *Colloquial.* synchronization; synchronism.

syn·chro·nism (siNG'krəniz,əm), *n.* the state of occurring at, existing in, or occupying the same space of time. —**syn·chron'ic,** *adj.*

syn·cre·tism (siNG'krətiz,əm), *n.* the reconciling of or attempt to reconcile diverse or opposite beliefs, practices, or groups, esp. in religion or philosophy.

syn·dac·tyl (sindak'til), *adj.* having some fingers or toes joined together completely or partially.

syn·de·re·sis (sindərē'sis), *n.* an inborn moral sense. Also **syn,te·re'sis.**

syn·des·mo·sis (sin'desmō'sis), *n.,* *pl.* **syn·des·mo·ses** (sin'desmō'sēz). a linkage of bones by ligaments or similar connective tissue other than at a joint and allowing little possibility of movement in relation to each other.

syn·det (sin'det), *n.* a synthetic detergent.

syn·det·ic (sindet'ik), *adj.* serving to link or join.

syn·dic (sin'dik), *n.* a person who officially represents and transacts business for a university or other corporate body. —**syn'di·cal**, *adj.*

syn·di·cal·ism (sin'dikəliz,əm), *n.* a movement, originating in France, seeking to transfer the control and ownership of the means of production and distribution, and ultimately the control of society, to workers' unions. —**syn'di·cal·ist**, *n.*, *adj.*

syn·drome (sin'drōm), *n.* a group of medical symptoms which when they occur together indicate a particular condition or disease.

syn·e·chism (sin'əkiz,əm), *n.* a philosophical inclination in thought to emphasize continuity, first recognized and recommended by the American philosopher C.S. Peirce (1839–1914).

syn·e·col·o·gy (sin,əkol'əjē), *n.* the ecology of a community of plants and animals as opposed to that of an individual species. See also **autecology.**

syn·ec·tics (sinek'tiks), *n.* the study of creativity, esp. creativity generated among a group of people and applied to solving problems.

synectics group, a group of diverse individuals who meet to try to find creative solutions to problems by the free play and interplay of their imaginations.

syn·er·get·ic (sin,əjet'ik), *adj.* working together. Also **syn,er·gis'tic.**

syn·er·gism (sin'əjiz,əm), *n.* the combined activity of two or more drugs, hormones, muscles, stimuli, or the like, which work towards the same end and produce an effect greater than the sum of effects of each acting alone.

syn·er·gy (sin'əjē), *n.* cooperative activity, esp. of two or more muscles, nerves, drugs hormones, or the like.

syn·ga·my (siNG'gəmē), *n.* the fusion of male and female gametes in fertilization.

syn·gen·e·sis (sinjen'isis), *n.* reproduction by fusion of male and female gametes; sexual reproduction.

syn·od (sin'əd, sin'od), *n.* any convention or council.

syn·od·ic (sinod'ik), *adj.* relating to similar positions of the moon or a planet relative to an imaginary line from the centre of the sun through the centre of the earth, and hence relating to the time between two instances of the moon or a planet apparently lying on this line.

sy·noe·cious, sy·ne·cious (sinē'sHəs), *adj.* See **synoicous.**

sy·noet·ic, sy·net·ic (sinet'ik), *adj.* in community or association with others.

syn·oi·cous (sinoi'kəs), *adj.* having male and female flowers on the same flower head, as in many composites such as the daisy and dandelion. Also **sy·ne'cious.**

syn·o·nym (sin'ənim), *n.* **1.** a word that means the same thing as another word, as *pigs* and *swine.* **2.** a word that has a meaning very close to that of another word or words, as *book*, *tome*, and *volume.* See also **antonym.** —**sy·non'y·mous,** *adj.*

syn·op·tic (sinop'tik), *adj.* of, relating to, taking, or giving a condensed but comprehensive statement or view of a subject.

syn·os·to·sis (sin,ostō'sis), *n.* the fusion of separate bones to form one bone.

syn·o·vi·a (sinō'vēə), *n.* a viscous fluid secreted by membranes lining certain joints and sheathing certain tendons and having the function of lubrication.

syn·tal·i·ty (sintal'itē), *n.* the mental and behavioural features of a group corresponding to the personality of the individual.

syn·the·sis (sin,thəsis), *n.*, *pl.* **syn·the·ses** (sin'thəsēz). the bringing together of two or more separate ingredients to create a single new substance, idea, etc. See also **analysis.** —**syn'the·size,** *v.*

synthetic philosophy, a philosophical system formulated and expounded by the English philosopher Herbert Spencer (1820–1903), and intended to comprehend and unify all knowledge on the basis of the evolutionary principle.

Syn·the·tism (sin,thətiz,əm), *n.* a style of painting developed in the late 19th century, making use of flat areas of strong colour in the manner of cloisonné enamel to convey abstract ideas in a simplified symbolic way. Also **Cloisonnisme.** See also **Nabi.**

sy·pher (sī'fə), *v.* to join edge to edge to form an even surface, as of slant-edged boards.

syr·inx (sir'iNGks), *n.*, *pl.* **sy·rin·ges** (sərin'jēz), **syr·inx·es.** the sound-producing organ of birds, situated at the point where the trachea divides to form the bronchi.

sys·sar·co·sis (sis,äkō'sis), *n.*, *pl.* **sys·sar·co·ses** (sis,äkō'sēz). the joining together of bones by intervening muscle, as the shoulder blade to ribs and vertebrae.

sys·tal·tic (sistal'tik), *adj.* contracting, esp. of rhythmic contraction alternating with dilatation.

sys·tem·a·tol·o·gy (sis,təmətol'əjē), *n.* the scientific study of systems and their development.

sys·tem·ic (sistem'ik), *adj.* relating to or affecting an organic system, as the whole body or one of the body's systems of organs.

sys·to·le (sis'təlē), *n.* that phase of the heartbeat when the ventricles contract, forcing the blood into the arteries. See also **diastole.**

syz·y·gy (siz'ijē), *n.* the point in orbit at which a heavenly body is in conjunction with or in opposition to the sun.

ta·bes (tā'bēz), *n.* a wasting away, usually resulting from chronic disease.

ta·bes·cent (təbes'ənt), *adj.* wasting away; becoming emaciated.

tab·o·ret (tab'ərit), *n.* 1. a stool. 2. a stand or frame for embroidery.

tab·u·la ra·sa (tab'yŏolə rä'sə), *n.* a mind on which no impressions have yet been made; a situation unhampered by preconceived ideas; something utterly without prejudice. [*Latin,* 'clean slate']

ta·chis·to·scope (təkis'təskōp,), *n.* an apparatus used to present various stimuli to the eye for a very brief period.

ta·chom·e·ter (takom'itə), *n.* 1. a device for measuring speed. 2. a device for measuring revolutions per minute made by a piece of machinery.

tach·y·aux·e·sis (tak,ēôgzē'sis), *n.* the growth of part of an organism at a faster rate than the whole. See also **isauxesis, bradyauxesis.**

tach·y·car·di·a (tak,ēkä'dēə), *n.* abnormally rapid beating of the heart.

ta·chym·e·ter (takim'itə), *n.* an instrument used in surveying for the rapid calculation of distances, directions, and differences in height.

ta·chym·e·try (takim'itrē), *n.* the technique of measuring distance, etc., with a tachymeter

tach·y·phy·lax·is (tak,ifilak'sis), *n.* temporary resistance to the effects of an injection of poison achieved by previous small injections of the poison. See also **mithridatism.**

tach·yp·noe·a (tak,ipnē'ə), *n.* abnormally fast breathing.

tach·y·tel·ic (tak,itel'ik), *adj.* relating to an abnormally fast rate of evolution. See also **horotelic, bradytelic.**

tac·it (tas'it), *adj.* expressed without words; implied; unspoken.

tac·i·turn (tas'itûn), *adj.* disinclined to talk; avoiding conversation. —**tac,i·turn'i·ty,** *n.*

ta·co (tä'kō), *n.* a tortilla rolled or folded over a filling.

tac·ti·cal (tak'tikəl), *adj.* relating to a manoeuvre or plan to achieve a desired purpose or temporary gain. See also **strategic.**

tac·tile (tak'tīl), *adj.* relating to the sense of touch.

tac·tion (tak'shən), *n.* contact; touch.

tac·tu·al (tak'choōəl), *adj.* relating to or arising from the sense of touch.

tae·ni·a·cide (tē'nēəsīd), *n.* any substance for destroying tapeworms.

tae·ni·a·fuge (tē'nēəfyŏoj,), *n.* any substance used to drive out tapeworms from the body.

tae·ni·a·sis (tēnī'əsis), *n.* infestation with tapeworms.

t'ai chi ch'uan (tī' jē chwän'), *n.* a form of callisthenics, originating in China, involving stylized rhythmical movements derived from martial arts. Often shortened to **t'ai chi.**

tai·ga (tī'gə), *n.* the coniferous forest, dominated by fir, pine, and spruce, that extends through the cold regions of the N. hemisphere. It is bounded by tundra to the north, and by grassland (e.g. steppe) to the south.

taille (tīl), *n.* the waist or bodice of a dress, robe, etc.

tail·leur (täyû'), *n.* a woman's tailored suit or costume.

tal·i·grade (tal'igrād), *adj.* putting the weight on the outer side of the foot when walking.

tal·i·on (tal'ēən), *n.* See **lex talionis.**

tal·i·ped (tal'iped,), *adj.* 1. distorted or twisted in the foot. 2. clubfooted.

tal·i·pes (tal'ipēz,), *n.* 1. a clubfoot. 2. clubfootedness.

tal·is·man (tal'ismən), *n.* a lucky charm.

ta·lus (tā'ləs), *n.* the anklebone; astragalus.

ta·ma·le (təmä'lē), *n.* a Mexican dish of meat wrapped in maizemeal dough and steamed.

ta·ma·sha (təmä'shə), *n.* (in the East Indies) a show; a spectacle; an entertainment.

tam·pon (tam'pon), *n.* a plug of lint, cotton, etc., to stop bleeding from an orifice.

tam·pon·ade (tam,pənäd'), *v.* 1. the application of a tampon to stop bleeding. 2. compression of the heart by fluid accumulated in the cavity surrounding it.

tan·ge·lo (tan'jəlō), *n.* a hybrid between the tangerine and the grapefruit.

tan·gen·tial (tanjen'shəl), *adj.* not essentially related to the main matter under consideration.

tan·gi·ble (tan'jibəl), *adj.* that can be touched; actual; substantial; real.

tan·go·re·cep·tor (tang,gōrisep'tə), *n.* a receptor responsive to touch.

tan·ta·lize (tan'təlīz), *v.* **tan·ta·lized, tan·ta·liz·ing.** to tease, esp. by showing something highly desirable to (someone) and then withdrawing it.

tan·ta·mount (tan'təmount,), *adj.* equal in

value, meaning, or effect to, as *His absence was tantamount to an admission of guilt.*

tan·tiv·y (tantiv'ē), *adv.* **1.** at the gallop; swiftly. —*adj.* **2.** fast; swift.

ta·pa (tä'pə), *n.* a cloth made from bark, used in the Pacific Islands.

tape·worm (tāp'wûm,), *n.* any of various parasitic flatworms inhabiting the intestines of vertebrate animals.

taph·e·pho·bi·a (taf,əfō'bēə), *n.* an abnormally excessive fear of being buried alive.

tap·is (tap'ē), *n.* a carpet or tapestry.

tap·ping (tap'iNG), *n.* See **paracentesis.**

tar·an·tel·la (tar,əntel'ə), *n.* a lively, whirling dance of southern Italy.

tar·ant·ism (tar'əntiz,əm), *n.* a nervous disorder producing an irresistible urge to dance.

tar·boosh (täbōōsH'), *n.* a brimless cap with a tassel, sometimes surrounded by a turban, worn by Muslim men.

tar·di·grade (tä'digrād,), *adj.* having a slow movement.

tare (ter), *n.* the weight of the receptacle, wrapping, etc., in which goods are packed.

tarn (tän), *n.* a small lake in a mountainous region.

ta·rot (tar'ō), *n.* a special set of playing cards used in fortune telling.

tar·pan (tä'pan), *n.* a variety of wild horse of eastern Europe and central Asia. Also **Przewalski's horse.**

tar·sal (tä'səl), *adj.* relating to the tarsus.

tar·si·a (tä'sēə), *n.* See **intarsia.**

tar·sus (tä'səs), *n.* the group of bones forming the heel and ankle in humans and the corresponding part in other vertebrates.

ta·sim·e·ter (təsim'itə), *n.* an electrical apparatus for recording very small changes in temperature and the like by means of pressure changes caused by expanding solids.

ta·ta·mi (tətä'mē), *n.* a kind of straw mat used in Japanese dwellings to partition off the interior.

tat·ter·de·mal·ion (tat,ədimāl'yən), *n.* a person dressed in ragged clothing.

tau·ri·form (tôr'ifôm,), *adj.* having the form of a bull.

tau·rine (tôr'īn), *adj.* relating to or resembling a bull.

tau·rom·a·chy (tôrom'əkē), *n.* the art of bullfighting.

tau·tol·o·gy (tôtol'əjē), *n.* unnecessary repetition of an idea in different words.

taw (tô), *v.* to dress a raw material, as an animal skin, for use.

taw·dry (tô'drē), *adj.* **taw·dri·er, taw·dri·est.** cheap, esp. in a showy, gaudy way.

tax·is (tak'sis), *n.* the response of an organism to an external stimulus by movement in a particular direction. See also **tropism.**

tax·on (tak'son), *n.* a taxonomic species, group, etc.

tax·on·o·my (takson'əmē), *n.* the scientific classification of living things. —**tax,o·nom'ic,** *adj.*

Tay-Sachs disease (tä'saks'), a rare disease characterized by gradual blindness and weight loss, and invariably fatal, usually affecting children of Jewish or eastern European origin.

teaching machine, an automatic device for presenting an item of information to a pupil and extracting a correct response before presenting further items.

tea·poy (tē'poi), *n.* a three-legged stand, esp. one used in serving tea.

tea·sel (tē'zəl), *v.* to raise a nap on cloth.

tech·noc·ra·cy (teknok'rəsē), *n.* government by those skilled in the uses of technology, as engineers, technical experts, etc.

tech·nog·ra·phy (teknog'rəfē), *n.* the description and study of the history and distribution of the arts and sciences.

tech·nol·o·gy (teknol'əjē), *n.* applied science; the industrial arts.

tec·ton·ic (tekton'ik), *adj.* relating to building or architecture.

tec·ton·ics (tekton'iks), *n. sing.* the art or science of construction, as of buildings, furniture, etc.

ted (ted), *v.* to spread out cut grass and the like to dry.

te·di·ous (tē'dēəs), *adj.* **1.** tiresome; boring; long-drawn-out, as *a tedious lecture on prunes.* **2.** tiring; exhausting, esp. because of boredom, as *a tedious trek through the desert.*

te·di·um (tē'dēəm), *n.* the quality of being irksome or wearisome.

teem (tēm), *v.* **1.** to be present in great quantity or abundance. **2.** to rain heavily for a long period.

teg·men (teg'mən), *n.* a top layer or covering.

teg·u·lar (teg'yōōlə), *adj.* relating to or consisting of tiles.

teg·u·ment (teg'yōōmənt), *n.* a covering of skin.

tek·non·y·my (teknon'əmē), *n.* the primitive custom of giving a child's name to its parent.

tek·tite (tek'tīt), *n.* a small, glassy body supposedly of meteoric origin.

tel·aes·the·si·a (tel,isthē'zēə), *n.* sensation received from a distance without normal use of the senses.

tel·e·gen·ic (tel,ijen'ik), *adj.* having an appearance or personality that shows to advantage on television. Also **videogenic.**

tel·eg·no·sis (tel,ənō'sis), *n.* knowledge acquired by supernatural means. —**tel,eg·nos'-tic,** *adj.*

te·leg·o·ny (təleg'ənē), n. the supposed continuation of the influence of a sire upon the offspring born to the mother after matings with subsequent sires.

tel·e·ki·ne·sis (tel,ikinē'sis), n. the causing of objects to move without physical contact or other normal force.

te·lem·e·ter (təlem'itə), n. an apparatus for measuring the value of a quantity and transmitting the results over a distance, usually by a radio device. —**te·lem'e·try**, n.

tel·en·ceph·a·lon (tel,ensef'əlon), n. the anterior part of the forebrain.

tel·e·ol·o·gy (tel,ēol'əjē), n. the doctrine that all things in nature are designed to fulfil a purpose.

te·lep·a·thy (təlep'əthē), n. communication of ideas, feelings, etc., by means other than the normal senses. —**te·lep'a·thist**, n.

te·leph·o·ny (tələf'ənē), n. the transmission of sounds by telephone or similar equipment.

tel·e·plasm (tel'əplaz,əm), n. the supposed emanation from a medium's body used to produce telekinesis.

Tel·e·promp·ter (tel'əpromptə), n. the trade name of a device for enabling a speaker on television to read a script while apparently speaking spontaneously.

tel·e·ran (tel'əran), n. a system of aerial navigation which transmits information by television to aeroplanes.

tel·ic (tel'ik), adj. tending towards a particular end.

tell·er (tel'ə), n. one entrusted with the counting of votes, money, etc.

tell·ing (tel'iNG), adj. effective; revealing.

tel·lu·ric (teloōr'ik), adj. relating to the earth; terrestrial.

tel·lu·ri·on (təloōr'ēon), n. an apparatus for demonstrating how the rotation of the earth causes day and night and seasonal changes.

tel·o·dy·nam·ic (tel,ōdīnam'ik), adj. relating to the transmission of power over a long distance.

tel·o·tax·is (tel,ətak'sis), n. movement of an organism in response to any of a number of simultaneous stimuli.

tel·pher, tel·fer (tel'fə), n. a car, etc., carried by means of telpherage.

tel·pher·age, tel·fer·age (tel'fərij), n. a transport system in which cars are suspended from or run on aerial cables.

tem·blor (tem'blə), n. Chiefly U.S. an earth tremor; an earthquake.

tem·er·ar·i·ous (tem,ərer'ēəs), adj. rash; reckless; impetuous.

te·mer·i·ty (təmer'itē), n. recklessness; daring; boldness.

tem·per·a (tem'pərə), n. a medium for painting consisting of powdered colours mixed with a natural or artificial emulsion, as egg yolk, oil, gum, etc.; the commonest painting medium before the invention of oil paint.

tem·plate (tem'plāt), n. a wooden or metal mould used as a guide in shaping or cutting wood, stone, or the like. Also **templet**.

tem·po·ral (tem'pərəl), adj. 1. relating to time. 2. relating to or concerning earthly life. 3. temporary; not eternal.

tem·po·rize (tem'pərīz), v. to avoid making a decision; be evasive.

tem·pu·ra (tempoōr'ə), n. a Japanese dish of seafood or vegetables coated with batter and deep-fried.

ten·a·ble (ten'əbəl), adj. that can be maintained, occupied, possessed, etc.

te·na·cious (tənā'sHəs), adj. having a firm hold or grip.

te·nac·i·ty (tənas'itē), n. the quality of being tenacious.

te·nac·u·lum (tənak'yoōləm), n. a small hook used by surgeons for holding parts, such as arteries, in operations.

Ten Commandments. See Decalogue.

ten·den·tious (tenden'sHəs), adj. having a bias; lacking impartiality; not fair or just.

ten·e·brif·ic (ten,əbrif'ik), adj. causing darkness.

ten·e·brous (ten'əbrəs), adj. gloomy; dark.

ten·ent (ten'ənt), adj. adapted for holding on or clinging with.

te·nes·mus (tənez'məs), n. an urge to evacuate the bowels or bladder but without the ability to do so.

ten·et (ten'it), n. a belief or doctrine held to be true.

te·nor·rha·phy (tənor'əfē), n. the surgical stitching of a tendon.

te·not·o·my (tənot'əmē), n. the surgical cutting of a tendon.

ten·seg·ri·ty (tenseg'ritē), n. (in architecture) the efficient use of continuous tension members and discontinuous compression members in skeleton structures.

ten·si·ble (ten'sibəl), adj. that may be pulled or stretched.

ten·sile (ten'sīl), adj. 1. relating to tension. 2. capable of being stretched.

tensile strength, the maximum longitudinal stress which a material can support without rupture.

ten·sim·e·ter (tensim'itə), n. an instrument which measures the pressure of vapour or gas.

ten·si·om·e·ter (ten,sēom'itə), n. 1. a device for measuring tensile stress in wires, beams, etc. 2. an instrument for measuring the surface tension of liquids.

ten·sor (ten'sə, ten'sô), n. a muscle that stretches any part of the body.

ten·ta·tion (tentā'sHən), n. the perfection of a

mechanical apparatus or the like by means of a series of tests of its functioning.

ten·u·i·ty (tənyōō'itē), *n.* the quality or state of being tenuous.

ten·u·ous (ten'yōōəs), *adj.* thin in form or consistency; rarefied; flimsy.

ten·ure (ten'yōōə, ten'yə), *n.* the act or right of holding or possessing something.

tep·id (tep'id), *adj.* lukewarm, as *tepid bathwater* or *tepid enthusiasm.*

ter·a·tism (ter'ətiz,əm), *n.* **1.** a biological freak. **2.** worship of the monstrous. See **teratosis.**

ter·a·to·gen·e·sis (ter,ətōjen'isis), *n.* the production of biological monstrosities or abnormal formations. Also **ter,a·tog'e·ny.**

ter·a·toid (ter'ətoid), *adj.* of monstrous or abnormal biological form.

ter·a·tol·o·gy (terətol'əjē), *n.* the study of malformations or monstrosities in organisms.

ter·a·to·sis (terətō'sis), *n.* a biological freak; a monstrosity. Also **teratism.**

ter·cen·te·nar·y (tû,sentē'nərē), *n.* **1.** a 300th anniversary. —*adj.* **2.** relating to a 300th anniversary.

te·rete (tərēt'), *adj.* slender and cylindrical with tapering ends.

ter·gi·ver·sate (tûjiv'əsāt,), *v.* to equivocate; to vacillate; to change one's opinions repeatedly.

ter·giv·er·sa·tion (tûrjiv,əsā'sHən), *n.* continual changing of one's mind; ambiguousness; equivocation.

ter·ma·gant (tû'məgənt), *n.* a violent, overbearing, or shrewish woman.

ter·mi·na·tor (tû'minā,tə), *n.* the dividing line between the lit and the unlit part of a planet.

ter·na·ry (tû'nərē), *adj.* **1.** involving or relating to three; triple. **2.** third in order or rank. **3.** using the number three as a base.

ter·nate (tû'nit), *adj.* having three parts; arranged in groups of three.

terne metal (tûn), an alloy of lead and tin.

terp·si·cho·re·an (tûp,sikərē'ən), *adj.* relating to dancing.

ter·ra·cot·ta (ter'əkot'ə), a hard earthenware, brownish in colour and usually unglazed.

ter·rane (tərān'), *n.* a connected group of rock formations.

ter·ra·que·ous (terā'kwēəs), *adj.* comprising both land and water.

ter·rar·i·um (terer'ēəm), *n., pl.* **ter·rar·i·ums, ter·rar·i·a. 1.** a vivarium for terrestrial animals. **2.** a glass container in which plants are grown.

ter·rene (ter'ēn, terēn'), *adj.* **1.** worldly; earthly; mundane. **2.** earthy.

ter·ric·o·lous (terik'ələs), *adj.* living on or in the ground.

ter·rig·e·nous (terij'ənəs), *adj.* **1.** produced by the earth. **2.** relating to sediment caused by the erosive action of tides, currents, etc., or to rocks formed from such sediment.

ter·rine (tərēn'), *n.* **1.** an earthenware casserole. **2.** a delicacy of meat or fish cooked in such a casserole.

terse (tûs), *adj.* concise; using few words.

ter·tian (tû'sHən), *adj.* of a fever marked by paroxysms which recur every second (or by inclusive reckoning every third) day, as some kinds of malaria. See also **quartan, quintan, sextan.**

ter·ti·ar·y (tû'sHərē), *adj.* **1.** third in rank or importance. **2.** (in geology) (cap. **T.**), relating to the earlier part of the Cenozoic era. See also **Neocene, Palaeocene.**

ter·ti·um quid (tû,sHēəm kwid'), something related to two things but distinct from each.

tes·sel·late (tes'əlāt), *v.* to pave with small blocks or squares, as a floor or pavement. —**tes,-sel·la'tion,** *n.*

tes·sel·lat·ed (tes'əlā,tid), *adj.* relating to or having the appearance of a mosaic; chequered.

tes·ser·a (tes'ərə), *n., pl.* **tes·ser·ae. 1.** a small piece used in mosaic work. **2.** a piece of bone or wood used by the ancients as a voucher, tally, ticket, etc.

tes·ta (tes'tə), *n., pl.* **tes·tae.** the hard external covering of a seed; integument.

tes·ta·cean (testā'sHən), *adj.* having a shell, as certain invertebrates.

tes·ta·ceous (testā'sHəs), *adj.* relating to shells; having a hard covering such as a shell.

tes·ta·men·ta·ry (tes,təmen'tərē), *adj.* **1.** relating to a will or testament. **2.** bequeathed by means of a will.

tes·tate (tes'tāt), *adj.* having left a valid will.

tes·ta·tor (tes'tātə), *n.* one who has made a will.

tes·ta·trix (testā'triks), *n., pl.* **tes·ta·tri·ces** (testā'trisēz). a female testator.

test ban, an agreement between nations not to test nuclear weapons or to test them only under certain prescribed conditions.

tes·ter (tes'tə), *n.* a canopy over a bed, pulpit, etc.

tes·ti·fi·ca·tion (tes,tifikā'sHən), *n.* the act of testifying; testimony.

tes·tu·di·nal (testyōō'dinəl), *adj.* relating to or resembling a tortoise or tortoise shell.

tes·tu·di·nate (testyōō'dināt), *adj.* shaped like a tortoise shell.

tes·ty (tes'tē), *adj.* irritable; easily annoyed.

tet·a·nus (tet'ənəs), *n.* **1.** an infectious disease caused by a particular bacterium entering open wounds and producing violent tonic spasms. See also **lockjaw. 2.** a condition in which muscles are contracted for a prolonged period.

tet·a·ny (tet'ənē), *n.* a medical condition marked by severe tonic spasms.

tête-a-tête (tāt'ətāt'), *n.* **1.** a close conversation or private interview, esp. between two people. **2.** a siamoise.

tet·rad (tot'rad), *n.* a set, group, or arrangement of four.

tet·ra·gon (tet'rəgon), *n.* a figure with four angles and four sides. —**te·trag'o·nal**, *adj.*

tet·ra·gram (tet'rəgram,), *n.* a word of four letters.

Tet·ra·gram·ma·ton (tet,rəgram'əton), *n.* the Hebrew word for God, written with four consonants usually transliterated as YHVH.

tet·ra·he·dral (tet,rəhē'drəl), *adj.* relating to or having the form of a tetrahedron.

tet·ra·he·dron (tet,rəhē'drən), *n.* a solid contained by four plane faces.

te·tral·o·gy (tetral'əjē), *n.*, *pl.* **te·tral·o·gies. 1.** a series of four connected works, as in literature or drama. **2.** (in classical Greek drama) a series of four plays, three tragic works and a concluding satirical work.

tet·ra·ple·gia (tet,rəplē'jēə), *n.* See **quadriplegia.**

tet·ra·pod (te'trəpod,), *n.* an object or device with four projections radiating from a central point at an angle of 120° to one another, so that if any three of the projections rest on a surface, the fourth will point upwards. See also **caltrop.**

thal·a·mus (thal'əmɔs), *n.* the middle part of the posterior subdivision of the forebrain.

tha·las·sic (thəlas'ik), *adj.* relating to, growing in, or living in the smaller seas, gulfs, etc.

thal·as·sog·ra·phy (thal,əsog'rəfē), *n.* the branch of oceanography dealing with coastal or smaller bodies of sea water.

thal·as·so·ther·a·py (thal,əsōther'əpē), *n.* treatment by sea-bathing, sea air, or a sea voyage.

thal·weg (täl'veg), *n.* a line joining the lowest points of a valley.

than·a·to·pho·bia (than,ətōfō'bēə), *n.* an abnormally excessive dread of death.

than·a·top·sis (than,ətop'sis), *n.* speculation about or contemplation of death.

thau·ma·tol·o·gy (thô,mətol'əjē), *n.* the study of miracles.

thau·ma·trope (thô'mətrōp), *n.* a card, disc, or the like with a different image on each side, which when swiftly rotated causes the two images to appear combined as one.

thau·ma·turge (thô'mətûj,), *n.* one who performs miracles. —**thau,ma·tur'gic,** *adj.*

thau·ma·tur·gy (thô'mətû,jē), *n.* the performance of miracles.

the·an·throp·ic (thē,anthrop'ik), *adj.* relating to both God and man; divine and human.

the·an·thro·pism (thēan'thrəpiz,əm), *n.* **1.** the union of the divine and human; the incarnation of God as man in Christ. **2.** the attributing of human characteristics to gods.

theatre of war, the whole area in which military forces are deployed and may be used in direct military action. See also **zone of interior.**

the·ba·ine (thē'bəēn), *n.* a substance obtained from opium but having poisonous effects similar to those of strychnine rather than narcotic effects.

the·ca (thē'kə), *n.* a cover or receptacle; sac.

the·ine (thē'ēn), *n.* caffeine, esp. as it occurs in tea.

the·ism (thē'izəm), *n.* **1.** belief in the existence of one god as the creator of the universe. **2.** belief in the existence of a god or gods.

the·lyt·o·ky (thilit'əkē), *n.* parthenogenesis resulting in the birth of female offspring only. Also **thel,y·ot'o·ky.** —**the·lyt'o·kous,** *adj.*

the·nar (thē'nä), *n.* **1.** the fleshy ball of the thumb. **2.** the fleshy outer side of the palm.

the·o·cen·tric (thē,ōsen'trik), *adj.* having God as the centre of all thoughts, feelings, etc.

the·oc·ra·cy (thēok'rəsē), *n.* a form of government in which the rulers, usually priests, claim to have or are regarded as having divine guidance.

the·oc·ra·sy (thēok'rəsē), *n.* a mixture of religious forms and deities as the object of worship by believers.

the·od·i·cy (thēod'isē), *n.*, *pl.* **the·od·i·cies.** the defence of the goodness of God in the face of arguments pointing to the ʼxistence of evil in the world. —**the·od·i·ce·an** (thēod,isē'ən), *n.*

the·od·o·lite (thēod'əlīt), *n.* a surveying instrument for checking gradients, angles, etc.

the·og·o·ny (thēog'ənē), *n.* **1.** a genealogy of the gods. **2.** an account of or poem dealing with the origin of the gods.

the·ol·a·try (thēol'ətrē), *n.* worship of a god.

the·om·a·chy (thēom'əkē), *n.* a conflict against or among the gods.

the·o·ma·ni·a (thē,ōmā'nēə), *n.* a form of madness in which the sufferer believes himself to be God or especially chosen by God.

the·o·mor·phic (thē,ōmô'fik), *adj.* resembling a god in appearance.

the·op·a·thy (thēop'əthē), *n.* strong emotion aroused by the contemplation of God.

the·oph·a·ny (thēof'ənē), *n.* the visible manifestation of God or a god to man.

theory-laden, *adj.* (of a concept, phrase, etc.) explicable only with reference to a particular theory.

the·os·o·phy (thēos'əfē), *n.* any religious belief or philosophy claiming mystical insight into the divine nature. —**the,o·soph'i·cal,** *adj.*

Ther·a·va·da (ther,əvä'də), *n.* See **Hinayana.**

ther·blig (thû'blig), *n.* any element in an operation or procedure that can be subjected to time and motion study. [anagram of F. B. Gilbreth (1868–1924), U.S. engineer]

the·ri·ac (thēr'ēak), *n.* **1.** treacle; molasses. **2.** an antidote to snake bites and other poisons, made of numerous drugs mixed with honey.

the·ri·an (thēr'ēən), *adj.* relating to marsupial and placental mammals.

the·ri·an·throp·ic (thēr,ēanthrop'ik), *adj.* partly animal and partly human in form.

the·ri·o·mor·phic (thēr,ēōmô'fik), *adj.* having the form of an animal, esp. of gods.

ther·mae (thû'mē), *n. pl.* hot springs.

therm·aes·the·si·a (thûm,isthē'zēə), the ability to feel heat or cold.

therm·al·ge·si·a (thûm,aljē'zēə), *n.* pain caused by heat.

therm·an·aes·the·si·a (thûm,anisthē'zēə), *n.* inability to feel heat or cold. Also **ther,mo·an,-es·the'sia.**

therm·i·on (thûm'ēən), *n.* an electrically charged particle, as an ion, emitted by an incandescent body. —**therm,i·on'ic,** *adj.*

therm·i·on·ics (thûm,ēon'iks), *n. sing.* the scientific study of thermionic phenomena.

ther·mis·tor (thûmis'tə), *n.* a resistor whose resistance varies with changes in temperature.

ther·mo·cline (thû'məklīn), *n.* a layer of water in a sea, lake, etc., marked by greater variations in temperature than the layers above and below it. See also **epilimnion, hypolimnion.**

ther·mo·cou·ple (thû'mōkup,əl), *n.* a device used to ascertain the temperature of a substance by measuring its electromotive force. Also **thermel, thermoelectric couple, thermoelectric thermometer.**

ther·mo·dur·ic (thû,mōdyŏŏr'ik), *adj.* resistant to high temperatures, as certain microorganisms.

ther·mo·dy·nam·ics (thû,mōdīnam'iks), *n.* the study of the relation between heat and mechanical energy and the conversion of one into the other. —**ther,mo·dy·nam'ic,** *adj.*

ther·mo·gen·e·sis (thû,mōjen'isis), *n.* the production of heat in an animal body. —**ther,-mo·ge·net'ic,** *adj.*

ther·mo·gen·ic (thû,mōjen'ik), *adj.* relating to or causing the production of heat.

ther·mog·e·nous (thûmoj'ənəs), *adj.* heat-producing.

ther·mo·ge·og·ra·phy (thû,mōjēog'rəfē), *n.* the study of variations in temperature according to geographical distribution.

ther·mog·ra·phy (thûmog'rəfē), *n.* a printing process in which the printed matter is dusted with powder and heated, fusing the ink to make the letters stand out in relief.

ther·mo·lu·mi·nes·cence (thû,mōlōō,mi-nes'əns), *n.* phosphorescence induced by the action of heat. Also **ther,mo·phos,pho·res'cence.** —**ther,mo·lu,mi·nes'cent,** *adj.*

ther·mol·y·sis (thûmol'isis), *n.* the dissipation of heat from the body.

ther·mom·e·try (thûmom'itrē), *n.* the science dealing with the measurement of temperature.

ther·mo·mo·tive (thû,mōmō'tiv), *adj.* relating to motion caused by heat.

ther·mo·nu·cle·ar (thû,mōnyōō'klēə), *adj.* relating to or involving a thermonuclear reaction or device.

thermonuclear reaction, a nuclear reaction between the atomic nuclei of a substance heated to a temperature of several million degrees.

ther·mo·phile (thû'mōfīl), *n.* an organism, as certain bacteria, that grows best in comparatively high temperatures, esp. between 50° and 60°C. —**ther,mo·phil'ic,** *adj.*

ther·mo·pile (thû'mōpīl), *n.* an apparatus consisting of a series of thermocouples joined together and used to generate electric current or to measure radiant energy.

ther·mo·plas·tic (thû,mōplas'tik), *adj.* having properties of softness and plasticity when heated.

ther·mo·re·cep·tor (thû,mōrisep'tə), *n.* a receptor sensitive to changes in temperature.

ther·mo·scope (thû'məskōp,), *n.* a device for measuring changes in temperature of a substance by noting the accompanying changes in its volume.

ther·mo·sen·si·tive (thû,mōsen'sitiv), *adj.* easily affected by a change, esp. a rise in temperature.

ther·mo·set·ting (thû'mōset,ING), *adj.* having the property of setting hard when heated and being incapable of remoulding.

ther·mo·sphere (thû'məsfē,ə), *n.* the region in the earth's atmosphere which lies above the mesosphere and in which temperature increases with altitude.

ther·mo·sta·ble (thû,mōstā'bəl), *adj.* retaining its characteristic properties when subjected to moderate heat.

ther·mo·stat (thû'məstat), *n.* a device for regulating a heating apparatus so as to maintain a constant temperature.

ther·mo·tax·is (thû,mōtak'sis), *n.* **1.** movement of an organism in response to a source of heat. **2.** the regulation of body temperature.

ther·mot·ro·pism (thûmot'rəpiz,əm), *n.* growth of an organism in a direction determined by a source of heat. —**ther,mo·trop'ic,** *adj.*

the·roid (thēr'oid), *adj.* having the characteristics or tendencies of an animal.

the·ro·phyte (thēr'əfīt,), *n.* a plant whose lifetime covers only one growing season.

ther·sit·i·cal (thûsit'ikəl), *adj.* abusive; foul-mouthed.

the·sis (thē'sis), *n.* a proposition put forward for discussion; a lengthy dissertation supporting such a proposition.

thes·pi·an (thes'pēən), *adj.* relating to the drama or to acting.

the·ur·gy (thē'ûjē), *n.* **1.** a system of magic or supernatural practices by those claiming to have the help of beneficent deities. **2.** the operation of divine or supernatural agency in human affairs.

thews (thyōōz), *n. pl.* sinew; muscle; muscular strength.

thi·a·sus (thī'əsəs), *n.* (in ancient Greece) a group holding a celebration or ceremony in honour of a patron god.

thig·mo·tax·is (thig,mōtak'sis), *n.* the movement of an organism in response to a mechanical stimulus. See **stereotaxis.**

thig·mo·tro·pism (thigmot'rəpiz,əm), *n.* growth of an organism in which the direction is determined by mechanical contact.

thill (thil), *n.* either of the two shafts of a vehicle which is drawn by one animal.

thim·ble·rig (thim'bəlrig), *n.* a game of deception in which a pea or the like, supposedly concealed under one of three thimbles, is palmed by one player while the other player guesses and lays bets on which thimble it is under.

thi·o·u·ra·cil (thī,ōyōōr'əsil), *n.* a crystalline powder used to reduce overactivity of the thyroid gland.

thix·ot·ro·py (thiksot'rəpē), *n.* the characteristic of certain gels to become liquid when stirred.

tho·rac·ic (thōras'ik), *adj.* of or relating to the thorax.

thrall (thrôl), *n.* one held in bondage; a slave.

thra·son·i·cal (thrəson'ikəl), *adj.* boastful; bragging.

threm·ma·tol·o·gy (threm,ətol'əjē), *n.* the breeding of animals and plants under domestication.

thren·o·dy (thren'ədē), *n.* a lament; funeral song; dirge. Also **thre·node** (thrē'nōd, thren'ōd).

thrive (thrīv), *v.* **thrived** or **throve, thrived** or **thriv·en, thriv·ing.** to grow or do well; flourish, as a person, a business, a crop, etc.

throe (thrō), *n.* a sharp spasm; a pang of emotion.

throm·bin (throm'bin), *n.* a substance that facilitates coagulation of the blood.

throm·bo·cyte (throm'bōsīt,), *n.* a nucleate cell that facilitates coagulation of blood in those vertebrates without blood platelets.

throm·bo·gen (throm'bōjen), *n.* See **pro·thrombin.**

throm·bol·y·sis (thrombol'isis), *n.* the dissolution of a thrombus. Also **throm·boc'la·sis.**

throm·bo·phle·bi·tis (throm,bōflibī'tis), *n.* inflammation of a vein with resulting occurrence of thrombosis in the affected part. See also **phlebothrombosis.**

throm·bo·sis (thrombō'sis), *n.* the clotting of blood in any part of the circulatory system.

throm·bus (throm'bəs), *n., pl.* **throm·bi** (throm'bī). a clot of blood which forms in a blood vessel.

throng (throNG), *n.* **1.** a great many, esp. of people; crowd. —*v.* **2.** to crowd; come together in one place in large numbers.

throw·ster (thrō'stə), *n.* a person who carries out the textile operation of twisting filaments, as of silk or synthetic fibre, into yarn without stretching them, an operation known as throwing.

thrum (thrum), *n.* one of the fringe of unwoven warp threads left on a loom after the web of fabric is cut off.

thug·gee (thugē'), *n.* (formerly in India) murder, usually by strangulation, and robbery by professional thugs.

thun·der·stone (thun'dəstōn,), *n.* any of various stones, as meteorites, etc., once believed to have fallen as thunderbolts.

thu·ri·ble (thōōr'ibəl), *n.* a vessel used for the burning of incense; censer.

thu·ri·fer (thōōr'ifə), *n.* a person who carries a thurible in religious services.

thurm (thûm), *v.* to shape or carve (wood) across the grain so as to make it appear to turn.

thwart (thwôt), *v.* to prevent (someone) from doing something or (something) from happening.

thy·la·cine (thī'ləsīn), *n.* a carnivorous, tan-coloured, black-striped, wolflike marsupial of Tasmania. Also **Tasmanian wolf, ursine dasyure.**

thy·ris·tor (thīris'tə), *n.* a semiconductor device used as a switching mechanism in electronic circuits. Also **sil'i·con con·trolled' rec'ti·fi·er.**

thy·roid (thī'roid), *n.* a ductless two-lobed endocrine gland situated in the neck of vertebrates, whose secretions regulate metabolism and growth. Also **thyroid gland.**

thy·ro·tox·i·co·sis (thī,rōtok,sikō'sis), *n.* an abnormal condition caused by excessive activity of the thyroid gland and characterized by enlargement of the thyroid, weight loss, protruding eyes, tremors, rapid pulse, etc.

tib·i·a (tib'ēə), *n.* the inner of the two bones between the knee and the ankle.

tic dou·lou·reux (tik, dōō,lōōrōō'), a form of neuralgia producing paroxysmal pain and muscular twitching in the face. Also **facial neuralgia.**

Tiffany glass. See **Favrile glass.**

ti·glon (tī'glon), *n.* the offspring of a mating between a tiger and a lioness.

ti·ki (tē'kē), *n.* a carved image of an ancestor, supernatural power, etc., worn as an amulet in some Polynesian cultures.

til·ak (til'ək), *n.* a coloured mark worn on the forehead by Hindu men and women.

til·de (til'də), *n.* **1.** a mark (~) placed over a letter, as over *n* in Spanish, to indicate a change in the sound of a letter. **2.** a similar mark used to indicate the omission of a syllable, word, or as a sign of negation in logic and mathematics, etc.

tim·bal, tym·bal (tim'bəl), *n.* **1.** a kettle-drum. **2.** a vibrating membrane found in certain insects.

tim·bale (tambäl'), *n.* **1.** a dish of meat, fish, or vegetables mixed in a rich sauce and baked in a mould. **2.** a small pastry filled with such a mixture. **3.** the straight-sided mould used in preparing such dishes.

tim·bre (tim'bə, tam'bə), *n.* the distinctive quality of a sound, as of a voice or of music produced by a particular instrument.

time-binding (tīm'bin,diNG), *n.* the preservation of memories and experiences by one generation for the use of succeeding generations.

tim·or·ous (tim'ərəs), *adj.* fearful; timid.

tim·pa·ni, tym·pa·ni (tim'pənē), *n. pl.* a set of kettledrums, as used by an orchestra.

tinc·to·ri·al (tiNGktôr'ēəl), *adj.* relating to colours, dyeing, or staining.

tin·e·a (tin'ēə), *n.* any of various fungal infections of the skin, hair, or nails, esp. ringworm. —**tin'e·al,** *adj.*

tin·ni·ent (tin'ēant), *adj.* having a ringing sound.

tin·ni·tus (tin'itəs), *n.* a sensation of ringing in the ears.

tin·tin·nab·u·lar (tin,tinab'yōōlə), *adj.* relating to bells or their sounds. Also **tin,tin·nab'u·lar·y, tin,tin·nab'u·lous.**

tin·tin·nab·u·la·tion (tin,tinab,yōōlā'sHən), *n.* the sound of bells ringing.

tint·om·e·ter (tintom'itə), *n.* a colorimeter for comparing a colour with a range of standard tints or colours.

tin·type (tin'tīp,), *n.* a photograph in the form of a positive made on a sensitized sheet of enamelled tin or iron.

tip·pet (tip'it), *n.* a cape or scarf of fur or wool worn with the two ends hanging loose in front.

tip·ple (tip'əl), *v.* **1.** to drink repeated small quantities of intoxicating liquor. —*n.* **2.** an alcoholic beverage.

ti·rade (tī'rād), *n.* a protracted speech of denunciation or abuse.

tire·some (tīr'səm), *adj.* boring; dull and exhausting.

ti·ro (ti'rō), *n.* See **tyro.**

ti·tan·o·saur (tītan'əsô), *n.* any herbivorous dinosaur of the genus *Titanosaurus* which belonged to the Cretaceous period.

tithe (tīTH), *n.* **1.** a tenth part of income or of agricultural produce paid to a Church or religious institution. **2.** any one-tenth tax or levy.

tit·i·vate (tit'ivāt), *v.* **1.** to dress up; to make smart; to adorn. **2.** to titillate; to tickle; to excite agreeably, as by stroking or flirtation.

ti·trate (tī'trāt), *v.* to determine the quantity of a constituent in a compound by adding a precise amount of a reagent.

tit·tle (tit'əl), *n.* **1.** a small dot in printing or writing. **2.** a very small part of anything; a minute quantity.

tit·u·ba·tion (tit,yōōbā'sHən), *n.* a disorder in bodily equilibrium causing an unsteady gait and trembling. —**tit'u·bant,** *adj.*

tit·u·lar (tit'yōōlə), *adj.* **1.** relating to or of the nature of a title. **2.** existing only in title; without the duties of office; nominal.

tme·sis (təmē'sis), *n.* the separation of parts of a compound word by the interposition of one or more other words, as *what deeds soever.*

TNT, a solid, high explosive not affected by normal friction or shock, used chiefly in explosive devices such as shells, and in the making of dyes and photographic chemicals. Also **trinitrotoluene, methyltrinitrobenzene.**

toad·y (tō'dē), *v.* **toad·ied, toad·y·ing. 1.** to flatter in a hypocritical way, so as to make a favourable impression, esp. for personal gain. —*n.* **2.** a person who fawns over or behaves in a servile manner to another, esp. for personal gain.

toc·ca·ta (təkä'tə), *n., pl.* **toc·ca·tas, toc·ca·te.** a musical composition intended to show the performer's technique.

toc·ol·o·gy, tok·ol·o·gy (tokol'əjē), *n.* obstetrics.

toc·sin (tok'sin), *n.* a warning signal; an alarm sounded by a bell.

to·gat·ed (tō'gātid), *adj.* peaceful.

to·hu·bo·hu (tō,hōōbō'hōō), *n.* disorder; chaos. [from Hebrew]

tok·a·mak (tok'əmak,), *n.* (in physics) a torus-shaped reactor, used for thermonuclear experiments, in which the extremely hot nuclear material is contained by powerful magnetic fields rather than the reactor walls.

to·ken·ism (tō'kəniz,əm), *n.* the practice of making only a token effort, as an employer who hires only sufficient persons of a racial minority to comply with the law.

tok·o·dy·na·mom·e·ter, toc·o·dy·na·mom·e·ter (tok,ōdī,nəmom'ətə), *n.* a device for measuring pressure within the uterus during labour. Also **toc·om'e·ter.**

tom·al·ley (tom'alē, təmal'ē), *n.* the liver of a lobster, as used in cookery.

tom·bo·lo (tom'bəlō), *n., pl.* **tombo·los.** a spit or bar of sand linking one island with another or with the mainland.

tome (tōm), *n.* a separate volume forming part of a set or a larger work; any learned or serious book.

to·men·tose (təmen'tōs), *adj.* densely covered with down or matted hair.

to·mo·gram (tō'məgram,), *n.* a photograph obtained by using tomography.

to·mo·graph (tō'məgräf,, tō'məgraf,), *n.* an apparatus for making tomograms.

to·mog·ra·phy (təmog'rəfē), *n.* the technique

of making x-ray photographs of a selected plane of the body.

to·net·ics (tōnet'iks), *n. sing.* the study of linguistic tones.

ton·neau (tunō'), *n., pl.* **ton·neaus, ton·neaux** (tunō'). **1. tonneau cover.** a cover that fits over the seats of an open car. **2.** the rear compartment of an car with passenger seating. See **millier.**

to·nom·e·ter (tōnom'itə), *n.* **1.** a device for measuring tonal frequency. **2.** any of several measuring instruments, as one for measuring tension inside the eyeball, for finding blood pressure, etc.

ton·sil·lec·to·my (ton,silek'təmē), *n.* the surgical excision of one or both tonsils.

ton·sil·li·tis (ton,silī'tis), *n.* inflammation of one or both tonsils.

ton·so·ri·al (tonsôr'ēəl), *adj.* relating to a barber or to shaving.

ton·sure (ton'sнə), *n.* the shaven part, usually the crown, of the head 'of a cleric.

ton·tine (ton'tēn), *n.* a form of annuity in which the amount left to each subscriber increases as other subscribers die.

to·nus (tō'nəs), *n.* a normal condition of moderate tension in muscle tissue.

tope (tōp), *v.* to drink any alcoholic beverages habitually in excessive quantities. —**top'er,** *n.*

to·pec·to·my (təpek'təmē), *n.* the surgical removal of a section of the cerebral cortex in order to relieve pain, etc.

to·phus (tō'fəs), *n., pl.* **to·phi** (tō'fī). a calcareous deposit in soft tissue around joints or on bone, esp. as a result of gout.

to·pi·ar·y (tō,pēərē), *n.* the art of clipping shrubs into ornamental shapes.

top·i·cal (top'ikəl), *adj.* **1.** relating to things of current or local interest. **2.** (in medicine) relating to a particular part of the body; local.

to·pog·ra·phy (təpog'rəfē), *n.* the detailed description or representation of the features of a particular region or district, esp. on a map or chart. —**to·pog'ra·pher,** *n.*

to·pol·o·gy (təpol'əjē), *n.* the branch of geometry that deals with those properties of forms which remain unchanged under conditions of deformation or transformation.

top·o·nym (top'ənim), *n.* a name which is derived from the name of a place.

to·pon·y·my (təpon'imē), *n.* **1.** the etymological study of place names. **2.** the classification of the names of the various parts of the body.

toque (tōk), *n.* a woman's close-fitting hat without a brim.

tor (tô), *n.* a rocky hill; a mass of rock reaching to a peak.

tor·chère (tôsнe'ə), *n.* a holder or stand for a candelabrum.

tor·e·a·dor (tor'ēədô), *n.* a bullfighter, usually mounted.

to·re·ro (torer'ō), *n.* a bullfighter, esp. a matador.

to·reu·tics (tərōō'tiks), *n. sing.* the technique of embossing or chasing metal or the like. —**to·reu'tic,** *adj.*

tor·ic (tor'ik), *adj.* relating to a lens having a surface forming part of a torus.

to·roid (tor'oid), *n.* a surface generated by a plane closed curve rotated about an axis lying in its plane. —**to·roi'dal,** *adj.*

tor·pid (tô'pid), *adj.* sluggish; lethargic; dull; dormant.

tor·por (tô'pə), *n.* a state of mental and physical inactivity; inertia; dormancy.

tor·por·if·ic (tôpərif'ik), *adj.* producing torpor.

tor·quate (tô'kwät), *adj.* having markings, distinctive feathers, etc., in a band around the neck.

torque (tôk), *n.* a force or movement which causes rotation.

tor·ques (tô'kwēz), *n. sing.* a marking or formation encircling the neck.

tor·re·fy (tôr'əfī), *v.* to parch or scorch; to dry with heat.

tor·sade (tôsād'), *n.* a twisted cord, esp. as used for ornamentation.

tor·si·bil·i·ty (tô,sibil'itē), *n.* the capability of being twisted.

tor·sion (tô'sнən), *n.* the act of twisting.

tort (tôt), *n.* a legal wrong in breaching a duty or infringing a right and for which the remedy lies in a civil action, as negligence, defamation. —**tor'tious,** *adj.*

torte (tôrt), *n.* a rich cake made of eggs, sugar, and ground nuts.

tor·ti·col·lis (tô,tikol'is), *n.* a condition in which the neck is twisted and the head carried in an abnormal position. Also **wryneck.**

tor·tile (tô'tīl), *adj.* twisted.

tor·til·la (tôtē'ə), *n.* a Mexican thin, flat cake of corn meal baked on a hot iron or earthenware plate.

tor·til·lon (tô,tēon'), *n.* a lump of paper twisted to a point.

tor·tu·ous (tô'снōōəs, tô'tyōōəs), *adj.* winding, twisting, or crooked; indirect; deceitful. See also **torturous.**

tor·tur·ous (tô'снərəs), *adj.* relating to or involving torture; extremely painful. See also **tortuous.**

to·rus (tôr'əs), *n.* **1.** (in architecture) a large convex moulding, commonly found at the base of a column. **2.** Also **anchor ring.** a doughnut-shaped surface described by the revolution of a conic section, esp. a circle, about an axis in its plane. —**to·roi'dal,** *adj.*

toss·pot (tos'pot,, tôs'pot,), *n.* a drunkard.

to·tal·i·tar·i·an·ism (tōtal,itər'ēəniz,əm), *n.* a system of government in which the state exerts absolute control over its citizens and does not tolerate differing opinions.

to·tem pole (tō'təm), a pole or post set up in front of a North American Indian dwelling, bearing carved or painted representations of the objects or creatures adopted as the emblems of the family or group.

to·ti·pal·mate (tō,tipal'mit) *adj.* having all toes fully webbed, as certain birds.

tour·bil·lion (tŏŏ,əbil'yən), *n.* a whirlwind or something resembling one, as a firework giving out spirally rising sparks.

tour de force (tŏŏ,əd fôrs'), *pl.* **tours de force** (tŏŏr də fôrs'). an outstanding achievement that is unlikely to be equalled or repeated.

tour·ne·dos (tŏŏ'ə'nidō), *n., sing.* and *pl.* thickly sliced fillet of beef served with any of several sauces.

tower of silence, a raised stone platform on which Parsees leave their dead to be eaten by vultures. Also **dakhma.**

tox·ae·mi·a (toksē'mēə), *n.* a diseased condition caused by the presence in the bloodstream of a poison of animal or vegetable origin. —**tox·ae'mic,** *adj.*

tox·i·co·gen·ic (tok,sikōjen'ik), *adj.* producing poisonous substances.

tox·i·col·o·gy (tok,sikol'əjē), *n.* the scientific study of poisons, their effects, and problems connected with them.

tox·i·co·sis (tok,sikō'sis), *n.* an abnormal bodily condition resulting from the action of a poison.

tox·in·an·ti·tox·in (tok'sinan'tītok,sin), *n.* a mixture of toxin and antitoxin formerly used to provide immunity against certain diseases.

tox·i·pho·bia (tok,sifō'bēə), *n.* an abnormally excessive fear of being poisoned.

tox·o·ca·ri·a·sis (tok,səkərī'əsis), *n.* disease caused by parasitic roundworms of the genus *Toxocara,* which mainly infest cats and dogs but can affect humans, causing liver damage and, sometimes chronic inflammation of the eyes.

tox·o·plas·mo·sis (tok,sōplazmō'sis), *n.* disease caused by parasitic protozoa of the genus *Toxoplasma,* which infect many animal species. In humans symptoms are generally mild, although infection during pregnancy can cause fetal abnormalities.

tox·oid (tok'soid), *n.* a toxin that has been treated to make it nontoxic, used to induce immunity against a specific disease by causing the formation of antibodies.

tra·be·at·ed (trā'bēā,tid), *adj.* designed or constructed with beams.

tra·bec·u·la (trəbek'yŏŏlə), *n.* a part of a botanical or other structure resembling a bar, rod, or small beam.

trac·er·y (trā'sərē), *n.* ornamentation consisting of a decorative interlacing of lines, bars, ribs, etc., esp. in architecture.

tra·che·a (trā'kēə), *n., pl.* **tra·che·ae** (trā'kiē).

the windpipe in man and other vertebrates, carrying air to and from the lungs.

tra·che·ot·o·my (trā,kēot'əmē), *n.* the surgical operation of making an incision in the trachea.

tra·cho·ma (trəkō'mə), *n.* a form of contagious conjunctivitis marked by granulations.

trac·tate (trak'tāt), *n.* a tract; treatise.

trac·tile (trak'tīl), *adj.* capable of being drawn out lengthways. See also **ductile, malleable.**

trac·tive (trak'tiv), *adj.* serving to pull; exerting traction.

trade-last (trād'last,), *n. U.S. informal.* a complimentary remark about a person repeated to him by a person who heard it in return for the repeating of a similar compliment paid to that person.

trade wind, the wind that blows almost constantly from the high-pressure areas of the subtropics to the low-pressure equatorial areas and, being deflected westwards by the earth's rotation, comes from a north-easterly direction in the northern hemisphere and a south-easterly direction in the southern hemisphere. Also **trade winds, trades.**

trad·i·tor (trad'itə), *n., pl.* **trad·i·to·res** (trad,-itôr'ēz). an early Christian who betrayed his coreligionists under Roman persecution.

tra·duce (trədyŏŏs'), *v.* to slander, malign, or blacken the reputation of.

tra·du·cian·ism (trədyŏŏ'sHəniz,əm), *n.* the doctrine that the soul as well as the body is born of one's parents. See also **creationism.**

trag·a·canth (trag'əkanth,), *n.* a kind of gum obtained from certain Asian plants and used to bind powders into pills, stiffen fabrics, etc. Also **gum tragacanth.**

trag·i·com·e·dy (traj,ikom'idē), *n.* a play, novel, etc., containing both tragic and comic elements.

tra·gus (trā'gəs), *n., pl.* **tra·gi** (trā'jī). a prominence in front of the external opening of the ear.

train oil, a thick oil obtained from marine animals, as whales, seals, etc.

trait (trāt), *n.* a characteristic, esp. one worthy of comment or mention as being responsible for a certain action, attitude, or behaviour.

tra·jec·to·ry (trəjek'tərē), *n.* the path of a missile, as a shell, rocket, arrow, etc., through the air.

tram·mel (tram'əl), *n.* **1.** (usually *pl.*) something that impedes action or progress; a restraint or check. **2.** an instrument for describing ellipses.

tra·mon·tane (trəmon'tān), *adj.* located or being beyond the mountains. Also **transmontane.**

tranche (tränCH), *n.* **1.** a fraction or instalment of a sum of money, such as an instalment of a loan. **2.** a block of shares, esp. as part of a phased issue.

tran·quil·lize (traNG'kwilīz), *v.* to calm or soothe; to become calm.

tran·quil·liz·er (traNG'kwilī,zə), *n.* a drug that calms; a sedative.

trans·ca·lent (transkā'lənt), *adj.* allowing the passage of heat.

trans·ceiv·er (transē'və), *n.* a radio set which combines a transmitter and a receiver.

tran·scend (transend'), *v.* (used figuratively) to pass or exceed; go further than.

tran·scend·ent (transen'dənt), *adj.* surpassing the normal limits; lying outside ordinary experience. **—tran·scend'ence,** *n.*

tran·scen·den·tal (tran,senden'təl), *adj.* **1.** transcendent. **2.** abstract; abstruse. **3.** idealistic; exaggerated.

trans·duc·er (transdyoo'sə), *n.* a device that transfers energy from one system to another, often in a different form.

tran·sect (transekt'), *v.* to cut across.

trans·el·e·ment (transel'əmənt), *v.* to transmute; change the nature of. Also **trans·el'e·ment·ate.**

trans·em·pir·i·cal (trans,empir'ikəl), *adj.* outside the limits of what can be learned by experience.

trans·fect (transfekt'), *v.* the introduction into a cell of genetic material derived from another cell or virus. **—trans·fec'tion,** *n.*

trans·fer·ence (trans'fərəns, trans'frəns), *n.* **1.** the act or instance of transferring or being transferred. **2.** (in psychology) the redirection of emotions and desires towards a new object, such as those of a client towards the psychoanalyst during therapy. **—trans·fer·en·tial** (trans,fərən'-sHəl), *adj.*

trans·fig·ure (transfig'ə), *v.* to change the form or appearance of; transform.

trans·form·er (transfô'mə), *n.* an apparatus that transforms electrical energy from one set of one or more circuits to another set of one or more circuits at the same frequency but usually at a different voltage.

trans·gen·ic (tranzjen'ik), *adj.* describing an organism whose genetic material contains genes from another species. Such organisms are produced by genetic engineering.

trans·hu·mance (transhyoo'məns), *n.* the seasonal movement of livestock and those who tend them.

tran·sil·i·ent (transil'ēənt), *adj.* moving rapidly from one state to another.

trans·il·lu·mi·nate (tranziloo'mənāt), *v.* to make light pass through.

tran·sis·tor (tranzis'tə), *n.* a very small electronic device which utilizes a semiconductor in order to control current flow between two terminals and is much used in electronic circuits.

tran·si·to·ry (tran'sitərē), *adj.* not lasting; short-lived; temporary.

trans·lit·er·ate (tranzlit'ərāt), *v.* to represent the letters, words, etc., of one language in the alphabet of another.

trans·lo·ca·tion (trans,lōkā'sHən, tranz,lōkā'-sHən), *n.* **1.** movement from one location to another. **2.** (in botany) the movement of nutrients, food reserves, etc., in solution between different parts of a plant. **3.** (in genetics) the transfer of part of a chromosome to another, dissimilar chromosome. **4.** (in cell biology) the movement of a ribosome along a molecule of messenger RNA as it translates the genetic transcript into successive components of the protein being assembled.

trans·lu·cent (tranzloo'sənt), *adj.* permitting the partial passage of light. Also **trans·lu'cid.**

trans·mi·grate (tranzmī'grāt), *v.* **1.** to go from one place to another, esp. to another country in order to settle there. **2.** (of the soul) to be reborn in another body after death. **—trans,mi·gra'tion,** *n.*

trans·mog·ri·fy (tranzmog'rəfī), *v.* **trans·mog·ri·fied, trans·mog·ri·fy·ing.** to change in form or appearance, esp. by becoming grotesque.

trans·mon·tane (tranz,montān'), *adj.* See **tramontane.**

trans·mun·dane (tranz,mundān'), *adj.* beyond the visible world.

tran·spic·u·ous (transpik'yooəs), *adj.* transparent.

tran·spon·der (transpon'də), *n.* a radio or radar set which automatically emits information on receipt of a certain signal.

trans·po·ni·ble (transpō'nibəl), *adj.* able to be transposed.

trans·po·son (transpō'zon), *n.* any of various genetic elements that can insert into a chromosome, thereby introducing new genes and altering the spatial relationships and possibly also the functions of adjacent chromosomal genes.

trans·pu·ter (transpyoo'tə, tranzpyoo'tə), *n.* a highly miniaturized microchip incorporating all the functions of a microprocessor, giving it computer-like capabilities.

tran·sub·stan·ti·ate (tran,səbstan'sHēāt), *v.* **1.** to change into another substance. **2.** to change (bread and wine) in essence, but not in appearance, into the body and blood of Christ.

trans·u·ran·ic (trans,yooran'ik), *adj.* having an atomic number greater than that of uranium.

trans·vec·tion (tranzvek'sHən), *n.* the conveyance of a witch by supernatural agency through the air.

tra·pe·zi·um (trəpē'zēəm), *n.,* *pl.* **tra·pe·ziums, tra·pe·zia. 1.** *Chiefly Brit.* a quadrilateral figure with two sides parallel but of unequal length. U.S. and Canadian name: **trapezoid. 2.** *Chiefly U.S. and Canadian* a quadrilateral figure in which no two sides are parallel.

trap·e·zoid (trap'izoid), *n.* **1.** a quadrilateral

figure in which no two sides are parallel. **2.** U.S. and Canadian name for **trapezium.**

tra·pun·to (trəpōōn'tō), *n.*, *pl.* **tra·pun·tos.** a type of quilting bearing a raised design made by outlining the design in running stitch and padding it underneath.

trau·ma (trô'mə), *n.*, *pl.* **trau·ma·ta** (trô'mətə), **trau·mas. 1.** an injury; a condition caused by injury. **2.** a severe and lasting emotional shock caused by an unpleasant or alarming experience. —**trau·mat'ic,** *adj.*

tra·vail (trəvāl'), *n.* work of a difficult or irksome nature; anguish; suffering.

trav·erse (trav'ûs, trəvûs'), *v.* to travel or pass along or through.

trav·er·tine, trav·er·tin (trav'ətin), *n.* a light-coloured limestone deposited around mineral springs, esp. hot springs, and used as a building material.

trav·es·ty (trav'istē), *n.* **1.** a ludicrous or ridiculous distortion; caricature or parody. —*v.* **2.** to make ridiculous by grotesque distortion.

tre·cen·to (trāCHen'tō), *n.* the 14th century in Italian art, literature, etc.

tre·en·ware (trē'ɔnwe,ə), *n.* kitchen utensils, household vessels, etc., made of wood.

tre·foil (trē'foil), *n.* an ornamental motif or structure resembling a clover leaf.

treil·lage (trā'lij), *n.* a trellis; lattice work.

trem·u·lant (trem'yōōlənt), *adj.* trembling; shaking.

trem·u·lous (trem'yōōlɔs), *adj.* affected with trembling as a result of nervousness, fear, etc.

trench·ant (tren'CHɔnt), *adj.* **1.** incisive; sharp; cutting. **2.** energetic; vigorously effective.

tre·pan (tripan'), *n.* a tool for gouging out cores so as to form small holes.

tre·phine (trəfēn', trifīn'), *n.* a circular saw with a guiding centre pin, used in surgery for cutting out circular sections of bone.

trep·i·da·tion (trep,idā'sHən), *n.* a state of fear or alarm; anxiety.

trep·o·ne·mi·a·sis (trep,ənimī'əsis), *n.* syphilis or a related disease.

tret (tret), *n.* an allowance of extra weight formerly given to a purchaser to make up for deterioration or waste of goods during transport.

tri·ad (trī'ad), *n.* a group of three closely associated persons or things.

tri·age (treäZH'), *n.* arrangement in order of urgency or importance, as in the sorting of battlefield casualties.

tri·ar·chy (trī'äkē), *n.* government or rule by three persons; a triumvirate.

Tri·as·sic (trīas'ik), *adj.* relating to the earliest period of the Mesozoic era, from about 220 million to 180 million years ago, distinguished by volcanic activity and the appearance of marine and amphibious reptiles.

trib·ade (trib'əd), *n.* a female homosexual.

trib·ad·ism (trib'ədiz,əm), *n.* homosexuality in females.

tri·bol·o·gy (trībol'əjē, tribol'əjē), *n.* the branch of engineering dealing with the characteristics of friction-bearing surfaces (e.g. bearings and gears), and with their design and lubrication. —**tri·bol'o·gist,** *n.* —**tri·bo·log·i·cal,** *adj.*

trib·u·la·tion (trib,yōōlā'sHən), *n.* suffering; distress; affliction.

tri·bu·nal (trībyōō'nəl), *n.* a court of justice; a judicial assembly.

trib·une (trib'yōōn), *n.* one who represents the ordinary people and defends their rights.

trice (trīs), *n.* a very short space of time; an instant; a moment.

tri·chi·a·sis (trikī'əsis), *n.* **1.** irritation due to ingrowing hair, esp. of the eye as a result of eyelashes growing inwards. **2.** the presence in the urine of hair-like filaments.

trich·oid (trik'oid), *adj.* resembling hair.

tri·chol·o·gy (trikol'əjē), *n.* the study of hair and its diseases.

tri·chot·o·my (trīkot'əmē), *n.* a division into three.

tri·chro·ma·tism (trīkrō'mətiz,əm), *n.* the condition of normal vision in which all the basic colours are perceived. Also **tri·chro,ma·top'si·a.**

tri·corn, tri·corne (trī'kôn), *n.* a hat having the brim turned up to form three sides.

tri·dent (trī'dənt), *n.* a three-pronged spear.

tri·fid (trī'fid), *adj.* divided into three.

tri·fling (trī'fliNG), *adj.* completely unimportant; not worth consideration, as *a trifling amount of money.*

tri·fo·cal (trīfō'kal), *adj.* (of spectacle lenses) having three parts one above the other, the lowest for near, the middle for mid, and the topmost for distant vision. See also **bifocal.**

tri·fur·cate (trīfû'kāt), *v.* to branch or fork into three parts.

trig·o·nal (trig'ənəl), *adj.* relating to or shaped like a triangle.

trig·o·nous (trig'ənəs), *adj.* having three angles; triangular.

tri·he·dral (trīhē'drəl), *adj.* having three surfaces meeting in a point.

tri·he·dron (trīhē'drən), *n.* the figure formed by three surfaces meeting in a point.

tri·lem·ma (trīlem'ə), *n.* a situation in which there are three unpleasant alternatives. See also **dilemma.**

tri·ma·ran (trī'məran,), *n.* a sailing vessel with three separate hulls.

trine (trīn), *adj.* triple; threefold.

trin·gle (triNG'gəl), *n.* a relatively narrow, straight, square-sectioned architectural moulding.

tri·ni·tro·tol·u·ene (trī,nītrōtol'yōōēn), *n.* See TNT. Also **tri·ni·tro·tol'u·ol.**

tripe (trīp), *n.* the lining of the first or second stomach of a ruminant mammal, used as food.

tri·phib·i·an (trīfib'ēən), *adj.* adept at or equipped for operations, warfare, etc., on land, sea, and in the air. Also **tri·phib'i·ous.**

triph·thong (trif'thoNG), *n.* a combination of three differing vowel qualities to form one sound.

trip·tych (trip'tik), *n.* a picture, carving, etc., on three panels side by side, esp. one in which the side panels fold over the central one. See also **diptych, pentaptych, polyptych.**

tri·que·tra (trīkwē'trə), *n.* a geometrical figure contained within three points, esp. one composed of three intersecting arcs, lobes, or ellipses. —**tri·que'trous,** *adj.*

tri·reme (trī'rēm), *n.* a war galley with three rows of oars on each side.

tri·sect (trīsekt'), *v.* to divide into three, esp. three equal parts.

tris·kel·i·on (triskel'ēon), *n., pl.* **tris·kel·i·a.** a figure composed of three branches, arms, or legs radiating from a centre. Also **tris'kele.**

tris·mus (triz'məs), *n.* an involuntary contraction of the jaw muscles.

tris·oc·ta·he·dron (trisok,təhē'drən), *n., pl.* **tris·oc·ta·he·drons, tris·oc·ta·he·dra.** a solid having 24 faces in three groups, each group corresponding to the face of an octahedron.

triste (trēst), *n. French.* mournful; sad.

tris·tesse (trēstes'), *n. French.* sadness; melancholy.

tri·tan·ope (trī'tənōp), *n.* one who suffers from tritanopia.

tri·tan·o·pi·a (trī,tənō'pēə), *n.* a defect in perception of colour in which the eye fails to distinguish properly blue and yellow.

trite (trīt), *adj.* overused and corny, as a phrase, joke, style, etc.

trit·u·rate (trit'yŏŏrāt), *v.* to grind to a fine powder; to pulverize. —**trit,u·ra'tion,** *n.*

tri·um·vi·rate (trīum'vərit), *n.* government by three men sharing power jointly. See also **qua·drumvirate.**

tri·une (tri'yŏŏn), *adj.* **1.** three in one constituting a unity. —*n.* **2. Triune,** the Trinity.

triv·et (triv'it), *n.* a stand with short legs placed under a hot dish to protect a table surface.

triv·i·al (triv'ēəl), *adj.* totally unimportant; insignificant; not worth considering, as *a trivial argument* or *a trivial idea.*

triv·i·um (triv'ēəm), *n., pl.* **triv·ia.** the lower division of the seven liberal arts studied in medieval schools, consisting of grammar, rhetoric, and logic. See also **quadrivium.**

troche (trōsH), *n.* a medicinal tablet, usually circular in shape.

trof·fer (trof'ə), *n.* a trough, usually fixed on a wall, for holding and reflecting upward the light of fluorescent lamps.

trog·lo·dyte (trog'lədīt), *n.* a cave dweller; a recluse; one who shuns the society of others.

troi·ka (troi'kə), *n.* a Russian carriage drawn by three horses harnessed abreast.

troil·ism (troil'izəm), *n.* a sexual relationship or encounter among three people.

trol·lop (trol'əp), *n.* a slovenly or loose-living woman.

trom·mel (trom'əl), *n.* a screen used for sifting ores, coal, gravel, etc., according to size.

trompe l'oeil (tromp, loi'), **1.** the attempt to deceive the eye into taking a painting of an object for real by means of perspective, foreshortening, and fine detail. **2.** a painting intended to create such an illusion.

tronc (troNGk), *n.* a fund into which are placed all tips received by the staff of a hotel, restaurant, etc., for subsequent sharing.

trope (trōp), *n.* the use of a word or phrase in a figurative sense; a figure of speech.

troph·ic (trof'ik), *adj.* **1.** relating to food, nutrition, or nourishment. **2.** (of a hormone) stimulating a particular tissue or process. —**troph'i·cal·ly,** *adv.*

tro·pism (trō'pizəm), *n.* the response of an organism to an external stimulus by growing towards or away from it. See also **taxis.**

tro·pol·o·gy (tropol'əjē), *n.* the use of figurative language in speech or writing.

trop·o·pause (trop'əpôz,), *n.* the upper boundary layer of the troposphere, separating it from the stratosphere.

tro·poph·i·lous (tropof'ələs), *adj.* adapted to a climate which has alternating periods favouring growth and dormancy.

trop·o·phyte (trop'əfīt,), *n.* a tropophilous plant.

trop·o·sphere (trop'əsfē,ə), *n.* that part of the atmosphere in which temperature decreases with height, lying below the stratosphere, separated from it by the tropopause, and extending about 6 to 12 miles above the surface of the earth.

Trot·sky·ism (trot'skēiz,əm), *n.* the theories advocated by the Russian revolutionary and writer Leon Trotsky (1879–1940), including the concept of immediate worldwide revolution. —**Trot'sky·ite,** *n.*

trou·blous (trub'ləs), *adj.* disturbed; full of troubles; agitated.

truck·le (truk'əl), *v.* to submit abjectly or tamely; to be servile.

truc·u·lent (truk'yŏŏlənt), *adj.* **1.** cruel; brutal; harsh. **2.** defiant or hostile.

truf·fle (truf'əl), *n.* a kind of edible subterranean fungus.

tru·ism (trŏŏ'izəm), *n.* something said that is unnecessary because it is so obvious that everyone knows it, as *Crime is dishonest.*

tru·meau (trŏŏmō'), *n., pl.* **tru·meaux.** a

carved or painted panel set together with a mirror, above or below it, in a frame.

trump·er·y (trump'ərē), *n.*, *pl.* **trump·er·ies.** **1.** a worthless or useless item. **2.** foolish or deceitful talk. —*adj.* **3.** cheap; tawdry; worthless.

trun·cate (trunG'kāt), *v.* to cut the top off; to shorten by cutting. —**trun·ca'tion,** *n.*

trun·cheon (trun'CHən), *n.* a short thick stick or club carried by a policeman.

trun·nion (trun'yən), *n.* one of a pair of barlike projections on the sides of a cannon, supporting it on its carriage and enabling it to swivel.

trus·sell, trus·sel (trus'əl), *n.* the upper die used in making coins by hand. See also **pile.**

truth serum, any drug, as scopolamine and some barbiturates, used in psychiatric treatment and criminal investigation to diminish a person's conscious or unconscious resistance to recalling experiences. Also **truth drug.** See also **narcoanalysis.**

truth-value, (in logic) either of the two values, true or false, that may apply to a sentence or logical proposition.

tryp·a·no·some (trip'ənəsōm), *n.* any of a genus of parasitic flagellate protozoans causing various kinds of disease in man and animals and usually transmitted by insects.

tryp·a·no·so·mi·a·sis (trip,ənōsōmī'əsis), *n.* any disease caused by trypanosomes.

tryp·sin (trip'sin), *n.* an enzyme produced by the pancreas and able to convert proteins into peptone.

tryst (trist), *n.* an agreement to meet at a certain time and place, esp. one made secretly between lovers.

tsar·e·vitch, czar·e·vitch (zär'əviCH), *n.* the son of a tsar.

tsa·rev·na, cza·rev·na (zärev'nə), *n.* the daughter of a tsar.

tsa·ri·na, cza·ri·na (zärē'nə), *n.* the wife of a tsar.

tsu·na·mi (tsoōnä'mē), *n.* a very large sea wave caused by a submarine earth movement or volcanic shock.

tu·ber·cle bacillus (tyōō'bəkəl), the bacterium, *Mycobacterium tuberculosis,* which causes tuberculosis.

tu·ber·cu·lin (tyōōbû'kyōolin), *n.* a sterile liquid prepared from the tubercle bacillus and used in diagnosing and treating tuberculosis.

tu·ber·os·i·ty (tyōōbərōs'itē), *n.* a large prominence or protuberance on a bone, usually serving to attach ligaments or muscle.

tu·fa (tyōō'fə), *n.* a porous limestone deposited around mineral springs. Also **calc-tufa, caltuff.**

tuff (tuf), *n.* rock composed of fine volcanic ash. Also **volcanic tuff.**

tuft·hun·ter (tuft'hun,tə), *n. Archaic.* one who

seeks to ingratiate himself with important people; a sycophant or toady.

tu·la·rae·mi·a (tōō,lərē'mēə), *n.* a bacterial disease of rabbits and other rodents, capable of being transmitted to man in the form of a fever of several weeks' duration. Also **deer fly fever, rabbit fever.**

tulle (tyōōl), *n.* a fine net fabric of silk or nylon used for dresses, veils, etc.

tum·brel, tum·bril (tum'brəl), *n.* a cart in which condemned persons were carried to the guillotine during the French Revolution.

tu·me·fa·cient (tyōō,məfā'sHənt), *adj.* swelling; causing to swell.

tu·me·fac·tion (tyōō,məfak'sHən), *n.* the action or process of making or becoming tumid.

tu·me·fy (tyōō'məfī), *v.* to cause to swell; to become swollen.

tu·mes·cent (tyōōmes'ənt), *adj.* becoming tumid; somewhat swollen.

tu·mid (tyōō'mid), *adj.* swollen; bloated; enlarged.

tum·mel·er, tum·mul·er (tōōm'ələ), *n. U.S. colloquial.* a person employed as entertainer and entertainment organizer by certain resorts.

tu·mult (tyōō'məlt), *n.* a commotion or great and noisy confusion; uproar, as *the tumult of the crowd.* —**tu·mul·tu·ous** (tōōməlcHōōəs, tyōōməl'tyōōəs), *adj.*

tu·mul·tu·ar·y (tyōōmul'cHərē, tyōōmul'-tyōōərē), *adj.* turbulent; lawless; disorderly.

tu·mu·lus (tyōō'myōoləs), *n., pl.* **tumu·lus·es, tu·mu·li.** **1.** an artificial mound or hillock, esp. over a grave. **2.** a rounded mound in congealed lava. —**tu'mu·lar, tu'mu·lous,** *adj.*

tun (tun), *n.* **1.** a large cask for holding wine, beer, etc. **2.** a unit of liquid capacity, esp. one equal to 252 wine gallons.

tur·ba·ry (tû'bərē), *n.* a piece of ground from which turf or peat may be taken.

tur·bid (tû'bid), *adj.* opaque; muddy; clouded; dense; confused.

tur·bi·nate (tû'binät), *adj.* shaped like a scroll; spiralled. Also **tur'bi·nat,ed.**

tur·bo·fan (tû'bōfan,), *n.* a turbojet engine having a turbine-driven fan which supplies air for combustion, cooling, etc.

tur·bo·jet (tû'bōjet,), *n.* **1.** an aeroplane equipped with turbojet engines. **2.** a turbojet engine.

turbojet engine, a jet propulsion engine using a turbine-driven compressor to compress air from the atmosphere for fuel combustion. Also **turbojet.**

tur·bo·prop (tû'bōprop,), *n.* **1.** an aeroplane using turbo-propeller engines. **2.** a turbo-propeller engine.

turbo-propeller engine, a jet engine fitted with a turbine-driven propeller, whose thrust is additional to that obtained by the thrust of the jet exhaust. Also **turboprop, turboprop engine, propjet engine.**

tur·di·form (tû'difôm,), *adj.* resembling a thrush in appearance.

tur·gent (tû'jənt), *adj.* turgid.

tur·ges·cent (tûjes'ənt), *adj.* becoming swollen or turgid.

tur·gid (tû'jid), *adj.* bloated; swollen; pompous.

tur·gor (tû'gə), *n.* the state of being turgid.

tur·moil (tû'moil), *n.* great confusion and disturbance; a completely mixed-up situation or state, as *the turmoil of war.*

turn·er·y (tû'nərē), *n.* 1. the shaping of articles on a lathe. 2. articles so made. 3. a place where such articles are made.

tur·pi·tude (tû'pityōod), *n.* wickedness of character; a wicked or depraved act.

tur·ri·cal (tû'ikəl), *adj.* relating to or resembling a turret.

tur·ric·u·late (tərik'yōolāt), *adj.* resembling or having a turret or turrets.

turt·let (tût'lit), *n.* a young turtle.

tusche (tōosH), *n.* a greasy substance used in lithography for its receptivity to lithographic ink and in etching and silk-screen printing as a resist.

tush·e·ry (tusH'ərē), *n.* an inferior style of writing characterized by the use of archaic language.

tus·sah (tus'ə), *n.* a coarse brownish silk from India. Also **tus'sore, wild silk.** See also **pongee, shantung.**

tus·sis (tus'is), *n.* a cough. —**tus'sal,** *adj.*

tu·te·lar·y (tyōot'ələē), *adj.* serving as a guardian or protector of a person or place.

tu·toy·er (tōo,twäyā'), *v.* to address or treat (a person) with familiarity, esp. where no familiarity exists.

tu·tu (tōo'tōo), *n., pl.* **tu·tus.** a short skirt of layers of stiffened tulle, worn by female ballet dancers.

tweet·er (twē'tə), *n.* a small loudspeaker which reproduces only high-frequency sounds. See also **woofer.**

tweet·er-woof·er (twē'təwōof'ə), *n.* a loudspeaker in which the tweeter is placed in front of the cone of the woofer.

tweeze, tweese (twēz), *n.* (formerly) a case holding surgical or similar instruments.

twi·bill (twī'bil,), *n.* a mattock with one end of the head like an adze-head and the other like an axe-head.

twit (twit), *v.* to tease or taunt; make fun of.

Ty·burn tree (tī'bûn trē'), the gallows. [after the site of the gallows near Marble Arch, London.]

ty·chism (tī'kizəm), *n.* the philosophical theory that chance plays an active part in the universe.

ty·cho·po·tam·ic (tī,kōpōtam'ik), *adj.* living or growing mainly in fresh and usually still rather than flowing water.

tym·bal (tim'bəl), *n.* See **timbal.**

tym·pa·ni (tim'pənē), *n. pl.* See **timpani.**

tym·pa·n·ist (tim'pənist), *n.* one who plays the timpani or other percussion instruments in an orchestra.

typh·lol·o·gy (tiflol'əjē), *n.* the body of scientific knowledge about blindness.

typh·lo·sis (tiflō'sis), *n.* blindness.

ty·pog·ra·phy (tīpog'rəfē), *n.* the art of printing with type; the work of designing and setting type and printing.

ty·pol·o·gy (tīpol'əjē), *n.* the theory or study of types or symbols; the systematic classification of objects according to type.

ty·poth·e·tae (tīpoth'itē), *n. pl.* an association of master printers.

ty·ro, ti·ro (tī'rō), *n.* a beginner.

ty·ro·thri·cin (tī,rōthrī'sin), *n.* a powdered antibiotic obtained from any of several soil bacilli and used for external treatment of localized bacterial infections.

U

u·bi·e·ty (yōōbī'itē), *n.* the state of being in a definite place.

u·biq·ui·tous (yōōbik'witəs), *adj.* omnipresent; being everywhere at once. —**u·biq'ui·tous·ly,** *adv.*

u·biq·ui·ty (yōōbik'witē), *n.* **1.** the state of being everywhere or in many places, esp. at the same time. **2.** (in theology) the omnipresence of God.

u·dom·e·ter (yōōdom'itə), *n.* an instrument for measuring rainfall; a rain gauge.

UHF, uhf. See **ultrahigh frequency.**

u·kase (yōōkāz'), *n.* a proclamation or edict given by an absolute authority. See also **fiat.** [from Russian]

u·lig·i·nous (yōōlij'ənəs), *adj.* growing in mud or swamps. Also **u·lig'i·nose.**

ul·lage (ul'ij), *n.* the amount by which contents, usually liquids, fall short of filling their container.

u·lot·ri·chous (yōōlo'trikəs), *adj.* belonging to a woolly-haired group of mankind.

u·lot·ri·chy (yōōlot'rikē), *n.* the condition of having woolly or very curly hair.

ul·ti·ma (ul'timə), *n.* the last syllable in a word. See also **penultima.**

ul·ti·mo·gen·i·ture (ul,timōjen'ichə), *n.* See **postremogeniture.**

ul·tra·high frequency (ul'trəhī,), any radio frequency between 300 and 3000 megahertz. *Abbr.:* **uhf, UHF.**

ul·tra·ism (ul'trəiz,əm), *n.* extremism; any manifestation of extremism.

ul·tra·ma·rine (ul,trəmərēn'), *adj.* **1.** beyond the sea. **2.** deep blue.

ul·tra·mon·tane (ul,trəmontān'), *adj.* situated beyond the mountains.

ul·tra·mon·ta·nism (ul,trəmon'tiniz,əm), *n.* the policy of one group within the Roman Catholic Church that favours increased authority for the pope. See also **Gallicanism.**

ul·tra·mun·dane (ul,trəmun'dān), *adj.* **1.** beyond the earth or the solar system. **2.** beyond the limits of physical existence; otherworldly.

ul·tra·son·ic (ul,trəson'ik), *adj.* of or denoting a sound frequency too high to be perceived by the human ear.

ul·tra·son·ics (ul,trəson'iks), *n., sing.* the scientific study of ultrasonic phenomena.

ul·tra·son·og·ra·phy (ul,trəsonog'rəfē), *n.* a technique that uses ultrasound to produce images of body tissues; it is used esp. to visualize the fetus during pregnancy. —**ul,tra·son,o·graph'ic,** *adj.* —**ul,tra·son,o·graph'i·cal·ly,** *adv.*

ul·tra vi·res (vī'rēz), exceeding the powers granted by law, esp. to a corporation or one of its officers.

ul·tra·vi·rus (ul,trəvī'rəs), *n., pl.* **ul·tra·vi·rus·es.** a virus so small that it can pass through the finest bacterial filters and can be seen only under a microscope specially adapted for viewing the minutest objects.

ul·u·late (yōōl'yōōlāt), *v.* **1.** to howl like a dog or hoot like an owl. **2.** to lament; wail, esp. shrilly. —**ul'u·lant,** *adj.*

um·bo (um'bō), *n., pl.* **um·bos, um·bones** (umbō'nēz). a boss on a shield, often at the centre. —**um'bo·nal, um'bo·nate,** *adj.*

um·bra (um'brə), *n., pl.* **um·brae** (um'brē). shadow; shade. See also **penumbra.**

um·brage (um'brij), *n.* a sense of slight or injury; the giving or taking of offence. —**um·bra'geous,** *adj.*

um·brif·er·ous (umbrif'ərəs), *adj.* giving or throwing shade.

un·bund·ling (unbund'ling), *n.* (in business) the dismantling of a conglomerate into its component companies, esp. in readiness to sell them.

un·can·ny (ənkan'ē), *adj.* **1.** extraordinary; highly unusual and outside normal expectations; not easily explained, as *He has an uncanny ability to play the violin.* **2.** unerring; completely accurate, as *He has an uncanny knack for saying the wrong thing.*

uncertainty principle, a concept of wave mechanics, formulated in 1927 by Heisenberg, that the precise position and the precise momentum of a particle in a given instant cannot both be known, and the more accurately the one is known the less accurately is the other known.

un·ci·al (un'sēəl, un'shəl), *adj.* pertaining to or written in a type of majuscule writing used in Latin and Greek manuscript between the 3rd and 9th centuries A.D. having more curves than monumental capitals and some ascending and descending strokes.

un·ci·form (un'sifôm,), *adj.* shaped like a hook. —*n.* See **hamate.**

un·ci·nate (un'sināt), *adj.* shaped like or furnished with a hook or hooks.

un·con·scion·a·ble (unkon'sнənəbəl), *adj.* not in keeping with the principles of one's conscience, or sense of what is proper and just, as *an unconscionable lack of courtesy.*

unc·tion (uNGk'sнən), *n.* the act of anointing, for medical or ritual purposes.

unc·tu·ous (uNGk'cнooəs), *adj.* 1. of the nature of ointment; greasy. 2. with an excessively moralizing, smooth, or complacent manner.

un·de·cil·lion (un,disil'yən), *n.* 1. (in Britain and Germany) the number represented by the figure 1 followed by 66 zeros. 2. (in the U.S.A. and Canada) the number represented by the figure 1 followed by 36 zeros.

un·der·croft (un'dəkroft,), *n.* an underground room or vault.

un·der·fur (un'dəfû,), *n.* the fine fur under the coarser outer fur in certain animals, as seals.

un·der·glaze (un'dəglāz,), *n.* a layer of colour applied to ceramic ware before it is glazed.

un·der·set (un'dəset,), *n.* an undercurrent in water, flowing in the opposite direction to the surface current.

un·du·late (un'dyoolāt), *v.* 1. to move or cause to move with a wavelike or winding motion. 2. to give a wave-like form to. 3. to have a wavy shape or surface. —*adj.* 4. wavy; winding. —**un'du·lat,ed**, **un'du·lant**, **un'du·la·tor·y**, *adj.* —**un,du·la'tion**, *n.*

un·ea·sy (unē'zē), *adj.* **un·eas·i·er**, **un·eas·i·est.** anxious, as *She was uneasy about meeting her future mother-in-law*; uncomfortable; restless, as *an uneasy situation in the Balkans.*

un·ex·cep·tion·a·ble (un,iksep'sнənəbəl), *adj.* beyond criticism; with which no fault can be found.

un·ex·cep·tion·al (un,iksep'sнənəl), *adj.* ordinary; not unusual.

un·fath·om·a·ble (unfaтн'əməbəl), *adj.* 1. too deep for the bottom to be reached. 2. impossible to understand or to get to the bottom of.

un·flag·ging (unflag'iNG), *adj.* without letup; constant, as *his unflagging love for his country.*

un·gual (uNG'gwəl), *adj.* relating to, shaped like, or furnished with a nail, claw, or hoof.

un·guent (uNG'gwənt), *n.* a soft or liquid ointment for wounds, etc.

un·guic·u·late (uNGgwik'yoolāt), *adj.* furnished with or resembling a nail or claw. Also **un·guic'u·lat,ed.**

un·gui·nous (uNG'gwinəs), *adj.* consisting of or like oil or fat; greasy.

un·guis (uNG'gwis), *n.*, *pl.* **un·gues** (uNG'gwēz). a nail, claw, or hoof.

un·gu·late (uNG'gyoolāt), *adj.* hoofed.

un·gu·li·grade (uNG'gyooligrād,), *adj.* walking on hooves, as a horse.

u·ni·cam·er·al (yoo,nikam'ərəl), *adj.* having only one (legislative) chamber.

u·ni·cos·tate (yoon,nikos'tāt), *adj.* with one rib or ridge.

un·in·ter·est·ed (unin'tərəstid), *adj.* not caring about; not interested. See also **disinterested.**

u·nip·ar·ous (yoonip'ərəs), *adj.* producing offspring or eggs only one at a time.

u·ni·pla·nar (yoo,niplā'nə), *adj.* restricted to one plane or two-dimensional continuum, as movement.

u·ni·tive (yoo'nitiv), *adj.* able or serving to unite; involving union.

u·ni·vo·cal (yoo,nivō'kəl), *adj.* 1. having only a single meaning; unambiguous. —*n.* 2. a word or construct with only one meaning. —**u,ni·vo'cal·ly**, *adv.*

un·kempt (unkempt'), *adj.* scruffy; sloppy; dishevelled; with the hair uncombed.

un·mit·i·gat·ed (unmit'igā,tid), *adj.* unrelieved; not reduced or made milder in intensity or severity; outright, as *an unmitigated fool.*

un·pro·pi·tious (un,prəpisн'əs), *adj.* unfavourable; disadvantageous, as *unpropitious weather for a picnic.*

un·sat·u·rat·ed (unsacн'ərā,tid), *adj.* denoting oils, esp. fish and vegetable oils, that are liquid at room temperatures, that are able to accept additional hydrogen atoms, and that do not raise cholesterol levels. See also **polyunsaturated.**

un·sa·vour·y (unsā'vərē), *adj.* 1. lacking flavouring; having an unpleasant flavouring or smell. 2. causing social or moral distaste or offence.

un·scram·bler (unskram'blə), *n.* a device to render scrambled telecommunications signals intelligible.

un·scru·pu·lous (unskroo'pyooləs), *adj.* without principles or scruples; having no concern for what is morally right, as *an unscrupulous businessman.*

un·seem·ly (unsēm'lē), *adj.* in bad form; not appropriate to or in keeping with proper behaviour or taste.

un·sul·lied (unsul'ēd), *adj.* not dirtied, disgraced, or contaminated; pure, or relatively so.

un·ten·a·ble (unten'əbəl), *adj.* indefensible, as an argument, etc. —**un·ten'a·bly**, *adv.*

un·touch·a·ble (untucн'əbəl), *n.* a person below the lowest social division of Hindu society, whom a caste man may not touch for fear of being defiled.

un·toward (untôd'), *adj.* not favourable; inappropriate; improper, as *an untoward remark.*

un·tram·melled (untram'əld), *adj.* not hampered or restrained, as *untrammelled joy.*

un·wit·ting (unwit'iNG), *adj.* not knowing or

thinking; not conscious, as *an unwitting mistake.*

un·wont·ed (unwŏnt'id), *adj.* unusual; remarkable. —**un·wont'ed·ly,** *adv.* —**un·wont'-ed·ness,** *n.*

u·pas (yōō'pəs), *n.* the poisonous sap of a Javanese tree, used on poison arrows.

up·braid (upbrād'), *v.* to scold in an angry way, as *She upbraided him for being late for dinner.*

up·per (up'ə), *n.* all that part of a boot or shoe which is above the sole.

up·stage (up,stāj'), *adv.* 1. at or towards the back of the stage. —*v.* 2. to move towards the rear of the stage, thus forcing another actor to turn his back to the audience and so overshadow his performance.

u·rae·mi·a (yōōrē'mēə), *n.* the presence in the blood of matter normally excreted in the urine, caused by malfunction of the kidneys. —**u·rae'-mic,** *adj.*

u·rae·us (yōōrē'əs), *n.*, *pl.* **u·rae·us·es.** the sacred asp or snake of ancient Egypt, used as an emblem of gods and rulers.

u·ran·ism (yōōər'əniz,əm), *n.* homosexuality, esp. male homosexuality.

u·ra·nog·ra·phy (yōōr,ənog'rəfē), *n.* the branch of astronomy devoted to describing and mapping the heavens, esp. fixed stars. Also **ura-nology.**

u·ra·nol·o·gy (yōōr,ənol'əjē), *n.* a treatise on stars. See **uranography.**

u·ra·nom·e·try (yōōr,ənom'itrē), *n.* 1. a chart showing the positions and sizes of stars on the celestial sphere. 2. the measurement of distances between stars.

ur·bane (ûbān'), *adj.* sophisticated; knowing how to behave in most social situations as a result of familiarity with life in large cities. —**ur·ban·i·ty** (ûban'itē), *n.*

ur·bi·cul·ture (û'bikul,CHə), *n.* the way of life in cities.

ur·ce·o·late (û'sēəlāt), *adj.* pitcher-shaped.

u·re·thra (yōōrē',thrə), *n.*, *pl.* **u·re·thrae** (yōōrē',thrē), **u·re·thras.** the tube which carries urine from the bladder out of the body and which in males also discharges semen.

ur·ic·ac·id·ae·mi·a (yōōr,ikas,idē'mēə), *n.* See **lithaemia.**

u·rol·o·gy (yōōrol'əjē), *n.* the medical study of urine and the genitourinary tract and of diseases affecting them.

u·ro·pyg·i·al gland (yōōr,ōpij'ēəl), a gland opening at the base of a bird's tail which secretes a fluid used in preening or cleaning the feathers. Also **oil gland, preen gland.**

u·ro·pyg·i·um (yōōrōpij'ēəm), *n.* the terminal

part of a bird's body, to which the tail feathers are attached.

ur·si·form (û'sifôm,), *adj.* bear-shaped.

ur·sine (û'sīn), *adj.* bearlike; of or relating to the bear.

ur·ti·car·i·a (û,tiker'ēə), *n.* a skin rash caused by an allergy, with raised pale areas on the skin and severe itching such as is caused by nettle stings; hives.

ur·ti·cate (û'tikāt), *v.* 1. to sting with or as if with nettles. 2. to whip with nettles or so as to cause a stinging sensation. —**ur'ti·cant,** *adj.* —**ur,ti·ca'tion,** *n.*

us·tu·late (us'tyōōlāt), *adj.* of scorched appearance. —**us,tu·la'tion,** *n.*

u·su·fruct (yōōs'yōōfrukt,), *n.* the right to use or benefit from something which belongs to another, short of destroying or harming it. —**u·su·fruc'tu·ar·y,** *n.*

u·surp (yōōzûp'), *v.* 1. to seize power illegally or by force. 2. to use without right. —**u,sur·pa'-tion,** *n.*

u·su·ry (yōō'zərē), *n.* 1. an extortionate, esp. illegally high, rate of interest. 2. the practice of lending money at such a high rate of interest. —**u'su·rer,** *n.* —**u·su'ri·ous,** *adj.*

u·til·i·tar·i·an (yōōtil,iter'ēən), *adj.* 1. relating to usefulness; useful rather than decorative. 2. supporting the doctrine of utilitarianism.

u·til·i·tar·i·an·ism (yōōtil,iter'ēəniz,əm), *n.* the doctrine that promoting the greatest happiness for the greatest number of people should be the principal concern of morality, a doctrine expounded by Jeremy Bentham and J.S. Mill.

u·ti pos·si·de·tis (yōō,tī pos,idē'tis), the principle of international law that at the conclusion of a war each side may claim as its own the territory it actually occupies.

u·tri·cle (yōō'trikəl), *n.* 1. a small, air-filled sac, as in a seaweed. 2. the larger of two sacs in the internal ear. —**u·tric'u·lar, u·tric'u·late,** *adj.*

u·tric·u·li·tis (yōōtrik,yōōlī'tis), *n.* inflammation of the utricle of the inner ear.

u·ve·i·tis (yōō,vēī'tis), *n.* inflammation of the uvea, i.e. the vascular layers making up the wall of the eyeball.

u·vu·la (yōō'vyōōlə), *n.*, *pl.* **u·vu·las, u·vu·lae** (yōō'vyōōlē). the conical flap of flesh that hangs down from the soft palate at the back of the mouth.

ux·o·ri·al (uksôr'ēəl), *adj.* of or befitting a wife.

ux·o·ri·cide (uksôr'isīd), *n.* 1. the act of killing one's wife. 2. a man who kills his wife.

ux·o·ri·lo·cal (uksôr,ilō'kəl), *adj.* See **matrilo-cal.**

ux·o·ri·ous (uksôr'ēəs), *adj.* excessively fond of or submissive to one's wife.

vac·il·late (vas'ilāt), *v.* **1.** to sway unsteadily; to fluctuate. **2.** to waver between different opinions; to be indecisive. —**vac'il·lant, vac'il·la·to·ry,** *adj.* —**vac·il·la'tion,** *n.*

va·cu·i·ty (vakyōo'itē), *n.* **1.** the state of being empty. **2.** a void; a vacuum. **3.** an absence of thought; something unintelligent or senseless.

vac·u·ous (vak'yōoəs), *adj.* empty; without ideas, intelligence, or purpose.

va·de me·cum (vā'dē mā'kəm), *pl.* **va·de me·cums.** something carried about the person constantly or frequently, esp. a book for reference.

va·dose (vā'dōs), *adj.* of, in, or from water situated above the water table.

va·gar·y (vā'gərē), *n.* **1.** an erratic or unpredictable occurrence or action. **2.** a whimsical, odd, or unusual idea. —**va·gar'i·ous,** *adj.*

vag·ile (vaj'īl), *adj.* able to move; having freedom of movement.

va·gi·na (vəjī'nə), *n.,* *pl.* **va·gi·nas, va·gi·nae** (vajī'nē). **1.** the passage leading from the womb to the exterior of most female mammals. **2.** a part or organ resembling a sheath, as that formed by the base of some leaves around a stem.

vag·i·nis·mus (vaj,iniz'məs), *n.* a painful involuntary contraction of the vagina.

va·got·o·my (vagot'əmē), *n.,* *pl.* **va·got·o·mies.** surgical cutting of the vagus nerve or its branches, performed in cases of gastric or duodenal ulcer to reduce secretory activity in the stomach.

val·e·tu·di·nar·i·an (val,ətyōo,d'iner'ēən), *n.* **1.** an invalid. **2.** someone obsessed with his poor health.

val·gus (val'gəs), *n.,* *pl.* **val·gus·es.** an abnormal position of part of the human bone structure, as a bowleg or a knock-knee, etc.

val·ine (vā'lēn), *n.* an amino acid, obtained by hydrolysis of plant or animal protein, used chiefly in medical nutrition and laboratory production of bacteria. Found in a meteorite in 1970.

val·late (val'āt), *adj.* surrounded or bordered by a ridge.

val·la·tion (vəlā'sHən), *n.* a rampart; the technique of building ramparts.

val·lec·u·la (vəlek'yōolə), *n.,* *pl.* **val·lec·u·lae** (valek'yōolē). a furrow; a hollow.

val·lec·u·late (vəlek'yōolāt), *adj.* having furrows or hollows.

val·or·ize (val'əriz), *v.* (of a government) to fix and maintain the price of a commodity by buying it at a fixed price. —**val,or·iz·a'tion,** *n.*

va·lu·ta (valōo'tə), *n.* the value of any currency expressed as its exchange rate with another currency.

van·quish (vaNG'kwisH), *v.* conquer; beat.

Van·sit·tart·ism (vansit'ətiz,əm), *n.* the doctrine that Germany is an aggressive country and should be demilitarized and undergo corrective education to prevent future aggression.

vap·id (vap'id), *adj.* insipid; dull; lifeless.

va·po·ret·to (vap,əret'ō), *n.,* *pl.* **va·po·ret·tos, va·po·ret·ti** (vap,əret'ē). a small steamboat used as part of a passenger transport service, esp. in Venice, Italy.

var·i·a (ver'ēə), *pl. n.* a compilation or miscellany, as of verse, stories, etc.

var·i·cel·la (var,isel'ə), *n.* chicken pox. —**var,i·cel'loid,** *adj.*

var·i·cel·late (var,isel'āt), *adj.* having longitudinal ridges showing the former positions of the rim of the aperture of a shell.

var·i·cel·la·tion (var,isəlā'sHən), *n.* inoculation with chicken pox virus.

var·i·ces (ver'isēz), *n. pl.* See **varix.**

var·i·e·gate (ver'ēəgāt), *v.* **1.** to vary the appearance of something, as by adding colours. **2.** to diversify; to make varied. —**var·i·e·ga'tion,** *n.*

var·i·e·gat·ed (ver'ēəgā,tid), *adj.* **1.** mottled; of different colours; patchy in colour. **2.** varied; of various natures.

va·ri·o·la (vərī'ələ), *n.* smallpox. —**var'i·o·late,** *adj.*

var·i·ole (ver'ēōl), *n.* **1.** a small depression resembling the marks left on the skin by smallpox. **2.** any of the light-coloured small spheres that resemble pockmarks found in several igneous rocks known as variolite.

var·i·o·rum (ver,ēôr'əm), *adj.* containing various versions of a text; containing many notes made by various critics or scholars.

var·is·tor (varis'tə), *n.* an electrical resistor, the resistance of which varies automatically in proportion to the voltage passing through it.

var·ix (ver'iks), *n.,* *pl.* **var·i·ces** (ver'isēz). **1.** a permanent abnormal dilatation and lengthening of a vein or artery, usually accompanied by the development of many twists. Also **var,i·cos'i·ty.**

2. a longitudinal ridge on a shell marking the former position of the rim.

var·let (vä'lit), *n.* a rascal; a scoundrel.

va·so·con·stric·tion (vä,zōkənstrik'sHən), *n.* constriction of the blood vessels. —**va,so·con·stric'tive,** *adj.*

va·so·con·stric·tor (vä,zōkənstrik'tə), *adj.* **1.** causing constriction of blood vessels. —*n.* **2.** a drug or nerve that causes constriction of blood vessels.

va·so·di·la·tor (vä,zōdīlā'tə), *adj.* **1.** causing blood vessels to relax or dilate. Also **va,so·de·pres'sor.** —*n.* **2.** a nerve or drug causing dilatation of the blood vessels.

va·so·in·hib·i·tor (vä,zōinhib'itə), *n.* anything that inhibits the performance of the vasomotor nerves, as a drug.

va·so·mo·tion (vä,zōmō'sHən), *n.* a change in diameter of a blood vessel.

va·so·mo·tor (vä,zōmō'tə), *adj.* controlling the diameter of blood vessels so as to regulate the flow of blood.

va·so·pres·sor (vä,zōpres'ə), *n.* a chemical, as adrenalin, that causes the muscular walls of arteries to contract, thus narrowing the arteries and increasing the blood pressure.

va·so·stim·u·lant (vä,zōstim'yōōlənt), *adj.* stimulating the vasomotor nerves.

va·so·ton·ic (vä,zōton'ik), *adj.* relating to or controlling the muscular tone of the blood vessels.

vas·sal (vas'əl), *n.* a subject; retainer; subordinate. —**vas'sal·age,** *n.*

vat·ic (vat'ik), *adj.* of, relating to, or of the nature of a prophet. Also **vat'i·cal.**

vat·i·cide (vat'isīd), *n.* **1.** someone who murders a prophet. **2.** the act of murdering a prophet.

va·tic·i·nal (vətis'ənəl), *adj.* of, relating to, or of the nature of prophesy; prophetic.

va·tic·i·nate (vətis'ināt), *v.* to prophesy; to foretell the future. —**va·ti,ci·na'tion,** *n.*

vaunt (vônt), *v.* **1.** to boast of; to brag about. —*n.* **2.** a boast.

vaunt·ed (vôn'tid), *adj.* praised to excess; boastfully praised.

vec·tion (vek'sHən), *n.* the passing on of a disease from one person to another.

vec·tor (vek'tə), *n.* **1.** a mathematical quantity having both magnitude and direction, represented by an arrow of a length proportional to the magnitude and pointing in the appropriate direction. See also **scalar.** **2.** the direction followed by a missile, aeroplane, etc. **3.** an organism, as an insect, that carries disease and transmits it from one host to another.

vec·tor·car·di·og·ra·phy (vek,təkä,dēog'rəfē), *n.* a method of finding the direction of the electrical forces of the heart and measuring their magnitude.

vegetable sponge. See **loofah.**

veg·e·tate (vej'ətāt), *v.* **veg·e·tat·ed, veg·e·tat·ing.** to remain inactive, esp. in the same place; resemble a vegetable.

ve·he·ment (vē'əmənt), *adj.* very strongly felt or expressed; with vigorous anger. —**ve'he·mence,** *n.*

veld, veldt (felt, velt), *n.* an area of open grassland characteristic of parts of South Africa, as on the plateau, and sometimes having scattered shrubs or trees.

vel·i·ta·tion (vel,ita'sHən), *n.* a minor argument or conflict.

vel·le·i·ty (vəlē'itē), *n.* a very weak volition prompting no action; wishfulness.

vel·li·cate (vel'ikāt), *v.* **1.** to twitch or cause to twitch. **2.** to pinch; to nip. **3.** to move convulsively.

ve·lou·té (vəlōō'tā, vəlōōtā'), *n.* a smooth white sauce made with any meat or fish stock.

ve·lu·ti·nous (vəlōō'tiənəs), *adj.* having a velvety surface, as some plants.

ve·na ca·va (vē'nə kä'və), *pl.* **ve·nae ca·vae.** either of the two large veins discharging blood into the right atrium of the heart.

ve·nal (vē'nəl), *adj.* able to be bribed; willing to use influence or authority improperly for mercenary gain. —**ve·nal'i·ty,** *adj.*

ve·nat·ic (vēnat'ik), *adj.* relating to hunting. Also **ve·nat'i·cal.**

ve·na·tion (vēnā'sHən), *n.* the arrangement of veins, as in an insect's wing or in a leaf.

ven·due (ven'dyōō), *n. U.S.* a public auction.

ven·e·nose (ven'ənōs), *adj.* poisonous.

ven·er·ate (ven'ərāt), *v.* **ven·er·at·ed, ven·er·at·ing.** to worship or revere. —**ven'er·a·ble,** *adj.* —**ven,er·a'tion,** *n.*

ve·ni·al (ve'nēal), *adj.* able to be pardoned or overlooked, as a sin or fault.

ven·in (ven'in), *n.* any of various poisonous substances present in snake venom. Also **ven'ene, ven'ine.**

ve·ni·re·man (vinī'rimən), *n.*, *pl.* **ve·ni·re·men.** (in the U.S.A.) someone summoned to act as a juror in a trial.

ven·om (ven'əm), *n.* **1.** poison, esp. that of a poisonous snake, spider, scorpion, etc. **2.** poisonous hatred, as *He regarded her with venom.* —**ven'om·ous,** *adj.*

vent·age (ven'tij), *n.* a small outlet giving on to a confined space, as a fingerhole in some wind instruments.

ven·ter (ven'tə), *n.* **1.** (in zoology) the abdomen or belly; a belly-like protuberance or concave part, as of bone. **2.** (in law) the womb, a wife, or a mother, as a source of progeny.

ven·tose (ven'tōs), *adj.* windy; given to empty talking.

ven·tral (ven'trəl), *adj.* relating to the abdomen or belly; on or relating to the front side or surface of the body.

ven·tri·cle (ven'trikəl), *n.* **1.** one of various hollow organs or parts of an animal body. **2.** either of the two lower chambers of the heart, which pump blood into the arteries. **3.** one of a series of communicating cavities in the brain. —ven·tric'u·lar, *adj.*

ven·tri·cose (ven'trikōs), *adj.* **1.** swollen, esp. on one side. **2.** with a large abdomen.

ven·ue (ven'yōō), *n.* the place where an event or action occurs.

ven·ule (ven'yōōl), *n.* a minute vein. —ven'u·lose, ven'u·lous, *adj.*

ve·rac·i·ty (vəras'itē), *n.* truthfulness; honesty. —ve·ra·cious (vərā'sнəs), *adj.*

ver·ba·tim (vûbā'tim), *adv.* word for word; in precisely the same words.

ver·bi·age (vû'bēij), *n.* wordiness; an unnecessary abundance of words.

ver·bose (vûbōs'), *adj.* wordy; using too many words. —ver·bos·i·ty (vûbos'itē), *n.*

ver·dant (vû'dənt), *adj.* covered with or green with vegetation.

ver·di·gris (vû'digrēs), *n.* a green or greenish-blue deposit formed on copper, brass, or bronze through prolonged exposure to air. Also **aerugo.**

ver·dure (vû'jə, vû'dyə), *n.* greenness, esp. of a mass of new vegetation; any green vegetation, as grass. —ver'dur·ous, *adj.*

ver·e·cund (ver'əkund), *adj.* diffidently embarrassed; shy; modest.

ve·rid·i·cal (vərid'ikəl), *adj.* truthful; true; genuine.

ver·i·si·mil·i·tude (ver,isimil'ityōōd), *n.* the appearance of truth or fact; probability. —ver,i·sim'i·lar, *adj.*

ver·ism (vēr'izəm), *n.* the theory that reality must be represented in art and literature, and therefore the ugly and vulgar must be portrayed.

ver·i·ta·ble (ver'itəbəl), *adj.* real; actual, as *a veritable genius.*

ver·juice (vû'jōōs), *n.* **1.** the acid juice of crab apples, unripe grapes, etc., used in cooking. **2.** sourness, as of disposition, etc.

ver·meil (vû'māl), *n.* any gilded metal, as silver gilt.

ver·mi·cide (vû'misīd), *n.* any substance used to kill worms, esp. parasitic intestinal worms.

ver·mic·u·lar (vûmik'yōōlə), *adj.* **1.** relating to or done by worms. **2.** marked with wavy lines resembling worms or their tracks.

ver·mic·u·late (vûmik'yōōlāt), *adj.* worm-eaten; of worm-eaten appearance.

ver·mi·form (vû'mifôm,), *adj.* worm-like in form.

vermiform appendix, a small, worm-like blind tube extending from the caecum in man and some other mammals, having no known purpose, and situated in man in the lower right-hand part of the abdomen.

ver·mi·fuge (vû'mifyōōj,), *adj.* having the effect of driving out parasites, as worms, from the intestines.

ver·nac·u·lar (vûnak'yōōlə), *adj.* native; local; not of foreign or learned origin, esp. of language.

ver·nal (vû'nəl), *adj.* relating to, occurring in, or coming in spring; springlike.

ver·nal·ize (vû'nəlīz), *v.* to accelerate the blossoming or seed bearing of a plant by chilling the seed or bulb.

ver·nis·sage (vû,nisäzн), *n.* the opening of an exhibition of paintings.

ver·ru·ca (vərōō'kə), *n.*, *pl.* **ver·ru·cae** (vərōō'sē). a wart or wart-like formation. —ver'ru·cous, *adj.*

ver·ru·cose (ver'ōōkōs), *adj.* warty; wart-like growths.

ver·sant (vû'sənt), *n.* the slope of a mountain or range of mountains; the general slope of a region or country disregarding interrupting features.

ver·sa·tile (vû'sətīl), *adj.* able to do many things well, as *a versatile cook.* —ver,sa·til'i·ty, *n.*

ver·si·col·our (vû'sikul,ə), *adj.* **1.** having various colours. **2.** changeable in colour. Also **ver'si·col,oured.**

ver·so (vû'sō), *n.*, *pl.* **ver·sos.** a left-hand page of a book, magazine, etc. See also **recto.**

ver·te·brate (vû'təbrāt), *adj.* **1.** having a backbone. —*n.* **2.** any animal with a backbone.

ver·tig·i·nous (vûtij'inəs), *adj.* **1.** whirling round. **2.** affected with or liable to affect with vertigo.

ver·ti·go (vû'tigō), *n.*, *pl.* **ver·ti·goes, ver·tig·i·nes** (vərtij'ənēz). dizziness; a disorder in which a person feels himself or his surroundings to be whirling round and often loses his balance.

ver·tu (vûtōō'), *n.* See **virtu.**

verve (vûv), *n.* enthusiasm; animation; vivaciousness, as of literature, art, personality, etc.

ve·si·ca (ves'ikə, visī'kə), *n.*, *pl.* **ve·si·cae** (vəsī'sē). a bladder. —ves'i·cal, *adj.*

ves·i·cate (ves'ikāt), *v.* to blister; to cause to blister. —ves'i·cant, *adj.*, *n.* —ves'i·ca·to·ry, *adj.*, *n.*

ves·i·cle (ves'ikəl), *n.* a small bladder-like sac or cyst. —ve·sic·u·lar (vəsik'yōōlə), *adj.*

ves·per·tine (ves'pətīn), *adj.* relating to or taking place in the evening.

ves·pi·ar·y (ves'pēər), *n.* a nest of wasps.

ves·pid (ves'pid), *n.* any insect of the wasp family.

ves·pine (ves'pīn), *adj.* relating to or resembling a wasp.

ves·tal (ves'təl), *adj.* vowed to chastity as the virgins who tended the temple of the Roman goddess Vesta; pure; chaste; virgin.

ves·ti·ar·y (ves'tēərē), *adj.* relating to garments or official vestments.

ves·tige (ves'tij), *n.* a lingering trace of something, practice, or state no longer in existence. —**ves·tig'i·al**, *adj.*

ves·tig·i·um (vestij'ēəm), *n.*, *pl.* **ves·tig·i·a** (vestij'ēə). a. vestigial anatomical structure or any other vestige.

ves·ture (ves'CHə), *n.* all that grows on and covers the land, with the exception of trees.

vet (vet), *v.* **vet·ted, vet·ting.** to evaluate and act according to the evaluation, as in screening candidates for a job, examining a manuscript, etc.

vet·i·ver (vet'ivə), *n.* the long aromatic roots of an East Indian grass used for screens and the like and in perfumery.

vex·il·lol·o·gy (veks,ilol'əjē), *n.* the study of flags. —**vex,il·lol'o·gist**, *n.* —**vex,il·lo·log'ic, vex,il·lo·log'ic·al**, *adj.*

vi·and (vī'ənd), *n.* any item of foodstuff.

vi·at·i·cum (vīat'ikəm), *n.*, *pl.* **vi·at·i·ca** (vīat'ikə), **vi·at·i·cums.** anything essential for a journey, as money, provisions, etc.

vi·a·tor (vīā'tə), *n.*, *pl.* **vi·a·to·res** (vī,ətôr'ēz). a traveller; a voyager.

vi·bra·tile (vī'brətīl), *adj.* relating to or like vibration; vibrating; capable of vibration.

vi·bris·sa (vībris'ə), *n.*, *pl.* **vi·bris·sae** (vībris'ē). one of the stiff hairs about the mouth of many animals, as rabbits, mice, etc.

vi·car·i·ous (viker'ēəs, vīker'ēəs), *adj.* acting, done, or suffered for another; experienced in the imagination through the words or deeds of another.

vice·ge·rent (vīs,jer'ənt), *n.* a deputy appointed by a ruler or supreme chief. —**vice,ge'ren·cy**, *n.*

vic·e·nar·y (vis,inərē), *adj.* consisting of or relating to 20.

vi·cen·nial (vīsen'ēəl), *adj.* relating to, lasting for, or happening every 20 years.

vice·re·gent (vīs,rē'jənt), *n.* one acting in place of a regent, sovereign, or governor.

vice·reine (vīs,rān'), *n.* the wife of a viceroy.

vice·roy (vīs'roi), *n.* a person appointed to act in the name of or in place of the sovereign in a dependent province or country.

vic·i·nage (vis'inij), *n.* **1.** a neighbourhood or surrounding district or its people. **2.** nearness.

vic·i·nal (vis'inəl), *adj.* **1.** belonging to or relating to a district. **2.** near; adjoining.

vi·cis·si·tude (visis'ityōod), *n.* **1.** a change during the course of something. **2.** *pl.* the ups and downs of fortune; successive changes or alternations of condition.

vic·to·rine (viktərēn'), *n.* a fur tippet.

vic·tress (vik'tris), *n.* a female victor.

vic·trix (vik'triks), *n.*, *pl.* **vic·tri·ces** (vik'trisēz). a victress.

vict·ual (vit'əl), *n.* **1.** food; provisions. Also **vict'ual·age.** —*v.* **2.** to supply with victuals. —**vict'ual·ler**, *n.*

vid·e·o·gen·ic (vid,ēōjen'ik), *adj.* See **telegenic.**

vi·du·i·ty (vidyōō'itē), *n.* widowhood or its duration.

vi·ges·i·mal (vījes'iməl), *adj.* relating to or based on 20; 20th; in 20s.

vi·gi·a (vijē'ə), *n.*, *pl.* **vi·gi·as. 1.** a warning mark on a navigational chart to indicate a likely hazard. **2.** an unknown feature sighted at sea and considered a likely hazard.

vi·gnette (vinyet'), *n.* **1.** an illustration or decorative design on the title page of a book or at the beginning or end of a chapter. **2.** a photograph or illustration with faded or dissolved margins. **3.** a brief, charming literary sketch. **4.** any beguiling scene, tableau, drawing, etc. **5.** ornamentation based on leaves, tendrils, etc., esp. vine leaves. —*v.* **6.** to finish (an illustration, photograph, etc.) in the manner of a vignette. **7.** to decorate with vignettes. **8.** to portray a subject in the style of a vignette. —**vi·gnet'tist**, *n.*

vig·or·ish (vig'ərisH), *n. U.S. slang.* **1.** a charge on a bet, payable to a bookie or the like. **2.** interest paid to a moneylender on a loan.

vi·gou·reux printing (vēgərōō'), a method of printing worsted fibres with colour before they are made into yarn, producing a multicoloured yarn.

vil·i·fy (vil'ifī), *v.* to speak ill of; to defame.

vil·i·pend (vil'ipend), *v.* **1.** to consider or treat as of little importance. **2.** to defame or slander.

vil·li·form (vil'ifôm,), *adj.* **1.** shaped like a villus. **2.** with fine close-set projections giving an appearance of velvet, as the teeth of some fishes.

vil·los·i·ty (vilos'itē), *n.* a villus; a group of or a covering of villi.

vil·lus (vil'əs), *n.*, *pl.* **vil·li** (vil'ī). a slender hairlike small projection on certain membranes, as on the lining of the small intestine. —**vil'lose, vil'lous**, *adj.*

vi·men (vī'men), *n.*, *pl.* **vim·i·na** (vim'inə). a long pliable plant shoot.

vi·min·e·ous (vimin'ēəs), *adj.* relating to, resembling, made of, or producing long pliable shoots or twigs.

vin·ci·ble (vin'sibəl), *adj.* conquerable.

vin·cu·lum (viNG'kyōōləm), *n.*, *pl.* **vin·cu·la** (viNG'kyōōlə). a bond or tie indicating unity, as may be printed over two numbers.

vin·di·cate (vin'dikāt), *v.* **vin·di·cat·ed, vin·di·cat·ing. 1.** to remove blame from someone, esp. by justifying his actions. **2.** to take revenge, or vengeance. —**vin,di·ca'tion**, *n.*

vin·dic·tive (vindik'tiv), *adj.* taking revenge or having a vengeful attitude.

vi·nic (vī'nik), *adj.* relating to, in, or from wine.

vin·i·cul·ture (vin'ikul,CHə), *n.* the study of winemaking.

vi·nif·er·ous (vīnif'ərəs), *adj.* suitable for or giving a heavy yield for wine-making.

vin·om·e·ter (vinom'itə), *n.* a device for measuring the alcoholic content of wine, usually as a percentage.

vi·nos·i·ty (vīnos'itē), *n.* the characteristics of a wine considered as a whole.

vi·nous (vī'nəs), *adj.* relating to or like wine; owing to, showing, or given to habitual wine-drinking.

vin·tag·er (vin'təjə), *n.* a helper at the grape harvest.

vi·o·la·ble (vī'ələbəl), *adj.* capable of being broken or infringed upon, as a promise, a code of behaviour, etc.

vi·o·les·cent (vī,əles'ənt), *adj.* 1. of a near-violet colour. 2. becoming violet in colour.

vi·rae·mi·a (vīrē'mēə), *n.* the presence of viruses in the blood.

vi·ra·go (virä'gō), *n.*, *pl.* **vi·ra·goes**, **vi·ra·gos**. a fiercely ill-tempered woman.

vi·res·cent (vīres'ənt), *adj.* becoming green. —**vi·res'cence**, *n.*

vir·ga (vû'gə), *n.*, *sing.* and *pl.* a streak of rain, hail, or snow that evaporates before it reaches the ground. See also **praecipitatio**.

vir·gate (vû'git), *adj.* rod-shaped; long, thin, and straight.

vir·gu·late (vû'gyŏŏlāt), *adj.* shaped like a rod.

vir·gule (vû'gyŏŏl), *n.* a short oblique stroke used in text between two alternative words, as *Dear Sir/Madam.* Also **solidus**, **shilling mark**.

vir·i·des·cent (vir,ides'ənt), *adj.* tinged with or somewhat green. —**vir,i·des'cence**, *n.*

vi·rid·i·ty (virid'itē), *n.* 1. greenness, esp. of vegetation. 2. mental or bodily inexperience or innocence; youth.

vir·i·lo·cal (vī,rilō'kəl), *adj.* See **patrilocal**.

vi·ri·no (virē'nō), *n.* a hypothetical infective particle, conceived as a rudimentary form of virus, proposed as the agent responsible for bovine spongiform encephalopathy and similar diseases. See also **prion**.

vi·ri·on (vī'rēən), *n.* the infective form of a virus, consisting of the viral nucleic acid (RNA or DNA) enclosed in a protein coat and in some cases an outer envelope.

vi·rol·o·gy (vīrol'əjē), *n.* the scientific study of viruses and the diseases they cause.

vi·ro·sis (vīrō'sis), *n.* any infection caused by a virus.

vir·tu, ver·tu (vûtŏŏ'), *n.* 1. excellence in objects of art. 2. *pl.* objects of art; antiques, or the like. 3. a knowledge of or a taste for such objects.

vir·tu·al (vû'CHŏŏəl, vû'tjŏŏəl), *adj.* being or having the effect or force of something without actually being it, as *She was a virtual prisoner in her own house.*

vi·ru·cide (vī'rŏŏsīd), *n.* a substance used for or capable of killing viruses.

vir·u·lent (vir'ŏŏlent, vir'yŏŏlənt), *adj.* 1. powerfully poisonous. 2. intensely hostile, bitter, or malignant.

vi·rus (vī'rəs), *n.*, *pl.* **vi·rus·es**. an organic particle, by far the smallest living organism known, existing only in animal and plant cells, and capable of causing various diseases.

vis·age (viz'ij), *n.* the face.

vis-à-vis (vēzəvē'), *adj.* face to face.

vis·cer·a (vis'ərə), *n. pl.*, *sing.* **vis·cus** (vis'kəs). the internal organs of the principal body cavities, esp. the abdominal cavity. —**vis'cer·al**, *adj.*

vis·cer·o·to·ni·a (vis,ərōtō'nēə), *n.* the personality pattern usually found in persons of endomorphic body type, exhibiting extroversion and love of comfort. See also **cerebrotonia**, **somatotonia**.

vis·cer·o·trop·ic (vis,ərōtrop'ik), *adj.* attracted to or affecting the viscera, esp. of a virus.

vis·cer·o·tro·pism (vis,ərōtrō'pizəm), *n.* infection of or attraction to the viscera.

vis·cid (vis'id), *adj.* of a thick, sticky consistency.

vis·co·e·las·tic (vis,kōilas'tik), *adj.* relating to a substance which is both viscous and elastic.

vis·coid (vis'koid), *adj.* slightly or tending to be viscous. Also **vis·coi'dal**.

vis·cos·i·ty (viskos'itē), *n.* 1. the condition or property of being viscous. 2. the property of a fluid of resistance against flowing.

vis·cous (vis'kəs), *adj.* of a sticky consistency or nature; thick in consistency.

vi·tal·ism (vīt'əliz,əm), *n.* the doctrine that phenomena are in essence self-determining and only partly controlled by mechanical forces. See also **dynamism**, **mechanism**.

vi·tel·line (vitel'īn), *adj.* relating to the egg yolk; resembling an egg yolk, in colour, shape, or the like.

vi·ti·ate (vish'ēāt), *v.* to impair; to corrupt; to invalidate in law. —**vi'ti·a·ble**, *adj.*

vit·i·cul·ture (vit'ikul,CHə), *n.* the scientific study or the cultivation of grapevines.

vit·i·li·go (vitilī'gō), *n.* an abnormality of skin pigmentation producing a piebald appearance, affecting the forearm principally. Also **leukoderma**, **piebald skin**.

vit·re·ous (vi'trēəs), *adj.* resembling glass in appearance and nature, as in lustre, composition, etc.

vi·tres·cent (vitres'ənt), *adj.* becoming, tending to become, or capable of becoming glass. Also **vi·tres'ci·ble**.

vit·ric (vit'rik), *adj.* relating to, resembling, or of the nature of glass.

vit·rics (vit'riks), *n.*, *sing.* and *pl.* 1. *sing.* the technique or art of making glassware. 2. *pl.* glassware or other vitreous articles.

vit·ri·form (vit'rifôm,), *adj.* glass-like in form or appearance.

vit·ri·fy (vi'trifī), v. to convert or be converted into glass or a glasslike substance. —**vit,ri·fi·ca'·tion,** n.

vi·trine (vitrēn'), n. a glass-fronted and often glass-sided display cabinet.

vit·ri·ol (vit'rēol), n. **1.** concentrated sulphuric acid. **2.** something severely hurtful in effect, as scathing sarcasm. —**vit·ri·ol'ic,** adj.

vit·ta (vit'ə), n., pl. **vit·tae** (vit'ē). a stripe or streak, as of colour on a plant or animal.

vit·tate (vit'āt), adj. having one or more longitudinal stripes.

vit·u·line (vit'yōolīn, vit'yōolin), adj. relating to or resembling a calf or veal.

vi·tu·per·ate (vītyōo'pərāt), v. to find fault with in harsh language; to speak to abusively or harshly.

vi·tu·per·a·tive (vītyōo'pərətiv), adj. abusively fault-finding; carping. —**vi·tu,per·a'tion,** n.

vi·va·cious (vīvā'sHəs), adj. lively and actively full of spirit; animated.

vi·var·i·um (vīver'ēəm, viver'ēəm), n., pl. **vi·var·i·ums, vi·var·i·a** (vīver'ēə, viver'ēə). a place for keeping living wild animals under conditions as near natural as possible, esp. for scientific purposes.

vi·va vo·ce (vī'və vō'CHē, vē'və), orally; by word of mouth.

vi·ver·rine (vīver'īn), adj. relating to an Asiatic and African family of small cat-like carnivores including civets, palm cats, etc.

viv·id (viv'id), adj. **1.** clear; true-to-life; realistic, as a vivid description. **2.** bright; brilliant, as the vivid colours in the painting.

viv·i·fy (viv'ifī), v. to give life to; to enliven.

vi·vip·ar·ous (vivip'ərəs, vīvip'ərəs), adj. giving birth to live young in a developed state rather than in eggs. See also **oviparous.**

viv·i·sect (viv'isekt), v. to dissect or make surgical experiments on live animals. —**viv,i·sec'·tion,** n.

vi·zier, vi·zir (vizē'ə, viz'ēə), n. a minister of state or other high official in various Muslim countries, esp. formerly.

vo·ca·ble (vō'kəbəl), n. **1.** a word or term. **2.** a word considered only as a form without regard to its meaning.

vo·cal·ic (vōkal'ik), adj. relating to, resembling, or rich in vowels.

vo·ca·tion (vōkā'sHən), n. one's work; what a person does for a living.

vo·cif·er·ate (vōsif'ərāt), v. to utter noisily; to shout. —**vo·cif·er·ance, vo·cif,er·a'tion,** n. —**vo·cif·er·ant, vo·cif·er·ous,** adj.

vo·coid (vō'koid), adj. **1.** resembling a vowel. n. **2.** a sound resembling a vowel. See also **contoid.**

voile (voil), n. a fine, semitransparent dress fabric of silk, cotton, wool, etc., with a plain open weave.

voir dire (vwä, dē'ə), **1.** an oath swearing a prospective juror or witness to tell the truth during questioning to ascertain his competence. **2.** such questioning.

vo·lant (vō'lənt), adj. **1.** flying or capable of flying. **2.** nimble in movement.

vo·lar (vō'lə), adj. **1.** relating to the palm of the hand or sole of the foot. **2.** relating to or for flight.

volcanic tuff. See **tuff.**

vol·can·ol·o·gy (vol,kənol'əjē), n. the scientific study of volcanoes and phenomena associated with them. Also **vulcanology.**

vole (vōl), n. the winning of all possible tricks in a deal by one player in a card game.

vol·i·tant (vol'itənt), adj. **1.** in the act of or capable of flying. **2.** moving; engaged in action.

vol·i·ta·tion (vol,itā'sHən), n. the act of or capacity for flying.

vo·li·tion (vōlisH'ən), n. the act or power of willing; a decision made by the will.

vol·i·tive (vol'itiv), adj. relating to or involving the will.

vol·plane (vol'plān), v. to glide earthwards in an unpowered aeroplane or one with the power cut off.

volt (vōlt), n. the unit used in measuring electric current, equivalent to the force or potential difference that will produce a steady flow of one ampere through a resistance of one ohm. Abbr.: V. —**volt'age,** n.

volte-face (volt,fäs'), n., sing. and pl. a complete reversal, as of opinion, policy, or the like.

vol·u·ble (vol'yōobəl), adj. with a ready flow of words; talkative.

vol·u·met·ric (vol,yōome'trik), adj. relating to measurement of or by volume.

vo·lup·tu·ar·y (vəlup'CHŌŌərē, vəlup'tyōo-ərē), n. one devoted to a life of luxurious and sensual self-indulgence.

vo·lute (vəlōot', vəlyōot'), n. a spiral or coiled object or form.

vom·i·to·ry (vom'itərē), n. **1.** an emetic. **2.** an opening, esp. one through which large numbers of people can enter or leave, as in a stadium. Also **vom,i·to'ri·um.**

voo·doo (vōō'dōō), n. a religious and ritual system centred on magic and several gods, practised mainly by West Indian Negroes.

vo·ra·cious (vorā'sHəs), adj. **1.** wanting or eating a large amount of food. **2.** eager, esp. excessively eager, to absorb or obtain. —**vo·rac'i·ty,** n.

vor·tex (vô'teks), n., pl. **vor·tex·es, vor·ti·ces** (vô'tisēz). a whirling, often suctional, mass of water, air, or fire. —**vor'tic·al, vor'ti·cose, vor·tig'i·nous,** adj.

vor·ti·cism (vô'tisiz,əm), n. an artistic movement, launched in Britain in 1913 by Wyndham Lewis, that combined elements of cubism and futurism in exploring the impact of the machine age. —**vor'ti·cist,** n.

vo·ta·ry (vō'tərē), n. a person bound by vows to religious life, as a nun.

vo·tive (vō'tiv), adj. given, consecrated, etc., in fulfilment of a vow.

vouch·safe (vouCHsāf'), v. to give or allow as a favour or by condescension.

vox bar·ba·ra (voks, bä'bərə), a questionable word formation or usage, esp. of pseudo-classical elements, as a Neo-Latin scientific term.

vox pop·u·li (voks' pop'yōōlī, pop'yəlē), n. the voice of the people; public opinion, esp. about what people say they want.

vo·yeur (vwäyû'), n. one who practises voyeurism.

vo·yeur·ism (vwäyû'izəm), n. the deriving of sexual gratification by looking at, esp. in secret, sexual organs, objects, or acts. —**voy·eur·is'tic,** adj.

voy·euse (vwäyûz'), n. French. a chair formerly used at gaming tables, with a padded rail across the top for spectators to lean on.

V/STOL (vē'stol), Abbr. for Vertical Short Take-Off and Landing.

V/TOL (vē'tul), Abbr. for Vertical Take-Off and Landing.

vul·can·ism (vul'kəniz,əm), n. the phenomena associated with the origin and movement of molten rock material.

vul·can·ol·o·gy (vul,kənol'əjē), n. See volcanology.

vul·gate (vul'gāt), n. **1.** any generally recognized version of a work. —adj. **2.** generally accepted or used.

vul·gus (vul'gəs), n. the common mass of people; the populace.

vul·ner·ar·y (vul'nərerē), adj. **1.** useful in healing wounds, as a drug, herb, etc. —n. **2.** any preparation or drug used to heal or promote healing of wounds.

vul·pec·u·lar (vulpek'yōōlə), adj. foxlike; relating to the fox.

vul·pi·cide, vul·pe·cide (vul'pisīd), n. the act of killing a fox other than by hunting.

vul·pine (vul'pīn), adj. relating to or characteristic of the fox; fox-like.

vul·tur·ine (vul'CHōōrīn), adj. vulture-like in behaviour, as in rapacity, etc.

vul·va (vul'və), n., pl. **vul·vae** (vul'vē), **vulvas.** the external female genital organs, including the clitoris, the openings of the urethra and vagina, and the labia majora and labia minora.

wad·dy (wod'ē), *n.* a heavy club used in war by the Australian aborigines.

wa·di, wa·dy (wä'dē), *n., pl.* **wa·dis.** a northern African watercourse that is dry except during the rainy season; the stream flowing through such a watercourse.

waf·ture (wäf'cнə), *n.* the act of wafting; a thing that is wafted.

wain (wān), *n.* a farm cart.

wald·glas (väld'gläs,), *n.* a type of unrefined Medieval and Renaissance glassware, greenish in colour.

wal·lah, wal·la (wo'lə), *n. Anglo-Indian.* a person in charge of, or connected with, a particular thing or function, as *a newspaper wallah* or *a government wallah.*

walled plain, a circular or nearly circular area on the moon, partially enclosed by walls that are usually lower than those of a crater. Also **ringed plain.**

wam·ble (wom'bəl), *v.* to move unsteadily; to stagger; to twist or roll about.

wam·pus (wom'pəs), *n.* a strange or disagreeable person; a lout.

wa·mus (wô'məs), *n.* a heavy, loosely knit cardigan jacket with a belt.

wan·i·gan (won'igən), *n. U.S.* **1.** a lumber camp's trunk, chest, etc., for storing supplies. **2.** a small office or shelter on wheels used in temporary lumber camps.

want·age (won'tij), *n.* that which is lacking, desired, or needed.

wan·ton (won'tən), *adj.* not justified; without reason; unrestrained by tact, morality, or conscience, as *a wanton disregard for others feelings.*

wap·pen·shaw, wap·in·shaw (wap'ənsнô, wop'ənsнô), *n.* a periodic review or muster of persons under arms formerly held by chiefs in certain areas of Scotland. Also **wap'pen·shaw,-ing, weaponshaw.**

war·i·san (war'isən), *n.* a note sounded to start an attack.

war·lock (wô'lok), *n.* a person, esp. a man, who practises black magic; a sorcerer.

warp (wôp), *n.* the set of threads running lengthways in a loom and crossed by and interlaced with the weft or woof.

war·ren (wor'ən), *n.* a place where rabbits breed or are numerous.

war·y (wer'ē), *adj.* **war·i·er, war·i·est.** very careful and cautious; watchful and alert.

wash sale, *U.S.* an illegal share transaction by buying and selling simultaneously through different brokers so that the shares appear to change ownership (but in reality do not) and trade in that stock appears active.

was·sail (wos'āl, wos'əl), *n.* **1.** a celebration with much drinking of healths. **2.** spiced ale or other liquor for drinking healths at festivities, as on Christmas Eve and Twelfth-night.

water hammer, a thumping sound caused by sudden stopping of a moving volume of water in a pipe.

wa·ter·proof (wô'təprōōf,), *adj.* impervious to water.

wa·ter·re·pel·lent (wô'təripel,ənt), *adj.* able to repel water but not impervious to it.

wa·ter·re·sist·ant (wô'tərizis,tənt), *adj.* able to resist water but not entirely prevent its penetration.

watt (wot), *n.* the unit of measurement of power, esp. electric power, equal to one joule per second or the energy expended per second by a steady electric current of one ampere flowing in a circuit across a potential difference of one volt. *Abbr.:* **W.** [named after Scottish engineer and inventor James *Watt* (1736–1819)]

wa·ver (wā'və), *v.* to hesitate or otherwise show indecision between two choices of things, actions, etc.

weal (wēl), *n.* well-being; welfare, as *the public weal.*

wea·sand (wē'zənd), *n.* **1.** the throat. **2.** the oesophagus. 3. the trachea.

we·ber (vā'bə), *n.* the SI unit of magnetic flux. *Symbol:* **Wb.**

web press, a rotary press into which paper is fed from a large roll, or web. Also **web-fed press.**

web·ster (web'stə), *n.* a weaver.

weft (weft), *n.* the yarns interwoven by a shuttle back and forth across the warp in weaving. Also **woof.**

weir (wē'ə), *n.* a small dam in a river.

welfare state, a state in which the welfare of its citizens with regard to employment, health and education, social security, etc., is the responsibility of the government.

Welt·an·schau·ung (velt'änsнou,ōōNG), *n. German.* a comprehensive philosophy or conception of the universe and of human life in relation to it.

wel·ter (wel'tə), *n.* a great many or a great deal; much, as *a welter of paperwork.*

wel·ter·weight (wel'tərwāt,), *n.* a boxer of the class between light welterweight and light middleweight in amateur boxing, lightweight and middleweight in professional boxing, and weighing 148 lbs. or less if an amateur, 147 lbs. or less if a professional.

Welt·po·li·tik (velt'politēk,), *n. German.* the policy of a nation towards the world.

Welt·schmerz (velt'sHmerts,), *n. German.* sentimental pessimism or melancholy over the state of the world.

weth·er (weTH'ə), *n.* a castrated male sheep.

wet·land (wet'land,), *n., usually pl.* a region of swamps, marshes, or bogs.

wharf·in·ger (wô'finjə, hwô'finjə), *n.* a person who owns or is in charge of a wharf.

wheal (wēl, hwēl), *n.* a small itching or burning swelling on the skin, as from an insect bite.

wheel·a·brate (wēl'əbrāt, hwēl'əbrāt), *v.* to harden the surface of steel by means of a rotating shot-peening device.

whelk (welk, hwelk), *n.* a pimple or pustule.

whelm (welm, hwelm), *v.* to submerge or engulf; to overcome.

whelp (welp, hwelp), *n.* **1.** the young of the dog, or of the lion, tiger, bear, leopard, wolf, etc. —*v.* **2.** to bring forth young, usually of a dog, lion, etc.

wher·ry (wer'ē, hwer'ē), *n.* a light rowboat used on rivers; skiff.

whick·er (wik'ə, hwik'ə), *v.* to neigh or whinny.

whif·fet (wif'it, hwif'it), *n.* a small dog.

whif·fle (wif'əl, hwif'əl), *v.* **1.** to blow in puffs or gusts, as the wind. **2.** to shift or veer about; to vacillate.

whif·fler (wif'lə, hwif'lə), *n.* **1.** a person who frequently shifts his opinions, interests, etc.; a person who vacillates or is evasive in an argument. **2.** an attendant, usually carrying a staff or sword, formerly employed to clear the way for a procession.

Whig (wig, hwig), *n.* **1.** (in British politics) **a.** a member of a political party which championed reform and held liberal principles, and later became the Liberal Party. **b.** one of the more conservative members of the Liberal Party. **2.** (in American history) **a.** a member of the party that supported the Revolution. **b.** a member of the party (*c.* 1834–1855) formed in opposition to the Democratic party and supporting a loose construction of the Constitution and tariff protection of industry.

whig·ma·lee·rie (wig,məlēr'ē, hwig,məlēr'ē), *n.* a fanciful idea; a whim.

whi·lom (wī'ləm, hwī'ləm), *adj. Archaic.* former; erstwhile, as *their whilom friends.*

white·a·cre (wīt'ā,kə, hwīt'ākə), *n.* a fanciful name for a hypothetical piece of land, esp. in law books to distinguish one piece of land from another. See also **blackacre.**

whited sepulchre, something or someone evil with the outward appearance of something good; a hypocrite. [Matt. 23:27]

white goods, *pl. n.* **1.** white fabrics. **2.** products (e.g. bed linen, tablecloths) typically manufactured from white fabric. **3.** household electrical appliances (e.g. washing machines, refrigerators) typically finished in white enamel. See also **brown goods.**

white man's burden, the alleged duty of the white race to look after the subject people of other races in its colonies.

white matter, *n.* (in anatomy) nerve tissue having a relatively whitish appearance owing to the preponderance of nerve fibres and their associated myelin sheaths. See also **grey matter.**

white noise, *n.* **1.** sound consisting of a completely random mix of frequencies over a wide frequency range. **2.** electrical interference consisting of signals distributed over a wide frequency band, as caused by thermal effects in a conductor or atmospheric disturbance.

white paper, an official report by a government.

white paternoster, an incantation used for warding off evil spirits and black magic. See also **black paternoster.**

white plague, tuberculosis, esp. of the lungs.

white primary, *U.S. history.* a primary election formerly held among the Democrats in those southern states in which only white people could vote.

white rainbow. See **fogbow.**

white sauce, a sauce made of butter or the like, flour, milk or stock, and seasoning.

white slave, a woman enticed or forced into prostitution.

white-smith (wīt'smith,, hwīt'smith,), *n.* a tin-smith.

white water, foaming water, as in rapids, etc.

whit·low (wit'lō, hwit'lō), *n.* an inflammation of a finger or toe, often with a discharge of pus. Also **agnail.**

whiz kid, *Colloquial.* a young and extremely intelligent, powerful, or successful executive, advisor, etc.

wid·der·shins (wid'əsHinz), *adv.* See **withershins.**

wid·get (wij'it), *n.* **1.** a knob, switch, or other similar small mechanism, esp. one of which the name is not known or has been forgotten. **2.** a typical or representative thing, as of a manufacturer's products.

widow's cruse, a supply that is inexhaustible. [1 Kings 17:10-16 and Kings 4:1-7]

wig·an (wig'ən), *n.* a canvas-like cloth for stiffening hems, lapels, etc.

wild·ing (wīl'diNG), *n.* any plant that grows wild.

wild silk. See tussah.

wile (wīl), *n.* **1. wiles,** a trick or ruse; a manoeuvre used to trap or lure someone. **2.** trickery.

will-o'-the-wisp (wil'əTHəwisp,), *n.* See ignis fatuus.

willow pattern, a design for china, originated in England in 1780 and picturing a willow tree, small bridge, pandas, etc., derived from Chinese sources and usually blue and white in colour.

wim·ble (wim'bəl), *n.* **1.** a device for extracting the rubbish from a bored hole, as in mining. **2.** any of various tools for boring.

wind·age (win'dij), *n.* the deflection of a projectile by the influence of the wind.

win·dow (win'dō), *n.* (in military usage). See chaff.

wind rose, a map symbol that shows for a particular place the frequency and strength of wind from different directions.

wind·row (wind'rō,), *n.* a row of hay, sheaves of grain, etc., raked or stacked together to dry.

wind shake, a flaw in wood supposedly caused by strong winds deforming the tree trunk. Also cupshake.

wind·ward (wind'wəd), *adv.* **1.** towards the side from which the wind blows. *—n.* **2.** the side facing into the wind.

win·kle·hawk (wiNG'kəlhôk,), *n.* an L-shaped tear in cloth.

win·now (win'ō), *v.* **1.** to separate grain from chaff, esp. by tossing it up so that the lighter chaff blows away and the grain falls back. **2.** to analyse critically; to separate or distinguish useful from useless parts.

win·some (win'səm), *adj.* attractive in an engaging way; charming.

winter lamb, a lamb born in the autumn or winter and sold for slaughter before May 20.

wi·sent (wē'zənt), *n.* the European bison, now nearly extinct.

wist·ful (wist'fəl), *adj.* characterized by longings or yearnings; pensive, esp. in a melancholy way.

witch ball, a ball of many mirrored facets hanging from the ceiling of a ballroom and rotated so that it sparkles in bright light.

with·al (wiTHôl'), *adv.* in addition; as well; in spite of all.

withdrawal symptom, any of the physiological and mental disturbances, as sweating, depression, etc., experienced by a drug addict deprived of drugs.

withe (with, wiTH, wīTH), *n.* a tough, flexible twig of willow, osier, or the like used for binding things together.

with·er·shins (wiTH'əSHinz), *adv.* in a direction contrary to the natural one, as anticlockwise, and supposed to bring bad luck. Also widdershins.

with·y (wiTH'ē), *n.* a flexible twig or stem; a withe.

wit·ling (wit'liNG), *n.* one who affects wittiness.

wit·tol (wit'əl), *n.* a man who knows of his wife's adultery and tolerates it. See also cuckold.

wi·vern (wī'vən), *n.* See wyvern.

wiz·ened (wiz'ənd), *adj.* dried up; shrivelled, as *a wizened old face.*

wold (wōld), *n.* a high, open tract of land.

wom·er·a (wŏŏm'ərə), *n.* a spear-throwing device used by Australian aborigines. Also woo'mer·a.

wont (wŏnt, wont), *n.* **1.** custom, habit, or practice, as *It was her wont to dine at eight.* *—adj.* **2.** accustomed, as *She was wont to dine at eight.*

wood·wind (wŏŏd'wind,), *n.* any of the group of musical instruments played by blowing and traditionally made of wood, as the flute, oboe, etc.

wood·wool (wŏŏd'wŏŏl,), *n.* fine wood shavings used in insulation, for packing breakable objects, as a binder in plaster, etc.

woof (wŏŏf), *n.* See weft.

woof·er (wŏŏf'ə), *n.* a large loudspeaker for reproducing low-frequency sounds. See also tweeter, tweeter-woofer.

wool·fell (wŏŏl'fel,), *n.* the pelt of a wool-bearing animal with the wool still on it.

wort (wût), *n.* **1.** a malt infusion, which after fermenting, becomes beer or mash. **2.** (in combination) a plant, vegetable, or herb, as *pearlwort, hornwort, navelwort.*

wrack (rak), *n.* a wreck; ruin; the remains or a vestige of something that has been destroyed.

wraith (rāth), *n.* an apparition of a person, supposed to foretell his death.

wran·gle (raNG'gəl), *v.* **1.** to argue noisily. **2.** to herd or round up, as livestock.

wreak (rēk), *v.* to inflict or give vent to, as harm, punishment, vengeance, etc.

wrick (rik), *v.* **1.** to sprain or wrench. *—n.* **2.** a sprain or wrench.

wrig·gle·work (rig'əlwûk,), *n.* decorative zigzags engraved on metal.

write-down (rīt'doun,), *n.* (in accounting) the reducing of the recorded value of an asset.

write-off (rit'ôf,), *n.* a cancellation from accounts as a loss.

wroth (rōth, roth), *adj.* angry; incensed as *He was wroth to discover the theft of his documents.*

wry (rī), *adj.* slightly askew; not straightforward, as *a wry smile or wry humour.*

wry·neck (rī'nek,), *n.* See **torticollis.**

wun·der·kind (wun'dəkind,, *German.* vōon'-dərkint,), *n., pl.* **wun·der·kinds, wun·der·kind·er** (wun'dəkind,ə). **1.** a child prodigy. **2.** one who achieves outstanding success while still young. [*German,* literally, wonder child]

wurst (wûst, wŏō'əst), *n.* sausage, esp. in combination as *liverwurst, bratwurst.*

wy·vern (wī'vən), *n.* a heraldic winged dragon with two legs like an eagle's and a barbed tail. Also **wivern.**

xan·thic (zan,*th*ik), *adj.* yellow or yellowish; relating to such a colour.

Xan·thip·pe (zantip'ē), *n.* a shrewish wife or woman.

xan·tho·chroid (zan'thōkroid), *adj.* belonging to or relating to those peoples of the white races with fair skin or hair.

xan·thous (zan'thəs), *adj.* yellow or yellowish.

xat (кнät), *n.* a totem pole.

X chromosome, a sex chromosome containing numerous genes including those which produce female characteristics, and usually found in pairs in females but in males singly or with a Y chromosome. See also **Y chromosome.**

xen·o·gen·e·sis (zen,ōjen'isis), *n.* the procreation of offspring with biological characteristics completely different from those of the parents, formerly but no longer thought possible.

xen·o·pho·bi·a (zen,ōfō'bēə), *n.* **1.** an abnormally excessive dread or dislike of foreign or strange people or things. **2.** an unreasonable dislike of foreigners. —**xen'o·phobe,** *n.*

xe·rarch (zēr'äk), *adj.* (of a sere) arising in a dry habitat.

xe·ric (zēr'ik), *adj.* of, relating to, or adapted to very dry conditions.

xe·ro·der·ma (zē,rōdû'mə), *n.* a condition involving dry, scaly skin; a mild form of ichthyosis. Also **xe·ro·der·mi·a** (zē,rōdû'mēə). —**xe,ro·der'ma·tous,** *adj.*

xe·rog·ra·phy (zirog'rəfē), *n.* a process for copying material from film or paper by means of charging with static electricity those areas of a plain paper corresponding to the printed areas of the original so that powdered resin carrying an opposite charge adheres to them and is then fused.

xe·roph·i·lous (zirof'ələs), *adj.* living or growing in very dry, and usually hot, conditions.

xe·roph·thal·mi·a (zēr,ofthal'mēə), *n.* abnormal dryness of the eyeball, a symptom of certain diseases, as conjunctivitis.

xe·ro·phyte (zēr'ōfīt,), *n.* a plant adapted to a very dry habitat.

xe·ro·sere (zēr'ōsē,ə), *n.* a sere arising under dry conditions.

xe·ro·sis (zirō'sis), *n.* **1.** a medical condition of abnormal dryness, as of the skin. **2.** the hardening of body tissues normal in old age.

x-height (eks'hīt,), *n.* (in typography) the height of the letter "x" in lower case of a given typeface.

x-high (eks'hī,), *adj.* (in typography) of a height equal to that of a lower-case "x" of the same typeface and body.

xiph·oid (zif'oid), *adj.* sword-shaped.

xy·lem (zī'ləm), *n.* the woody fibre or tissue of a tree.

xy·lo·graph (zī'ləgräf,, zī'ləgraf,), *n.* a design carved in wood; a print made from such a carving.

xy·log·ra·phy (zīlog'rəfē), *n.* the art of carving on wood or of making prints from such carving.

xy·loid (zī'loid), *n.* woody; resembling wood.

xy·lo·phage (zī'lōfāj), *n.* an insect that feeds on wood.

xy·loph·a·gous (zīlof'əgəs), *adj.* wood-eating. Also **hylophagous.**

xy·lot·o·mous (zīlot'əməs), *adj.* wood-boring or wood-cutting, as various insects.

xy·lot·o·my (zīlot'əmē), *n.* the technique of cutting thin slices of wood for examination under a microscope.

xys·ter (zis'tə), *n.* a surgical instrument used to scrape bones.

ya·hoo (yä'hŏŏ), *n.*, *pl.* **ya·hoos.** a bestial or coarse person.

Yang (yaNG), *n.* See **Yin and Yang.**

Yar·die (yä'dē), *n.* a member of a black criminal organization originating in Jamaica but now active in other countries.

yare (ye'ə), *adj.* quick; agile; easily handled, as a boat.

yar·mul·ke (yä'mŏŏlkə), *n.* a skullcap worn by Orthodox Jewish men and boys, esp. for prayer and religious study.

yar·o·vize (yär'əvīz), *v.* See **jarovize.**

yash·mak (yasH'mak), *n.* the veil worn by Muslim women in public to conceal the face below the eyes.

yaw (yô), *v.* (in rocketry) to deviate from a stable course because of oscillation about the longitudinal axis. See also **pitch.**

yaws (yôz), *n.* a contagious tropical disease caused by a particular bacterial species and characterized by warty red eruptions on the skin followed by the ulceration of tissue and destruction of bones. Also **framboesia.**

Y chromosome, a sex chromosome carrying the genes which produce male characteristics, occurring only in males, where it is paired with an X chromosome, and determining sex by its presence or absence. See also **X chromosome.**

yean (yēn), *v.* to give birth, as of ewes, nannygoats, or the like.

yean·ling (yēn'liNG), *n.* a newborn lamb, kid, or the like.

yegg (yeg), *n.* *Colloquial, chiefly U.S.* a travelling petty burglar; a vicious ruffian.

yellow-dog contract, *U.S.* a contract by which an employer agrees to employ a worker who in return agrees to remain outside or leave a labour union.

yellow fever, a severe, often fatal, virus infection occurring in tropical climates, transmitted by a mosquito, and characterized by fever, jaundice, vomiting, and haemorrhages. Also **yellow jack.**

yen·ta (yen'tə), *n.* *Colloquial.* an unpleasant, scandalmongering woman.

ye·shi·va (yəsHē'və), *n.*, *pl.* **ye·shi·vahs, ye·shi·voth** (yəsHē'vōt). an elementary school for Orthodox Jewish children; a school of higher education in Orthodox Jewish religious teaching, esp. for students intending to become rabbis.

yi (yē), *n.* the fulfilment of the particular obligations to society, specified in Chinese philosophy.

Yin and Yang (yin; yaNG), the two universal forces held in Chinese philosophy to be responsible for the harmonious balance of nature and to pervade and control the nature and destiny of all things, Yin being dark, cold, solid, and still, Yang being bright, warm, and active.

y·lem (ī'ləm), *n.* the primordial entity conceived in philosophy as the source from which all things in the universe have derived.

Yo·ga (yō'ga), *n.* union with the supreme spirit or any of the methods of attaining such union, esp. a Hindu system of asceticism, concentration, meditation, and exercise.

yo·gi (yo'gē), *n.* a person who practises or embraces Yoga.

yomp (yomp), *v.* to march or trek over arduous terrain, esp. when heavily laden.

young·ling (yuNG'liNG), *n.* a young person or animal; a beginner.

Young Turk, a rebellious member or adherent of a political party, usually agitating for more liberal policies.

youn·ker (yuNG'kə), *n.* a youngster.

yurt (yŏŏ'ət, yût), *n.* a portable circular hut or dwelling of the native tribes of northern and central Asia.

Z

za·ba·glio·ne (zabəlyō'nē), *n.* an Italian dessert made of egg yolks, sugar, and Marsala whipped to a thick foam in a bain-marie and served either hot or cold.

zaf·tig (zäf'tig), *adj. U.S. slang.* (of a woman) desirably plump and shapely.

zai·bat·su (zī'batsōō'), *n. sing.* and *pl. Japanese.* the large Japanese industrial or financial combines.

za·mar·ra (zəmar'ə), *n.* a coat made from sheepskin and resembling those worn by Spanish shepherds.

zap·ti·ah (zuptē'ə), *n.* a Turkish policeman.

za·re·ba (zərē'bə), *n.* a stockade, usually of growing thorn bushes, to protect a camp or village in the Sudan and neighbouring areas.

zarf (zäf), *n.* a decorative, usually metal, holder used in the Levant for handling coffee cups made without handles.

zar·zue·la (zäzwä'lə), *n.* a Spanish drama with music, frequently satirical and topical.

zax (zaks), *n.* a type of axe for making holes in slate through which nails can be driven.

zeal·ot (zel'ət), *n.* **1.** an enthusiastic or excessively enthusiastic supporter of a cause or person. **2.** a member of a fiercely patriotic Jewish resistance group which opposed the occupying Romans in Judea before and for some time after the fall of Jerusalem in A.D. 70.

zeal·ous (zel'əs), *adj.* eagerly enthusiastic; fanatical. —**zeal** (zēl), *n.*

ze·na·na (zenä'nə), *n.* the part of an Indian or Persian house where the females of the family were or are secluded; the females so secluded.

ze·nith (zē'ni*th*), *n.* the point on the celestial sphere directly above any observer or given location; the highest point. See also **nadir.**

zero gravity, the state in which there is no gravitational force, as in orbit outside the earth's atmosphere.

zero grazing, *n.* (in agriculture) a husbandry system in which cattle, sheep, etc. are permanently housed and supplied with freshly cut herbage.

ze·tet·ic (zətet'ik, zētet'ik), *adj.* proceeding by enquiry.

zib·el·ine, zib·el·line (zib'əlīn), *adj.* **1.** of or relating to the sable. —*n.* **2.** the dressed skin of the sable used as a fur for trimmings or garments.

zig·gu·rat (zig'ōōrat), *n.* a pyramidal temple of the ancient civilizations of Mesopotamia consisting of several superimposed stages, each smaller than the lower one, giving a terraced appearance, with a sanctuary at the top, or in the Assyrian version having a broad ramp winding around and up the pyramid to the sanctuary at the top.

zin·cog·ra·phy (ziNGkog'rəfē), *n.* the technique of making a printing plate of zinc by etching away the unwanted parts of its surface, leaving the part to be printed standing in relief.

zo·an·thro·py (zōan'thrəpē), *n.* a mental illness in which the patient believes he is an animal.

zo·e·trope (zō'itrōp), *n.* a device consisting of a drum inside which is placed, opposite slits, a series of images representing successive positions of a moving object so that when the drum is rotated rapidly the images seen through the slits give an illusion of motion. See also **mutoscope.**

zo·gan (zō'gan), *n.* Japanese inlaid metalwork used for decoration.

zo·ic (zō'ik), *adj.* **1.** of or possessing animal life. **2.** (in geology) (of rocks, etc.) containing animal fossils.

zone melting, a technique used to purify various metals and other minerals by passing a bar of the material through an induction coil to cause momentary melting of each part of the bar with consequent movement of impurities from the molten area to the area still to pass through the coil. Also **zone refining.** See also **cage zone melting.**

zone of interior, the entire area of a theatre of war except for the combat zone and its immediate communications zone.

zo·o·chem·is·try (zō,əkem'istrē), *n.* chemistry as it relates to the animal body.

zo·o·chore (zō'əkô), *n.* a plant so adapted in structure that it is spread by animals.

zo·o·ge·og·ra·phy (zō,əjēog'rəfē),· *n.* the scientific study of animal distribution and its causes and effects.

zo·og·ra·phy (zōog'rəfē), *n.* the scientific description of animals.

zo·oid (zō'oid), *n.* any organism capable of separate existence from the parent organism and either capable of spontaneous movement or produced by asexual reproduction.

zo·ol·a·try (zōol'ətrē), *n.* the worship of animals.

zo·ol·o·gy (zōol'əjē), *n.* the science of the study of animals. —**zo,o·log'i·cal**, *adj.* —**zo·ol'o·gist**, *n.*

zo·om·e·try (zōom'itrē), *n.* the scientific measurement and comparison of measurements of the parts of animals.

zo·o·mor·phic (zō,əmô'fik), *adj.* attributing animal form or nature to something, esp. to a deity. —**zo,o·mor'phism**, *n.*

zo·on·o·sis (zōon'əsis), *n.* an animal disease that can be passed on to man.

zo·oph·i·lism (zōof'iliz,əm), *n.* **1.** affection or emotional attachment to animals. **2.** attraction to or preference for animals, such as that exhibited by blood-sucking insects to their hosts. —**zo·o·phil·ic** (zō,əfil'ik), *adj.*

zo·oph·i·lous (zōof'ələs), *adj.* adapted to be pollinated by some animal that has been in contact with pollen.

zo·o·pho·bi·a (zō,əfō'bēə), *n.* an abnormal dread of animals.

zo·o·phyte (zō'əfīt,), *n.* any of various low forms of animal life, usually resembling a plant, as corals, sea anemones, and the like.

zo·o·plank·ton (zō,əplaNGk'tən), *n.* the minute animal organisms in plankton. See also **phytoplankton.**

zo·o·plas·ty (zō'əplas,tē), *n.* the transplanting into a human body of living tissue from another animal species.

zo·o·tech·nics (zō,ətek'niks), *n.* the science of breeding and keeping domesticated livestock.

zo·ot·o·my (zōot'əmē), *n.* the study of the bodily structure of animals, esp. by means of dissection; dissection for such a purpose.

zo·o·tox·in (zō,ətok'sin), *n.* a poisonous substance from an animal, as snake venom; a serum formed by the provocation of such a poison.

zo·ri (zô'rē), *n., pl.* **zo·ri.** a flat-soled Japanese sandal held on by a thong passing to each side of the foot from between the big and second toes.

Zo·ro·as·tri·an (zôr,ōas'trēən), *n.* a believer in a religion founded in Persia in the 7th century B.C. by Zoroaster and surviving in the Parsees of India, teaching that there is a supreme divine being, Ahura Mazda, of whom all nature, wisdom, and truth are part, and that there is a constant cosmic battle between good and evil spirits in which magic plays a predominant part. —**Zor,o·as'tri·an,ism**, *n.*

zos·ter (zos'tə), *n.* See **shingles.**

Zou·ave (zōōäv', zwäv), *n.* a member of a French infantry corps, originally of Algerian but now mainly of French soldiers, distinguished for their physique, dash, and picturesque uniform of baggy trousers, short open jacket, sash, and tasselled cap.

zuc·chet·to (zōōket'ō), *n.* a round skullcap worn by the Roman Catholic clergy, the pope's being white, a cardinal's red, a bishop's violet, and a priest's black.

zug·zwang (zōōg'zwaNG, *German.* tsōōk'-tsfäNG), *n.* a situation in a game of chess where all the moves open to one player will cause damage to his position.

zwie·back (zwē'bak), *n.* a rusk made of a light bread containing eggs.

zyg·a·poph·y·sis (zig,əpof'isis), *n., pl.* **zyg·a·poph·y·ses** (zig,əpof'isēz). one of the projections serving as joints to interlock each vertebra with the ones above and below it.

zy·go·dac·tyl (zī,gōdak'til), *adj.* with the toes of each foot arranged in pairs, one pair pointing forwards and one pair backwards, as in a parrot.

zy·go·mat·ic bone (zī,gōmat'ik), the cheek bone, forming the prominence of the cheek and the lower part of the eye socket.

zy·go·mor·phic (zī,gōmô'fik), *adj.* capable of being halved in one plane only to give two symmetrical halves, usually of flowers.

zy·mo·gen (zī'məjən), *n.* any substance capable of changing into an enzyme.

zy·mo·gen·e·sis (zī,mōjen'isis), *n.* the development of an enzyme from a zymogen.

zy·mol·o·gy (zīmol'əjē), *n.* the scientific study of enzymes and fermentation.

zy·mol·y·sis (zīmol'isis), *n.* the chemical reactions promoted by enzymes.

zy·mom·e·ter (zīmom'itə), *n.* an instrument for measuring the stage reached in fermentation, as in brewing, distilling, etc.

zy·mo·plas·tic (zī,mōplas'tik), *adj.* enzyme-producing.

zy·mo·sis (zīmō'sis), *n., pl.* **zy·mo·ses** (zīmō'sēz). any infectious or contagious disease.

zy·mos·then·ic (zī,mosthen'ik), *adj.* bringing about greater enzyme activity.

zy·mot·ic (zīmot'ik), *adj.* relating to, caused by, or as if caused by fermentation.

zy·mur·gy (zī'mûjē), *n.* the branch of applied chemistry that is concerned with fermentation, as in brewing, distilling, winemaking, and the like.